MANAGEMENT OF
PHYSICAL EDUCATION & ATHLETIC PROGRAMS

MANAGEMENT OF
PHYSICAL EDUCATION & ATHLETIC PROGRAMS

CHARLES A. BUCHER

Professor, School of Health, Physical Education, Recreation and Dance,
University of Nevada, Las Vegas
President, National Fitness Leaders Council
Consultant to the President's Council on Physical Fitness and Sports
Consultant to the National Fitness Foundation

NINTH EDITION
with 234 illustrations

TIMES MIRROR/MOSBY
COLLEGE PUBLISHING
ST. LOUIS • TORONTO • SANTA CLARA   1987

Editor: Nancy K. Roberson
Editorial assistant: Jeanne Hantak
Editing/production: CRACOM Corporation

NINTH EDITION

Library of Congress Cataloging-in-Publication Data

Bucher, Charles Augustus, 1912-
  Management of physical education and athletic
programs.

  Rev. ed. of: Administration of physical education &
athletic programs. 8th ed. 1983.
  Bibliography: p.
  Includes index.
  1. Physical education and training—Administration.
2. Sports—Organization and administration. I. Bucher,
Charles Augustus, 1912-   . Administration of
physical education & athletic programs. II. Title.
GB343.5.B77   1987   375′.6137   86-16391
ISBN 0-8016-0908-9

AC/D/D   9 8 7 6 5 4 3   02/C/237

*To my wife **Jackie***
and my children
Diana, Richard, Nancy,** and **Jerry

Preface

The ninth edition of *Management of Physical Education and Athletic Programs* is designed to provide a comprehensive, contemporary text for administration and management courses in the fields of physical education and athletics. This text has been completely revised based on changes that have taken place in physical education and athletic programs. This text represents the most current thinking and research evidence in these fields. Some of the changes that have taken place include:

Management information and use of computers. The key elements and purposes of management are discussed. Introduced are management techniques that have proven useful and successful in business and industry as well as the use that can be made of computers to help in planning and managing programs of physical education and athletics.

Chapter 15 is concerned with office management and computer use. It tells how the computer can be used with management tasks involving things such as bookkeeping, class schedules, and record keeping. More specifically, it can be used in handling payrolls, inventories, budgets, grades, use of building space, physical fitness records, team statistics, staff and faculty responsibilities, and personal data. In Appendix C the basics of the computer are outlined. The various components of a computer, the way it processes and stores information, and the nature and extent of software programs are discussed.

The emphasis on marketing. Limited funds for physical education and athletic programs make it imperative to introduce innovative fiscal practices. Funding resources, new marketing approaches, and better fiscal accountability are essential for effective management of physical education and athletic programs during the present period of economic uncertainty. Furthermore, marketing techniques are needed to win public support for these programs.

Chapter 14 is concerned with public relations and marketing in physical education and athletic programs. Information is presented to show how progressive programs today start with the needs of the consumer and with management oriented toward marketing rather than production. It emphasizes various factors that relate to getting the public to endorse and desire programs and services relating to physical education and athletics. It indicates the need to determine how well these programs and services meet the needs of the consumer.

Management of alternative physical education and athletic programs. With the fitness boom and the growth of sports and athletics, new settings for the conduct of such programs are appearing on the American scene. As a result, schools and colleges are no

vii

longer the only places for physical educators and athletic personnel to find employment as instructors and managers. In addition, organizations such as corporations, health clubs, senior citizen centers, and youth-serving agencies are expanding their fitness and recreation programs and hiring personnel to manage, teach, and conduct these programs. The descriptions and management responsibilities that relate to specific alternative physical education and athletic programs in places such as corporations, health clubs, and YMCAs are presented in Chapter 6.

Other changes

In preparing this edition of *Management of Physical Education and Athletic Programs* considerable market research was done by the publisher to determine what topics and material should be added and what information was outdated and unnecessary. In addition, the publishers asked several qualified individuals who teach administration/management of physical education courses to do a chapter-by-chapter critical evaluation of the eighth edition. Most of the comments and suggestions that were submitted by these reviewers were followed carefully. Some of the changes that resulted from these reviews include the reduction in the size of the text from 19 to 15 chapters, the consolidation of chapters that contained similar and relevant material, and less emphasis on topics such as adaptive physical education, health education, and evaluation that are covered in other courses in the professional preparation program.

Reasons why you should use this textbook
Comprehensive and systematic coverage

This text covers the essential elements of administration/management of physical education and athletic programs. First, it introduces the reader to the meaning of management and the various means of organizing and structuring a school or other organization in order to achieve the objectives of physical education and athletics. It then describes in detail management considerations in the conduct of physical education instructional programs: intramural, extramural, and club programs; interscholastic, intercollegiate club, and other competitive athletic programs. Next, it discusses the management of alternative physical educa-

tion and athletic programs such as industrial fitness. Finally, it covers various management functions such as personnel management and supervision, program development, facility management, fiscal and budget management, the purchase of supplies and equipment, legal liability, public relations, and office management.

Based on scientific theory

To the extent possible, this text discusses various concepts, management principles, and theories that are supported by scientific research, factual evidence, and sound logic. These have been drawn from the disciplines of sociology and psychology as well as the area of administrative theory.

Timely and practical material

The material in this text is up to date and timely, reflecting the latest trends and developments in the management of physical education and athletic programs. It has practical knowledge not only for the person managing these programs but also for those physical educators and athletic personnel who are instructors in such programs. The manuscript for the text was carefully reviewed by practicing management personnel and professors for accuracy, practicality, and information relevant to today's management courses.

Readable and interesting

The subject of management is presented in a readable style on the college student's level of understanding. Management is a fascinating subject, and I have tried to communicate my enthusiasm for the subject. Many new illustrations are used to provide a more interesting and meaningful text.

Pedagogical aids

The aids used in this text to facilitate its use by students and instructors include:

Instructional objectives: These are listed at the beginning of each chapter to introduce to the students the points that will be highlighted. Accomplishing the objectives indicates fulfilling the chapter's intent.

Introductory paragraphs: At the beginning of each chapter there is an introductory paragraph that provides a transition from the material and information discussed previously and the material and information to be discussed in the chapter that is currently under consideration.

Summary: Each chapter has a summary outlining the major points to assist the student in understanding and retaining the most important concepts covered.

Self-assessment exercises: These are exercises at the end of each chapter that will enable students to determine whether they understand the main points covered in the chapter.

References: At the end of each chapter references used in that chapter are listed so that readers who desire more information about subjects being discussed may find it.

Suggested readings: At the end of each chapter are listed other readings that relate to the topics discussed in that chapter. These annotated readings offer an opportunity for students to broaden their knowledge and understanding of the subject under discussion.

Figures, tables, photos: Essential points in each chapter are illustrated with clear visual materials.

Appendixes: Appendixes that offer information about crowd control, facility planning, computer basics, and adapted physical education are now included at the end of this edition.

Appendix A presents information regarding the causes of crowd control problems and some approaches to solutions. Solutions include suggested regulations and policies, adequate facilities, teaching concepts of good sportsmanship, community orientation, use of law enforcement and supervisory personnel, and communication with spectators and contestants.

Appendix B provides a checklist for managers interested in the planning of facilities for their physical education and athletic programs. It covers both indoor and outdoor facilities, including swimming pools, gymnasiums, dance studios, and provisions for the handicapped.

Appendix C presents computer basics, including such elements as input units, central processors, and output units. It also defines and describes such devices as keyboard, monitor, modem, printer, disc drive, software, program, and hardware.

Appendix D is concerned with adapted physical education and individual education program for special education and adapted physical education. It outlines and illustrates the various items to be included in such a program.

Instructor's Manual

An *Instructor's Manual* is available with this edition. It provides suggestions on how to use the text to its fullest potential. The manual includes chapter overviews, learning objectives, a topical teaching outline, key teaching points, and a test bank of multiple-choice and discussion questions for each chapter.

Charles A. Bucher

Acknowledgments

The secretarial staff of the School of Health, Physical Education, Recreation and Dance at the University of Nevada, Las Vegas, and particularly Joan Burns, have been most helpful in typing and retyping this manuscript.

I would like to say special thanks to the Times Mirror/Mosby Editor, Nancy K. Roberson, for her help and guidance in the preparation of this edition. Nancy used this text both when she was a major student in physical education and later when she became a college professor; now this text is her responsibility as an editor. This experience has provided Nancy with insights that few editors can provide. Again, my deep thanks to Nancy Roberson for all she has done to make this textbook the leading book in its field.

In addition, I would personally like to thank the following reviewers for their valuable input in making this edition better:

Dr. Betty Abercrombie
Oklahoma State University

Dr. David R. Laurie
Kansas State University

Dr. Diana Gray
Ohio State University

Dr. Dewayne Johnson
Florida State University

Contents

Chapter Five   **Interscholastic, Intercollegiate, and Other Competitive Athletic Programs,** 118

Part Three   Management of Alternative Physical Education and Athletic Programs

Part Four   **Management Functions**

Chapter Ten   Fiscal Management, 270

Chapter Eleven   The Purchase and Care of Supplies and Equipment, 295

Chapter Twelve   Management and the Athletic Training Program, 318

Chapter Thirteen   Legal Liability, Risk, and Insurance Management, 340

Chapter Fourteen **Public Relations,** 372

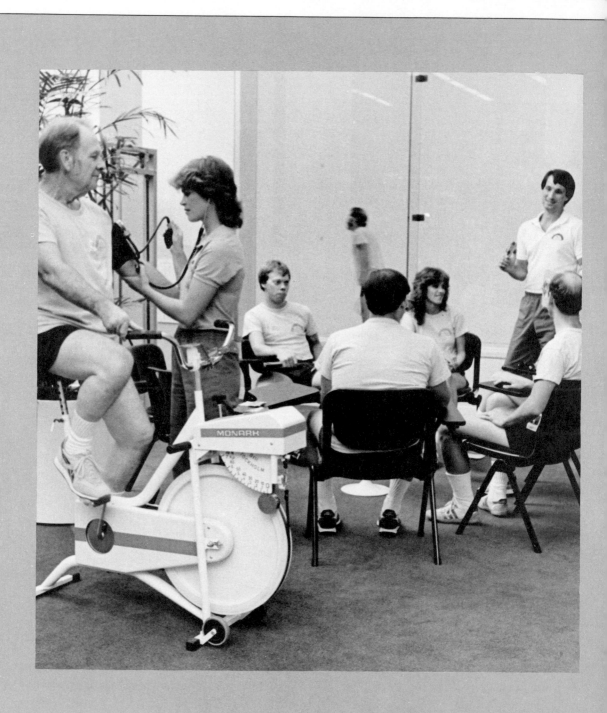

Part One
Administrative Theory and The Management Process

Chapter One

The Management Process

Instructional Objectives and Competencies to be Achieved
After reading this chapter the student should be able to

- Describe and contrast the *traditional view and the modern view of management.*
- Appreciate the advantages and the problems concerned *with a democratic and participatory management.*
- Discuss a modern philosophy of *management.*
- Identify the factors and qualifications *essential for an effective physical education and athletic management.*
- Enumerate the major duties of a *manager in a physical education program and in an athletic program.*
- Outline the preparation *necessary to be an effective manager.*
- Explain why a study of *management* is important to *the physical educator and athletic director.*

This text is concerned with the subject of management. Traditionally, the term administration has been used. However, the current emphasis and terminology uses the term management.

Management is an important consideration if physical education and athletic programs are to be conducted in an effective manner. It involves such important matters as personnel, programs, facilities, budgets, legal liability, and public relations. This text looks at these aspects of administration from a management point of view and explores ways they can be treated in an effective manner.

WHAT IS MANAGEMENT?

The American Association of School Administrators describes management as: "The total of the processes through which appropriate human and material resources are made available and made effective for accomplishing the purpose of an enterprise."

Zeigler and Bowie[9] give this definition: "Management involves the execution of managerial acts, involving conceptual, technical, human, and conjoined skills, while combining varying degrees of planning, organizing, staffing, directing, and controlling within the management process to assist an organization to achieve its goals."

By analyzing several definitions of management administration a reader will be better able to understand what a text in management is designed to cover. Some of the definitions proposed by experts in this field represent analyses of the management process based on research; others have been formulated as a result of the experience of managers or from observation of managers at work.

Halpin,[3] after analyzing administration management in education, industry, and government, states that administration refers to a human activity involving a minimum of four components: (1) the *functions or tasks* to be performed, (2) the *formal organization* within which administration must operate, (3) the *work group* or groups with which administration must be concerned, and (4) the *leader* or leaders within the organization. Administration (management) has also been defined as a means of bringing about effective cooperative activity to achieve the purposes of an enterprise.

Parkhouse and Lapin,[6] in their book *The Woman in Athletic Administration,* state that "successful management is working toward the achievement of objectives with and through people."

WHAT IS A MANAGER?

Clayton[1] presents the functions of a sports manager in these terms: "A sports manager has such a variety of duties that they touch on at least three career categories—communication, sales, and management . . . most important of these duties is the management aspect—the responsibility for decisions about personnel, finances, and facilities that affect the financial success of the enterprise."

A manager is a person who employs wise leadership in a manner that will enable an organization to function efficiently and effectively in achieving the goals for which that organization exists.

We have managers who are chairpersons of departments of physical education, directors of athletics, heads of Boys Clubs, managers of health clubs, directors of industrial fitness programs, and physical directors of Young Men's Christian Associations. All are involved with the business of management in their particular settings.

There are different kinds of managers. To carry out their duties some will manipulate members of their staffs, others are known for their inaction (seemingly waiting for problems to solve themselves), some are despots and authority figures, and others believe in providing democratic leadership for their organization. Some have warm, friendly personalities that fos-

ter a relaxed atmosphere and are popular with their staffs while others are cold and unresponsive to human needs. Each manager is different, characterized by such things as his or her training and preparation for the position, personality, experience, and beliefs.

Many managers are not trained to assume a management role. Although the trend is more and more toward having in important positions managers who have been prepared in this discipline, at the present time in physical education and athletics very few are. It is hoped that in the future more of the chairpersons and directors of programs in these special fields will be professionally prepared in management.

WHY SOME PERSONS GO INTO MANAGEMENT

Many reasons motivate individuals to go into management. Some persons like the recognition and prestige that frequently accompany a person who is a chairperson, director, dean, vice-president or president. The fact that management positions usually carry a higher salary than other positions in the organization can be a strong motivating factor for some people. Authority and power can also be reasons for seeking a management position. The manager usually has functions such as recommending salary increases, promotions, persons to fill job vacancies, and workloads, all of which appeal to some individuals. Some persons prefer management duties to those of teaching and coaching. Others want to contribute, build, and put into operation their own ideas for helping the organization grow and become better known. As can be seen readily, individuals enter management and become managers for many different reasons.

Whether or not individuals are successful in getting into the field of management depends upon the particular situation and other factors. A coach who is popular with players, the community, and staff may be selected. Sometimes a person is "kicked upstairs," that is, moved from one position to a higher managerial position. In Japan age at times provides opportunities for individuals to become managers. The reasons persons are selected for managerial positions should depend upon factors such as academic preparation for the position, experience in the field of management, and philosophy of management.

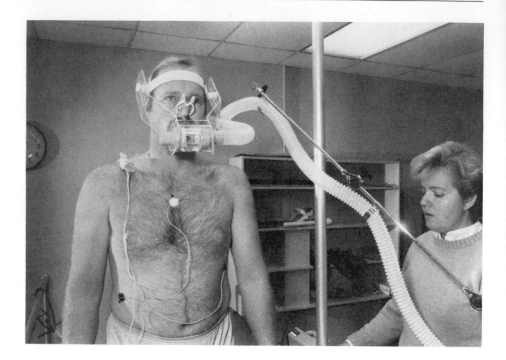

Much research is being done today in physical education and athletics.

THE IMPORTANCE OF MANAGEMENT

A study of management is important for all physical educators and athletic personnel. Some significant reasons physical educators should understand management follow:

The way in which organizations are managed determines the course of human lives. Human beings are affected by management. It affects the type of program offered, the climate in which the program takes place, the goals that are sought, and the health and happiness of members of the organization.

Management provides an understanding and appreciation of the underlying principles of the science of this field. Methods, techniques, and procedures used by the manager can be evaluated more accurately and objectively by staff members if they possess administrative understanding. Also, sound management will be better appreciated and unsound practices more easily recognized.

Studying management will help a person decide whether to select this field as a career. Increased understanding and appreciation of the management process will help an individual evaluate his or her personal qualifications and possible success.

Most physical educators perform some types of management work; therefore an understanding of management will contribute to better performance. Management is not restricted to one group of individuals. Most staff members have reports to complete, equipment to order, evaluations to make, and other duties to perform that are managerial in nature. An understanding of management will help in carrying out these assignments.

Management is fundamental to associated effort. Goals are reached, ideas are implemented, and an esprit de corps is developed with planning and cooperative action. A knowledge of management facilitates the achievement of such aims.

An understanding of management helps ensure continuity. A fundamental purpose of management is to carry on what has proved successful rather than destroy the old and attempt a new and untried path. An appreciation of this concept by all members of an organization will help to ensure the preservation of the best traditional practices that exist in the organization.

A knowledge of management helps further good human relations. An understanding of sound management principles will ensure the cooperation of the members of the organization and produce the greatest efficiency and productivity.

Management is gradually becoming a science, and the study of this science is essential to everyone. It can result in a better-ordered society through more efficiently run organizations. Every individual belongs to formal organizations. Through a democratic approach to management the individual can aid in carrying on what has proved to be good in the past.

THE SCOPE OF MANAGEMENT IN PHYSICAL EDUCATION AND ATHLETICS

It has been estimated that more than six million individuals in the United States today perform managerial work as their main function. This number is large, but as the technology and specialized functions of this country advance, more individuals will be needed to perform the myriad of managerial duties characteristic of the thousands of organizations in society. There are many more managerial positions in physical education and athletics than exist in schools and colleges. This, of course, runs into several thousands of positions. Many large educational institutions have several persons who assist in the management of physical education and athletic programs. Also, many organizations such as health spas, industrial fitness programs, senior citizen centers, YMCA's, and Boys' Clubs, also have management positions. Management offers many career opportunities for both women and men.

In these management positions physical educators, athletic directors, and others perform many managerial duties such as staffing, budgeting, coordinating, planning, communicating, reporting, and scheduling. It is essential that individuals who perform management work know the many aspects of this particular field. If they are not aware of certain basic facts and acceptable management procedures, they may make many errors, which could result in loss of efficiency, production, and staff morale and in poor human relations. Management is gradually becoming a science

with a body of specialized knowledge that should be known by all who would manage wisely and effectively.

A NEW PERSPECTIVE OF MANAGEMENT

The role of management has changed markedly in recent years. First, it is gradually becoming a science, but it is not currently a cut-and-dry science. Today, individuals who desire to prepare for management roles sometimes pursue college majors or graduate study in this discipline and do considerable work in areas such as the behavioral sciences as well as serving internships to become oriented to the various functions associated with their profession, just as physicians serve internships in hospitals to better understand the many medical problems they will have to face in their field. Such experiences as these enable managers to predict outcomes that will ensue from management actions.

Second, the manager who has special training in the field is many times more likely to be selected to fill a management position than the person who has no such training. For example, one of the fastest growing kinds of public administration is the city manager plan, in which the city manager is selected because of special training in public management. Also, the person selected today to be a superintendent of schools is most likely an individual who has majored in educational management. What is true in these cases may also be true in physical education and athletics in the future. Individuals need special preparation and expertise to help them perform managerial tasks more efficiently.

Third, managers have a greater responsibility to their staff members, faculty, and other members of the organization than was true many years ago. Today, managers serve the members of their organizations by trying to help all members accomplish their goals; that is, managers try to obtain the money, provide the facilities and equipment, and mobilize community support to get the job done. In other words, the manager is an implementor, an obstacle clearer, the person who tries to help the various people in the organization to achieve their goals, recognizing that as their goals are achieved so are the organization's goals achieved. As each individual achieves, so does the organization and the management.

Some differences between the old and the new manager

Differences between the old and the new manager include the following:

Years ago the manager had the greatest and sometimes the only voice in hiring new personnel. Today, a search committee is usually appointed to select personnel. Traditionally, the manager decided questions of promotion, tenure, rank, salary, and dismissal. Today, personnel evaluation is frequently the function of staff members. Traditionally, the manager had most to say about how the organization was to be governed. Today, staff have considerable influence on governance. Traditionally, the manager decided how the money was to be spent. Today, staff have a say, particularly with respect to the priorities and guidelines in funding. Traditionally, curriculum has been a faculty responsibility; however, managers have provided much of the curriculum leadership. Today, faculty members guard their curriculum rights very carefully and do not want any interference from the management.

Some of the reasons for this change in the attitude toward managers are the growing recognition of the importance and dignity of the individual, the existence of unions, and a growing concern among staff members regarding the excessive number of managers in the organization. Modern management is affected by bargaining agreements, whether union sup-

Fitness professionals learn new activities at Southeastern Regional Clinic on Physical Fitness and Sports.

ported or not, in determining the role of managers. It is also affected by such things as legislation and affirmative action.

MAJOR MANAGEMENT FUNCTIONS

The more commonly identified functions of management are planning, organizing, staffing, directing, and controlling.

Planning

Planning is the process of logically and purposefully outlining the work to be performed together with the methods to be used in the performance of this work. The total plan will result in the accomplishment of the purposes for which the organization is established. Of course this requires a clear conception of the aims of the organization. To accomplish this planning, the manager must have vision to look into the future and to prepare for what is seen. He or she must see the influences that will affect the organization and the requirements that will have to be met.

Organizing

Organizing refers to the development of the formal structure of the organization, whereby the various management coordinating centers and subdivisions of work are arranged in an integrated manner, with clearly defined lines of authority. The purpose behind this structure is the effective accomplishment of established objectives. Organizational charts aid in clarifying such organization.

The structure should be set up to avoid red tape and provide for the clear assignment of every necessary duty to a responsible individual. Whenever possible, standards should be established for acceptable performance for each duty assignment.

The coordinating centers of authority are developed and organized chiefly on the basis of the work to be done by the organization, services performed, individuals available in the light of incentives offered, and efficiency of operation. A single manager cannot perform all the functions necessary, except in the smallest organizations. Hence responsibility must be assigned to others logically. These individuals occupy positions along the line, each position being broken down in terms of its own area of specialization. The

higher up the line an individual goes, the more general the responsibility; the lower down the line an individual goes, the more specific the responsibility.

Staffing

The management duty of staffing refers to the entire personnel function of selection, assignment, training, and providing and maintaining favorable working conditions for all members of the organization. The manager must have thorough knowledge of staff members. He or she must select with care and ensure that each subdivision in the organization has a competent leader and that each employee is assigned to a job where he or she can be of greatest service. Personnel should possess energy, initiative, and loyalty. The duties of each position must be clearly outlined. All members of the organization must be encouraged to use their own initiative. They should be rewarded fairly for their services. The mistakes and blunders of employees must be brought to their attention and dealt with accordingly. Vested interests of individual employees must not be allowed to endanger the general interests of all. Work conditions should be made as pleasant and as nearly ideal as possible. Both physical and social factors should be provided for. Services rendered by personnel increase as the conditions under which they work improve.

Directing

Directing (leading is a more appropriate term) is a responsibility that falls to the manager as the leader. He or she must direct the operations of the organization. This means making distinct and precise decisions and embodying them in instructions that will ensure their completion. The manager must direct the work in an impersonal manner, avoid becoming involved in too many details, and see that the organization's purpose is fulfilled according to established principles. Executives have a duty to see that the quantity and quality of performance of each employee are maintained.

The manager is a leader. Success is determined by the ability to guide others successfully toward established goals. Individuals of weak responsibility and limited capability cannot perform this function successfully. The good manager should be superior in determination, persistence, endurance, and courage. He or she must clearly understand the organization's purposes and keep them in mind while guiding the way. Through direction, it is essential that he or she instill faith in cooperation, in success, in the achievement of personal ambitions, and in the integrity of the leadership.

Controlling

Controlling consists of several factors. Job standards should be established, and methods and procedures for measuring whether standards are met should be set. This should be done in light of the goals of the organization. When goals are not met, corrective action should be taken.

Controlling also means interrelating all the various phases of work within an organization; therefore the organization's structure must clearly provide close relationships and competent leadership in the coordinating centers of activity. The manager should meet regularly with chief assistants to make arrangements for unity of effort so that obstacles to coordinated work can be eliminated.

There should also be coordination with management units outside the organization where such responsibilities are necessary. Controlling means that subordinates must be kept informed through regular reports, research, and continual observation. In this respect the manager is a point of intercommunication. In addition to accepting the responsibility for reporting to higher authority, the manager must continually know what is going on in the area under his or her jurisdiction. Members of this organization must be informed on many topics of general interest, such as goals to be achieved, progress being made, strong and weak points, and new areas proposed for development.

OTHER APPROACHES TO MANAGEMENT FUNCTIONS

Peters and Waterman[7] suggest in their best-selling book, *In Search of Excellence,* that much can be learned about management functions by examining the best run industrial companies. The authors use a base of practical research as a foundation for their judg-

ments rather than material from the usual analytic pursuits of serious scholars.

Parkhouse and Lapin[6] list five functions or duties that are essential for the successful manager of athletics. According to the authors these managerial functions are interrelated and very important to successful administration. They are the following:

Planning. The wise administrator spends considerable time in planning how the organization and program can best meet its goals and objectives.

Decision making and problem solving. Informed decisions are necessary. Issues must be faced intelligently, rationally, objectively. The problem-solving approach is helpful in arriving at informed decisions.

Organization. The administrator should be able to organize and structure the organization so that personnel fit the existing job functions. Clear lines of authority and responsibility are essential.

Controlling and reappraising. There needs to be some accounting, some determination of whether set goals and objectives are being met. Then it is important to consider corrective action if these goals are not being met.

Communication. The administrator should be able to convey his or her correct viewpoint and ideas to others without them being garbled. Clear communication is necessary to gain mutual respect and trust for the administrator and his or her position and organization.

Two professors of physical education and former athletic directors see the following as management functions of the athletic director[2]:

Planning and budgeting—setting goals and planning for the achievement of these goals and carrying out the budgeting process from formulation to adoption.

Organizing, staffing, coordinating, and communicating—identifying positions within the organization and determining the duties and responsibilities of each.

Direction and delegation—facing problems and making decisions, putting well-thought through plans into action, and working with staff in achieving goals.

Controlling and reporting—measuring performance and guiding actions toward goals and then reporting progress.

Innovation—implementing new programs, ideas, and methods such as in coaching.

Representation—representing the athletic program to outside organizations, groups, and individuals.

U.S. OLYMPIC COMPLEX   OLYMPIC TRAINING CENTER   COLORADO SPRINGS

Olympic House—U.S. Olympic Committee Headquarters—Pikes Peak in rear

U.S. Olympic Sports Center/Facilities for 12 sports

U.S. Olympic Training Center.

Athletic Field at the U.S. Olympic Training Center

Photos by Robert F. George

THE NEW PERSPECTIVE OF MANAGEMENT IN PHYSICAL EDUCATION AND ATHLETICS

The management of physical education and athletic programs is directly affected by the new perspective of management. The person who seeks to hold a manager's role in such programs must recognize the importance of each individual in the organization and help in actively promoting each person's participation. The manager should recognize the need to help each person in the organization to develop and grow and become a force in helping the organization to achieve its goals. The manager must be interested in working for the department, division, school, corporation, or health club and in performing the many tasks involved in the organization.

Managers are involved with many tasks that involve the various members of their organization. Therefore it is very important that they be knowledgeable about group dynamics as well as about individual behavior. A need exists for considerable group interaction under the new style of management. To be successful, groups within an organization need to have common goals, a differentiation of roles, and shared values. For desirable change to take place management must be recognized as a social process that involves the interaction of people. Managers should recognize the importance of and be able to work within the framework of this social process.

If prospective managers of physical education and athletic programs are thinking about positions that have power over other individuals, places to force personal ideas on other members of the organization, or offices that provide opportunities for making unilateral decisions, then they should not go into management because they are doomed to failure. The formula for success is to generate power, adopt ideas, and make decisions with members of the organization. The power of the organization is important, not the power of the individual.

The new perspective of management also has implications for staff members. Because they now share in the many management tasks to be performed, they must also assume the responsibility that goes with such a role. This means such things as being knowledgeable about the issues being considered, partici-pating in the discussions, and making informed decisions. Not to accept such responsibilities is to cause irreparable harm to the organization of which one is a member.

THE MANAGER AS A LEADER

Being the head of a department, division, school of physical education or an industrial fitness program and also being the leader of these organizations are two different things. The head can be a person who takes care of the clerical details and occupies the main office in a department or division, but he or she may not necessarily be the leader of the organization. The manager should be one who helps and influences others in a certain direction as problems are solved and goals are achieved. In a school, college, business, or agency, the persons influenced are teachers, pupils, clerks, parents, custodians, and any person involved with the organization.

Knezevich[5] categorizes three kinds of leadership: (1) *symbolic leadership,* which is primarily a personality attribute; (2) *formal leadership,* which involves the use of a title, status, or position denoting a leadership role in a formal organization; and (3) *functional leadership,* or the role performed in an organized group. Knezevich points out that leadership is a social process involving working with people. Personality traits will not in themselves result in leadership. Furthermore, conferring a title does not necessarily provide leadership. Instead, the existing situation and the ability of the person to lead in that situation are critical. As a general rule, people will contribute most with leaders who are creative and imaginative.

The question of what makes a leader is a provocative one. Much research has been done concerning what constitutes the management leader. Years ago it was felt that combinations of personality characteristics or traits were the ingredients that determined who was a leader.

The qualities, characteristics, and skills required in a leader are determined to a large extent by the demands of the situation in which he is to function as a leader. In other words, a physical education management leader in one situation may not necessarily be a leader in another situation. Different styles of leader-

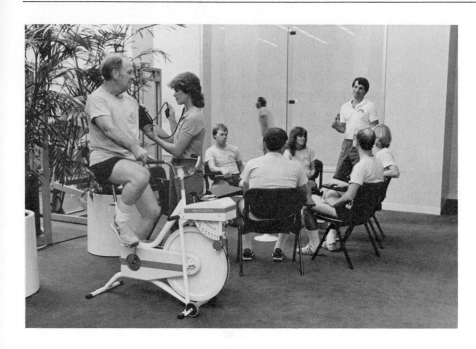

Tenneco Inc. fitness program.

ship are needed to meet the needs of different settings and situations. Therefore management is a social process.

Certain traits and attributes that influence leader behavior have been identified. Qualities such as popularity, originality, adaptability, judgment, ambition, persistence, emotional stability, social and economic status, and communicative skills are very important for persons to possess if they hope to lead. The traits found to be most significant are popularity, originality, and judgment. When these factors are related to physical education and athletic leaders, the following guidelines are worth considering:

The managers of physical education and athletic programs who possess such traits as ambition, ability to relate well to others, emotional stability, communicative skill, and judgment have greater potential for success in leadership than persons who do not possess these traits.

The managers of physical education and athletic programs who desire to be leaders of their organization must have a clear understanding of the goals of the organization. The direction in which they desire to

lead the organization must be within the broad framework of its goals and objectives and consonant with the needs of the community they serve.

The managers of physical education and athletic programs who desire to be leaders of their organizations must understand each of the persons who work with them, including their personal and professional needs.

The managers of physical education and athletic programs who desire to be leaders of their organizations need to establish a climate within which the organization's goals, personal needs of each staff member, and their own personality traits can operate harmoniously.

MANAGEMENT THEORY AND STYLES OF LEADERSHIP

Theories of management exist by which organizations are led by the persons holding executive positions. In some cases these theories have been referred to as styles of leadership. In determining which is the best theory or style of leadership it is important to evaluate each in terms of management theory.

Management theory in physical education and athletics

Many physical education and athletic programs are managed by persons who have practical experience. They have learned management through their own experience and understanding. Practical experience, although valuable, is not sufficient by itself. It is also important to know the research findings of academicians who have studied management and who, through their research, can provide insights into such areas as the structure of organizations, the role of leadership, and the human relations aspects that affect the achievement of goals. Most valuable is a combination of experience and an understanding and application of scientifically sound management theory. Physical and athletic educators, therefore, will enhance their productivity in the management process as they understand it from both a theoretical and a practical point of view.

Traditional theories

The traditional theories of management philosophy have usually had authoritarian, democratic, or laissez-faire orientations. A more recent theory of management or style of leadership involves the systems theory. The first three orientations may be considered traditional. Traditional philosophy views leaders as absolutes, which of course is unrealistic, because the nature of the human personality is seldom so extreme.

Authoritarian theory

The authoritarian philosophy usually implies a one-person leadership with decision making imposed by the leader on group members.

An example of this theory is the chairman of a physical education department who very seldom holds a staff meeting. Instead, he issues directives from his office indicating the policies and procedures that each staff member is expected to follow. Authority, this person feels, resides in his position as the head of the administrative unit. As a result, staff members frequently hesitate to disagree with him or suggest new ways of doing things.

Democratic or equalitarian theory

The democratic or equalitarian philosophy implies a leader who submits important matters to group discussion and involves group members in decision making.

An example of this theory is the head of a physical education department who holds regular staff meetings where items that affect the organization are discussed. Each member of the staff is respected as a person and for his or her suggestions and ideas. The staff helps in formulating goals and procedures that they are to follow. The head of the department realizes that for the organization to achieve its goals, all members must cooperate and help.

Laissez-faire theory

The laissez-faire philosophy implies a leader who gives little guidance and frequently leaves decision making to group members.

An example of this theory is the director of a program of physical education who doesn't provide active leadership. He or she feels that problems will solve themselves if given time. This individual frequently spends much time in activities that are personal in nature or do not have significant importance in the management of the organization. To a great degree staff members go their own separate ways because of the absence of leadership in the organization.

Systems theory

The systems theory of management has stemmed from the rapid growth of technology and management in recent years. By borrowing techniques from the business world, managers have constructed models that bring together the many facets of an organization. The systems theory is defined as a method designed to collect data on interrelated and interacting components that, when working in an integrated manner, help accomplish a predetermined goal or goals. The application of this strategy is called a systems theory of management.

Selected merits of the democratic or participatory theory

In the recommended democratic or participatory theory of management and style of leadership the manager follows certain steps in the democratic process and the staff members of an organization work together to accomplish group goals. Some of the steps that are considered follow:

Girls' volleyball, Riverside-Brookfield High School, Riverside, Ill.

Goals are developed through the group process; they are attainable, challenging, and adapted to the capacities of the members.

Good morale is developed among all staff members. This is essential to constructive group action. A climate of openness is established in group deliberations. All members feel a sense of belonging and recognize their important contributions in the undertaking. A feeling of oneness pervades the entire group.

Group planning is accomplished in a clearly defined manner. A stated procedure is followed. It is a cooperative undertaking, based on known needs, and flexible enough to allow for unforeseen develop-

ments. The fulfillment of plans brings satisfaction and a feeling of success to all who participated in their formulation and accomplishment. All members share in recognition for a completed job.

In staff meetings and group discussions the management applies democratic principles. Each member's contribution is encouraged and respected. Differences of opinion are based on principles rather than on personalities. The organization's objectives must be kept in mind at all times. All members are encouraged to facilitate the group process by accepting responsibility, alleviating conflict, making contributions, respecting the opinions of others, abiding by the will of the majority, and promoting good group morale.

Progress is evaluated periodically. The group evaluates itself from time to time on accomplishments in terms of the organization's goals and the effectiveness of the group process. Each individual evaluates his or her own role as a member of the organization with respect to contributions made to the group process and the accomplishments of the group.

Applying management theory

Management is not something that is hit or miss, trial and error, or a matter of expediency. Instead, a theory of management is emerging. A study of this management theory enhances the ability to act wisely in specific situations and provides a picture of how human beings work. Management theory also helps identify problems that need to be solved for an effective working organization to exist.

Textbooks and the professional literature on management indicate a search for its substance and for a framework of theory that would make the substance a meaningful whole. The traditional emphasis has been on the form rather than on the substance. Organizations such as the National Conference of Professors of Educational Administration, the Cooperative Program in Educational Administration, and the University Council for Educational Administration have helped to give impetus to this new movement and make management much more of a science than it has been in the past. It is thereby characterized by more objectivity, reliability, and a systematic structure of substance.

The traditional view of management revolved

around the idea that the manager existed to carry out the policies that had been developed by the duly constituted policy-forming group, such as a board of education. Modern management not only carries out policy but also plays an important role in developing policy, applying the knowledge and expertise that come from training and experience.

A study of the history of management shows that policy-forming groups, such as boards of education, once were held accountable for how the schools were managed, whereas the modern approach delegates responsibilities to the trained manager in many cases. The old concept of leadership in management was a passive leadership that remained in the background while the policy-forming group provided the strength and skill needed to run the organization. Under the modern view of management, however, strong leadership is required so that technical and expert judgments can be made to help organizations to achieve their objectives more effectively. The traditional view of management claimed that the best way to prepare to manage was to practice managing; experience was seen as the best teacher. However, the modern view of management recognizes the value of experience and at the same time maintains there exists a body of knowledge or theory that, when mastered, can help management play a more effective role in the organization with which it is associated.

According to Jenson and Clark,[4] new perspectives of administration (management) are the result of six phenomena:

1. Administration is a science, and the administrator is a professional person.
2. An intensive study of administration includes such phenomena as behaviors, social interactions, and human relationships.
3. Application of theory and model constructs are included in the study of administration.
4. Administration is differentiated into two dimensions: content and process.
5. New forces shape new perspectives in administration: new technologies, population trends, value systems, knowledge explosion, ideological conflicts, and so on.
6. Interest of scholars and researchers in the scientific study of the field of administration is increasing.

A PHILOSOPHY OF MANAGEMENT FOR PHYSICAL EDUCATION AND ATHLETICS

Human beings represent the most important consideration in the world. The real worth of a field of endeavor, organization, or idea is found in what it does for human beings. The most important and worthwhile thing that can be said about a particular vocation, organization, or movement is that it contributes to human betterment.

People have goals that represent a variety of human objectives. They include the need for health and security for oneself and one's family, the desire to obtain an education and to be employed in a worthwhile and gainful occupation, and the right to worship freely and to enjoy recreation.

People do not miraculously work together. They do not spontaneously band together and strive to accomplish common objectives. Because many groups of people have common goals, however, through associated effort they help each other achieve goals that would be impossible for them to accomplish alone. No one person can establish a school for his or her children's education, for example, but through cooperative effort and support, many people make a school possible. Thus individuals have similar goals that they will work together to attain.

Organizations, to function effectively, need machinery to help them run efficiently, to organize and execute their affairs, and to keep them operating smoothly, so that the goals for which they have been created will be achieved. This machinery is management, the framework of organizations and the part that helps organizations implement the purposes for which they have been established.

Management, therefore, exists to help people achieve the goals they desire to live happy, productive, healthful, and meaningful lives. It is not an end in itself; rather, it is a means to an end, the welfare of the people for whom the organization exists. Management exists for people, not people for management. Management can justify itself only as it serves the people who make up the organization, helping them to achieve the goals they have as human beings.

It can be seen, then, that in an organization, where the associated efforts of many individuals are necessary, it is essential to have human beings cooperate

Weight training and conditioning, Lyons Township High School, LaGrange, Ill.

and work together happily and purposefully to achieve an organization's goals. This is accomplished through direction, and management gives this direction.

To a considerable degree the actions of human beings in society are determined through their association with formal organizations. Formal organizations have leaders and purposes. They depend on cooperative efforts of individuals to achieve the objectives that have been set. Many times organizations have failed when their managers have lacked leadership ability, when there has been a lack of cooperative effort among members, or when the objectives have not been essential and good for society.

Management determines whether an organization is going to progress, operate efficiently, achieve its objectives, and have a group of individuals within its framework who are happy, cooperative, and productive. Management involves directing, guiding, and integrating the efforts of human beings so that specific aims may be accomplished. It refers particularly to a group of individuals, often called executives, who have as their major responsibility this direction, guidance, integration, and achievement.

Management is especially concerned with achievement, proof that the organization is attaining its goals. Achieving these results satisfactorily requires an understanding of human relationships and the ability to foresee the future and plan for any eventuality, and it demands the capacity to coordinate human personalities. Good management ensures that the associated efforts of individuals are productive. To accomplish this, managers must possess attributes that elicit the most creative efforts of the members of the organization.

Management also requires close supervision of the facilities, materials, supplies, and equipment essential to the life of the organization. It implies a logical formulation of policies and the effective operation of the organization.

QUALIFICATIONS OF MANAGERS

Although the qualities of a manager need to be considered in relation to the qualities of the persons in the organization he or she is attempting to lead, certain leadership characteristics arc also necessary for a successful manager. Identifying these qualities is essential to help determine whether one should go into this important field. This identification also helps evaluate the type of management that exists in a person's own organization, whether the person is a manager or not.

The qualifications of a manager are many. Some (conceptual skills, integrity, ability to instill good human relations, ability to make decisions, health and fitness for the job, willingness to accept responsibility, understanding of work, command of administrative skills, and intellectual capacity) are discussed in the following sections. No attempt has been made to list these in order of importance.

Conceptual skills

Conceptual skills include the abilities to see the organization as a whole, to originate ideas, to sense problems, and to work out solutions to these problems that will benefit the organization and establish the right priorities and organizational direction. Proper conceptual skills reduce the risk factor to a minimum.

A research project involving a self-analysis of nearly 1,000 executives, all of whom were presidents of industrial organizations, pointed out the following important considerations for the person who wants to be an efficient manager: using time effectively, motivating others, building a team, setting the direction, finding expert advice, making crisis decisions, negotiating, and undertaking effective self-improvement. Personal improvement, especially directed along lines involving public speaking, planning work, memory skills, conference leadership, writing, producing better ideas, and reading, was considered necessary.

Some individuals have qualities that perhaps have been developed through training and experience and that can be adapted to management work. These individuals are able to analyze situations objectively, to clarify generalizations, and to manage constructively rather than exploitatively. Such persons are sensitive to the important role human relations play in the successful functioning of any organization. These individuals think in imaginative terms. They are able to see into the future and plan a course of action with an open mind. They recognize problems in order of importance, are able to analyze a situation, develop various plans of action, and reach logical conclusions. They have the ability to organize.

Integrity

One of the most important qualifications of any manager is integrity. Whether or not a leader can inspire staff members, have their cooperation, and achieve the purposes of the organization will depend to a great degree on his or her integrity. Everyone likes to feel confident that a manager is honest and sincere, keeps promises, and can be trusted with confidential information. Such confidence cannot emanate from managers unless they have integrity. Failure to fulfill this one qualification will result in low morale and an inefficient organization.

Dance, Oak View Elementary School, Fairfax, Va.

Human relations skills

Human relations skills include the manager's ability to develop good working relationships among staff members, to get along with people, and to provide a working climate where individuals not only will produce but also will grow on the job.

A former president of the American Alliance for Health, Physical Education, Recreation, and Dance (AAHPERD) suggested the following as considerations for managers: "Be friendly and considerate, be alert to the opinions of others, be careful what you say and how you say it, be honest and fair, be wise enough to weigh and decide, tolerate human failings and inefficiency, acquire humility, and plan well for staff meetings."

The ability to get along with associates in work is an essential qualification for a manager. Only through cooperative effort is it possible for an organization to achieve its goals. This cooperative effort is greatest when those responsible for the coordination of human efforts have the welfare of the various members of the organization at heart. This means that a manager must be able to coordinate the abilities of many individuals. This is done in many ways. Some of these methods include setting a good example, inspiring confidence, selecting proper incentives, possessing poise, making the right decisions in tense moments, having an impersonal attitude, cooperating and helping others when necessary, and developing and practicing ethical standards. The manager must be adept at the art of persuasion, which takes into consideration such important items as the points of view, interests, and other factors characterizing those to be persuaded.

There is little associated effort without leadership. The manager must be a leader and possess the attributes and qualities that people expect if they are to achieve the purposes for which the organization has been established.

Ability to make decisions

The manager must be able to make decisions when necessary. This requires the ability to discern what is important and what is reasonable, what is in the best interests of the organization and what has the best chance for success, and then to foresee future developments as a result of the decision.

Decision is essential to accomplish objectives at the most opportune time. The manager should have the capacity and be willing to make a decision. Otherwise, lethargy, suspense, and poor morale result. The manager who procrastinates, is afraid of making the wrong decision, thinks only of his or her own welfare, and is oblivious to the organization's needs should never hold a management position.

Health and fitness for the job

Good health and physical fitness are essentials for the manager. They often have a bearing on making the right decisions. Socrates said that people in a state of bad health often made the wrong decisions in regard to affairs of state. H.S. Jennings, the famous biologist, pointed out that the body can attend to only one thing at a time. Therefore if attention is focused on a pain in

the chest, a stomach ailment, or a nervous condition, it is difficult to focus it on the functions that a manager must perform. Poor physical or mental health may cause poor management.

Vitality and endurance are essential to the manager. They affect his or her manner, personality, attractiveness, and disposition. Management duties often require long hours of tedious work under the most trying conditions. Failure to have the necessary strength and endurance under such conditions could mean the inability to perform tasks that are essential to the welfare of the organization. Members of an organization have confidence in those managers who watch over their interests at all times. It is possible for a manager to retain this confidence continuously only if he or she is in good health and physically fit to perform arduous duties.

Willingness to accept responsibility

Every manager must be willing to accept responsibility. The manager performs duties that influence the welfare of many individuals. Plans have to be fulfilled if the purposes of the organization are to be accomplished. Action is required to ensure production and render services. The person who accepts a management position is morally bound to assume the responsibility that goes with that position. An effective manager will be dissatisfied whenever he or she fails to meet responsibilities.

Understanding of work

The manager will benefit from having a thorough understanding of the specialized work in which the organization is engaged. If it concerns a particular industry, it will be advantageous to know the production process from the ground up. If it is government, knowledge of related legislative, executive, and judicial aspects will help. If it is education, familiarity with that particular field will be an asset. If it is a specialized field within education, it is necessary to have a knowledge of the particular specialty and also the part it plays in the total educational process. Guiding purposefully is difficult unless the individual knows his or her particular speciality and how it relates to other areas. One often reads about the Congressman who was once a page in the Senate, the

Sit and reach test, part of Health-Related Physical Fitness Test, Lyons Township High School, LaGrange, Ill.

railroad executive who was a yard worker, the bank president who started as a bookkeeper, and the superintendent of schools who started as a teacher. The technical knowledge and understanding of the total functioning of an organization are best gained through firsthand experience. A manager will find that detailed knowledge of an organization's work is invaluable in successfully guiding its operations.

Command of technical skills

Technical skills are similar in many ways to the first qualification listed—conceptual skills, but there is one essential difference. Conceptual skills refer more to the "know how" and temperament of the individual, whereas technical skills refer to the application of this knowledge and ability. An individual who possesses these skills can plan and budget his or her time and effort and also the time and work of others in the most effective way possible. Time is not spent on details when more important work should be done. Tasks are performed in a relaxed, efficient, calm, and logical manner. Work is accomplished in conformance with established standards. Duties are effectively executed, including those involving excess pressure and time.

It has been said that three conditions rapidly burn out a manager: performing his or her own duties in a tense, highly emotional manner; handling too many details; and being part of an organization not considerate of its administrators.

Intellectual capacity

Intellectual capacity in itself will not guarantee a good manager. In fact, the so-called intellectual often makes a very poor manager. Such traits as absentmindedness and tardiness, characteristic of some intellectual persons, are often not compatible with acceptance of responsibility. Intellectuals sometimes cannot make decisions because they visualize so many sides of an issue. Furthermore, such an individual is often not interested in people but in books, figures, or other data. This individual makes a poor leader because lack of interest in human beings results in poor followership.

However, intellectual capacity cannot be disregarded. To be an effective manager one must be intellectually competent. One should be able to think and reason logically, to apply knowledge effectively, to communicate efficiently, and to possess other abilities closely allied to the intellectual process. There have been many so-called brains who failed miserably as managers, whereas most effective managers have at least average intellectual capacities.

• • •

Space has not permitted a discussion of all the qualifications of the manager. Others, such as courage and initiative, are also important. There is in addition the ability to be an ambassador for the organization. Liaison work with higher echelon groups in the organization and also with outside groups is important. It is necessary at times to stand up and fight for a person's own department or division. To a great degree this will determine whether it is respected and has equal status with other management divisions.

THE PREPARATION OF MANAGERS

The modern view of management is that a professional preparation program for the person who desires to enter this field should include such essentials as taking foundation work in cognate fields, knowing himself or herself as an individual and as a potential manager, having technical and conceptual understanding of the community, recognizing the importance of instruction, studying and practicing decision making, and realizing the importance of human relations. Finally, there should be on-the-job learning experience closely supervised by an experienced individual.

Scott[8] has stated the type of preparation she feels persons need to become skilled in management practices and to be able to perform satisfactorily in light of the new perspective of management. Some areas she feels should occupy an important place in such preparation are the following:

A sound background in business practices. Included in this background should be an emphasis on budgeting and financial management.

Administrative use of computers. Today's administrator-manager needs to understand computer programmers.

Collective bargaining. To cope with unions it is important for today's manager to be conversant with collective bargaining and the skills needed in the negotiation process.

Public relations. Physical education and athletics need people who can articulate their positions eloquently, both verbally and in written form.

School law. The prevalence of litigation involving professional programs is such that the manager needs to be well informed about such things as liability, negligence, and product liability.

Interpersonal relations. Intensive work and study in personal relations is one of the most important requisites for an effective administrator-manager.

Tug-of-war taking place at Falmouth Elementary School, Falmouth, Va.

Some universities, as a part of the training and professional preparation of managers, include a course in sensitivity training or human awareness. The purpose of this course is to learn through an analysis of a person's own and other people's experiences. In human awareness training participants work together in small groups in an attempt to better understand themselves and other people. This group is frequently called a "T group," and the leader is called a trainer. His or her role is to help the group learn from its experiences. The group does not have a definite structure, and the leader initially stresses that the participants themselves will be the forces that determine how individual behavior is influenced. The leader also stresses that the data for learning will be the behavior of the group members.

SUMMARY

Management is the process by which key personnel provide leadership so that an organization functions efficiently and effectively in achieving the goals for which the organization exists. It involves such functions as planning, organizing, staffing, directing, and controlling. A philosophy of management for physical education and athletics should recognize that the welfare of the human beings who comprise the organization is the most important consideration and that managers need special qualifications including conceptual skills, integrity, intelligence, and good human relations together with a preparation that takes into account management theory.

SELF-ASSESSMENT TESTS

These tests will assist students in determining if material and competencies presented in this chapter have been mastered.

1. Take a sheet of paper and divide it into two halves as indicated here. On the left half list the characteristics of traditional management and on the right side the characteristics of the new perspective of management.

Characteristics of traditional management	Characteristics of the new perspective of management

2. Assume you are a manager who believes in the participatory theory of management. Describe how you would implement this theory as the manager of a program of physical education and athletics.
3. Discuss your philosophy of management.
4. You are superintendent of schools of a large school system interviewing applicants for the position of director of physical education and athletics. What qualifications would you look for among the many applicants who apply for the position?
5. List what you consider to be the major duties performed by a manager of a physical education and athletic program.
6. You aspire to be the manager of a large physical education and athletic program. To ensure that you will be well prepared to assume such a position, what type of preparation will you seek?
7. A classmate indicates that a study of management will not be of any use to him as a physical educator. Prepare a rebuttal to your classmate's statement.

REFERENCES

1. Clayton, R.D., and Clayton, J.A.: Concepts and careers in physical education, Minneapolis, 1982, Burgess Publishing Company.
2. Fuoss, D.E., and Troppmann, R.J.: Creative management techniques in interscholastic athletics, New York, 1977, John Wiley & Sons (1984, Krieger).
3. Halpin, A.W.: A paradigm for research on administrative behavior. In Campbell, R.F., and Gregg, R.T., editors: Administrative behavior in education, New York, 1957, Harper & Row, Publishers.
4. Jenson, T.J., and Clark, D.L.: Educational administration, New York, 1964, The Center for Applied Research in Education, Inc. (The Library of Education).
5. Knezevich, S.J.: Administration of public education, New York, 1981, Harper & Row, Publishers.
6. Parkhouse, B.L., and Lapin, J.: The woman in athletic administration, Santa Monica, Calif., 1980, Goodyear Publishing Company, Inc.
7. Peters, T.J., and Waterman, R.H., Jr.: In search of excellence, New York, 1982, Harper & Row, Publishers.
8. Scott, P.M.: The new administrator: a point of view, Journal of Physical Education and Recreation **50**:40, January 1979.
9. Zeigler, E.F., and Bowie, G.W.: Management competency development in sport and physical education, Philadelphia, 1983, Lea and Febiger.

SUGGESTED READINGS

- Eble, K.E.: The art of administration, San Francisco, 1978, Jossey-Bass Publishers.
  Offers practical assistance to administrators in carrying out their many responsibilities. Focuses on day-to-day tasks involving working with faculty and students. Discusses administrative skills, attitudes, and qualifications that can help in making a success of the management process.
- Kraus, R.G., and Curtis, J.E.: Creative management in recreation and parks, St. Louis, 1986, Times Mirror/Mosby College Publishing.
  Is concerned with the professional management of recreation and park agencies and programs; much of the material is equally applicable to physical education and athletic programs. Provides information and guidelines regarding contemporary management theory relating to such areas as personnel, facilities, and programs.
- Sergiovanni, T.J.: Handbook for effective department leadership, Boston, 1984, Allyn & Bacon, Inc.
  Discusses various resources and means of providing strong leadership at the department level. Applies the thinking of such authorities and management leaders as Peter Drucker, Abraham Maslow, and Max Weber to the role of department leadership.
- Shipman, N.J., et al.: Effective time management techniques for school administrators, Englewood Cliffs, N.J., 1983, Prentice-Hall, Inc.
  Authors use 60 years of cumulative experience as practicing administrators to offer suggestions and help in managing educational programs. Text is of particular value in providing help to managers in using their time to greatest advantage.
- Vander Zwaag, H.J.: Sport management in schools and colleges, New York, 1984, John Wiley & Sons, Inc.
  Covers the present structure of and functions in school and college sport programs. Tells how the fields of physical education and athletics are changing and how sport management is an emerging concept.
- Zeigler, E.F., and Spaeth, M.J.: Administrative theory and practice in physical education and athletics, Englewood Cliffs, N.J., 1975, Prentice-Hall, Inc.
  Discusses current management principles and theories of administration. Uses concrete guidelines for successful management. Stresses practical aspects of decision making, planning and evaluating, and concerns about finances, personnel, and public relations.

Chapter Two

Management Organization to Achieve Objectives of Physical Education and Athletics

Instructional Objectives and Competencies to be Achieved
After reading this chapter the student should be able to

- Discuss how and why management organization is important to the effectiveness of physical education and athletic programs.
- Identify the objectives of physical education and athletics for which the organization and structure exist.
- Outline the principles that should be followed in establishing an effective organization for physical education and athletic programs.
- Describe a formal and an informal type of organization and structure and provide the rationale for each.
- Outline the factors that need to be considered to develop a functional organization.
- Describe the organization and structure of physical education and athletic programs that exist in elementary and secondary schools, colleges and universities, and other organizations.
- Prepare a management organization chart for a physical education and an athletic program.

The first chapter was concerned with the nature and scope of management and such things as the duties and preparation of managers. This chapter discusses the objectives of physical education and athletics and the management organization and structure needed to accomplish these goals.

Schools, colleges, and other organizations do not function efficiently without some element that holds them together and gives them direction so they can

achieve the goals for which they exist. This element is management. It is the glue that binds the various units cohesively and provides the control and leadership needed to achieve success. To accomplish these functions a structure is needed that provides an efficient way of operating and carrying out the various responsibilities existing within the organization. The structure shows the roles various members of the organization play in achieving established goals. It shows to whom each member reports and who is responsible for carrying out duties. It shows a plan of action for getting the job done.

The primary purpose of structure in physical education and athletics is to make it possible to achieve goals and objectives. Unless the organization and structure perform this function as efficiently as possible, it is a failure and should be abandoned. The structure is a means to an end, not an end in itself. Because this is true, it follows that the goals or objectives of physical education and athletics must be clear in the mind of the management before establishing the organization and structure of the organization. Therefore the first task is to clarify what goals are being sought for physical education and athletics.

PHYSICAL EDUCATION OBJECTIVES TO BE ACHIEVED

The objectives of physical education discussed here pertain in general to all educational levels—elementary, secondary and college—although there could be further delineation of goals for each level. In addition, they also relate to most other agency and institutional programs.

A study of human beings reveals four general directions or phases in which growth and development take place: physical development, motor or skill development, cognitive development, and social development. Physical education contributes to each of these phases.

The physical development objective[2]

The physical development objective deals with the program of activities that builds physical power in an individual through the development of the various organ systems of the body. It results in the ability to sustain adaptive effort, the ability to recover, and the ability to resist fatigue. The value of this objective is based on the fact that an individual will be more active, have better performance, and be healthier if the organ systems of the body are adequately developed and functioning properly. It is sometimes called the physical fitness objective.

Muscular activity plays a major role in the development of the organ systems of the body, including the digestive, circulatory, excretory, heat regulatory, respiratory, and other systems. These systems are stimulated and developed through such activities as hanging, climbing, running, throwing, leaping, carrying, and jumping. Health is also related to muscular activity; therefore activities that bring into play all of the fundamental big muscle groups in the body should be vigorously engaged in regularly, so that the various organ systems are sufficiently stimulated.

Vigorous muscular activity produces several beneficial results. The developed heart provides better nourishment to the entire body. It beats more slowly and pumps more blood per stroke, delivering more food to the cells and more efficiently removing waste products. During exercise, the developed heart's speed increases more slowly and has a longer rest period between beats. After exercise it returns to normal much more rapidly. The individual who exercises regularly is able to perform work longer with less expenditure of energy and with much more efficiency than the individual who does not. This trained condition is necessary for a vigorous and abundant life.

The motor development objective[7]

The motor development objective is designed to make it possible to perform physical movement proficiently, gracefully, and esthetically, using as little energy as possible. This has implications for a person's work, play, and anything else that requires physical movement. The definition of the word *motor* involves the relationship of a nerve or nerve fiber that connects the central nervous system, or a ganglion, with a muscle. Movement results as a consequence of the impulse it transmits, which is known as the motor impulse.

Effective motor movement depends on a harmonious working together of muscular and nervous systems. It results in greater distance between fatigue and peak performance; it is found in activities involving running, hanging, jumping, dodging, leaping, kicking, bending, twisting, carrying, and throwing; and it will enable one to perform daily work efficiently without reaching the point of exhaustion so quickly.

In physical education activities the function of efficient body movement, or neuromuscular skill, is to provide the individual with the ability to perform pro-

Participants move to disco beat at Southeastern Regional Clinic on Physical Fitness and Sports, University of Tennessee, Chattanooga.

ficiently, which results in greater enjoyment of participation. The objective of physical education is to develop in each individual as many physical skills as possible so that interests will be wide and varied.

Physical skills are not developed in one lesson. It takes years to acquire coordination, and the most important period for development is during the formative years of a child's growth, when he or she attempts to synchronize the muscular and nervous systems for such movements as creeping, walking, running, and jumping. A study of kinesiology shows that many muscles of the body are used in even the simplest of coordinated movements. Therefore to obtain efficient motor movement or skill in many activities, it is necessary to start training early in life and to continue into adulthood.

The cognitive development objective[1]

The cognitive development objective involves the accumulation of a body of knowledge and the ability to think and interpret.

Physical activities must be learned. In movement one must think and coordinate muscular and nervous systems. Movement education, for example, is designed to provide an awareness of movement principles, such as the role of gravity, so that participants may better understand how to move efficiently.

The individual should also acquire a knowledge of rules, techniques, and strategies involved in physical activities. Basketball is an example. In this sport a person should know the rules, the strategy in offense and defense, the various types of passes, the difference between screening and blocking, and the values that are derived from playing this sport. Techniques learned through experience result in knowledge that is also acquired. For example, a ball travels faster and more accurately if one steps with a pass, and time is saved when the pass is made from the same position in which it is received. Furthermore, a knowledge of leadership, courage, self-reliance, assistance to others, safety, and adaptation to group patterns is important.

Knowledge concerning health should play an important part in the program. All individuals should know about their bodies, the importance of sanitation, factors in disease prevention, the importance of exercise, the need for a well-balanced diet, values of good health attitudes and habits, and the community and school agencies that provide health services. This knowledge contributes to physical prowess and to

Young men developing upper body strength.

general health. Through the accumulation of this knowledge, activities take on a new meaning and health practices are associated with definite purposes. This helps each individual to live a healthier and more purposeful life.

The social development objective[4]

The social development objective is designed to help an individual make personal adjustments, group adjustments, and adjustments as a member of society. Physical education activities offer valuable opportunities for making these adjustments, if there is proper leadership.

Social action is a result of certain hereditary traits and learned behavior. Interests, hungers, desires,

ideals, attitudes, and emotional drives are involved in everything we do. Play activities are one of the oldest and most fundamental drives in human nature. Therefore by providing individuals with satisfying experiences in activities in which they have a natural desire to engage, physical education presents the opportunity to develop desirable social traits. They key is qualified leadership.

All human beings should experience success, which can be realized through play. Through successful experience in play activities, a person develops self-confidence and finds happiness in achievement. Physical education can provide this satisfying experience by offering a variety of activities and developing the skills necessary for successful achievement.

In a democratic society all individuals should develop a sense of group consciousness and cooperative living, one of the most important objectives of the physical education program. Therefore in various play activities the following factors should be stressed: aid for the less skilled and weaker players, respect for the rights of others, subordination of one person's desires to the will of the group, and realization that cooperative living is essential to the success of society. The individual should be helped to feel that he or she belongs to the group and has the responsibility of directing his or her actions in its behalf. The rules of sportsmanship should be developed and practiced in all activities offered in the program. Courtesy, sympathy, truthfulness, fairness, honesty, respect for authority, and abiding by the rules help promote social efficiency.

THE OBJECTIVES OF ATHLETICS[8]

Although athletics in many cases is theoretically a part of the total physical education program and has the same general objectives as those already discussed for physical education, at the same time it has additional goals that relate directly to the achievement of a high degree of skill and competitive success. In certain situations some physical educators feel that the goals of some athletic programs are not compatible with the goals of physical education. Furthermore, the goals of highly competitive athletics differ in some respects for each educational level and agency programs.

Athletics in the elementary school

The athletics program in the elementary school should stress what is good for the child and provide opportunities for a variety of experiences. All athletic activities should be geared to the development level of the individual child and not just to his/her weight or chronological age. Children at this stage vary greatly in physical and psychological development; therefore an informal program which recognizes individual differences should be initiated.

The program should provide a wide variety of athletic experiences. Physical education activities that are selected should depend on the ability and skill level of each child. There should not be undue concentration on developing skill in just a few sports; nor should children be pressured into conforming to adult standards in a rigid, highly organized, and highly competitive athletic program. Body contact sports, particularly tackle football, are considered by many experts to have no place in programs for children of this age.

Athletic activities should be part of an overall school program, and competent medical supervision should be ensured.

Athletics in the junior high school

The junior high school athletic program should be adapted to the needs of boys and girls in grades 7, 8, and 9. This is a period of transition from elementary school to senior high school and from childhood to adolescence. It is a time when students are trying to understand their bodies, gain independence, achieve adult social status, acquire self-confidence, and establish a system of values. It is a time when an athletic program is needed to meet the abilities and broadening interests of the student.

Physiological maturity is one of the best criteria for determining whether a student is physiologically ready for participation in many interschool athletic sports, particularly body contact sports.

Interscholastic athletics of a varsity type, if offered, should be provided only after the prerequisites of a rich physical education class, adapted, and intramural and extramural program have been developed, and only when special controls in regard to such items as health, facilities, game adaptations, classification

of players, leadership, and officials have been provided.

Athletics in the senior high school

Representative goals of athletics in the senior high school have been stated by the Kent School District in Kent, Washington. They include such objectives as the promotion of physical excellence, an appreciation of competition, achievement by participants of goals such as self-assurance, an understanding of group loyalty and responsibility, an outlet for expression of emotions, ability to integrate various aspects of self (social, emotional, physical and intellectual)

Finals of Hershey's National Track & Field Youth Program. 500 youth from all 50 states and District of Columbia participated.

into action, qualities of good citizenship and other valuable personal qualities, and leadership ability. Goals also include providing an outlet for the release of personal energies in constructive ways, the use of sports as a unifying force for school and community, and the provision for activities that will help students live a balanced life.

Athletics in college, university, and agency programs

The objectives of highly organized athletic programs in many colleges, universities, and agency programs include: the development of excellence in athletic competition, providing a program that is financially self-sufficient, establishing a leadership position in athletics among other colleges and universities, satisfying spectators', athletes', community, and coaches' needs, and providing athletic programs for the gifted athlete. In other colleges and agencies athletics are low key, available for all individuals regardless of skill, and do not depend on spectators and gate receipts for support.

DEVELOPING A MANAGEMENT STRUCTURE THAT WILL ENABLE OBJECTIVES OF PHYSICAL EDUCATION AND ATHLETICS TO BE ACCOMPLISHED

After the goals and objectives for physical education and athletic programs have been identified, a management structure that will contribute to the achievement of these goals should be developed.

The structure refers to the framework whereby such things as titles of positions, role assignments, functions, and relationships are graphically illustrated. The structure implies lines of communication, coordination, and decision making.

Planning, developing, and organizing the structure for a physical education or athletic program are important management responsibilities. Efficient organization and structure result in the proper delegation of authority, effective assignment of responsibilities to staff members, adequate communication among the various units of the organization, and a high degree of morale among staff members. All of these factors determine whether or not the organization's goals are achieved.

PRINCIPLES AND GUIDELINES FOR MANAGEMENT ORGANIZATION AND STRUCTURE

Experts in many areas have developed principles to aid in effective management organization. Some of the most significant principles are given here.

The management structure of an organization should clarify the delegation of authority and responsibility. For the goals of the organization to be met efficiently and successfully, the management must delegate some of its powers to responsible individuals. These powers should be clearly defined to avoid overlapping authority.

Management work may be most effectively organized by function. This "doctrine of unity" maintains that all personnel engaged in a particular type of work should function under a single authority.

Span of control should be considered in organizational structure. The number of subordinates who can be supervised adequately by one individual determines the span of control.

Successful management depends on communication. Communication is essential to effective administration, because it helps avoid duplication and waste and promotes cooperation among departments.

Coordination and cooperation among various departments in an organization are essential to effective management. Coordination of departments keeps them well informed and working together in a complementary manner.

The manager must be an effective leader. An effective leader appreciates both the goals of the organization and the personnel working for the organization. Both are essential.

Staff specialization aids effective management. To achieve their objectives, organizations must perform many different tasks that require the abilities of various area specialists.

Authority must be commensurate with responsibilities, and lines of authority must be clearly drawn. An organization chart is a useful way to illustrate the lines of authority. These lines should be unambiguous.

Organization and social purpose cannot be separated. The structure of an organization is a means to an end and not an end in itself.

There is no single correct form of organization. Such things as size, personnel, and funds available often determine the best organization for a particular situation.

TRANSLATING THE MANAGEMENT STRUCTURE INTO GRAPHIC FORM (ORGANIZATION CHARTS)

Once the type of management structure desired has been determined, the next step is to prepare it in graphic form so it can be easily understood by members of the organization and by other interested individuals. As Parkhouse and Lapin[5] state regarding the woman in athletic administration: "An organization chart is an essential tool to an administrator. First, she must make a complete statement of the organization's objectives. Second, she develops a list of jobs and functions. Third, she determines whether each job is considered a line or staff position."

Charts are frequently used to illustrate and clarify the structure of an organization. These charts clearly depict the management setup of an organization and the key management positions and their functions.

They are used to orient new staff members to their responsibilities and their place in the total structure of the organization. They can also serve as a public relations medium and as a way to evaluate personnel performance. Finally, they are important in establishing accountability for the performance of specific duties of management personnel in an organization.

The procedure for developing an organization chart consists of six steps, according to Petersen and associates.[6]

Identify the objectives of the organization. These objectives determine the structure that needs to be developed. Therefore goals must be identified first.

Arrange objectives into meaningful functional units. This step requires assessing the organization with its differentiated parts and units and organizing it to effect a harmonious and integrated whole. If this step is successfully accomplished, it reduces friction and brings about a closely coordinated, smoothly functioning organization.

Arrange the identified functional units into appropriate management units, such as departments. This step varies in each organization but should represent

Skinfold test, part of Health-Related Physical Fitness Test, Lyons Township High School, LaGrange, Ill.

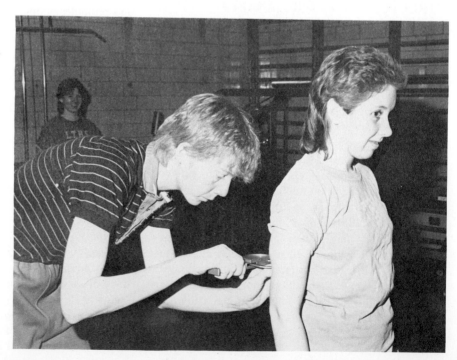

the most effective relationships for achieving the goals of the organization.

Prepare a model of the structure of the organization and give it a trial run. To make sure that the model represents the best management structure for the organization, it should be used initially on a trial basis.

Revise the model in light of input received. Views from personnel within and outside the organization should be sought and the model revised where necessary to achieve the most satisfactory structure possible.

Creative playground provides opportunities for various motoric exercises, Oak View Elementary School, Fairfax, Va.

Evaluate final design and assign persons who work within the organization to appropriate functional units. As a result of this final step, each member of the organization can see how he or she fits into the total plan.

Line and staff organization

The most common type of organization chart is a line and staff chart (see Fig. 2-1). A person in a line position has direct responsibility and authority for a specific objective or objectives of an organization. For example, an assistant director of physical education would be in a line position, with direct responsibility for duties assigned by the director. In turn, the assistant director would report directly to the director. A person in a staff position has an indirect relationship to a specific objective or objectives of an organization. Staff personnel often have advisory positions or are persons who are not responsible for carrying out the central mission of the organization. An example would be a ticket manager in the athletic administration of a college program. Staff personnel do not have authority over line personnel. Line positions are related to and derive authority from the chief administrator. Staff positions are usually indicated by broken lines and line positions by solid lines.

Line personnel are depicted in a vertical line in an organization chart reflecting the hierarchy of power, whereas staff personnel are depicted in a horizontal line.

In small management units such as departments of physical education or athletics that have only a few persons there is frequently little distinction between line and staff since very few, if any, staff positions per se exist.

FORMAL AND INFORMAL ORGANIZATION AND STRUCTURE

Organizational theory and structure require that first, there must be a need for an organization to exist, and second, the organization must know the goals it is trying to achieve. To accomplish these objectives a structure should be provided that enables the management to organize, direct, plan, motivate, and evaluate. These tasks can be performed through either a formal or an informal organization.

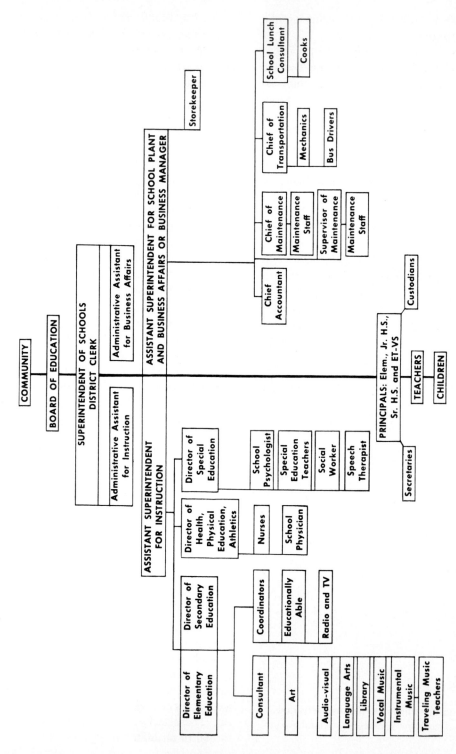

Fig. 2-1. The operational organization chart clarifies channels of communication for employees of school district. The superintendent administers school district policies through assistant superintendents, and they in turn use intermediate staff members in the process.

Formal organization

A formal organization is based on a hierarchal job organization, with tasks assigned by superior to subordinate, an organization seen in most organization charts with their job-task hierarchy and communications network (Fig. 2-1). Such an organization is concerned first with the positions to be filled and tasks to be accomplished and then with the persons to be assigned to these positions and tasks. Clearly delineated lines of authority and formal rules and regulations are earmarks of formal organization, as are dependence, obedience, discipline, reward, and chain of command.

Formal organization is used because it provides a clear picture of the positions that exist and the tasks to be performed. It represents a way to get things done by the use of authority. It places subordinates in a position where they must do what they are instructed to do; thus things get done. It assumes that control of behavior is accomplished through rational judgment and that the manager is the person most qualified to solve problems. It assumes that people should be instruments of production. It is strictly authoritarian.

Informal organization

Informal organization realizes that many relationships exist that cannot be illustrated in an organization chart. In other words, things get done outside the formal relationships that a chart reflects. It assumes that relationships occur in many informal settings where ideas are generated, productivity is enhanced, and high morale is developed.

Those who advocate informal organization contend this is how things are actually accomplished and thus oppose the formal, authoritarian type of organization. They also maintain that people who have rank in an organization do not always behave rationally nor do they have complete access to reliable information at all times. These advocates of informal organization also say that members of an organization are not merely instruments of production but instead have desires, values, needs, and aspirations that must be taken into consideration.

Modern theories of organization and structure indicate a shift away from the formal organization and structure toward the informal type with a greater human relations perspective. These modern theories are

College students engage in racquetball, University of Nevada, Las Vegas.

based on the fact that although most persons agree that some type of organizational framework is usually needed, most individuals are capable of some self-direction.

One aspect of informal organization is the formation of subgroups that do not appear on organization charts. For example, employee unions represent an important group with whom managers must work. In some organizations committees, commissions, and task forces also represent influential subgroups. Therefore the management must understand and appreciate what a staff member wants from his or her position, whether it is high wages, security, good working conditions, interesting work, or some other condition.

Modern theories of management are moving more and more toward a participatory philosophy, where both staff members and managers are involved in many organizational decisions. Employees will better identify with an organization if they are involved in the decision-making process.

MANAGEMENT STRUCTURES FOR PHYSICAL EDUCATION AND ATHLETIC PROGRAMS

The management structures currently used for physical education and athletic programs in many elementary and secondary schools, colleges and universities, and community organizations are discussed on the following pages.

The organization and structure of physical education and athletics in elementary and secondary schools (Fig. 2-2)

The school district is the basic management unit for the operation of elementary and secondary schools and is a quasi-municipal corporation established by the state. In the United States this basic educational unit ranges from a one-teacher rural system to a large metropolitan system serving thousands of pupils. A system may be an independent governmental unit or part of a state government or county or other local administrative unit. The governing body of the system is the school board. The chief administrative officer is the superintendent of schools.

The board of education* is the legal management authority created by the state legislature for each school district. The responsibility of the board is to act on behalf of the residents of the district it represents. It has the duty of appraising and planning the educational program on a local basis. It selects executive personnel and performs duties essential to the successful operation of the schools within the district. The board develops policies that are legal and in the interest of the people it serves. It devises financial means within the legal framework to support the cost of the educational plan. It keeps its constituents informed of the effectiveness and needs of the total program.

The key management personnel in a school system usually consist of the superintendent of schools, assistant superintendent, clerk of the board, principal, supervisor, and director.

Superintendent of schools

Within a large school system a superintendent has overall charge of the school program. Associate or assistant superintendents are in charge of technical detail, management, or various phases of the program, such as secondary education. There is also a superintendent's position associated with smaller schools. These officers are known as district superintendents; they are responsible for many schools extending over a wide geographical area.

The superintendent's job is to carry out the educational policies of the state and the board of education. The superintendent acts as the leader in educational matters in the community and also provides the board of education with the professional advice it needs as a lay organization.

Assistant superintendent for business services or school business manager

The business manager serves as director of business affairs and of operation and maintenance of buildings and grounds, usually directly supervising the business office staff and the building service and maintenance staff and indirectly supervising the custodial staff. He or she may perform the duties of the

---

*The term *board of education* is used in this discussion although *school committee, community-school boards,* and *board of directors* are used in some sections of the country.

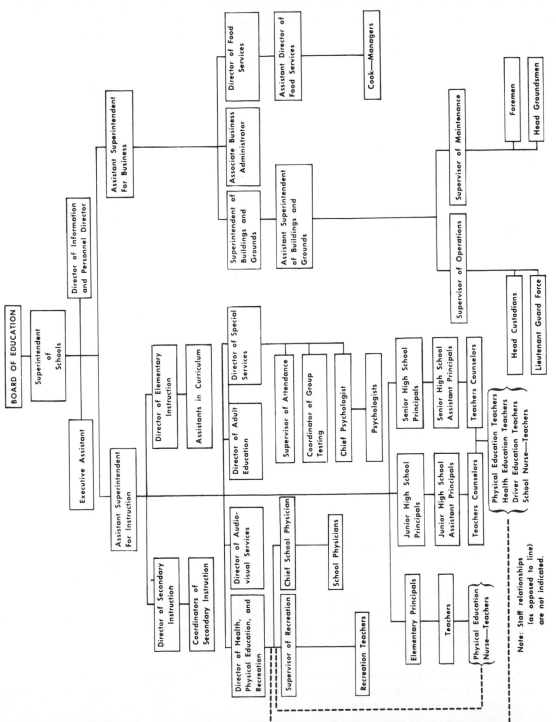

Fig. 2-2. Organization chart for public school system.

superintendent as directed in the superintendent's absence.

Assistant superintendent or director of instructional services

The director of instruction directly supervises the divisions of elementary education, secondary education, adult education, health and physical education, music education, vocational and practical arts, summer school education, and in-service training of teachers. He or she is involved in developing curriculum materials, organizing and supervising instruction, and teaching. The director of instruction may perform the duties of the superintendent of schools as directed in the superintendent's absence.

Assistant superintendent or director of personnel services

The director of personnel supervises both professional and nonprofessional employees and recruits and interviews candidates for positions. He or she is usually responsible for all pupil personnel services, guidance and psychological services, handicapped children and special services, as well as attendance and adjustment, including pupil accounting.

Clerk of the board

The clerk of the board of education is usually under the direction of the superintendent of schools. He or she has custody of the seal of the board, notifies members of the board of regular and special meetings, and has charge of files and records of the board. The clerk sees that all files and records are properly maintained, presents a periodic financial statement, and supervises accounting for tuition pupils.

Principal

The position of principal is similar to that of the superintendent; it differs mainly in the extent of responsibility. Whereas the superintendent is usually in charge of all the schools within a particular community, the principal is in charge of one particular school. The duties of the principal include executing educational policy as outlined by the superintendent, appraising the educational offering, making periodic reports on various aspects of the program, directing the instructional program, promoting good relationships between the community and the school, and supervising the maintenance of the physical plant.

Supervisor

The supervisor is generally responsible for improving instruction in a specific subject area, although sometimes a supervisor is responsible for the entire elementary or secondary instructional program.

Director

The director is responsible for functions of a specific subject matter area or a particular educational level. The responsibilities have administrative and supervisory implications.

Director of physical education and athletics. In most cases at the secondary school level the positions of director of physical education and director of athletics are consolidated into one position. There are communities, however, where the two responsibilities are separated into two positions.

In many cases the director of physical education has responsibilities that relate to grades K through 12. There is usually no formal structure per se for athletics at the elementary school level.

The director of physical education and athletics provides leadership, programs, facilities, and other essentials in these special areas. Specific responsibilities include the following: coordinating physical education and athletics; supervising inside and outside physical education facilities, equipment, and supplies concerned with special areas (this responsibility includes maintenance, safety, and replacement operations); maintaining liaison with community groups (this responsibility includes such duties as holding educational meetings to interpret and improve the program, scheduling school facilities for community groups, and serving on various community committees for youth needs); preparing periodic reports regarding areas of activity; supervising total physical education program (class, adapted, intramurals, extramurals, and varsity interscholastic or intercollegiate athletics); administering schedules, practice and game facilities, insurance, and equipment.

High school athletic councils

In some high schools athletic councils are formed to serve in an advisory capacity to boards of education and the administrative officers of the school. Membership includes such personnel as principals, athletic directors, physical education directors, students, athletic trainers, and coaches. These councils perform such functions as make and recommend policy, consider athletic problems, approve awards, determine eligibility regulations, approve budgets, and see that the athletic program is administered according to acceptable educational standards.

The organization and structure of physical education in colleges and universities
(Fig. 2-3)

A college or university is characterized by a governing board, usually known as a board of trustees, which is granted extensive powers of control by legislative enactment or by its charter. The governing board of a college usually delegates many of its powers to the management and faculty of the institution. The management officers, usually headed by a president, are commonly organized into such principal areas of administration as academic, student personnel services, business, and public relations. The members of the faculty are usually organized into colleges, schools, divisions, and departments of instruction and research. In large institutions one frequently finds a university senate that is the voice of the faculty and serves as a liaison between faculty and administration. The area of physical education can have school, division, or department status. The duties of a dean, director, or chairperson correspond in many ways to a principal, director, or chairperson in a high school.

Physical education is organized as one management unit for men and women in a majority of colleges and universities in the United States. The management unit may be either a college, school, division, or department; the manager in charge of the physical education program may be called a dean, director, supervisor, or chairperson. In many institutions of higher learning this manager is responsible directly to the president or to a dean, but in a few instances, he or she is responsible to the director of

athletics. (In some colleges, athletics are included as part of the same management setup with the rest of the physical education program.) In some cases the duties of the athletic director and the manager of the physical education program are assigned to the same person. Many colleges and universities have intramural athletic directors, and in most of these institutions intramural athletics are a part of the physical education program.

The various departments of physical education throughout the country have many different plans of organization. Several years ago it was common to see such titles as Department of Physical Culture or Hygiene. The term *physical training* was also used as a descriptive term for the work performed in this special area.

Today, one also sees a variety of titles associated with physical education, such as the ''Physical Education Department,'' ''Department of Ergonomics and Physical Education,'' the ''Department of Biokinetics,'' ''Health and Physical Education Department,'' the ''Health, Physical Education, and Recreation Division,'' ''School of Health, Physical Education, Recreation and Dance,'' and ''College of Health, Physical Education, Recreation and Dance.'' Camping and safety may also be included.

The titles given also show to some degree the particular work performed within these phases of the total program. In some schools and colleges physical education is organized into a separate unit with the various physical activities—intramural, extramural, and interschool or intercollegiate athletics—comprising this division. In other schools and colleges health and physical education are combined in one management unit.

The duties of the head of a physical education department may include coordinating the activities within the particular unit, requisitioning supplies and equipment, preparing schedules, making budgets, holding meetings, teaching classes, coaching, hiring and dismissing personnel, developing community relations, supervising the intramural, extramural, and intercollegiate athletic programs, evaluating and appraising the required class program, representing the department at meetings, and reporting to superiors.

Professional programs in physical education are a

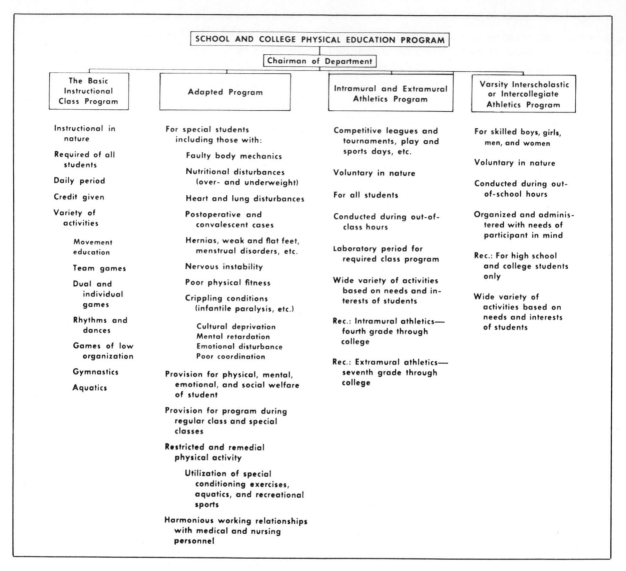

Fig. 2-3. Organization chart for school and college physical education program.

part of the physical education program at both the undergraduate and the graduate levels. Physical education and health *education* are frequently combined into the same administrative unit, but health *services,* as a general rule, are not organized as part of the physical education unit. Physical education is commonly responsible for the management of recreation programs for both students and faculty.

Surveys conducted indicate that most 2-year colleges require two hours weekly for one-half unit credit in physical education. Objectives in most cases stress the students' competence in maintaining good health and balanced personal adjustment. Some colleges are seriously attempting to meet these objectives, but others have not yet developed their programs sufficiently to accomplish this task. Athletics appear to be an especially strong point of physical education at the junior college level because of student and public interest. Some colleges provide broad programs of team competition in many sports, whereas others are limited.

Interviews with deans of instruction, faculty, and students of 2-year colleges indicate that they prefer to have one department chairperson in charge of both the health and physical education programs. The department chairperson usually is responsible to the dean of students or dean of instruction.

Physical education programs in colleges and in schools are commonly organized into four component parts: (1) the required class or basic instruction program, (2) the adapted program or program for the handicapped, (3) the intramural and extramural athletics program, and (4) the varsity interschool or intercollegiate athletics program. (Elementary schools usually do not have intramural and extramural athletics programs in the primary grades or varsity interscholastic athletics in either primary or intermediate grades.)

The *required class* or *basic instruction program* provides physical education for all students and teaches such things as the rules, strategies, and skills in the various activities that make up the program.

The *adapted program* meets the needs of individuals who are temporarily or permanently unable to take part in the regular physical education program because of some physical inadequacy, functional defect capable of being improved through exercise, or other deficiency.

The *intramural and extramural athletics program* is voluntary physical education for all students within one or a few schools or colleges that includes competitive leagues and tournaments and play and sports days and acts as a laboratory period for the required class program. In the intramural program students of only one school or college participate in activities, whereas in the extramural program students from more than one school or college participate.

The *varsity interschool* or *intercollegiate athletics program* is designed for the skilled individuals in one school or college who compete with skilled individuals from another school or college in selected physical education activities.

The organization and structure of athletics in colleges and universities

Because athletic programs are organized and administratively structured differently in colleges and universities than in high schools, the organization of athletics in colleges and universities requires further elaboration and discussion.

The athletic director

The athletic director in colleges and universities is responsible for the administration of the athletic program. In large institutions this is a full-time position, whereas in small institutions it may include other responsibilities involved with physical education and coaching.

Some of the key duties of many athletic directors include scheduling athletic contests and preparing contracts, arranging for team travel, supervising the coaching staff, making arrangements for home athletic contests, representing the institution at athletic association and league meetings, securing officials, checking and preparing eligibility player lists, preparing the athletic budget, and overseeing facility supervision and maintenance.

Faculty athletic committee

Most colleges with athletic programs of significant size have a faculty athletic committee. This committee serves in an advisory capacity to the president of the institution. In some cases, there are two such committees, one for women's athletics and one for men's athletics. The membership of such committees frequently includes representatives from the faculty, management, students, coaches, athletes, and alumni. The athletic director is usually a nonvoting member. The faculty athletic committee is involved in functions such as approving athletic budgets, developing eligibility standards, approving financial awards, authorizing schedules, acting on problems that arise, developing athletic policies, investigating Title IX infractions, reviewing the scholarship program, and deciding to what extent certain sports should be added or eliminated.

State College Board of Trustees

President of the College

Vice President

or

Dean of the College

Associate Dean or Head —————— Executive Committee: All Department Chairmen

School of Physical Education, Health, and Recreation

Chairman, Department of Physical Education, Men
- Advisory Committee
- Basic Instruction for Men
- Undergraduate Professional Curriculum
- Graduate Professional Curriculum
- Intramural Sports
- Supervision of Sports Facilities
- Supervision of Aquatics
- Faculty-Staff and Community Instructional Services
- Research Laboratory

Chairman, Department of Physical Education, Women
- Advisory Committee
- Basic Instruction for Women
- Undergraduate Professional Curriculum
- Graduate Professional Curriculum
- Intramural Sports
- Extramural Sports
- Dance Productions
- Faculty-Staff and Community Instructional Services
- Research Laboratory

Chairman, Department of Health Education
- Advisory Committee
- Undergraduate Professional Curriculum
- Service Courses in First Aid
- State Field Service
- Coordination With Community Health Services
- Health Education Institutes and Workshops
- Public and Private School Consultations

Chairman, Department of Recreation
- Advisory Committee
- Undergraduate Professional Curriculum
- Service Courses, General Elementary Teachers
- Campus Recreation
- State Field Service
- Administration of Outdoor Education Center
- Recreation Institutes and Workshops
- Coordination with Community Recreation Services
- Public, Private, and Commercial Recreation Consultations

Chairman, Department of Intercollegiate Athletics, Men (Director of Athletics)
- Advisory Committee
- Administration of Intercollegiate Athletics
- Coordination of Athletic Coaching Courses
- Coordination of Intercollegiate Athletic Schedules
- Coordination of Teaching Services of Coaches
- Coordination of Maintenance and Use of Athletic Facilities
- Coordination of Conference Affiliation, National Collegiate Athletic Association, American Amateur Athletic Union, etc.

Fig. 2-4. Organization chart for school of physical education, health, and recreation.

Faculty representative

Many colleges and universities have faculty athletic representatives. These are members of the faculty who represent the college or university at national association meetings such as the National Association of Intercollegiate Athletics (NAIA) and the National Collegiate Athletic Association (NCAA), as well as the conference to which the institution belongs. This faculty representative also is used in many institutions to check the eligibility of players in various sports, to attend faculty athletic committee meetings as a nonvoting member, and to give periodic reports to the faculty athletic committee.

Currently being discussed in some institutions of higher learning is the question of who should represent the women's athletic programs. Should the faculty representative be a man or woman? Most women feel strongly that a woman faculty representative should represent women's athletic programs.

Structure of the college or university athletic department

According to Parkhouse and Lapin,[5] there are four basic types of structure for athletic departments.

The first combines men and women in one department. A man is usually the athletic director, and a woman is an associate or assistant athletic director. In some cases the woman is called coordinator of women's athletics.

The second provides separate structures for men's and women's athletics. Each has its own athletic director, staff, and support services (Fig. 2-4).

The third provides that the athletic director is in charge of revenue-producing sports, that is, football, basketball, and ice hockey (frequently a man). An associate director is the business manager. Another associate director is in charge of all nonrevenue producing sports, both men's and women's (frequently a woman).

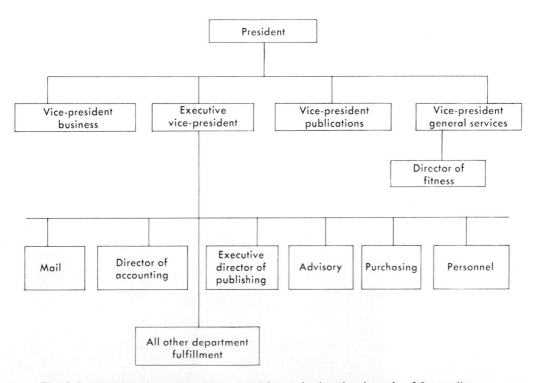

Fig. 2-5. Administrative structure of industrial organization showing role of fitness director.

The fourth brings together what were originally separate departments of physical education, intramurals, club sports, recreation, and athletics. All of these are combined into a single department.

The organization and structure of physical education in industry, health clubs, and organizations other than schools and colleges

Physical education programs exist in settings other than schools and colleges. Because of the current interest in health and physical fitness these settings are growing in number. The management structure for such programs varies with each organization (Fig. 2-5). In executive fitness programs in industry, for example, the physical education program may be structured so that it is responsible to the medical supervisor, president, or another officer in the organization. In health clubs the physical education program is often directly under the supervision of the owner or manager of the establishment. In correctional institutions the physical education program is usually under the direct supervision of the warden.

Because there is such a wide variation in the administration structure of physical education programs

in these organizations, it is impossible to describe a standard organization and structure. In a school or college some similarity exists between the type of management structure in use and the personnel who are identified with the structure. However, in health clubs, industry, and many other organizations the unique makeup and desires of each organization determine the structure.

These physical education and fitness programs, other than the ones in schools and colleges, are designed for the members of or clientele served by the organization. A few are conducted for profit, such as health clubs, whereas most are conducted for the benefit of the members, such as for the employees in industry.

These programs provide various activities, including stress testing to determine exercise tolerance, prescriptive exercises to develop and maintain physical fitness, a variety of sports and physical education activities, highly organized sports competition, and other forms of activity.

Equipment and facilities may include sophisticated Nautilus and Universal exercise equipment and facilities such as gymnasiums, exercise rooms, swimming pools, playfields, tennis courts, and jogging tracks.

College students in yoga class, University of Nevada, Las Vegas.

The physical education personnel involved in these programs include people trained in physical education specialities such as exercise physiology, biomechanics, athletic management, coaching, athletic training, and sports writing and public relations.

CONSIDERATIONS FOR A FUNCTIONAL AND EFFICIENT ORGANIZATION AND STRUCTURE

Developing a functional structure means delegating authority, resolving organizational conflicts, making meaningful decisions, and forming sound policies.

Delegating authority

The wise manager delegates responsibilities and with them the authority to make the necessary decisions for carrying out such responsibilities.

Most managers are overwhelmed with their assigned duties. In many cases it is humanly impossible for one person to discharge all of these duties. Therefore it is important to delegate some to qualified persons who can perform them efficiently.

There should be a clear understanding between the manager and the person to whom the duties are being delegated. The latter must be willing to assume such responsibilities and must know exactly what he or she is responsible for.

In physical education programs the director of physical education or chairperson often delegates to others responsibilities for the adapted program, intramurals, extramurals, and varsity sports. The director of athletics frequently delegates authority to the athletic trainer and to the coaches.

The manager should recognize that in delegating responsibilities, however, he or she is still responsible for the overall functioning of the unit, such as a school division, department, or program.

Resolving organizational conflicts

Within programs and departments conflicts do occur. Wherever human beings are involved, conflicts develop around such human needs as security, status, esteem, or self-actualization. When certain needs are not satisfied, conflict may arise. Persons have basic needs that can represent physical needs, such as the need for proper bodily comfort, psychological needs,

such as a feeling of belonging and recognition, or social needs, such as the desire to work with a certain group of people.

Organizational conflicts, as far as possible, should be solved effectively by the manager. This means creating an environment in which employees want to work and can achieve self-esteem and self-actualization. It means providing opportunities for personal growth. It means keeping channels of communication open at all times both to stifle rumors and to learn about employee complaints. It means making work as interesting as possible to guard against monotony. It means involving employees in decisions that affect their wellbeing.

Organizational conflicts are kept to a minimum if the management is aware of human needs and tries to satisfy these needs as far as possible.

Making and implementing meaningful decisions and assessing the results

Decision making in the management process requires that certain steps be followed. The traditional problem-solving approach includes the recognition of the problem, identifying the alternatives, gathering and organizing facts, weighing alternatives, and finally arriving at a decision. Management should not stop at the point of reaching a decision; it is essential to go on to the stages that involve implementation and assessment. The sequential stages of this process are well stated by Burr and associates.[3]

Deliberating. The problem is discussed, facts on the problem are gathered, and the problem is carefully analyzed.

Decision making. As a result of the deliberation a decision is made. Alternatives are carefully weighed, and a choice is made based on the facts.

Programming. After the decision is made, the program is developed so that it is ready for implementation. Questions are asked and actions taken with regard to the resources that are available, the planning that needs to be done, the budget, equipment, and material requirements that exist, and the needs in regard to staff and so on. In other words, information is researched that will provide a successful program and the right direction, in light of the decision that was made.

Stimulating. After the programming has been developed, it is set into operation. This requires the involvement of people, arousing interest, obtaining commitments, and initiating action. Motivation needs to be encouraged and attitudes developed in this process.

Coordinating. To effectively implement a program requires the coordination of staff efforts, material resources, proper communication, and other essentials that will assure that the program will be successfully launched.

Appraising. The last stage in the continuum is evaluating and appraising all stages of the process and the results obtained. This is an attempt to analyze where the process was successful or where it failed and the reasons for the success or failure. The information gathered will be used in future endeavors.

Forming sound policies

Policies are essential to the efficient management of any department, school, business, or other organization. Without them, there is little to guide the activities and conduct of the establishment in the pursuit of its goals. With well-reasoned policies the organization can function efficiently and effectively, and its members will better understand what is expected of them.

Policies are guides to action. Policies reflect procedures that, when adhered to, fulfill the best interests of the organization and the purposes for which it exists. If properly selected and developed, policies enable each member of an organization to know what duties are to be performed, the type of behavior that will result in the greatest productivity for the establishment, the best way the department goals can be accomplished, and the procedure by which accountability can be established and evaluated.

The efficient management of a physical education department requires the establishment of sound policies if it is to achieve its goals. During a school survey several years ago, the office of a director of physical education was visited. When he was asked to supply policies under which the department was managed, the director replied that no policies existed. Instead, the manager indicated that he dealt with each problem as it occurred. There were no set guidelines

established in advance, no written policies. As a result, chaos reigned in this program. Each faculty member had his or her own way of handling such things as student excuses from class, testing the skill level of boys and girls, and transporting players to athletic events.

The policies of the federal government are reflected in the laws of the land. They are developed in Congress and, after judicial and executive review and approval, become established policies by which the citizens and organizations of this country are guided. As a result, each person and organization knows whether selling heroin is legal or whether discriminating against people of another race is legal. Just as the national government has policies to guide the actions of its citizens and organizations, so also do the state and municipal divisions of government.

State and local systems of education also have established policies that provide guidelines for such important management considerations as the number of days school will be in session, what children and youth must attend school, and for whom educational programs are to be provided. Similarly, just as governmental organizations and their subdivisions establish policies to guide the workings of their organizations, so should physical education departments have policies to guide their actions and help achieve their objectives.

Management policies are statements of procedures that represent the legalistic framework under which the organization operates. As such, they are not changed frequently but have some sense of permanence. Therefore they are not developed on short notice or hastily written.

On the other hand, rules and regulations are usually more specific and are formulated to carry out the policy that has been established. For example, an established policy of a school might be that all athletes will be transported to interschool contests by school-owned transportation. Rules and regulations then could be established for such purposes as spelling out the nature and type of such transportation, the students who must comply with the policy, and when and how they will comply. Generally, rules and regulations can be changed much more readily than policies. In fact, some managers develop rules and regu-

Dance, Oak View Elementary
School, Fairfax, Va.

lations instead of policies so that they can be changed more easily.

Although policies are considered and formulated carefully, they should be reviewed periodically in light of any new developments that occur. For example, at present some schools are providing faculty and students with new freedoms, rights, and privileges that make some existing policies outdated and obsolete. Therefore change is needed.

How policy is developed. Policy emanates as a result of many phenomena. For example, the Constitution of the United States sets forth various conditions that affect policy development in organizations throughout the country. Educators, for example, must comply with such conditions as equal rights for all in the public schools, separation of church and state, various conditions inherent in the democratic process, and those included in Title IX.

Because education is a state responsibility, the state government also issues policies that must be adhered to by local education authorities. These policies include such items as the number of days schools must be in session, certification qualifications, subject requirements, and minimum salary schedules for teachers. Within the framework of these policies or guide-

lines established by federal and state agencies, however, local education authorities (such as boards of education) are permitted freedom to develop their own policies. Thus they establish policies on whether students can drive their automobiles to school and whether teachers can have sabbatical leaves. The department of physical education can develop policies within the framework of the higher echelons of authority previously mentioned. Sometimes local policies conflict with state policies; then local policies are declared invalid.

Policy is developed in many ways in physical education departments. In some organizations it is done autocratically with a manager establishing policy unilaterally. The process is devoid of deliberations and suggestions from the members of the organization. The trend now, however, is toward greater involvement of staff members in developing policy.

As a general rule, the cliché ''many heads are better than one'' is true in policy development. Policies must be carefully researched and thought through before being written. Therefore it is usually better to involve many people who look at education problems affecting policies from many different angles.

Although staff members may participate in policy

Weight lifting, Lyons
Township High School,
LaGrange, Ill.

development, it should be recognized that the formulation and development of policy is different from the execution of the policy. Execution of policy is usually a management responsibility and should be recognized as such.

Writing policies. Before policies are written, much research must be done to determine what goes into the substance of that policy. This can be done in several ways. One method is for the director of physical education to appoint a committee to research carefully and to recommend policy to the management.

When the committee has been formed to recommend policy, it will want to investigate the facts thoroughly. It may decide to research the state policies regarding this problem, what other organizations are doing, what policies already exist, the stand taken by selected national professional and athletic associations, views of other managers, the position of the American Civil Liberties Union, and other sources of information. After gathering all these facts, the committee will want to consider them carefully and then make a recommendation. If the recommendation is approved, the director of physical education may then recommend it to his or her superior for approval, who in turn, if he or she agrees, may recommend it to the board or other group for its final approval as the policy governing the organization.

The policy that finally emanates from the committee should be written clearly and concisely. There should be no ambiguities or possibilities for misinterpretation of what is intended by the policy statement. The statement of policy formulated by the committee should be reviewed carefully by the staff members and management to further determine that the statement says clearly what the organization's position is on this particular issue.

When policy is needed. Only the most important items facing the department of physical education should have policy statements. Policies on trivial matters should not be carried on the books, because confusion and failure to adhere to many of the policies can result when they are not known or understood. Furthermore, with too many policies, the important ones may be obscured by the proliferation of those less important. It is usually better to have only a few carefully researched policies that cover major management functions. The other matters, if they need attention, can be covered by rules and regulations or in some other manner.

SUMMARY

One of the functions of management is to develop an organizational structure through which the goals of physical education and athletics can be accomplished in an effective manner. The physical education and athletic objectives that are to be achieved include physical, motor, cognitive, and social development. To meet the needs of students the objectives of athletics will vary at each educational level.

Management structures for physical education and athletics are organized differently for elementary and secondary schools, colleges and universities, health clubs and organizations other than schools and colleges, and in industry. It is also important to recognize that an informal as well as a formal management organization and structure affect most programs of physical education and athletics. Furthermore, functions such as proper delegation of authority, decision making, and policy development and implementation should be considered when developing an organizational structure.

SELF-ASSESSMENT TESTS

These tests are to assist students in determining if material and competencies presented in this chapter have been mastered.

1. You have been asked by the chief manager of an organization to identify the objectives that physical education and athletics will be able to achieve for the members of that organization and to show how the management structure you have recommended will help achieve these objectives. Prepare a written statement for the chief manager of the organization that answers his or her questions.
2. Write an essay on the topic "Developing and Organizing the Structure for a Physical Education Program and for an Athletic Program is an Important Management Responsibility."
3. Cite at least six principles that should be observed in developing an effective management organization, and show how each of the following elements is essential to a sound management structure: delegation of authority, span of control, communication, and staff specialization.
4. You are an outside consultant with expertise in management organization and structure who has been hired by an organization with a physical education and athletic program to give advice about whether it should have a formal or informal structure. What advice would you give to this organization? Defend your decision.
5. Prepare a model for the management structure of a physical education or athletic program in an organization of your choice, and show why it is a sound structure.
6. Draw a structural organization chart for your college, showing the various management divisions. Discuss the responsibilities of each of the divisions.
7. Tell how the management organization and structure you recommended in item 4 would provide for each of the following: *delegating authority* to the heads of the instructional program, the program for the handicapped, intramurals and extramurals, and varsity athletics; *resolving a conflict* between the director of athletics and the director of intramurals; *determining budget allocations* for athletics; and *formulating policies* regarding Title IX.

REFERENCES

1. Barrow, H.M.: Man and movement: principles of physical education, Philadelphia, 1983, Lea & Febiger.
2. Bucher, C.A., and Prentice, W.E.: Fitness for college and life, St. Louis, 1985, Times Mirror/Mosby College Publishing.
3. Burr, J.B., et al.: Elementary school administration, Boston, 1963, Allyn & Bacon, Inc.
4. Gensemer, R.E.: Physical education: perspectives, inquiry, applications, Philadelphia, 1985, Saunders College Publishing.
5. Parkhouse, B.L., and Lapin, J.: The woman in athletic administration, Santa Monica, Calif., 1980, Goodyear Publishing Company, Inc.
6. Petersen, E., et al.: Business organization and management, Homewood, Ill., 1962, Richard D. Irwin, Inc.
7. Sage, G.H.: Motor learning and control—a neuropsychological approach, Dubuque, Iowa, 1984, Wm. C. Brown Publishers.
8. Vander Zwaag, H.J.: Sport management in schools and colleges, New York, 1984, John Wiley & Sons, Inc.

SUGGESTED READINGS

• Jewett, A.E., and Bain, L.L.: The curriculum process in physical education, Dubuque, Iowa, 1985, Wm. C. Brown (Publishers).
Contains theoretical and practical considerations for the implementation of physical education programs in school settings. Examines various curriculum models and the process involved in developing curricula materials. Indicates goals and objectives to be considered in the development of a curriculum.

• La Point, J.D.: Organization and management of sport, Dubuque, Iowa, 1980, Kendall/Hunt Publishing Company.
Provides an overview of many aspects of athletics involved in competitive sports. Discusses athletic problems encountered by athletes, parents, coaches, athletic directors, and school board members. Conceptualizes a philosophy of competitive athletics.

• Lawson, H.A.: Invitation to physical education, Champaign, Ill., 1984, Human Kinetics Publishers, Inc.
Covers such areas as qualifications that a person should have to make a success of physical education, describes nature and scope of the physical education profession, discusses challenges facing physical educators, identifies the organization of knowledge in the physical education profession into areas such as biomechanics, philosophy, physiology, psychology, history, and sociology, and provides a general overview of physical education as a career.

• Oxendine, J.B.: Psychology of motor learning, Englewood Cliffs, N.J., 1984, Prentice-Hall, Inc.
Covers the body of knowledge regarding motor skill learning including areas such as its nature and scope, learning theories and models, reinforcement and feedback, transfer of skill, retention and forgetting, readiness, arousal, practice, visual and kinesthetic perception, and reaction and movement speed.

• Siedentop, D.: Physical education, introductory analysis, Dubuque, Iowa, 1980, Wm. C. Brown Publishers.
Provides an introduction to physical education by discussing areas such as its historical foundations, its academic viability, programming trends, aims and objectives, and projects various ideas that will enable this field of endeavor to meet the challenges of the times.

• Zeigler, E.F.: Physical education and sport—an introduction, Philadelphia, 1982, Lea & Febiger.
Covers many aspects of physical education that a person going into this field needs to know and understand including discussions of the effects of physical activity on the human organism, sociocultural and behavioral aspects, motor learning and development, mechanical and muscular human functions, management theory and practice, program development, and measurement and evaluation.

Part Two
Management of Physical Education and Athletic Programs

Chapter Three

Physical Education Instructional Programs

Instructional Objectives and Competencies to be Achieved
After reading this chapter the student should be able to

- Provide a description of the nature, scope, purpose, and worth of instructional programs in physical education.
- Outline management guidelines for preschool, elementary school, secondary school, and college and university physical education instructional programs.
- Describe management instructional strategies for physical education programs resulting from Title IX legislation.
- Justify the need for certain management procedures, such as scheduling, time allotment for classes, size of classes, instructional loads, class management, uniforms, taking roll, selecting physical education activities, grouping, and area of student involvement.
- Understand the professional nature of selected management problems in instructional programs such as having physical education required or elective, substitutions, credit, class attendance, excuses, instruction by specialist or classroom teacher, dressing and showering, records, and evaluation.
- Discuss what is meant by an adapted program of physical education.
- Describe the various elements that make up an individualized education program (IEP).
- Describe administrative procedures to follow in order to comply with and implement Public Law 94-142.

Thus far in this text we have concerned ourselves with the nature and scope of management as they relate to physical education and athletics. We have also discussed the objectives these programs are designed to achieve and the organizational structure needed to accomplish these goals. This chapter now looks at instructional programs and identifies guidelines and problems associated with these instructional programs.

Years ago the basic instructional program was graphically represented as the base of an isosceles triangle. The parts above the base were the adapted, intramural, and extramural programs, and the apex of the triangle was the varsity athletic program. What the isosceles triangle symbolized is still true today. To have a sound physical education program it is essential to have a firm and solid base.

The instructional program in physical education is

the place to teach skills, strategies, understandings, and essential knowledge concerning the relation of physical activity to physical, mental, emotional, and social development. It is also a place to get participants to achieve an optimum state of physical fitness.

Skills should be taught from a scientific approach, so that the various biomechanical factors that affect movement are understood clearly by the participant. Demonstrations, super-8 films, loop films, models, slide films, videotapes, posters, and other visual aids and materials can help in instruction.

The material presented throughout the school life of the student should be sequential in development and progressive in application. A physical fitness program should also be developmental, starting with the individual's present state of fitness and gradually moving to a higher level of fitness.

Performance objectives should be established for individual student achievement. When boys and girls advance from one grade to another, they should have achieved certain objectives in various physical education activities, just as they master various levels of skills and understandings in other subjects.

Physical education should involve more than physical activity. As the participant understands more fully the importance of sports and activities in life, what happens to the human body during exercise, the relation of physical activity to one's biological, psychological, and sociological development, the history of various activities, and the role of physical activity in the cultures of the world, physical education acquires more intellectual respectability and meaning.

Just as textbooks are used in other courses in the educational system, so should they be used in physical education in a school program, with regular assignments given. Textbooks not only should contain material on physical skills but also should cover the subject matter of physical education.

Records that follow a student from grade to grade should be kept throughout his or her school life. These records will indicate the degree to which the objectives have been achieved by the student, his or her physical status, skill achievement, knowledge about the field, and social conduct, all of which help interpret what physical education has done for the student and what still needs to be done. There should

Karate class, University of Nevada, Las Vegas.

also be homework in physical education to help master subject matter, improve skills, and achieve physical fitness.

The basic instructional physical education period cannot be conducted in a "hit-or-miss" fashion. It must be planned in accordance with the needs and interests of the individuals it serves.

SCHOOL AND COLLEGE PHYSICAL EDUCATION PROGRAMS

Physical education programs in schools and colleges have had a prominent place in educational systems since the turn of the century. These programs exist at the preschool, elementary school, junior high school, senior high school, and college and university educational levels.

Preschool physical education programs

The concept of early schooling is no longer regarded as a custodial or compensatory undertaking. Instead it is viewed as a necessary provision for the normal growth and development of children. This change has come about because of research on the growth and development of children from birth to 6 years, as well as the change in family life, as indicated by such developments as more mothers entering the workforce. Research by such professionals as psychologists and sociologists has indicated that the early years are crucial for the child intellectually, physically, and socially. In light of such developments, play schools and nursery schools have gained wide popularity.

Preschool educational programs involve indoor and outdoor play-learning activities. Physical education activities include the development of fundamental movement skills, fitness and self-testing activities, music and rhythmic activities, and rhymes and story plays. The program of selected physical activities helps the child develop a positive self-concept, develop social skills, enhance physical fitness, and improve cognitive and sensorimotor skills.

Research maintains that a relationship exists between perception and motor development and that perception is related to cognition; therefore physical movement experiences play a part in cognitive development.

Preschool programs are becoming an important part of educational systems in this country, and physical education is playing an important role in such programs.

Elementary school physical education programs[3]

The elementary schools of the nation are stressing movement education. Experts do not agree on a single definition for movement education. They do agree, however, that movement education depends on physical factors in the environment and on the individual's ability to react intellectually and physically to these factors. Movement education attempts to help the student become mentally and physically aware of his or her bodily movements. It is based on a conceptual approach to human movement. Through movement education, the individual develops his or her own techniques for dealing with the environmental factors of force, time, space, and flow as they relate to various movement problems.

Movement education employs the problem-solving approach. Each skill to be explored presents a challenge to the student. Learning results as the student accepts and solves increasingly more difficult problems. For this reason, the natural movements of childhood are considered to be the first challenges that should be presented to the student.

Traditional physical education emphasizes the learning of specific skills through demonstration, drill, and practice. Movement education emphasizes learning skill patterns through individual exploration of the body's movement potential. Traditional physical education stresses the teacher's standard of performance. Movement education stresses the individual child's standard of performance.

Management guidelines for elementary school physical education programs

Elementary schools stress perceptual motor development and, in addition, an interdisciplinary approach whereby the subject matter of physical education is integrated with certain other subjects such as music, science, and art.

Some management guidelines that should be recognized in elementary school physical education programs follow. The program should meet the needs of all children, including the handicapped, slow learner,

Physical education classes, Falmouth Elementary School, Falmouth, Va.

culturally deprived, gifted, and normal. The program should stress movement education, perceptual-motor development, and interdisciplinary analysis. It should include a variety of experiences that will help the child form a sound foundation on which to build more complex skills, strategies, and techniques. It should provide developmental and progressive experiences. The program should stress such factors as creativity, self-expression, positive self-concept, social development, and safety.

Secondary school physical education programs

The junior high and senior high schools of the nation should build on the physical education provided at the elementary school level. Some management guidelines that represent important considerations in secondary school physical education programs follow. Most of the guidelines set for the elementary school also have merit in developing programs for secondary schools. The program should be based on the developmental tasks of secondary school students. The program should consist of a variety of activities, including gymnastics, self-testing activities, rhythm and dance, aquatics, dual and individual sports, team sports, movement skills, and physical fitness activities. The program should provide an understanding of the human body and the impact of physical activity on its various organic systems. Basic Stuff Series I and II that include concepts, principles, and developmental ideas extracted from the body of knowledge for physical education and sports should be used. The program should teach skills progressively and eliminate excessive repetition of activities. Title IX regulations should be adhered to. Handicapped students should be provided a program in the least restrictive environment. The program should encourage vigorous physical activity and develop an optimum state of physical fitness.

In addition to the management guidelines above the following points should be stressed:

The physical education class is a place to teach the skills, strategy, appreciation, understanding, knowledge, rules, regulations, and other material and information that are part of the program. It is not a place for free play, intramurals, and varsity competition. It is a place for instruction. Every minute of the class period should be devoted to teaching boys and girls the skills and subject matter of physical education.

Instruction should be basic and interesting. Skills should be broken down into simple components and taught so that each individual may understand clearly what he or she is expected to accomplish and how it should be done. Use of demonstrations, loop films,

models, slide films, posters, and other visual aids and materials can help to make the instruction more meaningful and interesting.

Instruction should be progressive. There should be a definite progression from simple to complex skills. Just as a student progresses in mathematics from simple arithmetic to algebra, geometry, and calculus, so the pupil should progress in physical education from basic skills and materials to more complex and involved skills and strategies.

Instruction should involve definite standards. Students should be expected to reach individualized standards of achievement in the class program. A reasonable amount of skill—whether it is in swimming, tennis, or another activity—should be mastered, depending on individual differences. Laxity and indifference to achievement should not be tolerated any more in physical education than in any other subject area in the curriculum. When boys and girls graduate from high school they should have met definite standards that indicate that they are *physically educated.*

Instruction should involve more than physical activity. All physical education classes do not have to be held in the gymnasium where physical activity predominates. A reasonable proportion of class time,

Sit-ups to develop abdominal strength, Lyons Township High School, LaGrange, Ill.

perhaps as much as 10% to 20%, can be devoted to discussions, lectures, independent study, Basic Stuff Series I and II, working on learning packages, and meaningful classroom activity. Outstanding coaches often have chalk talks for their players, in which they study rules and regulations, strategies, execution of skills, and other materials essential to playing the game effectively. This same principle can be applied to the physical education class period. Physical activity should not be conducted in a vacuum; if it is, it has no meaning and will not be applied when the student leaves the class and school. As the student understands more fully the importance of sports and activities in life, what happens to the body during exercise, the history of the various activities in which he or she engages, and the role of physical activity in the culture of the world, the class takes on new meaning and physical education takes on new respect and prestige.

There should be records. The instructor should keep adequate records to provide tangible evidence of the degree to which objectives are being met by the students. This means that data on physical fitness, skill achievement, knowledge of rules and other information, and social conduct—such as sportsmanship—should be a part of the record.

There should be homework. It is just as reasonable to assign homework in physical education as in general science. Much subject matter is to be learned, and many skills are to be mastered. If teachers would require their students to work on various activity skills and knowledge outside of class, there would be more time in class for meaningful teaching.

Each student should have a health examination before participating in the physical education program. An annual health examination should be regarded as a minimum essential to determining the amount and nature of physical activity that best meets each student's needs.

The teaching load of physical educators should be determined not only by the number of instructional class periods assigned but also by the total number of activities handled by the teacher both in class and outside of class. To do efficient work a teacher should have a normal work load—not an overload. Some professional standards have established that class instruction should not exceed 5 hours, or the equivalent of five class periods each day.

Innovative ideas in secondary school physical education[1]

Many innovative instructional programs are being used in physical education at the secondary school level. These include programs stressing personalized and individualized learning; those emphasizing performance objectives, competency packages, and goal setting; those concerning themselves with career and leadership opportunities; those including electives; those stressing flexibility in scheduling; and those concentrating on such specialized types of experiences as cycling, exercise physiology, and the environment.

Management guidelines for college and university physical education programs

Colleges and universities should provide instruction in physical education that meets the following management criteria: The program should be available to all students. The program should not be a repetition of the high school program but should offer more advanced work in physical education. The program should include innovative features to meet the needs of students and at the same time be interesting and challenging to them. The program should not allow ROTC, band, athletics, or other activities to be a substitute for physical education. The program should provide electives. The program should stress knowledge and understanding of the value of physical activity. The program should stress the study and practice of the science and art of movement. The program should stress lifetime skills. The program should be conducted by qualified faculty members.

A survey of the status of required physical education in colleges and universities in the United States indicates that many institutions require physical education for students. Also, many institutions have made physical education voluntary for students. A few have a requirement for students only in certain departments or schools. The majority of the institutions requiring physical education indicate that the requirement is for a 2-year period. The survey indicates the trend is toward more emphasis on recreation and fitness activities and on coeducational classes.

The college and university physical education program is the end of formal physical education for

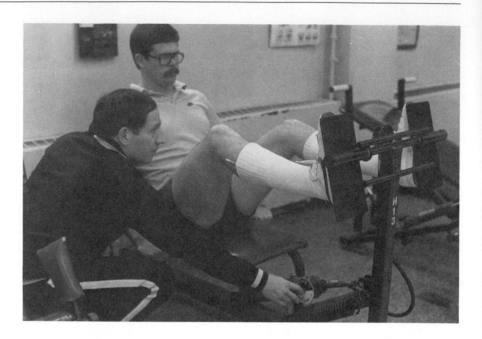

Physical education activity, Riverside-Brookfield High School, Riverside, Ill.

many students. The age range of individuals in colleges and universities is wide, incorporating those from 16 to 60 years of age. However, most college students are in their late teens or early twenties. These individuals have matured in many ways. They are entering the period of greatest physical efficiency. They have developed the various organ systems of the body. They possess strength, stamina, and coordination. College and university students have many interests. They want to prepare themselves for successful vocations, an objective that requires the physical educator to show how the physical education program can contribute to success in their work. College students are interested in the opposite sex. They want to develop socially. This has implications for a broad coeducational program, as does Title IX. They are interested in developing skills that they can use and enjoy throughout life. They are interested in becoming physically fit.

In formulating a program at the college and university level, one needs to remember that many students enter with limited activity backgrounds. Therefore the program should be broad and varied at the start, with opportunities to elect activities later. Considerable opportunity should exist for instruction and practice in those activities in which a student desires to specialize. As much individual attention as possible should be given to ensure necessary skill and fitness development.

Most colleges offer physical education twice a week for 2 years. Some colleges and universities have few requirements, whereas others state that certain physical standards of achievement must be met.

The program of activities should be based on the interests and needs of students and the facilities and staff available. Some colleges have introduced "Foundations" courses, getting at the subject matter of physical education.[2] An important place for coeducation exists at the college level in activities such as tennis, dancing, swimming, badminton, volleyball, golf, softball, racquetball, aquatics, dance, bowling, table tennis, skating, archery, horseback riding, mountaineering, orienteering, snow skiing, skydiving, judo, hiking, tumbling, and camping.

In college physical education programs physical achievement tests should be used to assess student needs and assure progress. Special help and prescribed programs should be offered to help physically underdeveloped students. Another suggestion has been made to institute a requirement that all students

Dance class, Lyons Township
High School, LaGrange, Ill.

demonstrate proficiency in swimming and physical fitness.

The growth of the 2-year college has been significant. In many respects the activities for the 2-year college are the same as those for the 4-year institution. However, because many community college students end their education after 2 years of study, they need to develop skills to enrich their leisure time and to stimulate a desire to keep themselves fit throughout their lifetime.

Most of the 2-year colleges require students to take physical education both years. Most of the programs require 2 hours each week and stress the successful completion of the service program as a requirement for graduation. Activities required in one California junior college include aquatics, archery, badminton, bowling, fencing, folk and square dance, golf, ice skating, modern dance, sailing, social dance, tennis, tumbling, gymnastics, trampoline, and volleyball.

Management factors relating to one or more educational levels

Certain factors relate to one or more educational levels (elementary, secondary, college). Some of the more pertinent factors include interrelationships of

elementary, secondary, and college and university programs; teaching aids and materials; class management; implications of Title IX for instructional strategies; and implications of Public Law 94-142 for instructional strategies.

Interrelationships of elementary, secondary, and college and university programs

The physical education programs at the elementary, secondary, and college levels should be interrelated. Continuity and progression should characterize the program from the time the student enters school until graduation. Overall planning is essential to ensure that each student becomes physically educated and to guarantee that duplication of effort, waste of time, omissions, and shortages do not occur.

Continuity and progression do not exist today in many of the school systems of the United States. To a great degree each institutional level is autonomous, setting up its own program with little regard for what has preceded and what will follow. If the focus of attention is on the student—the consumer of the product—then program planning will provide the student with a continuous program, developed in light of his or her needs and interests, from the time he or she starts school until graduation. Consideration also should be given to adult years. Directors of physical education for the entire community should shoulder this responsibility and ensure that such a program exists. Some communities have directors of school and community physical education and recreation programs, ensuring a continuous program for the entire population.

MANAGEMENT GUIDELINES FOR SELECTING TEACHING AIDS AND MATERIALS

When selecting audiovisual aids or other resources and materials, physical educators should consider the following principles that make using these aids effective and valuable:

Materials should be carefully selected and screened. The teacher should preview the materials to make sure they are appropriate for the unit and age level of the students and that they present information in an interesting and stimulating manner.

Proper preparation of materials should be made. The teacher should check all equipment that may be necessary for the presentation of materials to make sure that it is in operating condition. Record players and movie projectors, in particular, need to be carefully checked before they are used.

The presentation of materials should be planned and integrated into the lesson. Students should be properly introduced to the materials so that they know what to expect and so that they understand their relationship to the unit of study.

Materials should be presented to the students in a proper learning situation. Students should be located so that all may hear, see, and learn from the material being presented to them. They should realize that they will be held responsible for the information being presented.

Materials should be varied. Different types of materials should be chosen for presentation to stimulate the varying interests of the students. A teacher using films or slide films exclusively does not take full advantage of supplementary materials available for widespread appeal.

Use of supplementary materials should be limited. The teacher should place a reasonable limit on the use of extra teaching materials to maintain a balance between supplementary learnings and those gained from regular instructional materials.

Care should be taken to avoid excessive expenses. A reasonable part of the instructional budget should be set aside for supplementary materials. This amount should be in accordance with the emphasis placed on this phase of the teaching program.

Records and evaluations of materials should be maintained. All supplementary materials should be carefully evaluated and records kept on file for future reference. This should save the unnecessary expense involved in reordering or duplicating materials and in maintaining outdated materials.

By following these principles the teacher is able to supplement learnings with materials that are valuable and interesting to the students.

Various types of materials, activities, and personnel that can be used in the instructional process include the following:

Reading materials: textbooks, magazines, booklets, pamphlets

Audiovisual aids: motion pictures, slide films, learning loops, television, videotape, phonographs and audiotape records, records

Special aids: charts, photographic materials, bulletin boards, magnetic boards

Professional personnel: from professional associations and organizations

Community activities: recreational activities, PTA-sponsored events

Clinics: special games and programs put on by visiting teams, teaching organizations, community organizations

CLASS MANAGEMENT[4]

Good management does not just happen. It requires careful thought, good judgment, and planning before the class begins to have a group of participants act in an orderly manner, accomplish the tasks that have been established, and have an enjoyable, satisfying, and worthwhile experience. The leader who is in charge of a class where these optimal conditions exist has spent considerable time planning the details of the class from start to finish.

The following reasons for good organization

Dance class, University of Nevada, Las Vegas.

should be recognized by every teacher and administrator:

- It helps to eliminate discipline problems.
- It gives meaning and purpose to instruction and to the activities.
- It results in efficiency, the right emphasis, and the best use of the time available.
- It more fully ensures that the needs and interests of the participants will be satisfied.
- It more fully ensures progression and continuity in the program.
- It provides for measurement and progress toward objectives.
- It ensures participants' health and safety.
- It encourages program adaptations to each individual's needs and interests.
- It reduces errors and omissions.

- It helps to conserve the instructor's time and strength and aids in giving the instructor a sense of accomplishment.

Management guidelines

- Long-term planning for the semester and the year, as well as daily, weekly, and seasonal planning, should be done.
- A definite time schedule should be planned for each period, considering time to be devoted to showering and dressing, taking roll, class activity, and other essentials.
- The activity should be carefully planned so that it proceeds with precision and dispatch, with a minimum amount of standing around and a maximum amount of activity for each student.
- The classroom environment should be one of safety.

The equipment should be in good condition, and line markings, arrangements for activities, and other essential details should be attended to.

- Procedures to be followed in the locker room should be established to provide for traffic, valuables, clothes, and dressing and showering.
- The instructor should always be punctual for class meetings.
- Participants should be encouraged and motivated to do their best.
- A planned program of measurement and evaluation should be provided to determine progress being made by participants and the effectiveness of teaching.
- The instructor should wear suitable clothing.
- The instructor should have a good command of the subject, recognizing the values of demonstrations, visual aids, and other techniques to promote learning.
- Desirable attitudes and understandings toward physical fitness, skill learning, good sportsmanship, and other concepts inherent in physical education should be stressed at all times.

TITLE IX

Today's relevant physical education program must take into account the passage of an important law by the national government, namely, Title IX. On May 27, 1975, the president of the United States signed into law Title IX of the Education Amendments Act of 1972, which prohibits sex discrimination in educational programs that are federally assisted. The effective date of the regulation was July 21, 1975.

Title IX affects nearly all public elementary, secondary, and postsecondary educational institutions. This includes the nation's 16,000 public school systems and nearly 2700 postsecondary institutions. As a first step the regulations provide that educators should perform a searching self-examination of policies and practices in their institutions and take whatever remedial action is needed to bring their institutions into compliance with the federal law.

Reason for Title IX. The main reason for the enactment of Title IX was such testimony before Congressional and other committees as the following: Girls were frequently denied the opportunity to enroll in traditionally male courses and activities, and girls and women were frequently denied equal opportunity. A national survey conducted by the National Education Association showed that although women constituted a majority of all public school teachers, they accounted for only 3.5% of the junior high school principals and 3% of the senior high school principals.

Implications of Title IX for physical education instructional programs

Physical education classes must be organized on a coeducational basis. This regulation does not mean that activities must be taught coeducationally. Within classes, students may be grouped by sex for such contact sports as wrestling, basketball, and football. Also, within physical education classes, students may be grouped on an ability basis even though such grouping results in a single-sex grouping. However, sex must *not* be the criterion for grouping. It must be something other than sex. Furthermore, if an evaluation standard has an adverse impact on one sex, such as a standard of accomplishment in a physical fitness test, different evaluation requirements must be used.

Schools and colleges must provide equal opportunities for both sexes. This is true in respect to such items as facilities, equipment and supplies, practice and games, medical and training services, coaching and academic tutoring opportunities, travel and per diem allowances, and housing and dining facilities.

Equal opportunity means that the activities offered must reflect the interests and abilities of students of both sexes.

Adequate facilities and equipment must be available for both sexes in every sport. Furthermore, one sex cannot dominate the facilities or the new equipment.

Also, adequate time for practice and games must be provided for both sexes. Again, one sex cannot dominate.

Schools and colleges must spend funds in an equitable manner. Although equal aggregate expenditures are not required, an educational institution cannot discriminate on the basis of sex in providing proper equipment and supplies.

Title IX takes precedence over all state and local laws and conference regulations that might be in conflict with this federal regulation.

Yoga class, University of Nevada, Las Vegas.

If an institution receives federal aid, it must be in compliance with Title IX, even though its athletic or physical education program does not directly receive any of this aid. The Grove decision overturned this ruling.

There can be no discrimination in respect to personnel standards. No discrimination can exist in respect to personnel standards by sex, including marital or parental status, for employment, promotion, salary, recruitment, job classification, or fringe benefits.

Scholarships must be awarded equitably. The regulations require an institution to select students to be awarded financial aid on the basis of criteria other than a student's sex.

Interpretation of Title IX regulations

Some interpretations of Title IX regulations that affect physical education instructional programs are listed here. Interpretations such as the following have come from various sources. Sex designations associated with class schedules, activities, and budgets are not permitted. The term *girls' gymnasium* can be used; however, the scheduling of this facility must be nondiscriminatory in respect to each sex. Policies and procedures in regard to items such as uniforms and attendance must apply to both sexes. Sex-segregated administrative units, such as departments, do not necessarily have to be merged, although having faculty of men and women in integrated offices in newly combined administrative units is encouraged. If a significantly greater number of one sex is enrolled in a particular physical education class, the administration, if called on, should be prepared to provide the rationale for such organization. Supervision of locker rooms may be assigned to teacher aides, paraprofessionals, or teachers in other departments. Marks or grades given in physical education classes should reflect individual growth and performance and not compare sexes with one another. Standards of performance that provide an unfair comparison for one sex should not be used. In some cases separate standards might be used for each sex; for example, on a physical fitness rating, where boys may be taller and stronger than girls, separate standards may be used.

Coeducational physical education classes. Because the provision for coeducational classes is one of the key implications of Title IX regulations, this topic is discussed further here.

Problems in physical education classes have been cited in the professional literature. Weber[8] indicates that problems such as the following have developed

Coeducational volleyball,
Hampton Institute, Hampton,
Va.

as a result of Title IX: the teacher is not professionally prepared to teach various activities in a coeducational setting; male and female teachers who traditionally made decisions on their own are finding it difficult to function as a team with the other sex and share the decision-making process; students are also finding problems such as being unable in some activities to perform satisfactorily in front of members of the opposite sex, and thus lose face; and girls with poor skills are excluded from participation on highly skilled coeducational teams.

Weber also points out how many of these problems can be solved by such means as teachers getting rid of their personal sex biases, using new techniques, seeking a balance between female teachers' and male teachers' instructional methods, and reexamining philosophies regarding the teaching of physical education.

Other problems that have arisen in physical education classes as a result of Title IX include assignment of office space, scheduling a gymnasium for various activities, teaching certain activities such as wrestling, the danger of being accused of making sexual advances against students, supervision of locker rooms, and dressing standards.

The main consideration in establishing coeducational sports programs is to respond to the interests and ability levels of the participants. Because of their level of skill and other reasons, some males and females will not wish to participate in coeducational sports programs, even on an intramural or recreational level. Opportunities should be provided for these individuals to participate on separate teams. When conducting sports on a coeducational basis, appropriate modifications should be made in the rules and conduct of the activities to equalize competition between the sexes.

Compliance with Title IX. Title IX is being enforced by the Office for Civil Rights of the federal government. The first step seeks to have voluntary compliance. If violations are found, federal financial support may be cut off and other legal measures taken, such as referring the violation to the Department of Justice for appropriate court action.

The Office of Civil Rights is trying to approach Title IX constructively. It wishes to achieve the goals of Title IX, that is, to end discrimination against women, in the shortest time possible. Opportunity for women is the law of the land and must be enforced. The aim will be to use the Department's enforcement

Coeducational dance, Oak
View Elementary School,
Fairfax, Va.

machinery by giving priority to systemic forms of discrimination rather than following an approach whereby individual complaints assume priority. This means that the total picture of noncompliance will be assessed, taking into consideration information received from individuals and groups, as a means of determining enforcement priorities and compliance reviews.

Title IX regulations have been evolving for a long time. They should result in increased physical education opportunities for all students.

The question whether Title IX applies to all programs in an educational institution or whether it applies only to programs that get direct federal aid has been referred to the courts. The Grove decision (see p. 61) ruled that Title IX applies only to programs that get direct federal aid. Although the courts favor the latter, many institutions impose Title IX regulations on all programs within their jurisdiction.[5]

THE ADAPTED PROGRAM AND PHYSICAL EDUCATION FOR HANDICAPPED PERSONS

The adapted program refers to the phase of physical education that meets the needs of the individual who,

because of some physical inadequacy, functional defect capable of being improved through physical activity, or other deficiency, is temporarily or permanently unable to take part in the regular physical education program or in which special provisions are made for handicapped students in regular physical education classes. It also refers to students of a school or college student population who do not fall into the "average" or "normal" classification for their age or grade. These students deviate from their peers in physical, mental, emotional, or social characteristics or in a combination of these traits.

The principle of individual differences that applies to education as a whole also applies to physical education. Most administrators believe that as long as a student can attend school or college, he or she should be required to participate in physical education. If this tenet is adhered to, it means that programs must be adapted to individual needs. Many children and young adults who are recuperating from long illnesses or operations or who are suffering from other physical or emotional conditions require special consideration in their programs.

It cannot be assumed that all individuals in physical education classes are not handicapped. Unfortunate-

Physical education instructor helping handicapped student.

ly, many programs are administered on this basis. One estimate has been made that one out of every eight students in our schools is handicapped to the extent that special provision should be made in the educational program.

Schools and colleges will always have students who, because of many factors such as heredity, environment, disease, accident, or some other reason, have physical or other impairments. Many of these students have difficulty adjusting to the demands society places on them. The responsibility of physical education programs is to help each individual who comes into class. Even though a person may be atypical, this is not cause for neglect. In fact, it should represent an even greater challenge to see that he or she enjoys the benefits of participating in physical activities adapted to his or her needs. Provision for a sound adapted program has been a shortcoming of physical education throughout the nation because of a lack of properly trained teachers, because of the financial cost of remedial instruction, and because many administrators and teachers are not aware of their responsibility and the contribution they can make in this phase of physical education. These obstacles should be overcome as the public becomes aware of the need to educate *all* individuals in *all* phases of the total education program.

The nation's handicapped persons

The nation's estimated 50 million handicapped persons have engaged in an aggressive civil rights movement. These actions were aimed at obtaining the equal protection promised under the Fourteenth Amendment to the Constitution of the United States.

As a result of the actions on the part of handicapped persons, the nation is finally awakening to their needs. Until recently in the nation's history, handicapped persons were viewed as nonproductive. As a result, it has been common for handicapped persons to be discouraged. Today, however, the picture has changed. The handicapped are achieving their rights under the Constitution and are being employed in gainful jobs and taking their rightful place in society.

Definitions relating to the adapted program and physical education for handicapped persons[7]
Handicapped

Handicapped persons include those who have been identified as being mentally retarded, emotionally disturbed, deaf or hearing impaired, visually impaired, orthopedically impaired, speech impaired, learning disabled, multihandicapped, or otherwise health impaired.

Physical education

Physical education as it relates to the handicapped under federal law is the development of (1) physical and motor fitness, (2) fundamental motor skills and patterns, and (3) skills in aquatics, dance, and individual and group games and sports (including intramural and lifetime sports).

Special education

Under federal law special education means specially designed instruction, at no cost to parents or guardians, to meet the unique needs of a handicapped child, including classroom instruction, physical education instruction, home instruction, and instruction in hospitals and institutions.

Individualized education program (IEP)

The individualized education program (IEP) is the program or prescription written for each child in rela-

tion to his or her specific disability. It will be discussed in more detail later in this chapter (also see Appendices).

Least restrictive environment

In essence the least restrictive environment means the handicapped child is placed in a class or setting that is as similar to a normal class as possible and where the child can function safely. This location ranges from a full-time regular physical education class, to a regular physical education class with consultation from specialists in adapted physical education, to part-time regular physical education and part-time adapted physical education, to adapted physical education with regular physical education only for specific activities, to full-time adapted physical education in a regular school, to adapted physical education in a special school.

Types of handicapped individuals

Many terms have been used to classify and define handicapped individuals. These terms vary from publication to publication. Categories of children designated by the United States Congress in relation to legislation for handicapped persons will be the primary classifications used in this text. These categories include the mentally retarded, hard-of-hearing, deaf, speech impaired, visually handicapped, seriously emotionally disturbed, crippled, and other health impaired or learning disabled children who may require educational services out of the ordinary.

Functional physical education goals for handicapped persons

Selected goals that give direction to the physical education program for the handicapped student and that translate into objectives for each participant, as outlined by the AAHPERD, are presented here in the following adapted form[7]:
- Inform each student of his or her capacities and limitations
- Provide each student within his or her capabilities the opportunities to develop organic vigor, muscular strength, joint function, and endurance
- Provide each student with opportunities for social development in recreational sports and games

- Provide each student with opportunities to develop skills in recreational sports and games
- Help students meet demands of day-to-day living
- Help students with permanent disabilities in their social development
- Develop personal pride in overcoming disabilities or other forms of impairment
- Develop an appreciation for individual differences and being able to accept limitations and still be a part of the group

Public Law 94-142[6]

A milestone in legislative proposals providing for the handicapped was the passage of the Education of All Handicapped Children Act of 1975, which was signed into law by the President of the United States as PL 94-142. This legislation spells out the federal government's commitment to educating handicapped children and provides for annual funding on a sliding scale for this purpose. It provides educational services to handicapped children not receiving a free and appropriate public education and assistance for severely handicapped children receiving inadequate help.

There are specific implications in PL 94-142 for physical education. Special education has been defined within this legislation as "specially designed instruction, at no cost to parents or guardians, to meet the unique needs of a handicapped child including classroom instruction, instruction in *physical education,* home instruction, and instruction in hospitals and institutions."

Handicapped children, as defined in PL 94-142, are those who require some type of special education and related services. Related services, under the act, are defined as "transportation and developmental, corrective, and other supportive services, including occupational therapy, recreation, and medical and counseling services." Although gifted children might need special education and related services, they are not covered under the law.

Other specific stipulations of PL 94-142 require the following:

- State and local educational agencies initiate policies to ensure all handicapped boys and girls the right to a free and appropriate education.
- Planning of individualized educational programs,

with conferences among parents, teachers, representatives of local educational agencies, and where appropriate, children themselves. These conferences must be held at least once a year.

- Due process for parents and children, to ensure that their rights are not abrogated.
- A per pupil expenditure that is at least equal to the amount spent on nonhandicapped children in the state or local school district.
- The state and local agency shall carry out the mandates of the law according to specific timetables provided therein.
- The development of a comprehensive system of personnel training, including preservice and inservice training for teachers.
- That handicapped students will be educated in the "least restrictive environment." This means that they will be mainstreamed into the regular class whenever possible.

Aspects of PL 94-142 related to physical education. Section 121a.307 of the regulations of PL 94-142, which spells out the requirements for physical education, follows:

121a.307 Physical education

(a) *General.* Physical education services, specially designed if necessary, must be made available to every handicapped child receiving a free appropriate public education.

(b) *Regular physical education.* Each handicapped child must be afforded the opportunity to participate in the regular physical education program available to nonhandicapped children unless:

    (1) The child is enrolled full-time in a separate facility; or

    (2) The child needs specially designed physical education, as prescribed in the child's individualized education program.

(c) *Special physical education.* If specially designed physical education is prescribed in a child's individualized education program, the public agency responsible for the education of that child shall provide the services directly, or make arrangements for it to be provided through other public or private programs.

(d) *Education in separate facilities.* The public agency responsible for the education of a handicapped child who is enrolled in a separate facility shall insure that the child receives appropriate physical education services in compliance with paragraphs (a) and (c) of this section.

Individualized education programs for handicapped persons

After identification and eligibility have been determined for handicapped students, an individualized education program (IEP) must be developed for each individual. PL 94-142 specifies the requirements for the development of such programs. Section 4(19) provides the following (also see Appendices):

The term individualized education program means a written statement for each handicapped child developed in any meeting by a representative of the local educational agency or an intermediate educational unit who shall be qualified to provide, or supervise, the provision of specially designed instruction to meet the unique needs of handicapped children, the teacher, the parents or guardians of such child, and wherever appropriate, such child, which statement shall include:

A. A statement of the present levels of educational performance of such child;

B. A statement of annual goals, including short-term instructional objectives;

C. A statement of the specific educational services to be provided such child, and the extent to which such child will be able to participate in regular educational programs;

D. The projected date for initiation and anticipated duration of such services; and

E. Appropriate objective criteria and evaluation procedures and schedules for determining, on at least an annual basis, whether instructional objectives are being achieved.

The comprehensive IEP should be developed using the team approach. The following persons should be represented on the team: parent, teacher (classroom or physical education teacher, special education teacher), student, and, when appropriate, person responsible for supervising special education, related services such as guidance; and other necessary agencies.

Facilities, equipment, and supplies

Appropriate and adequate facilities, equipment, and supplies are important to successful programs of physical education for handicapped persons. However, these items must be emphasized in special or adapted physical education programs because facilities and equipment are designed for students in the regular class. Adaptations are often necessary when

Special fitness awards for the mentally retarded, AAHPERD–Kennedy Foundation.

handicapped students are mainstreamed into regular programs.

The passage of recent legislation and the results of various legal decisions have prompted school districts to make available the necessary facilities, equipment, and supplies to ensure a quality education for handicapped students. There is some question, however, about whether handicapped students are being provided with adequate facilities, equipment, and supplies.

The types of facilities and equipment needed for adapted physical education will vary according to the nature of the program (adapted sports, remedial or corrective exercises, or rest and relaxation), the type of student (mentally retarded, physically handicapped, or some other), and the school level at which the program is conducted. For example, the elementary school program in adapted physical education may be taught in the regular gymnasium, or in less desirable circumstances, in the classroom. In secondary schools and colleges, however, a special room for adapted physical education should be provided.

The Virginia State Department of Education, in its instructional booklet of *Physical Education for Handicapped Students,* outlines some of the factors that should be taken into consideration for handicapped students. A few of these factors are as follows:

Within building
Doors easy to open
Ramps with handrails on both sides
Elevators or chair lifts when necessary
Floors with nonslip surfaces
Toilet seats of proper height with rails provided
Outside building
Loading and parking areas close to entrances
Convenient parking places
Ramps suitable for wheelchairs
Doorways wide enough for wheelchairs
Emergency exits for wheelchairs
Adaptive physical education equipment (for bowling)
Providing a wheelchair student with a bowling ball ramp
Providing a blind student with a bowling rail
Providing a student with limited strength with lightweight, plastic bowling balls and pins

MANAGEMENT MATTERS RELATED TO PHYSICAL EDUCATION INSTRUCTIONAL PROGRAMS
Scheduling

The manner in which physical education is scheduled reflects the physical education leadership and the attitude of the central administration. Physical education is more meaningful for participants when the schedule reflects their interests, rather than administrative convenience.

Scheduling should be done according to a definite plan. Physical education should not be inserted in the overall master scheduling plan whenever there is time left over after all the other subjects have been provided for. This important responsibility cannot be handled on a hit-and-miss basis because that disregards the interests and needs of the students. Instead, physical education should be scheduled first on the master plan, along with subjects such as English and science that are required of all students most of the time they are in school. This allows for progression and for grouping according to the interests and needs of the individual participants. The three important items to consider in scheduling classes are (1) the number of teachers available, (2) the number of teaching stations available, and (3) the number of students who must be scheduled. This formula should be applied to most subjects in the school offering. Physical education will normally be scheduled correctly, as will other subjects, if this formula is followed.

All students should be scheduled, with no exceptions. If the student can go to school or college, he or she should be enrolled in physical education. Special attention should be given, however, to the handicapped or gifted individual to ensure that he or she is placed in a program suited to his or her individual needs. Also, special attention should be given to the weak student who needs extra help developing physical skills.

Special attention should be given to the availability of facilities, equipment, and supplies, and the weather. Planned units of work usually become increasingly longer as the student progresses to the next grade level, because of the student's longer interest span and greater maturity, and the increased complexity of the activities.

Every physical educator should make a point of presenting to the central administration his or her plans for scheduling physical education classes. The need for special consideration should be discussed with the principal and the scheduling committee. Through persistent action, progress will be made. The logic and reasoning behind the formula of scheduling classes according to the number of teachers and teaching stations available and the number of students who must be scheduled cannot be denied. It must be planned this way to ensure progression in instruction.

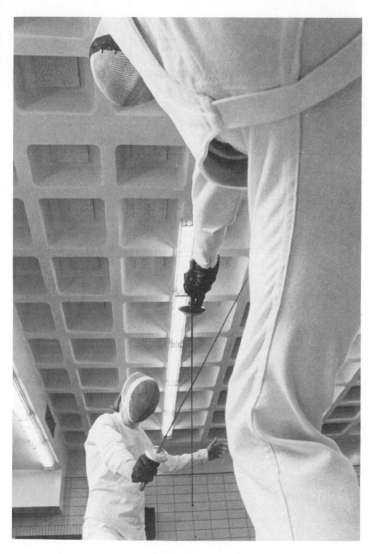

Fencing is one activity in the physical education program at Florissant Valley Community College in St. Louis.

Flexible scheduling. The introduction of flexible scheduling into school programs has implications for the administration of school physical education programs. Flexible scheduling assumes that the traditional system of having all subjects meet the same number of times each week for the same amount of time each period is passé. Flexible scheduling provides class periods of varying lengths, depending on the type of work being covered by the students, methods of instruction, and other factors pertinent to such a system. Whereas the traditional master plan makes it difficult to have flexible scheduling, the advent of the computer has made such an innovation practical and common.

Flexible scheduling also makes it possible to schedule activities for students of differing abilities differently so that all are not required to have a similar schedule based on a standard format of the school day. Under the traditional system, all students who were the slowest, for example, took as many courses as the brightest. Under flexible scheduling, some students may take as few as four courses and some as many as eight.

Modular scheduling breaks the school day into periods of time called modules. In a high school in Illinois the school day is composed of 20-minute modules, and classes may vary from one to five modules, depending on the purpose of the course. The school is on a 6-day cycle and operates by day one, two, or three rather than the traditional days of the week. In physical education, each grade level meets for three modules per day, 4 days each week. Each grade level also has a two-module group meeting once every cycle. In this meeting students hear guest speakers and lectures concerned with physical education concepts.

In other schools using modular scheduling, students frequently have unscheduled modules that can be used for swimming pool or gymnasium activities. Intramurals, open lab sessions (free time to use facilities), sport clubs, and demonstrations also provide incentives for students to use the skills they have learned.

Dress

Dress does not have to be elaborate. An important concern is that the uniform ensure safety when students are engaged in physical activity. For girls and women simple washable shorts and blouses or one-piece suits are suitable. For boys and men white cotton jerseys and trunks suffice. Of course, appropriate footwear also should be worn. An important consideration is to keep the uniform clean. The instructor should establish a policy on clean uniforms and work diligently to see that hygienic standards are met by all.

Time allotment

Just as scheduling practices vary from school to school, college to college, and state to state, so does the time allotment. In some states there are mandatory laws that require that a certain amount of time each day or week be devoted to physical education, whereas in others permissive legislation exists. For grades one to twelve the requirement varies in different states from none, or very little, to a daily 1-hour program. Some require 20 minutes daily and others 30 minutes daily. Other states specify the time by the week, ranging from 50 minutes to 300 minutes. Colleges and universities do not usually require as much time in

physical education as do grades one to twelve. One practice in higher education is to require physical education two times a week for 2 years.

The general consensus among physical education leaders is that for physical education to be of value, it must be given with regularity. For most individuals this means daily periods. Health experts also agree that exercise is essential to everyone throughout life.

Some individuals feel that, especially in the elementary schools, a program cannot be adapted to a fixed time schedule. However, as a standard, there seems to be agreement that a daily experience in such a program is needed. Such a recommendation is made and should always be justified on the basis of value and contribution to the student's needs. There should be regular instructional class periods and, in addition, laboratory periods where the skills may be put to use.

On the secondary level especially, it is recommended that sufficient time be allotted for dressing and showering in addition to the time needed for participation in physical education activities. Some leaders in physical education have suggested a double period every other day rather than a single period each day. This might be feasible if the daily class periods are too short. However, the importance of daily periods should be recognized and achieved wherever possible. Administrators should work toward providing adequate staff members and facilities to allow for a daily period.

The amount of time suggested for adults to spend in exercise programs is a minimum of three times a week (not on consecutive days). However, a daily exercise period is considered best.

Class size

Some school and college administrators feel that physical education classes can accommodate more students than the so-called academic classes. This is a misconception that has developed over the years and needs to be corrected.

The problem of class size seems to be more pertinent at the secondary level than at other educational levels. At the elementary level, for example, the classroom situation represents a unit for activity, and the number of students in this teaching unit is usually reasonable. However, some schools combine various

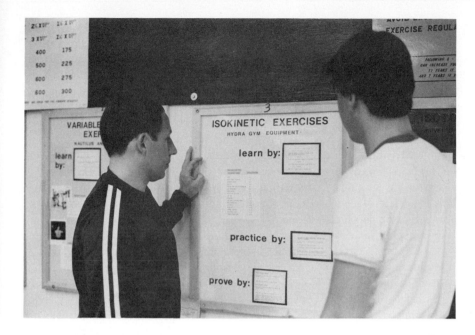

Instructor and student
examining plan for isokinetic
exercises, Riverside-
Brookfield High School,
Riverside, Ill.

classrooms for physical education, resulting in large classes that are not desirable.

Classes in physical education should be approximately the same size as classes in other subjects in the school or college offering. This is just as essential for effective teaching, individualized instruction, and progression in physical education as it is in other subjects. Physical education contributes to educational objectives on an equal basis with other subjects in the curriculum. Therefore the size of the class should be comparable so that an effective teaching job can be accomplished and the objectives of education attained.

After much research, many committees established a standard for an acceptable size of physical education classes. They recommend not more than 35 students as the suitable size for activity classes. Normal classes should never exceed 45 for one instructor. Of course, if there is a lecture or other activity scheduled adaptable to greater numbers, it may be possible to have more persons in the class. For remedial work, the suitable class size is from one-on-one to 20 to 25 and should never exceed 30. With flexible scheduling, the size of classes can be varied to meet the needs of the teacher, facilities, and type of activity being offered.

Instructional loads and staffing

The load of the physical educator should be of prime concern to the administrator. To maintain a top level of enthusiasm and strength, it is important that the load be adjusted so that the physical educator is not overworked.

A few years ago one state recommended that one full-time physical education teacher should be provided for every 240 elementary pupils and one for every 190 secondary pupils enrolled. If such a requirement is implemented, it would provide adequate staff members in this field and avoid an overload for many of the teachers.

Professional recommendations regarding teaching load at precollege educational levels have been made that would limit class instruction per teacher to 5 hours or the equivalent in class periods per day, or 1500 minutes per week. The maximum would be 6 hours per day or 1800 minutes a week, including afterschool responsibilities. A daily load of 200 students per teacher is recommended and never should exceed 250. Finally, each teacher should have at least one free period daily for consultation and conferences with students.

It is generally agreed that the normal teaching load

in colleges and universities should not exceed 15 hours per week.

The work load in a health spa or industrial physical fitness center is usually an 8 hour or 9 AM to 5 PM shift 5 days each week. Many stay open at night so the staff may have other work hours.

Differentiated staffing

Many innovations, such as differentiated staffing, are directed toward aiding the teacher in the performance of his or her duties. Paraprofessionals, certified undergraduate interns, and student teachers provide a school in Minnesota with valuable staff members.

Differentiated staffing relates to increased responsibilities or differentiation of functions among staff members. For example, in team teaching, higher salaries are given to team leaders or head teachers. Staff members who assume such roles as heads of departments or staff assistants are usually compensated accordingly. Outstanding, competent staff members with expertise in certain areas are assigned to special projects in some systems and compensated accordingly.

The benefits derived from differentiated staffing are obvious from the responsibilities given to various staff members. In schools, for example, the teacher is able to devote more time to help students, and he or she can also be free to work with small groups in different skills. Differentiated staffing allows the teacher to be free to teach and not be directly involved in clerical and physical responsibilities.

Paraprofessionals. Responsibilities include (1) supervised instructional assistance, (2) assisting in swimming pool, (3) clerical duties, (4) student conduct supervision, and (5) preparation of learning materials.

Certified undergraduate interns. Responsibilities include (1) clerical assistance, (2) record keeping, (3) material preparation, (4) conduct supervision in noninstructional areas, (5) individual assistance, and (6) observation.

Student teachers. Responsibilities include (1) observation, (2) supervised clerical teaching experience, (3) assisting supervising teachers, (4) preparation of learning materials, (5) individual assistance, and (6) extracurricular guidance.

Cross-country obstacle runs provide large muscle and endurance activity for children, Oak View Elementary School, Fairfax, Va.

Taking roll

There are many methods of taking roll. If a method satisfies the following three criteria, it is usually satisfactory. (1) It is efficient—roll taking should not consume too much time. (2) It is accurate—after the class has been held, it is important to know who was present and who was not and who came late or left early. (3) It should be uncomplicated—any system that is used should be easy to administer.

Some methods for roll taking follow:

1. *Having numbers on the floor*—each member of the class is assigned a number that he or she must stand on at the time the signal for "fall in" is given. The person taking attendance records the numbers not covered.
2. *Reciting numbers orally*—each member of the class is assigned a number that he or she must say out loud at the time the signal for "fall in" is given. The person taking attendance then records the numbers not given.
3. *Tag board*—each member of the class has a number recorded on a cardboard or metal tag that hangs on a peg on a board in a central place. Each member of the class who is present removes his or her tag from the board and places it in a box. The person taking attendance records the absentees from the board.
4. *Delaney system*—a special system developed by Delaney involves using a folder with cards that are turned over when a person is absent. It is a cumulative system that records the attendance of pupils over time. Adaptations of this system are used elsewhere.
5. *Squad system*—the class is divided into squads and the squad leader takes the roll for his or her squad and in turn reports to the instructor.
6. *Issuing towels and equipment*—the roll is taken when a towel is issued to each student or when it is turned in, or when a basket with uniform is issued or returned.
7. *Signing a book or register*—students are required to write their names in a book or register at the beginning of the class. Some systems require the writing of a name at the beginning of a period and crossing it out at the end of a period. The person taking attendance records the names not entered.

Selecting physical education activities

Physical education activities represent the heart of the program. They are the means for accomplishing objectives and achieving life's goals. Because activities are so important to the physical education profession, they must be selected with considerable care.

Criteria for selection

Activities should be selected in terms of the values they have in achieving the objectives of physical education. This means they should develop not only body awareness, movement fundamentals, and physical fitness, but also the cognitive, affective, and social makeup of the individual.

Activities should be interesting and challenging. They should appeal to the participants and present them with problem-solving activities and situations that challenge their skill and ability. For example, golf always presents the challenge of getting a lower score.

They should be adaptable to the growth and developmental needs and interests of children, youth, and adults. The needs of individuals vary from age to age. Consequently, movement activities and the pattern of organization must also change to meet these needs. The activity must be suited to the person, not the person to the activity. Wherever possible, participants should be allowed some choice in their activities.

Activities should be modifications of fundamental movements such as running, jumping, throwing, walking, and climbing.

Activities must be selected in light of the facilities, supplies, equipment, and other resources available in the school, college, or community. One cannot plan an extensive tennis program if only one court is available.

Activities should be selected not only with a view to their present value while the child is in school but also with a view to postschool and adult living. Skills learned during school and college days can be used throughout life, thus contributing to enriched living. Patterns for many skills used in adult leisure hours are developed while the individual is in the formative years of childhood.

Health and safety factors must be considered when selecting activities. An activity such as boxing has

Creative playground provides opportunities for various motoric experiences, Oak View Elementary School, Fairfax, Va.

been questioned because of its effect on the health and safety of individuals.

The local education philosophy, policies, and school or college organization must be considered.

School activities should provide situations similar to those that children experience in natural play situations outside school.

Activities should provide the participant with opportunities for creative self-expression.

Activities selected should elicit the correct social and moral responses through high-quality leadership.

Activities should reflect the democratic way of life.

One survey produced a list of physical education activities offered throughout the country, here classified into various categories. These do not necessarily meet criteria that have been listed. They merely indicate current offerings in physical education programs in the United States:

Team games

Baseball	Soccer
Basketball	Softball
Codeball	Speedball
Field hockey	Touch football
Flag football	Volleyball
Football	

Outdoor winter sports

Ice hockey	Snow games
Roller skating	Snowshoeing
Skating	Tobogganing
Skiing	

Other activities

Camping and outdoor activities	Jogging
Combatives (judo, karate)	Kayaking
Correctives	Mountaineering
Fly-tying	Movement education
Games of low organization	Orienteering
	Relays
	Self-testing activities
	Yoga

Rhythms and dancing

Folk dancing	Rhythms
Gymnastic dancing	Square dancing
Modern dancing	Social dancing
Movement fundamentals	Tap dancing

Formal activities

Calisthenics	Marching

Water activities

Canoeing	Scuba diving
Diving	Surfing
Lifesaving	Swimming
Rowing	Water games
Sailing	Water skiing

Gymnastics

Acrobatics	Rope climbing
Apparatus	Stunts
Obstacle course	Trampoline
Pyramid building	Tumbling

Dual and individual sports

Archery	Paddle tennis
Badminton	Racquetball
Bait and fly casting	Rifle
Bowling	Rope skipping
Checkers	Shuffleboard
Cycling	Skeet shooting
Darts	Skish
Deck tennis	Table tennis
Fencing	Tennis
Fishing	Tether ball
Golf	Track and field
Handball	Trap shooting
Horseback riding	Wrestling
Horseshoes	

Grouping participants

Homogeneous grouping in physical education classes is desirable. To render the most valuable contribution to participants, factors influencing performance must be considered when organizing physical education groups. The lack of scientific knowledge and measuring techniques to obtain such information and the management problems of scheduling have handicapped the achievement of this goal in many programs.

The reasons for grouping are sound. Placing individuals with similar capacities and characteristics in the same class makes it possible to better meet the needs of each individual. Grouping individuals with similar skill, ability, and other factors aids in equalizing competition. This helps the student realize more satisfaction and benefit from playing. Grouping promotes more effective teaching. Instruction can be better organized and adapted to the level of the student. Grouping facilitates progression and continuity in the program. Furthermore, grouping creates a better learning situation. Being in a group with persons of similar physical characteristics and skills ensures some success, a chance to excel, recognition, a feeling of belonging, and security. Consequently, this helps the social and personality development of the

Outdoor survival activity being practiced, Lyons Township High School, LaGrange, Ill.

individual. Finally, homogeneous grouping helps protect the participant physically, emotionally, and socially.

The problem of grouping is not so pertinent in the elementary school, especially in the lower grades, as it is in the junior high school and upper levels. At the lower levels the grade classification serves the needs of most children. As children grow older, the complexity of the program increases, social growth becomes more diversified, competition becomes more intense, and consequently, a greater need for homogeneous grouping exists.

At present students are grouped on such bases as

grade, health, physical fitness, multiples of age-height-weight, abilities, physical capacity, motor ability, interests, educability speed, skill, and previous experience. Techniques such as the following are used to obtain the needed information: health examinations; tests of motor ability, physical capacity, achievement, and social efficiency; conferences with participants; and determination of physiological age.

The ideal grouping organization would consider all factors that affect performance—intelligence, capacity, interest, knowledge, age, height, weight, and so on. To apply all these factors, however, is not administratively feasible at the present time. Some form of grouping is essential to provide a program that promotes educational objectives and protects the student. On the secondary and college levels, the most feasible procedure is to organize subgroups within the regular physical education class. Classification within the physical education class should be based on age, height, weight, and other factors, such as interest and skill, which are developed after observing the activity. For those individuals who desire greater refinement in respect to grouping, motor capacity, motor ability, attitude, appreciation, and sports-skills tests may be used.

To abide by Title IX regulations, physical educators should not group by sex. Some physical education departments have adopted a nongraded curriculum that places students in learning situations according to present levels of skill achievement and physical maturity. A child's chronological age or grade level attainment is not a factor in the nongraded physical education curriculum. This allows for individual student differences and interests.

Areas of student leadership and involvement

In recent years students have been demanding greater involvement in the educational process, and in most cases this increased involvement has been satisfactory to both students and administrators. Some of these areas of involvement are discussed briefly here.

General planning. Students should be involved in planning meetings that discuss schedule changes, curriculum innovations, and recent changes in educational methods. Students might be invited to attend school board meetings and parent association meetings and could also accompany teachers and administrators to other schools where certain innovations may be directly observed. Some schools and colleges have instituted student advisory boards that meet with staff members to discuss problems, changes, and future planning ideas.

Curriculum planning. Student surveys reveal the extent of curriculum changes desired by the student body. Administrators, teachers, and students should carefully weigh this information in light of the current literature, research studies, and actual curriculum changes in other schools and colleges. Student participation and feedback are essential; however, students do have limited experience in educational matters, and this must also be considered. Frequently the use of experimental programs on a limited basis can test the change before implementing it on a larger scale.

In a high school in Massachusetts students take an active role in curriculum planning. Students plan what they are going to learn and how they would like to learn the gymnastics unit of the physical education class. Several days are set aside for students to set goals, plan the steps needed to reach a specific goal, and make a commitment to learning and improvement. The students put their goals in writing and then set about to achieve them. Instruction is provided, and grading is a cooperative venture between students and teachers.

Leadership training programs. An innovative student leadership program is the Physical Education Leadership Training Program sponsored by a school in Virginia. As part of an elective course in the physiology of exercise, juniors and seniors can relate their learning experiences to leadership experiences in elementary schools.

The program has as its primary objectives (1) to assist in instruction, particularly when the physical education teacher is absent; (2) to provide in-depth study of health and physical education for students who want to teach as a career; (3) to provide students with leadership opportunities; and (4) to provide individualized instruction. The content and leadership experiences are developed and coordinated by the eleventh and twelfth grade classes. Supervision of the program is provided by the elementary physical education teacher, elementary classroom teacher, senior high school physical education teacher, head of the senior high school physical education department, and supervisor of physical education.

The four phases of the program are (1) in-service training, (2) observation, (3) teaching, and (4) teaching without supervision. This program is valuable to both teachers and students and helps the elementary grade teachers provide individualized help for each student.

Selecting student leaders. Several methods are used by physical educators to select student leaders. Some advocate appointing temporary leaders during the first few sessions of a class until the students become better known to their classmates and instructor. Some selection methods are discussed in the following paragraphs.

Volunteers. Students are asked to volunteer to become a student leader. It may happen that the least qualified persons are the ones who volunteer. If this method is used, it should be with the understanding that the student leader will serve for only a relatively short time.

Appointment by the instructor. The physical education instructor may appoint the student leader. One of the limitations of this procedure is that it is not democratic because it does not involve the students who are going to be exposed to the student leader. However, if the teacher's objective is to let each student in the class have a student leadership experience, this limitation can be overcome.

Election by the class. The students in the class may elect the persons they would like to have as leaders. A limitation of this method is that the persons selected are often the most popular students as a result of participation in sports or student government. Being the most popular does not mean that they are qualified to be leaders. This is a democratic procedure, however, and if the guidelines for selecting leaders are established and if the proper climate prevails, it can be effective.

Volleyball practice, Riverside-Brookfield High School, Riverside, Ill.

Selection based on test results. A battery of tests is sometimes used by physical educators to select student leaders. Tests of physical fitness, motor ability, sports skills, and leadership and personality characteristics yield useful information. They provide tangible evidence that a person has some of the desirable qualifications needed by a student leader in a physical education class. In addition, if the physical educator desires to have the entire class participate in the student leadership program, the test results may also be valuable to the teacher in helping each student identify weaknesses that need to be overcome during the training period.

Selection by Leaders' Club. Physical educators sometimes organize Leaders' Clubs to provide a continuing process for selecting student leaders. The members of the Leaders' Club, under the supervision of a faculty advisor, select new students to participate as leaders-in-training. Then, after a period of training, these students in turn become full-fledged student leaders.

The role of the Leaders' Club in training student leaders. One method of training student leaders is through a Leaders' Club. These clubs commonly have their own constitution, governing body, faculty advisor, and training sessions.

The written constitution of a Leaders' Club usually states the purpose of the club, requirements for membership, qualifications and duties of officers, financial stipulations, procedures for giving awards and honors, and other rules governing the organization.

The governing body of the Leaders' Club may consist of a president, vice-president, treasurer, and secretary, all of whom are elected by the members of the club.

The faculty advisor works closely with the leaders to ensure that the objectives of the Leaders' Club are accomplished. The faculty advisor supervises the affairs of the club and provides inspiration and motivation to the leaders, encouraging creativity and helping the students achieve their goals.

The Leaders' Club usually has regular meetings weekly, biweekly, or monthly. The students who are interested in becoming student leaders apply for membership in the Leaders' Club. Certain eligibility requirements are usually established for membership in the club.

Using the student leader. Student leaders may be used in the physical education program in several capacities.

Class leaders. There are many opportunities in the basic physical education instructional class period where student leaders can be effective. These include duties such as: acting as squad leader; being a leader for warm-up exercises; demonstrating how skills, games, and strategies are to be performed; taking attendance; supervising the locker room; and providing safety measures for class participation, such as acting as a spotter, checking equipment and play areas, and providing supervision.

Officials, captains, and other positions. Student leaders can gain valuable experience by serving as officials within the class and intramural program, being captains of all-star or other teams, coaching intramural or club teams, and acting as scorers and timekeepers.

Committee members. Many committee assignments should be filled by student leaders so that they gain valuable experience. These include being a member of a *rules committee,* where rules are established and interpreted for games and sports, serving on an *equipment and grounds committee,* where standards are established for the storage, maintenance, and use of these facilities and equipment, and participating on a *committee for planning special events* in the physical education program, such as play, sports, or field days.

Supply and equipment manager. Supplies and special equipment including basketballs, archery, golf, and hockey equipment, and audiovisual aids, are needed in the physical education program. The equipment must be taken from the storage areas, transferred to the place where the activity will be conducted, and then returned to the storage area. The student leader can help immeasurably in this process and profit from such an experience.

Program planner. Various aspects of the physical education program need to be planned, and students should be involved. Student leaders, because of their special qualifications and interest, are logical choices to participate in such planning and curriculum development. Their knowledge and advice can ensure that the program meets the needs and interests of the students who participate in the program.

Record keeper and officer manager. Attendance records and inventories must be taken, filing and recording done, bulletin boards kept up to date, visitors met, and other responsibilities attended to. These necessary functions provide worthwhile experiences for the student leader and benefit the program.

Special events coordinator. A multitude of details always are involved in play days, sports days, demonstrations, and exhibitions. Student leaders should be involved in planning and conducting these events.

Evaluating the program. The student leadership program should be evaluated periodically to determine the degree to which the program is achieving its stated goals. Students should be involved in this evaluation. Questions such as the following might be asked: "Are the experiences provided worthwhile?" "Are the students developing leadership qualities?" "Is the teacher providing the necessary leadership to make the program effective?" "Are any of the assigned tasks incompatible with the objectives sought?" "Is the Leaders' Club helping to create a better leaders' program?"

SELECTED MANAGEMENT PROBLEMS IN INSTRUCTIONAL PROGRAMS

The manager of any physical education program is perennially confronted with questions such as: Should physical education be required or elective? How much credit should be given? Is it possible to substitute some other activity for physical education? What should be the policy on class attendance? How should an instructor deal with excuses? These and other questions are answered in the following discussion.

Should physical education be required or elective?

General agreement that physical education should be required at the elementary level exists. However, there are many advocates on both sides of the question of whether it should be required or elective on the secondary and college levels. Both groups are sincere and feel their beliefs represent what is best for the student. Probably most specialists feel the program should be required. Some school administrators feel it should be elective. Following are some of the arguments presented by each.

Required

Physical education is a basic need of every student.

The student is compelled to take so many required courses that the choice of electives is limited, if not entirely eliminated, in some cases.

The student considers required subjects most important and most necessary for success.

Various subjects in the curriculum would not be provided unless they were required. This is probably true of physical education. Until state legislatures passed laws requiring physical education, this subject was ignored by many school administrators. If physical education were elective, the course of some administrative action would be obvious. Either the subject would not be offered at all or the administrative philosophy would so dampen its value that it would have to be eliminated because of low enrollment.

Even under a required program, physical education is not meeting the physical, social, and cognitive needs of students. If an elective program were instituted, deficiencies and shortages would increase, further handicapping the attempt to meet the needs of the student.

Elective

Physical education "carries its own drive." If a good basic program is developed in the elementary school, with students acquiring the necessary skills and attitudes, the drive for such activity will carry through in the secondary school and college. There will be no need to require such a course, because students will want to take it voluntarily.

Objectives of physical education are focused on developing skills and learning activities that have carry-over value, living a healthful life, and recognizing the importance of developing and maintaining one's body in its best possible condition. These goals cannot be legislated. They must become a part of each individual's attitudes and desires if they are to be realized.

Some children and young adults do not like physical education. This is indicated in their manner, attitude, and desire to get excused from the program and to substitute something else for the course. Under such circumstances the values that accrue to these individuals are not great. Therefore it would be best to place physical education on an elective basis where

Outdoor recreation activities, Portage High School, Portage, Ind.

only those students who participate actually desire to do so.

Should substitutions be allowed for physical education?

A practice exists in some school and college systems that allows students to substitute some other activity for their physical education requirement. This practice should be scrutinized and resisted aggressively by every administrator.

Some of the activities used as substitutions for physical education are athletic participation, Reserve Officers' Training Corps, and band.

No substitute for a sound program of physical education exists. In addition to healthful physical activity, it is concerned also with developing an individual socially, emotionally, and mentally. The individual develops many skills that can be applied throughout life. These essentials are lost if a student is permitted to take some other activity in place of physical education.

Should credit be given for physical education?

Whether credit should be given for physical education is another controversial problem with which the profession is continually confronted. Here again advo-

cates can be found on both sides. Some feel the joy of the activity and the values derived from participation are sufficient in themselves without giving credit. On the other hand, some feel that physical education is the same as any other subject in the curriculum and also should be granted credit.

The general consensus among physical education leaders is that if physical education is required for graduation and if it enriches a person's education, credit should be given, just as for other subjects.

What policy should be established on class attendance?

It is important for every department of physical education to have a definite policy on class attendance that covers absenteeism and tardiness. Because it is felt that students should attend school and college regularly, it follows that they should also attend physical education classes regularly. However, time for independent study should be included in the schedule.

Regular participation in physical education is essential to the value of the program; therefore every physical education department should have a clear-cut policy on attendance regulations. These regulations should be few and clearly stated in writing so that they are recognized, understood, and strictly enforced by teachers and students. They should allow a reasonable number of absences and tardinesses. Perfect attendance at school or college should not be stressed. Many harmful results can develop if students feel obligated to attend classes when they are ill and should be at home. There should probably be some provision for makeup work when important experiences are missed. However, makeup work should be planned and conducted so that the student derives essential values from such participation, rather than enduring it as a disciplinary measure. There should also be provision for the readmission of students who have been ill.

A final point to remember is the importance of keeping accurate, up-to-date attendance records to minimize administrative problems.

What about excuses?

The principal, nurse, or physical educator frequently receives a note from a parent or family physician asking that a student be excused from physical education. Many abuses develop if all such requests are granted. Many times for minor reasons the student does not want to participate and obtains the parent's or family physician's support.

One survey showed that high schools permitted a student to be excused on the basis of a parental note, a memorandum from the family physician, or the discretion of the physical education teacher. Although some schools would accept the recommendation of any of these three persons, other schools would accept only an excuse from the school physician. At the college level most programs accept the college physician's excuse or permit the instructor of each class to use his or her own discretion in granting excuses to students.

Those surveyed listed reasons for granting excuses in physical education. Secondary schools grant most of their excuses for participation in athletics and for being in the school band. Some schools permit their athletes to be excused only on the day of the game, whereas others grant a blanket excuse for the entire sports season. Other reasons for excuses on the secondary level included makeup tests, driver training, counseling, a too-heavy extracurricular load, and medical reasons. At the college level excuses were granted to athletes, veterans, students who could pass physical fitness tests, honor students, and older students, for medical reasons, in "hardship cases," and so on.

The survey also reported what was done with the students who were excused. Students in secondary schools were required to attend study halls; to score, officiate, or help around the physical education department; to write reports; to remain on the sidelines; or to report after school. At the college level most colleges did nothing except follow a pattern of failing a student in some cases if he or she exceeded the legal number of excused absences each semester. A few either required the student to observe the class, substitute a health class, or study in the gymnasium; some left it up to the instructor's discretion.

Some school systems have controlled the indiscriminate granting of requests for excuses from physical education. Policies have been established, sometimes through conferences and rulings of the board of education, requiring that all excuses be reviewed and approved by the school physician before they are granted. Furthermore, family physicians have been asked to state specific reasons for requesting excuses from physical education. This procedure has worked satisfactorily in some communities. In other places physical educators have taken particular pains to work closely with physicians. They have established a physical education program in collaboration with the school physician so the needs of each individual are met, regardless of his or her physical condition. They have met with the local medical society in an attempt to clear up misunderstandings about the purpose and conduct of the program. Family physicians have been brought into the planning. As a result of such planning, problems with excuses from physical education have been considerably reduced. It has been found that in those communities where parents, family physicians, and the lay public in general understand physical education, the number of requests for excuses is relatively small. In such communities the values derived from participation in the program are clearly recognized, and because most parents and physicians want children to have worthwhile experiences, they encourage rather than limit such participation.

A few years ago, a conference concerned with close cooperation between physical education and

Scuba diving class, University of Nevada, Las Vegas.

medical doctors drew up this list of statements in respect to the problem under discussion:

• Orient the student, parent, and physician at an early date in regard to the objectives of the physical education program.
• Route all requests for excuse through the school physician. In the absence of the physician, the school nurse should have this responsibility.
• Discard permanent and blanket excuses. Instead of being categorically excused, boys and girls can be given an activity in keeping with their special needs.
• Students involved in the excuse request should have a periodic recheck on the need for excuse.
• Conferences between the school physicians and the head of the physical education department on the local level need to be emphasized.
• The problem of excuse from physical education should be tied in with the total guidance program of the school.

Who should conduct the elementary school physical education class?

The question of who should conduct the elementary school physical education class has been continually discussed for many years. Some educators advocate that the classroom teacher handle physical education classes, and many supporters want a specialist to take over this responsibility. The classroom teacher has limited professional education in physical education. Some classroom teachers are not interested in teaching physical education. Furthermore, there is increased interest in physical education today, which implies that qualified and interested persons should handle these classes. The trend is toward more emphasis on movement education, perceptual motor development, physical fitness, skills, and other aspects of education with which physical education is concerned. More research is needed on physical education programs as they relate to the learning and growth of children. There is an increased emphasis on looking to the specialist in physical education for help and advice in planning and conducting the elementary school program. These developments have implications for a sound in-service program to help the classroom teacher do a better job in physical education.

In light of the present status of physical education in the elementary schools of this country, such recommendations as the following should be very carefully considered. Each elementary school should be staffed with a specialist in physical education. The classroom teacher may find his or her best contribution to physical education programs in kindergarten to grade three, but to do the best job he or she needs preparation in this special field and the advice and help of a physical education specialist. Although the classroom teacher can contribute much to the physical education program in grades four to six, factors such as the growth changes and interests taking place in boys and girls and the more specialized program that exists at this level make it imperative to seek the help of a specialist who possesses the ability, experience, and training required to meet the needs of growing boys and girls and to gain their respect and interest. The specialist and the classroom teacher should pool their experience to provide the most desirable learning experience. Each teacher has much to contribute and should be encouraged to do so.

Dressing and showering

Such factors as the age of the participant, time allowed, grade participating, and type of activity should be considered in a discussion of dressing and showering for physical education classes.

The problem of showering and dressing is not so pertinent at the lower elementary level where the age of the participants and type of activities as a general rule do not require special dress and showering. Also the time allotted is too short in many cases. In the upper elementary and at the junior and senior high school and college levels, however, it is a problem.

Physical education embodies activities that require considerable movement, resulting in perspiration. In the interests of comfort and good hygiene practices, provisions should be made for special clothing and showering. The unpleasantness of a student's returning to class after participating in a physical education activity, with clothes malodorous and wet from perspiration, does not establish habits of personal cleanliness and good grooming. Therefore all schools should make special provisions for places to dress in comfortable uniforms and for showering. Such places should be convenient to the physical education areas, be comfortable, and afford privacy. Although boys and girls are increasingly becoming accustomed to using a group shower, many still prefer private showers. In the interests of these individuals, such facil-

ities should be provided. There should also be a towel service. Many schools have facilities for laundering towels that have proved satisfactory.

Records

Records are essential in keeping valuable information regarding the participants' welfare. They also are essential to efficient program planning and administration. They should, however, be kept to a minimum and should be practical and functional. They should not be maintained merely as busy work and for the sake of filling files.

Some of the records should be concerned directly with the welfare of the participant and others with certain administrative factors.

Records that concern the welfare of the participant are the health records, the cumulative physical education form, attendance reports, grades, and accident reports.

Health records are essential. They contain information on the health examination and other appraisal techniques, health counseling, and any other data pertaining to the person's health.

The cumulative physical education record should contain information about activities engaged in, after-school play, tests, interests, needs, and other pertinent information about the student's participation in the physical education program.

There should be special records for attendance, grades, and any special occurrences with a bearing on the participant that are not recorded in other records.

If a student is involved in an accident, a full account of the circumstances surrounding the accident should be recorded. Usually special forms are provided for such purposes.

Management records provide general information and equipment records, including a list of the year's events, activities, records of teams, play days, sports days, intramurals, events of special interest, techniques that have been helpful, budget information, and any other data that would be helpful in planning for succeeding years. Memory often fails over time, with the result that many good ideas are lost and many activities and techniques of special value are not used because they are forgotten.

There should be records of equipment, facilities, and supplies that show the material needing repair,

CRITERIA FOR EVALUATING PHYSICAL EDUCATION INSTRUCTIONAL PROGRAMS

	Poor (1)	Fair (2)	Good (3)	Very good (4)	Excellent (5)
Meeting physical education objectives					
1. Does the class activity contribute to the development of physical fitness?	☐	☐	☐	☐	☐
2. Does the class activity foster the growth of ethical character, desirable emotional and social characteristics?	☐	☐	☐	☐	☐
3. Does the class activity contain recreational value?	☐	☐	☐	☐	☐
4. Does the class activity contain carryover value for later life?	☐	☐	☐	☐	☐
5. Is the class activity accepted as a regular part of the curriculum?	☐	☐	☐	☐	☐
6. Does the class activity meet the needs of *all* participants in the group?	☐	☐	☐	☐	☐
7. Does the class activity encourage the development of leadership?	☐	☐	☐	☐	☐
8. Does the class activity fulfill the safety objective in physical education?	☐	☐	☐	☐	☐
9. Does the class activity and conduct foster a better understanding of democratic living?	☐	☐	☐	☐	☐
10. Does the class activity and conduct cultivate a better understanding and appreciation for exercise and sports?	☐	☐	☐	☐	☐

PERFECT SCORE: *50*   ACTUAL SCORE: _____

Leadership (teacher conduct)					
1. Is the teacher appropriately and neatly dressed for the class activity?	☐	☐	☐	☐	☐
2. Does the teacher know the activity thoroughly?	☐	☐	☐	☐	☐
3. Does the teacher possess an audible and pleasing voice?	☐	☐	☐	☐	☐
4. Does the teacher project an enthusiastic and dynamic attitude in class presentation?	☐	☐	☐	☐	☐
5. Does the teacher maintain discipline?	☐	☐	☐	☐	☐
6. Does the teacher identify, analyze, and correct faulty performance in guiding pupils?	☐	☐	☐	☐	☐
7. Does the teacher present a sound, logical method of teaching motor skills, for example, explanation, demonstration, participation, and testing?	☐	☐	☐	☐	☐
8. Does the teacher avoid the use of destructive criticism, sarcasm, and ridicule with students?	☐	☐	☐	☐	☐
9. Does the teacher maintain emotional stability and poise?	☐	☐	☐	☐	☐
10. Does the teacher possess high standards and ideals of work?	☐	☐	☐	☐	☐

PERFECT SCORE: *50*   ACTUAL SCORE: _____

Adapted from Piscopo, J.

CRITERIA FOR EVALUATING PHYSICAL EDUCATION INSTRUCTIONAL PROGRAMS—cont'd

	Poor (1)	Fair (2)	Good (3)	Very good (4)	Excellent (5)
General class procedures, methods, and techniques					
1. Does class conduct yield evidence of preplanning?	☐	☐	☐	☐	☐
2. Does the organization of the class allow for individual differences?	☐	☐	☐	☐	☐
3. Does the class exhibit maximum activity and minimum teacher participation (e.g., overemphasis on explanation and/or demonstration)?	☐	☐	☐	☐	☐
4. Are adequate motivational devices such as teaching aids and audiovisual techniques effectively utilized?	☐	☐	☐	☐	☐
5. Are squad leaders effectively employed where appropriate?	☐	☐	☐	☐	☐
6. Does the class start promptly at the scheduled time?	☐	☐	☐	☐	☐
7. Are students with medical excuses from the regular class supervised and channelled into appropriate activities?	☐	☐	☐	☐	☐
8. Is the class roll taken quickly and accurately?	☐	☐	☐	☐	☐
9. Are accurate records of progress and achievements maintained?	☐	☐	☐	☐	☐
10. Are supplies and equipment quickly issued and stored?	☐	☐	☐	☐	☐

PERFECT SCORE: *50*   ACTUAL SCORE: _____

	Poor (1)	Fair (2)	Good (3)	Very good (4)	Excellent (5)
Participant conduct					
1. Are the objectives of the activity or sport clearly known to the learner?	☐	☐	☐	☐	☐
2. Are the students interested in the class activities?	☐	☐	☐	☐	☐
3. Do the students really enjoy their physical education class?	☐	☐	☐	☐	☐
4. Are the students thoroughly familiar with routine regulations of class roll, excuses, and dismissals?	☐	☐	☐	☐	☐
5. Are the students appropriately dressed for the class activity?	☐	☐	☐	☐	☐
6. Does the class exhibit a spirit of friendly rivalry in learning new skills?	☐	☐	☐	☐	☐
7. Do students avoid mischief or "horseplay"?	☐	☐	☐	☐	☐
8. Do students take showers where facilities and nature of activity permit?	☐	☐	☐	☐	☐
9. Do slow learners participate as much as fast learners?	☐	☐	☐	☐	☐
10. Do students show respect for the teacher?	☐	☐	☐	☐	☐

PERFECT SCORE: *50*   ACTUAL SCORE: _____

Continued.

CRITERIA FOR EVALUATING PHYSICAL EDUCATION INSTRUCTIONAL PROGRAMS—cont'd

	Poor (1)	Fair (2)	Good (3)	Very good (4)	Excellent (5)
Safe and healthful environment					
1. Is the area large enough for the activity and number of participants in the class?	☐	☐	☐	☐	☐
2. Does the class possess adequate equipment and/or supplies?	☐	☐	☐	☐	☐
3. Are adequate shower and locker facilities available and readily accessible?	☐	☐	☐	☐	☐
4. Is the equipment and/or apparatus clean and in good working order?	☐	☐	☐	☐	☐
5. Does the activity area contain good lighting and ventilation?	☐	☐	☐	☐	☐
6. Are all safety hazards eliminated or reduced where possible?	☐	☐	☐	☐	☐
7. Is first aid and safety equipment readily accessible?	☐	☐	☐	☐	☐
8. Is the storage area adequate for supplies and equipment?	☐	☐	☐	☐	☐
9. Does the activity area contain a properly equipped rest room for use in injury, illness, or rest periods?	☐	☐	☐	☐	☐
10. Does the activity area contain adequate toilet facilities?	☐	☐	☐	☐	☐

PERFECT SCORE: *50*　　　　　　　　　ACTUAL SCORE: _____

Criteria	Perfect score	Actual score
Meeting physical education objectives	50	_____
Leadership (teacher conduct)	50	_____
General class procedures, methods, and techniques	50	_____
Pupil conduct	50	_____
Safe and healthful environment	50	_____
TOTAL	250	_____

new materials needed, and the location of various materials, so that they can be found easily.

Records of such items as locker or basket assignments are essential to the efficient running of a physical education program.

Providing for the health of the participant

Physical education staff members must safeguard the health of all individuals in the program. To accomplish this objective, the staff members in the health program must have a close working relationship.

Every participant should have periodic health examinations with the results of these examinations scrutinized by the physical educator. A physical education program must be adapted to the needs and interests of each person. The physical educator is responsible for health guidance and health supervision in the physical education activities. The physician should be consulted when persons return after periods of illness, when accidents occur, and at any other time that such qualified advice is needed.

SUMMARY

The instructional program in physical education is the place to teach such things as skills, strategies, and understandings concerning the contribution of physical activity to total well-being.

Physical education instructional programs exist at all educational levels and in several community agencies. Management guidelines exist for teaching physical education in all of these settings and for selecting teaching aids and materials.

Effective class management aids the successful management of a physical education organization.

Title IX affects the implementation of physical education instructional programs in educational institutions receiving federal aid.

The adapted physical education program is designed to meet the needs of all individuals. Public Law 94-142 provides educational services for handicapped students in the adapted physical education program.

Management matters that relate to physical education instructional programs include scheduling, dress, class size, differentiated staffing, selection of activities, grouping participants, and student leadership.

Selected management problems related to the instructional programs involve whether physical education should be required, and whether substitutions should be permitted and credit given. These problems also include the development of policies on class attendance, excuses, dressing and showering, and record keeping.

CRITERIA FOR EVALUATING PHYSICAL EDUCATION INSTRUCTIONAL PROGRAMS

Piscopo has developed the checklist at the end of this chapter for evaluating physical education instructional programs.

SELF-ASSESSMENT TESTS

These tests will assist students in determining if material and competencies presented in this chapter have been mastered:

1. You are a member of a physical education staff in a high school where the instructional program is under attack by the faculty. It has been suggested that the instructional program be abolished. Prepare a brief in defense of the instructional physical education program that describes its nature, scope, and worth in the educational process.
2. You have been invited to speak to the Parent Teachers Association in your community on the topic, ''Physical Education from Preschool through the College Years.'' Prepare a speech that describes the various instructional physical education programs at each educational level and the purpose and nature of each. Present your speech to your class.
3. Develop a model for a high school instructional physical education program as a result of Title IX legislation.
4. Compare how traditional physical education instructional programs are conducted with respect to handicapped students and how it is proposed they should be conducted as a result of mainstreaming and the passage of Public Law 94-142.
5. Develop a list of principles for physical education instructional programs that would serve as guides for each of the following: scheduling, time allotment for classes, size of classes, instructional loads, class management, uniforms, taking roll, selecting activities, grouping, and areas of student involvement.
6. What is meant by an adapted physical education program?
7. You are a director of a school physical education program and have been asked by the superintendent of schools to plan an adapted program of physical education for the entire school system, elementary school through high school. Prepare the plan you will submit to the superintendent, including the objectives you will strive to achieve, the guidelines you will follow, how you plan to schedule the students, and the activities you will offer.
8. You are a member of a school physical education staff and have been selected by your college to see that PL 94-142 is fully implemented in your program. Prepare a plan that will ensure that your school physical education program has fully complied with this law.

REFERENCES

1. Bucher, C.A., and Keonig, C.R.: Methods and materials for secondary school physical education, ed. 6, St. Louis, 1983, The C.V. Mosby Company.
2. Bucher, C.A., and Prentice, W.E.: Fitness for college and life, St. Louis, 1985, Times Mirror/Mosby College Publishing.
3. Graham, G., et al.: Children moving, Palo Alto, Calif., 1980, Mayfield Publishing Company.
4. Jensen, C.R.: Administrative management of physical education and athletic programs, Philadelphia, 1983, Lea & Febiger.
5. Mirga, T.: Reynolds claims Grove City measure unjustifiably extends federal power, Education Week, March 13, 1985.
6. Singer, J.D.: 10th anniversary of P.L. 94-142: a 'visionary' law that has worked, Education Week, February 27, 1985.
7. Stein, J.U.: A clarification of terms, Journal of Health, Physical Education, and Recreation **42**:63, September 1971.
8. Weber, M.: Title IX in action, Journal of Physical Education and Recreation **51**:20, May 1980.

SUGGESTED READINGS

• Arnheim, D.D., and Sinclair, W.A.: Physical education for special populations, Englewood Cliffs, N.J., 1985, Prentice-Hall, Inc.
  Provides valuable information for the professional physical educator working as a generalist or specialist in adapted physical education. Practical strategies and desirable activities for specific populations are provided. Covers areas such as teacher qualifications, sports competition and physical education for the disabled, learning disabled, mentally retarded, and other forms of handicapping conditions. Sets forth guidelines for areas such as program development and financial support.

• Harrison, J.M.: Instructional strategies for physical education, Dubuque, Iowa, 1983, Wm. C. Brown Company.
  Designed to help physical educators acquire skills necessary to design and carry out effective instructional programs in their field of expertise. Presents skills essential for instruction, covers classroom management, and outlines how unit planning can take place. Ties together cognitive, psychomotor and affective learning domains as a basis for the design and implementation of instructional strategies. Provides learning aids to help students and provides practical examples in such areas as performance objectives, evaluation, and discipline.

• Kleinman, M.: The acquisition of motor skill, Princeton, N.J., 1983, Princeton Book Company, Publishers.
  Discusses theoretical foundations of motor learning and establishes the basic psychological foundations of motor learning. Covers such important items as transfer of learning, distribution of practice, knowledge of results, motor retention, and motor control. Contributes to the instructional program in physical education by providing basic information about how motor skills can best be taught.

• Rink, J.E.: Teaching physical education for learning, St. Louis, 1985, Times Mirror/Mosby College Publishing.
  Promotes teaching practices that make a difference in the learning of students. Guidelines and suggestions offered will help the preservice or experienced teacher in their instructional roles. Task complexity and difficulty, learner readiness, and relatedness of sequential learning experiences are taken into consideration. Helps students become competent teachers by improving their skills and effectiveness in achieving desirable goals. Identifies the major components of the instructional process and then describes, analyzes, and interprets the instructional process in light of the teacher's role.

• Willgoose, C.E.: The curriculum in physical education, Englewood Cliffs, N.J., 1984, Prentice-Hall, Inc.
  Discusses the curriculum of physical education in various educational levels. Against a background of societal needs and educational foundations, student characteristics, and research findings, it discusses curriculum planning, program organization, the curriculum guide, individualizing physical education, and curriculum evaluation.

Chapter Four

Intramural, Extramural, and Club Programs

Instructional Objectives and Competencies to be Achieved
After reading this chapter the student should be able to

- Define *intramural, extramural,* and *club programs* and name the objectives each is designed to achieve.
- Prepare a list of policies that, if followed, will enable a person to organize and administer intramural, extramural, and club physical education programs.
- Understand the roles played by various administrative personnel in conducting intramural, extramural, and club programs.
- Discuss how intramural, extramural, and club programs are administered in elementary schools, secondary schools, colleges, universities, and other organizations.
- Organize various types of competition for intramural and extramural activities.
- Show the importance of and the procedures for administering sport clubs, corecreation, and programs for handicapped students and faculty members.

Chapter Three was concerned with basic instructional physical education programs, one of the components of a well-rounded offering for students in schools and members of other organizations. This chapter is concerned with a second component, the intramural, extramural and club phase of the physical education program. This component offers competitive and other types of physical activities for individuals of all levels of skills and abilities.

Intramurals and extramurals comprise that phase of a physical education program in a school, college, industry, or other organization geared to the abilities and skills of the entire student body or the members of the organization. It consists of voluntary participation in games, sports, and other activities. This phase offers intramural activities within a single school or other institution and such extramural activities as play and sports days that bring together participants from several institutions.

A club program is usually devoted to one activity such as tennis, skiing, or mountain climbing, and it encourages students and other individuals to participate at all levels of skill. It may be managed by members of an organization, such as students in schools and colleges, or by the central management of an organization. Members, advisors, or community volunteers provide instruction. Clubs are popular in schools and colleges, as well as in other organizations. Many communities have tennis, swimming, racquetball, riding, and other types of clubs.

Intramurals were started many years ago as a result of student motivation in schools and colleges. Initially, they received little management support and were poorly organized. However, as student interest grew the demand for departmental control grew. In 1913 intramural sports came under faculty control at the University of Michigan and Ohio State University. Since that time intramurals, extramurals, and club programs have continued to grow and in most educational institutions today are under the management and direction of faculty personnel. The National Intramural Sports Council was organized in Washington, D.C., May 27-28, 1965, and held its first meeting in 1966.

INTRAMURAL AND EXTRAMURAL PROGRAMS
Objectives

The objectives of intramural and extramural programs are one indication of why such programs have expanded greatly throughout the country.

The objectives of intramural and extramural activities are compatible with the overall objectives of physical education and also with those of education in general.

The objectives of the intramural and extramural programs may be classified under four headings: (1) health, (2) skill, (3) social development, and (4) recreation.

Health. Intramural and extramural activities contribute to the physical, social, and emotional health of the individual. They contribute to physical health through participation in activities offering healthful exercise. Such characteristics as strength, agility, speed, and body control are developed. They contribute to social health through group participation and work toward achievement of group goals. They contribute to emotional health by helping a person achieve self-confidence and improve his or her self-concept.

Skill. Intramural and extramural activities offer the opportunity for every individual to display and develop his or her skills in various physical education activities. Through specialization and voluntary par-

ticipation they offer people the opportunity to excel and to experience the thrill of competition. It is generally agreed that an individual enjoys activities in which he or she has developed skill. Participation in athletics offers the opportunity to develop proficiency in group activities where each person is equated according to skill, thus providing for equality of competition, which helps guarantee greater success and enjoyment. Intramurals also enable many persons to spend leisure moments profitably and happily.

Social development. Opportunities for social development are numerous in intramural and extramural activities. Through many social contacts, coeducational experiences, playing on teams, and other situations, desirable qualities are developed. Individuals learn to subordinate their desires to the will of the group and to develop sportsmanship; they also learn fair play, courage, group loyalty, social poise, and other desirable traits. Voluntary participation exists in such a program, and persons who desire to play under such conditions will live by group codes of conduct. These experiences offer training for citizenship, adult living, and human relations.

Recreation. Intramural and extramural programs help develop an interest in many sports and physical education activities; this interest carries over into adult living and provides the basis for many happy leisure hours. These programs also provide excellent recreational activities during school days, when idle moments have the potential to foster antisocial behavior.

RELATION TO BASIC INSTRUCTIONAL AND HIGHLY ORGANIZED ATHLETIC PROGRAMS

Intramural and extramural activities and interscholastic and intercollegiate athletics are integral phases of the total physical education program in a school or college, which consists of the instructional program, the adapted program, the intramural and extramural program, and the varsity athletic program. Each has an important contribution to make to the achievement of physical education objectives. It is important to maintain a proper balance so each phase enhances and does not restrict the other phases of the total program.

The basic instructional program in physical education is looked on by most physical education leaders as the foundation on which the adapted, intramural and extramural, and highly organized athletic programs rest. The instructional program includes teaching such things as concepts, skills, and strategies. Intramural, extramural, and club programs provide opportunities for students and others to use these concepts, skills, and strategies in games and contests that are usually competitive. This part of the total physical education program is often referred to as the laboratory where the individual has an opportunity to experiment and test what has been learned in the instructional program.

Whereas intramurals and extramurals are for everyone, varsity athletics are usually for those individuals skilled in various physical activities. Intramurals are conducted on an intrainstitutional basis, whereas varsity athletics and extramurals are conducted on an interinstitutional basis.

Very little conflict will exist between these two phases of the program if the facilities, time, personnel, money, and other factors are apportioned according to the degree to which each phase achieves the desired outcome, rather than the degree of public appeal and interest stimulated. One should not be designed as a training ground for the other. It should be possible for a person to move from one to the other, but this should be incidental rather than planned.

If conducted properly, each phase of the program can contribute to the other, and through an overall, well-balanced program the entire student body or members of an organization will come to respect sports and the great potentials they have for improving physical, mental, social, and emotional growth. When a physical education program is initially developed, it seems logical first to provide an intramural program for the majority of persons, with the varsity athletic program becoming an outgrowth of it. The first concern should be for the majority. This is characteristic of the democratic way of life. Although the intramural and extramural athletic programs in a school or college are designed for every student, in practice they generally attract poorly skilled and moderately skilled individuals. The skilled person finds a niche in the varsity athletic program. This has its benefits in that it is an equalizer for competition.

The philosophical model[6] depicted in Fig. 4-1, *A*, illustrates one basis for the placement of intramurals in physical education programs. This triangular model displays an interdependency and a building of skills from the instructional level to the intramural level and finally to the athletic attainment level. This model conveys the philosophy that instruction is basic to the other programs and that intramural skills are essential to producing the athletic skills found in varsity play.

The model in Fig. 4-1, *B*, is presented because of its implications for viewing the phases of the physical education program as both interdependent and equal. It establishes each phase as independent of the others. Intramurals and athletics are placed close to each other because each is related to the other more closely than are recreation and instruction. Recreation has been added to the model because of its contribution to intramural activities and because both have as a primary objective the satisfaction derived from participation.

MANAGEMENT PERSONNEL

Many management personnel are needed if an intramural and extramural program is to be a success. Some key persons involved are the director, student leaders, student directors and unit managers, intramural and extramural council members, and officials.

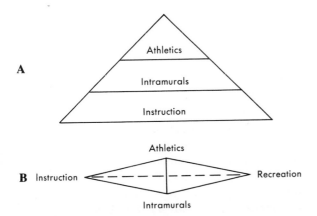

Fig. 4-1. A, Traditional triangular concept of physical education and intramurals. **B,** A modern conceptualization of physical education and intramurals.

Intramural competition at elementary school level.

The director

Many larger schools, colleges, businesses, and other organizations have established the position of director of intramurals and extramurals. In some cases other titles are used. The director is responsible for establishing programs, getting adequate funding, involving the community, and evaluating the success of the program. Some of the more specific duties of the director include planning programs; organizing tournaments and other forms of competition; supervising the maintenance of facilities, equipment, and supplies; attending and planning intramural council meetings; interpreting the program to the membership, the management, and the public in general; supervising the program in action; preparing budgets; and evaluating the worth of the program.

Place in management structure. The director or person in charge of intramurals in a school is usually responsible to the director of physical education. In some cases, not all of these various components are under the same department. However, intramural programs are usually a responsibility of the physical education department. Several colleges appoint one person to administer the entire campus recreation program of which intramurals, extramurals, and club activities are a part. In some cases control of intramurals is delegated to students themselves.

Intramural and extramural activities are part of the physical education program. However, in most cases they should be separate divisions of the overall program, receiving equal consideration with the other athletic divisions concerning staff members, finances, facilities, equipment, supplies, and other essentials. One staff member who is well trained in physical education and whose chief interest is intramural and extramural activities should be directly responsible for the program. Working with the director where conditions warrant should be assistant directors, supervisors, student managers, and other staff members as needed, depending on the size of the organization. There should also be an adequate number of officials.

Student leaders

Student involvement in all phases of education has been steadily increasing. Involvement in the management of intramurals and extramurals is happening in high schools and on college campuses. Roles of student leaders may range from serving as officials to being managers and office assistants. For example, many colleges have ''drop-in'' centers where student supervisors are available to establish programs, reserve equipment, and arrange for the gymnasium or swimming pool to be open for additional hours. Some schools have student managers who supervise intramural activity.

Student directors and unit managers

In some school programs the director of intramurals and extramurals appoints an upperclass student who has been involved with the program as student director. This student director may have such responsibilities as contacting officials, working with managers, issuing supplies, and scheduling.

Student unit managers have an important responsibility because they are in charge of a particular sport or activity. They usually work closely with the team captains and manage supplies and equipment, team rosters, and entry sheets, notifying teams of the time and date of contests and clarifying eligibility rules.

Intramural and extramural council members

An important feature of the overall management of an intramural or extramural program is an intramural and extramural council, which is usually an elected council with representatives from the participants, central administration, intramural staff, health department, and staff. The council is influential in establishing policy and practices for a broad athletic program. The council assists and advises the person in charge and the staff members. In some cases it plays an important role in the decision-making process. Councils usually have representatives from the various participating units who communicate information to the participating teams. The council also helps make decisions about program operation and serves as a sounding board for ways in which the program may be improved.

Officials

Excellent officials are necessary for a sound intramural program. They should have special qualifications, including a knowledge of the activity, the participants, the goals of the program, and the organization's philosophy of competition. Some of the responsibilities of the managers of the intramural program are to find sources for good officials and then to select and train them so they enhance the program. Some of the duties performed by officials are to have game equipment ready before the contest, see that accurate score sheets are prepared, check for any safety hazards, prepare accident reports if needed, and officiate the game or activity objectively and impartially. Some institutions put officials through a training program, supervise them during the playing season, and evaluate their performance after the season is over. Studies have shown that most colleges pay their intramural officials. Elementary and secondary schools usually do not have the money to pay officials, so they seek voluntary help from students, parents, and community workers. At the same time it is recognized that these volunteers need close supervision.

POLICIES FOR ORGANIZATION AND MANAGEMENT

A list of policies governing the various features of the program should be in writing and well publicized, perhaps as a handbook.

Policies for intramurals and extramurals should be developed in at least the following areas: student involvement in the organization and management of these programs, health and welfare of all participants, activities that meet the interests and needs of the participants, officiating, protests, eligibility standards, fees, postponements, point systems, and awards.

MANAGEMENT CONCERNS IN ELEMENTARY AND SECONDARY SCHOOLS

The management of intramurals at the elementary and secondary school levels presents some problems that are peculiar to these programs. Whereas in many colleges and universities students live in dormitories and on campus, this is not the case in elementary and secondary schools. Some students in the lower edu-

Recreational and intramural activities for children.

cational levels have to work after school or catch a bus to take them home and cannot stay after school to participate in intramurals, whereas the college student more often is able to participate because he or she is not faced with such a problem, at least in institutions where dormitory living exists. Also, many times the parents of elementary and secondary school students do not see the value of intramurals and so do not have their sons and daughters participating in them after school. College students, on the other hand, make their own decisions in most cases. Another problem faced by managers of elementary and secondary school intramural programs is the unavailability of facilities. Most schools have only one gymnasium and limited outdoor space. Varsity sports often are given priority in the use of these facilities, which works a hardship on the intramural program. The question of financial support also exists in many schools.

In light of these problems the physical educators in charge of intramural programs need to be creative when trying to manage such a program. In some schools, for example, they use community parks, YMCA swimming pools, and Boys Clubs facilities to help them provide a program that meets the needs of their students.[9]

ORGANIZATIONAL CONSIDERATIONS

The organization of an intramural or extramural program involves selecting activities, scheduling, determining eligibility, establishing awards and point systems, maintaining records, planning health examinations, financing, and directing publicity and promotion.

Activities.[7] The activities constituting the intramural and extramural program determine the amount of resulting participation. It is therefore important to select the right activities. Some management guidelines that will help in selecting activities follow:

- Activities should be selected in accordance with the season of the year and local conditions and influences.
- Activities should reflect the needs and interests of the students or the members of the organization.
- Coeducational recreational activities should be provided.

- The activities included in the physical education school instructional program should be coordinated with the activities included in the intramural and extramural program. The latter should act as a laboratory for the former.
- Many desirable activities require little special equipment and do not require long periods of training to get the participant in appropriate physical condition.
- Consideration should be given to such recreational activities as field trips, dramatics, hiking, and handicrafts.
- Activities should be selected with special attention to the ability and safety of the participant.

Self-directed intramural activities should have a place. Opportunities should be provided for students to come to a facility and work out without having to enter a competitive tournament. This is particularly necessary in light of the physical fitness movement and today's busy life-style.

The following are some activities that have been used successfully in various intramural and extramural programs throughout the nation:

Selected individual activities

Archery	Racquetball
Badminton	Rope climbing
Billiards	Scuba diving
Bowling	Shooting
Curling	Shuffleboard
Cycling	Skiing
Deck tennis	Swimming
Golf	Table tennis
Gymnastics	Tennis
Handball	Track and field
Horseshoes	Tumbling
Paddle tennis	Weight lifting
Physical fitness	Wrestling

Selected recreational activities

Camping and cookouts	Hosteling
Canoeing	Ice skating
Cycling	Rifle
Dancing	Roller skating
Figure skating	Rowing
Fishing	Sailing
Hiking	Tumbling
Horseback riding	

Selected team sports

Baseball	Softball
Basketball	Speedball
Field hockey	Swimming
Football	Touch (or flag) football
Gymnastics	Track and field
Ice hockey	Volleyball
Lacrosse	Water games
Soccer	

Scheduling. The time when intramural and extramural activities are scheduled will depend on the facilities, season of year, community, faculty availability, student needs, and budget requirements.

One of the most popular and convenient times for schools is late afternoon. This has proved best for many elementary, junior high, and senior high schools. In the spring and fall it has also been popular in colleges. It is an economical time because lights are not required and the outdoors is available. It also ensures more faculty supervision.

Evenings have been used quite extensively at colleges during the winter. This is not recommended for elementary, junior high, or senior high schools.

Some schools use hours during the school day. The physical education class is primarily an instructional period, however, and use of this period for intramurals or extramurals does not seem to be in conformance with the standards set by the profession. However, some schools have satisfactorily used free periods, activity periods, and club periods for the program when facilities are available.

The noon hour has been popular in some schools, especially in elementary and secondary schools and particularly in rural schools where students do not go home for lunch. Because students will be active anyway, such a period offers possibilities in selected situations, if strenuous activities are not offered.

Saturdays have also been used in some situations. Although the weekend is a problem in some localities because many individuals have to work or have planned this time to be with their families, it has worked successfully in many communities.

The time before school in the morning has also been satisfactory in a few schools.

Special days are set aside in some schools for field days when all the students participate in a day or a half-day devoted entirely to the program's activities.

In recent years the computer has been used with greater frequency in scheduling intramural events. Most schools, especially colleges, have a computer for registration or financial procedures, and this computer may also be used for scheduling.

Intramural activities in industry, youth-serving agencies, and other organizations are scheduled at various times to meet the convenience of the members. Activities might be scheduled at any time during the day and the night.

Eligibility. A few simple eligibility rules are needed. These should be kept to a minimum, because the intramural and extramural programs should offer something for the vast majority of students.

It is generally agreed that in schools and colleges players should not be allowed to participate in activities when they are on the varsity team or squad. Professionals should be barred from those activities in which they are professional. A student should be allowed to participate on only one team in a given activity during the season. Students, of course, should be regularly enrolled in the school and carrying what the institution rules is a normal load. Unsportsmanlike conduct should be dealt with in a manner that is in the best interests of the individual concerned, the program, and the established goals. Certain activities by their very nature should not be engaged in by individuals with certain health problems. Therefore such individuals should be cleared by the health department of the school before participation is allowed in such activities.

Recently, several states have instituted policies linking academic achievement and attendance of students with their eligibility to participate in extracurricular activities.[1] However, some controversy has developed about whether a student should be denied the right to participate in such activities because of low grades. In some cases state officials have threatened to challenge such action in the courts.

Awards. There are arguments pro and con concerning granting awards for intramural and extramural competition. Some argue that awards stimulate inter-

Intramural tug-of-war in the Clark County Public Schools, Las Vegas, Nevada.

est, are an incentive for participation, and recognize achievement. Some argue that awards make the program more expensive, that a few individuals win most of the awards, and that they are unnecessary because individuals would participate even if no awards were given. Leaders who oppose awards also stress that there should be no expectation of awards for voluntary, leisure-time participation and that it is difficult to make awards on the basis of all factors that should be considered. Their belief is that the joy and satisfaction received are reward enough.

One study indicates that approximately four out of five intramural directors give awards. Letters, numerals, and similar awards are used most frequently in schools; medals and trophies are given more extensively at junior colleges, 4-year colleges, and in other organizations.

Awards, if given, should be inexpensive, such as medals, ribbons, certificates, plaques, cups, or letters.

Point systems. Most intramural programs have a cumulative point system figured on an all-year basis, which maintains interest and enthusiasm over the course of the school year and encourages greater participation.

A system of keeping points should be developed that stimulates wholesome competition, maintains continued interest, and is in conformance with the objectives of the total program. The system should be readily understood by all and easy to administer. Under such conditions, points should be awarded on the basis of contests won, championships gained, standing in a league or order of finishing, participation, sportsmanship, and contribution to the objectives of the program.

A point system might be based on the following items:
Each entry, 10 points
Each win, 2 points
Each loss, 1 point
Forfeits, 0 points
Each team championship, 10 points
Second-place team championship, 6 points
Third-place team championship, 3 points
Each individual championship, 6 points
Second-place individual championship, 4 points

Trophies awarded by Youth Services Section, Los Angeles City Schools.

Third-place individual championship, 3 points
Each game an official works, 3 points
Being homeroom representative, 10 points
Each meeting attended by homeroom representative, 2 points

Protests of forfeitures.[10] Procedures should be established in advance so that all persons involved know what the rules are when a protest is made and forfeitures of contests take place. The circumstances under which protests and forfeitures will be acted upon, who will make the decision, and the penalties that will be assessed should be clearly set forth. An attempt should be made to have established policies that help to prevent and discourage protests of forfeitures since a great deal of time and effort are involved in such actions, and they also frequently result in bad feelings and negative public relations.

Records. Efficient management of the program will necessitate keeping records. These should not be extensive but should contain the information needed to determine the worth of the program and the progress being made.

Such records allow for comparison with other similar organizations. They show the degree to which the program is providing for the needs of the entire membership and the extent of participation. They show the activities that are popular and the ones that are not so popular. They focus attention on the best units of competition, needs of the program, effective management procedures, and leadership strengths and weaknesses. Record keeping is an important phase of the program that should not be overlooked.

Use of computers in intramurals.[2] Intramurals can be managed much more efficiently using some of the versatile programs now available for the computer. Information such as the following can be stored in the computer: team statistics (names, addresses, and telephone numbers), team win-loss records, eligibility facts, officials, and team history. In this way such things as eligibility of players can be checked quickly, team records can be determined on short notice, faculty availability is known, schedules can be reproduced easily, and program evaluation can be conducted effectively. Particularly in large programs use of the computer can result in the elimination of much book work and the rendering of greater service to students and other clientele.

Health examinations. Health examinations should be required of all participants as a safeguard to their health. Sometimes this is taken care of through an annual health examination and at other times through special examinations given before a seasonal activity starts.

Finances. The finances involved in intramural and extramural programs are raised in various ways. Because these programs have as many, or more, contributions to make to educational objectives as other parts of the educational program, they should be financed out of board of education and central administration funds, just as other phases of the program are financed. They should be included in the regular physical education budget and supported through regularly budgeted school or college income.

Another method of financing the programs that has proved satisfactory in some high schools and colleges incorporates the cost of running the programs in the regular activity fee that includes student activities such as dramatics, the interscholastic athletic program, musicals, and band concerts. This provides funds in proportion to the student enrollment and can be anticipated in advance. Also, this method eliminates any additional charges to the student.

Other methods of financing used by some organizations include using money taken from athletic gate receipts, equipment rental, required participant entry fee, and special fund-raising projects such as athletic nights, carnivals, and presenting talented athletic and other groups. Some argue that such practices create an overemphasis on gate receipts, that they discourage spectators from attending and persons from participating, and that they require special projects to raise money, which should not be necessary for such a valuable phase of the program.

Publicity and promotion. Members of an organization and the public in general must understand the intramural and extramural programs, the individuals they service, the activities offered, and their objec-

tives. Such information can be disseminated to the right individuals only through a well-planned publicity and promotion program.

Newspapers should be encouraged to give appropriate space to these activities. Brochures, bulletin boards, posters, and the school or organization's newspaper can help focus attention on the program. Notices can be prepared and sent home to parents in elementary and secondary schools. A handbook can be prepared that explains all the various aspects of the total program and can be given to all who are interested. Record boards can be constructed and placed in conspicuous settings. Clinics can be held on the various sports. Orientation talks and discussions can be held in school and college assemblies and at other gatherings. Special days can be held with considerable publicity, and such catch slogans as "It Pays to Play" can be adopted. A good job of publicity and promotion will result in greater student participation and better public understanding.

At Downers Grove (Illinois) North High School, where they offer 40 activities a year, the organizers feel they have the ingredients to publicize the program. These ingredients include a *Weekly Trojans Intramural Report,* T-shirts for champions, team uniforms paid for by local merchants, pictures of winners on the Intramural Bulletin Board, community-oriented events such as the Trojan mile for runners, and an annual Intramural Champions Pizza Party.

PATTERNS OF ORGANIZATION
Intramural and extramural programs in the elementary school

The intramural and extramural programs in the elementary school should be outgrowths of the instructional program. They should consist of a broad variety of activities including stunts, rhythmic activities, relays, and tumbling. They should be suited to the ages and interests of children at this level and should be carefully supervised. The younger children in the primary grades probably will benefit most from free play. In the upper elementary grades, recess periods and afterschool activities can take place on both intragrade and intergrade bases. The programs should be broad, varied, and progressive, with participants similar in maturity and ability.

Guidelines for intramural and extramural programs in the elementary school follow:

- A basic instructional offering geared to the needs, interests, and growth and developmental levels of elementary school children should be prerequisite to and foundational for intramural and extramural programs.
- Qualified leadership should be provided, including competencies involving understanding the physical, mental, emotional, and social needs of elementary school children.
- Competition should involve only children compatible in maturity, size, and ability.

SUGGESTED PROGRAM OF ACTIVITIES FOR ELEMENTARY SCHOOLS[4]

Fall and spring

Beat the runner	Prisoner out
Bicycle distance race	Punchball
Cosom hockey	Relays
Dodge ball	Rope jumping
Endball	Soccer
Fitness day	Soccer kick
Flag football	Softball
Foursquare	Speedball
Hopscotch	Stealing sticks
Kickball	Tetherball
Longball	Track and field
Playdays	Wiffleball

Winter

Badminton	Newcomb
Basket shooting	Relays
Basketball	Rhythms
Battleball	Rope climbing
Bowling	Shuffleboard
Cageball	Trampolining
Cosom bowling	Tug-of-war
Cosom hockey	Tumbling
Dodge ball	Volleyball
Gym scooters	Wiffleball
Gymnastics	Wrestling
Ice skating	

From Hyatt, R.W.

- Intramurals and extramurals should be limited to grades four through six in the elementary school. In grades kindergarten through three the regular basic instructional physical education program provides sufficient competition.
- Desirable social, emotional, physical, and health outcomes for students should be the aim of intramural and extramural programs.
- Activities such as tackle football and boxing should not be permitted.
- The planning of the program should involve students, parents, and community.

Intramural and extramural programs in the middle school and junior high school

The main concentration in athletics should be on intramurals in the middle school and intramurals and extramurals in the junior high school. At these educational levels students are taking a special interest in sports, but at the same time their immaturity makes it unwise to allow them to engage in a highly organized interscholastic program. The program should involve both boys and girls, appeal to the entire student body, have good supervision by a trained physical educator, and be adapted to the needs and interests of the pupils.

Many authoritative and professional groups favor broad intramural and extramural programs and oppose a varsity interscholastic, competitive program in junior high school. They feel this is in the best interests of youths at this age.

The junior high school provides a setting for giving students fundamental skills in many sports and activities. It is a time of limitless energy when physiological changes and rapid growth are taking place. Youths in junior high schools should have proper outlets to develop themselves healthfully.

Intramural and extramural programs in the senior high school, college, and university[3]

At senior high schools, colleges, and universities the intramural and extramural programs should receive a major emphasis. At this time the interests and needs of students require such a program. These students want and need to experience the joy and satisfaction that are a part of playing on a team, excelling in an

Inner-city youths in Los
Angeles enjoy and benefit
from recreational
experiences.

activity with one's own peers, and developing skill. Every high school, college, and university should see to it that a broad and varied program is part of the total physical education plan.

The intramural and extramural programs should receive more emphasis than they are now getting at senior high schools and colleges. They are basic to sound education. They are settings where the skills learned and developed in the instructional program can be put to use in a practical situation, with all the fun that comes from such competition. They should form a basis for applying skills that will be used during leisure time, both in the present and in the future.

Personnel for such programs should be adequate. Good leadership is needed if the programs are to prosper. Each school should be concerned with developing a plan where proper supervision and leadership are available for afterschool hours. Qualified officials are also a necessity to ensure equal and sound competition. Facilities, equipment, and supplies should be apportioned equitably for the entire physical educa-

tion program. No part of any group or any program should monopolize facilities and equipment.

The college and university level offers an ideal setting for play and sports days for both men and women.

Sports clubs should be encouraged in those activities having special appeal to groups of students. Through such clubs, greater skill is developed in the activity, and the social experiences are worthwhile.

Coeducational recreational activities should play a prominent part in the program, and Title IX ensures that this will take place. Girls and boys need to participate together. Many of the activities in the high school and college programs adapt well to both sexes. Such activities include volleyball, softball, tennis, badminton, table tennis, folk and square dancing, bowling, swimming, and skating. In some cases the rules of the games will need to be modified. The play and sports days also offer a setting where both sexes can participate and enjoy worthwhile competition together.

SUGGESTED ACTIVITIES FOR JUNIOR HIGH AND MIDDLE SCHOOLS

F = fall
W = winter
S = spring
A = all seasons (popular sport)

Team sports

A	Basketball	W	Ice hockey	A	Speedball
S	Baseball (boys)	FS	Kickball	F	Touch (or flag) football
A	Dodge ball	W	Newcomb ball	S	Track and field
S	Fieldball	A	Soccer	F	Tug-of-war
FS	Field hockey	S	Softball	W	Volleyball
W	Gymnastics				

Individual and dual sports

FS	Archery	FS	Horseshoes	A	Table tennis
A	Badminton	FS	Paddle tennis	FS	Tennis
A	Basketball goal shooting	A	Paddleball	A	Tetherball
A	Bounce ball	FS	Paddle tetherball	FS	Track and field
A	Bowling	A	Quoits	AW	Tumbling
W	Deck tennis	A	Rope climbing	W	Wrestling (boys)
A	Handball (1-wall)	A	Shuffleboard		

Corecreational activities

A	Badminton	FS	Golf	W	Skiing
A	Bicycling	FS	Horseshoes	A	Table tennis
A	Bowling	W	Ice skating	FS	Tennis
FS	Canoeing	FS	Roller skating	FS	Track and field
A	Dance (social and folk)	A	Shuffleboard	AW	Volleyball
W	Deck tennis				

Club activities

A	Bicycling	FS	Fishing	S	Outings
S	Canoeing	A	Hiking	FS	Roller skating
A	Dance (social, folk, square, modern)	W	Ice skating	A	Tumbling

Special events

FS	Track-and-field meet	FS	Field day	WS	Relay carnival
WA	Basketball skills contest	S	Baseball and softball field meet		

From Hyatt, R.W.

SUGGESTED PROGRAM OF ACTIVITIES FOR SENIOR HIGH SCHOOLS*

Aerial darts	Gymnastics	Social, square, and folk dancing
Archery	Handball	Softball
Badminton	Hiking	Speedball
Basketball	Horseshoes	Swimming
Basket shooting	Ice skating	Table tennis
Bicycle distance race	Jogging	Tennis
Bowling	Kickball	Touch, or flag, football
Chess and/or checkers	Paddleball	Track and field
Cross-country	Physical fitness	Trampolining
Deck tennis	Roller skating	Tug-of-war
Field hockey	Rope climbing	Tumbling
Fitness day	Shuffleboard	Volleyball
Golf	Skating	Water polo
GRA	Soccer	Wrestling

From Hyatt, R.W.

Intramural and extramural programs in other organizations

Intramural and extramural programs play a major role in many organizations outside the educational domain. For example, in industry there are many intramural leagues for employees in a variety of sports and other physical activities. In many instances baseball diamonds, basketball courts, jogging areas, platform and lawn tennis courts, swimming pools, and even golf courses are provided. Employees usually take an active role in these programs, which contribute much to their morale and well-being.

Students enjoying a golf game during their leisure hours, Colgate University, Hamilton, N.Y.

MIAMI-DADE COMMUNITY COLLEGE[4]
Miami, Florida

Men's events	Women's events
Fall	
Water polo	Speed and novelty
Swimming	swimming
Bowling	Golf
Flag football	Volleyball
Archery	Bowling
Volleyball	Scavenger hunt
Biliards	Kickball
Tug-of-war	Sit-down volleyball
Turkey run	Turkey run
Wrestling	Badminton
Winter	
Novelty swim	Games night
Basketball	Basketball and free throw
Falcon 50 (bicycle race)	contest
Track and field	Filly 440
Table tennis	Track and field
Racquetball	Frisbee
Golf	Archery
Softball	Deck tennis
Badminton	Softball
Gym hockey	Speed and novelty swim
Tennis	Easter egg throw

From Hyatt, R.W.

What is true in business is also true in YMCAs, Boys Clubs, and other youth- and adult-serving agencies. Intramurals represent an important part of their curricular offering.

The same types of tournaments and forms of competition employed in schools and colleges are used in these nonschool organizations.

UNITS AND TYPES OF COMPETITION

The careful selection of appropriate units and types of competition will help enhance the values that accrue from intramural and extramural activities.

Units of competition. Many ways exist for organizing competition for the intramural and extramural programs. The units of competition should lend inter-est, create enthusiasm, and allow for identity with some group where an esprit de corps can be developed and where a healthy attitude is added to the competition.

At the elementary school level, the classroom provides a basis for such activity. It may be desirable in some cases to organize on some other basis, but the basic structure of the homeroom lends itself readily to this purpose.

At middle, junior high, and senior high schools, several units of organization are possible. Organization may be by grades or classes, homerooms, age, height, weight, clubs, societies, residential districts, physical education classes, study groups, or the arbitrary establishment of groups by staff members. The type of unit organization will vary from school to school and from community to community. The staff member in charge of the program should try to determine the method of organization best suited to the local situation.

At a college or university or in an industry or other organization several units for organization are also possible. Organization may be on the basis of fraternities or sororities, classes, colleges within a university, departments, clubs, societies, physical education classes, boarding clubs, churches, residential districts, geographic units or zones of the campus, dormitories, marital status, social organization, assignment by lot, honorary societies, or groups set up arbitrarily. Again, the best type of organization will vary from situation to situation.

Types of competition. Several different ways of organizing competition are possible. Three of the most common are leagues, tournaments, and meets. These methods of organization take many forms, with league play popular in the major sports, elimination tournaments used to a great extent after league play has terminated, and meets held to culminate a season or year of sports activity.

Individual and group competition may be provided. Individual competition is adaptable to such team activities as basketball, softball, and field hockey.

Various types of tournament competition have been written up widely in books specializing in intramurals and other aspects of sports. For this reason only a brief discussion of these items will be included here.

The round robin tournament is probably one of the most widely used and one of the best types of competition, because it allows for maximum play. It is frequently used in leagues, where it works best with no more than eight teams. Each team plays every other team at least once during the tournament. Each team continues to play to the completion of the tournament, and the winner is the one who has the highest percentage, based on wins and losses, at the end of scheduled play.

The elimination tournament does not allow for maximum play; the winners continue to play, while the losers drop out. A team or individual is automatically out when it or he or she loses. However, this is the most economical form of organization from the standpoint of time in determining the winning player or team.

The single or straight elimination tournament is set up so that one defeat eliminates a player or team (Fig. 4-2). Usually a drawing for positions takes place, with provisions for seeding the better players or teams on the basis of past experience. Such seeding provides more intense competition as the tournament moves toward the finals. Under such an organization, byes are awarded in the first round of play whenever the number of entrants is not even. Although such a tournament is a timesaver, it is weak because it does not adequately select the second- and third-place winners. The actual winner may achieve the championship because another player who is better has a bad day. Another weakness is that the majority of participants play only once or twice in the tournament.

The double elimination tournament does not have some of the weaknesses of the single elimination, because it is necessary for a team or individual to lose twice before being eliminated.[5] This is also characteristic of various types of consolation elimination tournaments that permit the player or team to play more than once (Fig. 4-3).

In some consolation tournaments all the players who lose in the first round and those who, because they received a bye, did not lose until the second round get to play again to determine a consolation winner. In other similar tournaments any player or team who loses once, regardless of the round in which

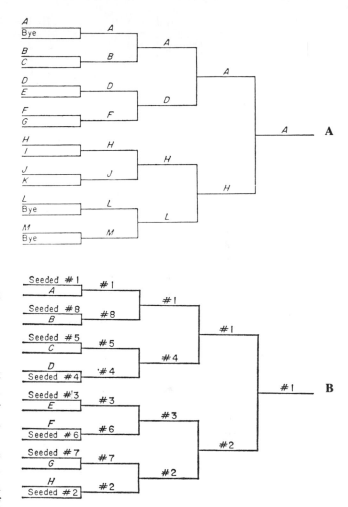

Fig. 4-2. A, Single elimination tournament. **B,** Single elimination tournament with seedings.

the loss occurs, is allowed to play again. There are also other tournaments, such as the Bagnall-Wild Elimination Tournament, that place emphasis on second and third places.

The ladder tournament adapts well to individual competition. Here the contestants are arranged in ladder, or vertical, formation with rankings established arbitrarily or on the basis of previous performance. Each contestant may challenge the one directly above or in some cases two above, and if he or she

I. 1 vs. 5
   2 vs. 6
   3 vs. 7
   4 vs. 8

II. 1 vs. 2
    3 vs. 5
    4 vs. 6
    8 vs. 7

III. 1 vs. 3
     4 vs. 2
     8 vs. 5
     7 vs. 6

IV. 1 vs. 4
    8 vs. 3
    7 vs. 2
    6 vs. 5

V. 1 vs. 8
   7 vs. 4
   6 vs. 3
   5 vs. 2

VI. 1 vs. 7
    6 vs. 8
    5 vs. 4
    2 vs. 3

VII. 1 vs. 6
     5 vs. 7
     2 vs. 8
     3 vs. 4

A

B

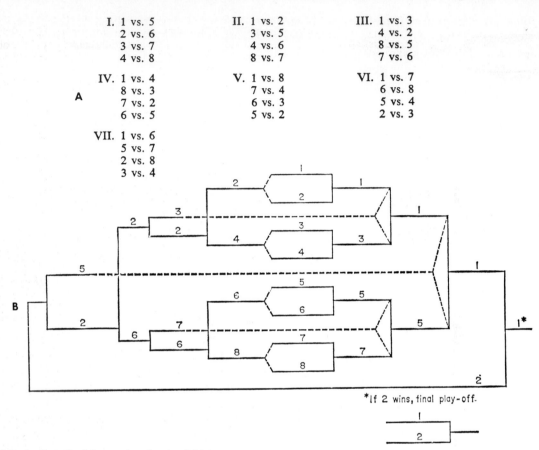

*If 2 wins, final play-off.

Fig. 4-3. **A,** Round robin rotation for an eight-team league. **B,** Double elimination tournament. **C,** Consolation tournament–teams. **D,** Ladder tournament.

C

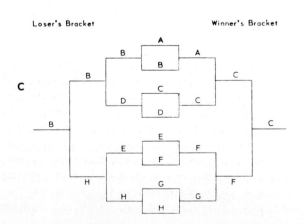

D

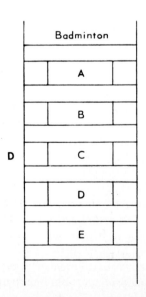

UNIVERSITY OF TENNESSEE[4]

Men	Women	Faculty/staff	Corecreation
Fall			
Team:	Team:		
Football	Football	Football	Paddleball
Bowling	Tug-of-war	Golf	Racquetball
Handball	Volleyball	Handball	Tennis
Tug-of-war	Badminton	Paddleball	Badminton
Volleyball		Racquetball	
Golf		Squash	
		Tennis	
Individual and dual:	Individual and dual:	Badminton	
Handball	Paddleball	Turkey trot	
Paddleball	Racquetball		
Racquetball	Squash		
Squash	Tennis		
Tennis	Golf (par 3)		
Golf (par 3)	Pass, punt, and kick		
Pass, punt, and kick	Turkey trot		
Turkey trot			
Winter			
Team:	Team:		
Basketball	Basketball	Three-player basketball	Paddleball
Racquetball	Inner tube water polo	Handball	Racquetball
Inner tube water polo	Swimming and diving	Paddleball	Badminton
Swimming and diving	Bowling	Racquetball	Table tennis
Track relays		Squash	
Individual and dual:	Individual and dual:		
Handball	Paddleball		
Paddleball	Racquetball		
Racquetball	Squash		
Squash	Badminton		
Badminton	Basketball free throw		
Basketball free throw			
Wrestling			

From Hyatt, R.W.

wins, the names change places on the ladder. This is a continuous type of tournament that does not eliminate any participants. However, it is weak because it may drag and interest may wane.

The pyramid tournament is similar to the ladder variety (Fig. 4-4). Here, instead of having one name on a rung or step, several names are on the lower steps, gradually pyramiding to the top-ranking individual. A player may challenge anyone in the same horizontal row, and then the winner may challenge anyone in the row above him or her.

The spider web tournament takes its name from the

bracket design, which is the shape of a spider's web (Fig. 4-5). The championship position is at the center of the web. The bracket consists of five (or any other selected number) lines drawn radially from the center, and the participants' names are placed on concentric lines crossing these radial lines. Challenges may be made by persons on any concentric line to any person on the next line closer to the center. This tournament provides more opportunity for activity.

The type of tournament organization adopted should be the one best for the group, activity, and local interests. The goal should be to have as much participation as possible for the facilities and time available. Tournaments encourage participant interest and enthusiasm and are an important part of intramural and extramural athletic programs.

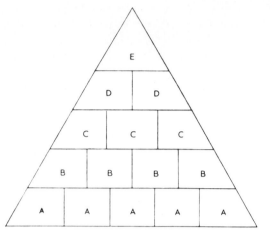

Any A may challenge any B.
Any B may challenge any C.
Any C may challenge any D.
Either D may challenge E.

Fig. 4-4. Pyramid tournament.

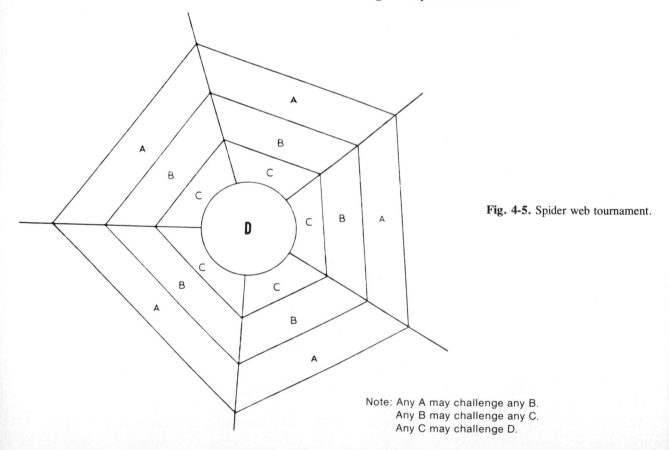

Fig. 4-5. Spider web tournament.

Note: Any A may challenge any B.
Any B may challenge any C.
Any C may challenge D.

EXTRAMURALS

Extramurals are a part of the total physical education program that represent an increase in the intensity of competition above that of intramurals. Whereas intramurals are conducted within a school, college, or other organization, extramurals represent informal competition with other schools, colleges, and organizations. Extramurals usually involve participants regardless of their skills and abilities. Also, they are less highly organized than varsity athletic programs. Furthermore, the emphasis is more on social outcomes than on winning. Three types of extramurals are discussed here: sports days, play days, and invitation days.

Sports days, play days, and invitation days

Sports days, play days, and invitation days are rapidly growing in popularity and deserve a prominent place in the extramural athletic program of any school, college, or other organization. Although they have been used mainly by girls' and women's physical education programs, they are equally important for boys and men. They have received the endorsement of AAHPERD, the National Association for Girls and Women in Sport, and many other prominent associations concerned with physical education.

Sports days refer to a program when one or several schools, colleges, or other organizations participate in physical education activities. They may enter several teams in various sports. When thus organized, each team is identified with the institution it represents. Sports days may also be used to culminate a season of activity for participants within, for example, the same school or college. When several schools or colleges participate in a sports day, the number of activities may range from one to eight, although it is generally agreed that having too many activities is sometimes a disadvantage. No significant awards are granted for the various events, and the publicity does not encourage fierce competition.

Play days usually refer to a day or part of a day set aside for participation in physical education activities. It may be for participants from the same school, college, or organizations ranging from several institutions in the same community, or from many schools and colleges in various communities and organizations. In the play day each team is composed of individuals from different organizations. Here the organization loses its identity, whereas it is maintained in the sports day. The teams are usually labeled by distinctively colored uniforms, arm bands, numbers, or some other device. The activities can be individual or team and competitive or noncompetitive. It would be noncompetitive, for example, if several students desired to engage in horseback riding, not for the purpose of competing against one another but simply for the sociability of the occasion.

Invitation days refer to a time when two schools, colleges, or other organizations usually meet for competition in an activity. This practice has worked out successfully at the end of a seasonal activity, when the winning intramural team or representatives from several teams compete against a similar group from another school, college, or other organization. The emphasis, however, is not on placing selected, highly skilled players on one team to enhance the chances of winning but on the social benefits and fun that can be gained from the occasion.

The advantages of sports days, play days, and invitation days are evident. They offer opportunities for all members of a school or an organization to participate in wholesome competition regardless of skill. They offer the individual an opportunity to participate in many varied activities in a spirit of friendly rivalry. They stress both social and physical values. They eliminate the pressures and undesirable practices associated with highly competitive athletics. They are available to all. They are especially adaptable for immature youngsters who should not be exposed to the practices and pressures of high-level competition. They add interest to student participation and offer innumerable opportunities for leadership.

SPORTS CLUBS

The concept of a sports club originated in Europe where many community sports clubs exist. A sports club specializes in a particular activity. Club teams are often established, and equipment and other expenses are usually paid for by the club members. The administration of the club is composed of voluntary or paid coaches, managers, and officers.

Some advantages of sports clubs include the following: they provide opportunities for students and others to engage in activities of interest to them but not available in other parts of the physical education program; they provide opportunities for self-administration, self-financing, and self-planning; and they provide opportunities for students and faculty members to participate together.

A definite plan is needed whereby sports clubs can be readily organized and readily disbanded if sufficient interest is not evident. Some suggested items to consider include the need for a faculty or other responsible person to provide leadership for the club, obtaining needed funds, establishing rules and regulations, securing necessary equipment, and electing a committee to recommend policies.

Sports clubs provide interested participants an opportunity for social group experiences and for the enjoyment of a particular sports activity. Clubs have many different interests, including water ballet, table tennis, boating, and ice skating. Most sports clubs in schools and colleges provide for student administration and financing. Financing may be derived from students through student fees, dances, and exhibition games. The club should provide for some relationship with the athletic administration of the institution. Procedures and policies clarifying this relationship should be a part of the club's bylaws. Such a relationship is necessary in matters of equipment and facility use, eligibility insurance, travel, injuries, and program assistance.

Sports clubs in operation today include those concerned with activities such as the following: skiing, soccer, karate, trap and skeet shooting, weight lifting, archery, bowling, boxing, canoeing, cricket, racquetball, judo, lacrosse, dance, mountaineering, parachuting, hang gliding, rifle and pistol target practice, rodeo, rugby, sailing, scuba, fencing, and flying.

Sports clubs are the responsibility of the intramural manager in many organizations. As such, the manager sees that constitution and bylaws, membership qualifications, fees, advisors, officers, coaches, scheduling, and financing are provided for.

In some cases clubs are financially self-sufficient as

Chess as a recreational activity, Milwaukee, Wis.

a result of fees and assessments of the members of the organization. In other instances the school, college, business, or other organization underwrites the cost of operating the club. In other cases finances are provided by the members themselves.

Equipment and facilities for clubs may be provided by the organization or may be rented. Travel and transportation may be provided by the organization or paid for by the participants.

The responsibility for insurance usually rests with the club member. Some organizations obtain reduced group insurance rates for their members.

COEDUCATIONAL RECREATION

In light of Title IX and in view of the desire and interest on the part of girls and women to engage in sports, physical education, and recreation activities, coeducational recreation (corecreation) is growing very rapidly, not only in schools and colleges, but also in community recreation and other organizational programs.

According to Hyatt[4] the objectives of corecreational sports in adapted form are as follows: (1) to provide opportunities for both sexes to engage in wholesome play experiences; (2) to provide opportunities for cooperative efforts of both sexes; (3) to provide new programs and activities for couples; (4) to enable participants to enjoy themselves, have fun, and develop friendships; (5) to provide opportunities for both sexes to experience new activities and develop skills; and (6) to provide the skills and information needed for spending leisure hours constructively in physical pursuits.

The corecreational program should offer opportunities for participation in many types of activities, including individual sports, team sports, noncompetitive activities, social activities, and both indoor and outdoor activities. Activities such as golf, tennis, swimming, archery, raquetball, dance, and skating are especially suited to corecreational programs. Competition, when offered, should meet the needs, abilities, and interests of both sexes. In certain cases modification of the rules of some sports may be necessary.

One southern educational institution offers the following corecreational activities:

Fall quarter—tennis, shuffleboard, horseshoes, turkey trot
Winter quarter—paddleball, racquetball, badminton, table tennis
Spring quarter—basketball, softball, volleyball, paddleball, racquetball
Summer quarter—softball, volleyball, paddleball, racquetball, tennis

The corecreational program will enhance intramural, extramural, and club activities. It is greatly needed and should represent an important part of these programs in the future.

FACULTY, STAFF, AND FAMILY PROGRAMS

Faculty members, staff members, and families of members of educational institutions and other organizations need to have opportunities to engage in recreational activities. In some institutions programs that include activities such as volleyball, softball, basketball, tennis, golf, handball, racquetball, badminton, swimming, jogging, and bowling have been very popular. Sometimes teams and leagues are organized to add variety to the competition. Faculty sports clubs and fitness programs have been exceptionally well received. Faculty-family recreation nights or Saturday or Sunday afternoons are favorites. In such cases children usually are not admitted unless accompanied by their parents. Faculty-student activities and sports nights are also scheduled in some schools and colleges.

In institutions where the faculty members, staff members, and families have been provided for in the recreational program, dividends have accrued for these programs in the form of support and financial help. Participants greatly appreciate it if dressing and locker room facilities can also be furnished.

INTRAMURALS FOR THE HANDICAPPED

In the same way that instructional physical education programs are provided for the handicapped so should intramural, extramural, and club programs be provided for them. The University of New Mexico has shown how this objective can be accomplished. After assessing the needs of the handicapped at this institution it was determined that a variety of recreational

CHECKLIST FOR SCHOOL CLUB AND ACTIVITY PROGRAMS

	Yes	No
1. Are club activity programs a normal outgrowth of the regular school program?		
2. Are there clearly stated objectives for the club or activity program?		
3. Does the club program supplement the formal curriculum by increasing knowledge and skills?		
4. Are clubs organized in terms of educational value rather than administrative convenience?		
5. Does the administration set adequate policies to guide the program?		
6. Have the aims and objectives of the club or activity program been determined?		
7. Can any student join a club?		
8. Is a student limited to the number of clubs he or she may join?		
9. Does each club have a simple constitution and bylaws that can guide students in the conduct of the organization?		
10. Do the clubs prepare the student for democratic living?		
11. Do the activities help to develop school spirit?		
12. Does the school schedule club activities so that they do not conflict with regularly scheduled school activities?		
13. Does the school administrator guarantee the program adequate space and funds to carry on a worthwhile program?		
14. Can a student discover and develop special attitudes and abilities through the club and activity program?		
15. Does the club and activity program offer opportunities for vocational exploration?		
16. Is the individual student able to develop socially acceptable attitudes and ideals through the club program?		
17. Does the club experience provide situations that will contribute to the formation of improved behavior patterns in the student?		
18. Do all club members actively participate in program planning?		
19. Are the projects and activities of the club initiated primarily by the students?		
20. Do the activities performed pertain to the club purposes?		
21. Are students allowed to select clubs and activities according to interests?		
22. Are students issued a calendar of events?		
23. Does the school library make available books and periodicals needed by club and activity groups?		
24. Does the club faculty advisor enlist the confidence of boys and girls?		
25. Is the club faculty advisor willing to give time and thought to making the club or activity program a success?		
26. Is the club faculty advisor able to find his or her chief satisfaction in pupil growth and not in appreciation of personal efforts?		
27. Does the administration of the school evaluate the club periodically?		
28. Does the club allow time for the evaluation of activities?		

Skiing as a recreational activity, Colgate University, Hamilton, N.Y.

Physical education programs are needed for inner-city youths. A baseball game offered by Youth Services Section, Los Angeles City Schools.

AN INTRAMURAL PROGRAM EVALUATION CHECKLIST[8]

A program can be evaluated in terms of the stated principles and objectives or according to prevalent acceptable standards.

How does the intramural program measure up to the acceptable minimum standards? By taking a few minutes to check off the items listed below, a quick evaluation can be made of the present status of the excellence of the program.

Philosophy and objectives   Yes   No

1. Is a written philosophy or a set of objectives available to the participants?   _____   _____

Organization and administration

1. Is the director professionally qualified to administer the program?   _____   _____
2. Does the director devote sufficient time per week to administering his or her program? _____   _____
3. Are participants included in the management of the program?   _____   _____
4. Is there an advisory committee?   _____   _____

Units of competition

1. Are participants classified according to ability, age, height, or weight within the competitive unit? _____   _____
2. Within the basic unit, are participants permitted to choose the members of their teams? _____   _____

Program activities

1. Does the director consult with the participants to make sure that their interests are of prime consideration in the selection of activities for the program? _____   _____
2. Are there both strenuous and nonstrenuous sports in the program?   _____   _____
3. Are there both team and individual sports in the program?   _____   _____
4. Are there at least five different sports making up the program?   _____   _____
5. Do corecreational activities make up part of the program?   _____   _____

Time periods

1. Do the hours that participants are free receive top priority for scheduling?   _____   _____
2. Is the noon hour used for intramurals?   _____   _____

Methods of organizing competition

1. Is the round robin tournament used whenever possible in preference to others?   _____   _____

Point system of awards

1. Is recognition of any kind given to the participants for their achievements?   _____   _____
2. Is the award primarily for achievement instead of incentive for participants?   _____   _____

Rules and regulations

1. Are the rules defining such things as eligibility, health, safety, forfeits, postponements, and team membership distributed to all participants? _____   _____
2. Is the lack of good sportsmanship regarded as a rule violated?   _____   _____
3. Is equipment provided for all the activities offered?   _____   _____

From Matthews, D.O.

AN INTRAMURAL PROGRAM EVALUATION CHECKLIST—cont'd

Publicity

1. Is there a special bulletin board for intramural information?　　　　　　————　————

Finances

1. Does the organization provide funds for the operation of the program?　　————　————

Rating scale

A "yes" answer must be given in each category if a program is to be considered *good* or *excellent*.

Excellent	15 to 22
Good	13 to 14
Fair	10 to 12
Poor	9 or below

---

activities should be available for the handicapped population on campus. It was felt that the involvement of the handicapped in sports and related activities would be of great value to these students because they would be provided with this means of relaxation, the constructive use of leisure, and the means for maintaining good health. Next, facilities were sought that met the specialized needs of the disabled person. Then, when needed, rule modifications were made in the activities to be offered. For example, wheelchair tennis was played as doubles in the singles court, and the ball was allowed to bounce twice before being returned over the net.

Sports activities at the University of New Mexico include swimming, tennis, archery, table tennis, badminton, bowling, and chess. These activities are scheduled at the same time as the rest of the intramural program. In this way handicapped students feel a part of the regular program and social environment and at the same time the other students become aware of the needs and interests of the handicapped students.

An important effort is put forth by the intramural staff members to contact personally all of the handicapped students on campus and urge them to participate in this program.

Funding for such programs comes from student fees, because such fees are appropriated for all students regardless of abilities and skills.

EVALUATION

One of the most important functions of the intramurals manager is the continual evaluation of the program to see if its goals are being met. It also must be evaluated in terms of budget and numbers of persons participating in programs. If a program has few participants and a relatively high cost of operation, it may have to be phased out.

Evaluation techniques will differ, but generally speaking the process should include: (1) definition of program objectives; (2) data collection and evaluation including participation count, team numbers, and games played and forfeited; (3) appraisal forms, including player ratings, scores, and team surveys; (4) study groups and consultant advice; and (5) participant opinion about specific activities.

Recent forms of evaluation have used consultants on a voluntary, advisory basis. Consultants are usually objective and can provide information without prejudice. Evaluation score cards, such as Ridgeway's Scorecard for Evaluation of Men's Intramural Sports Programs in Colleges and Universities, have also been found to be functional. In addition, many schools have used computers in evaluating intramural programs. In some cases the cost of using computers for evaluations is not practical.

SUMMARY

Intramural, extramural, and club programs represent a very important component of the total physical education program. They contribute to important qualities such as skill, health, social development, and recreation. In addition, they provide an opportunity for all students to participate on a voluntary basis. Activities should be selected that reflect the basic instructional program and student interests. The management of intramurals at lower education levels is sometimes difficult because of a lack of transportation for students during after-school hours and a lack of facilities, finances, and parental support. In order to have a well-run program the management of intramurals should be concerned with things such as scheduling, awards, point systems, eligibility requirements, and officials so that the best interests of the student and the educational process will be served. There are many different types of tournaments that can be used in intramurals to increase the flavor of the competition. Intramural programs should be evaluated periodically to determine how they can be improved to better serve the clientele for which they have been established.

SELF-ASSESSMENT TESTS

These tests will assist students to determine if material and competencies presented in this chapter have been mastered.

1. In terms of their objectives and activities, justify the place of intramural, extramural, and club programs in the total physical education plan of a school, college, or other organization.
2. Imagine you are the director of physical education in a high school, college, or other organization. You have been requested by your superior to develop a list of policies for a newly organized intramural and extramural program in your organization. Prepare the policies and submit them to your class for their critical evaluation.
3. Conduct a job analysis of the roles played by various administrative personnel involved with the intramural and extramural program of the college you are attending. Compare it to the personnel discussed in this chapter.
4. Develop what you consider to be a model intramural and extramural program for an elementary school, high school, college, and large corporation.
5. Identify the following: round robin tournament, straight elimination tournament, ladder tournament, pyramid tournament, and double elimination tournament. Using one of these tournaments, prepare a hypothetical competitive program for 16 teams in basketball.
6. Describe the procedure you would use for organizing a scuba diving club in your school.

SELECTED REFERENCES

1. Bridgman, A.: Backlash: Its efforts to tie achievement with extracurriculars, Education News, March 13, 1985.
2. Dougherty, N.J., and Bonanno, D.: Management principles in sport and leisure activities, Minneapolis, 1985, Burgess Publishing Company.
3. Hammitt, S.A., and Hammitt, W.E.: Campus recreation activities—planning for better use, Journal of Physical Education, Recreation and Dance **56**:23, January 1985.
4. Hyatt, R.W.: Intramural sports: organization and administration, St. Louis, 1977, The C.V. Mosby Company.
5. Intramurals for senior high schools, The Athletic Institute, Chicago.
6. Jones, T.R.: Needed, a new philosophical model for intramurals, Journal of Health, Physical Education, and Recreation **43**:34, 1971.
7. Malsam, M., and Nelson, L.: Integrating curriculum objectives into your outdoor education program, Journal of Physical Education, Recreation and Dance **55**:52, September 1984.
8. Matthews, D.O.: Intramural administration principles, The Athletic Journal **46**:82, 1966. Reproduced courtesy The Athletic Journal, adapted and updated, 1979.
9. Nave, J.L., and Saidak, D.: Physical education programs with out facilities, Journal of Physical Education, Recreation and Dance **54**:57, November/December 1983.
10. Sims, D., and Fabian, L.: Eliminate volleyball forfeits, Journal of Physical Education, Recreation and Dance **54**:57, March 1983.

SUGGESTED READINGS

• Fairman, L.S., and Nitchman, J.: A complete bowling program in our gymnasium, Journal of Physical Education, Recreation and Dance **54**:59, March 1983.
Presents an innovative approach to bowling that is being used at Sheffield Middle School in Lorain, Ohio. The authors brought the bowling to the students in their gymnasium rather than paying the expense of taking them to

the bowling alley. Tells how one of the authors built a complete, portable, eight-lane bowling alley for use in school's physical education program.

- Imergot, L.S.: Get those skeletons out of the closet . . . and use them in intramurals, Journal of Physical Education, Recreation and Dance **54**:64, June 1983.

Rather than being held on a specific date and time intramurals were scheduled with a deadline date with one week to complete contests. This change increased time for other activities such as coed badminton, made it easier to supervise matches, and caused the number of forfeits to decrease because players could play at their convenience. Provides some good suggestions that should be taken into consideration when scheduling intramurals.

- McLellan, R.W.: Intramural-recreational programs—selecting qualified coordinators, Journal of Physical Education, Recreation and Dance **55**:57, August 1984.

Depicts how out of physical education and organized recreational sport programs have come the intramural and recreational sport programs of today. These programs represent an important aspect of the overall educational program. Points out the many educational values of such programs.

- Ross, J.G., et al.: Physical activity outside of school physical education, Journal of Physical Education, Recreation and Dance **56**:35, January 1985.

Provides the results and cites the need to be aware of national trends and patterns of participation in physical activity sources for students other than the school physical education programs, since the typical student spends more than 80% of his or her physical activity time in other settings. Shows the amount of time spent in such places as community organizations, the types of activity engaged in, and their contribution to fitness.

- Turner, E.T.: Helter-skelter tournament, Journal of Physical Education, Recreation and Dance **54**:61, March 1983.

Indicates how most appropriate tournament should be selected in intramurals in order to have maximum participation and interest. Describes the Helter-Skelter Tournament, which is designed for classroom use and has been in use for 7 years. The Helter-Skelter Tournament provides the student with maximum participation in tournament play as well as many opportunities to experience success-failure situations. A meaningful, flexible, enjoyable and educationally sound tournament.

Chapter Five

Interscholastic, Intercollegiate, and Other Competitive Athletic Programs

Instructional Objectives and Competencies to be Achieved
After reading this chapter the student should be able to

- Discuss the purpose of and the values derived from participating in competitive athletic programs.
- Specify the duties performed by such key management personnel in athletic programs as the athletic director, coach, athletic trainer, and members of the athletic council.
- Explain some of the management considerations involved in athletic programs relating to scheduling, providing for the health of participants, contracts, officials, transportation, game management, crowd control, protests and forfeitures, awards, and records.
- Understand some of the central issues involved in such management problems concerned with athletics as recruitment, eligibility, proselyting, scouting, finances, and extra pay for coaching.
- Describe the nature and scope of athletic programs in elementary, junior high, and senior high schools, colleges and universities, and in other organizations.
- Identify some of the key athletic associations and the role they play in influencing highly organized athletic competition in schools, colleges, and other organizations.
- Outline key provisions of Title IX.

Three components of a physical education program have been discussed—namely the basic instructional program, the adapted program, and intramural and extramural offerings. The remaining component of a physical education program will be discussed in this chapter. It involves competitive athletics in schools, colleges, and other organizations.

Interscholastic, intercollegiate, and other highly organized athletic programs represent an integral part of the total physical education program. In most cases they should evolve from the intramural and extramural athletic programs.

Athletics, with their appeal to both youths and adults, should be the heart of physical education and should help achieve goals that will enrich living for all who participate.

The interschool athletic program is designed for individuals most highly skilled in sports. It is one of

Women's intercollegiate basketball, University of Nevada, Las Vegas.

the most interesting and receives more publicity than the other phases of physical education. The reason for this is not that it is more important or renders a greater contribution; instead, it is largely the result of popular appeal. That sportswriters and others discuss it in glowing terms and that it involves competition pitting one school or college against another school or college also increases its public appeal. A spirit of rivalry develops, which seems to be characteristic of American culture.

Interscholastic and intercollegiate athletics programs have probably had more difficulties attached to them than to any other phase of the physical education program. The desire to win and to increase gate receipts has resulted in some unfortunate practices, such as unethical recruitment procedures, changing transcripts to make players eligible, admitting students who may be academically unqualified, and extensive public relations programs. Large stadiums and sports palaces that require huge financial outlays for their upkeep have been constructed.

The challenge of providing sound educational programs in varsity interscholastic and intercollegiate athletics is one that all physical education personnel recognize. The challenge can be met and resolved if physical educators bring to the attention of administrators and the general public the true purposes of athletics in a physical education program. It is important to stress that a need exists for having an athletic program that meets the needs of everyone; that such a program is organized and administered with the welfare of the individual in mind; that it is conducted in a manner where educational objectives are not compromised when they are exposed to pressures from sportswriters, alumni, and community members; and that it has leaders who are trained in physical education.

WHAT SPORT DOES FOR PEOPLE

Wilkerson and Dodder[16] have conducted research to determine what sport does for people. They found that sport has the following seven functions in society:

Emotional release—Sport releases emotions, acts as a safety valve, and relieves aggressive tendencies.

Affirmation of identity—Sport offers opportunities to be recognized and to express one's individual qualities.

Social control—In a society where deviance is prevalent, sport provides a means of control over people.

Socialization—Sport serves as a means of socializing those individuals who identify with it.

Change agent—Sport results in social change, introduces new behavior patterns, and changes the course of history (for example, it allows for interaction of all kinds of people and for upward mobility based on ability).

Collective conscience—Sport creates a communal spirit that brings people together in search of common goals.

Success—Sport provides a feeling of success both for the participant and for the spectator when a player or team with whom one identifies achieves. To win in sport is also to win in life.

VALUES CLAIMED FOR COMPETITIVE ATHLETICS

The values of athletics are discussed under the headings of physical fitness, skill, individual development, and social development.

Physical fitness

Athletics contribute to physical fitness by developing organic vigor, neuromuscular skill, and desirable attitudes toward play and exercise. To develop and maintain a high degree of physical fitness, the individual must voluntarily submit to a vigorous program of exercise. Perhaps the strongest force capable of motivating a person to engage in strenuous conditioning programs is the desire to excel in athletic competition to enhance their peer status. The contribution to a high degree of physical fitness is an obvious concomitant.

Skill

To achieve success in athletics, an individual must develop neuromuscular skills that will enable him or her to respond instantly and effectively in a game situation. The resulting skill development will enable the individual to respond to situations requiring strength, endurance, speed, or coordination.

Acquiring skill through athletics also leads to a high level of proficiency and a desire to engage in physical activity. Some research shows that persons who engage in sports when they are young are more likely to lead physically active lives when they are older. The development of physical skill has many other benefits for the individual, such as feelings of accomplishment, recognition, and belonging, a more positive self-image, and less expenditure of energy.

Individual development

Self-realization, self-sufficiency, self-control, and self-discipline are individual qualities frequently developed through athletics. An individual's self-image is gained through comparing himself or herself with others; athletics provides many such opportunities for comparison.

Self-sufficiency and self-reliance are developed because athletics provides opportunities for a person to make decisions and to profit from mistakes, thereby also gaining self-direction.

Self-control may be developed; the ability to withstand or to adjust to emotional stress is believed to be a result of the stress adaptation mechanism conditioned by exercise. The increased adrenal activity that follows exercise increases the reserve of steroids available to counter stress. Furthermore, the highly charged atmosphere inherent in athletic contests provides opportunities for participants to test and develop their ability to exercise self-control.

Athletic competition develops self-discipline. Participation and success in athletics require a great deal of self-sacrifice. The individual is called on to subordinate personal wishes and desires to those of the group and to submit to strenuous conditioning programs and rigid training rules. Such sacrifices can lead to the development of both mental and physical discipline.

Social development[6]

Athletics provides opportunities for competition and cooperation. Although competition is a part of our way of life, at the same time our way of life demands cooperation, self-sacrifice, and respect for other persons. Competition and cooperation therefore must be interdependent. Athletics provides a natural opportu-

Men's intercollegiate baseball, University of Nevada, Las Vegas.

nity to achieve this dual objective, because individuals must be both competitive and cooperative.

Athletics also stresses fairness, adherence to the rules, ability to accept defeat, and respect for other players.

KEY MANAGEMENT PERSONNEL INVOLVED IN ATHLETIC PROGRAMS*

Key management personnel involved in athletic programs include the director of athletics, the coach, the athletic trainer, and members of the athletic council.

The following additional personnel are involved in athletic programs, particularly at the college level: assistant or associate athletic directors, sports information director, athletic business manager, facility

director, travel coordinator, administrative assistant, fund raiser, equipment manager, game manager, ticket manager, and coordinator of special events. Only the four major management positions applicable to high school and college will be discussed here.

The director of athletics

The director of athletics implements the athletic policies as established by the council, board, or committee. Responsibilities of the athletic director include preparing the budget for the sports program, purchasing equipment and supplies, scheduling athletic contests, arranging for officials, supervising eligibility requirements, making arrangements for transportation, seeing that medical examinations of athletes and proper insurance coverage coverage are adequate, and generally supervising the program.

---

*For the role of officials in the athletic programs, see p. 129.

The athletic director should be prepared in physical education and athletics. The best qualifications include a major in physical education, as well as experience as a player and as an athletic coach.

In a large school, college, or other organization with a large athletic program, the athletic director might work closely with a faculty manager or business manager of athletics. This manager might handle officials, hire ticket sellers and ticket takers, develop programs, keep financial records, pay guarantees, and be in charge of security.

The director of athletics in some large programs might also have an assistant to help with such responsibilities as scheduling, staff supervision, eligibility, budgets, purchasing, travel, and insurance.

There might also be a director of sports information who handles media releases, develops brochures, and handles such things as athletic statistics and photography.

The coach[5]

One of the most popular positions in physical education is coaching. Many students who show exceptional skill in an interscholastic sport feel they would make good candidates for various coaching positions. They feel that because they have proved themselves outstanding athletes in high school, they will be successful in coaching. This, however, is not necessarily true. There is insufficient evidence to show that exceptional skill in any activity necessarily guarantees success in teaching that activity. Many other factors such as personality, interest in youths, knowledge of human growth and development, psychology, intelligence, integrity, leadership, character, and a sympathetic attitude are essential to coaching success.

Coaching should be recognized as teaching. Because of the nature of the position, a coach may be in a better position to teach concepts that affect daily living than any other member of a school facility. Youths, with their inherent drive for activity and action and their quest for the excitement and competition found in sports, look up to the coach and in many cases feel that the coach is a person to emulate. Therefore the coach should recognize his or her influence and see the value of such attributes as character, per-

sonality, and integrity. Although a coach must know thoroughly the game he or she is coaching, these other characteristics are equally important.

Coaching is regarded by some organizations as a position of insecurity. Coaching offers an interesting and profitable career for many individuals. However, the coach should recognize the possibility of finding himself or herself in a situation where the pressure to produce winning teams may be so great as to cause unhappiness, insecurity, and even the loss of a job.

Of the qualifications needed to be a coach, there are four that should be displayed by all coaches. First, the coach is able to teach the fundamentals and strategies of the sport; he or she *must* be a good teacher. Second, the coach needs to understand the player: how a person functions at a particular level of development—with a full appreciation of skeletal growth, muscular development, and physical and emotional limitations. Third, the coach understands the game coached; thorough knowledge of techniques, rules, and similar information is basic. Fourth, the coach has a desirable personality and character. Patience, understanding, kindness, honesty, sportsmanship, sense of right and wrong, courage, cheerfulness, affection, humor, energy, and enthusiasm are imperative.

The only qualification some coaches have is that they have played the game or sport in high school, college, or professionally. It is generally recognized that the best preparation a coach can have is training in physical education. In light of this, several states are attempting to see that coaches, particularly at the precollege level, have at least some training in physical education.

Certification of coaches

Standards for coaching certification were identified by the AAHPERD through their Task Force on Certification of High School Coaches. The essential areas identified by the Task Force were (1) medical aspects of athletic coaching, (2) sociological and psychological aspects of coaching, (3) theory and techniques of coaching, (4) kinesiological foundations of coaching, and (5) physiological foundations of coaching.

Coaches should be encouraged to seek training

One of the most popular phases of physical education is coaching. Coach teaching tennis, University of Nevada, Las Vegas.

even if certification standards have not yet been required by their particular state. The trend toward certification is growing, but more important, the thorough training of all coaches is essential to the health and performance of athletes.

Nobel and Sigle[11] surveyed the 50 states and Washington, D.C., regarding the certification of coaches. The responses provide the following information:

In 34 states nonteachers are allowed to coach either regularly or in an emergency.

In 20 states there are no minimum requirements other than age.

In 8 states a teaching certificate is required.

In 1 state a Red Cross First Aid course is required.

In 1 state attendance at a rules clinic in the particular sport coached is required.

In 1 state a knowledge of developmental skills of the sport coached is required.

In 5 states (Iowa, Minnesota, Pennsylvania, South Dakota, and Wyoming) paraprofessionals are required to complete a coaching preparation program.

In 15 states limitations are placed on nonteaching coaches, such as not allowing them to be head coaches or that a teacher must be present on road trips.

In 8 states (Arkansas, Iowa, Minnesota, New York, Oklahoma, Oregon, South Dakota, and Wyoming) additional requirements are necessary, such as taking certain courses, having work in physical education, being versed in first aid, having coaching experience, and being certified in physical education.

Evaluation of coaches

As an example of the evaluation of coaches, the Beaverton (Oregon) School District's[12] form for evaluating their coaches is depicted in Fig. 5-1.

The athletic trainer

The profession of athletic training has taken on greater significance in recent years with the increase in sports programs and the recognition that the health of the athlete is an important consideration.

Today's athletic trainers need special preparation to carry out their duties, which include prevention of injuries, first aid and postinjury treatment, and rehabilitation work. Such preparation, if possible, should include a major in physical education, certification by the National Athletic Trainers Association or being a registered physical therapist. Also needed are such personal qualifications as emotional stability under

DEPARTMENT OF ATHLETICS

Name_____ SCHOOL DISTRICT NO. 48   Evaluator _____

Assignment _____ Beaverton, Oregon   Date _____

COACH'S EVALUATION

COACH'S SELF-EVALUATION (To be completed prior to the start of coaching assignment.)

1. Statement of personal goals and/or program goals as they relate to your coaching
    assignment.

    _____   _____
    _____
    _____
    _____

2. Statement of self-evaluation on applicable criteria relative to completion of goals
    statement. (To be completed at the conclusion of your coaching assignment.)

    _____   _____
    _____
    _____
    _____

3. ATHLETIC COORDINATORS EVALUATION (To be completed subsequent to the coaching assign-
    ment then reviewed with the coach.)
    CODE: Scale of 1 to 5, with 5 highest competency. If blank, not applicable.

    A. Administration   Circle one
        1. Care of equipment (issue, inventory, cleaning, etc.)   1 2 3 4 5
        2. Organization of staff   1 2 3 4 5
        3. Organization of practices   1 2 3 4 5
        4. Communication with coaches   1 2 3 4 5
        5. Adherence to district and school philosophy and policies
            (eligibility reports, inventories, budgets, rosters,
            insurance forms, and follow-up, scores reported)
        6. Public relations   1 2 3 4 5
        7. Supervision   1 2 3 4 5
    B. Skills
        1. Knowledge of fundamentals   1 2 3 4 5
        2. Presentation of fundamentals   1 2 3 4 5
        3. Conditioning   1 2 3 4 5
        4. Game preparation   1 2 3 4 5
        5. Prevention and care of injuries (follow-up with parents) 1 2 3 4 5
    C. Relationships
        1. Enthusiasm   1 2 3 4 5
            a. For working with students   1 2 3 4 5
            b. For working with staff (support of other programs) 1 2 3 4 5
            c. For working with academic staff   1 2 3 4 5
            d. For the sport itself   1 2 3 4 5
        2. Discipline   1 2 3 4 5
            a. Firm but fair   1 2 3 4 5
            b. Consistent   1 2 3 4 5
        3. Communication with players
            a. Individual   1 2 3 4 5
            b. As a team   1 2 3 4 5
    D. Performance
        1. Appearance of team on the field or floor   1 2 3 4 5
        2. Execution of the team on the field or floor   1 2 3 4 5
        3. Attitude of the team   1 2 3 4 5
        4. Conduct of coach during game   1 2 3 4 5
    E. Self-improvement
        1. Attends in-district meetings and clinics   1 2 3 4 5
        2. Attends out-of-district clinics   1 2 3 4 5
        3. Keeps updated by reading current literature   1 2 3 4 5
4. Review by Building Athletic Coordinator with Coach
    (District Athletic Coordinator will review all evaluations before
    forwarding to principal.)

    _____
    _____
    _____
    _____

5. To be placed in working papers of principal and forwarded to the personnel office
    with yearly teaching evaluation.

Original-Building Principal
  Canary-District Athletic Coordinator   _____
    Pink-Building Athletic Coordinator   Signed by Coach
    Gold-Coach

                                               _____
                                               Signed by Evaluator

Fig. 5-1. An example of a form for evaluating coaches.

stress, ability to act rationally when injuries occur, and a standard of ethics that places the welfare of the participant uppermost.

In many schools and colleges the financial situation does not permit hiring a full-time athletic trainer. Some schools and colleges therefore find that if a full-time athletic trainer is not a possibility, it may be feasible to provide such a service by hiring a person who is a part-time teacher and a part-time trainer; is a secretary or nurse and is also a trainer; is a trainer–assistant athletic director; is a trainer–health service person; is a trainer who can also teach in the adapted physical education program; or is a teacher on the faculty who instructs in an athletic training degree program and who also is an athletic trainer.

Special qualifications for athletic trainers

Athletic trainers should complete a 4-year college curriculum that emphasizes the biological and physical sciences, psychology, coaching techniques, first aid and safety, nutrition, and other courses in physical education. The athletic trainer should be competent in accident prevention, emergency treatment, and rehabilitation of injured athletes. The athletic trainer should be able to work closely with administrators, coaches, physicians, the school nurse, students, and parents in a cooperative effort to provide the best possible health care for all athletes under his or her jurisdiction. He or she is also responsible in many college programs for development and supervision of a student athletic training staff.

Arnheim[2] lists the following as the personal qualifications needed by athletic trainers: good health, sense of fair play, maturity and emotional stability, good appearance, leadership, compassion, intellectual capacity, sense of humor, kindness and understanding, competence and responsibility, and a sound philosophy of life.

The courses required in professional preparation programs for athletic trainers also indicate some of the competencies needed. These courses include anatomy, physiology, physiology of exercise, applied anatomy and kinesiology, psychology, first aid and safety, nutrition, remedial exercise, health, techniques of athletic training, and laboratory practice in the techniques of athletic training.

More women need to become involved in athletic training. In many undergraduate physical education programs, women have not received adequate preparation in athletic training courses. Most athletic training in women's competitive sports is performed by men who often cannot handle the physical and

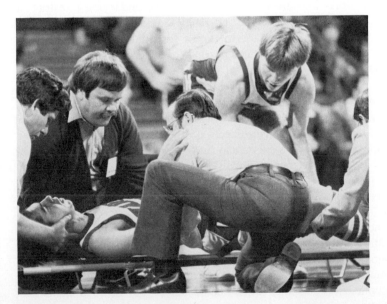

Athletic trainer at work.

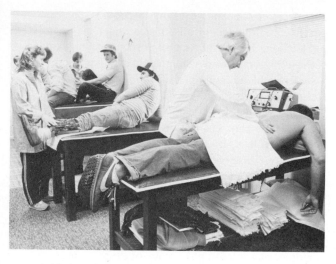

Athletic trainer at work.

emotional trauma suffered by female athletes. In addition, a female athlete may be reluctant to seek the services of a male athletic trainer. Women are more likely to be open about personal problems with other women. Athletic training is important in all sports, male and female. Injuries and other related problems occur regularly in women's sports, and women should be adequately trained to handle these situations.

The athletic council

Most colleges and many schools have some type of athletic council, board, or committee that establishes athletic policies for the institution. It may involve only faculty members, or it may also involve students. Such councils, boards, or committees are responsible for giving the athletic program proper direction in the educational program.

The composition of such committees or councils varies widely from school to school and college to college. In a school, the principal may serve as chairperson, or the director of physical education or other faculty member may hold this position. The committee may include coaches, members of the board of education, faculty members, students, or members of the community at large. In a college or university, the composition of the committee may

consist of administrators, faculty members, students, athletic directors, coaches, and others.

Some of the functions of athletic councils at the high school and college levels include making policy, approving awards, advising athletic department on problems, endorsing and approving schedules and budgets, evaluating the athletic program, investigating complaints, interviewing and recommending coaches to athletic directors, developing eligibility guidelines, considering postseason play, approving codes of ethics, reviewing scholarship programs, and deciding if various sports programs should be added or dropped.

SELECTED MANAGEMENT FUNCTIONS IN ATHLETIC PROGRAMS

Many management functions are pertinent to the directing of a highly organized athletic program, including schedules and practice periods, contracts, health of the players, officials, transportation, game management, crowd control, protests and forfeitures, awards, and records.

Schedules and practice periods

Scheduling involves maintaining a proper balance between home and away contests, seeking contests with organizations and institutions of approximately the same size and caliber of play, and trying to restrict the scope of the geographical area where contests are held to keep transportation costs to a minimum.

Where leagues and conferences are in place, schedules are usually made many months or years in advance and have representatives from each of the institutions involved.

Athletic directors frequently have the coaches or in many instances permit the coaches to schedule their own sports and limit their activity to negotiating the contracts involved.

Limits for the length of seasons should be defined. These should have the approval of school, college, or other organizational authorities. The length of seasons should be arranged so they interfere as little as possible with other school and college work. Practice before the first game should be adequate so the players are in good physical condition. Depending on the sport, limits should be set on the total number of games and also on the number of games played in any

ATHLETIC EVENTS AGREEMENT
Department of Intercollegiate Athletics
University of Nevada, Las Vegas

ATHLETIC ACTIVITY _____

_____ VS UNIVERSITY OF NEVADA, LAS VEGAS

I. THE PARTIES HERETO HEREBY AGREE AS FOLLOWS:

(1) _____
        (Location)   (Date)   (Time)

(2) _____
        (Location)   (Date)   (Time)

(3) _____
        (Location)   (Date)   (Time)

(4) _____
        (Location)   (Date)   (Time)

II. THE FINANCIAL AGREEMENT SHALL BE SPECIFIED SUBSEQUENTLY:

(1) _____
      (Financial Sum)

(2) _____
      (Complimentary Tickets)

(3) _____
      (Other)

FOR: UNIVERSITY OF NEVADA, LAS VEGAS   **FOR: VISITING TEAM**

Signature: _____   Signature: _____

Title: _____   Title: _____

Date: _____   Date: _____

DISTRIBUTION:
    WHITE: University of Nevada, Las Vegas
    PINK: Visiting Team

Fig. 5-2. Athletic events agreement.

one week. Postseason games are not considered advisable by many educators.

Some factors that may affect scheduling include climatic conditions, maximizing gate receipts, number of participants, state playoffs and invitational tournaments, transportation, school facilities available, different sports that appeal to the same students, and maximum number of games or contests permitted.

Practice periods should be scheduled equitably and according to Title IX regulations. All coaches and other personnel involved in using the facilities should be involved in decision making.

Contracts

Written contracts are usually essential in the management of interscholastic and intercollegiate athletics (Fig. 5-2). On the college level, in particular, games are scheduled many months or years in advance. Memories and facts tend to fade and become obscure with time. To avoid misunderstanding and confusion, it is best to have in writing a contract between the schools or colleges concerned.

Contracts should be properly executed and signed by official representatives of both schools or colleges. Many athletic associations provide specially prepared forms for use by member schools or colleges. Such forms usually contain the names of the schools, dates, and circumstances and conditions under which the contests will be held. In addition, they usually provide for penalties if contracts are not fulfilled by either party.

Health of the players

Athletics should contribute to the health of the players. Through wholesome physical activity the participant should become more physically, mentally, emotionally, and socially fit.

Medical examination

One of the first requirements for every participant in an athletic program should be a medical examination to determine physical fitness and capacity to engage in such a program. The strenuous nature of athletics and the demands placed on the participant make this examination imperative.

Safety

Everything possible should be done to ensure the safety of the participant. A coach should always conduct the program with the health of the players in mind. He or she will have a knowledge of first aid and will continually be alert to stop players from further participation if they are unduly fatigued; have received head, spine, or neck injuries; or are dazed. He or she will not allow a player who has been unconscious as a result of injury to resume play until a thorough check and approval have been given by a qualified physician. The coach will also work closely with the team or school physician, trying to make every effort possible to guard the health of the players.

Proper conditioning and training should take place before any player is subjected to competition. Such conditioning and training should be progressive and gradual. There should always be enough players on the squad to allow for substitutions in the event a person is not physically or otherwise fit for play.

Proper facilities and equipment should be available to guard the safety and health of the players. This means that facilities are constructed according to recommended standards concerning size, surfacing, and various safety features. Protective equipment should be provided as needed in the various sports. If desirable facilities and equipment are not available, such competition should not be provided.

Games should be scheduled that result in equal and safe competition. The desire of small schools to defeat larger schools, where the competition is not equal, often brings disastrous results to the health and welfare of the players. Under such circumstances, one often hears the remark, "They really took a beating." Competition should be as equitable as possible.

Prompt attention should be given to all injuries. Injured players should be examined by a physician and given proper treatment. There should be complete medical supervision of the athletic program. The trainer is not a substitute. A physician should be present at all games and practices involving the most strenuous contact sports. The physician should determine the extent of injury. After being ill or hurt, a player should not be permitted to participate again until the coach receives an approved statement from the family, school, or college physician.

Proper sanitary measures should be taken. Individual towels and drinking cups should be provided; the day of the team towel and the team drinking cup has passed. Equipment and uniforms should be cleaned as often as necessary. Locker, dressing, shower, toilet, and other rooms used by players should be kept clean and sanitary. Playing areas should be kept clean and safe. Gymnasiums should be properly heated, and every measure taken to ensure conditions are as nearly ideal as possible.

Injuries and insurance

The state athletic association in many states sponsors an athletic insurance plan. Such plans pay various medical, x-ray examination, dental, hospitalization, and other expenses according to the terms of the plan. Some private insurance companies also have such plans. Their purposes are to provide enrolled athletes with benefits that will help meet the cost of medical, dental, and hospital care in the event of accidental injury resulting from participation in physical education or athletics sponsored by a participating school. The amount of any payment for an injury is only the amount of the actual expenses incurred but not in excess of the amounts listed in the schedule of allowance for such injury. To collect benefits, plan requirements must be met.

The insurance provided by various state and independent plans usually includes benefits for accidental death or dismemberment, hospital expenses, x-ray examination fees, physicians' fees, and surgical and dental expenses. Dental benefits may or may not be included in the schedule of surgical benefits. In some plans catastrophe benefits are also available for injuries requiring extensive medical care and long-term hospitalization. Coverage is normally provided on a deductible basis, with the insurance company paying 75% to 80% of the total cost over the deductible amount up to a maximum amount.

State high school athletic associations in a few states operate successful benefit plans, primarily by adopting many of the benefits used by the insurance industry—nonallocated benefits, catastrophic coverage, and nonduplication of benefits.

Every school, college, and other organization should have a written policy concerning financial and other responsibilities associated with injuries. The administrator, parents, and players should be thoroughly familiar with the responsibilities of each regarding injuries.

Officials

Officials greatly influence the athletic program and determine whether it is conducted for the benefit of the players. Officials should be well qualified. They should know the rules and be able to interpret them accurately; recognize their responsibility to the players; be good sportsmen; and be courteous, honest,

Intercollegiate football, University of Nevada, Las Vegas.

Officials play a very important role in athletic contests.

friendly, cooperative, impartial, and able to control the game at all times.

To ensure that only the best officials are used, procedures should be established to register and determine those who are qualified. Officials should be required to pass examinations on rules and to demonstrate their competency. Rating scales have been developed to help make such estimates. Most athletic associations have some method of registering and certifying acceptable officials. The National Association for Girls and Women in Sport of the AAHPERD has a rating committee that certifies officials. In some states the officials who are used then rate the schools or colleges regarding facilities, environment, and circumstances surrounding the game.

Subject to contract differences, officials are frequently chosen by the home team with approval of opponents. The practice of the home team selecting

officials without any consideration of the wishes of other organizations or regard for impartial officiating has resulted in relations that have not been in the best interests of players or of athletics in general. A growing practice of having the conference or association select officials has many points in its favor.

Officials should be duly notified of the date and time of the contests to which they have been assigned. Officials' fees vary from school to school, although some associations have set up standard rates. It is usually considered best to pay a flat fee that includes salary and expenses, rather than to list both separately.

Transportation

Transporting athletes to games and contests presents many management problems, such as: Who should be transported? In what kinds of vehicles should athletes

Umpires play a major role in baseball competition.

be transported? Are athletics part of a regular program? Should private vehicles or school- and college-owned vehicles be used? What are the legal implications involved in transporting athletes to school-sponsored and college-sponsored events?

The present trend is to view athletics as an integral part of the educational program so that public funds may be used for transportation. At the same time, however, statutes vary from state to state, and persons managing athletic programs should examine carefully the statutes in their own state.

Many managers feel that athletes and representatives of the school or college concerned, such as band members and cheerleaders, should travel only in transportation provided by the school. Where private cars belonging to coaches, students, or other persons are used, the manager should be sure to determine whether the procedures are in conformity with the state statutes regarding liability. Under no circumstances should students or other representatives be permitted to drive unless they are licensed drivers. Under most circumstances students should not be used as drivers.

The business manager is usually responsible for the transportation program. He or she will make a provision in the transportation program for buses to carry athletic teams to sport contests so they will arrive safely on time. The director of athletics must be informed of the mode of transportation that will be available so he or she can plan accordingly. This involves a direct relationship between the director of athletics and the transportation supervisor. All requests for special athletic trips should be in writing and acknowledged by the secondary school principal or college administrator where he or she is involved. This is necessary because the principal or college administrator will be aware of any conflicts with other parts of his or her program. The business administrator finds it difficult to schedule special athletic trips on a moment's notice, although this situation can arise when games are canceled because of the weather or other unforeseen events. The director of athletics should submit a monthly calendar of athletic events, listing the date, time and place of departure, event, destination, number of participants, time of pickup, and remarks.

As the boxed material below shows, the events scheduled on April 8 are routine, and the transporta-

---

MONTH OF APRIL

April 8

Depart: 3:00 PM
From: Senior High School
Team: Junior Varsity Baseball
To: Jones High School
Students: 35
Pickup: 5:30 PM
Remarks

April 9

Depart: 3:00 PM
From: Junior High School
Team: Varsity Tennis
To: Albany High School
Students: 5
Pickup: 5:00 PM
Remarks: Station wagon requested; Coach Lewis will drive.

April 10

Depart: 3:00 PM
From: Senior High School
Team: Varsity Baseball and Varsity Tennis
To: Baseball to Jones High School
   Tennis to Albany High School
Students: 40
Pickup: Baseball—5:00 PM
   Tennis—5:30 PM
Remarks: One bus for both teams—drop off baseball first.

---

tion supervisor can request a bus accordingly. The events on April 9 are more complex, and the director of athletics can state a preference for a station wagon. It is more economical for a school district or college to furnish a station wagon rather than a 60-passenger bus to transport five students. The events on April 10 are more complex, and the remarks indicate that one bus can be used for both teams. It is necessary to list the number of participants so the proper size bus, or buses, can be assigned. This calendar should be submitted in triplicate (carbons) to the business administrator. After the transportation department has scheduled the trips, the business manager initials all three copies and returns two copies to the athletic director. The director keeps one copy, and the other copy is sent to the principal or college manager. The procedure for submitting transportation requests could vary in different schools. The manager might receive the schedule for approval before the business office.

Game management[15]

Because so many details are connected with game management, it is possible to include only a brief statement of the more important items. To have an efficiently conducted contest, it is important to have good organization. Someone must be responsible. There must be planning. Many details must be attended to, including (1) before-game responsibilities, (2) game responsibilities, (3) after-game responsibilities, and (4) preparation for out-of-town games. Before a home game details such as contracts, eligibility records, equipment, facilities, tickets, public relations, medical supervision, officials, and physical examinations must be thoroughly checked. Game responsibilities at home games include checking such items as supplies and equipment, entertainment, tickets and ushers, scoreboards, public-address system, presence of physician, and quarters for visiting teams. The responsibilities after a home game consist of checking such items as payments to officials and visiting school, records of officials, and participation records. When preparing for an out-of-town game, important details such as parents' permissions, transportation, funding, contracts, personnel, and records must be attended to (Fig. 5-3).

UNIVERSITY OF NEVADA, LAS VEGAS

Controller's Office
Accounts Payable Department
CLAIM FOR GROUP TRAVEL EXPENSES

Note: Do not use this form for submitting Travel expenses for individual faculty/staff of UNLV.

Department to Travel: _____

Destination: _____

Dates of Travel: _____

Number of Students and Staff Members: _____

SUMMARY OF EXPENDITURES

Transportation:

Method: _____

Cost (Do not enter cost of any agency vehicle.) _____

Meals, lodging, and miscellaneous:

Dates						Total
Breakfasts						
Lunches						
Dinners						
Lodging						
Other						
Student Allowance						

Total Meals, Lodging, and Miscellaneous: . . . .

Total All Expenditures and/or Student Allowances. . . . .
(Must be substantiated by receipts)

Advance Received: . . . .

Balance Due or to be reimbursed. . . . .
(If balance is to be reimbursed to the traveler submit a request
for check in the amount of reimbursement.)

Account to be Charged: _____

Signed by: _____

Approved by: _____
Department Head

(1) Controller's Office
(2) Controller's Office
(3) Department

UNLV AP 270 4-76

Fig. 5-3. Claim for group travel expenses.

Crowd control

Crowd control at athletic contests is becoming increasingly important in light of dissent, riots, violence, and disturbances on high school and college campuses and in public gathering places. The elimination of night athletic activities has been on the increase, particularly in large cities. School districts and college authorities are taking increased precautions to avoid any disturbances. More police are being brought in to help supervise the crowds at athletic contests, sportsmanship assemblies are being held, townspeople are being informed, administrators are discussing the matter, and careful plans are being developed.

The California Interscholastic Federation—Southern Section published crowd management guidelines after several years of research into crowd control problems in southern California. The suggested guidelines were general and not specifically applicable to all communities. In substance these guidelines urged civic leaders to meet first with local school administrators to determine precisely in what athletic activities civic group assistance would be most helpful. The guidelines would then be expanded or revised to suit the situation. (See Appendixes for further guidelines on crowd control.)

Protests and forfeitures

Procedures for handling protests and forfeitures in connection with athletic contests should be set. Of course, careful preventive action should be taken beforehand to avoid a situation when such protests and forfeitures occur. Proper interpretation of the rules, good officiating, elimination of undue pressures, and proper education of coaches on the objectives of athletics will help prevent such action.

However, the procedure for filing protest and forfeitures should be established. This procedure should be clearly stated in writing and contain all the details, such as the person to whom the protest should be sent, time limits involved, person or group responsible for action, and any other necessary information. A frequent reason for a protest is the use of ineligible players. Most associations require the forfeiture of any game in which ineligible players participate.

Awards

The basis for awards in interscholastic and intercollegiate athletics is the same as that for intramural and extramural athletics. There are arguments for and against giving awards. Some individuals feel that the values derived from playing a sport—joy and satisfaction and physical, social, and other values—are sufficient and that no awards should be given. Others argue that awards are traditional and symbolic of achievement and should be given.

The awards policy should be determined locally. A definite policy that cuts across all the affairs of the school or college should be established. The practice of giving awards in the form of letters, insignia, or some other symbol is almost universal. When awards are given they should be simple and inexpensive. Some state athletic associations, for example, have stated that the award should not cost more than $1.00. Furthermore, it seems wise not to distinguish between so-called major and minor sports when giving awards. They should be treated equally.

Intercollegiate basketball, University of Nevada, Las Vegas

Records

The wise manager and coach will keep accurate records of all the details concerned with the management of athletics. The following records should be kept: records of participation for eligibility purposes and records that show the extent of the program; records on the conduct of various sports from year to year so they can be compared over time and also compared with other organizations; statistical summaries of player and game performance that will help the coach determine weaknesses in game strategy or identify players' performances and other items essential to well-organized play; records of equipment and supplies; officials' records; financial records; and other records related to conducting the total program. Sound business and management demand record keeping.

SELECTED MANAGEMENT PROBLEMS ASSOCIATED WITH ATHLETICS

The director of athletics or other manager responsible for interscholastic, intercollegiate, or other competitive athletic programs is bound to encounter many problems, including recruitment, eligibility, scholarships, proselyting, scouting, finances, drugs, and extra pay for coaching. In addition, certain problems arise in school situations when working with the business administrator.

Recruitment

Recruiting athletes is a controversial issue. Some educational institutions indicate that they do not condone recruiting for the primary purpose of developing winning teams. They feel the procedure for admittance should be the same for all students, regardless of whether they are athletes, chemistry students, music students, or others. No special consideration should be shown to any particular group. The same standards, academic and otherwise, should prevail.

Some educational institutions, however, actively recruit athletes for their varsity teams. The main consideration here is to live up to rules of the league, the conference, the NCAA, or other organizations in which the institution participates. To do otherwise is not condoned.

In schools and colleges athletic teams should be composed of matriculated students attracted to the school or college because of its educational advantages.

The management can do much to see that acceptable academic standards are observed in the recruitment process. It should be made clear in writing that established rules will be observed and that any violation will be dealt with severely. Also, the management might find it helpful to conduct seminars for the coaching staff on effective recruiting practices.

Eligibility

Standards regarding the eligibility of contestants are essential. These should be in writing, disseminated widely, and clearly understood by all concerned. They should be established well ahead of a season's or a year's play so players, coaches, and others will not become emotional when they suddenly realize they will not win a championship because they cannot use a star player who is ineligible.

Standards of eligibility in interscholastic circles usually include an age limit of not more than 19 or 20 years of age; a requirement that an athlete be a bona fide student; rules on transfer students that frequently require their being residents in the community served by the school; satisfactory grades; a limit of three or four on number of seasons of competition allowed (playing in one game usually constitutes a season); regular attendance at school; permission to play on only one team during a season; and a requirement that the participant have a medical examination, amateur status, and parent's consent. These regulations vary from school to school and state to state.

The National Federation of State High School Athletic Associations considers a student ineligible for amateur standing if the student (1) has accepted money or compensation for playing in an athletic contest, (2) has played under an assumed name, (3) has competed with a team whose players were paid, or (4) has signed a contract to play with a professional team.

Eligibility requirements at the college and university level include rules about residence, undergraduate status, academic average, amateur status, limits of participation, and transfer. In some cases players must have been in residence for at least 1 year, whereas in others they can play as freshmen. Furthermore, they must be carefully matriculated students carrying a full program of studies, have a satisfactory grade point average, and have had only so many years of competition. Also, a student cannot participate after the expiration of four consecutive 12-month periods following the date of initial enrollment in an institution of higher learning. Amateur status is also a requirement.

Scholarships

Should athletes receive scholarships or special financial assistance from schools and colleges? This subject is argued and is mainly a problem at the college level. Those in favor of scholarships and financial assistance claim that a student who excels in sports should receive aid just as much as one who excels in music or any other subject. They claim that such inducements are justified in the educational picture. Those opposed point out that scholarships should be awarded on the basis of the need and general academic qualifications of a student, rather than skill in some sport. Another controversy concerns the right of women to receive athletic scholarships, although Title IX states that women are to receive scholarships the same as men.

One solution is to list criteria for making such grants and have them handled by an all-school or all-college committee. This plan is based on the premise that scholarships and student aid should not be granted to the athletic or to any other department. Instead, they should be handled on an all-school or all-college basis and given to students who need them most and are best qualified. In this way those students who need assistance, regardless of the area in which they specialize, will be the ones to receive aid.

Proselyting

Proselyting is a term applied to a high school or college that has so strongly overemphasized athletics that it has stooped to unethical behavior to secure outstanding talent for winning teams. High schools are not troubled with this problem as much as colleges are, but sometimes they also have difficulties. In some incidents a father was provided employment so he would move his family to a particular section of a city or a particular community so his child would be

eligible to play with the local team. However, thanks to vigilant state athletic associations, such incidents have been kept to a minimum. The following represent some of the rules in force in many states to eliminate special inducements to attract athletes. Rules that have been established by many state high school athletic associations include:

- Only acceptable forms of recognition should be presented to athletes. These usually include letters, monograms, or school insignias.
- The educational institution or athletic association should be the only source of awards to athletes.
- No student should be the recipient of special treatment from any outside organization.
- Complimentary dinners (from local organizations) may be accepted by athletic teams if approved by the superintendent of schools.

Scouting

Scouting has become an accepted practice at high school and college levels. By watching another team perform, one will learn the formations and plays used and discover certain weaknesses. One coach said his scouting consisted of watching players to determine little mannerisms they had that would give away the play going to be used.

Many schools and colleges are spending considerable money on scouting. Some scout a rival team every game during the season, using three or four persons on the same scouting assignment and taking moving pictures at length so the opponent's play can be studied in great detail. It is felt by some physical educators that money could be spent more wisely if used to enhance the value of the game for the participants, rather than to further any all-important effort to win.

Many unethical practices have entered into scouting. Coaches have been known to have scouts observe secret practice sessions. Scouting is considered unethical under any circumstances except by means of observing regularly scheduled games. If scouting does occur, the head coach at the institution has direct responsibility for the action.

Many coaches say the only reason they scout is that they themselves are being scouted. Therefore they feel it will work to their disadvantage unless they follow the same procedure. If something could be done to eliminate or restrict scouting, considerable time and money could be put to much better use.

Finances

Throughout the country interscholastic and intercollegiate athletic programs are financed through many different sources. These include gate receipts, board of education and central university funds, donations, special projects, students' fees, physical education department funds, magazine subscriptions, and concessions. In high schools a "general organization" frequently handles the funds for athletics. Some colleges finance part of the program through endowment funds.

It has long been argued by leaders in physical education that athletic programs have great educational potential. They are curricular in nature rather than extracurricular. This means they contribute to the welfare of students like any other subject in the curriculum. On this basis therefore the finances necessary to support such a program should come from board of education or central university funds. Athletic programs should not be self-supporting or used as a means to support part or all of the other so-called extracurricular activities of a school or college. They represent an integral part of the educational program and as such deserve to be treated the same as other aspects of the program. This procedure is followed in some schools and colleges with benefits to all concerned and should be an ideal toward which all should strive.

Gate receipts are the source of many unfortunate practices in athletics. Too often they become the point of emphasis rather than the valuable educational outcomes that can accrue to the participant. When this occurs, athletics cannot justify their existence in the educational program. Furthermore, the emphasis on

Interscholastic gymnastics, Thornwood High School, South Holland, Ill.

gate receipts is a vicious cycle—the money increases the desire for winning teams so there will be greater financial return, which in turn results in greater financial outlays to secure and develop even better teams. This goes on and on, resulting in a false set of standards forming the basis of the program.

One survey indicates that one out of every five U.S. schools has cut back athletic programs or may soon do so as a result of budgetary difficulties. Declining athletic support has also resulted in lessened support for other nonacademic activities.

In some school districts a fee is collected from students who desire to participate in interscholastic athletics.

Drug abuse

Drug abuse among high school and college students is a reality, one that must be recognized and treated. The athlete is no exception to the growing use of drugs among students. Many coaches and physical educators assume the rigid training and health requirements of athletes somehow protect them from drug abuse. However, athletes are a part of the whole school social environment, and intense peer group pressures are exerted on them just as they are on other students.

The drug abuse problem in the world of professional and college sports is of great concern to Americans. The news media, public, and particularly educators and coaches, should be even more concerned about the young athlete and drug abuse. Drug use and addiction is not limited to the adult world. It has also snared the younger generation.

The Drug Education Committee of the National Collegiate Athletic Association has indicated that most athletes bring their drug use habits with them when they come to the (college) campus.

Therefore they conclude that "it may be more effective to deal with the problem at the secondary school level." Dr. Roy T. Bergman,[3] team physician for high school teams in Escanaba, Mich., points out, "(Drugs) have made their way into high school and junior high school athletes and substance abuse among these age groups is on the increase."

Alcohol is the most commonly used drug with 93 out of every 100 young athletes 11 to 14 years of age

coming in contact with this element. Marijuana is the next most popular drug on the list. The United States Department of Health and Human Services has pointed out that approximately one out of every three high school seniors had tried marijuana before entering high school.

Other agents used by young athletes who hope to give themselves more energy include cocaine and "uppers" such as amphetamines, caffeine, and ephedrine. Anabolic steroids are also being used by these sport neophytes who hope to make themselves bigger and stronger for sports competition.

These drugs are taking their toll among our young athletes. Growth potential and maturity are being hampered, side effects are causing poor health. Instead of improving athletic performance these drugs are resulting in slower reaction times, improper coordination with poor execution of movement, altered perception of speed, and in impairment of motor function in general. In addition, they also are resulting in academic and vocational failure.

According to the report in the September 1984 *Athletic Business,* the Milton, Wisconsin, School District is coming to grips with drug abuse. Their program is designed to identify those students who come to school under the influence of alcohol or other drugs. If students exhibit overt behavior of drug abuse they are referred to the principal of the school. If they voluntarily admit use of drugs, they are then referred to the student assistance and counseling program. However, if they claim they are not involved, they are given a urinalysis test. If the test is positive, they are assigned to a state licensed assessment program. If students refuse to take the test, they are placed on a 3-day suspension and assigned to a licensed assessment program and must get treatment before returning to school.

The Milton, Wisconsin, program applies to all students. Players and cheerleaders are informed that the use of alcohol and other drugs is strictly forbidden. They are also told that voluntary self-referral to the student assistance program for drug abuse is not a violation of the athletic code.

The Arkadelphia, Arkansas, School District program for drug abuse is more punitive in nature. Stiff penalties are imposed when students are caught: *first offense,* withdrawal from school for one semester or suspension; *second offense,* suspension for 12 months; *third offense,* permanent expulsion.

Bruce Durbin, Executive Director of the National Federation of State High School Associations (which represents 20,000 schools and has 93,000 individual members), feels that a drug program should stress education rather than enforcement. Such programs should reach coaches, officials, students, and educators in general.

The state of Minnesota is using an education program with the help of the Hazelden Foundation, the Kroc Foundation, and the Minnesota State High School League. As a team they are sponsoring several projects, such as chemical awareness seminars. This program is building a model for other state associations to follow.

The drug abuse program called Operation Cork was founded by Joan Kroc, widow of McDonald's founder Ray Kroc, for the purpose of coping with the problems of athletes and drugs. The Hazelden-Kroc Foundations are now investing $7 million in a facility that will focus its efforts on drug education and drug abuse prevention.

Extra pay for coaching

A frequent topic of discussion at school meetings is whether teachers should receive extra pay for extra services. Parents, taxpayers, and school boards have been trying to decide whether athletic coaches, band leaders, dramatics supervisors, publication consultants, and others who do work in addition to their teaching load should receive additional compensation for such services.

A sensible solution to this problem is essential to the good morale of a school staff. Because school systems are demanding more and more services, a policy must be formulated to cover the extra duties being heaped on the shoulders of teachers.

The many faceted problem of extra pay for extra services concerns a large number of educators, administrators, and laymen. Following are ideas that represent the thinking of many teachers and administrators throughout the country.

The educational program in all school systems should rest on a sound financial base. Coaches' sal-

aries should be sufficient to provide a comfortable living. They should not have to seek extra work in school or elsewhere to make ends meet.

If possible, there should be enough staff members in every school to make it unnecessary for anyone to take on an extra load.

Extra work means loss of efficiency. A teacher or coach can perform at his or her best for only a certain number of hours a day; then the law of diminishing returns sets in.

All teachers and coaches work beyond the school day. They prepare teaching assignments, grade

Interscholastic volleyball, Riverside-Brookfield High School, Riverside, Ill.

papers, keep records, and take on other professional responsibilities. It is difficult therefore to determine what is "extra work."

Extra work in education is not comparable to extra work in business or industry. Professional ethics dictate that positions in public service cannot be categorized in the same way as many other types of work.

Coaching loads should be equalized as far as possible. If inequalities exist that cannot be corrected through extra staff, extra pay is justified.

Where extra pay is provided, it should be distributed equitably to all who work beyond a normal school day. Teachers and coaches should perform extra work only in areas where they are qualified.

The most acceptable form of compensation for additional duties is extra pay. The practice of released time does not seem to meet the wishes of most coaches.

The problem of extra pay for extra service is not easy to resolve. Convincing arguments can be given for both sides. Because local needs differ, a nationwide solution cannot be prescribed. However, any community wrestling with this problem may well be guided by the foregoing points.

Problems created by the rapid growth of girls' and women's sports and Title IX

The number of girls and women participating in sports has grown by leaps and bounds, but so have the problems, most of which are the result of this growth.

One problem relates to the need to achieve and maintain high-quality athletic programs. The budget crunch and distressed economy have not provided for needed additional facilities such as locker rooms, gymnasia, athletic fields, and equipment. Although girls and women are entitled to an equitable share of these necessities, these items exist in insufficient number to accommodate the expanded girls' and women's sport programs.

Girls' and women's athletic programs are beginning to be faced with the same concerns that boys' and men's programs have faced over the years: emphasis on winning, recruiting, unethical means of obtaining star players, and the demand for scholarships. Some women physical educators, as a result, are being exposed to the same temptations to produce winning teams.

Present practices indicate that women leaders in physical education and athletics are encountering the

Women's intercollegiate athletics, University of Kansas, Lawrence, Kan.

same problems that beset the men when they were deciding whether to go "big time" in athletics. In an effort to gain parity with athletic programs for men, some practices that have been adopted by men are now being endorsed by women.

Coaches in girls' and women's programs also are finding it difficult in some instances to be prepared adequately for their coaching responsibilities. Title IX has brought about so many changes in such a short period, that many noncoaching women are assigned to coaching responsibilities, and they are finding that coaching is different from teaching. During many years of teaching and little varsity team coaching they have developed philosophies that at times are in conflict with the demands on them to coach highly skilled varsity teams who are supposed to win games.

Girls' and women's programs are also being engulfed in publicity and promotion of a magnitude they never experienced before the present emphasis on highly organized competition for women. Girls' and

women's sports are featured in the newspaper headlines, television coverage, and radio news. They have become "big time." As a result of such exposure, girls and women are having difficulty keeping their sports programs in proper perspective and observing sound ethical practices.

MANAGEMENT GUIDELINES FOR COMPETITIVE ATHLETIC PROGRAMS

Competitive athletic programs exist in schools, colleges, universities, and other organizations.

Elementary and junior high schools[5]

Since athletics was first introduced into the education picture, pushing these competitive experiences down into the lower education levels has been continual. Educational athletics started at the college level with a crew race between Harvard and Yale in 1852. Then other sports were introduced to campuses throughout the United States. As higher education athletic pro-

---

ATHLETIC PROBLEMS BUSINESS ADMINISTRATORS ENCOUNTER

Some of the pitfalls and problems encountered by business administrators in working with athletic directors and coaches, as seen through the eyes of business administrators, follow:
- Overestimation of budget requests with the expectation of a reduction in the request
- Not being able to justify budget requests as they relate to the total educational program
- Deadlines not met for submitting requests for transportation, supplies, and other needs
- Lack of awareness of the school district or college philosophy regarding the place of the athletic program in the curriculum, which leads to budget complications
- Lack of cooperative planning regarding the transportation, equipment available, and the scheduling of special athletic events away from school or college, necessitating the use of buses
- Late notification to the business administrator's office of cancellation of special athletic event that requires cancellation of a prearranged bus
- Negligence in filing accident reports on students injured in sports or classes, no matter how insignificant an accident may seem at the time
- Incomplete records on students participating in sports—especially regarding the requirement that all students receive a physical examination *before* trying out for the sport
- Lack of concern for accident victims
- Lack of knowledge of an injured student's rights and privileges under the student accident policy
- Failure to realize that the educational goals represented in the philosophy of the school or college take priority over selfish, petty, and political interests
- Lack of respect for the chain of command—a physical education teacher or coach should not bypass the director of the department when communicating with the business office
- Lack of interest in the facilities at his or her disposal, causing breakdowns and extra added expense

Cheerleaders at intercollegiate athletic competition, University of Nevada, Las Vegas.

grams expanded and gained recognition and popularity, the high schools felt sports should also be a part of their educational offerings. As a result, most high schools in America today have some form of interscholastic athletics. In recent years junior high schools have also felt the impact of interscholastic athletic programs. A survey made by the National Association of Secondary School Principals (which included 2296 junior high schools) showed 85.2% had some program of interscholastic athletics, whereas 14.8% did not.

Interscholastic athletics should not be present at the elementary school level. In kindergarten through grade six, physical activities should be geared to the developmental level of the child. Starting with grade four it may be possible to initiate an informal intramural program. However, developing skill in only a few sports or requiring children to conform to adult standards of athletic competition should not be emphasized.

The special nature of grades seven through nine, representing a transition period between the elementary school and the senior high school and between

childhood and adolescence, has raised a question in the minds of many educators about whether an interscholastic athletic program is in the best interests of the students concerned.

Management guidelines for elementary school athletics

Many of the guidelines of the American Academy of Pediatrics apply at the elementary school level and to the type of athletic competition that should be offered:

All children should have opportunities to develop skill in a variety of activities.

All such activities should take into account the age and developmental level of the child.

Athletic activities of elementary school children should be part of an overall school program.

Competent medical supervision of each child should be ensured.

Health observation by teachers and others should be encouraged and help given by the physician.

Athletic activities outside the school program should be on an entirely voluntary basis without undue emphasis on any special program or sport and without undue emphasis on winning. These programs should also include competent medical supervision.

Competitive programs organized on school, neighborhood, and community levels will meet the needs of children 12 years of age and under. State, regional, and national tournaments and bowl, charity, and exhibition games are not recommended for this age group. Commercial exploitation in any form is unequivocally condemned.

Body-contact sports, particularly tackle football and boxing, are considered to have no place in programs for children of this age.

Competition is an inherent characteristic of growing, developing children. Properly guided, it is beneficial and not harmful to their development.

Schools and communities as a whole must be made aware of the needs for personnel, facilities, equipment, and supplies, which will assure an adequate program for children in this age group.

All competitive athletic programs should be organized with the cooperation of interested medical groups, who will ensure adequate medical care before and during such programs. This should include thorough physical examinations at specified intervals, teaching health observation to teachers and coaches as well as attention to factors such as (1) injury, (2) response to fatigue, (3) individual emotional needs, and (4) the risks of undue emotional strains.

Muscle testing is not, per se, a valid estimate of physical fitness or of good health.

Participation in group activities is expected of every child. When there is a failure to do so or lack of interest, underlying physical or emotional causes could be suspect.

Leadership for young children should be such that highly organized, highly competitive programs are avoided. The primary consideration should be a diversity of wholesome childhood experiences that will aid in the proper physical and emotional development of the child into a secure and well-integrated adult.

Management guidelines for junior high school athletics

The research regarding a highly organized athletics program at the junior high school level indicates the following points of substantial agreement:

The junior high school educational program should be adapted to the needs of boys and girls in grades seven, eight, and nine. This is a period of transition from elementary school to senior high school and from childhood to adolescence. It is a time when students are trying to understand their bodies, gain independence, achieve adult social status, acquire self-confidence, and establish a system of values. It is a time when a program of education unique to this age group is needed to meet the abilities and broadening interests of students.

The best educational program at the junior high school level provides program enrichment to meet the needs of students in grades seven through nine, rather than using the senior high school or other educational level as a blueprint to follow.

A distinct and separate educational climate for these grades is needed to ensure the program will not be influenced unduly by either the elementary or the senior high school.

Coaches are needed whose full responsibilities involve working with grades seven, eight, and nine and whose training has included an understanding of the needs of these students and of the educational program required to meet those needs.

The junior high school should provide for exploratory experiences with specialization delayed until senior high school and college.

The junior high school should provide for the mental, physical, social, and emotional development of students.

Out-of-class, as well as in-class, experiences should be provided.

Concern for the development of a sound standard of values in each student should be present.

The principal and other members of the administration have the responsibility for providing sound educational leadership in all school matters. The type of physical education and athletic programs offered will reflect the type of leadership provided.

The physical education program at the junior high school level should consist of a class program, an adapted program, and intramural and extramural programs. The interscholastic athletics program is controversial.

The interscholastic athletics program, if offered,

Water polo, Lyons Township
High School, LaGrange, Ill.

should be provided only after the prerequisites of physical education, adapted, intramural, and extramural programs have been developed, and only as special controls regarding health, facilities, game adaptations, classification of players, leadership, and officials have been provided.

The physical education program should be adapted to the needs of the student. There is a need for a wide variety of activities, based on physical and neuromuscular maturation, that will contribute to the development of body control, enable each student to experience success, provide for recognition of energy output and fatigue, and take into consideration the growth spurt of early adolescence.

The physical education program should provide a favorable social and emotional climate for the student. There should be freedom from anxiety and fear, absence of tensions and strains, a feeling of belonging for each student, a social awareness that contributes to the development of such important traits as respect for the rights of others, and an atmosphere conducive to growing into social and emotional maturity.

Personal health instruction should be closely integrated into the physical education program.

Coeducational activities should be provided.

All physical activities should be carefully supervised by a physician and conducted under optimal health and safety conditions.

Students who are not physiologically mature should not engage in activities that are highly competitive or require body contact, a high degree of skill, or great amounts of endurance.

Physiological maturity is the best criterion for determining whether a student is physiologically ready for participation in most interscholastic athletic activities.

Competition itself is not the factor that makes athletics dangerous to the physiologically mature student. Instead, items such as the manner in which the program is conducted, type of activity, facilities, leadership, and physical condition of students are the determining factors.

Physiological fitness can be developed without exposure to an interscholastic athletic program.

Competitive athletics, if properly conducted, have the potential for satisfying such basic psychological needs as recognition, belonging, self-respect, the feeling of achievement, as well as providing a wholesome outlet for the physical activity drive. However, if conducted in light of adult interests, community pressure, and other questionable influences, they can prove psychologically harmful.

Interscholastic athletics, when conducted in accordance with desirable standards of leadership, educational philosophy, activities, and other pertinent factors, have the potential for realizing beneficial social effects for the student; but when not conducted in accordance with desirable standards, they can be socially detrimental to the student.

Tackle football, ice hockey, and boxing have questionable value for junior high school students.

Management guidelines for interscholastic (high school) and intercollegiate athletic programs[8]

Selected recommended standards for high school and college athletic programs follow:

Organization

The wholesome conduct of the athletic programs should be the ultimate responsibility of the school administration.

Athletic policy should be adapted, evaluated, and supervised by a faculty committee.

Athletic policy should be implemented by the director of physical education and the director of athletics.

Athletics should be organized as an integral part of the department of physical education.

Staff

All members of the coaching staff should be members of the faculty.

All coaches should be hired on their qualifications to assume educational responsibilities and not on their ability to produce winning teams.

All coaches should enjoy the same privileges of tenure, rank, and salary accorded other similarly qualified faculty members.

All public school coaches should be certified in physical education.

Finances

The financing of interscholastic and intercollegiate athletics should be governed by the same policies that control the financing of all other educational activities within an institution.

Gate receipts should be considered an incidental source of revenue.

Health and safety

An annual physical examination should be required of all participants; a physical examination on a seasonal basis would be preferable.

Each school should have a written policy for the implementation of an injury-care program.

Each school should have a written policy concerning the responsibility for athletic injuries and should provide or make available athletic accident insurance.

All coaches should be well qualified in the care and prevention of athletic injuries.

A physician should be present at all contests at which injury is possible.

Only that equipment offering the best protection should be purchased.

All protective equipment should fit players properly.

Competition should be scheduled only between teams of comparable ability.

Games should not be played until players have had a minimum of 3 weeks of physical conditioning and drill.

Playing fields should meet standards for size and safety.

Eligibility

All schools should honor and respect the eligibility rules and regulations of respective local, state, and national athletic associations.

A student who is not making normal progress toward a degree or diploma should not be allowed to participate.

Recruiting

The athletic teams of each school should be composed of bona fide students who live in the school district or who were attracted to the institution by its educational program.

All candidates for admission to a school should be evaluated according to the same high standards.

All financial aid should be administered with regard to need and according to the same standards for all students. The recipient of financial aid should be

EVALUATION OF A HIGH SCHOOL ATHLETIC PROGRAM[10]

	Yes	No
1. Athletic program an integral part of total curriculum		
a. The sports are an outgrowth of the physical education program	_____	_____
b. A variety of sports are available for all students	_____	_____
c. The educational values of sport are foremost in the philosophy	_____	_____
d. All students have an opportunity to participate in a sport	_____	_____
e. Athletics are used appropriately as a school's unifying force	_____	_____
f. Athletes are not excused from courses, including physical education, because of athletic participation	_____	_____
2. Coaches as faculty members		
a. Coaches have an adequate opportunity to exercise the same rights and privileges as other faculty members in determining school and curricular matters	_____	_____
b. Coaches attend, and they are scheduled so they may attend faculty meetings	_____	_____
c. Coaches are not expected to assume more duties of a general nature than are other faculty members	_____	_____
d. Teaching tenure and other faculty privileges are available to athletic personnel	_____	_____
e. Assignments for extra duties are made for coaches on the same basis as for other teachers	_____	_____
3. Participants encouraged by activities to perform adequately in academic areas		
a. Athletes are held accountable scholastically at the same level as other students	_____	_____
b. Practices are of such length and intensity that they do not deter students' academic pursuits	_____	_____
c. Game trips do not cause the students to miss an excessive number of classes	_____	_____
d. Counseling services emphasize the importance of academic records in regard to career education	_____	_____
e. Athletes are required to attend classes on days of contests	_____	_____
4. Meeting philosophy of school board		
a. New coaches are made aware of the board policies and informed that they will be expected to follow them in spirit as well as letter	_____	_____
b. All coaches are regularly informed by the principal and athletic director that they must practice within the framework of board policy	_____	_____
c. A procedure is available for the athletic director and coaches to make recommendations regarding policy change	_____	_____
d. Noncoaching faculty members are made aware of board policy regarding athletics so they may discuss it from a base of fact	_____	_____
e. The philosophy of the board is written and made available to all personnel	_____	_____
5. Awards		
a. Only those intrinsic awards authorized by local conferences and state athletic associations are given	_____	_____
b. Diligence is exercised to ensure that outside groups do not cause violations of the award regulations	_____	_____
c. Care is taken to assure that athletes are not granted privileges not available to the general student body	_____	_____
6. Projected program outcomes		
a. It is emphasized that participation in athletics is a privilege	_____	_____

From National Council of Secondary School Athletic Directors.

EVALUATION OF A HIGH SCHOOL ATHLETIC PROGRAM—cont'd

	Yes	No
b. Development of critical thinking as well as athletic performance is planned into the program	_____	_____
c. Development of self-direction and individual motivation is a real part of the athletic experience	_____	_____
d. The athletes are allowed to develop at their own cognitive, psychomotor, and effective readiness level	_____	_____
e. The accepted social values are used as standards of behavior both on and off the playing area	_____	_____
7. Guarding against student exploitation		
a. The student is not used in athletic performance to provide an activity that has as its main purpose entertainment of the community	_____	_____
b. The student's academic program is in no way altered to allow him to maintain eligibility with less than normal effort on his part	_____	_____
c. The student is not given a false impression of his athletic ability through the device of suggesting the possibility of a college scholarship	_____	_____
d. The athletes are not given a false image of the value of their athletic prowess to the material and cultural success within the school and community	_____	_____

---

given a statement of the amount, duration, and conditions of the award.

Awards

The value of athletic awards should be limited.

There should be no discrimination between awards for different varsity sports.

The presentation of all-star and most valuable player awards should be discouraged.

The checklist above provides an evaluation aid in determining the relationship of the high school athletic program to the total educational program.

Management guidelines for competitive athletic programs in other organizations

Other organizations also have highly competitive athletic programs. These are frequently found in such organizations and businesses as the YMCA, commercial clubs that specialize in one or more sports, and Police Athletic Leagues.

The main consideration in such athletic programs is to gear them to the age and needs of the participants. Youth-serving agencies, for example, should observe the established standards for interscholastic programs, whereas adults might follow the standards applicable at the college and university level.

Many advantages accrue from belonging to leagues and conferences rather than playing independently. Leagues and conferences cause several people to get together and establish procedures, rules, and regulations that are more likely to benefit the participant than if a team were organized independently.

Usually athletics sponsored by educational institutions take special pains to provide for the health of the participants. They frequently have insurance, athletic trainers, physicians in attendance, and other provisions that help guarantee safer participation for the players. Sometimes in highly competitive athletic programs in other organizations, there is not the same concern for the safety and well-being of the players; as a result, players sometimes participate at their own risk.

It would be helpful if organizations would think through and apply many of the procedures and standards set forth in this chapter for educational institutions.

Management guidelines for athletics for handicapped persons

Persons with handicaps can receive the same benefits from a program of competitive sports as nonhandicapped persons. The following reasons for including adapted sports activities in the physical education program are listed by Crowe, Auxter, and Pyfer.[4]

Many students assigned to an adapted physical education class are unable to correct an existing condition and also are unable to participate in regular physical education. A program of adapted sports would be ideal for such students because it would give them some form of physical activity.

Students in the adapted physical education program need activities that have carry-over value. They may continue exercise programs in the future, but they also need training in carry-over types of sports and games that will be useful to them in later life.

Adapted sports activities may have a therapeutic value if they are carefully structured for the student.

Adapted sports and games should help the handicapped individual learn to handle his or her body under a variety of circumstances.

There are recreational values in games and sports activities for the student who is facing the problem of overcoming some type of handicap; some of his or her special needs can best be met through recreational kinds of activities.

A certain amount of emotional release takes place in play activities, and this is important to the student with a disability.

The Joseph P. Kennedy Jr. Foundation probably has focused more attention on sports for handicapped persons than any other single organization or legislation. The most visible activity promoted by the Kennedy Foundation is the Special Olympics, which was organized in 1968. It was designed to provide mentally retarded youths, 8 years of age and over, with opportunities to participate in a variety of sports and games on local, state, regional, national, and international levels.

The basic objectives of the Special Olympics are to:

Encourage development of comprehensive physical education and recreation programs for the mentally retarded in schools, day-care centers, and residential facilities in every community.

Prepare the retarded for sports competition—particularly where no opportunities and programs now exist.

Supplement existing activities and programs in schools, communities, day-care centers, and residential facilities.

Provide training for volunteer coaches to enable them to work with youngsters in physical fitness, recreation, and sports activities.[14]

TITLE IX AND THE CHANGING ROLE OF GIRLS' AND WOMEN'S ATHLETIC COMPETITION

The women's movement, proponents of equality in girls' and women's sports, and Title IX have altered the concept of women's sports in recent years. Women are becoming more and more accepted as athletes, with a full right to experience all kinds of sports activities. Many persons wrongly interpret this kind of statement to mean that women want to compete with men in all sports activities. Although women may compete with men in certain coeducational activities, such as bowling, tennis, and volleyball, they also want separate but equal athletic programs, including equal funding, equipment, and facility use.

Procedures and practices concerning interscholastic and intercollegiate athletic competition for girls vary from state to state. Some schools and colleges have broad programs of interscholastic athletics, others have few, and some have modified programs. Most states do not set up specific requirements for girls' athletics but feel that their established regulations apply to both girls and boys. A few states have athletic associations for girls that are similar to those for boys.

The National Association for Girls and Women in Sport (NAGWS) of the AAHPERD believes that teams should be provided for all girls and women desiring competitive athletic participation. Adequate funds, facilities, and staff should be provided for these programs.

Title IX*

One of the major reasons Title IX came into being was to ensure that girls and women receive the same rights as boys and men. Testimony before congressional committees before the enactment of this legislation indicated that girls and women were being discriminated against in many education programs, including physical education and athletics.

Although Title IX applies to all types of educational programs, probably the most dramatically affected have been sport and physical education programs. Girls' and women's athletic programs, in particular, have grown rapidly in only a few years. In the early 1970s there were comparatively few varsity interscholastic and intercollegiate teams for girls and women. Today, however, as a result of the federal regulation banning sex discrimination, it is a different story. Girls' and women's sport teams have come into their own and are in evidence throughout the nation.

Provisions of Title IX affecting athletic programs

Some of the provisions of Title IX affecting athletic programs include the following:

Separate teams for boys and girls, or a coeducational team, must be provided in schools and colleges. For example, if there is only one team in a particular school, such as swimming, then students of both sexes must be permitted to try out for this team.

Equal opportunities must be provided for both sexes in educational institutions in equipment and supplies, use of facilities for practice and games, medical and training services, coaching and academic tutoring, travel allowances, housing and dining facilities, compensation of coaches, and publicity.

Equal aggregate expenditures are not required; however, equal opportunity for men and women is mandated.

Where men are given the opportunity for athletic scholarships, women must also be given the same opportunity.

Contact sports such as football, basketball, boxing, wrestling, rugby, and ice hockey may be offered either separately or on a unitary basis.

The emphasis of Title IX is to provide equal opportunity for both sexes. In determining whether equal opportunity is provided, it is important to know whether the interests and abilities of students of both sexes have been met and whether such things as adequate facilities and equipment are available to both sexes in each sport.

Title IX guidelines provide that expenditures on men's and women's athletics be proportional to the number of men and women participating in athletics. This standard of substantially equal per capita expenditures must be met unless the institution can demonstrate that the differences are based on nondiscriminatory factors, such as the costs of a particular sport (for example, the equipment required) or the scope of the competition (national rather than regional or local). This proportional standard applies to athletic scholarships, recruitment, and other readily measurable financial benefits such as equipment, supplies, travel, and publicity.

According to the Department of Health and Human Services, the policy is designed to eliminate, over a reasonable period of time, the discriminatory effects, particularly at the college level, of the historic emphasis on men's sports and to facilitate the continued growth of women's athletics. It requires colleges and universities to take specific steps to provide additional athletic opportunities for women—opportunities that will fully accommodate the rising interests of women participating in athletics.

Procedures for assuring compliance with Title IX

To make sure the provisions of Title IX have been complied with by an educational institution, certain

---

*Parts of this section have been taken directly from government documents relating to Title IX, particularly the following documents:

U.S. Department of Health, Education, and Welfare, Office for Civil Rights: Final Title IX regulation implementing education amendments of 1972—prohibiting sex discrimination in education, Washington, D.C., July 21, 1975, Government Printing Office.

U.S. Department of Health, Education, and Welfare, Office for Civil Rights: Memorandum to chief state school officers, superintendents of local educational agencies and college and university presidents. Subject: Elimination of sex discrimination in athletic programs, Washington, D.C., September 1975, Government Printing Office.

procedures are followed. Each educational institution usually has some member of the faculty or staff coordinate a self-evaluation and assure compliance.

The steps that have been followed in some physical education and athletic programs involve first developing a statement of physical education philosophy that provides a guide for equality of opportunity for both sexes. Then student interest is determined regarding the activities they desire in the physical education and athletic program. In addition, all written materials concerned with items such as curriculum, employment, administration, and course content are reviewed to see that needed changes are made to ensure that physical education activities are being taught coeducationally. Also, such things as practice times for all teams, provision for supplies and equipment, travel expenses, number of coaches assigned to teams, and salaries of coaches are examined to see if any discrepancies exist between the sexes. The membership requirements for clubs and other student organizations associated with physical education and athletics are reviewed. The amount of publicity and information services provided for physical education and athletic programs are checked. Eligibility requirements for scholarships and financial aid, medical and accident policies, award systems, and employment procedures are examined. Teaching loads, coaching assignments, and facility assignments are also included in such an appraisal.

According to the AAHPERD,[1] many questions can be asked to determine if equality exists between men and women. For example, under *employment conditions* the question might be asked, ''Are men and women paid the same salaries for essentially the same work for both teaching and coaching?'' Under *physical education classes* the question might be asked, ''Are physical education requirements for graduation the same for boys and girls, men and women?'' Under *recreational opportunities,* ''Are intramural programs provided for both sexes?'' Under *athletics,* ''Does the total budget reflect comparable support to both the men's and women's programs?'' Many other questions are listed in their publication to determine if equality exists.

In some cases where equality does not exist be-

tween men and women, litigation is initiated. For example, in one case a high school girl wanted to participate on the boys' golf team. There was no golf team for girls, and the court ruled in favor of the girl and allowed her to participate. Another case involved girls who wanted to play on the high school football team, thus challenging a state athletic association rule excluding girls. The court ruled in favor of the girls and said the association rule discriminated on the basis of sex.

The publication *In the Running,*[13] a project of the Women's Equity Action League Educational and Legal Defense Fund, has indicated the following pros and cons of bringing a legal suit:

Some *pros of filing a complaint* are: It is possible to win. You may convince other women to take legal action for other complaints. You may change discriminatory practices at your school or college. Many girls and women may benefit from your action. Your action may result in the Title IX compliance plan at your school becoming the subject of scrutiny. Schools that have been cited for complaints are more likely to be closer to compliance with the law.

Some *cons of filing a complaint* are: You can lose. You may lose your position or scholarship. You may become frustrated in dealing with the many organizations involved. The procedure sometimes takes years to resolve. You may be labeled a trouble-maker.

Organizations that will be of help in case you find that inequality exists are: Department of Health and Human Services; Office for Civil Rights; Equal Employment Opportunity Commission; Office of Federal Contract Compliance; and the U.S. Department of Labor—Wage and Hour Division of the Employment Standards Administration.

Title IX athletics complaints have been filed against several institutions. The complaints were filed with regional Office of Civil Rights (OCR) offices and have been referred to the national OCR headquarters office in Washington, D.C.

Coeducational sports and Title IX

Coeducational sports should be provided for students in schools and institutions of higher education because of the benefits (mainly sociological and cultural) that can accrue from such participation. However, coeducational sports, in some cases, should be limited to the intramural and recreational levels.

In instances where one or two highly skilled females would not otherwise have the opportunity to participate in a particular sport, they must be allowed to participate with males.

The main reason for not advocating coeducational sports participation on interscholastic and intercollegiate levels in many sports is the physiological differences between males and females. The ratio of strength to weight is greater in males than in females. Females thus would be at a decided disadvantage in those sports requiring speed and strength, including all contact sports and some noncontact sports such as track and field and volleyball.

Other reasons exist for advocating separate teams for males and females. For instance, if coeducational varsity teams were encouraged, males would comprise most of the teams. Because of the "speed, size, and strength" factors, girls would not be able to make varsity teams in any great numbers. Consequently, teams would be mostly male dominated.

The impact of Title IX on girls and women in sports

During the year before the birth of Title IX, 3,366,000 boys and 294,000 girls competed in interscholastic sports in the United States. Seven years later the figures showed 4,109,000 boys and 1,645,000 girls in the same activities. The figures are even larger today. Girls' participation in interscholastic sports increased 460% during the interim. Furthermore, the participation of girls increased from 7% of the total number of students involved to 29%. In addition, approximately 500 colleges offer athletic scholarships to women athletes. The Association for Intercollegiate Athletics for Women (AIAW), now defunct, had more than 1000 member schools a few years ago and was the largest collegiate athletic association in the United States. Since that time, however, the NCAA has taken over control of women's athletics in many colleges and universities. The AIAW is no longer active in governing women's intercollegiate athletics.

The situation on the secondary school level is about the same as it is on the college level; males are participating in organized athletic programs in greater numbers than females. Although girls on the secondary school level have made tremendous gains insofar as the total number of participants in interscholastic athletics, they still represent only about half the total number of boys who participate in interscholastic athletics.

The National Federation of State High School Associations indicates there are approximately two million female participants in athletics on the high school level. Girls participate in a total of 29 high school sports. The three most popular sports, in terms of schools sponsoring teams and number of participants, are basketball, track and field, and volleyball. Budgets for boys' sport activities at the interscholastic level were on the average larger than the budgets for girls' sport activities.

Although sports programs for men and women are still not equal in terms of funding, legislation such as Title IX has had a positive impact. Sports programs for males and females on all levels are much more equal in the 1980s.

Title IX, the courts, and prospects for the future[7,9]

The courts have caused some changes in Title IX. The United States Supreme Court decision regarding Grove City College has changed the interpretation of Title IX as formerly held. The court ruled that only the student aid office at Grove City College was covered by law barring sex bias, because the only federal money that the institution received came through the Pell Grants that its students received. In the case of private institutions that receive direct federal aid, the U.S. Commission on Civil Rights said that only the program or activity that actually receives the aid now must abide by Title IX regulations. In other words, the federal law barring sex discrimination in education, according to the Grove City ruling, does not apply to schools and colleges as a whole but only to those parts of an institution that receive federal aid directly. The court ruling means, for example, that if the athletic and physical education programs do not receive federal aid directly, they are not covered by Title IX. This ruling has raised a storm of protest from the Office of Civil Rights and other organizations supporting the original concept of Title IX—if an institution received federal aid, then all programs within that organization are covered by Title IX regulations.

After the Grove City decision there was action in Congress to introduce new language to resurrect the kinds of protection afforded by Title IX, but that legislation did not pass the Senate. There is more support for and acceptance of women's sports than ever before, but the mechanism that opened those doors is gone. Each school district and each college or university or other institution is unique and as a result must develop its own plan for compliance with Title IX. Noncompliance can present many problems and difficulties. This nation can no longer justify inequities in the manner in which both sexes are treated.

. Each institution and each educational program will face many problems in complying with Title IX. This is true particularly in light of the budget crises that many schools and colleges face at present. For example, it will be difficult for many institutions to increase items such as course offerings, budgets, and facilities for an expanded athletic program for girls without curtailing some other parts of the educational program at the same time, possibly that of the boys. It will be difficult to bear the increased costs of adding faculty, facilities, supplies and equipment, and scholarships to provide girls and women with a physical education and athletics program comparable to what boys and men now possess.

All of these problems can be solved, however, as they are being solved in thousands of educational institutions from coast to coast. For example, in many schools and colleges athletic and physical education activities are being modified so students may engage in them on a coeducational basis. Basketball is being played with modifications such as three women and two men on a team, with field goals scored by women counting four points and those by men two points, and with men not being permitted to enter the free-throw lane at any time at either end of the court. Volleyball is being played with four men and four

women; men are not permitted to spike and must serve underhand. Furthermore, at least one woman must touch the ball before it is volleyed back over the net by her team. Adaptations and modifications can be developed in most activities to make them suitable for coeducational use.

Instructors of physical education classes and coaches of athletic teams, when assigned to teams of the opposite sex or on a coeducational basis, have proved successful. Budgets have been increased for girls' and women's programs in many cases without harming the overall physical education and athletic program. Schedules have been revised so that both males and females have equitable access to facilities. Many other changes have also taken place to comply with the spirit of Title IX.

Compliance may be achieved according to the spirit of the federal mandate if there is a willingness to comply and a desire to cooperate with other members of an educational institution. The first and foremost way to achieve desirable results is to work through the system in one's local situation. It should be recognized that resistance in some cases will be encountered because change seldom comes easily. However, there should be equity for both sexes, and as a result such changes will eventually take place. The Office for Civil Rights is willing to assist school officials in meeting their Title IX responsibilities. Regional offices exist in ten different locations throughout the nation where help may be secured.

SELECTED ATHLETIC ASSOCIATIONS

An individual school or college, by itself, finds it difficult to develop standards and control athletics in a sound educational manner. However, uniting with other schools and colleges makes such a project possible. This has been done on local, state, and national levels in the interest of better athletics for high schools and colleges. Establishing rules and procedures well in advance of playing seasons provides educators and coaches the necessary control for conducting a sound athletic program. It helps them resist pressures of alumni, students, spectators, townspeople, and others who do not always have the best interests of the program in mind.

Various types of athletic associations exist. The ones most prevalent in high schools and colleges are student athletic associations, local conferences or leagues, state high school athletic associations, National Federation of State High School Athletic Associations, National Collegiate Athletic Association, and various conferences that exist throughout the nation.

The student athletic association is an organization within a school designed to promote and participate in the conduct of the athletic program of that school. It is usually open to all students in attendance. Through the payment of fees, it often helps support the athletics program. Such associations are found in many high schools throughout the country. They can be helpful in the development of a sound athletic program.

Various associations, conferences, or leagues bind together athletically several high schools within a particular geographical area. These are designed to regulate and promote wholesome competition among the member schools. They usually draw up schedules, approve officials, handle disputes, and have general supervision over the athletic programs.

The state high school athletic association that now exists in almost every state is a major influence in high school athletics. It is open to all professionally accredited high schools within the state. It has a constitution, administrative officers to conduct the business, and a board of control. The number of members on the board of control usually varies from six to nine. Fees are usually paid to the association on a flat basis or according to the size of the school. In some states there are no fees, because the necessary revenue is derived from the gate receipts of tournament competition. State associations are interested in a sound program of athletic competition within the confines of the state. They concern themselves with the usual problems that have to do with athletics, such as rules of eligibility, officials, disputes, and similar items. They are interested in promoting sound high school athletics, equalizing athletic competition, protecting participants, and guarding the health of players. They are an influence for good and have won the respect of educators.

National Association for Girls and Women in Sports (NAGWS)

The National Association for Girls and Women in Sport is one of the seven associations of the American Alliance for Health, Physical Education, Recreation, and Dance and is concerned with the governance of sports for girls and women.

The specific functions of the NAGWS are the following:

To formulate and publicize guiding principles and standards for the administrator, leader, official, and player.

To publish and interpret rules governing sports for girls and women.

To provide the means for training, evaluating, and rating officials.

To disseminate information on the conduct of girls' and women's sports.

To stimulate, evaluate, and disseminate research in the field of girls' and women's sports.

To cooperate with allied groups interested in girls' and women's sports in order to formulate policies and rules that affect the conduct of women's sports.

To provide opportunities for the development of leadership among girls and women for the conduct of their sports programs.

The National Council of Secondary School Athletic Directors

The American Alliance for Health, Physical Education, Recreation, and Dance established the National Council of Secondary School Athletic Directors. The increased emphasis on sports and the important position of athletic directors in the nation's secondary schools warranted an association where increased services could be rendered to enhance the services given to the nation's youth. The membership in the National Council is open to members of AAHPERD who have primary responsibility in directing, administering, or coordinating interscholastic athletic programs.

The purposes of the Council follow:

To improve the educational aspects of interscholastic athletics and their articulation in the total educational program

To foster high standards of professional proficiency and ethics

To improve understanding of athletics throughout the nation

To establish closer working relationships with related professional groups

To promote greater unity, good will, and fellowship among all members

To provide for an exchange of ideas

To assist and cooperate with existing state athletic directors' organizations

To make available to members special resource materials through publications, conferences, and consultant services

The National Federation of State High School Athletic Associations

The National Federation of State High School Athletic Associations was established in 1920 with five states participating. At present nearly all states are members. The National Federation is particularly concerned with the control of interstate athletics. Its constitution states this purpose:

The object of this Federation shall be to protect and supervise the interstate athletic interests of the high schools belonging to the state associations, to assist in those activities of state associations, which can best be operated on a nationwide scale, to sponsor meetings, publications and activities which will permit each state association to profit by the experience of all other member associations, and to coordinate the work so that waste effort and unnecessary duplication will be avoided.

The National Federation has been responsible for many improvements in athletics on a national basis, such as eliminating national tournaments and working toward a uniformity of standards.

The National Collegiate Athletic Association (NCAA)

The National Collegiate Athletic Association was formed in the early 1900s. The alarming number of football injuries and the fact that there was no national control of the game of football led to a conference of representatives of universities and colleges, primarily from the eastern United States, on December 12, 1905. Preliminary plans were made for a national agency to assist in the formulation of sound require-ments for intercollegiate athletics, particularly football, and the name Intercollegiate Athletic Association was suggested. At a meeting March 31, 1906, a constitution and bylaws were adopted and issued. On December 29, 1910, the name of the association was changed to National Collegiate Athletic Association. The purposes of the NCAA are to uphold the principle of institutional control of all collegiate sports; to maintain a uniform code of amateurism in conjunction with sound eligibility rules, scholarship requirements, and good sportsmanship; to promote and assist in the expansion of intercollegiate and intramural sports; to formulate, copyright, and publish the official rules of play; to sponsor and supervise regional and national meets and tournaments for member institutions; to preserve athletic records; and to serve as headquarters for national collegiate athletic matters.

Membership in the NCAA requires that an institution be accredited and compete in a minimum of four sports each year on an intercollegiate level. At least one sport must be competed in during the normal three major sport seasons.

The services provided by the NCAA are as extensive as its stated purposes for existence. These services include publication of official guides in various sports, provision of a film library, establishment of an eligibility code for athletes and provisions for the enforcement of this code, provisions for national meets and tournaments in 12 sports with appropriate eligibility rules for competition, provision of financial and other assistance to groups interested in the promotion and encouragement of intercollegiate and intramural athletics, and provision of administrative services for universities and colleges of the United States on matters of international athletes. The NCAA now offers women's, as well as men's, championships in various sports.

The National Association of Intercollegiate Athletics (NAIA)

Also on the college and university levels is the National Association of Intercollegiate Athletics, which has a large membership, especially among the smaller colleges. This organization has become affiliated with AAHPERD.

The National Junior College Athletic Association (NJCAA)

The National Junior College Athletic Association is an organization of junior colleges that sponsors athletic programs. It has regional offices with an elected regional director for each. Regional business matters are carried on within the framework of the constitution and bylaws of the parent organization. The regional directors, who are run by an executive committee, hold an annual legislative assembly in Hutchinson, Kansas, and determine the policies, programs, and procedures for the organization. The *Juco Review* is the official publication of the organization. Standing and special committees are appointed each year to cover special items and problems that develop. Membership entitles each member to the services provided by the NJCAA.

National championships are conducted in sports such as basketball, cross country, football, wrestling, baseball, track and field, golf, and tennis. National invitation events are also conducted in activities such as soccer, swimming, and gymnastics.

The NJCAA is affiliated with the National Federation of State High School Athletic Associations and the National Association of Intercollegiate Athletics.

It is also a member of the United States Track and Field Federation, Basketball Federation, the United States Collegiate Sports Council, United States Olympic Committee, United States Gymnastics Federation, National Basketball Committee, and American Alliance for Health, Physical Education, Recreation, and Dance.

Some of the services offered by the NJCAA to its members include an insurance plan for athletics, recognition in official records, publications, film library, and participation in events sponsored by the association.

Amateur Athletic Union (AAU) of the United States

Founded in 1888, the Amateur Athletic Union of the United States is probably the oldest, as well as the largest, single organization designed to regulate and promote the conduct of amateur athletics. Certainly it is the most influential organization governing amateur sports in the world. The AAU is a federation of athletic clubs, national and district associations, educational institutions, and amateur athletic organizations.

Many persons associate the AAU only with track and field events. However, it is concerned with many

Everything possible should be done to guard safety of players. NCAA championship competition in lacrosse.

more sports and activities, including basketball, baton twirling, bobsledding, boxing, diving, gymnastics, handball, judo, karate, luge, power lifting, swimming, synchronized swimming, water polo, weightlifting, and wrestling. In addition to governing the multiplicity of sports and activities, the AAU is vitally concerned with ensuring that the amateur status of athletes is maintained at all times when participating in amateur sports. To this end, the leaders of the AAU have developed and promulgated a precise set of guidelines describing amateurism.

Some of the other activities of the AAU include registering athletes to identify and control the amateur status of participants in sports events, sponsoring national championships in many sports, raising funds for American athletes in international competition and the Olympic Games, conducting tryouts for the selection of Olympic competitors, and sponsoring Junior Olympic competition. The AAU has established a number of committees for the various sports and activities (for example, Age Group Diving, Track and Field, Youth Activities, Swimming) to help with the monumental task of performing the myriad duties associated with governing such a large number of sports and activities. An executive director directs and coordinates all activities of the AAU.

Other organizations

In higher education there are also many leagues, conferences, and associations formed by a limited number of schools for athletic competition. Examples are the Ivy League and the Big Ten Conferences. These associations regulate athletic competition among their members and settle problems that may arise in connection with such competition.

SUMMARY

The standards for competitive athletics in schools, colleges, and other organizations have been clearly stated. There should be no doubt in any individual's mind about the types of interscholastic and intercollegiate programs that are sound educationally and in the best interests of students and other individuals who will participate in them. It is the responsibility of managers and others concerned with such programs to implement the various standards that have been estab-lished. In every case it is not a question of deemphasis but a question of reemphasis along educational lines. Good leadership will make the interscholastic and intercollegiate programs forces for good education that have no equal.

Athletics are a part of a total physical education program. The objectives stated earlier in this text for physical education also apply to interschool and intercollegiate athletics. The manager can evaluate his or her program in terms of the extent to which the listed objectives are being achieved.

Athletics have value if they are conducted in a sound educational manner. The management in charge of athletics is largely responsible to see that they are conducted in accordance with the standards that have been set forth. In so doing, they may be confronted with many problems that periodically occur in these programs because of their public exposure and money involved. However, management knows the goals to be achieved and the standards to be observed. Therefore it is its responsibility to see that the athletic program is conducted accordingly.

SELF-ASSESSMENT TESTS

These tests will assist students in determining if material and competencies presented in this chapter have been mastered:

1. Imagine you are at a school budget hearing where a taxpayer attacks the varsity athletic program as costing too much money for the values derived from such a program. As a member of the physical education staff you are asked to react to the taxpayer's statement. What values can you cite to support the need for a varsity athletic program?
2. Write a profile of what you consider to be an ideal athletic director, coach, and athletic trainer.
3. List some essential points to keep in mind concerning each of the following: contracts, officials, protests and forfeitures, game management, awards, schedules, records, and medical examinations for athletes.
4. As a director of athletics, what administrative policy would you recommend regarding the following: gate receipts, tournaments and champi-

onships, eligibility, scholarships, recruiting, proselyting, and scouting?

5. Develop a set of standards that could be used to appraise an athletic program in an elementary school, a high school, a college, or other organization.

6. What is the role of the athletic association in the conduct of athletics? Identify three athletics associations and the role each plays.

7. Prepare a report that provides pertinent facts regarding the impact of Title IX on girls' and women's sports. Identify the various aspects of Title IX legislation.

REFERENCES

1. American Alliance for Health, Physical Education, Recreation, and Dance: Equality in sports for women, Reston, Va., 1977, The Alliance.

2. Arnheim, D.D.: Modern principles of athletic training, ed. 6, St. Louis, 1985, Times Mirror/Mosby College Publishing.

3. Athletic business, September 1984.

4. Auxter, D., and Pyfer, J.: Principles and methods of adapted physical education and recreation, ed. 5, St. Louis, 1985, Times Mirror/Mosby College Publishing.

5. Bucher, C.A., and Thaxton, N.: Physical education and sport: change and challenge, St. Louis, 1981, The C.V. Mosby Company.

6. Cratty, B.J.: Social psychology in athletics, Englewood Cliffs, N.J., 1981, Prentice-Hall, Inc.

7. Evans, G.: Civil rights panel assails bill to override Grove City ruling, Chronicle of Higher Education, March 13, 1985.

8. Frey, J., editor: The governance of intercollegiate sports, West Point, N.Y., 1982, Leisure Press.

9. Mirga, T.: Reynolds claims Grove City measure unjustifiably extends federal power, Education Week, March 13, 1985.

10. National Council of Secondary School Athletic Directors: Evaluating the high school athletic program, Washington, D.C., 1973, American Association for Health, Physical Education, Recreation, and Dance.

11. Noble, L., and Sigle, G.: Minimum requirements for interscholastic coaches, Journal of Physical Education and Recreation **51**:32, November/December 1980.

12. Pflug, J.: Evaluating high school coaches, Journal of Physical Education and Recreation **51**:76, April 1980. Courtesy of the American Alliance for Health, Physical Education, Recreation, and Dance, 1900 Association Dr., Reston, Va.

13. Rosensweig, M.: Want to file a Title IX complaint? In The Running **1**:1, Fall 1978.

14. Stein, J.U., and Klappholz, L.A.: Special olympics instructional manual, Washington, D.C., 1977, American Associa-

tion for Health, Physical Education, Recreation, and Dance and the Kennedy Foundation.

15. Vander Zwaag, H.J.: Sport management in schools and colleges, New York, 1984, John Wiley and Sons.

16. Wilkerson, M., and Dodder, R.A.: What does sport do for people? Journal of Physical Education and Recreation **50**:50, February 1979.

SUGGESTED READINGS

- Bird, A.M., and Cripe, B.K.: Psychology and sport behavior, St. Louis, 1986, Times Mirror/Mosby College Publishing.
  Introduces the student to the field of sport psychology and the basic concepts of scientific inquiry. Discusses such topics as behaviorism, cognitive sport psychology, sport aggression, group performance, trait psychology, coaching behavior, and arousal.

- Cratty, B.J.: Psychology in contemporary sport, Englewood Cliffs, N.J., 1983, Prentice-Hall, Inc.
  Provides guidelines for coaches and athletes regarding various aspects of the psychology of sports, including psychological assessment in athletics, motivation, activation, aggression, and mental states. It also discusses characteristics and concerns for women and children in sports, the coach, teammates, and spectators. It concludes with a review of how effectively sport practices should and can be conducted.

- Howell, F.M., et al.: Do high school athletics pay? The effects of varsity participation on socioeconomic attainment, Sociology of Sport Journal **1**:15, 1984.
  Reports on a study that evaluates the hypothesis that participation in high school athletics has a positive effect on education, occupational status attainment, and earnings. Based on a national sample of 1,628 males who were surveyed during high school years and one and five years after graduation, it was found that the hypothesis could not be supported.

- Morris, A.F.: Sports medicine, prevention of athletic injuries, Dubuque, Iowa, 1984, Wm. C. Brown Publishers.
  Covers various aspects of sports medicine, including contribution of sports to health, concepts of human skeletal muscles, athletic training and conditioning for sports, strength training programs, power development, endurance training, flexibility development, athletic injuries, nutrition, drugs, and environmental factors. Also deals with the female athlete, the young athlete, and the psychology of sports.

- Northrip, J.W., et al.: Analysis of sport motion, 1983, Dubque, Iowa, Wm. C. Brown Publishers.
  Introduces the physical educator to the exercise sciences

of anatomic kinesiology and biomechanics. Helps students to understand relationship between these two sciences as they are used in analyzing sport motions. Book is especially concerned with the teaching-coaching of individual skills in sport and athletics. Helps student in applying concepts and principles from these exercise sciences to the actual practice of conducting teaching-coaching assignments.

- Paterno, J., et al.: Crystal balling with America's sports leaders, Athletic Business, January 1985.

Nationally known sport leaders predict what the future holds for college sports, women's athletic programs, youth sports, and the Olympics. Discusses topics such as academic standards and athletics, recruiting, economic problems, and Title IX.

- Robinson, J.G.: Reaching your athletic potential, Tigard, Ore., 1981, Quality Publications.

Written for men and women who are serious about a career in sports. Maintains athletic development is an organized process that requires planning and persistence. Devotes chapters to the following areas: goals, planning, motivation, attitude, conditioning, self-image, practicing, and performing. Provides suggestions for reaching your athletic potential.

- Roy, S., and Irvin, R.: Sports medicine, Englewood Cliffs, N.J., 1983, Prentice-Hall, Inc.

This text, coauthored by a sports medicine team who have reviewed much of the literature relating to sports medicine and then organized the material into a practical presentation. Is especially appropriate for athletic trainers, sports medicine physicians, and coaches. Covers important areas such as the prevention and treatment of athletic injuries, specific athletic injuries and related problems, the female athlete, nutrition, and thermal injuries.

Part Three
Management of Alternative Physical Education and Athletic Programs

Chapter Six

Alternative Physical Education and Athletic Programs

Instructional Objectives and Competencies to be Achieved
After reading this chapter the student should be able to

- Identify alternative physical education and athletic programs providing employment opportunities for physical educators
- Understand some of the management and program responsibilities in alternative settings
- Describe the role of physical education and athletics in alternative physical education and athletic programs
- Determine qualifications and preparation needed to successfully fulfill management responsibilities in alternative settings

This text is devoted in great measure to management responsibilities and information regarding physical education and athletic programs in educational institutions at the elementary, secondary, and college levels. However, in recent years many promising careers and employment opportunities have developed in settings other than schools and colleges. Organizations such as industrial establishments, health clubs, senior citizen centers, YMCA's and fitness centers have provided new avenues of employment for physical educators.

This chapter is designed to provide the reader with information about selected organizations where physical educators may find employment as instructors and managers.

Information is presented on specific corporate fitness programs, health clubs, fitness centers, Boys Clubs of America, athletic clubs, governor's councils on physical fitness and sports, Young Men's and Women's Christian Associations, and senior citizen centers.

CORPORATE FITNESS PROGRAMS

In the past few years many large and small corporations have begun to offer employee health and fitness programs. In turn, physical educators have found corporate fitness to be an attractive employment opportunity that offers work in fitness and recreation activities outside of the educational teaching field. Indeed, the position of Fitness Director is an exciting and, at times, lucrative occupation and offers many opportunities for employment of physical educators.

In the following pages are descriptions of corporate fitness programs that presently exist. Information regarding these programs has been taken from several sources including professional literature, publications prepared by the corporation or company, and from personnel employed by the organization. Names of the managers and administrative personnel were correct at the time this manuscript was being prepared for publication. Further information may be obtained by writing directly to the company itself.

My thanks to Ms. Lori Dry for her help in gathering much of this information on corporate fitness programs.

Xerox Corporation
Source of information

Xerox Corporation

General information

The Xerox Corporation offers an internship program for students majoring in recreation management or physical education. Lately Xerox has begun to lean more toward physical fitness than simply recreation for its employees.

When hiring new fitness staff members, Xerox first looks at those applicants who have completed the internship program; however, the internship program is not a prerequisite.

Objectives of Xerox's physical fitness program

To provide optimum physical and mental fitness for its employees through organized fitness and recreation programs

To promote the constructive use of leisure time and provide relief for harmful stress

Staff

Xerox employs 28 physical education and recreation people and 16 physicians.

Managers

W. Brent Arnold: Manager, Physical Fitness & Recreation B.S./M.S. in Recreation Management

Peter De Franco: Supervisor, Fitness & Recreation B.S. in Recreation Management

Catherine Roach: Health Management Program Administrator B.S. in Physical Education M.S. in Exercise Physiology

Jeffrey McCall: Equipment Coordinator A.A.S. in Recreation Administration

Management and program responsibilities

These responsibilities are listed in the Student Fieldwork Manual prepared by the Xerox Corporation. Included in this list are:

Organize and supervise activities

Implement the fitness center's policies

Provide coverage of the equipment room

Administrative duties (review financial procedures, bookkeeping, attend various meetings, compile monthly participant statistics, correspond with various employees)

Four specific programs at Xerox

XICTMD: Xerox International Center For Training and Management Development

XLRA: Xerox Leesburg Recreation Association

XHMP: Xerox Health Management Program

FRC: Fitness and Recreation Center

These programs are fully explained in the Student Fieldwork Manual.

Equipment and facilities

Xerox has a number of both indoor and outdoor facilities that are listed in the Student Fieldwork Manual. They range from courts, tracks, and pools to weights and other exercise equipment.

Exer-trail program

This program, which consists of a series of exercise stations, is designed to work on total fitness (including cardiovascular endurance, flexibility, muscular endurance, and strength).

Before participating in any programs that Xerox offers, workers must be examined by a physician. Xerox employs physicians so that periodic examinations may also be conducted.

Job outlook

Xerox is accepting applications.

Address

Xerox Corporation
Senior Specialist Fitness & Recreation
P.O. Box 2000
Leesburg, Virginia 22075

Kimberly-Clark
Source of information

Information pamphlet, phone conversation with Connie Smoczyk, Health Education and Exercise Programs Manager, and *Management Review Journal,* 1982.

General information

The Kimberly-Clark program began in April of 1977. Today it has grown to a $2.5 million employee fitness program. It has a 7,000 square-foot multiphasic health testing center and a 32,000 square-foot fitness center.

In past years Kimberly-Clark has basically concentrated on health education rather than physical education. Programs such as smoking cessation, weight control through diet, and CPR courses, are a major focus in their program. Only very recently has the company started to stress physical fitness through exercise. Specific individualized weight programs are currently being offered, and exercise classes are also becoming more organized.

In 1982 Kimberly-Clark's Health Management Program developed the Student Assistant Program. The program gives students the opportunity to receive practical training for their careers as health care professionals. The program has expanded to allow physical education majors the same opportunity. Further information regarding the student assistantships can be found in the company's literature.

Objectives of the program

To achieve a higher level of wellness and productivity in employees and to reduce absenteeism and the rate of escalation of health care costs

Staff members playing racquetball at Xerox Corporation Fitness and Recreation Center.

Fitness participants jogging at Xerox Corporation Fitness and Recreation Center.

Fitness participants running at Xerox Corporation Fitness and Recreation Center.

Gymnasium at Xerox
Corporation Fitness and
Recreation Center,
Leesburg, Va.

Staff

Kimberly-Clark employed 15 full-time employees in 1984 with an emphasis being placed on health educators. However, they have recently hired two full-time physical educators to help develop the physical fitness aspect of the program. The top managers are:

Connie Smoczyk: Health Education and Exercise Manager
Sharon Sorensen: Fitness Program Assistant
Bill Boles:　　　 Supervisor of Exercise Facility
Patrick Lord:　　 Exercise Coordinator

Kimberly-Clark also employs a 22-person medical staff headed by Dr. Robert Dedmon.

Four components of the program

Medical screening with exercise testing
Health education
Aerobic exercise and cardiac rehabilitation
Employee assistance program

These components are outlined in the pamphlets received from the Kimberly-Clark Corporation.

Programs offered

Health education classes
Exercise classes
Nutrition and weight counseling
Stress management and relaxation skills
Specific training in exercise
Activity classes

Computerized records and reports are used to record statistical data regarding participants in the program.

Job outlook

The program is continuing to grow and more physical education people will be needed in the future.

Address

Kimberly-Clark
401 North Lake Street
Neenah, Wisconsin 54956

Tenneco Incorporated
Source of information

Tenneco Incorporated

General information

Tenneco Incorporated is a diversified, energy-related company with over 100,000 employees world wide. The Tenneco Health and Fitness Center occupies 25,000 square feet.

Why was the program developed

To preserve Tenneco's most important asset, its innovative skilled employees

Core goal

To increase awareness of and commitment to positive health habits and improve the overall quality of life

Six main objectives

To increase the level of cardiovascular fitness

To increase employees' knowledge of positive health habits and reduce coronary risk factors

To obtain employee ownership in the program and promote self responsibility

To motivate employees to improve and/or maintain their optimum standard of health

To further develop the above objective within interested Tenneco divisions outside of the Houston area

To further develop program adherence by involving the employee's support groups (families)

Staff

8 full-time fitness professionals

5 part-time nurse practitioners

1 part-time cardiologist

1 part-time dietitian

1 part-time counselor

Tenneco's medical director, vice-president, and corporate officer supervise the Health and Fitness Department.

Program statistics

The program's 3318 participants are full-time regular Tenneco employees who have completed a medical and fitness screening process. They range in age from 17 to 70 years; 79% are under 40 years of age. Of the present active participants, 52% are female and 48% male. On the average, more than 100 new members are screened each month.

Equipment and facilities

32 pieces of Nautilus weight-training equipment

12 bicycle ergometers

Stretching apparatus

Racquetball/handball courts

Large aerobics room

A track that encircles the entire building

A computer-based information system stores individual exercise data and provides participants feedback.

Evaluation process

Health and Fitness Monthly Statistics: Consists of a computer-generated report that converts participants' exercise data to enable the staff to evaluate the effectiveness of promotional campaigns or special events.

Fitness and Wellness Program Evaluation: Uses participant surveys and questionnaires to gather information. These tools provide direct feedback from the participants.

Special Projects: These projects do not have a longitudinal design. Provide information that can be used immediately.

Longitudinal Projects: Possibly the most important area. The most important undertaking is a study designed to measure the impact of the program on the participants compared to nonparticipants.

Job outlook

Memberships in the fitness program are growing rapidly, which is a good sign for those hoping to seek a position at this company.

Address

Tenneco Health and Fitness Department

% William B. Baun

P.O. Box 2511

TEL 826

Houston, Texas 77001

Lockheed Missiles and Space Company

The company organized a fitness program now known as Lockheed Employee Recreation Association (LERA).

Employees playing volleyball, Tenneco Health and Fitness Department.

The computer as an aid to fitness in the Tenneco Health and Fitness Department.

The computer as an aid to fitness in the Tenneco Health and Fitness Department.

Source of information

Parks and Recreation, August 1984; pamphlet from LERA, telephone conversation with Mitch Sudy, Fitness Administrator.

General information

The LERA is located in the heart of the Silicon Valley and serves the needs of 23,000 employees, their families, and retirees. The center is a 3,200 square-foot multiuse facility.

In 1983 the Lockheed Corporation employed three full-time and three part-time people to operate the fitness center. By the mid-1980s the program had grown and LERA was operated by 14 full-time and nine part-time fitness personnel.

The top four managers of the program are the Executive Director and three other program managers (Fitness Program, Senior Recreation Manager, and the Recreation Senior Clerk). The other contracts are arranged with special interest instructors, who provide a variety of physical education and recreation activity classes.

LERA also has a Student Internship program.

Funding

The funding for the program is derived from two main sources. Lockheed Missiles and Space Company cover the salaries and fringe benefits of LERA employees, insurance costs, and building maintenance. LERA generates money from merchandise sales, fee programs, commissions, and recreational vehicle parking lots to support the programs and services on a self-sustaining basis.

Fitness staff responsibilities

To teach health and physical fitness classes, general conditioning classes, aerobics, cardiovascular programs, and exercise and weight control programs
Each class lasts 6 to 8 weeks.
To organize special teams and tournaments
To present education-oriented seminars
To publish sports and fitness newsletters
To supervise and assist
Administrative duties: Collecting fees, keeping records, recording statistics

Equipment and facilities

This information is listed in the informat-sheets sent by LERA. They range from courts, fields, and multipurpose rooms to weights, 10-station circuit training, and exercise bikes.

LERA's personal fitness evaluation

The test evaluates:

Resting heart rate	Cardiovascular fitness
Resting blood pressure	Muscular endurance
Percent body fat	Flexibility

The test is not diagnostic in nature, and it is recommended that all persons entering the program seek medical clearance first. All persons 35 years of age or older *must* have a doctor's release form before entering any program. (LERA does not employ a personal physician.)

Results and benefits of the LERA program

There has been a dramatic reduction in:
Absenteeism
Turnover
Lost productivity

Job outlook

Since the program is growing rapidly, the future outlook is quite promising.

Address

Lockheed Employee's Recreation Association
P.O. Box 504
Sunnyvale, California 94086

Phillips Petroleum Company
Source of information

Telephone conversation with Sharon (secretary to Charles Kittrell, Executive Vice-President) and Employee Benefit Plan Review, August 1982.

General information

Phillips Petroleum Company has been sponsoring fitness programs for its employees since the 1930s. In the beginning the company paid one half of each employee's membership at the local YMCA and the swimming pool; interest grew rapidly. In 1950 Phillips incorporated athletic facilities in a new office building so that employees could use the facility during the lunch hour. Over 60% of all employees now participate in the fitness program.

Philosophy of the program

Being fit makes a difference in how you feel about yourself, your job, and the people around you. Healthier people are happier, more productive people. They do a better job, and when they do a better job, it benefits them and the company as a whole.

Staff

The company employs a fitness staff consisting of eight people. These employees are basically physical fitness professionals who assist, supervise, and organize special event programs.

Specific programs offered

Weight lifting and muscle toning programs
Aerobic and other exercise classes
Diet and weight control programs
Bowling, tennis, and golf teams (leagues)

"Operation Lifestyle"

This program combines exercise, stress management, and diet (weight control) under staff supervision.

Job outlook

This program is not as extensive as some others established by larger corporations. However, it has been doing well, and interest in the program grows yearly. Physical education majors are hired when job openings are available.

Address

Phillips Petroleum Company
Hershey, Pennsylvania

PepsiCo, Inc.
Source of information

Dynamic Years, January-February 1984, and telephone conversation with Director Dennis Colacino.

General information

The PepsiCo programs have grown dramatically in recent years, and as a result the company has built an extensive fitness facility.

Employees entering the programs are evaluated regarding aerobic capacity, strength, flexibility, body composition, and risk analysis. Exercise programs are then prescribed and each exerciser is closely supervised and monitored.

Staff

15 to 20 full-time fitness personnel
A number of part-time fitness employees
A medical staff

Responsibilities of fitness staff

To organize individual exercise programs
To supervise and assist participants in their programs
To record participants' statistics
To teach classes in physical education and health education
To motivate participants

Job outlook

This is a large company that grows yearly. It employs many physical educators, therefore the job outlook is very good.

Address

PepsiCo, Inc.
Anderson Hill Road
Purchase, New York 10577

Bonne Bell Incorporated
Source of information

Telephone conversation with Connie Schafer, Consumer Relations, and information found in Bonne Bell information pamphlet.

General information

At the present time Bonnie Bell does have a fitness program, but they do not employ a fitness staff. Facilities are available to employees, but supervision and assistance from a trained staff are not included. However, the company indicated that it is in the process of developing a fitness program operated from within the company itself. Within the next year they plan to hire a fitness director and an assistant administrator to help organize specific programs. The starting date and the exact number of fitness personnel that would be hired have not been decided. Prospective fitness employees will include physical education and exercise physiology majors.

Plans are presently being worked on to increase the facilities available at the Lakewood branch offices (especially exercise rooms and a weight room). Some of the branches already have some facilities, but there is no structured program and no one to assist participants. Even with no assistance, employees are becoming involved in fitness programs on their own, thus the Bonne Bell Company wishes to encourage exercise by organizing their own program.

Industrial physical fitness program.

It is hoped that the new program will be free to all Bonne Bell employees with a minimal fee being charged to family members who wish to participate.

Goals

To increase loss of weight
To increase productivity
To enhance their philosophy, which is "Be Fit, Look Good"

Job outlook

As soon as the new plans are implemented the employment outlook for physical education majors is very good.

Address

Bonne Bell Incorporated
Georgetown Row
Lakewood, Ohio 44107

General Dynamics
General information

The Health and Fitness Center and its programs are not officially mandated by the corporate office. The center operates under the jurisdiction of the Convair Recreation Association that also oversees 52 clubs. Also, there is a 33,000 square-foot clubhouse located in Kearny Mesa, California.

Equipment and facilities

The 4,000 square-foot fitness facility includes lockers, showers, saunas, complete weight training and machinery.
The fitness center offers a wide variety of programs to meet the needs of all General Dynamics employees, retirees, and their families. An $80 annual fee is charged.
Shape Up programs are available: An exercise and education class emphasizing a balanced life-style. Over 800 people have participated in or are currently participating in the Shape Up programs.
 Prefitness and postfitness profiles are administered to participants of each session.

Objectives of the program

To provide General Dynamics' employees with an awareness of health and well-being factors
To help General Dynamics' employees change their health behavior to facilitate well-being and disease prevention
To create a supportive environment to consistently reinforce positive life-style behaviors
 In order to meet these objectives, the center designed a program that includes testing, screening, referrals, films, newsletters, incentive programs, and lectures on health and well-being issues.

Staff

3 full-time members (director, assistant director, program coordinator)
1 part-time weight trainer/fitness specialist
4 consultants (on an annual basis)
15 to 18 graduate and undergraduate student interns

Address

General Dynamics
Convair Recreation Association
9115 Clairemont Mesa Boulevard
San Diego, California 92123
Telephone: (619) 227-8900

HEALTH CLUBS AND FITNESS CENTERS

The health club and fitness center business has increased significantly in the last decade. Membership consists of both men and women in most clubs and fitness centers although some are for the exclusive use of only one sex. Their facilities include exercise rooms, resistive-type exercise equipment of the Universal or Nautilus design, treadmills, stationary bicycles, swimming pools, saunas, steam rooms, cold plunges, oil baths, and locker and shower areas. Their programs include. items such as fitness testing and prescription, weight training, yoga, aerobics of various types, and athletic competition. Their instructors include physical educators, business executives, and sales personnel.

 Several existing health clubs and fitness centers are described in this section.

Intramural racquetball, part of the industrial fitness program at Forbes Magazine Fitness Center, New York.

Organization

Lifestyles Total Fitness

Clientele served

Center draws people interested in both fitness and physical therapy.

Goals of organization

To provide quality service
To promote more community involvement
To develop ability to give official certification to prospective aerobic instructors

Management

Manager:
  Brent F. Hamblin
  B.S., Zoology, Brigham Young University
  B.S., Physical Therapy, University of Utah
  Experience: 2 years Lifestyles Manager
    1 year College Park Medical Offices
  Salary: $20,000 to $40,000 range
  Advancement Prospects: Next move would be to area supervisor and then to regional director
    1. Manager
    2. Area supervisor
    3. Regional director
    4. Vice president
    5. President
    6. Part ownership

Personnel

The staff consists of a manager, exercise supervisor, and secretary.

There are nine to 10 aerobic instructors, which includes an aerobic manager.

Management duties

Management of physical therapy patients
Staffing
Supervision of clients in exercise area
Management and supervision of outside programs sponsored by center (runs, tournaments, etc.)
Occasional public relations with area doctors concerning center's role

Management aspects of organization

Organizational structure: See Figure 6-1.
Budget: Yearly income at present is $90,000.
Operational Management Policies: They have a handbook with policies and job descriptions, but it is not for public use.

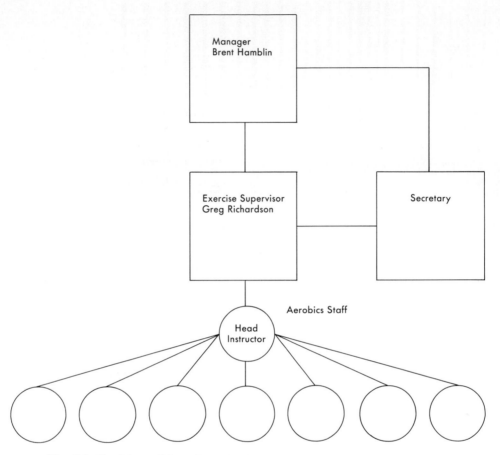

Fig. 6-1. Graphic rendition of organizational structure of Lifestyles Total Fitness.

Facility Management: One person is in charge of all aspects of the center. The three full-time persons are in charge of all cleaning, upkeep, and maintenance of equipment and facility.

Programs offered

Conditioning
Fitness maintenance
Videotape educational programming
Medical problem exercise programming
Aerobic dance classes
Aerobic specialties (senior citizens, for example)

Organization

Golden Venus

Clientele served

Women ages 14 to 23 years
    Approximately 1000 women per day use the facilities.

Goals of organization

To provide opportunity for women to achieve individual fitness goals.
To provide a schedule which meets need of clientele

in terms of hours of operation and types of classes offered.

To provide privacy for women engaging in various fitness routines.

Management

President/Manager: Norman Attenhofer

Norman Attenhofer—Doctorate in kinesiology from Tulane University, master's degree in speech pathology from Louisiana State. Taught speech and coached debate for 15 years. Developed a weight training program system (1948) for football training. A contemporary of Vic Tanney and Jack La Lanne and began as an instructor with Golden Venus and worked his way up through the system to a managerial position. Eventually he supervised nine studios in the greater Houston area.

Personnel

The staff consists of 22 personnel, with 7 support personnel. The concept of management is a team concept with great emphasis placed on listening to the concerns and ideas expressed by the personnel and the clientele. Management type is characterized as "from the bottom up."

Advancement prospects for personnel are good. The organization's president proposes to train all instructors as managers so that they can handle all situations that might arise, especially emergencies.

Management duties

Planning, promotions, budget, general administration, some personnel supervision.

Management aspects of the organization

Revenue is approximately $100,000 each month with $92,000 being put back into the business.

Programs offered

Fitness Programs

Other options are being considered besides aerobics since aerobics seems to take a tremendous toll on the body over a long period of time. Future program developments include providing a diagnostic service for the individual client based on medical and scientific procedures. This would allow each person to be measured by computer concerning specific fitness needs. This could then be coded on a small credit card–type disk. Members would be allowed to do what would be healthful and beneficial for them in terms of a fitness workout.

Organization

Keys to Fitness

Clientele served

Approximately 150 women per day

Goals of the organization

To offer a safe program of physical fitness for female clients, including individualized workouts, classes, diet and nutritional advice, and specific plans for dealing with special health problems (arthritis, back problems, obesity).

Management

Owner/Business Manager: Richard Keyes

Head Instructor/Manager: T.J. Willis

Experience: T.J. Willis is a certified instructor and consultant for Aerobics and Fitness Association of America. He has several years experience working in health spas.

Salary: 10% of all sales plus an hourly wage

Personnel

There are three instructors/assistants. The organization would like to have all instructors certified before they are allowed to teach.

Management duties

The owner/business manager is responsible for payroll, scheduling, promotion, and budget.

The head instructor/manager is responsible for training, supervision, and evaluation of instructors; supervision and monitoring of clients' workout programs; supervision of facility; conducting of advanced classes.

Management aspects of the organization

All instructors should be certified fitness instructors.

All instructors participate in the maintenance of the facility.

All instructors place injury prevention as primary in dealing with clients' program.

Since the operation is new, most of the incoming cash is used for the growth of the business, salaries, and overhead.

Programs offered

Thirty-three aerobic classes are offered per week targeting various fitness levels. Individual workout plans are designed and monitored for the clients.

Organization

Bodystyles

Clientele served

Open to men and women 18 years and older.
At the time of this writing there were over 250 members.

Goals of the organization

To be the finest, most advanced operation of its kind on the West Coast. Although small in size, the operational layout is precise and based on exercising the various body parts in sequence. The amount of analytical aerobics equipment on hand coupled with planned acquisitions lend credence to the owner's vow to achieve these goals.

Management

Manager: John Szarko
          B.S. in Marketing (St. John's University)
Experience: Has been involved with bodybuilding and health-oriented type clubs since his late teens. He currently owns and manages his own marketing firm.

Personnel

The on-site staff consists of four individuals, a supervisor and three instructors. There is currently no requirement for personnel to possess a formal educational background in physical education.
Salary of staff members: 4% commission plus an hourly wage

Advancement prospects: Personnel will receive preference for promotion to various management or franchise/license opportunities

Management duties

Szarko takes responsibility for all management decisions and duties.

Management aspects of the organization

No written management policy currently exists. The facility is operated on a ''memo'' format, that is, a list of things to do each week.

Programs for adult fitness are growing rapidly.

Monthly budget

Minimum: $3,000
Maximum: $6,000
    This includes salaries, utilities, lease payments for equipment, miscellaneous.

Organization

Gold's Gym and Fitness Center

Clientele served

A cross section of individuals with weight problems and those wishing to maintain or improve present fitness levels

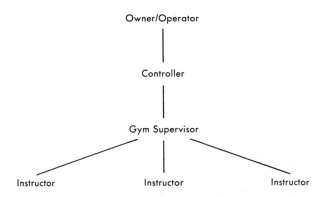

Fig. 6-2. Organizational structure of Bodystyles.

Goals of the organization

To develop Gold's Gym into a highly profitable operation
To create a high public awareness of the facility

Management

Supervisor and Co-owner of center: Zach Franzi
Education: Bachelor's degree plus some graduate classes. Attended University of Pittsburgh and University of Nevada, Las Vegas; majored in physical education and took some exercise physiology classes.
Experience: Owner of a small health and fitness center before Gold's Gym
Salary: $500 to $800 a week
Duties: Sales manager, public relations director, and supervisor of staff
Advancement prospects: Fair to good

Personnel

Twenty-two individuals are on staff. Facility management staff consists of janitors, who provide equipment maintenance and repair along with facility cleanup.

Management aspects of organization

Organizational Structure: See Figure 6-3.
Budget: Revenue is derived from membership sales, vitamins, clothing, and snack bar, along with aerobic memberships and suntan sales.

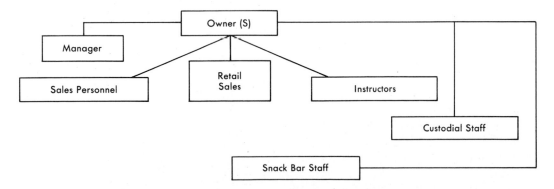

Fig. 6-3. Organizational structure of Gold's Gym and Fitness Center.

Policies: Staff is expected to abide by a handbook (pamphlet) containing standards for dress, demeanor, and training.

Program offered

Incoming clients are tested in areas of strength and cardiovascular fitness. They are then given individual programs that are monitored and upgraded every three weeks.

Organization

Stewart/Mojave Recreation Center

Clientele served

Men, women, and children

Goals of the organization

Perry Coyle would like the center to be run more like a fitness club than a recreation center.

Management

Recreation Center Supervisor: Perry Coyle

Education: Bachelor's degree plus some graduate classes. Attended University of Montana, San Jose State, and University of Nevada, Las Vegas (major—Recreation)

Administrative experience: This is Perry Coyle's first supervisory job and his tenth year in this city.

Salary: $25,000 a year

Advancement prospects: Two administrative positions above the supervisor role and four positions above that within the system

Personnel

Twelve staff members are employed. The city provides upkeep and maintenance for the center.

Management aspects of organization

Organizational structure: See Figure 6-4.

Budget: City expends a minimal amount for the center. Community membership funds along with racquetball rental facilities provide the bulk of money for the budget.

Policies: Staff is expected to abide by a booklet of policies and procedures outlining lesson plans, dress code, etc.

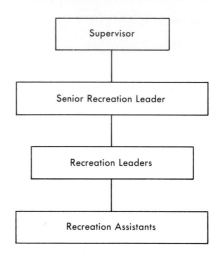

Fig. 6-4. Organizational structure of Stewart/Mohave Recreation Center.

Program offered

The overall program contains beginning and intermediate classes ranging from aerobics and gymnastics to weight lifting and a variety of other sports activities.

OTHER ALTERNATIVE PHYSICAL EDUCATION AND ATHLETIC CENTERS

In addition to corporate fitness and health clubs and fitness centers there are other settings in which physical educators are finding employment and assuming management responsibilities. These include Boys Clubs of America, athletic clubs, Young Men's and Women's Christian Associations, and Senior Citizens' Centers. A representative establishment in each of these categories is described.

Organization

Boys Clubs of America

Clientele served

Boys and girls, ages 7 to 18

872 members

Primarily for the financially or socially disadvantaged youth

Goals of the organization

To provide programs for the disadvantaged youth of the community who are between the ages of 7 through 18.

Six core services are offered:
Personal adjustment
Citizenship and leadership development
Cultural enrichment
Health and physical education
Social recreation
Outdoor and environmental education

Management

Manager: Ben Montoya, Director of Operations
Education: Bachelor of Arts in Education
Master's in Educational Administration
Experience in management:
1 year as Department Head of Physical Education in a junior high school
4 years as the Director of Operations for Boys' and Girls' Club

Management duties

To hire, train, and supervise staff
To implement and evaluate programs that are within the guidelines established by the board of directors
Salary range: $25,000 to $30,000 per year
Prospects for advancement: Excellent

Management policies

Policies are set by board of directors and administered by director of operations
Hours of operation: 2:30 PM-8:30 PM Monday through Friday, 10 AM-5 PM Saturdays and holidays, closed Sundays.
Facility management through unit directors
Program staff supervises participants

Budget

Set by board of directors
Executive director raises funds through various projects that he/she implements
70% of funds raised by the community
30% of funds comes from the United Way

Facility management

Through unit directors facilities are maintained
Each facility has two janitors to clean and repair
Program staffers supervise participants in the facility

Programs offered

Programs include camping, general daily activity (for example, pool, basketball, weights), individual services, (for example, counseling), special events program (for example, job search, leadership development, and pet raising).

Organization

Senior Citizens' Center

Clientele

Senior citizens

Management

Robert C. Light—54 years old. Former minister. B.A. in Religious Studies, M.A. in Management, M.A. in Gerontology
Experience: Administrator at senior center complex in Minneapolis
Duties: See Figure 6-5
Salary: $35,000 to $40,000 range
Advancement: He is now the head of a division in the organization. Next step would be to head the Recreation Department.

Responsibilities and duties

Under the administrative direction of the deputy city manager for community services, the director of the Senior Citizen's Center is responsible for planning, organizing, and directing the implementation of all activities falling within the purview of that department.

Responsible for the administration of the following activities: development and administration of a comprehensive program of activities and services for senior citizens, management of schedules and activities within the center, development of new center programs, satellite programs for senior citizens, and referral assistance to other support agencies (functions as liaison with center advisory board).

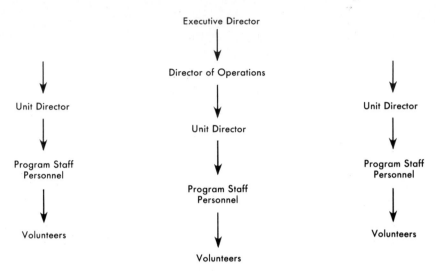

Fig. 6-5. Organizational structure of Boys Club of America.

Administrative duties include participation with the city manager's office in the development of broad departmental policy; preparation and administration of annual departmental budget; expenditure control, provision of information to the city manager's office regarding departmental progress, coordination of departmental activities with those of other city departments; identification and implementation of innovative programs and procedures for the staff. As a manager, the director is responsible for continued evaluation and development of all departmental personnel, for task assignment, and for assuring timeliness and quality of all departmental work products.

Personnel

12 full-time personnel
6 full-time personnel paid directly by city
20 contractual personnel paid for teaching classes
2 students performing work-study
Number of students doing actual field study in social work
Number of people from the community doing volunteer work

Organization

Young Men's Christian Association

Clientele served

The YMCA is basically a family-oriented organization providing assorted programs for children of all ages, teens, and adults.

Goals of the organization

The goals of the YMCA are to aid in the development of Christian standards of living, conduct, and life purpose in its members and constituency. It is dedicated to the concept of wellness, helping each individual develop a positive attitude toward life and to accept responsibility for his or her own life and to focus on the joys of living life to its fullest.

Management

The director of the YMCA is Bob. His educational background consists of having a bachelor's degree in physical education and a master's degree in exercise physiology. Additional training consisted of the YMCA Career Development Program. The director is in charge of all the programs and hires the staff to

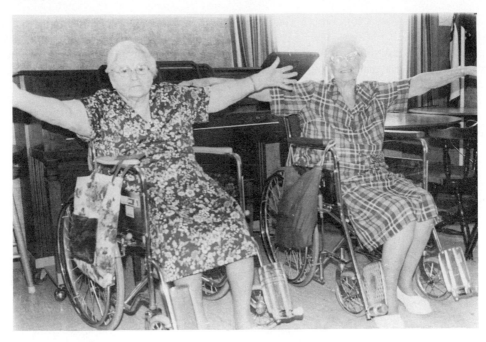

Part of square dance call, "Take your arms out to the side, like you can hold the ocean tide."

direct the various classes and programs in their particular field.

He also conducts seminars and does public relations work. Teaching is of great interest to Bob, so he specializes in teaching various classes at the YMCA. Bob's salary is $25,000 a year. After serving as a physical director of the YMCA he may move up the administrative ladder if he so chooses, depending on the type of job he has been doing. The director chooses to work closer with the people as he finds it satisfying to see the results and the advancements of people's efforts.

Personnel

The number of personnel involved varies due to the fact that the YMCA is a nonprofit organization. It uses volunteers to help run many of the programs. The total hired are 34. The personnel is broken down as follows:

Executive staff: 7
Professional staff: 7
Support staff: 7 to 8
Life Guards: 5
Maintenance: 6 to 7
Instructors: They are hired on part-time basis and are specialists in their areas, which include aerobics, gymnastics, swimming, fitness classes, diving, lifesaving, scuba diving, prenatal care, basketball, racquetball, and tennis. Volunteers help teach some classes and help in special events, which include coaching of kids' sports, slumber parties, and ski trips.

Equipment and facilities

The facilities of the YMCA consist of an olympic size swimming pool, diving area, instructional pool, plus a whirlpool all in one area, which is enclosed by surrounding glass doors and an outdoor patio. The gym area is large and is separated by curtain dividers. This provides separate instruction or workout areas for various activities. There is a basketball area, gymnastics area, exercise area for aerobic classes, and ping pong area.

The offices and lounge are on the second level. A viewing area is provided for parents. The back area includes racquetball and handball courts. The facility also includes six outdoor tennis courts and an outdoor running track. The locker rooms are separate for women, men, boys, and girls.

Six to seven maintenance people take care of the facility. They do general cleaning and upkeep of the building and do maintenance repairs when needed. Each instructor is responsible for setting up the equipment for their class and putting it away. The supervisor of each program sees that each instructor's duties are carried out properly.

The lifeguards are responsible in checking the chlo-

Bicycling is excellent exercise for old and young alike.

rine and chemical balance of the pool and jacuzzi to maintain the proper level.

Operational management polices

Each staff member is required to prepare 17 specific goals to be accomplished each year. The person is then evaluated on the results once a year.

Budget

The total budget of operating the YMCA averages around $700,000 per year. Salaries amount to about $400,000 per year. Another expense is maintenance, approximately $190,000.

Program development

The YMCA program is continuously growing. The swim program is strong and is set up according to the YMCA National Progressive Swimming Program. When the required skills are mastered, the student progresses to the next higher level. Other areas of the swim program include Tiny Tot swim classes and Baby Gym and Swim classes. A new class that has been added is a prenatal swim class. The gymnastics program is relatively new. Because of the popularity of the sport the classes are growing. Other areas that are growing are the aerobics classes and physical fitness classes. More classes have been added to the program. The YMCA does a good job in providing the proper programs to keep a person of any age physically fit.

Organizaton

Athletic Club East

Clientele served

4100 members: 60% male, 40% female

Goals of the organization

To provide the community with a quality facility for health fitness and recreation program

Management

Manager: Ed Peterson
Education: B.S. in Exercise Physiology
Experience in management: Five years at present position

Salary range: $18,000 to $30,000 per year
Prospects for advancement: Fair to good

Management duties

To hire, train, and supervise staff
Oversee the maintenance of all equipment
Develop and implement athletic programs
Sell memberships

Personnel

Facility manager
Director of maintenance: Oversees cleaning and repairs
Activities director: Oversees all participation programs, aerobics, weight training, dances, and a variety of vacation trips
Front desk personnel: Maintain the phones and reservations for court time

Management aspects of organization

Graphic rendition of organizational structure: See Figure 6-6.
Policies are set by the general manager with some input by the board of owners.
Policies are carried out by the managers.
Operational hours are 24 hours a day, 7 days a week.

Programs that exist and program development

Existing programs are aerobics, day-care service, ski trips, weight training, racquetball leagues and tournaments, handball, cycling club and stationary bicycles, Diet Control Club, social functions, and jogging club. Programs are developed and implemented by club managers.

SUMMARY

Physical education and athletic programs are not limited to schools, colleges, and other educational institutions. Many other programs and settings exist in the larger community in places such as corporate enterprises, health clubs, athletic clubs, YMCAs, Boys Clubs of America, and senior citizen centers. These alternate settings represent new opportunities for physical educators seeking employment as instructors and managers.

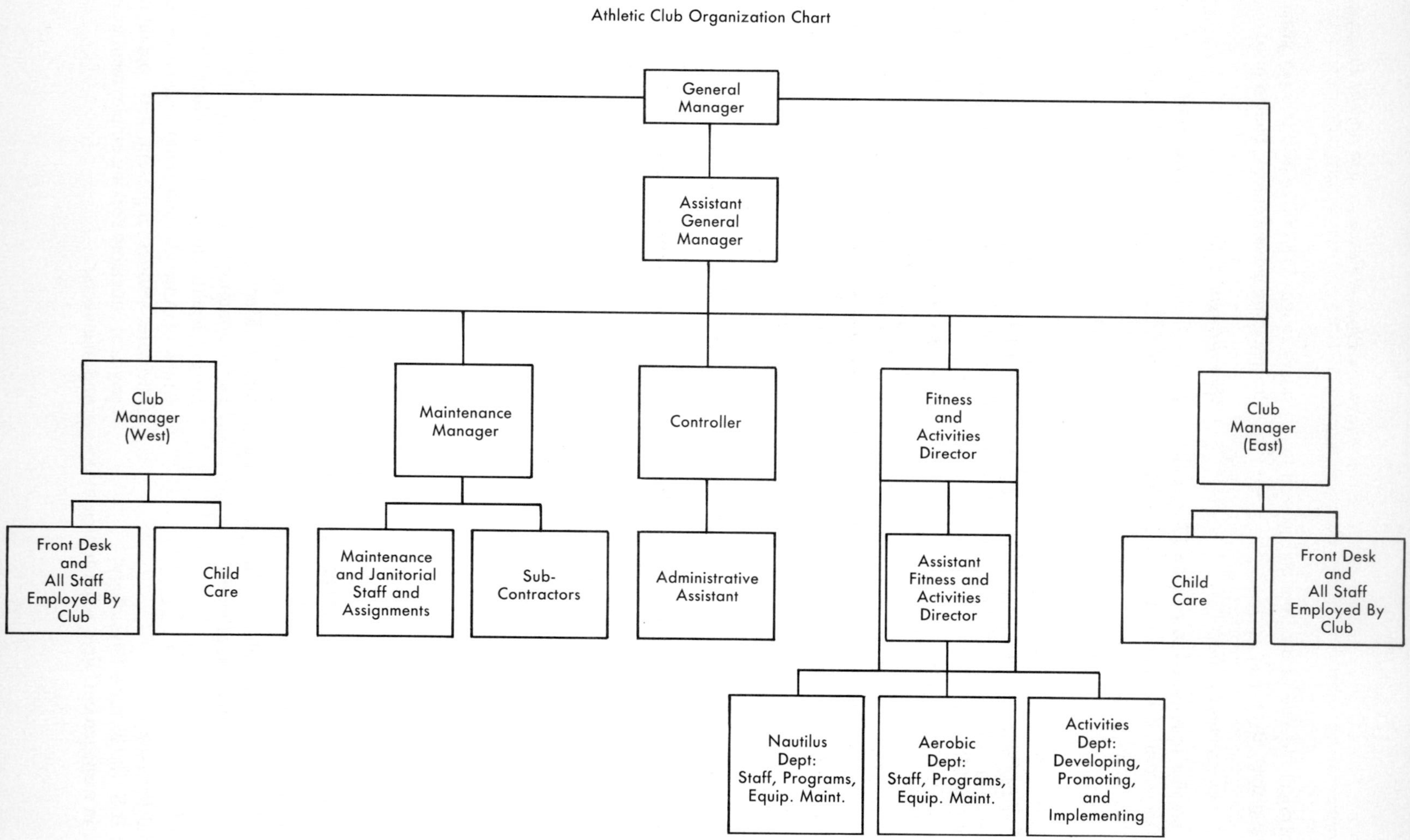

Athletic Club Organization Chart

Fig. 6-6. Athletic club organization chart.

SELF-ASSESSMENT TESTS

These tests will assist students in determining if material and competencies in this chapter have been mastered:

1. Conduct a survey of your county and state to determine alternative physical education and athletic programs providing employment opportunities for physical educators.

2. Prepare a set of guidelines you would follow if you were asked to manage an industrial fitness program, a health club, and a center for senior citizens.

3. What physical education objectives can be accomplished in alternative physical education and athletic programs?

4. Identify the preparation and qualifications needed to successfully fulfill management responsibilities in alternative settings for physical education and athletics.

SUGGESTED READINGS

- Bucher, C.A.: Foundations of physical education and sport, ed. St. Louis, 1987, Times Mirror/Mosby College Publishing.
  Includes a large section on alternative careers in physical education and sport. Discusses various organizations and professions together with preparation and qualifications needed to be employed in these areas.

- Clayton, R.D., and Clayton, J.A.: Concepts and careers in physical education, Minneapolis, 1982, Burgess Publishing Company.
  Designed for students who are considering a career in physical education. The appendix lists organizations of all types that are of interest to physical educators, together with addresses of organizations to contact if more information is desired.

- Kraus, R.: Recreation and leisure in modern society, Glenview, Ill., 1984, Scott, Foresman and Company.
  Describes recreation and leisure programs in voluntary and special-interest organizations, in commercial and private recreation, and for special populations. In many of these programs physical education and athletic activities are conducted and physical educators and athletic personnel may find employment.

- Pestolesi, R.A., and Baker, C.: Introduction to physical education: a contemporary careers approach, Glenview, Ill., 1984, Scott, Foresman and Company.
  Provides physical educators with an orientation to many diverse careers.

- Zeigler, E.F., and Bowie, G.W.: Management competency development in sport and physical education, Philadelphia, 1983, Lea & Febiger.
  Discusses the personal skills, human skills, conceptual skills, technical skills, and conjoined skills needed to be a success in the field of management.

Part Four
Management Functions

Chapter Seven

Personnel Management and Supervision

Instructional Objectives and Competencies to be Achieved
After reading this chapter the student should be able to

- Understand the need for personnel policies.
- State the basic principles underlying effective personnel management.
- Summarize the qualifications needed by physical educators who work in settings such as educational institutions, health clubs, industrial fitness programs, centers for the aged, and youth-serving agencies.
- Trace the process for recruitment, selection, orientation, and in-service training of new staff members.
- Discuss the subject of supervision, including the qualities needed by supervisory personnel, the role of group dynamics in the supervisory process, and the basic principles that should guide effective supervisory working relationships with staff members.
- Describe various methods of evaluating physical educators and other personnel in physical education programs.

This text has been concerned thus far with a discussion of management theory, organization, and structure and the management of various kinds of physical education and athletic programs. Part Four contains a discussion of the main functions and duties that managers must perform within these programs. The first of these is personnel management and supervision.

Personnel management originally was mainly concerned with selecting, placing, and retaining people who were staff members of an organization. Today, however, personnel management has taken on a more mature connotation. It does not involve manipulating

people to get them to produce as much as possible. Instead it involves the entire organization and the procedures by which the organization can best achieve its goals. Recruitment, selection, morale, and other considerations become the responsibility not only of management but also of all staff members. As a result, it depends on various individuals and groups understanding and accepting each other and working closely together to ultimately achieve the organization's goals.

The nature of personnel management and supervision is changing. Students, faculty, and employees are participating more in managing and supervising.

Managers and supervisors are consulting with staff members before making final decisions on curriculum, scheduling, evaluations, and working conditions. Managers are also being required to negotiate with unions in collective bargaining sessions. Management and supervisory positions are no longer considered to be the only positions where decision-making takes place. Now, various staff members have a voice in departmental policy making.

For all these reasons personnel management and supervision are perhaps the most challenging responsibilities of an effective leader. A leader who does not have the cooperation of his or her personnel will have great difficulty implementing any decision or policy.

PERSONNEL POLICIES

With the help of staff members the management should see that a detailed list of personnel policies is developed. These policies should be sound, up to date, and consistent with the best thinking on personnel management. Furthermore, after careful thought and deliberation, these policies should also be put into writing and be made available to all staff members and managers. Selected areas that should be covered by personnel policies include assignments, promotions, separations, evaluations, hours of work, compensation, fringe benefits, absences, leaves, travel, in-service training, and conduct on the job.

In some cases personnel policies are not developed by the management but rather by a bargaining contract. In such cases the bargaining contract will probably affect the flexibility with which the manager and management may operate. It is very important that management understand such a practice.

PRINCIPLES OF PERSONNEL AND SUPERVISORY MANAGEMENT

Productive personnel management and supervision do not just happen. They occur only as a result of adhering to a prescribed set of basic principles.

Cooperation

To achieve cooperation, the specialties and unique abilities of individuals must be noted and used when their services will be most effective. Maintaining co-operation among the staff will largely depend on staff satisfaction in the work environment, and fulfillment of the organizations goals. The function of supervision is to see that these essentials are accomplished.

The individual as a member of an organization

Management and supervision should seek to imbue the organization with the idea that every individual has a stake in the enterprise. The undertakings can be successful only if all persons contribute by working to their fullest potential; then success brings satisfaction to all. Submergence of self is necessary for achievement of the organization's goals.

Final authority

The existing authority belongs to the job and not to the person. The manager and supervisor should never feel powerful and all-important. Authority does not reside in one human being but in the best thinking, judgment, and imagination the organization can command. Each individual has only the authority that goes with his or her position. In turn, this authority is respected by other members whose work is closely allied to achieving the objectives for which the organization exists. Authority comes from those who perform the more technical aspects of the organization's work and from those who, because of their positions, are responsible for ultimate decisions. Department heads and staff consultants issue reports interpreting the facts. Their judgments, conclusions, and recommendations contribute to the formulation of the final decisions, which are the responsibility of the manager. If these interpretations, judgments, conclusions, and recommendations are not accepted, the organization may fail. Its best thinking has been ignored. Furthermore, individuals cannot be induced to contribute their efforts to an organization that has little respect for their thinking. Authority permeates the entire organization from top to bottom.

Staff morale

The management should continually strive to create conditions that contribute to good staff morale. The degree to which high staff morale exists will be in direct proportion to the degree to which such conditions are satisfied.

The class instructor is a very important consideration in personnel management.

Leadership. The quality of the leader will determine staff morale to a great degree. From the top down, all leaders should be carefully selected. Other things being equal, individuals will contribute better service, produce more, have an overall better morale, and have more respect for individuals who are leaders in the true sense of the word.

Physical and social environment. A healthful physical and social environment is essential to good staff morale. The organization must provide for the physical health of the worker. It must also make provisions for mental health, including proper supervision, opportunity for advancement, emergency plans, and avenues for intellectual improvement.

The social environment is also an important consideration. The individuals with whom a person works and the activities in which he or she engages can strengthen or dampen the human spirit. An individual's performance can be greatly effected by his or her interactions with others. Therefore, to improve oneself, it is important to associate with those who can contribute to this improvement. Because the working day represents, to a great degree, the majority of an individual's social relationships, it is important that these relationships be wholesome and conducive to individual improvement.

Advancement. Human beings like to feel that they are getting ahead in the world. Each member of an organization must know what is essential for progress and promotion. Opportunities should be provided for learning new skills, gaining new knowledge, and having new experiences. Encouragement should be given to those who are anxious to improve and are willing to devote extra time and effort to this end.

Recognition of meritorious service. All human beings need to be recognized. Those who make outstanding contributions to the organization should be so honored. This is important to further greater achievements.

Individual differences. An important principle of personnel management is recognizing individual differences and different types of work. Individuals differ in many ways—abilities, skills, training, and physical, mental, and social qualities. Also, various types of work require different skills, abilities, and training. These differences must be recognized by the

Recruiting the right personnel for faculty positions is an important function of management.

manager, who must make sure that the right person is in the right position. An individual who is a round peg in a square hole does not contribute to their or the organization's welfare. To be placed in a position that should be held by a person with lesser qualifications or vice versa is unjust and devastating.

It is important for the manager and supervisor to recognize the individual differences existing in the organization. To develop efficient communication, a sense of responsibility, and the basis for personnel improvement and advancement within the organization, such status systems must be readily understood, authoritative, and authentic. The status granted any one person should be in line with the capacities and importance of the function he or she performs. Many disruptive features can develop in status systems if individual abilities are not recognized, if the system is allowed to become an end rather than a means to an end, and if proper incentives are not provided at each level.

Differentiated staffing. Management must recognize staff members' interests, talents, and general suitability for each position. Teachers should be as-

signed activities where they demonstrate particular skills. Schools are also employing persons such as paraprofessionals, activity specialists, interns, teacher aids, clerks, custodians, and equipment and facility managers, to perform specialized tasks.

PERSONNEL RECRUITMENT AND SELECTION

Personnel recruitment and selection are important functions of management. They include consideration of the special qualifications for teaching, the general qualifications of physical educators, and the special qualifications of those working in health clubs, industrial fitness centers, and other agencies. Orientation and in-service training are also responsibilities that go with staff recruitment and selection.

SPECIAL QUALIFICATIONS FOR TEACHING

Several persons were interviewed to find out what characteristics they thought existed in the most qualified instructors they had contact with. These qualities most frequently mentioned were:

Instructor knew the subject matter well

Instructor took a personal interest in each student

Instructor was well respected and respected the students

Instructor stimulated the students to think

Instructor was interesting and made the subject matter come to life

Instructor was an original thinker and creative in his or her methods

Instructor was a fine speaker, presented a neat, well-groomed appearance

Instructor has a good sense of humor

Instructor was fair and honest in dealings with students

Instructor was understanding and kind

Beginning instructors need considerable encouragement and help. The management should be aware of these needs and work to ensure that they are met. A survey of 50 instructors indicated the following problems of beginning instructors:

Difficulties arising from a lack of facilities

Large size of classes, making it difficult to instruct effectively

Instructional assignments in addition to the primary responsibility of teaching physical education

Discipline problems with students

Conflicting methods between what was taught the beginning instructor in his or her training institution and the established patterns of experienced instructors

Clerical work—difficulty keeping records up to date

Problems encountered in obtaining books and supplies

Problems encountered in obtaining cooperative attitude from other instructors

Lack of departmental meetings to discuss common problems

Failure to find time for personal recreation

GENERAL QUALIFICATIONS FOR PHYSICAL EDUCATORS

The most important consideration in management is selecting the best qualified personnel. The members of an organization determine whether it will succeed or fail. Therefore the management must recognize the following qualifications of physical educators.

The physical educator should be a graduate of an approved training institution that prepares persons for physical education. The college or university should be selected with care.

Because physical education is based on the foundation sciences of anatomy, physiology, biology, ki-

nesiology and biomechanics, sociology, psychology, and research, the physical education leader should be well versed in these disciplines.

The general education of physical educators is under continuous scrutiny and criticism. Speech, knowledge of world affairs, mastery of the arts, and other educational considerations are important in the preparation of the physical educator. Because the position requires frequent appearances in public, communication skills are essential.

Physical education work is strenuous and therefore demands that members of the profession be in good physical condition in order to carry out their duties efficiently and effectively. Physical educators are supposed to help build healthy bodies, and therefore should be in good physical condition themselves.

Many moral and spiritual values are developed through participation in games and other physical education activities. Therefore it is essential that the physical educator stress fair play, good sportsmanship, and sound values. His or her leadership should develop a recognition of the importance of high moral and spiritual values.

The physical educator should have a sincere interest in physical education: he or she must enjoy teaching, participating in the activities, helping others realize the thrill of participation and becoming physically fit. Unless the individual has a firm belief in the value of his or her work and a desire to help extend the benefits of such an endeavor to others, he or she will not be an asset to the profession.

The physical educator should possess an acceptable standard of motor ability. To teach various games and activities to others, it is necessary to have the skills to participate in them. The physical educator must enjoy working with people, for there is continuous informal association when teaching physical education activities. The values of such a program will be greatly increased if the physical educator elicits sportsmanship, cooperation, and a spirit of friendship.

SPECIAL QUALIFICATIONS FOR PHYSICAL EDUCATORS IN OTHER SETTINGS

The physical educator who seeks employment in settings other than schools and colleges needs to possess the general qualifications listed, and in addition, the

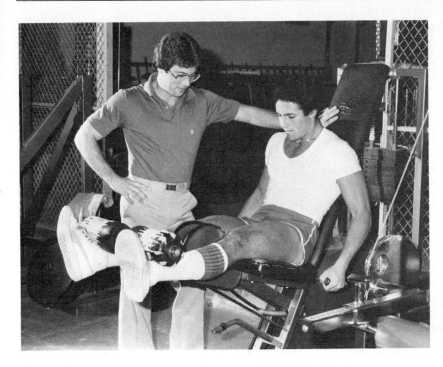

Special qualifications are needed by strength coaches.

special training and qualifications needed for work in the agency or area where he or she seeks employment. For example, a physical educator who seeks employment in an industrial executive fitness program should have as much experience as possible in exercise physiology, because many of the duties will involve helping assess the physical status of employees and planning and supervising programs to develop and maintain an optimum state of physical fitness in employees. It would also be helpful to be familiar with the various types of exercise equipment that are used in these programs. If the physical educator plans to seek a position in the employee recreation program in industry, he or she should have a wide variety of skills in activities that will interest adults. Furthermore, he or she will need special qualifications in program planning, scheduling, facility maintenance, public relations and promotion, conducting various types of tournaments, and physical fitness evaluation.

To be successful in such settings as health clubs, nursing homes, centers for the aged, and youth-serving agencies, the physical educator should know the characteristics and needs of the special population being served. For example, a physical educator working with the elderly must understand senior citizens— their lifestyles, interests, needs, physical fitness status, and the activities and programs that will contribute to their well-being.

In a health club the educator must be able to assess, to the best of his or her ability, the physical fitness of the patrons, of their remedial physical needs, and then supervise their fitness programs.

GUIDELINES FOR STAFF RECRUITMENT

Several guidelines regarding the recruitment of qualified personnel follow:

A job description that includes the various duties and qualifications the position requires should be prepared. These items should be spelled out in detail, including things such as the title of the position, a list of specific duties involved, salary, and educational and experience requirements. In addition, it is a practice to declare that the organization is an Equal Opportunity Employer.

Notices of the position vacancy should be widely

distributed within the organization itself and to professional programs and placement offices in colleges and universities, to respected leaders and colleagues in the field, and professional organizations such as the AAHPERD. Some organizations also advertise such positions in newspapers and professional journals.

Members of the management can also obtain excellent recommendations through personal contacts with professional colleagues in other institutions and agencies and through people who know of individuals with outstanding qualifications for such positions. Furthermore, confidential information that cannot be obtained through a phone conversation can be given in writing.

Candidates for the position should be asked to send their credentials, including college transcripts, confidential references (or persons who can be contacted by the employing organization), and a record of work and professional experiences.

A file should be prepared on each candidate being considered.

GUIDELINES FOR SELECTION

Many organizations have a search or personnel committee that recruits and interviews candidates for vacancies and makes recommendations to the administration. Guidelines for the selection of personnel follow:

The search, personnel, or other committee or individual should review the files of all candidates, select the three to five best prospects for the position, and then invite them for a personal interview.

Persons within the organization who apply for the position should be evaluated according to the same criteria applied to candidates from outside the organization.

The personal interview offers an opportunity to see the candidate firsthand and to discuss the position with him or her. During a personal interview it is important to assess the candidate's personality, character, education, experience, and qualifications. Questions asked might revolve around his or her interest in the position, qualifications, understanding of the employing organization, involvement in various professional activities, and background experience and education.

Based on personal interviews and a further examination of credentials, a recommendation should be made to the management that includes either one or several applicants, giving the administration the prerogative to select the best-qualified person.

The fringe benefits that go with a position should be discussed with prospective employees. These could be the deciding factor that prompt an outstanding person to accept a position. Such benefits as health insurance, retirement benefits, sick leave, annual leave, and travel allowances are an important consideration in the minds of many prospective employees.

Another consideration that should be discussed is contracts. Contractual items such as salary, length of employment, duties, tenure considerations, job details, and vacation time should be made very clear to the prospective employee. Managers should make sure applicants clearly understand all aspects of the position for which a person is being hired.

Offers of employment and acceptance can be made orally first but should be followed up in written form.

ORIENTATION OF THE NEW STAFF MEMBER

The new staff member needs considerable orientation and help in adjusting satisfactorily to the new position. Therefore management should provide guidance and assistance during the first days on the job. Help should be provided if needed with housing, transportation, and getting settled. An orientation familiarizing the person with the organization and top personnel should be conducted. The first staff meeting also offers an opportunity to introduce the new staff member to the group.

The management will want to discuss and clarify the new staff member's duties and responsibilities. The new member should know the person to whom he or she is responsible, as well as the lines of communication within the organization and any protocol that should be observed. The new person will have many questions; these should be expected and answered frankly. Salary and fringe benefits should be further clarified by the manager. Proper orientation will result in a happier and more productive member of the organization.

The newly employed staff member needs considerable orientation and help in adjusting satisfactorily to the new position. First aid being administered by teacher at Portage High School, Portage, Ind.

IN-SERVICE TRAINING

Because of the various changes occuring within this profession, staff members should periodically attend in-service training programs. New methods of management, programming, and evaluating have implications for physical education. Physical educators should weigh these innovations carefully and incorporate them into their programs. The public expects physicians, lawyers, architects, and other professionals to incorporate the latest techniques and knowledge into their practice, and physical educators should do the same.

Some suggestions for in-service training include the following:

- Conducting workshops for staff members in which new trends and developments in physical education are examined
- Urging consultants and professional colleagues who are specialists in facilities, curriculum development, methods, activity skills, and visual aids to meet with staff members to discuss these new developments
- Encouraging staff members to take graduate courses in their fields of specialization

- Developing a professional library with the latest books and periodicals in physical education and making them readily accessible to staff members
- Devoting some staff meetings to discussions of new developments in physical education
- Encouraging staff members to attend professional meetings and, if possible, subsidizing some of the costs
- Using staff members with special talents to upgrade the knowledge and competence levels of other staff members
- Providing preschool or summer orientation sessions for staff members
- Conducting research and experimentation within the organization's own program in such areas as facilities and methods

SUPERVISION

Supervisors must recognize each individual staff member and the contribution he or she makes to the organization, see that staff members are assigned to tasks in line with their abilities, be willing to delegate responsibility, establish high, attainable standards, provide a complete analysis of each position in the organization, establish accountability for each staff

The coach of a college team at Smith College, Northampton, Mass., discusses strategy with her players.

member, and help each member to feel a sense of accomplishment.

Supervision will be effective if sound leadership is provided within the organization.

Qualities of the supervisor who is a leader

Years ago it was believed that certain beliefs or qualities indicated who the leaders would be, that leaders are born and not made, and that some people will lead and others will follow. These statements are not exactly true. Instead, personal characteristics, experience, and the ability to work independently of others helps in determining the person with leadership qualities.

Some research has shown the relationship of personality factors to leadership and found that the leader of a group exceeds the other staff members in such areas as scholarship, acceptance of responsibility, participation, and socioeconomic status.

Other research has shown that the closer an individual conforms to the accepted norms of the group, the better liked he or she will be; the style of the leader is determined more by the expectations of the

membership and the requirements of the situation than by the personal traits of the leader; the leader will be followed more faithfully the more he or she makes it possible for the members to achieve their private goals along with the group goals; and in a small group, authoritarian leadership is less effective than democratic leadership in holding the group together and getting its work done.

Hersey and Blanchard's Situational Leadership Theory[4] suggests that to be an outstanding leader, the individual will change behavior with each situation. Also, the theory is based on things such as the interaction between the one who aspires to be a leader and the followers, the group's socioemotional support, two-way communication with the group, maturity level of followers, and education and experience of individuals or groups who are being led.

The physical educator who desires to exercise a leadership and supervisory role in an organization should study the management theory reflected in the research studies available on supervision. This will help ensure success as a leader in any particular situation.

The physical educator should also recognize that various personal qualities are essential for providing supervisory leadership. These personal qualities include a sense of humor, empathy, sensitivity, feeling of adequacy, ability to win confidence and respect, enthusiasm, originality, sincerity, and resourcefulness. Supervision requires the ability to assist staff members to see their own strengths and weaknesses, provide assistance in helping them to solve problems, resolve personnel conflicts, improve morale, and judge objectively personal performance and make recommendations for promotions and other rewards. To accomplish these tasks the supervisor must be able to promote staff development, create effective channels of communication, establish whose accountable for what, set goals, and provide adequate rewards.

GROUP DYNAMICS

Group dynamics are important in supervision. They are concerned with understanding the nature and role of groups in modern living. As used in this text, they are considered in light of the supervisory role in physical education programs. Research has revolved around the structure of groups, how groups operate, the relationships of members within a group and between groups, the factors that affect group attitudes and productivity, and what types of leadership are most effective in varying group relationships.

Physical educators can benefit from a study of group dynamics because they work with various groups of people in their programs, and they are interested in getting groups to enter and participate in their activities and support their programs. Teamwork is essential when working with other professional groups, and managers and supervisors must work closely with various groups both inside and outside the organization.

Shaw[9] has noted the following research approaches to the study of groups:

Formal models research: theoretical models of the structure and behavior of groups are developed.
Field theory: the behavior of groups and individuals within a group results from many interrelated and interdependent phenomena.
Sociometric research: the choices of the group on an interpersonal basis among members play a major role.

Systems approach: the group is viewed as a structure of interlocking elements, and group inputs and outputs are analyzed.
Psychoanalytic approach: the factors that groups and individuals use for motivation and defensive actions form the basis for investigation.
Empirical approach: groups are observed, observations are recorded, and statistical procedures are used to develop basic concepts and guidelines regarding group decisions.

Research has shown that supervisors must understand certain factors concerning groups in order to work effectively with them. These factors include an understanding of the group's mission in working with other groups, the power the group has over its own members, whether the group's activities are informal or highly structured, and the satisfaction derived by members of the group as a result of such group association. Other factors include the similarities of members of the group, the relationship of members with each other, the degree to which members actively participate in group activities, the ease of access to group membership, significance of the group to its members, overall stability of the group, and the structure of the group as it effects the status of each of its members.

Shaw[9] suggests the following five reasons why groups are effective:

Group performance provides increased motivation over individual performance. Groups usually produce better solutions to problems than do persons working alone. Groups are able to learn faster than individuals by themselves. More new and different ideas are generated by both individuals and groups where there is an absence of critical evaluation.

An understanding of group dynamics can enhance the physical educator's role in the supervisory process. It is an evolving area that has great potential for increasing the productivity and interpersonal relationships of any organization.

THE WORKING RELATIONSHIP BETWEEN SUPERVISORS AND STAFF

Effective working relationships between supervisors and staff members will be discussed under four sections: (1) responsibilities of supervisors, (2) responsibilities of staff members, (3) common points of conflict, and (4) checklist for effective working relationships.

Responsibilities of supervisors

Supervisors should possess a sound understanding of human nature to work effectively with people. Physical educators should not look on supervising as impersonal but should always keep in mind human dimensions and give human problems high priority.

Supervisors should understand their own behavior. They should see conflicts where they exist and not fabricate them where they do not exist. They should give an accurate account of group expectations although they may not be in agreement with them. They should recognize the differences and rationale between their own views and those of other people.

Supervisors should exercise wisely the authority vested in their positions. The authority goes with the office and not with the person. Supervisors should recognize that the position exists to further the goals of the organization and that it should never be used for personal reasons.

Supervisors should establish effective means of communication among members of the organization. Opportunities should be readily available to discuss personal and professional problems, new ideas, and ways to improve the effective functioning of the organization.

Supervisors should provide maximum opportunity for personal self-fulfillment. Each person has a basic psychological need to be recognized, to have self-respect, and to belong. Within organization requirements, supervisors should make this possible for every member of the organization.

Supervisors should provide leadership. Supervising requires leadership qualities that bring out the best individual effort of each staff member and a total coordinated effort working toward common goals.

Supervisors should provide clear-cut procedures. Sound procedures are essential to the efficient functioning of an organization; therefore they should be carefully developed, thoroughly discussed with those concerned, written in clear, concise language, and then followed.

Supervisors should plan meaningful meetings. Staff meetings should be carefully planned and efficiently conducted. Meetings should not be called on impulse or dominated by the supervisor. Plans and procedures agreed on should be carried out.

Supervisors should recommend promotions only on the basis of merit, without politics or favoritism. Recommendations for promotions, when requested, should be arrived at through careful evaluation of each person's qualifications and objective criteria.

Supervisors should protect and enhance the mental and physical health of staff members. In carrying out this responsibility, the supervisor should attempt to eliminate petty annoyances and worries that can weigh heavily on staff members, increase the satisfactions each person derives from the organization, promote friendly relationships, develop an esprit de corps, improve respect for the status of staff members, and establish a climate of understanding that promotes good will.

Responsibilities of staff members

Physical educators should support the total program. Each staff member must see his or her responsibility to the program. This means serving on committees, attending meetings, contributing ideas, and giving support to worthy new developments regardless of the phase of the program to which he or she belongs. Also, staff members should view their own fields of specialization in proper perspective with the total endeavor.

Physical educators should take an interest in supervision by participating in policy and decision making, role playing the problems and pressures faced by the supervisor, and contributing ideas that will help cut down on red tape and thus streamline the process.

Physical educators should carry out their individual responsibilities efficiently. If each job is performed effectively, the total organization will function more efficiently.

Physical educators should get their reports in on time. Purchase requisitions, attendance, excuse and accident reports, and the multitude of other forms and reports that have to be completed and then collated in the supervisor's office must be done on time. Punctuality makes supervising easier.

Physical educators should be loyal. Each staff member has the responsibility to be loyal to his or her organization. Disagreement about the supervision can exist, but loyalty to the leaders and the organization is essential.

Physical educators should observe proper protocol. Administrators and supervisors do not appreciate a staff member going over their heads to a higher authority without their knowing about it. Lines of authority must be recognized and followed in every organization.

COMMON POINTS OF CONFLICT BETWEEN SUPERVISORS AND STAFF MEMBERS

Areas where poor working relationships occur include the following:

- The failure of supervisors to recognize physical education as a vital subject
- The existence of authoritarian and undemocratic supervision
- The failure to clarify goals and responsibilities of the organization and for each member of the organization
- The failure of supervisors to provide dynamic leadership
- The failure of supervisors to provide clearly defined procedures
- The practice of supervisors encroaching on classes and schedules without good reason or adequate previous announcement
- The assignment of unreasonable work loads and assignments
- The failure of staff members to read bulletins that contain important announcements
- The failure of supervisors to assume conscientiously the duties and responsibilities associated with supervision
- The existence of unsatisfactory working conditions
- The lack of adequate materials, supplies, and equipment

Physical educators should be professional. In relationships with colleagues, supervisors, or the general public, a staff member should recognize that there is a professional way of behaving. Confidences are not betrayed, professional problems are ironed out with the people concerned, and personality conflicts are discussed with discretion.

PERSONNEL PROBLEMS REQUIRING SPECIAL ATTENTION

Selected personnel problems needing special attention are teacher burnout, stress management, unionism, affirmative action, and use of certified and noncertified personnel.

Teacher burnout

Teacher burnout has been defined by one person as "a physical, emotional, and attitudinal exhaustion." More stable school and college faculties, shrinking employment opportunities, austere budgets, back-to-basics movements, public criticism, lack of community support, heavier teaching loads, accountability, discipline problems, and inadequate salaries are a few of the conditions resulting in teacher burnout.

Some teachers are tired of their work and the many educational problems they face. As a result, in many cases the students are being shortchanged and the teachers are complacent, dissatisfied, restless, and suffering emotionally and sometimes physically.

What can be done to cope with teacher burnout? How can teachers who are suffering from it be helped? What procedures will result in self-renewal for teachers? More important, how can teacher burnout be prevented?

Many suggestions have been made for eliminating and avoiding teacher burnout. They are listed here so beginning teachers and those on the job will be familiar with ways to avoid it or, if already afflicted, can find a cure for it.

Langlois[8] has found that fitness is the answer. She has initiated faculty fitness classes at her college that have paid dividends in eliminating and avoiding teacher burnout.

Crase[5] suggests the following activities as antidotes to teacher burnout and complacency: reassess teaching technologies, reevaluate curricular offerings, participate in visitations and exchange programs, participate in structured learning experiences, become involved in professional organizations, reassess reading habits, contribute to professional publications, develop a quest for new knowledge, get involved in local service functions, and explore additional development opportunities.

Wendt[11] implies that change may help in avoiding teacher burnout.

Austin[1] lists several possible solutions: use holidays and vacations for personal and professional revitalization, change the way material is taught, transfer to another school, transfer to another position within the educational system, find a job outside education, or participate in in-service education.

Horton[6] points out that teacher burnout must be attacked on several fronts since no single cause or solution exists. Therefore a teacher experiencing burnout must recognize the problem and then develop a meaningful plan of correction.

Stress management

Stress can be harmful or beneficial depending on the nature of the stimulus or stressor, as the causal agent is called. Harmful stress affects the ability of the body to maintain stable conditions within itself. Beneficial stress can result in euphoria and greater personal achievements. Negative stress should be reduced to avoid developing physical or emotional health problems. In many cases physical activity provides an excellent means of stress reduction.

Some symptoms of stress that may represent danger signs are irritability, headaches, pain in the back, loss of appetite, nightmares, depression, emotional tension, and heart palpitations.

The late Dr. Hans Seyle, biologist, endocrinologist, and a pioneer in modern stress theory, defined stress as the ''nonspecific response of the body to any demand placed upon it.'' He indicated the body's response to stress follows a three-stage pattern:

Alarm State—the body mobilizes its resources to fight the hostile stressor.

Athletic trainer wrapping athlete's ankle.

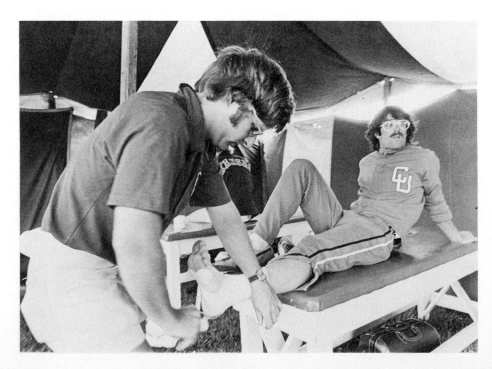

Resistance State—the body adjusts to stress by using its maximum ability to withstand the stressor.

Exhaustion State—the body becomes devitalized and loses ablty to resist stress, leading to serious illness and even death.

Many mental and physical reasons have been set forth proclaiming the benefits of physical activity in stress reduction. Through physical activity a person can improve mind-body harmony and thus reduce harmful stress, thereby contributing to his or her own health and fitness.

Exactly how physical activity reduces stress is not completely understood. It has been generally established that the mind can influence the body and the body influences the mind. Research suggests that physical activity can result in a positive psychological response. This is similar to when a negative mental state is changed, resulting in an improved physical condition with less risk of psychosomatic and other disorders.

One theory is that exercise burns up stress hormones. The human body reacts to stress by a response known as "fight or flight." As a result, a number of hormonal and physiological changes take place as stress by-products are created.

If one responds to the stressor by engaging in physical activity, the stress by-products are used. Seyle suggested that the person who exercises regularly is able to resist stressors better, and that stressful situations do not represent as much harm to the physically active person as to the sedentary individual.

A second explanation is that activity helps to release the tension that can accumulate when one is under stress. As a result, hormone-induced tension is alleviated by physical activity. A stress-regulated and controlled life-style should provide a balance between work, exercise, rest, and structured relaxation training.

De Vries, a respected physiologist from the University of Southern California, found in his research that activities such as jogging, bicycling, and walking from 5 to 30 minutes producing an increased heart and respiration rate, resulted in significant relaxation for tense persons. Physical activity appears to provide a mental diversion from problems and activities that cause stress.

GENERAL GUIDELINES FOR STRESS REDUCTION

Try not to be a perfectionist—instead, perform and work within your capabilities

Spend your time in ways other than trying to befriend those persons who don't want to experience your love and friendship

Enjoy the simple things of life

Strive and fight only for those things that are really worthwhile

Accent the positive and the pleasant side of life

On experiencing a defeat or setback, maintain your self-confidence by remembering past accomplishments and successes

Don't delay tackling the unpleasant tasks that must be done; instead, get at them immediately

Evaluate people's progress on the basis of their performance

Recognize that leaders, to be leaders, must have the respect of their followers

Adopt a motto that you will live in a way that will earn your neighbor's love

Try to live your life in such a way that your existence may be useful to someone

Clarify your values

Take constructive action to eliminate a source of stress

Other suggestions

Maintain good physical and mental health

Accept what you cannot change

Serve other people and some worthy cause

Share worries with someone you can trust

Pay attention to your body

Balance work and recreation

Improve your qualifications for the realistic goals you aspire to

Avoid reliance on things such as drugs and alcohol

Don't be narcissistic

Manage your time effectively

Laugh at yourself

Get enough rest and sleep

Don't be too hard on yourself

Improve your self-esteem

Seyle, H. (1974).

Another researcher found that physical activity provides a low type of stress for the adrenal glands that in turn strengthens them so that they can more effectively counter severe stress. Increased adrenal activity as a result of exercise appears to result in the creation and formation of reserves of steroids which counteract stress.

Some experts feel that an important point to make is that endurance exercise promotes the secretion of hormones called endorphins that produce the "jogger's high." Endorphins are 200 times more powerful than morphine and are nature's way of rendering negative psychological feelings inert and producing a natural feeling of well-being.

Other experts point out that regular and adequate amounts of exercise help reduce stress by contributing to a lower heart rate, lower blood pressure, improved condition of blood vessels, fewer circulatory disorders, and better body composition.

The negative image of the human body held by some persons, whether it is caused by overweight, weak muscular development, or poor posture, can be a stressor. Exercise can improve body development and in turn a person's self-image.

Stress can be managed in other ways, such as various kinds of relaxation techniques, biofeedback, and meditation. Seyle's guidelines for stress reduction are outlined on the previous page.[3]

Physical education teacher discussing physical education contract with student in Omaha (Neb.) Public Schools.

Unionism

Unionism is widespread, and administrators, teachers, and other staff members should understand and be able to work effectively with unions.

The emphasis in physical education over the years has been for professionals to know their professional organizations. The student and manager are well oriented to these organizations. But how much orientation is there to unionism? It would seem very little, yet teacher, labor, and other unions are calling on physical educators to strike, to agree to binding arbitration agreements, and to give allegiance to union leaders who may or may not act in the best interests of physical education and sports.

Managers, especially, need to understand unionism and to be able to work with unions. Some recommendations for managers to follow if involved with professional negotiations are: look on negotiations as a time to attempt to improve relationships rather than harm such relationships, adjust to negotiations and make the best of their working relationship, advance the organization and improve its democratic atmosphere, insist on being a part of the negotiation process, protect the right to be the professional leader of the organization, and strive to promote mutual respect, cooperation, and shared decision making in the negotiation process. Managers should know what their responsibilities are in professional negotiations, and these should be spelled out in a written job description. If managers perform within the responsibilities as stated, then they should receive solid backing from their superiors.

Affirmative action

Managers need to understand and conform to affirmative action guidelines. Among other things, these guidelines indicate that no discrimination can exist on the basis of sex, race, ethnic background, or creed. All individuals must be afforded equal opportunities to achieve their destinies. In hiring personnel for instance, attention must be given to adequate publicity of vacancies, consideration of all applications, and selection based on each individual's qualifications. No discrimination can exist against minority groups in employment, salary, or promotion. Also, organizations should strive for balance and a representative number of staff members who are, for example, male and female, nonwhite and white, handicapped and nonhandicapped.

Many organizations have individuals whose responsibilities include promoting and overseeing the process of equal opportunity within their department, school, or division. Managers should consult with these individuals periodically to see that affirmative action guidelines are being met. If no such individual exists in an organization, then the manager should see that proper conditions exist.

Use of certified and noncertified personnel

A trend in recent years has been to use noncertified personnel in physical education to teach activities when permanent certified personnel do not have the proper expertise or when work loads have become too heavy for the full-time faculty. The profession has suggested the following guidelines.

New activities in which students and other consumers are interested in participating need to be taught by regular full-time faculty members. In hiring new faculty attention should be given to applicants who have the qualifications to teach new activities. If no faculty member is available to teach a new activity, noncertified personnel can be hired. Such a person should have expertise in the activity to be taught. Proper supervision should be provided for the noncertified person. The noncertified person will be replaced when regular full-time faculty become qualified to teach the new activities.

There is considerable discussion in athletic programs whether or not athletic coaches should be certified. Broderick, Kelly and Brightwell[2,7] have explored this question and, among other recommendations, feel that coaches need to be qualified since tasks such as training and conditioning programs, and injuries can lead to health and medical problems if the coaches are not qualified. Also, the growth in sport and athletic programs has increased the need for more coaches for both girls' and women's and boys' and men's programs.

Grievance and due process

In most educational organizations a prescribed procedure is set forth to be followed by a staff member or other person who has a *grievance*. Grievance implies that the person feels he or she has been wronged and

CHECKLIST FOR EFFECTIVE WORKING RELATIONSHIPS AMONG MANAGERS, SUPERVISORS, AND PHYSICAL EDUCATORS

	Yes	No
1. Job descriptions of all positions are formulated, written, and disseminated to each individual involved.	_____	_____
2. Polices are cooperatively formulated.	_____	_____
3. Staff members are encouraged to participate in the determination of policies. Management uses faculty committees to develop policies.	_____	_____
4. Policies cover priorities in the use of physical education facilities.	_____	_____
5. Policies have been developed and are in writing for the major areas of the enterprise, as well as specifically for physical education.	_____	_____
6. Departmental policies and procedures are up to date and complete.	_____	_____
7. Board establishes and approves policies and programs.	_____	_____
8. Physical educators know the policies of their organization and work within this framework.	_____	_____
9. Open channels of communication are maintained between manager, supervisor, and staff.	_____	_____
10. In-service education is provided.	_____	_____
11. Staff members are encouraged to participate in the activities of professional organizations.	_____	_____
12. Supervisors act in an advisory and not a managerial capacity.	_____	_____
13. The teaching load of all instructors is equitable in that such factors as the following are considered: work hours per week and number of clientele per week.	_____	_____
14. Athletics are open to all and conducted according to sound educational principles.	_____	_____
15. Policies are in writing and disseminated and cover the organization and management of athletics.	_____	_____
16. Coaches are certified in physical education.	_____	_____
17. The group process is effectively used in staff and committee meetings.	_____	_____
18. There is a strong belief in and a willingness to have a democratic management.	_____	_____
19. Staff meetings are well organized.	_____	_____
20. New staff members are oriented with respect to responsibilities, policies, and other items essential to their effective functioning in the organization.	_____	_____
21. Departmental budgets and other reports are submitted on time and in proper form.	_____	_____
22. Staff members attend meetings regularly.	_____	_____
23. Staff members participate in curriculum studies.	_____	_____
24. Class interruptions are kept to an absolute minimum.	_____	_____
25. Proper management channels are followed.	_____	_____
26. Relationships with colleagues are based on mutual integrity, understanding, and respect.	_____	_____
27. Management is interested in the human problems of the organization.	_____	_____
28. Maximum opportunity is provided for personal self-fulfillment consistent with organization requirements.	_____	_____
29. Department heads are selected on the basis of qualifications rather than seniority.	_____	_____
30. Staff members are enthusiastic about their work.	_____	_____
31. All personnel are provided opportunities to contribute to the improved functioning of the organization.	_____	_____

CHECKLIST FOR EFFECTIVE WORKING RELATIONSHIPS AMONG MANAGERS, SUPERVISORS, AND PHYSICAL EDUCATORS—cont'd

	Yes	No
32. The board's executive officer executes policy.	____	____
33. Faculty and staff assignments are educationally sound.	____	____
34. Management works continually to improve the working conditions of personnel.	____	____
35. Responsibilites are equitably distributed.	____	____
36. Management provides recreational and social outlets for the staff.	____	____
37. Management recognizes and records quality work.	____	____
38. Physical educators seek to improve themselves professionally.	____	____
39. Physical educators view with proper perspective their special fields in the total enterprise.	____	____
40. Physical educators organize and plan their programs to best meet the needs and interests of the participants.	____	____
41. Health and physical educators continually evaluate themselves and the professional job they are doing in the organization.	____	____
42. Budgetary allocations are equitably made among departments.	____	____
43. Management is sensitive to the specific abilities and interests of staff.	____	____
44. Physical educators take an active role in planning.	____	____
45. Physical education objectives are consistent with general education objectives.	____	____
46. Management recognizes and gives respect and prestige to each area of specialization in the organization.	____	____
47. Physical educators are consulted when new facilities are planned in their areas of specialization.	____	____
48. Funds are available for professional libraries, professional travel, and other essentials for a good in-service program.	____	____
49. Physical educators carefully consider constructive criticism when given by the administration.	____	____
50. Management is skilled in organization and administration.	____	____

has a just cause for protest and complaint; a hardship or harm has been caused.

The established procedure usually includes discussing the grievance with various persons in the chain of command and trying to solve the problem at the lowest possible level. If the problem cannot be solved at the lowest level, it moves on to a higher level or is given to a grievance committee. This committee discusses all the facts in the case and tries to arrive at a solution that is right and, if possible, satisfactory to all concerned.

The management should always be alert to situations where grievances may occur and try to solve personal and other problems before they reach the grievance stage. At the same time, it may not always be possible to solve some problems, and therefore it is essential to have an established grievance procedure.

Due process refers to an established procedure that is designed to safeguard the legal rights of the individual. For example, when a person is accused of some wrong doing, he or she is protected legally by having the right to pursue a judicial procedure that enables the facts to be presented thoroughly before a final decision is made.

EVALUATION

Managers and supervisors need to establish methods to measure staff effectiveness, to make sound decisions for retention, salary adjustments, and promotion, as well as to help staff members improve. The management should encourage a program of evaluation. Staff members need to be helped to improve their own effectiveness. Records should be kept to determine progress.

Some guidelines for evaluating staff members follow:

Appraisal should involve staff members themselves. Evaluation is a cooperative venture, and staff members should be involved in developing the criteria for evaluation because they need to understand the process.

Evaluation should be centered on performance. The job to be accomplished should be the point of focus with extraneous factors omitted.

Evaluation should be concerned with helping staff members grow on the job. The purpose of evaluation is to help the person evaluate himself or herself and maintain strengths and reduce weaknesses.

Evaluation should look to the future. It should be concerned with developing a better physical education program and a better organization.

Evaluation of staff members should be well organized and administered. The step-by-step approach should be clearly outlined.

Sturtevant[10] suggests that the use of management techniques can be very helpful in assessing programs. Problems such as depressed economic conditions, changing enrollments, cost-effectiveness, and increased competition can be analyzed more objectively by using management techniques to do things such as improve productivity, increase efficiency, and reduce costs. When such techniques are used and departmental and programmatic assessment has taken place and has been examined by administrators, then informed decision making can take place.

METHODS OF EVALUATION

Some methods of evaluating instructors follow.

Observation of teachers in the classroom or in the gymnasium. Teachers can be notified in advance that the observation will take place, and a conference should follow the observation, with the teachers' performances being discussed and evaluated.

Student progress. With this method standardized tests are used to determine what progress the student has made as a result of exposure to the teacher.

Ratings. Ratings vary and may consist of an overall estimate of a teacher's effectiveness or consist of separate evaluations of specific teacher behaviors and traits. Self-ratings may also be used. Ratings may be conducted by the teacher's peers, by students, or by management personnel and may include judgments based on observation of student progress. To be effective, rating scales must be based on criteria such as objectivity, reliability, sensitivity, validity, and utility.

At colleges and universities the evaluation of teacher performance is sometimes more difficult than at other schools because of the unwillingness of the faculty to permit managers or others to observe them. Various methods have been devised to rate faculty members, including statements from department heads, ratings by colleagues, ratings by students, and ratings by deans and other administrators.

What constitutes effective evaluation as it relates to an instructor in a particular school or college? Several studies have been conducted with some interesting findings. For example, only a slight correlation exists between intelligence and the rated success of an instructor. Therefore, within reasonable limits, the degree of intelligence a teacher has seems to have little value as a criterion. The relation of knowledge of subject matter to effectiveness appears to depend on the particular teaching situation. A teachers' demonstration of good scholarship while in college appears to have little relationship to good teaching. Some evidence shows that teachers who have demonstrated high levels of professional knowledge on National Teachers Examinations are more effective teachers. However, the evidence here is rather sparse. The relationship of experience to effectiveness also seems to have questionable value. Experience during the first five years of teaching seems to enhance teacher effectiveness but then levels off. Little, if any, relationship exists between effectiveness and cultural background, socioeconomic status, sex, and marital status. Finally, little evidence shows that any specified aptitude for teaching exists. More research needs to be done to establish what constitutes teacher effectiveness on the job.

Accountability. Accountability may be simply defined as a means of holding the instructor (and other staff members) responsible for what the students or other individuals learn or achieve. The emphasis behind accountability must be learning. For accountability to be valid, curriculum revision must take place to allow for the best possible student progress. Once this has been accomplished (continuous program evaluation is essential), the instructor can direct his or her time and energy toward learning motivation. When an atmosphere of enjoyment is created, learning comes more naturally.

How can accountability be assessed? The first obstacle that must be overcome to have a valid accountability program is the acceptance by instructors of certain objectives that must be met. This can usually be accomplished by developing performance objectives. Once objectives have been developed, both the student and instructor know what is expected of them. Accountability can be based on how well the students satisfy the stated performance objectives for each unit. Some have suggested that student performance should be a basis for instructor bonuses. This method of accountability has many pros and cons.

Student evaluations. The student is the one most exposed to the teacher and his or her method. Therefore the student should have some say about whether the teacher is doing a satisfactory job of teaching.

Some factors that students feel relate to teacher effectiveness include knowledge of subject, fairness, interest in students, patience, leadership that was amicable but firm, enthusiasm, and skill in activities.

Many teachers are using a student questionnaire for teacher evaluation. The student is asked to respond to multiple choice questions that indicate items such as (1) interest level in activity, (2) skills learned, (3) time spent outside of class on activity, (4) knowledge gained, and (5) rating of instructor regarding understandability of his or her instructions, organization of presentation, enthusiasm, knowledge, skill, and interest in students. A space is often left for the student to express himself or herself in paragraph form concerning changes in curriculum or teaching methods.

Self-evaluation. An area of evaluation often overlooked is self-evaluation, which is often the key to self-improvement. One should ask himself or herself some of the following questions: Have I been innovative? Do I alter my teaching to meet the different ability levels I encounter? Are my classes planned well in advance to be sure of teaching space, equipment, and facility use? Do I involve all my students in activities? Do I stress cognitive, social, and behavioral objectives? Do I change my activities from year to year and try new concepts such as contact grading, performance objectives, self-directed learning, and resource centers? Do I continually evaluate my activity programs? Do I try to improve myself by continuing my education?

Questions such as these can help the instructor begin to evaluate himself or herself. Self-evaluation is

Veterans' Administration employees in the nation's capital get in physical shape to provide better personnel management in their programs.

The coach of an athletic team can have a
strong influence on his players.

not easy but can be valuable in improving an instructor's teaching.

Independent evaluators

In recent years the trend has been toward using independent evaluators because they may be more objective in assessing a teacher's abilities. Independent evaluators should be thoroughly trained and familiar with the subject they are evaluating and should have a teaching and administrative background. Often evaluators are drawn from education consultant groups, education specialists in civil service positions, or university or college professors.

Evaluating the prospective teacher

The competence of the prospective teacher is an important facet of the total educational evaluation system. Traditionally the undergraduate education major was evaluated in terms of grade point average, completion of required course work, and a minimum grade level in major subjects. Obviously, such evaluation techniques are not sufficient to produce quality teachers. New criteria of assessment must be established to include such factors as (1) comprehensive

testing to ascertain mastery of both general and specific knowledge, as well as teacher education objectives; (2) performance testing based on teaching task analysis; and (3) an internship to develop teaching skills.

The prospective teacher should be field oriented, with much of his or her 4 years spent in school involving school-related tasks. During undergraduate years, the individual should have experience in grading papers, keeping records, individual tutoring, and actual classroom teaching. The teacher who has graduated from such a program and has satisfied the assessment criteria will be a better teacher and will also have an easier and more enjoyable adjustment to the first few years of teaching.

Performance-based teacher education

The trend today, as has been pointed out earlier in this text, is toward performance-based teacher education. Under this plan the prospective teacher is evaluated, not in terms of courses taken, but in terms of certain competencies (skills, knowledge, abilities) that have been determined essential to satisfactory teaching. The prospective teacher is evaluated by scientific assessment techniques, and the stress is on his or her performance. A major consideration is whether this prospective teacher can change student behavior through his or her teaching.

Evaluation of physical educators in other settings

Much of what has been said about the evaluation of teachers of physical education is also true about the evaluation of physical educators who work in other capacities. They are held accountable for the effective performance of assigned duties. This accountability is determined by observing physical educators on the job, by eliciting opinions from persons who have been served by them, and by their productivity. One form of productivity in a commercial establishment, such as a health club, unfortunately, is how many customers are attracted to the organization and the bottom line profit or loss figure for the business.

The main concern of all physical educators wherever they are employed is to do the best job possible, and let the evaluation take care of itself. In other words, one should be enthusiastic, develop as much expertise as possible concerning the position and re-sponsibilities one has, and provide the best service possible to the persons being served. One should also develop good human relations with everyone concerned. If these suggestions are adhered to, the physical educator should not have to worry about the evaluation process; professional advancement will result.

SUMMARY

One of the most important functions that management has to perform is that of personnel management. Management is responsible for such actions as establishing policies under which the staff will operate, seeing that staff morale is at a high level, recruiting qualified members for the organization, providing adequate supervision, using group dynamics in the achievement of organization goals, and providing ways to prevent such personnel problems as undue stress and teacher burnout. Furthermore, managers must be able to work harmoniously with unions and the public in general. Finally, staff members need to be evaluated periodically in an objective manner so that performance can be improved and deserving staff are compensated and promoted.

With the individualized approach to learning in Omaha Public Schools, each student meets with teacher for evaluation of prescribed task.

SELF-ASSESSMENT TESTS

These tests will assist students in determining if material and competencies presented in this chapter have been mastered:

1. Define what is meant by *personnel management* and *supervision* and the principles you would follow if you were a supervisor of a physical education staff.

2. If you were the employing officer hiring a physical educator in a school, college, health club, or corporation, what qualifications would you look for in the person you desire to employ?

3. Prepare a step-by-step procedure for the recruitment, selection, orientation, and in-service training of a new member of a physical education staff.

4. You are scheduled to be interviewed by a superintendent of schools who is looking for a person to supervise the work of some physical educators who teach at the elementary school level in her school system. During the interview she asks you to state your qualifications for such a position, how you will use group dynamics in the position, and how you plan to work most harmoniously and productively with staff members. Tell your class what you told the superintendent of schools. Then, have the class decide whether or not you were hired for the position.

5. Develop a rating sheet you would use to evaluate the work of a physical educator teaching at the high school level and a health club or industrial physical fitness employee.

REFERENCES

1. Austin, D.A.: Renewal, Journal of Physical Education and Recreation **51**:57, 1980.
2. Broderick, R.: Non-certified coaches, Journal of Physical Education, Recreation and Dance **55**:38, May/June 1984.
3. Bucher, C.A., and Prentice, W.E.: Fitness for college and life, St. Louis, 1985, Times Mirror/Mosby College Publishing.
4. Case, R.W.: Leadership in sport—the situational leadership theory, Journal of Physical Education, Recreation and Dance **55**:15, January 1984.
5. Crase, D.: Development activities: a hedge against complacency, Journal of Physical Education and Recreation **51**:53, November/December 1980.
6. Horton, L.: What to do about teacher burnout? Journal of Physical Education, Recreation and Dance **55**:69, March 1984.
7. Kelley, J.E., and Brightwell, S.: Should interscholastic coaches be certified? Journal of Physical Education, Recreation and Dance **55**:49, March 1984.
8. Langlois, S.: Faculty fitness: a program to combat teacher burnout, Update, March 1981.
9. Shaw, M.: Group dynamics: the psychology of small group behavior, New York, 1971, McGraw-Hill Book Company.
10. Sturtevant, M.: Use management techniques to assess programs, Journal of Physical Education, Recreation and Dance **55**:48, May/June 1984.
11. Wendt, J.: Resistance to change, Journal of Physical Education and Recreation **51**:56, November/December 1980.

SUGGESTED READINGS

- Cratty, B.J.: Social psychology in athletics, Englewood Cliffs, N.J., 1981, Prentice-Hall, Inc.
  Looks at various ways social psychologists have studied group interaction and social influences. Helps in anticipating problems when working with groups, rather than simply reacting to unfortunate situations after they arise.

- Iacocca, L.: Iacocca—an autobiography, New York, 1984, Bantam Books, Inc.
  Tells the story of one of the most successful managers in industry today. As Chief Executive Officer of the Chrysler Corporation he transformed a dying company into a great success. Relates how he works with his staff in achieving results.

- Jackson, J.J.: Sport administration, Springfield, Ill., 1981, Charles C Thomas, Publisher.
  Describes management concerns regarding personnel in such areas as concepts of power and authority, leadership, supervision of workers and clients. Provides valuable suggestions for personnel management.

- Kraus, R.G., and Curtis, J.E.: Creative management in recreation, parks, and leisure services, St. Louis, 1986, Times Mirror/Mosby College Publishing.
  Chapter 3 discusses the scope and process of personnel management. Includes information concerning such items as job descriptions, competency-based approaches to hiring personnel, professional preparation, employment standards, supervisory practices, training approaches, and working with unions.

- Lehr, C.: Meeting staff development needs of teachers, Journal of Physical Education, Recreation and Dance **55**:73, August 1984.
  Tells what mature professional teachers want in the way of staff development. Such things as interaction with

peers, self-awakening and how to improve their teaching are what they desire most.

- Rogers, E.J.: Getting hired, Englewood Cliffs, N.J., 1982, Prentice-Hall, Inc.
  The author as Vice President and Director of Personnel for a large corporation discusses the importance of such things as resumes, interviews, planning, and how to get off to a good start in a new position.

- Sergiovanni, T.J.: Handbook for effective department leadership, Boston, 1984, Allyn & Bacon, Inc.
  Covers role of chairpersons as department heads. Discusses job descriptions, leadership role, department structure, teacher satisfaction, facilitating change, supervision, and the importance of personal health.

Chapter Eight
Program Development

Instructional Objectives and Competencies to be Achieved
After reading this chapter the student should be able to

- Explain why program development is an important part of the management process and what the program of physical education should accomplish.
- Identify the factors that influence program development.
- Outline a step-by-step process for program development, including the people or groups who will be involved.
- Describe a systems and competency-based approach to program development.
- Discuss significant developments in program development.
- Develop a procedure for evaluating a program.

Chapter 7 was concerned with personnel management, one of the most important functions that chairpersons and other individuals involved with administrative functions in physical education and athletics have to assume.

Chapter 8 presents another important function of management—to provide the leadership and support needed to develop a program that will achieve the objectives of physical education.

The term *program development* as used in this text refers to the total learning experiences provided to consumers to achieve the objectives of physical education. It is concerned with the component parts of the physical education program as well as with the resources (such as personnel, facilities, and money) involved in implementing these learning experiences. Physical education management is involved with programs in schools, colleges, industry, and other organizations. Today the trend is to provide programs

planned in light of the following considerations: (1) the needs and abilities of the consumer, (2) the needs of society, (3) the practical usefulness of various knowledge and skills, and (4) the psychology of learning.

WHAT PROGRAM GOALS SHOULD THE PHYSICAL EDUCATION MANAGEMENT SUPPORT?

In brief, the main goals the physical education program should strive to accomplish pertain to four areas. The physical education curriculum should (1) develop physical powers, (2) develop skill in activities, (3) develop an understanding of physical activity, and (4) provide a meaningful social experience.

Develop physical powers

The physical education program should develop such physical characteristics as adequate cardiovascular function, proper body composition, strength, flexibility, body awareness, endurance, muscular power, coordination, speed, balance, accuracy, and proper posture.

Develop skill in activities

The physical education program should develop skill in activities such as movement fundamentals, fundamental activities (running, jumping, skipping), individual sports, team sports, gymnastics, aquatics, and rhythmic activities such as dance. The management should also provide support for activities that will assist in the development of the various components of health-related physical fitness.

Develop an understanding of physical activity

The physical education program should develop an understanding of among other things the contribution of physical activity to physical health (weight control, absence of fatigue), of biomechanical principles (role of gravity, force), and of mental health (relief of nervous tension, body image). Also, the physical education management should help students and other individuals to assess their own fitness needs and to solve their fitness problems.

Provide a meaningful social experience

The physical education program should provide for such social goals as the human desire for affiliation with other people, success in play activities, a feeling of belonging, recognition of ability, and respect for leadership and followership.

IMPORTANCE OF PROGRAM DEVELOPMENT AND THE ROLE OF MANAGEMENT

Sergiovanni[6] indicates that management should pay attention to three simple concerns regarding program development. The first is what ought to be taught (the ideal program), the second is what is being taught (the real program), and the third is determining what can be taught (the practical program).

Program development should determine what needs to be learned and achieved and should provide the means for seeing that these are accomplished. Because no two persons are exactly alike, flexibility

and a wide range of experiences that meet the requirements of all individuals are needed.

The management plays an important part in program planning. The goal of management is to provide better teaching, better learning situations, and better experiences and activities to achieve the established objectives. Because new problems constantly arise and unmet needs continue to exist or go unrecognized, continuous planning is urgently needed. The manager provides the required leadership.

Program construction requires the selection, guidance, and evaluation of experiences and activities to achieve both long-term and more immediate goals. It provides for a periodic evaluation of the entire program to make changes whenever necessary. It considers factors such as participants, the community, the organization, existing facilities, personnel, time allotments, national trends, and state rules and regulations. It sets up a framework for orderly progression. It offers a guide to physical education personnel so they are better able to achieve educational goals.

Although program development is in many cases a staff and faculty responsibility, the management plays a very important role in effecting program reform. The management assesses the organization's needs and sees that the wheels are set in motion to develop a program meeting the organization's objectives.

PEOPLE INVOLVED IN PROGRAM DEVELOPMENT

Program planning should be characterized by broad participation of many people. The considerations of managers, staff members, state groups, consumers, parents and community leaders, and other individuals are important.

Managers

Managers are key personnel in program planning. They serve as the catalytic forces that set curriculum studies into motion; the leadership that encourages and stimulates interest in providing better learning experiences; the obstacle clearers who provide the time, place, and materials to do an effective job; and the implementors who help carry out appropriate recommendations of such studies.

McNeil[4] for example, points to the roles of prin-

Students doing early morning jogging routine on the track, University of Nevada, Las Vegas.

cipals and superintendents of schools in program development. Principals are primarily middlemen between the central office, parents and staff when it comes to program development. Superintendents of schools influence program development by discussing curriculum with boards of education, by seeing that state and federal government mandates are implemented, and by providing for in-service training of teachers.

Staff

At the grass roots level of the program, staff members actually know what is feasible. The staff member can contribute his or her experiences and knowledge and present data to support recommendations of desired changes. Teachers' comments based on their many experiences and understanding of students' needs and interests can make a valuable contribution. Committees are an effective way to use staff members. They can be established to study philosophy, specific instructional areas, pertinent case studies, immediate and specific objectives, needs of participants, means of implementing changes, and the program of evaluation.

State groups

Throughout most states are many people and agencies who can help in physical education planning. These include the state department of public instruction or education, the state department of health, colleges and universities, industrial groups, and voluntary health agencies. These groups may provide program guides, courses of study, teaching aids and materials, and advice that will prove to be invaluable.

The consumer

Consumers can play a part in program development. Their thinking in regard to what constitutes desirable activities and methods of instruction, for example, is worthwhile. Students today are more actively expressing their program desires. They want to be heard and to be identified with the various courses and activities that the program provides.

Parents and community leaders

Discussions with parents and other interested citizens can sometimes help communicate to the public what the school is trying to achieve and how it can best be accomplished. Parents and other community-minded people can make significant contributions in evaluating participant behavior in terms of desired outcomes. Along with students they are actively expressing their program desires.

Other individuals from specialized areas

Program development should use the services of interested individuals, such as physicians, nurses, recreation leaders, and industrial leaders, who can make worthwhile contributions by looking at the program from all sides and angles.

COOPERATIVE PLANNING BY PEOPLE INVOLVED IN PROGRAM DEVELOPMENT

Many areas are to be considered in cooperative planning of the physical education program: finding a group of individuals committed to work cooperatively in the study and organization of program-related materials; formulating a philosophy of physical education related to consumer needs and goals; understanding thoroughly the objectives of physical education; analyzing the consumer and the organization in reference to their needs, attitudes, values, and objectives in terms of programs and facilities; formulating objectives consistent with consumer needs and general principles of the planning group; selecting activity units that satisfy the statement of objectives; developing teaching aids and resource materials; developing evaluation techniques and provisions for continuous program assessment.

FACTORS THAT INFLUENCE PROGRAM DEVELOPMENT

Factors that directly and indirectly influence program development in physical education include (1) the community, (2) federal and state legislation, (3) research, (4) professional organizations, (5) attitudes of managers, faculty, students, and consumers, (6) facilities and equipment, (7) scheduling classes, (8) class size, (9) physical education staff members, (10) climate and geographical considerations, and (11) social forces.

The community

The community has considerable influence on physical education program development. In public schools and other institutions in particular, where the community provides the funds for the program, there are implications for program development. The community wants to be involved.

Smith[7] points out the extent of community involvement in Darien, Connecticut public schools. She notes how various groups within this community were involved in a curriculum study project. A task force on physical education was appointed by the board of education; it consisted of 13 members who were active in the community and business life. The task force established the objectives they wished to accomplish and the strategy they would use to achieve these goals. The strategy provided for a survey of 600 students in the school system, coaches and staff members, 1000 Darien residents selected from tax rolls, and 40 organizations with a direct or indirect interest in athletics and recreation. Furthermore, the task force established evaluation criteria for program assessment.

The result of this community involvement project was rewriting curriculum guides for each level of instruction from kindergarden through grade twelve, setting up student advisory boards and student intramural councils, creating a physical education inventory system, creating faculty manager positions in the secondary school, instituting a full-day in-service workshop for physical education teachers, holding regular meetings with community agencies, and developing a coaches' handbook.

Federal legislation

Although the governmental authority primarily responsible for education is the state, the federal government is active in shaping educational programs. The Department of Health and Human Services is responsible for recommending many legislative changes in various fields, including education.

Title IX had a profound effect on educational programs by prohibiting sex discrimination in educational programs. As a result, many school districts have had to revise their curricula to meet the mandate. For example, those schools with separate classes for boys and girls must now have coeducational classes.*

PL 94-142 also has had an effect on school programs in physical education by requiring schools to provide educational services for handicapped students.†

State legislation

The state is the governmental authority primarily responsible for education. Local boards of education

---

*For further information on Title IX see Chapters 3 and 4.
†For further information on PL 94-142 see Chapter 3.

are responsible to the state for operating schools in their respective local school districts. They must adhere to the rules and regulations established by state departments of education.

State departments of education set policies concerning credits to be earned for graduation, courses to be included in the curriculum, and the number of days and the amount of time to be spent in class.

In most cases the regulations adopted by state departments of education set minimum standards. Ideally, school administrators will go beyond these minimum standards.

Research

Although some school districts rely on research to aid them in developing and revising their physical education curricula, too many schools fail to be guided by the latest research in developing their curricula.

Important research studies that affect curriculum offerings in physical education are being conducted by people in a variety of disciplines. An example of the results of research that have influenced physical education curricula are studies relating to the fitness of American children and youths. The results have

University of Nevada student practicing on balance beam.

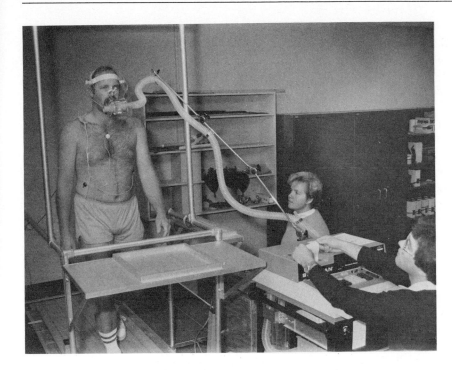

Research going on in exercise physiology laboratory, University of Nevada, Las Vegas.

shown that American children and youths are lacking in many fitness components, and curricula have been revised accordingly to upgrade their physical fitness status.

Relevant research in the social, psychological, and physical sciences, as well as in physical education, should guide physical education program planning. Researchers are investigating motor learning, learning theory, and movement education, and their research has implications for curriculum development in elementary school physical education.

Professional organizations

National, state, and local professional organizations are constantly engaged in activities that influence physical education programs. Through such activities as workshops, conferences, research, and publications, these organizations provide needed information in developing curricula.

The AAHPERD for example, sponsors many national conferences of vital importance to physical education. Research studies, panels, and a general exchange of ideas are presented at these conferences. Also, on request the AAHPERD will suggest knowledgeable consultants to work with school personnel in curriculum development and revision.

The Young Men's and Young Women's Christian Associations (YMCA, YWCA), American College of Sports Medicine, and National Education Association (NEA), as a result of their research and deliberations, have an impact on physical education programs.

State and local professional organizations also provide valuable professional information. Individuals responsible for program development and revision should keep abreast of the latest activities of their state and local professional organizations.

Attitudes of managers, faculty, students, and consumers

In education the scope and content of physical education programs are influenced by school managers and teachers. If physical education is viewed as an integral part of the school program, attempts will be made to provide the necessary support, financial and otherwise, for a quality program. If, on the other hand, it is viewed as extraneous, attempts to create and administer sound programs may be thwarted. The attitudes of teachers and students toward physical education can also affect the kind of program offered.

Management has the responsibility for interpreting the program to students, faculty, school boards, and the community. A written statement of philosophy and policies should be provided and included in the curriculum guide.

Students' and consumers' attitudes should not be overlooked by program planners. The way students and consumers feel about physical education will influence their participation in the program. A questionnaire written in language that students and consumers can understand is one way of assessing attitudes toward physical education.

Facilities and equipment

The provision of adequate facilities and equipment can help in determining the success of the physical education program. Both indoor and outdoor facilities help in providing a quality program. The extent and nature of the facilities depend on such factors as the number of students and the geographical location of the school.

Class schedules

The number of classes of physical education provided each week and the length of these classes effect the program. The minimum time for all subjects is set by state departments of education. However, local school managers can increase the amount of time spent in physical education classes, as in other subjects.

Class size

The type of activity being taught and the number of instructors will determine the class size. It is recommended that under normal circumstances the number of children in a physical education class not exceed 30. Classes in adapted physical education should be limited to 20 or less. In school districts where physi-

cal education is accepted as an integral part of the school curriculum, class size is kept at a level that promotes optimum learning. The school management can do much in seeing that this goal is achieved.

Physical education staff members

The number and qualifications of physical education staff members influence the program. Are there qualified teachers of physical education? Is there a supervisor of physical education to coordinate physical education in the school district? These are important questions that need to be considered because a sound physical education program will depend on the quality of its teaching staff. The faculty of every school should include personnel who have expertise in physical education.

The physical education specialist responsible for physical education should have completed a sequence of courses relating to his or her specialty. Too often physical education specialists with only two or three courses in physical education are assigned to teach or coach in the school program. The management should see that only qualified personnel are hired.

Climate and geographical considerations

The content of the program in physical education is also influenced by weather conditions and the geographical location of the school. Program designers should emphasize the environmental aspects of school locations. For example, many outdoor activities can be scheduled in schools in areas where the weather is normally warm for most of the year, and schools in areas with an abundance of water can stress aquatic activities.

Social forces and pressure groups

Social forces such as the civil rights movement, the feminist movement, automation, mass communication, student activism, and sports promotion have implications for program development. Times change, customs change, habits change, and the role of institutions and their responsibilities to society also change.

Pressure groups such as the John Birch Society, the National Rifle Association, labor unions, ROTC,

MANAGEMENT PRINCIPLES TO CONSIDER IN PROGRAM DEVELOPMENT

Although program development varies from organization to organization, the following general principles are applicable to all situations:

Learning experiences and activities should be selected and developed to achieve desired outcomes.

The value of program development is determined by improved instruction and results.

Program development is a continuous effort rather than one accomplished at periodic intervals.

The leadership in program development rests primarily with managers and supervisors.

The management should consult (wherever possible and practical) teachers, laymen, students, participants, state consultants, and other persons who can contribute to the development of the best program possible. The work should not, however, place an unreasonable demand on any person's time and effort.

Program development depends on a thorough knowledge of the needs and characteristics, developmental levels, capacities, and maturity levels of participants as well as an understanding of their environments and life-styles.

Program development should permit staff members to explore sound principles of learning when selecting and developing experiences.

Physical education should be viewed in its broadest scope and include all programs provided by the physical education department.

Physical education should be integrated with other areas in the organization.

Physical education activities should be selected using valid criteria.

and the Council for Basic Education often influence physical education programming in some communities.

STEPS IN PROGRAM DEVELOPMENT

The major steps involved in program development include (1) determining the objectives, (2) analyzing the objectives in terms of the program, (3) analyzing the objectives in terms of activities, (4) providing program guides and teaching aids, and (5) assessing the program.

Determining the objectives

Determining the objectives involves studying such factors as the nature of society, developmental program trends, the learning process, and the needs of the consumer so that objectives may be clearly formulated.

According to Sergiovanni,[6] objectives should originate from studies of society and its needs, studies of learners and their needs and learning styles, concepts, content, and ideas that specialists in the area under study consider important.

Analyzing the objectives in terms of the program

Having determined the objectives and knowing the characteristics of the consumer, those developing a program can outline and analyze broad categories of experiences and activities and assign relative emphases to the various phases of the process. The specialized fields of physical education and athletics should be viewed as part of the total organizational program. Consequently, their specific objectives should relate to the overall objectives of the organization.

Analyzing the objectives in terms of activities

The next step is to focus attention on the activities needed to achieve the set objectives. Obviously, for example, the physiological needs of the consumer necessitate providing a wide range of physical activities. Growth and developmental characteristics of children and physical capacities and abilities need to be studied in the school.

Providing program guides and teaching aids

Curriculum and program guides and teaching aids such as books and visual aids offer opportunities to

Creative playground provides opportunities for various motoric experiences.

use educationally sound materials to achieve objectives.

Assessing the program

Evaluation represents the culmination of the programs development process—what actually takes place in the classroom, gymnasium, fitness center, or swimming pool. The learning that takes place, the physical fitness achieved, the aids, methods, and materials used, and the outcomes accomplished determine the success or failure of program development.

SELECTED APPROACHES TO ORGANIZING CURRICULUM EXPERIENCES

Many approaches and models have been designed for the development and organization of curriculum experiences. For example, Jewett and Bain[3] describe what they feel are curriculum designs for the 1980s. They are listed under the titles of: Developmental Education, Humanistic Physical Education, Fitness, Movement Education, Kinesiological Studies, Play Education, and Personal Meaning.

Three approaches that have been used to organize curriculum experiences are the systems, conceptual, and competency-based approaches.

Systems approach

In recent years many physical educators have tried to develop a more logical means of determining what activities to include in a program. In some cases formulas have been created; in other cases step-by-step procedures have been developed to match activities to goals. Such methods of program development are encouraging because they represent an attempt to make program development in physical education a more scientific procedure.

A systems approach for developing a physical education program may be helpful to the physical educator because it provides a scientific, logical method for preparing a program of physical education that meets the needs of children and adults. This sytems approach to program development is composed of the following seven steps:

1. *Identify the developmental objectives* to be achieved in physical education (for example, organic development, skill development, cognitive development, and social-affective development).

2. *Divide each of the developmental objectives listed in the first step into subobjectives.* Identifying the subobjectives brings into sharper focus what needs to be accomplished and makes more manage-

able the achievement of the developmental objective. The following are examples of subobjectives of each of the developmental objectives:

Organic Developmental Objective

Subobjectives
   Cardiorespiratory endurance
   Muscular strength and endurance
   Coordination
   Balance
   Posture
   Flexibility
   Speed
   Agility
   Accuracy

Skill Developmental Objective

Subobjectives
   Locomotor and nonlocomotor skills
   Movement fundamentals
   General motor ability
   Specific motor ability in game and sport skills

Cognitive Developmental Objective

Subobjectives
   Understanding the principles of movement (role of gravity, force)
   Knowledge of rules and strategies of games and sports
   Knowledge of contribution of physical activity to health
   Awareness of contribution of physical activity to academic achievement
   Problem-solving ability

Social-Affective Developmental Objective

Subobjectives
   Sportsmanship
   Clarifying values
   Cooperation in group work
   Positive attitude toward physical education
   Respect for other students and leadership

3. *Identify the characteristics of the participants in terms of each subobjective identified in step 2.* A cardiorespiratory endurance characteristic, for example, of students in grades seven to nine under the developmental objective of organic development is that they tire easily because of their rapid, uneven growth, whereas in grades ten to twelve, students

Dance class, Oak View Elementary School, Fairfax, Va.

have or nearly have reached physiological maturity and therefore are better equipped to engage in extended vigorous activity.

The characteristics of students at each educational level must be determined in terms of each of the subobjectives identified in step 2. Where pertinent, characteristics of boys and girls should be differentiated. It is now possible to see the relationship between the goals and the specific characteristics of the students.

4. *Determine students' needs in relation to the characteristics outlined in step 3.* For each subobjective, the needs of the students concerned must be identified. For example, a cardiorespiratory endur-

Dance class, University of Nevada, Las Vegas.

ance characteristic of students in grades seven to nine indicates that they tire easily because of their rapid, uneven growth. Therefore a need exists for physical education experiences that overcome fatiguing factors associated with time, distance, and game pressures. On the other hand, because a characteristic of students in grades ten to twelve is greater physiological maturity, more vigorous activities are required. Students also need guidance related to such items as amounts of activity, food habits, rest, and sleep.

5. *Identify appropriate activities.* For example, the activities scheduled for students in grades seven to nine that meet their needs should include such sports as soccer or field hockey, depending on the school's facilities, using modified rules, including shortened periods of play, smaller playing areas, frequent time-outs, and unlimited substitutions.

6. *List specific performance objectives for the participants in relation to their objectives, characteristics, and needs and the activities appropriate to their age, physical condition, and ability.* For each of the subobjectives, specific performance objectives

will be listed. For example, a performance objective for the cardiorespiratory endurance subobjective for seventh to ninth grade students could be an exercise that measures cardiorespiratory endurance (for example, running a quarter mile), where the student is able to perform without undue fatigue and with a quick heart rate recovery. A performance objective for tenth to twelfth grade students might be having the student run one-half mile and be able to perform without undue fatigue and with a quick recovery of pulse and heart rate. Of course, all performance objectives should consider the characteristics and needs of the specific students in question. Performance objectives provide specific levels of accomplishment that indicate whether the desired goals have been accomplished.

7. *Identify the teaching methods and procedures that will most effectively achieve the desired goals.* These methods provide variety and apply sound motor learning theories (mass versus distributed practice, for example). They reinforce concepts related to accomplishing the objectives (for example, follow-

through helps guarantee accuracy, a concept in skill development).

Methods that can be used to develop the subobjective of cardiorespiratory endurance for seventh to ninth graders include a laboratory experiment with conditioned and nonconditioned animals, an explanation of the role and worth of cardiorespiratory endurance in organic development and physical fitness, a discussion of research that outlines the physical fitness status of their age group, and actual participation in activities that develop this endurance, together with an explanation of performance objectives and practice to accomplish them.

The seven-step systems approach to curriculum development provides a logical, scientific, step-by-step method for determining the activities that will achieve the objectives, meet the characteristics and needs of participants, and provide the performance objectives to assess whether or not students have met each objective. A systems approach may provide a meaningful physical education program aimed at helping participants become truly physically educated and making physical education a viable, well-planned offering that achieves specific developmental goals.

Conceptual approach

During the past two decades many disciplines have instituted major curriculum reforms that emphasize the concept approach to curriculum development. New curriculum models based on the conceptual approach have been designed for mathematics, science, biology, social studies, and health education.

In addition to studying national curriculum models, physical education curriculum planners and other educators interested in the conceptual approach to curriculum development should also become acquainted with the theoretical aspects of concept development.

To better understand the conceptual approach to curriculum development a definition of a concept is presented. Woodruff defines a concept as follows:

. . . some amount of meaning more or less organized in an individual's mind as a result of sensory perception of external objects or events and the cognitive interpretation of the perceived data.[8]

According to Woodruff, several kinds of concepts can be identified. He indicates that a concept might be a mental construct, an abstraction, a symbolic response, or some other connotation. It should be added that although a concept might be a high-level abstraction, many concepts might also be presented as concrete, easy-to-understand ideas. For example, a concept in applied exercise physiology could be related to the cardiac response to exercise: the heart rate increases during exercise. It can be illustrated by having students take their resting pulse rate, engage in exercise, and then take their pulse rate again to note the increase as a result of exercise. Another concept is related to energy metabolism whereby the body must provide energy compounds needed for the function of any active tissue. This concept is somewhat more abstract than the first. These and other concepts have been tested and found useful for students in the upper elementary school level.

The following example of the concept approach is based on movement activities. It is broken down into the key concept, the concept, and subconcepts. Some conceptual statements are then given.

Key concept: Individual development can be enhanced through movement activities.
Concept: The development of locomotor skills is necessary for effective and efficient movement. These skills are also necessary for later development of competency in specialized sports and other activities.
Subconcept: Sprints and distance running are two specialized forms of one locomotor movement—running.

Examples of conceptual statements in physical education

Proper techniques and skill in starting are necessary for mastery of sprint running. The ability to understand and carry out the concept of pacing (the idea of running at a gradually increased speed to have enough energy left to sprint the last part of the race) is necessary for distance running. Proper leg strength is important in sprint running. Proper leg strength, endurance, and cardiovascular-respiratory endurance are important in distance running. A knowledge of the cognitive aspects related to both sprint and distance running and a proper attitude about running are necessary to the development of these running skills.

Basic Stuff Series I and II

The National Association of Physical Education and Sport of the AAHPERD has created Basic Stuff Series I and II.* The purpose behind this project has been to identify the basic knowledge that applies to physical education programs and organize it in a manner that can be used by physical educators. It is applicable to elementary and secondary school children and youth at a time when the foundations are being laid down for adult years. It stresses basic concepts presented in simple, concise language involved with the six areas of exercise physiology, kinesiology, motor learning, psychosocial aspects of physical education (movement), humanities (art, history, and philosophy), and motor development. A booklet has been prepared covering the basic concepts in each of the six areas; it is designed for pre-service and in-service teachers. Series I represents the body of knowledge that supports the worth of physical educa-

---

*Basic Stuff Series I and II may be ordered through AAHPERD Publications, P.O. Box 870, Lanham, MD 20801.

tion. The chapters in each pamphlet in the series share a similar organizational format relating to questions asked by students, such as (1) What do you have to help me? (2) How do I get it? (3) Why does it happen this way? Concepts are presented and then the student is shown how it can best be accomplished. It also explains why the concept is valid and works.

In Series II, which has been designed for teachers in the field, examples of instructional activities are provided for early childhood (ages 3 to 8), childhood (ages 9 to 12), and adolescence (ages 13 to 18). The scientific knowledge in the six areas in Series I is related directly to the physical education class and enables the physical education practitioner to have at his or her disposal the basic information and learning activities that will make it possible to educate the students. General concepts such as how to learn a new skill, how to better one's performance, and the beneficial effects of exercise are identified. Then the series shows how they may be included in activity programs and presented to students by showing them why these concepts are important. This is accomplished by relat-

Research is a very important part of physical education and athletics.

ing the concepts to the motives most children and young people desire for themselves. These motives are health (they want to feel good), appearance (they want to look good), achievement (they want to achieve), social (they want to develop esthetic and affective qualities), and coping with the environment (they want to survive). Furthermore, the Basic Stuff Series makes it possible for teachers to tell and show students what concepts are important in physical education and how and why they are important.

Basic Stuff Series I and II have been developed by scholars and teachers who are experts in their particular disciplines. Heitmann[2] has presented a plan for integrating Basic Stuff Series I and II into curriculum models.

Competency-based approach

Competency-based learning has evolved because of a public and professional concern for accountability. Students are taught by means of defined performance objectives based on psychomotor, cognitive, and affective tasks. Students are not in competition with each other but with themselves. The teacher becomes an aid to learning rather than a demonstrator, and each student proceeds at his or her own rate. In addition, resource materials are made available to students to help further their behavioral and cognitive skills.

How competency-based instruction or learning actually takes place can better be understood by reviewing the competency-based instruction at a university in Texas. This program is used in the physical education department with prospective teachers.

In this approach the professor explicitly outlines all factors essential for success in the program. Objectives are thoroughly defined and understood by students entering the program. This helps to focus professor-student effort toward a specific training result rather than toward nonproductive work. Students are tested before entering a particular program to assess present competencies. Learning units are individualized to suit the needs of each student. Instruction is divided into psychomotor, cognitive, and affective tasks, and students must attain competencies in each. Resource material is available to aid students in attaining competency. At the completion of a unit students are tested for psychomotor, cognitive, and affective performance.

Competency-based learning is also used as a grad-

Dance is an important activity in a physical education program.

ing method. For example, in a high school in Illinois the performance objectives were written by a group of physical educators and were based on general, organic, neuromuscular, emotional, social, and cognitive goals. A competency-based learning unit for freshman gymnastics, for example, was divided into a 10-day introductory unit and a 3-week advanced unit. A lecture and demonstration of the 40 selected gymnastic stunts were presented to the students, followed by an introductory unit in instruction and practice. The grading system for the introductory unit was as follows, based on satisfactory performance as predetermined by the instructor:

16 to 28 stunts = A
10 to 15 stunts = B
6 to 9 stunts = C
3 to 5 stunts = D
0 to 2 stunts = F

The advanced unit required a 3-week instruction-demonstration period with the students, continuing from the introductory unit. A student who satisfactorily completed 20 to 40 stunts received an A, 16 to 27 stunts a B, and 10 to 15 stunts a C. A performance objective unit was also prepared for sophomores required to take a 3-week unit in soccer.

The committee wrote performance objectives for all activities in the 4-year high school curriculum. The freshmen and sophomores started in the program with teachers who desired to work with the performance objective concept. The initial evaluation was positive for both students and teachers.

Other competency-based programs in physical education have been developed in such places as North Haven, Connecticut (Cripton Project), Florida, Michigan, and Oregon. The Cripton Project curriculum, entitled "Continuous Progress, K-12," consists of a comprehensive set of competencies and provides

Dance class, State University College, Potsdam, N.Y.

AAHPERD HEALTH-RELATED PHYSICAL FITNESS TEST

Item A: Distance run

Fitness component: Cardiorespiratory fitness
Purpose: To measure the maximal function and endurance of the cardiorespiratory system
Item description:

Procedures and norms are provided for two optional distance run tests: the mile run for time and the nine minute run for distance. The decision as to which of the two tests to administer should be based on facilities, equipment, time limitations, and personal preference of the teacher. For students 13 years of age and older, the 1.5 mile run for time or the 12 minute run for distance may be utilized as the distance run items.

Item B: Sum of skinfolds (triceps and subscapular)

Fitness component: Body composition
Purpose: To evaluate the level of body fatness
Item description:

In a number of regions of the body, the subcutaneous adipose tissue may be lifted with the fingers to form a skinfold. The skinfold consists of a double layer of subcutaneous fat and skin whose thickness may be measured with a skinfold caliper. The skinfold sites (triceps and subscapular) have been chosen for this test because they are easily measured and are highly correlated with total body fat.

Item C: Sit-ups

Fitness component: Muscular strength/endurance
Purpose: To test muscular strength and endurance of the abdominal muscles.
Item description:

The pupil lies on his back with knees flexed, feet on floor with the heels between twelve and eighteen inches from buttocks. The pupil crosses arms on chest placing hands on the opposite shoulder. His feet are held by his partner to keep them in touch with the testing surface. The pupil, by tightening his abdominal muscles, curls to the sitting position. Arm contact with the chest must be maintained. The sit-up is completed when elbows tough the thighs. The pupil returns to down position until the midback makes contact with the testing surface.

Item D: Sit and reach

Fitness component: Flexibility
Purpose: To test the flexibility of the low back and posterior thigh
Item description:

The pupil removes his shoes and assumes the sitting position with the knees fully extended and the feet against the apparatus shoulder width apart. The arms are extended forward with the hands placed one on top of the other. The pupil reaches directly forward, palms down, along the measuring scale. In this position, the pupil slowly stretches forward four times and holds the position of maximum reach on the fourth count. The position of maximum reach must be held for one second with knees in full extension while the feet are in contact with the apparatus.

From American Alliance for Health, Physical Education, Recreation, and Dance.

for student levels of achievement to be assessed periodically and a student profile card that tracts each student's progress throughout his or her school experience. The competencies are grouped into 10 clusters consisting of 44 competency packages.

OTHER SELECTED CONSIDERATIONS FOR PROGRAM PLANNING
Health-related physical fitness

The AAHPERD through its Task Force on Youth Fitness has advocated for the general population the need for health-related physical fitness consisting of an emphasis on cardiovascular function, body composition, strength, and flexibility. These components also represent the ingredients for performance-related fitness. Curriculum designers will want to keep health-related and performance-related fitness in mind in developing programs for various segments of the population. Pate and Corbin[5] have indicated some implications for curriculum development in physical education of health-related physical fitness.

The wellness movement

The emphasis today on the wellness movement has implications for curriculum development in physical education. The trend today is toward an emphasis on seeing how humans can stay well and fit. Self-help medicine is the answer. People need to follow a personal health regimen and adopt a life-style that stresses fitness. Physical activity, physical fitness, and physical education programs thus have an increased value and importance for all segments of the population. Curriculum designers in physical education therefore should take the wellness movement into consideration in developing their programs.

Mastery learning

Mastery learning is based on the assumption that nearly all students and other people can master material if they are given sufficient time and the material is presented in an understandable way. First material is presented to a group of students, for example. Then an evaluation is conducted and those students who have not mastered the material are given a second chance. The material is presented again but in a different way and in a manner that can be better understood by the students who didn't master the material in the first place. This procedure can be repeated until all students have mastered the material. Mastery learning operates under the assumption that there are few failures—everyone succeeds. Curriculum designers should take this new development into consideration in developing physical education programs.

Movement education

Movement education has been of value in elementary school physical education programs (Fig. 8-1). Therefore it should be seriously considered by physical educators developing curricula for elementary school children. A discussion of movement education is presented in Chapter 3.

Title IX and PL 94-142

Chapters 3 and 4 discuss at length Title IX and PL 94-142 and the manner in which they affect curriculum development in physical education. Because these are federally mandated laws, physical educators must abide by them.

Humanistic education

Change is needed in our society to humanize schools and other organizations so students and other persons feel a sense of identity and belonging and are actively involved in the decision-making processes that affect them. Physical education curriculum designers need to be concerned with humanization and involvement processes.

Olympic curriculum*

The education committee of the United States Olympic Committee has prepared booklets designed to incorporate the ideals associated with the Olympic Games into the curriculum of several subjects in elementary, junior high, and senior high schools. One of the subjects in which these Olympic concepts can be taught is physical education. Curriculum designers will want to review these booklets and determine if this material should be a part of their program.

---

*United States Olympic Committee: The Olympics: an educational opportunity, enrichment units K-6 and enrichment units 7-9, Colorado Springs, Colo., 1981, U.S. Olympic Committee.

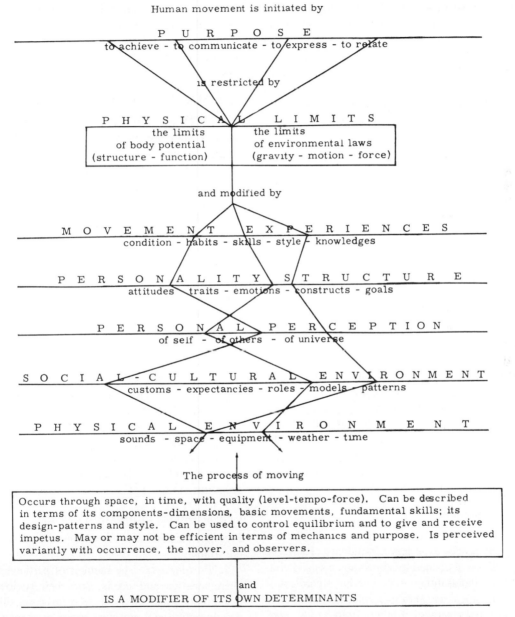

Human movement is initiated by

P U R P O S E

to achieve - to communicate - to express - to relate

is restricted by

P H Y S I C A L   L I M I T S

the limits	the limits
of body potential	of environmental laws
(structure - function)	(gravity - motion - force)

and modified by

M O V E M E N T   E X P E R I E N C E S

condition - habits - skills - style - knowledges

P E R S O N A L I T Y   S T R U C T U R E

attitudes - traits - emotions - constructs - goals

P E R S O N A L   P E R C E P T I O N

of self - of others - of universe

S O C I A L - C U L T U R A L   E N V I R O N M E N T

customs - expectancies - roles - models - patterns

P H Y S I C A L   E N V I R O N M E N T

sounds - space - equipment - weather - time

The process of moving

Occurs through space, in time, with quality (level-tempo-force). Can be described in terms of its components-dimensions, basic movements, fundamental skills; its design-patterns and style. Can be used to control equilibrium and to give and receive impetus. May or may not be efficient in terms of mechanics and purpose. Is perceived variantly with occurrence, the mover, and observers.

and

IS A MODIFIER OF ITS OWN DETERMINANTS

Fig. 8-1. Movement education, an approach to the study of observable movement, is an objective of many elementary school physical education programs.

New Games

New Games represents an innovative approach being used by some physical educators. It is based on such concepts as ''any game can be a new game,'' ''anyone can play,'' ''creating a new game is part of the fun,'' ''we play for the fun of it,'' ''it is the process of finding a game that we will want to play,'' and ''we learn about play by playing.'' The New Games organization holds training sessions for individuals who are interested in learning more about this movement.

Lifetime sports

Today considerable emphasis is placed on the importance of including lifetime sports in a physical education curriculum. The term *lifetime sports* refers to sports that can be engaged in throughout a person's life, such as tennis, golf, and swimming. A significant part of the physical education curriculum should be devoted to these activities.

High adventure leisure activities

More people today are engaging in such high adventure leisure activities as skydiving, hang-gliding, and rock climbing. The risks involved in participating in such activities appeal to some individuals who want to be challenged, desire a thrill, and are looking for excitement. It is questionable whether such activities should be a part of any school physical education curriculum. If they are a part of the curriculum in an adult organization other than schools, there should be considerable stress on participants knowing the fundamentals of the activity and on their being fit to cope successfully with these activities.

Nongraded curricula

Nongraded schools are based on the premise that individual differences exist among students. Therefore grade levels are abolished in some subjects, and children with similar abilities study together regardless of their chronological age. For example, a science class might have students ranging in age from 5 to 8 years. A student progresses as rapidly as desired, based on individual potential. The desirability of nongrading in physical education is controversial.

Accountability

Accountability generally denotes various ways of making persons answerable for their performance. Performance or productivity may be measured by pre-specified goals, the outcomes of which must meet certain standards. Accountability in education may include students as well as teachers and administrators.

THE MANAGEMENT AND PROGRAM CHANGE

Because so many factors continually influence programs, the physical educator must assess the recommended changes to make informed and wise decisions. Four questions that managers might ask themselves in evaluating changes follow:

1. *What are the functions of the organization?* How does the suggested change conform to the philosophy and purpose of the organization?

2. *Am I sufficiently well informed so I can make an intelligent decision?* Managers need to be knowledgeable about the learning process, the patterns of human growth and development, current program needs, and the needs and interests of the people in the local community.

3. *How does the change relate to staff, plant, budget, and other important administrative considerations?* The change must be practical to implement and make the best use of staff and plant.

4. *What do the experts say?* What is the thinking of professionals who have done research, studied the problem intensively, and tested the proposal widely? Expert opinion may be helpful in making a wise program decision.

Considerations in program change

Program revision cannot occur without considering the following:

1. *Participants.* The number of participants, their characteristics and needs, and their socioeconomic backgrounds and interests need to be considered before initiating any pertinent program change.

2. *Staff members.* Staff members play a key role in program revision. For example, the attitude of the faculty in a school toward change, present teaching

loads, comprehension of goals of the school, attitudes toward in-class and out-of-class programs, competencies in curriculum revision, and past training and experience are a few important considerations. Change in curriculum might mean new members being added to the faculty or a different type of competency being represented on the staff.

3. *Physical plant.* The adequacy of the physical plant for present and future programs must be considered. Information should be available on capabilities and limitations of the present plant. New demands may be placed on facilities through a program revision that brings about changes in class size.

4. *Budget.* The budget is another important consideration. What will the new program cost? What are the sources of support? Before staff members expend time and effort to study program change, they need reasonable assurance that proposed changes are economically feasible. In systems using PPBS, budgets are formulated considering the objectives of the program; PPBS also provides for evaluation techniques that require curriculum change if goals are not being met.

5. *Program.* Because any new proposal is likely to reflect present practices to some degree, it seems logical that the present program needs careful scrutiny to determine what has happened over the years, the degree to which staff members have brought about change, and the general direction in which the institution is moving.

6. *Management.* Staff members must take a hard look at the managerial leadership. The philosophy of the management and its views toward change should be carefully weighed. Managers will need to approve budgetary allocations and necessary expenditures, as well as pass on the proposed changes.

Research in physical education and program change

Advancing the frontiers of knowledge in physical education and athletics is urgently needed. Too many unsupported claims on the value of physical education have been made. There is a need to determine its worth through valid research findings—basic research that will advance knowledge and applied research that will determine the best ways to use this knowledge.

Many questions are still unanswered, such as: What is the best way to develop physical fitness? What activities are most effective for weight control? How much can retarded children learn? What activities can the employee on the job perform to promote his or her physical fitness? What are the most important biomechanics of human movement? What areas of exercise physiology need the greatest attention and research? What activities are best conducted coeducationally? What is the relationship of personality development to motor performance? What is the relationship of scholastic achievement to physical fitness? What is the therapeutic value of physical activity? What instructional strategies are most effective in mainstreaming?

EVALUATION

Once a program has been developed, evaluation is essential to determine the extent to which the experiences provided have produced desirable outcomes for participants. Unless the outcomes are acceptable, the program cannot be considered successful. Essential characteristics of an evaluation program follow.

The relationship between program planning and evaluation is recognized and understood by all individuals involved in the program. Changes are based on evaluation techniques and results. All learning experiences are evaluated. Evaluation is primarily concerned with: (1) meeting consumer needs, (2) meeting the objectives of the program, and (3) considering the requirements of parents, staff members, and organization members.

Goodlad[1] indicates that program evaluation to date has used the following four means to determine the worth of a new program: (1) observing individuals who have been exposed to the new program and the progress they have made, (2) systematic questioning of persons involved in the program, (3) testing participants periodically to determine their progress, and (4) comparative testing of participants under both the new and old programs to determine the progress of each.

Program management evaluation

Evaluation of program management may be a yearly procedure, handled by members of a department for the purpose of curriculum organization, or it may be an examination of the whole organization by a visiting team of specialists. The process of evaluation itself involves rating or judging the program according to selected criteria and standards. Some standardized forms have been developed to evaluate various phases of the physical education curriculum.

Where standardized tests are not available to judge program management, criteria based on authoritative textbook sources or the judgment of experts in the field must be established.

The following are sample questions, which may be answered "poor," "fair," "good," or "excellent" or be scored on a scale of one to ten. Sample areas of the program are listed with questions concerning the various factors.

Instructional program

Does the program devote equitable time to team sports, individual sports, rhythms and dance, and gymnastic activities?

Are the available equipment and facilities adequate to allow maximum participation?

Are reasonable budgetary allotments made for the program?

Are accurate evaluation procedures carried out and are worthwhile records kept?

Are minimal participation requirements met by all students?

Are participants meeting proper physical education requirements in regard to dressing and showering?

Are proper safety measures taken in all activities?

Are opportunities for developing student leadership being provided in the class program?

Adapted program

Do adequate screening procedures determine all possible participants in this program?

Are adequate facilities, equipment, time, and space made available to the program?

Are proper supervision and instruction afforded each individual participant?

Is medical approval obtained for each individual's regimen of activity?

Do participants engage in some of the regular class work, as well as remedial classes, when advisable?

Are careful records and progress notes kept on each student?

Is the financial allotment to the program reasonable?

Does student achievement indicate the value of the program?

Intramural and extramural sport programs

Are intramural and extramural sports offered to all students in as many activities as possible?

Has participation in these programs increased during the past year?

Is maximum coaching supervision available to players?

Is adequate financial assistance given to this phase of the program?

Are accurate records maintained concerning the participants, their honors, award, and electives?

Does the reward or point system emphasize the joys of participation rather than stress the value of the reward?

Is equipment well cared for and properly stored to gain the most use from it?

Are competitive experiences wholesome and worthwhile for all participants?

Interscholastic sport program

Is financial support for this program provided by the physical education budget?

Is there equitable financial support for all sports in the interscholastic program?

Are interscholastic sports available to all students, boys and girls alike?

Are adequate health standards being met in respect to number of practices and games, fitness of participants, and type of competition?

Is competition provided by schools of a similar size?

Is the program justifiable as an important educational tool?

High school girl performing on the bar, Ridgewood High School, Norridge, Ill.

Are academic standards for participants maintained?

Are good public relations with the community furthered through this program?

Staff

Is the teaching staff well qualified and capable of carrying out the program?

Is the program run efficiently, with little loss of teaching time or space, and is maximum use made of facilities?

Are professional standards maintained regarding class size and teacher assignment?

Is the departmental organization on a democratic basis, with members sharing in the decisions?

Do members of the staff have a professional outlook, attend professional meetings, and keep up with the latest developments in the field?

In what areas have scientific tests and research been made for contribution to the profession?

These are just a few sample questions that may be used in evaluating program management. The key to successful evaluation of this type lies in the follow-up steps for improvement.

Whatever method of program evaluation is selected, it should be realistic, functional, and continuous, in order to fulfill its major purpose of benefiting the participants.

SUMMARY

Management has the responsibility to see that outstanding physical education programs are developed, periodically reviewed, and changed when necessary to better meet the needs of the consumer. This responsibility includes deciding on what goals should be supported, enlisting the help of key individuals in

SUGGESTED OUTLINE OF A SCHOOL CURRICULUM EVALUATION CHECKLIST

The following evaluation checklist for physical education programs suggests methods of assessing curriculum development in this area.

	Yes	No
1. Does the physical education curriculum meet the established objectives?		
2. Does the physical education curriculum provide for the keeping of records to show student progress?		
3. Is evaluation used to help each student in the physical education program find out where he or she is in relation to the program objectives?		
4. Are objective as well as subjective measures used to determine the progress of students in attaining program objectives?		
5. Are the students protected by periodical medical examinations to see if they have health deficiencies?		
6. Does the physical education curriculum provide for the administration of physical fitness tests to evaluate the fitness of each student?		
7. Does the physical education program provide for the testing of skills and use specific ability tests?		
8. Does the physical education curriculum provide for cognitive testing of students?		
9. Does the physical education curriculum provide for the testing of the social adjustment of each student?		
10. Are the attitudes and interests of the students evaluated?		
11. If scientific methods of testing are not feasible, does the physical education curriculum provide for teacher-made tests?		
12. Does the physical education program use test results in planning and assessing units of activity?		
13. Does the physical education curriculum provide for mobility of students based on evaluation results?		
14. Does the physical education curriculum provide for student evaluation as well as teacher evaluation?		
15. Does the physical education program provide for the recognition of curriculum problems and then try to bring about change?		
16. Once change in the curriculum is recognized, is it easy to bring about change?		
17. Is the physical education staff receptive to change?		
18. Is there a provision for ongoing evaluation of programs in reference to satisfying objectives according to an established schedule?		

the construction of the program, taking into account the factors and groups who influence and are influenced by the program, following the proper procedure and selecting the best approach in the development of the program, and being aware of what is happening in the special field for which a program is being developed. In other words, management is responsible for providing effective leadership and support in the developmental process.

SELF-ASSESSMENT TESTS

These tests will assist students in determining if material and competencies presented in this chapter have been mastered.

1. Explain to the class what is meant by program development, the role of the administration in this process, and the ways in which program change occurs.
2. If you were an administrator in a junior high school, what factors would influence the various activities included in your program?
3. You have been assigned to chair a committee to develop a physical education program for a particular school or organization. What people would you select to serve on the committee with you?
4. List and discuss several principles you would observe in developing the curriculum to which you have been assigned in number 3.
5. Trace program development using the systems approach for a high school.
6. You have been hired as a consultant to evaluate a physical education program. Develop a method you will follow in conducting this evaluation.

REFERENCES

1. Goodlad, J.I.: School curriculum in the United States.
2. Heitmann, H.M.: Integrating concepts into curricular models, Journal of Physical Education and Recreation **54**:42, February 1981.
3. Jewett, A.E., and Bain, L.L.: The curriculum process in physical education, Dubuque, Iowa, 1985, Wm. C. Brown Publishers.
4. McNeil, J.D.: Curriculum: a comprehensive introduction, Boston, 1981, Little, Brown & Co., Inc.
5. Pate, R., and Corbin, C.: Implications for curriculum, Journal of Physical Education and Recreation **52**:36, January 1981.
6. Sergiovanni, T.J.: Effective department leadership, Newton, Mass., 1984, Allyn & Bacon, Inc.
7. Smith, N.W.: Community involvement through a curriculum study project, Journal of Physical Education and Recreation **52**:16, June 1981.
8. Woodruff, A.D.: The use of concepts in teaching and learning, Journal of Teacher Education **20**:84, March 1964.

SUGGESTED READINGS

• Gensemer, R.E.: Physical education: perspectives, inquiry, applications, Philadelphia, 1985, Sanders College Publishing.
  Discusses perspectives of the philosophies and principles of physical education and the science of this field of endeavor. Presents information about how the knowledge base of physical education relates to career potentials. Tells what physical education is, what it studies, and how it is used.
• Oliva, P.F.: Developing the curriculum, Boston, 1982, Little, Brown & Co., Inc.
  Provides a comprehensive analysis of the process of curriculum development, curriculum planning, and curriculum improvement. Management personnel will find the book to be a practical guide to curriculum development.
• Rink, J.E.: Teaching physical education for learning, St. Louis, 1985, Times Mirror/Mosby College Publishing.
  Has implications for the implementation of the curriculum in physical education through the improvement of the efficiency of instruction, quality of teaching, and other factors that should be considered in seeing that students reap the greatest benefits from the curriculum. Covers such things as sequential learning experiences.
• Sanborn, M.A., and Hartman, B.G.: Issues in physical education, Philadelphia, 1982, Lea & Febiger.
  Helpful for management personnel who need to make curricular decisions involving types of programs to be supported. Recognizes the issues and resultant problems that can occur.
• Willgoose, C.E.: The curriculum in physical education, Englewood Cliffs, N.J., 1984, Prentice-Hall, Inc.
  Provides help in the development of a curriculum in physical education for all educational levels. Covers such topics as objectives, curriculum planning, research, program organization, the curriculum guide, evaluation, and management guidelines for programs at each educational level.

Chapter Nine

Facility Management

Instructional Objectives and Competencies to be Achieved
After reading this chapter the student should be able to

- Prepare a list of principles that could be used by the management in planning, constructing, and using facilities for physical education and athletic programs.
- List the procedure involved in working with an architect.
- Describe the indoor facilities (type, size, location) needed in physical education and athletic programs and prepare guidelines for managers to follow in planning such facilities.
- Describe the outdoor facilities (type, size, location) needed in physical education and athletic programs and prepare guidelines for managers to follow in planning such facilities.
- Compute the number of teaching stations needed, given the total number of participants, size of classes, and periods per week.
- Discuss new features and developments in the construction of physical education and athletic facilities.
- Show how to provide facilities that will be conducive to a healthful and safe environment for conducting physical education and athletic programs.

Facility management is usually a responsibility of those persons who are in charge of physical education and athletic programs. The facilities for which they are responsible include outdoor facilities such as playgrounds and football fields and indoor facilities such as locker and shower rooms and gymnasia. Facility management includes not only the effective maintenance of such facilities but also at times planning new structures to enhance their programs.

Some recent developments have implications for facility management. The cost of materials and labor is rising as a result of inflation. High interest rates make it difficult to get bond issues passed for facility construction. Facilities must be available to girls, women, and minorities. PL 94-142 and other legislation for the handicapped mandate certain facility changes for the disabled. Energy conservation and costs must be taken into consideration. Community involvement must be given priority in many facility projects.

That little or no money is available in some situations has resulted in alternative methods for seeing that physical education and athletic programs have the necessary facilities to conduct excellent programs.

Methods such as renovating existing structures and instituting multiple use of present facilities are being adopted. Where funds are limited, cost-cutting involves following construction plans that are most economical in cost and in the use of energy.

Physical plants require careful planning and consultation with specialists in architectural planning. Managers, physical educators, and other personnel should participate in planning new facilities and be knowledgeable about their structure and functions. Trends and innovative structural concepts should be thoroughly examined to provide a healthful and efficient physical plant.

The physical plant is a major consideration in most physical education, athletic, and recreational programs. New architectural ideas are being introduced and new concepts developed to have a more economical and functional plant. Some building concepts include *convertibility,* for example, rearranging interiors by using movable walls and partitions and using the gymnasium and ampitheater for a variety of activities such as basketball, ice skating, and baseball. Such versatility is needed to accommodate a number of different activities so small and large group instruction and independent study spaces may be provided. This flexibility also ensures such important functions as team teaching and proper installation and use of electronic aids.

Many excellent books are devoted exclusively to facilities for physical education and athletics. Some of these are listed at the end of this chapter. They should be consulted by physical educators who desire a more thorough treatment of this subject.

PLANNING THE FACILITY

At the outset two principles relating to facility management should be uppermost in the minds of physical educators: (1) facilities emanate as a result of program needs, and (2) cooperative planning is essential to avoid common mistakes. The objectives, activities, teaching methods and materials, management policies, equipment and supplies represent program considerations regarding facilities. The educational and recreational needs of both the school and community, the thinking of both managers and physical educators, and the advice of both architects and lay

persons are other considerations if facilities are to be planned wisely.

Management guidelines and principles for facility planning that apply to all educational levels and organizations include the following:

All planning should be based on goals that recognize that the total physical and nonphysical environments must be safe, attractive, comfortable, clean, practical, and adapted to the needs of the individual.

Facilities should be economical to maintain.

The planning should include a consideration of the total school health and physical education facilities and the recreational facilities of the community. The programs and facilities of these areas are essential to any community. Because they are closely allied, they should be planned coordinately and based on the needs of the community. Each should be a part of the overall community pattern.

Facilities should be geared to health standards, which are important in protecting the health of individuals and in determining the outcomes.

Facilities should be easily accessible for individuals who will be using them.

Facilities play a part in disease control. The extent to which organizations provide ample play area space, sanitary considerations, proper ventilation, heating, and cleanliness will to some extent determine how effectively disease is controlled.

Managers must make plans for facilities long before an architect is consulted. Technical information can be obtained in the forms of standards and guides from various sources, such as state departments of education, professional literature, building score cards, and various manuals. Information can also be secured from important groups such as the American Association of School Administrators and the American Institute of Architects.

Standards used as guides and as a starting point will prove helpful. However, it is important to keep in mind that standards cannot always be used entirely as developed. They usually have to be modified in light of local needs, conditions, and resources.

Building and sanitary codes administered by the local and state departments of public health and the technical advice and consultation services available through these sources should be known and used by

U.S. Olympic Training
Center.

U.S. OLYMPIC COMPLEX   **OLYMPIC TRAINING CENTER**   **COLORADO SPRINGS**

U.S. Olympic Training Center—Colorado Springs, Colorado

Boxing facilities at the U.S. Olympic Training Center

Photos by Dave Black

managers during the planning and construction of facilities. Information concerned with acceptable building materials, specifications, minimum standards of sanitation, and other details may be procured from these sources.

Physical education and recreation personnel should play important roles in planning and operating facilities. The specialized knowledge that such individuals have is important. Provisions should be made so their expert opinion will be used to promote a healthful and proper environment.

Facilities should be planned with an eye to the future. Too often, facilities are constructed and outgrown within a very short time. Units should be large enough to accommodate peak-load participation for various activities. The peak-load estimates should be made with future growth in mind.

Planning should provide adequate allotment of space to the activity and program areas, which should receive priority in space allotment. The management offices and service units, although important, should not be planned and developed in a spacious and luxurious manner that goes beyond efficiency and necessity.

Geographical and climatic conditions should be considered when planning facilities. By doing this, the full potential for conducting activities outdoors as well as indoors can be realized.

Architects do not always pay as much attention as they should to the educational and health features when planning buildings and facilities. Therefore it is important that they be briefed on certain requirements that physical educators feel are essential so the health and welfare of children, youth, and adults may be provided for. Such a procedure is usually welcomed by the architect and will aid him or her in rendering a greater service to the community.

Facilities should include all the safety features essential in physical education programs. Health service substations near the gymnasium and other play areas, proper surfacing of activity areas, adequate space, and proper lighting are a few of these considerations.

The construction of school physical education facilities often tends to set a pattern that will influence parents, civic leaders, and others. This in turn promotes a healthful and safe environment for the entire community.

The physically handicapped should be considered in the planning.

Facilities should be planned primarily for the participants.

Planning for schools should take into consideration the types of activities in the programs at each educational level.

SELECTED HEALTH CONSIDERATIONS IN FACILITY PLANNING

The participant must be given a safe, healthful, pleasant, and emotionally secure environment. The environment also includes the outdoors, where everything possible should be done to control land, water, and air pollution. The total environment must also be healthful and pleasant for staff members, faculty members, and employees.

Another set of principles basic to facility planning concerns the optimal promotion of a healthful environment for participants. Included in this set of principles is the provision for facilities that consider the physiological needs of the participant, including proper temperature control, lighting, water supply, and noise level. A second principle is to provide safe facilities. The facilities should be planned so the danger of fire, the possibility of mechanical accidents, and the hazards involved in traffic would be eliminated or kept to a minimum. A third principle is concerned with protection against disease. This means attention to items such as proper sewage disposal, sanitation procedures, and water supply. Finally, a fourth principle is the need to provide a healthful psychological environment. This has implications for space, location of activities, color schemes, and elimination of distractions through such means as soundproof construction.

The general health features of the physical environment include site, building, lighting, heating and ventilation, plant sanitation, and acoustics.

Site. There are many aspects to consider in selecting a suitable site. These considerations will differ, depending on the community. Whether it is a rural or an urban community will have a bearing on the location of the site. In an urban community it is desirable to have a school situated near transportation facilities but at the same time located away from industrial concerns, railroads, noise, heavy traffic, fumes, and

America's Olympic hopefuls call Colorado Springs home.

U.S. OLYMPIC COMPLEX **OLYMPIC TRAINING CENTER** **COLORADO SPRINGS**

America's Olympic Hopefuls Call Colorado Springs Home

Photo by Robert F. George

U.S. Olympic Sports Center at the Olympic Complex in Colorado Springs

Photo by Dave Black

smoke. Consideration should be given to the trends in population movements and future development of the area in which the buildings are planned. Adequate space for play and recreation should be provided. Some standards concerning schools recommend 5 acres of land for elementary schools, 10 to 12 acres for junior high schools, and 20 acres for senior high schools. The play area should consist of a minimum of 100 square feet for every child.

Attention should be given to the esthetic features of a site because of its effect on the physical and emotional well-being of participants and staff members. The surroundings should be well landscaped, attractive, and free from disturbing noises or odors.

Building. The trend in schools is toward one-story construction at the precollege level where possible, with stress on planning from a functional rather than an ornamental point of view. The building should be constructed for *use*. The materials used should make the building attractive and safe. Every precaution should be taken to protect against accidents, fire, slippery floors, and other dangers. The walls should be painted with light colors and treated acoustically. Doors should open outward. Space for clothing should be provided. Provisions for handicapped persons, including ramps and toilet facilities, are major considerations.

Lighting. Proper lighting is important to conserve vision, prevent fatigue, and improve morale. In the past it had been recommended that natural light should come into the room from the left and that artificial light should be provided as needed. There is a trend now toward allowing natural light from more than one direction. Artificial light, moreover, should come from many sources rather than one to prevent too much concentration of light in one place. Switches for artificial light should be located in many parts of the room.

In gymnasiums and swimming pools light intensity should range from 10 to 80 footcandles, depending on the activity being conducted.

Glare is undesirable and should be eliminated. Fluorescent lights should be properly installed and adjusted for best results. Strong contrasts of color

Fitness center at Riverside-Brookfield High School, Riverside, Ill.

such as light walls and dark floors should be avoided if possible.

Heating and ventilation. Efficiency in the classroom, gymnasium, special activities rooms, and other places is determined to some extent by thermal comfort, which is mainly determined by heating and ventilation.

The purposes of heating and ventilation are to remove excess heat, unpleasant odors, and, in some cases, gases, vapors, fumes, and dust from the room; to prevent rapid temperature fluctuations; to diffuse the heat within a room; and to supply heat to counteract loss from the human body through radiation and otherwise.

Heating standards vary according to the activities engaged in, the clothing worn by the participants, and the section of the country.

Concerning ventilation, the range of recommendations is from 8 to 21 cubic feet of fresh air per minute per occupant. Adequate ventilating systems are especially needed in dressing, shower, and locker rooms, toilet rooms, gymnasiums, and swimming pools. The recommended humidity ranges from 35% to 60%. The type and amount of ventilation will vary with the specific needs of the particular area.

Plant sanitation. Plant sanitation should not be overlooked. Sanitation facilities should be well planned and maintained. The water supply should be safe and adequate. If any question exists, the health department should be consulted. Concerning water supply, one authority suggests that at least 20 gallons per individual per day is needed for all purposes.

Drinking fountains of various heights should be recessed in corridor walls and should be of material that is easily cleaned. A stream of water should flow from the fountain so it is not necessary for the mouth of the drinker to get too near the drain bowl.

Water closets, urinals, lavatories, and washroom equipment such as soap dispensers, toilet paper holders, waste containers, mirrors, bookshelves, and hand-drying facilities should be provided as needed, also keeping the handicapped person in mind.

Waste disposal should be adequately cared for. There should be provision for cleanup and removal of paper and other materials that make the grounds and buildings a health and safety hazard, as well as unsightly. Proper sewage disposal and prompt garbage disposal should also be provided.

Acoustics. Noise distracts, causes nervous strain, and results in the loss of many of the activity's benefits. Therefore noise should be eliminated as effectively as possible. This can be achieved by acoustical treatment of such important places as corridors, gymnasiums, and swimming pools.

Acoustical materials include plasters, fibers, boards, tiles, and various fabrics. Floor covering that reduces noise can be used in corridors, and acoustical material can be used in walls. Swimming pools and gymnasiums need special treatment to control the various noises associated with enthusiastic play partici-

Varsity crew in rowing tank with mirrors.

ROLE OF MANAGEMENT IN FACILITY ADMINISTRATION

Kraus and Curtis[8] have indicated the role of administrators in facility management. They are presented here in the following adapted form:

- The administration should familiarize itself with background information pertinent to the facility plan and should be actively involved in all planning sessions.
- The administration should meet and discuss the facility project with all people who have a stake in the project. The administration should be familiar with the views of such people and consider their suggestions carefully.
- The administration should insist on being involved in selecting the architect or engineer who is going to do the plan. The administration should press strongly for selecting competent and qualified people to do the job rather than the lowest bidder or firm with political connections.
- The administration should be at all planning conferences to present the department's point of view and programs to be considered.
- The administration should visit the site regularly after construction begins. All problems should be noted and a follow-up of recognized errors made.
- The administration should insist that all details and standards incorporated in the project plan be carried out exactly as specified. The administration should not approve any facility or authorize payment unless this has been done.

---

pation. Ceiling and wall acoustical treatment helps control noises in the gymnasium, whereas mineral acoustical material, which will not be affected by high humidity, is helpful in the swimming pool.

DETERMINING NUMBER OF TEACHING STATIONS NEEDED

The teaching station concept should be considered when scheduling physical education classes. A teaching station is the space or setting where one teacher or staff member can carry on physical education activities for one group of students. The number and size of teaching stations available together with the number of teachers on the staff, the size of the group, the number of times the group meets, the number of periods in the school or college day, and the program of activities are important items to consider when planning.

According to the participants in the National Facilities Conference,[3] the following formulas help determine the number of teaching stations needed.

Elementary schools

The formula for computing the number of teaching stations needed for physical education in the elementary schools is:

$$\text{Minimum number of teaching stations} = \frac{\text{Number of classrooms of students} \times \dfrac{\text{Number of physical education periods per week per class}}{\text{Total periods in school week}}}{}$$

For example, in an elementary school with six grades, with three classes at each level (approximately 450 to 540 students), ten 30-minute physical education periods per day, and physical education conducted on a daily basis, the teaching station needs are calculated as follows:

$$\text{Minimum number of teaching stations} = 18 \text{ classroom units} \times \frac{5 \text{ periods per week}}{50 \text{ periods per week}} = \frac{90}{50} = 1.8$$

Secondary schools and colleges

The formula for computing the number of teaching stations needed for physical education in colleges and secondary schools is as follows:

$$\text{Minimum number of teaching stations} = \frac{\text{Number of students}}{\text{Average number of students per instructor}} \times \frac{\text{Number of periods class meets each week}}{\text{Total number of class periods in school week}}$$

For example, if a school system projects its enrollment to 700 students and plans six class periods a day with an average class size of 30 students, and physical education is required daily, the formula is as follows:

$$\text{Minimum number of teaching stations} = \frac{700 \text{ students}}{30 \text{ per class}} \times$$

$$\frac{5 \text{ periods per week}}{30 \text{ periods per week}} = \frac{3,500}{900} = 3.9$$

Colleges should substitute pertinent facts into the same formula to determine the number of teaching stations they would need.

THE TEAM APPROACH TO FACILITY PLANNING

Facility planning requires a team approach that includes the architect, consultants, and physical education and athletic professionals. Flynn[7] has indicated the steps that should be followed in achieving the best results from the team approach. *First,* form a planning team that will identify needs and prepare a project proposal. Included on this team would be the project coordinator for the organization for whom the facility is being planned, the architect, and a specialist from physical education. Team members should understand the role each plays in the planning process. *Second,* hire a consultant during the early stages of the project because the other team members usually do not have expertise in all aspects of programming and design. The consultant can help in closing the gap between architectural theory and physical education and athletic practice. *Third,* stress faculty and staff member involvement to provide information about special areas and facilities for which they are responsible. For example, a biomechanist, exercise physiologist, adapted physical education teacher, or dance instructor could provide information about his or her projected laboratory or other facility. *Fourth,* visit other facilities in other locations to obtain ideas that may contribute to a better facility. The planning team should also be alert when making recommendations for controlling maintenance and operational costs as much as possible after the facility has been built. When construction is underway, not only the architect and consultant but also the physical education and athletic specialist should monitor the work

going on. By doing this many errors can be avoided or corrected.

WORKING WITH THE ARCHITECT

The architect is the specialist in facility planning and the leader in designing physical education facilities. The architect, through his or her training and experience, is a specialist who is competent to give advisory service in all aspects of facility management.

Ferreri,[6] a chief operations officer for a group of architects in Illinois, points out that a successful relationship between the architect and the school is a very important consideration. Lines of communication within the school, between the school and the architect, and within the architect's office must be based on mutual understanding. Communication about program needs and space requirements must be continual. These are the hallmarks, he says, of the happy and successful facility planner.

Physical educators should carefully think through their own ideas and plans for their special facilities and submit them in writing to the architect during the early stages of planning. The architect and physical education specialist should have several conferences in which they exchange views and consider architectural possibilities.

Many architects know little about physical education programs and therefore welcome the advice of specialists. The architect might be furnished with such information as the names of plants where excellent facilities exist, kinds of activities that will constitute the program, space requirements for various activities, storage and equipment areas needed, temperature requirements, relation of dressing, showering, and toilet facilities to program, teaching stations needed, best construction materials for activities, and lighting requirements. The physical educator may not have all this information readily available, including some of the latest trends and standards recommended for his or her field. However, such information can be obtained through professional organizations, other schools and organizations where excellent facilities have been developed, and facility books developed by experts in the area.

Mr. William Haroldson, former Director of Health and Physical Education for the Seattle, Washington, public schools, developed a procedural outline in co-operation with three architectural firms, which lists some essential considerations for physical educators when planning with architects. Some of the main points from this outline are discussed here.

Educational specifications. Adequate educational specifications provide the basis for good planning by the architect:

1. General description of the program, such as the number of teaching stations necessary to service the physical education program for a total student body of approximately _____ boys and _____ girls
2. Basic criteria that pertain to the gymnasium: the number of teaching periods per day, capacities, number, and size of courts, lockers, and projected total uses contemplated for the facility
   a. Availability to the community
   b. Proximity to parks
   c. Parking
   d. Size of groups that will use gymnasium after school hours
   e. Whether locker rooms will or will not be made available for public use
3. Specific description of aspects of the physical education program that affect the architects
   a. Class size and scheduling, both present and future; number of instructors, present and future
   b. Preferred method of handling students, for example, flow of traffic in classrooms, locker rooms, shower rooms, and going to outside play area (This item has a direct bearing on the design of this area.)
   c. Storage requirements and preferred method of handling all permanent equipment and supplies (Here, unless a standard has been established, requirements should be specific—for example, request should state number and size of each item rather than "ample storage.")
   d. Team and other extracurricular use of facilities (It helps the architect if the educational specifications can describe a typical week's use of the proposed facility, which would include a broad daily program, afterschool use, and potential community use.)

Meeting with the architect. At this point, it is advisable to meet with the architect to discuss specifications to ensure complete understanding and to allow the architect to point out certain restrictions or limitations that may be anticipated even before the first preliminary plan is made.

Design. The factors to be considered in the design of the facility and discussed with the architect should include the following:

1. *Budget.* An adequate budget should be allowed. Gymnasiums are subject to extremely hard use, and durability should not be sacrificed for economy.
2. *Acoustics.* Use the service of acoustical consultants.
3. *Public address system.* How is it to be used—for instruction, athletic events, general communication?
4. *Color and design.* Compatible with surrounding neighborhood.
5. *Fenestration* (window treatment). Consider light control, potential window breakage, vision panel; gymnasium areas should have safety glass (preferred) or wire protectors.
6. *Ventilation.* The area should be zoned for flexibility of use. This means greater ventilation when a larger number of spectators are present, or a reduction for single class groups, or isolated areas, such as locker rooms. Special attention must be given to proper ventilation of uniform drying rooms, gymnasium storage areas, locker and shower areas. (Current and off-season uniform storage areas require constant ventilation when plant is shut down.) Ventilation equipment should have a low noise level.
7. *Supplementary equipment in the gymnasium.* Such equipment should be held to a minimum. Supplementary equipment, such as fire boxes, should be recessed.
8. *Compactness and integration.* Keep volume compact—large, barnlike spaces are unpleasant and are costly to heat and maintain. Integrate as far as budget permits.
9. *Mechanical or electrical features.* Special attention should be given to location of panel boards, chalk boards, fire alarm, and folding doors.

Further critique with the architect. The architect begins to develop plans from an understanding of the initial requirements he or she has considered in relation to the design factors listed.

When the basic plan is set, the architect will usually call in consulting engineers to discuss the structural and mechanical systems before approval of the plan. These systems will have been outlined by the architect but cannot be discussed with the consultants other

Super tent at LaVerne College, Calif.

than in generalities before the plan is in approximate final form.

More meetings are then held regarding approval of preliminary plans and proposed structural and mechanical systems and the use of materials after the incorporation in the preliminary plans.

If supplementary financing by governmental agencies is involved, the drawing or set of drawings will have been submitted to those agencies with a project outline or specifications as soon as the plan has been sufficiently developed to establish the area. If the agency approves the application as submitted by the architect, the final preliminary working drawings are started.

Final processing. It is advisable to settle all matters that can be settled during preliminary planning to save time. If this method is used, greater clarity is assured and less changing or misunderstanding results. Preliminary plans are drawn with the intent of illustrating the plan; working drawings are technical and often difficult to interpret. However, if physical educators from the school wish to check the working drawings before their completion, they should be welcome to do so.

INDOOR FACILITIES

Several special areas and facilities are needed by physical education and athletic programs.

Management and staff offices

It is important, as far as practical and possible, for physical educators and athletic directors to have a section of a building set aside for management and staff offices. The minimum area should be a large central office with a waiting room. The central office provides a place where secretarial and clerical work can be performed, space for keeping records and files, and storage closets for office supplies. The waiting room can serve as a reception point where persons can wait until staff members are ready to see them.

Separate offices for the staff members should be provided, if possible. This provides a place where conferences can be held in private and without interruption. This is an important consideration for health counseling and for discussing scholastic, family, recreational, and other problems. If separate offices are not practical, a desk should be provided for each staff member. There should then be a private room available to staff members for conferences.

Other facilities that make the administrative and staff setup more efficient and enjoyable are staff dressing rooms, department library, conference room, and toilet and lavatory facilities.

Locker, shower, and drying rooms

Physical education and athletic activities require facilities for storage of clothes, showering, and drying. These are essential to good health and a well-organized program.

Locker and shower rooms should be readily accessible to activity areas. Locker rooms should not be congested places that persons want to get out of as soon as possible. Instead, they should provide ample room for storage and dressing lockers, stationary benches, mirrors, recessed lighting fixtures, and drinking fountains.

An average of 14 square feet per individual at peak load exclusive of the locker space is generally required to provide proper space.

Storage lockers should be provided for each individual. An additional 10% should be installed for expanded enrollments or membership. These lockers are for the permanent use of each individual and can be used to hold essential clothing and other supplies. They can be smaller than the dressing lockers; some recommended sizes are 7½ by 12 by 24 inches, 6 by 12 by 36 inches, and 7½ by 12 by 18 inches. Basket lockers are not favored by many experts because of hygiene problems, because an attendant is required for good administration of this system, and because of the necessity of carting the baskets from place to place.

Dressing lockers are used by participants only when actually engaging in activity. They are large, usually 12 by 12 by 54 inches or 12 by 12 by 48 inches in elementary schools, and 12 by 12 by 72 inches for secondary schools and colleges and for community recreation programs.

Shower rooms that have both group and cubicle showers should be provided. Some facility planners recommend that girls and women have a number of shower heads equal to 40% of the enrollment at peak load, and boys and men, 30% of the enrollment at peak load. Another recommendation is one shower head for four boys or men and one for three girls or

---

COMMON ERRORS MADE BY PHYSICAL EDUCATORS IN FACILITY MANAGEMENT

Some common mistakes made by physical educators and athletic directors in facility planning and management include the following:

- Failure to adequately project enrollments and program needs into the future (Facilities are difficult to expand or change, so this is a significant error.)
- Failure to provide for multiple use of facilities
- Failure to provide for adequate accessibility for students in physical education classes and also for community groups for recreation
- Failure to observe basic health factors regarding lighting, safety, and ventilation when planning facilities
- Failure to provide adequate space for the conduct of a comprehensive program of physical education activities
- Failure to provide appropriate accommodations for spectators
- Failure to soundproof areas of the building where noise will interfere with educational functions
- Failure to meet with the architect to present views on program needs
- Failure to provide adequate staff offices
- Failure to provide adequate storage space
- Failure to provide adequate space and privacy for medical examinations
- Failure to provide entrances large enough to transport equipment
- Failure to observe desirable current professional standards
- Failure to provide for adequate study of cost in terms of durability, time, money, and effective instruction
- Failure to properly locate teaching stations with service facilities

Locker room at the University of
Notre Dame accents a healthy
environment for athletes.

Gymnasium, McPherson High
School, McPherson, Kan.

women at peak load. These should be 4 feet apart. If showers are installed where a graded change of water temperature is provided and where the individual progresses through such a gradation, the number of shower heads can be reduced. The shower rooms should also be equipped with liquid soap dispensers, good ventilation and heating, nonslip floors, and recessed plumbing. The ceiling should be dome-shaped so it will more readily shed water.

The drying room adjacent to the shower room is essential. This should be equipped with proper drainage, good ventilation, towel bar, and a ledge that can be used to place a foot on while drying.

Special attention should be paid to the health aspects of shower facilities. The shower room should be kept clean, and soap and warm water should be available. Proper heating and ventilation should be provided; a nonslip floor surface should be installed; and ceilings should be constructed to prevent condensation. The drying area should be washed daily to prevent athlete's foot and other contaminations. A towel service should be initiated if it does not already exist.

Locker rooms should provide dressing and storage lockers for all participants. Adequate space should be provided so dressing is not done in cramped quarters.

Gymnasiums

The type and number of gymnasiums that should be part of a school or organizational plant depend on the number of individuals who will be participating and the variety of activities that will be conducted in this area.

The publication *Athletic Business*[2] lists some suggestions to consider when building or renovating a gymnasium. One of the major suggestions is to save money on the square footage, not on dollars per square foot. The wrong time to save money, they point out, is when considering building materials. With careful planning it is possible to buy the best materials and finishes. The publication also suggests that it is important to visit other facilities to find out the advantages and disadvantages of those in use.

General construction features include smooth walls, hardwood floors (maple preferred—laid lengthwise), recessed lights, recessed radiators, adequately screened windows, and storage space for the apparatus and other equipment. It is also generally agreed that in schools it is best to have the gymnasium located in a separate wing of the building to isolate the noise and to provide convenient location for community groups that will be anxious to use such facilities.

COMMON ERRORS IN PHYSICAL EDUCATION SERVICE FACILITIES*

- Failure to provide adequate locker and dressing space
- Failure to plan dressing and shower area so as to reduce foot traffic to a minimum and establish clean, dry aisles for bare feet
- Failure to provide a nonskid surface on dressing, shower, and toweling room floors
- Failure to properly relate teaching stations with service facilities
- Inadequate provision for drinking fountains
- Failure to provide acoustical treatment where needed
- Failure to provide and properly locate toilet facilities to serve all participants and spectators
- Failure to provide doorways, hallways, or ramps so that equipment may be moved easily
- Failure to design equipment rooms for convenient and quick check-in and check-out
- Failure to provide mirrors and shelving for boys' and girls' dressing facilities
- Failure to plan locker and dressing rooms with correct traffic pattern to swimming pool
- Failure to construct shower, toilet, and dressing rooms with sufficient floor slope and properly located drains
- Failure to place shower heads low enough and in such a position that the spray is kept within the shower room
- Failure to provide shelves in the toilet room

*A report of a conference sponsored by the Athletic Institute and the AAHPERD on the planning of facilities for health, physical education, and recreation.

GUIDELINES FOR GYMNASIUM PLANNING

- Hard maple flooring that is resilient and nonslippery
- Smooth interior walls to a height of 10 or 12 feet, upper walls need not be smooth
- The ceiling should reflect light and absorb sound, and there should be at least 22 to 24 feet from the floor to exposed beams
- Windows should be 10 to 12 feet above floor and placed on long side of room
- Heating should be thermostatically controlled, radiators recessed with protecting grill or grate if placed at floor level
- Subflooring should be moisture- and termite-resistant and well ventilated
- Suspension of apparatus from the ceiling and the erection of wall-type apparatus must be well planned
- Mechanical ventilation may be necessary
- Proper illumination meeting approved standards and selectively controlled for various activities must be designed
- Floor plates for standards and apparatus must be planned, as well as such items as blackboards, electric clocks and scoreboards, public address system, and provisions for press and radio
- Floor markings for various games should be placed after prime coat of seal has been applied and before application of the finishing coats

---

Many gymnasiums have folding doors that divide them into halves, thirds, or fourths and allow activities to be conducted simultaneously on each side. This has proved satisfactory where separate gymnasiums could not be provided.

In elementary schools that need only one teaching station, a minimum floor space of 36 by 52 feet is suggested. Where two teaching stations are desired, floor space of 54 by 90 feet may be divided by a folding partition.

In junior and senior high schools where only one teaching station is desired, a minimum floor space of 48 by 66 feet is necessary. An area 66 by 96 feet exclusive of bleachers will provide two teaching stations of minimum size. The folding partition that provides the two teaching stations should be motor driven. Where seating capacity is desired, additional space will be needed. If more than two teaching stations are desired, the gymnasium area may be extended to provide an additional station or activity rooms may be added. Of course, the addition of a swimming pool also provides an additional teaching station.

Other considerations for gymnasiums should include provisions for basketball backboards, mountings for various apparatus that will be used, recessed drinking fountains, places for hanging mats, outlets for various electric appliances and cleaning devices, proper line markings for activities, bulletin boards, and other essentials of a well-rounded program.

Just as safe and properly constructed equipment should be a part of outdoor facilities, so should they be a part of indoor physical education facilities. Adequate space should be provided for all the activity phases of the program, whether they are in the gymnasium, swimming pool, or auxiliary areas. Mats should be used as a protective measure on walls and other areas where participants may be injured. Drinking fountains should be recessed and doors should open away from the playing floor. Proper flooring should be used—tile-cement floors are sometimes undesirable where activity takes place. Space should be provided for the handicapped where persons in wheelchairs and on crutches can be accommodated.

Clothing and equipment used in physical education activities should meet health standards. If not, odors and germs will thrive, causing an unpleasant environment that may help spread disease. Gymnasium mats, for example, should be kept clean. Regular physical education clothing, not street clothes, should be worn except in social dancing or similar activities. Clean clothing, including all types of athletic costumes, should be required. Footwear should be fitted properly, and socks should be clean.

Guidelines in gymnasium planning. The following guidelines are valid for administrators, architects, board members, and other persons involved in gymnasium planning. Many of these guidelines are overlooked by those responsible for gymnasium construction.

The roof. If the roof is not properly designed before construction, costly changes in equipment installation may occur later. Ceiling support beams are also essential for the physical educator to make maximal use of the facility. The design of the roof should allow for support beams strong enough to absorb the stress placed on them in various activities. Support beams should be placed to allow maximal flexibility in the location of apparatus. The design should also consider the placement of gymnastic apparatus so students are saved from obstructions in the event of falls.

The floor. The floor is a vital part of the gymnasium and should be constructed from hardwood, not tile. Although expensive, hardwood is safer, does not become slick, and is better for athletic performance. Plates for floor apparatus such as the high bar should be designed with safety and flexibility in mind.

The walls. Electrical outlets should be provided throughout the gymnasium so audiovisual areas can be used at each activity station. Walls behind baskets should be recessed and padded. This is safer than hanging pads near glazed tile walls. It is a good idea to provide a wall for participants to practice their tennis skills. A line should be painted along the wall to indicate the height of the tennis net. The wall can also be used for hardball and other ball skills.

Lighting. Adequate durable lighting with recessed fixtures is essential. This helps prevent bulb breakage from ball activities.

Acoustics. Noise control should be a primary consideration in any gymnasium construction. Acoustic treatment of ceilings and walls can help reduce or eliminate noise.

Special activity areas. Although gymnasiums take up considerable space, there should still be additional areas for activities essential to physical education and athletic programs.

Wherever possible, additional activity areas should be provided for remedial or adapted activities, apparatus, handball, squash, weight lifting, dancing, rhythms, fencing, dramatics, and for various recreational activities, such as arts and crafts, lounging and resting, and bowling. The activities to be provided will depend on interests of participants and type of program. The recommended size of such auxiliary gymnasiums is 30 by 50 by 24 feet, or 40 by 60 by 24 feet. A 75 by 90 foot auxiliary gymnasium is ideal.

It should also be pointed out that regulation class-

Special tennis structure, Brigham Young University, Provo, Utah.

Tennis courts, Sinclair Community College, Dayton, Ohio.

rooms and other space can be converted into these special rooms. This may be feasible where the actual construction of such costly facilities may not be practical.

The remedial or adapted activities room should be equipped with items such as horizontal ladders, mirrors, mats, climbing ropes, stall bars and benches, pulley weights, dumbbells, Indian clubs, shoulder wheels, and other equipment suited to the needs of the individuals participating.

Auxiliary rooms. The main auxiliary rooms are supply, check-out, custodial, and laundry rooms.

Supply rooms should be easily accessible from the gymnasium and other activity areas. In these rooms balls, nets, standards, and other equipment needed for the program are stored. The size of these rooms varies according to the number of activities offered and the number of participants.

Check-out rooms should be provided seasonally. They house the equipment and supplies used in various seasonal activities.

Custodial rooms provide a place for storing equipment and supplies used to maintain these specialized facilities.

Laundries should be large enough to accommodate the washing of such essential items as towels, uniforms, and swimsuits.

Indoor swimming pools

Major design decisions must be made if an organization decides to construct a pool. These include items such as the nature of the program to be conducted in a pool, type of overflow system, dimensions and shape of pool, depth of the water, type of finish, type of filters and water treatment system, construction material, amount of deck area, climate control, illumination, and number of spectators to be accommodated.

Some mistakes that should be avoided in the construction of a pool include entrances to the pool from the locker rooms opening onto the deep rather than the shallow end of the pool, pool base finished with slippery material such as glazed tile, insufficient depth of water for diving, improper placement of ladders, insufficient rate of recirculation of water to accommodate peak bathing loads, inadequate storage space, failure to use acoustic material on ceiling and walls, insufficient illumination, slippery tile on decks, and an inadequate overflow system at the ends of the pool.

Some trends and innovations in pool design and operation include: the Rim-Flow Overflow System, inflatable roof structure, the skydome design, pool tent cover, floating swimming pool complex, prefabrication of pool tanks, automation of pool recirculating and filter systems, regenerative cycle filter system, adjustable height diving platform, variable depth bottoms, fluorescent underwater lights, automatic cleaning systems, and wave-making machines.

Swimming pools have two main objectives: to provide instructional and competitive programs and to provide recreation.

The swimming pool should be located on or above the ground level, have a southern exposure, be isolated from other units in the building, and be easily accessible from the central dressing and locker rooms. Materials that have been found most adaptive to swimming pools are smooth, glazed, light-colored tile or brick.

The standard indoor pool is 75 feet long. The width should be a multiple of 7 feet, with a minimum of 35 feet. Depths vary from 2 feet 6 inches at the shallow end to 4 feet 6 inches at the outer limits of the shallow area. The shallow or instructional area should comprise about two thirds of the pool. The deeper areas taper to 9 to 12 feet deep. An added but important factor is a movable bulkhead that can be used to divide the pool into various instructional areas.

The deck space around the pool should be constructed of a nonslip material and provide ample space for land drills and demonstrations. The area above the water should be unobstructed. The ceiling should be at least 25 feet above the water if a 3-meter diving board will be used. The walls and the ceiling of the pool area should be acoustically treated.

The swimming pool should be constructed to receive as much natural light as possible, with the windows located on the sides rather than on the ends. Artificial lighting should be recessed in the ceilings. Good lighting is especially important near the diving boards. Underwater lighting is beautiful but not essential.

There should be an efficient system for adequately heating and circulating the water. The temperature of the water should range from 75° to 80° F.

If spectators are to be provided for, a gallery sepa-

Swimming pool complex, Brigham Young University, Provo, Utah.

Swimming pool, Sinclair
Community College,
Dayton, Ohio.

SUGGESTED SWIMMING POOL REGULATIONS*

- Everyone using the pool should have a bath with soap and water.
- Pupils should expectorate only in the overflow trough.
- Boys and men should swim in the nude or wear sanitized trunks. Girls and women should wear sanitized tank suits.
- Girls and boys with long hair should wear rubber bathing caps. Caps keep hair, dandruff, and hair oil from contaminating the water and also keep hair out of the eyes.
- Pupils with evidence of skin infection, eye infection, respiratory disease, open cuts or sores, or bandages should be excluded from using the pool.
- There must be no rough or boisterous play and no running or playing tag in or around the pool area.
- Pupils should wear ear plugs or nose clips if these have been recommended by their physicians. Some pupils, on medical recommendation, may need to be excused at least temporarily from participation in the aquatic program.
- A qualified person, either the instructor or other person qualified as a lifeguard, should be on duty whenever the pool is in use. No pupil should enter the pool unless a guard is present. All doors leading to the pool should be locked when the pool is not in use and a guard is not on duty.
- Since dirt from shoes may be tracked into the pool and contaminate the water, spectators should be prohibited from entering the pool deck.

*Pool regulations advocated by the National Education Association and the American Medical Association.

rate from the pool room proper should be erected along the length of the pool.

An office adjacent to the pool where records and first aid supplies can be kept is advisable. Such an office should be equipped with windows that overlook the entire length of the pool. Also, lavatory and toilet facilities should be available.

The swimming pool is a costly operation. Therefore it is essential that it be planned with the help of the best advice obtainable. Specialists who are well acquainted with such facilities and who conduct swimming activities should be brought into conferences with the architect, a representative from the public health department, and experts in essentials such as lighting, heating, construction, and acoustics.

Health considerations for swimming pools

Swimming pools need special attention whether indoor or outdoor. First, the pool should be properly constructed to provide for adequate filtration, circulation, and chlorination. A daily diary should be kept on things such as water temperature, hydrogen ion concentration, residual chlorine, and other important matters. Regulations for pool use should be established, and students should be acquainted with them.

Athletic training and health service facilities

Athletic training and health services are an important part of the program and require adequate facilities. They are discussed in Chapter 12.

OUTDOOR FACILITIES

The outdoor facilities discussed in this section are play areas, game areas, outdoor swimming pools, and camps.

Play areas

Many factors must be considered when planning outdoor facilities for schools and colleges. Before a site is selected, it is important to appraise the location, topography, soil drainage, water supply, size, shape, and natural features. The outdoor facilities should be as near the gymnasium and locker rooms as possible and yet far enough from the classrooms so the noise will not be disturbing.

The play areas should serve the needs and interests of the students for the entire school year and at the same time should provide a setting for activities during vacation periods. The needs and interests of the community must also be considered, for the play areas can be used for some community recreation programs. This is especially important in some communities where facilities such as education and recreation centers can be planned. Because the community uses the areas after the school day is over, the plan is feasible.

The size of the playground area should be determined on the basis of activities offered in the program and the number of individuals who will be using the facilities at peak load. Possibilities for expansion should also be kept in mind. Playing fields and playgrounds should have good turf and be clear of rocks, holes, and uneven surfaces. A dirty, dusty surface, for example, can aggravate conditions such as emphysema, chronic bronchitis, and allergies. Artificial turf is now being used more and more; however, it needs several improvements to reduce injuries and other problems associated with it. Safety precautions should also be provided in terms of well-lined areas, regularly inspected equipment, and fenced-in playfields and playgrounds, particularly where there is heavy traffic adjoining these facilities. Rubber asphalt, synthetic materials, and other substances that require little maintenance and help to free an area from cinders, gravel, stones, and dust are being used on outdoor surfaces. In some sections of the country limited shelters are also being used to provide protection from the rain, wind, and sun. All outdoor areas should have sanitary drinking fountains and toilet facilities as needed.

Elementary school. The activities program in the elementary school suggests what facilities should be available. Children in the primary grades engage in big muscle activity involving adaptations of climbing, jumping, skipping, kicking, throwing, leaping, and catching. Children in the intermediate and upper elementary grades perform these activities and others in games of low organization, team games, and fundamental skills used in playing these games.

The playground area for an elementary school should be located near the building and should be easily accessible from the elementary classrooms.

The University of Idaho has a portable football field. The tartan turf is 200 × 370 feet and can be rolled up and stored on a 210-foot long steel drum.

The kindergarten children should have a section of the playground for their exclusive use. This should be at least 5000 square feet and separated from the rest of the playground. It should consist of a surfaced area, a grass area, and a place for sand and digging. The sand area should be enclosed to prevent the sand from being scattered. It is also wise to have a shaded area where storytelling and similar activities may be conducted. Some essential equipment includes swings, slides, seesaws, climbing structures, tables, and seats.

The children older than kindergarten age in the elementary school should have play space that includes surfaced and grass areas, play equipment, and a shaded area.

The grass area provides space for many field and team games. Provisions for speedball, soccer, field hockey, softball, and fieldball could be included.

The play area should provide equipment such as climbing bars in the form of a jungle gym, horizontal bars, and Giant Strides. There should be ample space to provide for the safety of the participants.

The shaded area may provide space for activities such as marbles, hopscotch, ring toss, and storytelling.

The surfaced area may serve a variety of purposes and activities year-round for both school and community. It can house basketball, tennis, and handball courts, games of minimum organization, and other activities. This area should be paved with material that provides resiliency, safety, and durability. Rapid and efficient drainage is essential. Lines may be painted on the area for various games. Schools should allow additional space adjacent to this area for possible future expansion.

Other recreation areas that have important implications for the community are a landscaped, parklike area, a place for quiet activities such as dramatics and informal gatherings, a wading pool, a place for older adults to congregate, and a place for children to have gardening opportunities.

Junior high school. The junior high school play and recreation area, planned and developed for the children who attend the school and also for the adults in the community, should be located on a larger site than that for the elementary school. The site should have 10 to 25 acres on it. Local conditions will determine the amount of area available.

Many of the facilities of the elementary school will be used in the junior high school. In many cases, however, the various areas should be increased in size. The necessary facilities should provide for those activities that will be part of the regular physical education class and of the intramural program.

A landscaped, parklike area should be provided for various recreational activities for the community, such as walking, picnicking, skating, and fly casting.

Senior high school. The senior high school physical education program is characterized by a team game program in various activities. This emphasis, together with the fact that facilities are needed for the recreational use by the community, requires an even larger area than those for the two previous educational levels. Estimates range from 10 to 40 acres for such a site.

Most of the areas that have been listed in discussing the elementary and junior high schools should be included at the senior high school.

Considerably more space for physical education class instruction in the various field games is necessary to provide full-sized official fields for softball, field hockey, soccer, speedball, lacrosse, football, and baseball. The intramural and the interscholastic programs, as well as the community recreation program, could use these facilities.

Football and track can be provided for in an area of approximately 4 acres, with the football field placed within the track oval. A baseball field is questionable in such an area, because track and baseball are both spring sports. Baseball needs an area about 350 feet square. This allows a minimum of 50 feet from home plate to the backstop and also allows adequate space outside the first and third base lines.

Game areas

The recommended dimensions for game areas for school physical education programs have been outlined by a group of experts as shown in Table 9-1. One acre will accommodate four tennis courts, four handball courts, three badminton courts, and two volleyball courts.

The game area should permit basic physical education instructional classes to be held and also provide fields for softball, field hockey, soccer, speedball, lacrosse, and court areas that include basketball, softball, and other activities. There should be proper space for track if desired, an oval one-fourth mile around or at least a straightaway of 380 feet and 15 to 20 feet wide. Of course, an interschool athletic area, which usually includes football, track, baseball, and soccer, is also needed.

The winter activities should not be forgotten. With such activities gaining increased popularity, provisions should be made for skiing, sledding, skating, and other winter activities.

One state recommends the outdoor facilities for the basic needs of a physical education and recreation program, from kindergarten to grade twelve, should consist of a minimum of 12 acres. This area should be divided into an elementary area of 3 acres; courts area of 1 acre; high school girls' and boys' intramural area of 5 acres, and an interschool athletic area of 3 acres. With the trend toward coeducational activities, the boys' and girls' areas are combined.

A concept in play areas is the multipurpose sports court. This small, self-contained, fenced-in court provides for a variety of activities in a small area. The average sports court is 12 by 24 by 10½ feet and is completely enclosed (including top) with a weatherproofed steel tube and link fence that rests like a box on the floor of the court. Low-cost lighting and canvas covering can be used for evening and colder weather activities. The floor is frequently a raised wooden deck that allows for quick drainage and a weather-resistant playing surface. However, pads of other playing surfaces can be laid over the wooden deck. The court can be used for basketball, volleyball, paddle tennis, handball, and other activities. This type of court is excellent for crowded urban

Table 9-1. Recommended dimensions for game areas[3]

	Elementary	Upper grades	High school (adults)	Area size (sq. ft.)
Basketball	40′ × 60′	42′ × 74′	50′ × 84′	5,000
Volleyball	69′ × 50′	25′ × 50′	30′ × 60′	2,800
Badminton			20′ × 44′	1,800
Paddle tennis			20′ × 44′	1,800
Deck tennis			18′ × 40′	1,800
Tennis		36′ × 78′	36′ × 78′	7,200
Ice hockey			85′ × 200′	17,000
Field hockey			180′ × 300′	54,000
Horseshoes		10′ × 40′	10′ × 50′	1,000
Shuffleboard			6′ × 52′	648
Lawn bowling			14′ × 110′	7,800
Tetherball	10′ circle	12′ circle	12′ circle	144
Croquet	38′ × 60′	38′ × 60′	38′ × 60′	2,275
Handball	18′ × 26′	18′ × 26′	20′ × 34′	1,280
Baseball			350′ × 350′	122,500
Archery		50′ × 150′	50′ × 300′	20,000
Softball (12″ ball)	150′ × 150′	200′ × 200′	250′ − 250′	62,500
Football—with 440-yard track—220-yard straightaway			300′ × 600′	180,000
Touch football		120′ × 300′	160′ × 360′	68,400
6-man football			120′ × 300′	49,500
Soccer			165′ × 300′	57,600

areas, industrial recreation programs, schools, apartments, and individual homes.

Outdoor swimming pools

The outdoor swimming pool is a popular and important facility in many communities. To a great degree climatic conditions determine the advisability of such a facility.

Outdoor pools are built in various shapes, including oval, circular, T-shaped, and rectangular. Rectangular pools are most popular because of easier construction and because they lend themselves better to competitive swimming events.

The size of pools varies, depending on the number of persons they are to serve. One recommendation has been made that 12 square feet of water space per swimmer be allotted for swimming purposes or, if the deck is taken into consideration, 20 square feet of space for swimming and walking area per swimmer.

The decks for outdoor pools should be larger than those for indoor pools. This larger space will accommodate more people and also provide space for sunbathing.

Shower facilities should be provided to ensure that every swimmer takes a soapy shower in the nude before entering the water. A basket system for storing clothes has been found practical, but when the pool is located adjacent to a school, it is sometimes practical to use the locker and shower facilities of the school. However, it is strongly advised that wherever possible, separate shower and basket facilities be provided. Toilets should also be provided.

Because swimming is popular at night as well as in the daytime, lights should be provided so a great percentage of the population may participate in this healthful and enjoyable activity.

Diving boards generally are of wood or metal, but in recent years fiberglass and plastic ones have proved popular. The standard heights of boards are 1 and 3 meters. The 1-meter board should be over water 9 to

10 feet deep and the 3-meter board over 10 to 12 feet deep. The board or any diving takeoff area should have a nonskid covering. The boards should be securely fastened to the ground or foundation.

The rules and regulations concerning diving equipment should be clearly posted near the diving areas. Roping off and patrolling the area are good safety precautions.

Camps

Because camping is becoming an increasingly popular activity in both school and recreational programs, it should receive consideration.

Camps should be located within easy reach of the school and community. They should be in locations desirable from the standpoints of scenic beauty, safety, accessibility, water, and natural resources pertinent to the program offered. Activities usually offered include fishing, hiking, swimming, campcraft, boating, nature study, and appropriate winter sports. The natural terrain and other resources can contribute much toward such a program.

There should be adequate housing, eating, sanitation, waterfront, and other facilities essential to camp life. These do not have to be as elaborate as those in the home or school. Adequate protection against the elements is essential, however. Facilities should also meet acceptable standards of health and sanitation. In general, camp structures should be adapted to the climatic conditions of the particular area in which the camp is located. It is wise to consult public health authorities when selecting a campsite. Sometimes existing facilities can be converted to camp use. The campsite should be purchased outright or a long-term lease acquired.

FACILITIES FOR THE HANDICAPPED[4]
(Figs. 9-1, 9-2, and 9-3)

Since the passage of PL 94-142 more consideration has been given to the facility needs of the handicapped. These facilities in particular are concerned with the student's program of developmental exercises, perceptual-motor activities, modified sports, and rest and relaxation. These facilities usually vary from school to school and according to the type of handicapped persons served.

The Timpany Center[1] in San Jose, California, is a model facility for a variety of handicapped persons. This excellent facility is barrier-free and humanistic in design, provides an assortment of regular and wheelchair sports, has a water-readiness swimming pool, and contains special equipment in the gymnastics area to provide challenges. The facility provides physical education, recreation, and athletic opportunities for handicapped individuals.

Facilities in elementary schools for the adapted program vary from a classroom to a gymnasium, swimming pool, or outside play area. Some schools

The University of Notre Dame's Athletic and Convocation Center provides a healthful environment for part of its athletic program.

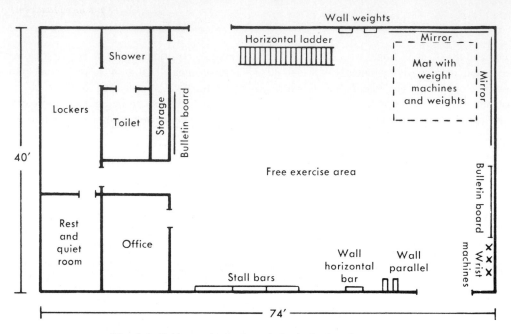

Fig. 9-1. Self-contained adapted physical education room.

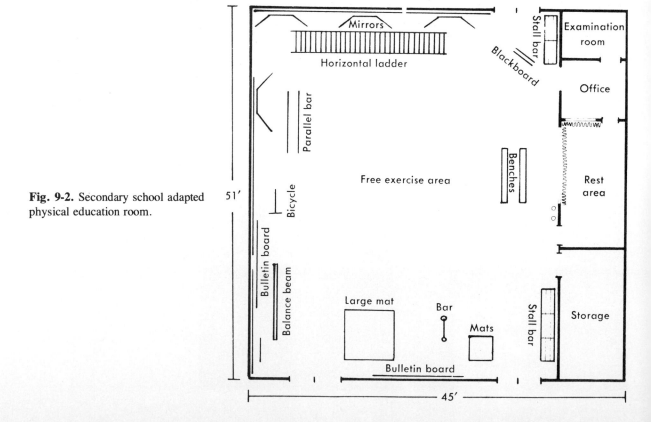

Fig. 9-2. Secondary school adapted physical education room.

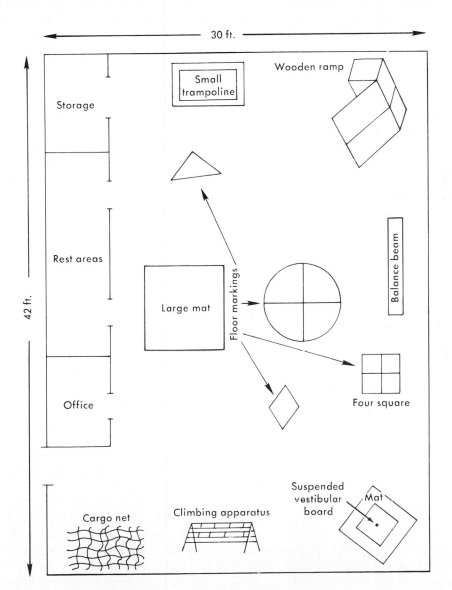

Fig. 9-3. Elementary school adapted physical education room.

take their students to special centers for the handicapped or to another school within the district. The minimum facility for the elementary school would be ample space to enable a program of adapted physical education involving things such as performing special exercises, playing with balls and hoops, and participating on various pieces of climbing apparatus.

Facilities in secondary schools should include an adapted physical education room large enough to accommodate things such as specialized equipment (horizontal ladder, pulleys), exercises, and play activities. The minimum size for a junior or senior high school room would be 40 by 60 feet. There should also be an adapted sports area located adjacent to the adapted physical education room. In this sports area activities such as volleyball, paddle tennis, badminton, table tennis, shuffleboard, and croquet would be conducted. A swimming pool at any educational level would be especially desirable because most handicapped persons enjoy and profit from swimming activities. As in the case with elementary school students, secondary schools and colleges sometimes use locations in the community, private facilities, or recreation centers to carry on their program.

OTHER SPECIAL FACILITIES

Other facilities needing special attention include those in dance, gymnastics, weight training, wrestling, martial arts, racquetball, and other sports and research and teaching areas.

Dance facilities

Because dance is becoming very popular as an activity, special facilities should be provided. It is recommended that a minimum of 100 square feet per student be provided with full-length mirrors, a speaker system, and a control system for record players and microphones. Practice bars should be on one wall at heights of 34 and 42 inches. The floor is an important consideration and it is recommended it be of sealed and buffed hard northern maple.

Special activity and other areas

Where possible, special activity and other areas, such as a gymnastic area of 120 by 90 feet with a minimum ceiling height of 23 feet, should be provided. A weight training area will receive considerable use if provided.

It is recommended that such a room contain a minimum of 2500 square feet. A wrestling and martial arts area of a minimum 50 by 100 feet will provide for two square mats 42 by 42 feet each. Racquetball and handball courts are common, particularly in colleges. Each four-wall court is 40 feet long and 20 feet wide with a ceiling height of 20 feet.

Other areas that may be considered are squash courts, multipurpose activity area, fencing area, indoor tennis facilities, indoor archery range, indoor rifle range, and golf practice area.

Research and teaching areas to be considered include laboratories for human performance projects, motor learning, biomechanics, the sociology of sport, and instructional media.

TRENDS IN THE CONSTRUCTION OF PHYSICAL EDUCATION FACILITIES

There are many new trends in facilities and materials for physical education programs including new paving materials, new types of equipment, improved landscapes, new construction materials, new shapes for swimming pools, partial shelters, and synthetic grass. Combination indoor-outdoor pools, physical fitness equipment for outdoor use, all-weather tennis courts, and lines that now come in multicolors for various games and activities are other new developments.

In gymnasium construction some of the new features include using modern engineering techniques and materials, which has resulted in welded steel and laminated wood modular frames; arched and gabled roofs; domes that provide areas completely free from internal supports; exterior surfaces of aluminum, steel, fiberglass, and plastics; different window patterns and styles; several kinds of floor surfaces of nonslip material; prefabricated wall surfaces; better lighting systems with improved quality and quantity and less glare. Facilities are moving from using regular glass to either a plastic and fiberglass panel or to an overhead skydome. Lightweight fiberglass, sandwich panels, or fabricated sheets of translucent fiberglass laminated over an aluminum framework are proving popular. They require no painting, the cost of labor and materials is lower, shades or blinds are not needed to eliminate glare, and the breakage problem is reduced or eliminated.

Locker rooms and service areas are including built-in locks with combination changers that permit staff members to change combinations when needed. Ceramic tile is used more extensively because of its durability and low-cost maintenance. Wallhung toilet compartment features permit easier maintenance and sanitation with no chance for rust to start from the floor. Odor control is being effectively handled by new dispensers. New thin-profile heating, ventilating, and air-conditioning fan coil units are now being used.

The athletic training and health suite is being modernized by making it more attractive and serviceable. Also, the trend is toward better ventilation, heating, and lighting and more easily cleaned materials on walls and floors to guarantee improved sanitation.

New developments concerning indoor swimming pools include automatic control boards, where one person can have direct control over all filters, chlorinators, chemical pumps, and lever controllers; much larger deck space area constructed of nonslip ceramic tile; greater use of diatomaceous earth rather than sand filters to filter out small particles of matter including some bacteria; underwater lighting; water-level deck pools (where the overflow gutters are placed in the deck surrounding the pool instead of in the pool's side walls and provision is made for grating designed so the water that overflows is drained to a trench under the deck without the possibility of debris returning to the pool); air-supported roofs that can serve as removable tops in a combination indoor-outdoor pool; and movable bulkheads.

New developments concerning outdoor swimming pools involve new shapes—including oval, wedge, kidney, figure-8, cloverleaf, and bean shaped—as well as modern accessories, including wave-making machines, gas heaters, automatic water levelers, and retractable roofs and sides. More supplemental recreational facilities, such as shuffleboard courts, volleyball, and horseshoes, and more deck equipment, including guard rails, slides, and pool covers, are being included around larger pools.

New concepts have been put to good use in the physical plants of the following schools:

Oak Grove High School, San Jose, California. This school has a movable interior partitioning system with adjustable lighting, acoustics, and air conditioning that can accommodate different types of activities on short notice.

Nova High School, Fort Lauderdale, Florida. This school spent 10% of the school's total cost on teaching aids so all types of audiovisual materials could be used or piped into most classrooms and teaching stations in the school.

Andrews Senior High School, Andrews, Texas. Here the open court has a windowless exterior and faces inward to a concourse and a domed rotunda. Along the concourse are a swimming pool and gymnasium, and under the rotunda is an assembly area.

Holland High School, Holland, Michigan. This school built its plant on the compass plan with four small schools. Physical education facilities are shared by all schools.

New Haven, Connecticut, Public Schools. This city adapted its facilities to the community school concept with each school including community facilities involving the city's social and welfare agencies where such problems as health, family relations, and unemployment are major concerns.

Portland State University, Oregon. Here the roof of the physical education building was covered with artificial surfacing to provide tennis courts and a general sports area.

Brooklyn Polytech, New York City. A bubble was erected on top of the physics building for a gymnasium.

University of Texas at El Paso. This university covered its outdoor swimming pool with prefabricated material to have an all-weather, year-round facility.

LaVerne College, California. Here what some persons call a super tent, involving a cable-supported fabric roof structure made of fiberglass and Teflon, houses theater, gymnasium, cafeteria, bookstore, and health clinic.

Cuyahoga Falls, Ohio. Here a roof was installed over the swimming pool so it could be used all throughout the year. In the summer months the roof is removed.

Thomas Jefferson Junior High School, Arlington, Virginia. This school has implemented the shared facilities concept by housing together performing arts, recreation, and physical education.

A, Graceland Fieldhouse, Lamoni, Iowa. **B,** Forman School, Litchfield, Conn.

Harvard University, Massachusetts. Here the largest air-supported structure for a new track facility has been erected; it is 250 feet wide, 300 feet long, and 60 feet high.

Lewis and Clark Elementary School, St. Louis, Missouri. A physical education partial shelter has been erected with the sides of the open structure protected by banks of shrubbery.

Boston College, Massachusetts. A roof design of hyperbolic parabaloids is used. This efficient structure spans a large area—42,000 square feet of floor space.

Limited shelters for physical education

The shelter or limited shelter provides protection from extremes of climate, uses the desirable elements of the natural environment, and creates an interesting background for physical education activities.

The actual design of the shelter is determined by climate, use, and activity program. Methods of controlling air movement may be developed by using natural elements (trees and plantings), architectural elements (wall, roofs, and screens), and mechanical devices (fan, moving walls, and screens). Solar radiation may be controlled with natural shading and moving walls. These shelters cost about half as much as the traditional gymnasium.

Air-supported structures

An air-supported structure consists of a large plastic bubble that is inflated and supported by continuous air pressure. It is the least expensive building that can be erected, costing from one fifth to one half of what a solid structure would cost. These facilities have housed military equipment and served as theaters, factories, swimming pools, tennis courts, and gymnasiums.

The outside construction is usually made of vinyl-coated or Dacron polyester, which is lightweight, strong, and flexible. The fabric is flame-retardant, waterproof, tear-resistant, mildew-resistant, and sunlight-resistant. Installation is simple and may be completed in a few hours by a minimum crew. The installation process includes placement of vinyl envelope and inflation. The bubble is supported by a blower that provides a constant flow of air pressure. The bubble may be easily dismantled by stopping the blower, opening the door, unhitching the attachments, and folding the bubble compactly.

Minigyms and fitness corners

Most schoolchildren must confine their physical activities to the physical education class, which may not meet every day. Even in gym classes students are often required to participate amid an atmosphere of formality when time is taken up in attendance lineups, exercises, testing, and other planned activities. How can this be changed?

The answer may be found in minigyms, which can be operated in the halls and alcoves of the school building. They may consist of climbing, pulling, and hanging apparatus that the students use between classes, at study hours, lunch, and recess. This idea is to distribute the gymnasium throughout the school. Some other suggestions include mats, chinning bars, inclines, walls to throw balls against, and carpeted corridors for stunts and tumbling.

Classrooms can also be turned into minigyms with fitness corners for exercise and equipment such as stationary bicycles, rowing machines, and stand-up desks to promote activity.

Tennis courts and other facilities

Rubber-cushioned tennis courts are being used in some places. They consist of tough durable material about 4 inches thick, which has the individual advantages of clay, turf, and composition courts combined in one surface.

Other new developments in physical education facilities are numerous. Sculptured play apparatus has been produced by a number of firms. It is designed to be more conducive to imaginative movements and creativity than conventional equipment. Hard-surfaced, rubberized, all-weather running tracks, radiant heating of decks on swimming pools, floating roofs that eliminate non-load-bearing walls, interior climate control, better indoor and outdoor lighting, rubber

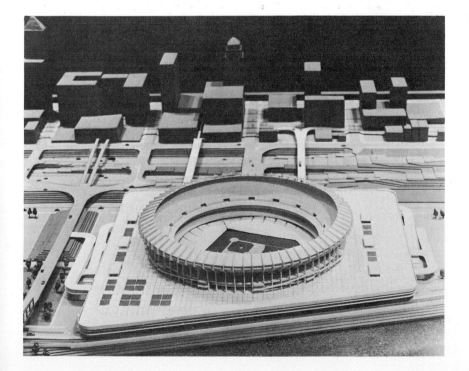

Home of the Cincinnati Reds.

Graceland Fieldhouse,
Lamoni, Iowa.

padding for use under apparatus, the park-school concept with land being used for school and recreational purposes, outdoor skating rinks, translucent plastic materials for swimming pool canopies and other uses, electrically operated machinery to move equipment and partitions and bleachers, and auxiliary gymnasiums for both activity and classroom use are more of the new developments in facilities for physical education programs.

A LOOK INTO THE FUTURE OF SPORTS FACILITIES

Bellemare[5] lists 40 of the latest facility developments for sports. Some of these are: synthetic ice, snowless ski hills, climbing walls, turntable skating, convertible roofs, mobile locker rooms, illuminated game lines, folding racquet courts, moveable pool floors, and wave pools.

PARK-SCHOOL FACILITIES

In the park-school complex the school is erected near a park, and the park facilities are used by both the school and the community. This has implications particularly for physical education and recreation programs, for the school usually uses the park facilities

during school hours and the recreation department uses them after school hours, on weekends, and during vacation periods.

The T. Wendall Williams Community Education Center in Flint, Michigan, is situated on a two-block site that adjoins a 72-acre park. The area consists of 30 classrooms, a lower elementary group activity area, a large sunken learning resources center, five team-teaching rooms, and a large gymnasium. The recreation area is located on park property and administered by the Flint Recreation and Park Department. Facilities are provided for baseball, softball, soccer, football, basketball, and picnicking. Swimming areas, tennis courts, and activity areas for small children are included. In the winter the pool is covered for all-year swimming, and the tennis courts are converted into a large artificial ice-skating rink. The park also provides natural areas for learning and recreation for all.

MAINTENANCE OF FACILITIES

Planning and constructing facilities are important administrative functions. An equally important responsibility is maintaining facilities. With proper maintenance a facility will last longer, provide a healthier environment, be less costly, and provide a more satisfying experience for participants. Just as planning and constructing facilities in physical education and athletics are team efforts, so is maintaining these facilities. The custodial staff, the participants, and the physical education and athletic staffs must all work together in taking pride in their facility and putting forth a special effort to see that it is maintained in perfect condition.

COMMUNITY USE OF SCHOOL AND COLLEGE FACILITIES

Schools and colleges continually receive requests to open their facilities to various community groups. It is therefore imperative for the administration to establish guidelines ensuring that appropriate precautions are taken and such facilities are used properly when approval is given.

First, the administration should see that a written policy is established and approved by proper authorities regarding community use of facilities (who can use, at what times, under what conditions). Second, the administrative procedure regarding community use should be established. This usually includes such things as making a proper application, obtaining the liability insurance coverage necessary, setting the fee payment, and making stipulations regarding maintenance and security. Third, administrative controls should be established to see that administrative policies and procedures are carried out as specified.

Schools using community resources

Such facilities as parks, bowling alleys, swimming pools, ski slopes, and skating arenas can extend the school physical education program and related sports activities. Most community facilities can be used during off-hours and after school, and the charge is frequently nominal.

SUMMARY

Facility management is an important administrative responsibility. It involves such things as planning in light of physical education program needs, taking health conditions into consideration, working with the architect, and being aware of the latest developments in facility construction. A knowledge of the basic requirements of both indoor and outdoor facilities is important for both regular and handicapped persons so that the needs of all participants may be met. The management should also be concerned with the main-

Louisiana's Superdome, New Orleans, La.

Houston's Astrodome.

tenance of the facilities since this is a very important management function. Furthermore, most physical education and athletic facilities are used by more than students and members of one organization. It is common practice for community residents and other organizations also to use such facilities. Therefore consideration should be given to the development of policies for such usage.

SELF-ASSESSMENT TESTS

These tests will assist students in determining if material and competencies presented in this chapter have been mastered.

1. State 10 basic considerations that should be followed by administrators in planning physical education and athletic facilities.
2. As an administrator of a physical education and athletic program, what steps would you follow in working with an architect in the construction of a gymnasium?
3. Prepare a sketch of what you consider to be an ideal indoor physical education plant.
4. Develop a list of standards for outdoor areas in physical education and athletics, including play areas and swimming pools, for an elementary school and for a high school.
5. You are a director of physical education in a secondary school with 500 students. There are five class periods a day with an average class size of 30 students, and physical education is required daily. What is the minimum number of teaching stations you will need?
6. Describe some new features being used in the construction of physical education and athletic facilities. What are the advantages of these new features?
7. Prepare a checklist for a physical education and athletic plant that will ensure that it is safe and healthful for all participants.

REFERENCES

1. Athletic Business, January 1982, p. 52.
2. Athletic Business, July 1984, p. 20.
3. Athletic Institute and AAHPERD, Planning facilities for athletics, physical education and recreation. Flynn, Richard B., Editor, North Palm Beach, Fla., 1985, The Athletic Institute.
4. Auxter, D., and Pyfer, J.: Principles and methods of adapted physical education and creation, ed. 5, St. Louis, 1985, Times Mirror/Mosby College Publishing.
5. Bellemare, H.K.: Athletic purchasing and facilities, October 1983, p. 20.
6. Ferreri, J.P.: Successful strategies for facility planning, Athletic Business, January 1985, p. 64.
7. Flynn, R.B.: The team approach to facility planning, Athletic purchasing and facilities **5:**12, June 1981.
8. Kraus, R.G., and Curtis, J.E.: Creative administration in recreation and parks, ed. 4, St. Louis, 1986, Times Mirror/Mosby College Publishing.

SUGGESTED READINGS

- Arnheim, D.D., and Sinclair, W.A.: physical education for special populations, Englewood Cliffs, N.J., 1985, Prentice-Hall, Inc.
  Discusses, suggests, and provides guidelines for adapted physical education facilities. Outlines how facilities can be modified and planned to meet the needs of handicapped individuals.
- Athletic Business, "A Gym By Any Other Name Is A Multipurpose Area," March 1985, p. 46.
  Describes how modern technology and proper design principles make it possible to have a gymnasium that is multipurpose in construction as well as in usage.
- Dougherty, N.J., and Bonanno, D.: Management principles in sport and leisure services, Minneapolis, 1985, Burgess Publishing Company.
  Chapter 7 in this book is concerned with facility development and management. Lists the steps in the process of facility development, the role of the manager, the planning process, operational considerations, and policies needed.
- McGuire, M.: Skylit cluster design: efficient space combined with aesthetic form, Athletic Business, July 1984, p. 32.
  Describes the multipurpose 130,000 square foot physical education facility at the College of Du Page.
- Penman, K.A.: What's what in sports surfaces? Athletic Business, August 1984, p. 8.
  Discusses the various options in sport facility surfaces available in today's market and the management guidelines that should be used in selecting the surface to be used.
- Vander Zwaag, H.J.: Sport management in schools and colleges, New York, 1984, John Wiley & Sons, Inc.
  Discusses items such as financing, management, procedures for use, and facility management as a part of program planning.

Chapter Ten

Fiscal Management

Instructional Objectives and Competencies to be Achieved
After reading this chapter the student should be able to

- Support the need for sound fiscal management in physical education and athletic programs.
- Explain the budgeting process and formulate a physical education and athletic budget.
- Apply a planning-programming-budgeting-evaluation system (PPBES) in the management of physical education and athletic programs and also a zero base budget.
- Understand the role of school and college business managers or administrators in fiscal management.
- Outline the principles necessary for managers to follow to ensure financial accountability in a physical education and athletic program.

Another very important function of management involves finding the funds necessary to provide sound physical education and athletic programs. Adequate funding must be procured, programs implemented, and accountability for funds established. This chapter deals with this managerial function.

Fiscal management has become an increasingly important responsibility for management in light of current financial problems. In recent years these financial problems have made it much more difficult to fund physical education and athletic programs. Some of the reasons for this difficulty include the high price of supplies and equipment; the need to finance an increasing number of girls and women who are participating in sports; crowd control costs at athletic events as a result of violence; expensive product liability and lawyer contingency funds; and an inflation rate that is resulting in rising costs for labor, teachers, coaches, officials, and other personnel.

An analysis of the responses of directors of physical education and athletics in New York (more than 1000 questionnaires were sent) regarding the effect of budget cuts and austerity budgets on their programs, highlights the difficulties managers of physical education and athletic programs are having today. The survey resulted in the following findings:

67% of the directors said they had to cut supplies, transportation, specific sports, and levels of sports to balance the budget.

29 athletic programs were conducted with private funds during the time they were on austerity budgets.

40% of the directors conducted athletic programs using volunteer coaches in parts of their programs.

Fund-raising activities for athletics included booster club memberships, participation fees, sales, student work projects, and promotional activities such as lotteries.

Regarding support for their athletic programs, the teachers' association was the least supportive and the students the most supportive. The school administration and the community were also highly supportive of their programs.

Efficient fiscal management is an essential management function that ensures proper money accountability. Therefore the manager must understand thoroughly the fiscal needs and objectives of all the departments under his or her supervision. Budgeting must deal with departmental requests. The fiscal management of an institution or department is a difficult, challenging responsibility.

IMPORTANCE AND FUNCTION OF FISCAL MANAGEMENT

The services a program provides, whether personnel, facilities, or other items, usually involve the disbursement of funds. This money must be secured from proper sources, be expended for proper purposes, and be accounted for item by item. The budget, the master financial plan for the organization, is constructed with these purposes in mind.

Policies for raising and spending money must be set within specific limits. Persons responsible should know the procedures for handling such funds with integrity, the basic purposes for which the program exists, the laws, and the codes and regulations concerning fiscal management. Only as the funds are used wisely and in the best interests of all people concerned can the outlay of monies be justified.

Place of fiscal management in physical education and athletic programs

In schools, colleges, or other organizations, physical education and athletics have a major outlay of funds. Personnel, health services, facilities, supplies and equipment are only a few of the items that amount to large sums of money. As much as 25% of many school and college plants is devoted to these programs. Probably as many as 400,000 physical educators and coaches are collectively paid millions of dollars annually in salaries. More than 60 million students participate in school physical education and athletic programs.

Gymnasiums, swimming pools, athletic training rooms, playgrounds, and other facilities are being constructed at huge costs to the taxpayers.

What is true of schools and colleges regarding fiscal management is also true of recreation, industrial, and other settings where physical education and athletic programs exist.

Responsibility

The responsibility for fiscal management, although falling largely on the shoulders of the management, involves every member of the staff.

Formulating and preparing the budget are cooperative enterprises. They are based on information and reports that have been forwarded by staff members from various departments and subdivisions of the organization. These reports must contain information on programs, projects, obligations that exist, funds that have been spent, and monies that have been received from various sources. Managers must have an overall picture of the entire enterprise at their finger-

---

PURPOSES OF FISCAL MANAGEMENT

Some of the principal purposes of financial management in physical education and athletic programs are the following:

To prevent misuse and waste of funds that have been allocated to these special fields

To help coordinate and relate the objectives of physical education and athletic programs with the money appropriated for achieving such outcomes

To ensure that monies allocated to physical education will be based on research, study, and a careful analysis of the pertinent conditions that influence such a process

To involve the entire staff in formulating policies and procedures and in preparing budgetary items that will help ensure that the right program directions are taken

To use funds to develop the best physical education programs possible

To exercise control over the process of fiscal management to guarantee that the entire financial process has integrity and purpose

To make the greatest use of personnel, facilities, supplies, equipment, and other factors involved in accomplishing organizational objectives

Girls' and women's physical education and athletic programs are expanding.

tips. They must be cognizant of the work being done throughout the establishment, functions that should be carried out, needs of every facet of the organization, and other items that must be considered in preparing the budget. The larger the organization, the larger should be the budget organization under the manager. The efficiency of the enterprise depends on expert judgment in fiscal matters. In schools and colleges, students themselves play a part. For example, through general organizations, budgets are prepared and outlays of funds relating to many activities, such as plays and athletics, are approved, amended, or rejected. Fiscal management involves many people, but the job of leadership and direction falls on the management.

BUDGETING

Budgeting is the formulation of a financial plan in terms of work to be accomplished and services to be performed. All expenditures should be closely related to the objectives the organization is trying to achieve. In this aspect the management plays an important part in budgeting.

Budgets should be planned and prepared with thought to the future. They are an important part of management's 3-year, 5-year, or 7-year plan and the program of accomplishment outlined for a fiscal period. Projects of any size should be integrated progressively over many years. Thus the outlay of monies to realize such aims requires long-term planning.

According to the strict interpretation of the word, a budget is merely a record of receipts and expenditures. As used here, however, it reflects the long-term planning of the organization, pointing up the needs with their estimated costs, and then ensuring that a realistic program is planned that will fit into the estimated income.

The budget forecasts revenues and expenses for a period of 1 year, known as the fiscal year.

Types of budgets

There are short-term and long-term budgets. The short-term is usually the annual budget. The long-term budget represents long-term fiscal planning, possibly for a 10-year period. Most physical education and athletic personnel will be concerned with short-term or annual budgets whereby they plan their financial needs for a period covering the school year.

Responsibility for budgets

The responsibility for the preparation of the budget may vary from one locality to another. In most school systems the superintendent of schools is responsible. In colleges it is the responsibility of the president and the dean. In other organizations the department head plays a key role. It is often possible for school managers, department heads, teachers, professors, and members of the organization to participate in preparing the budget by submitting various requests for budget items. In other situations a comprehensive budget may first be prepared and then submitted to the subdivisions for consideration.

In some large school systems the superintendent of schools frequently delegates much of the budget responsibility to a business administrator, a clerk, or an assistant or associate superintendent.

The final official school authority concerned with school budgets is the board of education. In some organizations other than schools it is the controller.

This agent or person can approve, reject, or amend. Beyond the board of education rests the authority of the people, who in most communities have the right to approve or reject the budget.

In colleges the budget may be handled in the dean's office, or the director or chairperson of the physical education department may have the responsibility. In some cases the director of athletics is responsible for the athletic budget.

Within school departments of physical education and athletics the chairperson, supervisor, or director is the person responsible for the budget. However, he or she will usually consult with members of the department and receive their suggestions.

Criteria for a good budget

A budget for physical education and athletics should meet the following criteria: The budget will clearly present the financial needs of the entire program in relation to the objectives sought. Key persons in the organization have been consulted. The budget will provide a realistic estimate of income to balance the expenditures anticipated. The budget should reflect equitable allocations to boys' and girls' athletic programs. The possibility of emergencies is recognized through flexibility in the financial plan. The budget will be prepared well in advance of the fiscal year to leave ample time for analysis, thought, criticism, and review. Budget requests are realistic, not padded. The budget meets the essential requirements of students, faculty, staff members, and administrators.

Budget preparation and planning

The budget process is continuous. One authority on business management indicates the following seven basic steps to this process:[5]

Planning: Administration uses the brain power of the staff members and community in creative planning.

Coordinating: Administration coordinates and integrates staff members and community suggestions and recommendations into a unified whole.

Interpreting: To have support for the budget, proper interpretation of plans and actions are a continual part of the budgetary process.

Presenting: The administration presents the budget in a simplified version so it can be readily understood. Pictures, diagrams, graphs, and other materials make such a presentation more interesting and informative.

PURPOSES OF BUDGETS

They express the plan and program for physical education and athletics. They determine things such as (a) size of classes, (b) supplies, equipment, and facilities, (c) methods used, (d) results and educational values sought, and (e) personnel available.

They reflect the philosophy and policies of the professions of physical education and athletics. They provide an overview of these specialized areas.

They determine what phases of the program are to be emphasized and help analyze all aspects of physical education and athletic programs.

They interpret the need and the funds necessary for physical education and athletics.

In a school program they help determine, together with the budgets of other subdivisions, the tax levy for the school district.

They make it possible to administer the physical education and athletic programs economically by improving accounting procedures.

They make it possible, on approval by officials, to authorize expenditures for the program of physical education and athletics.

Approving: Adoption of the budget is but the formal approval of many projects that have been studied and considered throughout the year. The administration is continually planning, researching, and studying various budgetary items.

Administering: The budget, when approved, serves as an administrative guide throughout the year as to how monies will be spent and what activities will be conducted.

Appraising: Appraisal is a continuous process indicating how the budget is functioning. Methods used include daily observation, cost accounting records and reports, surveys, audits, checklists, and staff studies.

Four general procedures in budget planning that physical education and athletic personnel might consider include the following: First, actual preparation of the budget by the chairperson of the department with his or her staff, listing the various estimated receipts, expenditures, and any other information that needs to be included. Second, presentation of the budget to the principal, superintendent, dean, board of education, or other person or group that represents the proper authority and has the responsibility for reviewing it. Third, after formal approval of the budget, its use as a guide for the financial management and administration of the department or organization. Fourth, critical evaluation of the budget periodically to determine its effectiveness in meeting organizational needs, with notations being made for the next year's budget.

The preparation of the budget, representing the first step, is a long-term endeavor that cannot be accomplished in 1 or 2 days. The budget can be prepared well only after a careful review of program effectiveness and extensive appraisal. However, the actual completion of the budget usually is accomplished in the early spring after a detailed inventory of program needs has been taken. The director of physical education or athletics, after close consultation with staff members and the principal, dean, superintendent of schools, or other responsible administrative officer, should formulate the budget.

Involvement of staff members

Involving staff members in the budget-making process is very important. Klappholz[3] provides some suggestions that follow:

- Teachers and coaches should maintain inventory forms indicating supplies and equipment on hand.
- Teachers, coaches, and directors should keep accurate records of all costs for each activity or sport.
- Teaching staff members and coaches should determine the items that were not a part of this year's budget but that should be included in the budget for the coming year.

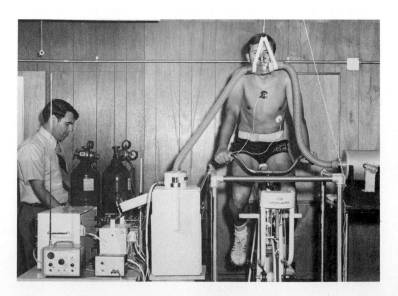

Physical fitness research being carried on in the exercise physiology laboratory at the University of Nevada, Las Vegas.

- Accurate records should be kept by staff members regarding funds allocated and spent each year. Then it should be determined if funds were spent for purposes that were initially listed.
- When all pertinent information has been collected and analyzed, the administration should meet with all staff members and go over requests.
- The administration should prepare total physical education or athletic budgets including all valid requests. The budget should not be padded, but provision should be made for emergencies.

Klappholz also stresses that administrators and staff members should do their homework by having the latest prices for supplies and equipment; number of students or other personnel in the program; cost of such items as officials, travel, meals, lodging, insurance, and medical supervision; money needed for teaching aids and other materials; and cost of attending professional meetings.

Many records and reports are essential to budget preparation. The inventory of equipment and supplies on hand will be useful, and copies of inventories and budgets from previous years will provide good references. Comparison of budgetary items with those in other organizations of similar size may be of help. Accounting records will be valuable.

The preparation of the budget should allow some flexibility for readjustment, if necessary. It is difficult to accurately and specifically list each detail in the way it will be needed and executed.

The budget should represent a schedule that can be justified. This means that each budgetary item must satisfy the needs and interests of everyone concerned. Furthermore, each item that constitutes an expenditure should be reflected in budget specifications.

Girls' interscholastic basketball in progress in the Clark County Public Schools, Las Vegas, Nev.

A SCHOOL BUDGET

Proposed budget classification by major function

	Salaries fees, and benefits	Equipment and supplies	Services and other expenses	Totals
Board of education and district administration				
Board/district administration	$ 183,400	$ 11,400	$ 45,900	$ 240,700
District insurance			74,600	74,600
Claims, property tax, administration costs			78,300	78,300
Category total				$ 393,600
Instruction				
Building administration	302,600	19,700	8,600	330,900
Salaries and materials	3,178,300	169,000	439,700	3,787,000
Guidance and health	264,200	2,900	14,600	281,700
Student activities	57,300	22,900	6,700	86,900
Category total				$4,486,500
Support services				
Transportation	287,600	106,500	36,300	430,400
Operation and maintenance	362,000	42,900	378,400	783,300
School lunch			5,000	5,000
Category total				$1,218,700
Employees benefits	1,293,400			$1,293,400
Total operating expenses	$5,928,800	$375,300	$1,088,100	$7,392,200
Debt service			765,600	765,600
TOTAL BUDGET				
				$8,157,800

Budget organization

Budgets can be organized in many ways. One pattern that can prove useful for the physical education and athletic manager might include four sections. First, an introductory message enables the administration to present the financial proposals in terms a person outside the specialized fields might readily understand. This section offers to physical education specialists an opportunity to discuss some aspects of the program in lay terms and some of the directions that need to be taken to provide for the physical fitness of the students.

The second section presents an overall view of the budget, with expenditures and anticipated revenues arranged clearly and systematically so any person can compare the two.

A third section, with an estimate of receipts and expenditures in much more detail, enables a principal, superintendent of schools, board of education, or other interested person or group to understand the budget specifically and to follow up any item of cost.

A fourth section might include supporting schedules to provide additional evidence for the requests outlined in the budget. Many times a budget will have a better chance of approval if there is sufficient documentation to support some items. For example, extra pay for coaching may be supported by presenting salary schedules for coaches in other school systems.

Another type of budget organization might be one that consists of the following three parts: (1) an introductory statement of the objectives, policies, and programs of the physical education department; (2) a résumé of the objectives, policies, and programs interpreted in terms of proposed expenditures; and (3) a financial plan for meeting the needs during the fiscal period.

Not all budgets are broken down into these three or four divisions. All budgets do, however, give an itemized account of receipts and expenditures.

In a physical education budget common inclusions are items concerning instruction, such as extra compensation for coaches; matters of capital outlay, such as a new swimming pool or handball court; replacement of expendable equipment, such as basketballs and baseball bats; and provision for maintenance and repair, such as refurbishing football uniforms or resurfacing the playground. It is difficult to estimate many of these items without making a careful inventory and analysis of the condition of the facilities and equipment.

BREAKDOWN OF BUDGETARY ALLOCATIONS FOR REGULAR INSTRUCTIONAL PROGRAMS

The programs listed below describe the funding for regular classroom instruction. The costs of general classroom teachers in grades one through five are divided among the language arts, mathematics, and environment programs, according to the estimated percentage of instructional time each subject receives in the classroom curriculum.

Program costs in grades six through twelve are based on the division of staff members by academic specialization.

The unclassified code contains those general supply and equipment items that support the entire program and cannot be allocated by program.

	Salaries	Benefits	Equipment	Supplies	Services	Total
Art	$ 136,761	$ 38,434	$ 522	$ 10,401	$ 677	$ 186,795
Business education	66,465	18,681	2,150	1,638	1,350	90,284
Driver education	4,410	1,239	550	10,850	—	17,049
Environment	151,747	42,650	—	1,999	300	196,696
Health education	2,290	627	—	400	420	3,737
Home economics	39,609	11,313	—	3,341	447	54,528
Industrial arts	70,837	19,910	471	5,335	675	97,228
Kindergarten	47,203	13,267	—	1,255	—	61,725
Language arts	613,255	172,365	—	14,375	2,900	802,895
Foreign languages	158,078	44,430	—	5,361	1,715	209,584
Mathematics	452,918	127,291	710	7,489	560	588,968
Music	141,035	39,635	516	2,439	850	184,485
Physical education	233,176	65,552	2,147	6,069	2,590	309,534
Reading (special)	83,162	23,372	—	915	400	107,849
Science	333,804	87,083	3,124	11,140	1,850	437,001
Speech	10,751	3,018	—	261	—	14,030
Social studies	283,827	79,774		4,509	3,500	371,610
Unclassified	146,898	41,286	1,737	22,009	9,080	221,010
TOTAL	$2,976,226	$829,745	$11,927	$109,786	$27,314	$3,954,998

METHODS OF FUND RAISING FOR PHYSICAL EDUCATION AND ATHLETIC PROGRAMS

The sources of income for most school and college physical education and athletic programs include the general school or college fund, gate receipts, and general organization and activity fees. However, these do not provide sufficient monies to run quality programs.

The budget crunch in many school districts and institutions of higher learning has caused physical education and athletic directors to find ways of raising revenues for their programs. In Massachusetts, for example,[6] they are getting business organizations to provide matching funds for specific programs, conducting fund-raising campaigns among alumni, soliciting local citizens to make tax-free donations and to make provision in their wills, and selling passes to the public for athletic contests.

Other sources of additional revenue are special foundation, governmental, or individual grants or gifts; sale of television and radio rights; concessions at athletic contests and physical education events; and special fund-raising events such as a faculty-varsity basketball game.

Aufsesser and Mechikoff[1] have provided some excellent suggestions for physical educators who are looking to replenish their funds with grantsmanship and external funding. They point out that govenmental sources are minimal but with well-written proposals physical educators can obtain corporate dollars. Such proposals should clearly outline the proposed project, goals, and outcomes of the project itself, then carefully select a number of funding groups to be contacted and be persistent in following up each source.

The principles of fund raising are simple and easy to apply. A successful campaign is the combination of a good cause, careful planning, fact-finding, and skillful communication. Good public relations are essential. Secondary schools have a product with which many people like to be associated, and that is athletics. Physical education is not quite as attractive to most individuals. However, if presented in the right way with students as a point of focus, it also can be a recipient of fund-raising drives.

To be effective, a program of fund raising should

have excellent organization, sound objectives, effective leadership on the part of management, and a philosophy that is compatible with a sound education.

Some illustrations of successful fund raising are associated with booster clubs. The question of using booster clubs is controversial since sometimes such clubs want to have a say in the running of physical education and athletic programs. Of course, this should not be permitted.

Christian Brothers High School in Sacramento, California, has the La Salle Club, which raises money for the athletic and physical education programs by means such as the Old Timer Baseball Night, a golf tourney, and a fireworks booth on the 4th of July. Davis Senior High School in Davis, California, has an annual Lift-A-Thon for their football program to raise money. Notre Dame High School in Sherman Oaks, California, uses their booster club membership as a major contributor to their athletic fund. The Dell Rapids, South Dakota, school system sells advertising on their scoreboards to help finance their programs.

Some high schools across the country use professional organizations to do their fund raising. For example, the Revere Company has helped many schools to raise funds. Parke Techniques is a company that works through the schools selling everything from bookends to paper weights. Another company is the American Cap Company, which prints painter's caps. Win Craft Incorporated makes pom-poms, buttons, balloons, megaphones, cushions, and many other items.

PAY TO PLAY POLICY

A recent development in high school athletic programs is to require students who wish to participate in these activities to pay fees.[4] This plan is being initiated because school sports programs are being cut back drastically due to lack of funds. Pete Altieri, President of the National Council of Secondary School Athletic Directors indicates that the average high school athletic budget has been reduced by at least 25% and some even by 75%. This cut in funds in combination with increased costs is prompting some schools to say that students must pay if they are going to play.

The arts and crafts program is one of the many daily club activities for members of the Boys' and Girls' Club in Las Vegas, Nev.

Although some states such as Iowa and Michigan have ruled against such a practice, California courts have upheld the fees. A citizens' group called "The Coalition Opposing Student Fees" lost a suit against the Santa Barbara School Board. The ruling stated that fees were permissible since sports took place outside the regular school day, students engage voluntarily in sports, fees are used only to pay the cost of running such a program, and fees do not violate the equal opportunity clauses of federal and state constitutions, that is, financially disadvantaged students are exempt from fees.

If a school institutes a "pay to play" policy, they should make sure that the fee charged is reasonable, disadvantaged students (those who are financially unable to pay) are exempt, fees are used solely to cover costs of running the program, and participation is voluntary.

TRADITIONAL SOURCES OF INCOME

General school or college fund. In elementary and secondary schools, the physical education and athletic program would be financed through the general fund to a large extent. At colleges and universities, the general fund of the institution would also represent a major source of income.

Gate receipts. Gate receipts play an important part in some schools in financing at least part of the physical education and athletic program. Although gate receipts are usually less important at lower educational levels, colleges and universities sometimes finance their entire athletic, intramural, and physical education programs through such a method. At a few high schools throughout the country, gate receipts have been abolished because of the feeling that if athletics represent an important part of the education program, they should be paid for in the same way that science and mathematics programs are financed.

General organization and activity fees. Some high schools either require or make available to students separate general organization or activity fees and tickets or some other inducement that enables them to attend athletic, dramatic, and musical events. In colleges and universities a similar plan is generally used, thus providing students with reduced rates to the various out-of-class activities offered by the institution. Table 10-1 shows a general organization financial statement.

Table 10-1. General organization athletic account—financial report (September-December)

EXPENSES		
Football		
Officials (four home games)	$ 480.00	
Equipment and supplies	2364.02	
Transportation	175.00	
Supervision (police, ticket sellers and takers)	952.00	
Reconditioning and cleaning equipment	1313.20	
Medical supplies	125.40	
Scouting	60.00	
Film	31.36	
Guarantees	520.00	
Football dinner	231.00	
Miscellaneous (printing tickets, meetings)	172.00	
Total football expense		$6423.98
Cross country		
State and county entry fees	$ 10.00	
Transportation	64.00	
Total cross country expense		$ 74.00
Basketball		
Supervision (three games)	$ 36.00	
Custodian (three games)	26.00	
Police (one game)	12.00	
Total basketball expense		$ 74.00
Cheerleaders		
Transportation	52.20	
Sixteen sweaters	320.00	
Cleaning sweaters	96.00	
Total cheerleader expense		$ 468.20
TOTAL EXPENSES		7040.18
RECEIPTS		
Football		
Newburgh game	$1311.70	
Norwalk game	1819.60	
Yonkers game	1129.50	
Bridgeport game	1100.00	
Guarantee (New Haven)	120.00	
TOTAL RECEIPTS		$5480.80

ESTIMATING RECEIPTS

Some steps that might be followed for estimating receipts in the general school budget and that also have application to the physical education budget include gathering and analyzing all pertinent data, including past and current information, estimating all income based on a comprehensive view of income sources, organizing and classifying receipts in appropriate categories, estimating revenue from all gathered data, comparing estimates with previous years, and drawing up a final draft of receipts.

EXPENDITURES

In physical education and athletic budgets, typical examples of expenditures are items of *capital outlay,* such as a swimming pool; *expendable equipment,* such as basketballs; and a *maintenance and repair provision,* such as towel and laundry service and the refurbishing of uniforms. See Table 10-3 for a sample list of expenditures for athletics.

Some expenditures are easy to estimate but others are more difficult, requiring accurate inventories, past records, and careful analysis of the condition of the equipment. Some items and services will need to be figured by averaging costs over a period of years, such as cleaning and mending athletic equipment. Awards, new equipment needed, guarantees to visiting teams, and medical services for emergencies are other expenditures that must be included.

Some sound procedures to follow in estimating expenditures include: determining objectives and goals of program; analyzing expenditures in terms of program objectives; preparing a budgetary calendar that states what accomplishments are expected and by what date; estimating expenditures by also considering past, present, and future needs; comparing estimates with expenditures from previous years; and thoroughly evaluating estimates before preparing a final draft.

Cost-cutting procedures

In light of current economic problems some managers are cutting costs, according to the survey of directors of physical education and athletics in New York. This is being accomplished by such means as cutting referees' pay, eliminating insurance, having fewer athletic contests, doing away with low participation sports, using volunteer coaches, discontinuing the purchase of personally used items, reducing the number of coaches, lowering coaches' salaries, eliminating sports where rental facilities are used, scheduling different teams on the same day and combining transportation for these teams, and sharing uniforms by several teams.

BUDGET PRESENTATION AND ADOPTION

In a school, physical education budgets after being prepared should usually be submitted to the superintendent through the principal's office. The principal is the person in charge of his or her particular building; therefore subdivision budgets should be presented to him or her for approval. Good management means, furthermore, that the budgetary items have been reviewed with the principal during their preparation, so that approval is usually routine.

In colleges and universities, the proper channels should be followed. This might mean clearance through a dean or other management officer. Each person who is responsible for budget preparation and presentation should be familiar with the proper working channels.

For successful presentation and adoption, the budget should be prepared in final form only after careful consideration so that little change will be needed. Requests for funds should be justifiable, and ample preliminary discussion of the budget with persons and groups most directly concerned should be held so needless difficulty will be avoided.

BUDGET MANAGEMENT

After the presentation and approval of the budget, the next step is to see that it is managed properly. This means it should be followed closely with periodic checks on expenditures to see that they fall within the budget appropriations provided. The budget should be a guide to economical and efficient administration.

BUDGET APPRAISAL

Periodic appraisal calls for an audit of the accounts and an evaluation of the school program resulting from the management of the current budget. Such appraisal should be done honestly and with a view to eliminating weaknesses in current budgets and strengthening future ones. It should also be remembered that the budget will be only as good as the management makes it and that the budget will improve only as the management improves.

ZERO BASE BUDGETING

Zero base budgeting, a procedure and system that is based on a justification for all expenditures of an organization at the time the budget is formulated, was developed and introduced by the Texas Instruments Company in 1969.

The traditional method of developing a budget is to use the previous year's budget as a base and then require a justification for any increase that is requested for the ensuing year. For example, if $500 had been allocated for intramurals the previous year and the intramural director asked for $600 this year, then only the $100 increase would have to be justified.

Zero base budgeting, on the other hand, requires a justification of all expenditures that are requested. In the example above, the entire $600 would have to be justified. In other words, each element or subdivision of an organization that is allocated funds starts from zero and any and all funds requested must be justified in light of their contribution to the achievement of the objectives of the organization.

Zero base budgeting requires each subdivision or program of an organization to justify its request for funds, requires planning regarding how these subdivisions can contribute to the achievement of the organization's goals, and brings decision making into the procedure. Zero base budgeting could mean that some elements of an organization have outgrown their usefulness and no longer will receive any funds whatsoever. Also, it could mean that new programs would be more likely to receive funds if they can be shown to be in line with and capable of contributing to organization goals.

The steps followed in zero base budgeting include identifying the goals of the organization, planning a program to meet goals, identifying alternative ways to achieve goals in light of budgetary constraints, doing a cost analysis of the alternatives, and then arriving at a decision in light of the analysis regarding what functions or alternatives should receive funding.

Zero base budgeting could be especially valuable to organizations so steeped in tradition that they are not capitalizing on current trends and developments and need to implement new ideas and projects. This type of budgeting can also make it possible to see that funds are used in the most effective way to achieve organizational goals.

PPBES—PLANNING-PROGRAMMING-BUDGETING AND EVALUATION SYSTEM

PPBES came about as a solution to problems of fiscal accountability and optimal use of limited resources.

A history of PPBES

PPBS, as it was originally known, started in 1949 when the Hoover Commission report on the organization of the executive branch recommended that the government adopt a budget based on function, activities, and objectives. In 1954 the Rand Corporation developed a performance budget for use in military spending. Planning-Programming-Budgeting System (PPBS) was the title given to this system. The DuPont Corporation and the Ford Motor Company were among the first to use PPBS. In the early 1960s Robert McNamara introduced the system to the Defense Department. The results of the system were so impressive that President Johnson ordered all federal departments and agencies to adopt PPBES by August 1965. Presently, many schools, colleges, and other organizations are using this system, and many more are researching the feasibility of using it in their particular cases. PPBS became PPBES when the function of *evaluation* was added.

Definition of PPBES

PPBES may be defined as a long-range plan to accomplish an organization's objectives, using continual feedback and updating of information to allow for greater efficiency in the decision-making process. The four elements of PPBES are as follows:

1. Planning—establishing objectives
2. Programming—combining activities and events to produce distinguishable results
3. Budgeting—allocating resources, the financial plan for meeting program needs
4. Evaluation—determining how adequately the

budget fits the program, the program meets the objectives; and the relationship of accomplishments to cost

First, the objectives of the organization must be clearly defined. All activities that contribute to the same objective, regardless of placement in the organization, are grouped together. A financial plan designed to reach these objectives is formulated for a particular time period. An analysis document discusses long-range needs and evaluates the adequacy, effectiveness, costs, benefits, and difficulties inherent in the proposed program. Under PPBES, funds must be used with definitive goals in mind. In this way accountability for expenditures is stressed. In using PPBES each activity and educational program is considered, not only by itself but also with respect to other educational programs that comprise the whole system. In this way the needs of the entire school system or organization are considered.

The PPBES cycle[2] (Fig. 10-1)

The steps necessary to apply PPBES follow:

1. *Goals and objectives must be determined.* Goals and objectives should be stated in terms of behavior and performance. The deserved results of the program should also be determined in relation to knowledge, skills, and attitudes.
2. *Statement of needs and problems.* Needs and problems of the particular organization must be adequately defined.
3. *A determination of expected satisfaction of needs is essential.* Numbers of persons and skills needed must also be determined.
4. *Constraints and feasibility.* Both of these items must be evaluated to determine whether the system can overcome certain limitations (personnel, materials, facilities). The system may need modification in terms of needs or objectives to overcome the existing limitations.
5. *Alternative programs.* These programs outline the different ways the organization can reach its goals. Alternative programs should be evaluated in terms of needs, goals, and constraints of the system.
6. *Resource requirements must be estimated.* The resource needs of each alternative must be computed. The easiest way to do this is to derive the faculty teaching cost per student credit hour and then add department costs, counseling, administration, equipment, and clerical costs.
7. *Estimate benefits to be gained from each alternative.* The benefits of the program must be determined in relationship to student accomplishment at present and in the future.
8. *Develop an operating plan.* From the data collected, all alternatives should be weighed against fixed criteria such as cost of implementation and risk in-

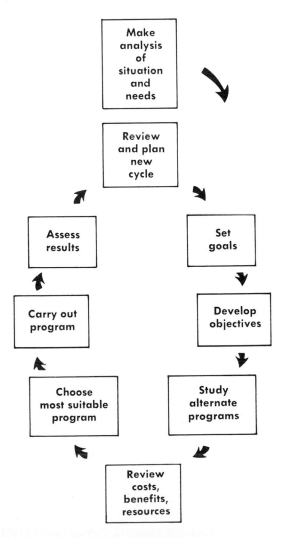

Fig. 10-1. The PPBES Cycle.

volved, estimated benefits, and future budget allocations.

9. *Pilot implementation of best alternative*. A pilot program should be conducted at a level where it could be modified or changed without involved or costly effort.

10. *Evaluation*. The data from the pilot program should be used in determining whether it is meeting the objectives of the organization. It should be modified accordingly.

11. *Feedback and further modification*. Once PPBES is in process, it should be continually reevaluated and modified to ensure that the goals and objectives agreed on are being met.

Advantages and disadvantages of PPBES

Before implementing PPBES in an institution, the management must be thoroughly familiar with the advantages and disadvantages of such a system. Each situation differs, and careful analysis before implementation is essential.

Some of the advantages of PPBES follow:

1. The system aids in formulating goals, objectives, and skills.
2. Curriculum can be designed to meet the objectives formulated.
3. Staff members can be provided with prior planning and resource material.
4. Alternative plans can be more systematically analyzed.
5. Costs and accomplishments may be compared.
6. Staff members are more involved in decision making.
7. Instructional costs may be easily identified.
8. Innovation can be promoted in programs.
9. Evaluating criteria is continually applied to the system.
10. Public awareness and understanding are increased.

The disadvantages of such a system:

1. Staff time is limited, and staff members with sufficient technical skills in these areas are also limited.
2. Implementation may lead to conflict and resistance from community members.
3. Cost-benefit analysis is difficult to quantitate; some benefits from education are not easily measurable.
4. Communication among staff members may be limited as a result of centralization of system planning.

5. PPBES is a method of indicating the best use of funds; however, in doing so, funds are also expended, and limited budgets may not be able to implement such a system.
6. The vocabulary is vague to those who are not directly involved in using such a system.
7. PPBES may be mistakenly seen as a substitute for management rather than a tool of management.
8. Alternatives with great potential are passed up because of their high chance of failure according to PPBES criteria.
9. Some persons may feel that they are answerable to the ''system'' for their program; however, the ''system'' should be an aid, not a deterrent.

Using PPBES

Surveys indicate that more than 1000 schools in the United States use PPBES with their budgets. Michigan and California are two examples.

The Michigan program. Michigan has adopted PPBES in its publicly funded institutions of higher learning. Although the system costs more money, it enables administrators to have greater information for decision making and gives taxpayers a better indication of where their money is being spent.

The California program. Under the director of the Advisory Commission on School District Budgeting and Accounting, 15 pilot school districts used PPBES. They simplified plans so they were readily understandable to voters in the hope that the public's understanding would help the passage of school bond issues. When explained in terms of objectives and expected accomplishments, the voters supported budgets and approved programs.

It is obvious from the California and Michigan examples that PPBES is a process that can help use available funds wisely, point up problem areas, and improve program defects. In addition, the public is given clear and understandable data to aid in deciding on budgets.

How can PPBES be applied to physical education and athletic programs?

Physical education has much to gain by implementing PPBES. If this system is used, physical education programs and budget requests cannot be arbitrarily dropped or refused because of inadequate funding. Each segment of the curriculum must be given equal emphasis according to objectives and benefits derived from meeting these objectives.

Physical education and athletic budgets before PPBES were considered in terms of bats and balls rather than total program needs and benefits. PPBES is now used by physical education departments to comprehensively present needed information required by administrators. PPBES provides management with a detailed list of goals and objectives, an analysis of problems, alternatives, solutions, and recommendations. The most important accomplishment of PPBES is the way it relates program costs to expected accomplishments.

COST ANALYSIS

Cost analysis of materials used in a program is a derivative of cost accounting. Cost analysis is needed to help the manager evaluate present operations as well as project future planning. Cost analysis is limited to the types of accounting systems being used as well as designating the unit to be compared. It is particularly applicable to schools and colleges. For example, some schools operate on grades one to eight, kindergarten to grade twelve, or some other educational pattern. Naturally, a great difference in expenditures per pupil would occur in the various patterns of organization.

Various units are used in cost analysis in a school's general education fund. The number of pupils in attendance, the census, average daily attendance, and average daily membership are some of those used. Each of the various units has advantages and disadvantages.

As a raw measure of educational costs, the aver-

Joggers going through their routines at the Institute for Aerobics Research in Dallas, Texas.

age daily membership is a better measure than the average daily attendance. Teachers' salaries must be paid whether pupils are in 90% or 100% attendance, and desks and school books must be available whether pupils are in attendance or not. With respect to raw per capita units, the average daily membership is a better unit to measure the educational costs than the more commonly used average daily attendance unit. Tradition, however, has favored the average daily attendance unit over average daily membership.

Cost analysis as it relates to equipment and supplies for physical education and athletics may be simply handled by allowing a certain number of dollars per pupil or per participant, depending on whether one is concerned with a school or another organizational program.

Some experts in fiscal management feel a per capita expenditure allocation for physical education and athletics represents a good foundation program. However, they recommend in addition (1) an extra percentage allocation for program enrichment, (2) an extra percentage allocation for variation in enrollment, and (3) a reference to a commodity index (current prices of equipment and supplies) that may indicate need for changes in the per capita expenditure because of current increase or decrease in the value of the items being purchased.

To determine the amount of money needed for physical education and athletic programs the following example can be used as a guideline. The director of health and physical education submits and substantiates the needs for the coming school year; increased expenditures—a sound estimate of projected increases regarding pupil program participation based on increased enrollments, pupil interest, program changes, and the anticipated cost of equipment and supplies to be used; inventory—present equipment and supplies on hand and the condition of these items; and the previous year's budget—amounts allocated in previous year or years. These items represent the basis on which most allocations of funds to physical education and athletic programs are determined.

Directors of physical education and athletic programs surveyed felt that when they were granted increases in per capita allocations it was the result of such factors as increase in the number of participants,

a careful evaluation of the number of participants and the time they spent using the equipment and supplies, the cost per hour, and an excellent working rapport with the board of education.

THE BUSINESS ADMINISTRATOR AND FISCAL MANAGEMENT IN SCHOOLS AND COLLEGES

Schools and colleges today are in the business of education. The size of the physical plant and the large expenditures require the talents of a qualified business administrator. The school or college business administrator is an integral part of the entire management team and ideally should have experience in both business administration and education. He or she is primarily responsible for the efficient and economic management of business matters concerning the educational institution.

Physical education and athletic directors must understand and appreciate the vital role of the business administrator. Many management functions of physical educators, including fiscal management, fall within the responsibility of the business administrator. The business administrator is a specialist in this area, and educators should work closely with this individual in reference to business-related matters.

The school or college business administrator is an important member of the management team who has a significant contribution to make in the decision-making process, as well as in executing business functions. He or she is well versed in educational matters, as well as in business management. He or she is in a position to participate under the superintendent's or president's leadership in making decisions concerned with fiscal matters.

The college business manager, or the vice-president for business affairs, as the person is sometimes called, is responsible for budget preparation and fiscal accounting, investment of endowment and other monies, planning and construction of buildings, data processing, management of research and other contracts, business aspects of student loans, and intercollegiate activities.

Most key business officers have earned a master's or a doctor's degree, usually in business administration. However, some are certified public accountants and some have taken courses in management institutes. Most college business managers are recruited outside the academic world.

For the purposes of this text, the term *business administrator* is used, and the duties of such an educational officer are discussed in terms of schools and the school district. However, the functions outlined for the business administrator, the problems discussed, and the working relationship with physical education personnel are similar to or have implications for physical educators in colleges and other organizations.

Function

The business administrator's function is strictly limited by the size of the educational triangle—program, receipts, expenditures (Fig. 10-2). The greater the perimeter of the triangle, the larger the sphere of operations. This applies to all departments in the system. Likewise, in times of inflation, the expenditures and receipts may increase, and as a result, the program side may also increase, but the actual program could remain the same. Hence, it is obvious that the business administrator must project both expenditures and receipts if a constant program is going to be maintained.

The business office represents a means to an end and it can be evaluated in terms of how well it contributes to the realization of the objectives of education.

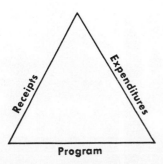

Fig. 10-2. The business administrator's isosceles triangle.

Objectives

In serving schools and colleges, the business administrator constantly has the goal of helping them obtain the greatest educational service possible from each tax or aid dollar spent. He or she should take a democratic approach on decisions affecting others. A decision will then be reached that will be for the best, with the assurance that the educational benefits are worth the cost.

The business administrator is part of the team of administrators—along with presidents, principals, superintendents, and board members—who may be expected to look into the years ahead and have some ideas regarding the future plans of the school or college.

Responsibilities

The business administrator's responsibilities are varied. He or she is as familiar with employee health insurance problems as with state and federal allocations for education. In the smaller school district the business responsibilities are incorporated into the duties of the chief school administrator. As districts enlarge, they need to hire a person to oversee all the nonteaching areas of the district so the chief school administrator is free to devote more time to the educational programs of the district. No two districts are alike in handling business responsibilities.

Following are some of the administrator's duties as listed by Frederick W. Hill, a past president of the Association of School Business Officials:

Budget and financial planning. This is an area in which the business official has to be sensitive to the needs of staff members to carry out a program. One also must have a sixth sense to understand how much the community can expend on the program. This can be related to the accompanying isosceles triangle. A direct relationship must exist among all the components that make up the three sides of the triangle.

Purchasing and supply management. The business official must use the best purchasing techniques to obtain maximum value for every dollar spent. After purchases are made and goods received, he or she is responsible for warehousing, storage, and inventory control. An article offered at the cheapest price is not always the most economical to purchase.

Plans. The business official works with administrators, teachers, architects, attorneys, and citizens of the community in developing plans for expansion of building facilities.

Personnel. The business official's duties vary in relation to the size of the district. In a large district he or she may be in charge of the nonteaching personnel, and in a small district he or she may be in charge of all personnel. In this capacity the official has to maintain records, pay schedules, retirement reports, and other personnel records.

Staff improvement. The business official is always interested in upgrading the people under his or her jurisdiction by providing workshops and in-service courses concerning latest developments in the field.

Community relations. Without community support the school would not operate. Some administrators tend to forget this when they become too far removed from the community. There is always a need to interpret the business area to the public.

Transportation. It has often been said that boards of education find themselves spending too much time on the three Bs—buses, buildings, and bonds. When this occurs, it is time to look into hiring a business official.

Food services. The business official is responsible for the efficient management of food services.

Accounting and reporting. The business official establishes and supervises the financial records and accounting procedures.

Debt service. The business official is involved with various capital developments and financial planning through short-term and long-term programs. Part of the financial rating of a school or a college district is judged on the way its debt service is handled.

Insurance. The business official must be familiar with a large schedule of insurance provisions ranging from fire and liability to health insurance. He or she must maintain records for proof in case of loss.

Legal matters. The business official has to be fa-

Checking for fitness at PepsiCo in Purchase, New York. The key factors in the success of PepsiCo's program are an atmosphere in which fitness and health are encouraged and personal examples are set by top level management, the availability of a professional staff, and the accessibility of facilities and supervision to all employees.

Table 10-2. Sample sports program, general organization, and board of education report of expenditures and receipts

Sports	Board of education	General organization	Total
TOTAL EXPENDITURES			
Baseball	$ 765.75		$ 765.75
Basketball	890.70	$ 106.34	997.04
Football	847.68	3943.09	4340.77
Cross country	129.00	37.00	166.00
Cheerleaders	126.58	249.10	375.68
Golf	91.50		91.50
Hockey	842.25	48.95	891.20
Soccer	343.20		343.20
Swimming	456.10	41.10	497.20
Tennis	40.00	4.00	44.00
Track	516.27	15.03	531.30
TOTAL	$5049.03	$3994.61	$9043.64
TOTAL GENERAL ORGANIZATION RECEIPTS			
Football		$2740.40	
Basketball		381.30	
TOTAL			$3121.70

miliar with education law, and he or she must know when to consult with attorneys.

System analysis. The business official must constantly question existing systems to see if they can be changed so the job can be done more efficiently. New methods are being introduced using data processing that will be a challenge, as well as an aid, to the business official.

Money raising. The business administrator is frequently called on to lead fund-raising drives for colleges and universities.

Grants and financial aid. The business official must be aware of money available for programs through private, state, and federal grants and money available for scholarship candidates from private and public sources.

FINANCIAL ACCOUNTABILITY

The large amount of money involved in physical education and athletic programs makes strict accountability mandatory. This includes the maintenance of accurate records, proper distribution of materials, and adequate appraisal and evaluation of procedures. Financial accounting should provide a record of receipts

Table 10-3. A sample list of expenditures for athletics

	Baseball	Basketball	Football	Cross country	Golf	Hockey	Soccer	Swimming	Tennis	Track	Total
Equipment and supplies	$369.55	$158.30	$279.68	$ 45.80	$36.01	$251.65	$ 70.40	$ 80.05	$ 27.20	$231.77	$1549.50
Transportation	208.50	248.70	39.60	83.20	48.40	495.00	63.70	108.80	93.78	120.90	1510.48
Officials	122.00	391.35	50.00				52.00				615.35
Cleaning	65.70	30.95	129.40			95.60	57.20			141.10	519.95
Supervision		66.00									66.00
Custodian		37.00									37.00
Additional coaching			350.00				100.00				450.00
Entry fees					7.00			17.21	4.00	22.50	50.75
Rental, club pool								250.00			250.00
TOTALS	$765.75	$932.30	$847.68	$129.00	$91.50	$842.25	$343.20	$456.10	$124.78	$516.27	$5049.03

REASONS FOR FINANCIAL ACCOUNTING

To provide a method of authorizing expenditures for items that have been included and approved in the budget. This means proper accounting records are being used.

To provide authorized procedures for making purchases of equipment, supplies, and other materials and to let contracts for various services

To provide authorized procedures for paying the proper amounts (a) for purchases of equipment, supplies, and other materials, which have been checked upon receipt, (b) for actual labor, and (c) for other services rendered

To provide a record of each payment made, including the date, to whom, for what purpose, and other pertinent material

To provide authorized procedures for handling various receipts and sources of income

To provide the detailed information essential for properly auditing accounts, such as confirmation that money has been spent for accurately specified items

To provide material and information for the preparation of future budgets

To provide a tangible base for developing future policies relating to financial planning

and expenditures for all departmental transactions, a permanent record of all financial transactions for future reference, a pattern for expenditures closely related to the approved budget, a tangible documentation of compliance with mandates and requests imposed either by law or by administrative action, an evaluation procedure to ensure that funds are dealt with honestly, and proper management with respect to control, analysis of costs, and reporting.

Management policies for financial accounting

The management has the final responsibility for accountability for all equipment and supplies. Departments should establish and enforce policies covering loss, damage, theft, misappropriation, or destruction of equipment and supplies or other materials. A system of accurate record keeping should be established and be uniform throughout the organization. The person to whom equipment and supplies are issued should be held accountable for these materials. Accurate inventories should be kept.

Accounting for receipts and expenditures

A centralized accounting system is advantageous, with all funds being deposited with the treasurer, business manager, or other responsible person. Purchase orders and other procedures are usually then countersigned or certified by the proper official, thus better guaranteeing integrity in the use of funds. A system of bookkeeping wherein books are housed in the central office by the finance officer helps ensure better control of finances and allows all subdivisions or departments in a system to be financially controlled in the same manner. Such a procedure also provides better and more centralized record keeping. The central accounting system fund accounts, in which the physical education and athletic funds are located, should be audited annually by qualified persons. Finally, an annual financial report should be made and publicized to indicate receipts, expenditures, and other pertinent data associated with the enterprise.

All receipts and expenditures should be recorded in the ledger properly, providing such important information as the fund in which it has been deposited, or from which it was withdrawn, and the money received from sources such as athletics and organization dues should be shown with sufficient cross references and detailed information. Supporting vouchers should also be at hand. Tickets to athletic and other events should be numbered consecutively and checked to get an accurate record of ticket sales. Students should not be permitted to handle funds except under the supervision of some member of the administrative staff or faculty. All accounts should be properly audited at appropriate intervals.

Purchase orders on regular authorized forms issued by the organization should be used, so accurate records may be kept. To order verbally is a questionable policy. Preparing written purchase orders, on regular forms and according to good accountability procedure, better ensures legality of contract together with prompt delivery and payment.

THE ROLE OF THE MANAGER IN BUDGETING

A. Preliminary considerations in preparing the budget
 1. Program additions or deletions
 2. Staff changes
 3. Inventory of equipment on hand
B. Budget preparation: additional considerations
 1. Athletic gate receipts and expenditures—athletic association fund
 2. Board of education budget—allocations for physical education, including athletics
 3. Coaches' request and requests of teachers and department heads
 4. Comparison of requests with inventories
 5. Itemizing and coding requests
 6. Budget conferences with administration
 7. Justification of requests
C. Athletic association funds: considerations
 1. Estimated income
  a. Gate receipts
  b. Student activities tickets
  c. Tournament receipts
 2. Estimated expenditures
  a. Awards
  b. Tournament fees
  c. Films
  d. Miscellaneous
  e. Surplus
D. General budget: considerations
 1. Breakdown
  a. By sport or activity
  b. Transportation
  c. Salaries of personnel
  d. Insurance
  e. Reconditioning of equipment
  f. Supervision
  g. General and miscellaneous
  h. Equipment
  i. Officials
 2. Codes
  a. Advertising
  b. Travel
  c. Conferences
  d. Others
E. Postbudget procedures
 1. Selection of equipment and supplies
 2. Preparation of list of dealers to bid
 3. Request for price quotations
 4. Requisitions
 5. Care of equipment

6. Notification of teachers and coaches of amounts approved
F. Ordering procedures
 1. Study the quality of various products
 2. Accept no substitutes for items ordered
 3. Submit request for price quotations
 4. Select low quotes or jusify higher quotes
 5. Submit purchase orders
 6. Check and count all shipments
 7. Record items received on inventory cards
 8. Provide for equipment and supply accountability
G. Relationships with administration
 1. Consultation—program plans with building principal and/or superintendent
 2. Make budget recommendations to administration
 3. Advise business manager of procedures followed
 4. Discuss items approved and deleted with business manager
 5. Advise teachers and coaches of amounts available and adjust requests
H. Suggestions for prospective directors of physical education programs
 1. Develop a philosophy and approach to budgeting
 2. Consult with staff for their suggestions
 3. Select quality merchandise
 4. Provide proper care and maintenance of equipment and supplies
 5. Provide for all programs on an equitable basis
 6. Budget adequately but not elaborately
 7. Provide a sound, well-rounded program of physical education
 8. Emphasize equality for girls and boys
 9. Provide for basic instructional, adapted, intramural and extramural, and interscholastic parts of the program
 10. Conduct a year-round public relations program
 11. Try to overcome these possible shortcomings:
  a. Board of education not oriented to needs of physical education
  b. Program not achieving established goals
  c. Staff not adequately informed and involved in administrative process

CHECKLIST FOR BUDGETING AND FINANCIAL ACCOUNTING

	Yes	No
1. Has a complete inventory been taken and itemized on proper forms as a guide in estimating equipment needs?		
2. Does the equipment inventory include a detailed account of the number of items on hand, size and quantity, type, condition, etc.?		
3. Is the inventory complete, current, and up-to-date?		
4. Are budgetary estimates as accurate and realistic as possible without padding?		
5. Are provisions made in the budget for increases expected in enrollments, increased pupil participation, and changes in the cost of equipment and supplies?		
6. Have supply house and the business administrator been consulted on the cost of new equipment?		
7. Has the Director of Physical Education and Athletics consulted with the staff on various budget items?		
8. Has the Director of Physical Education and Athletics consulted with the school business administrator in respect to the total budget for the department?		
9. Are new equipment and supply needs for physical education and athletics determined and budgeted at least one year in advance?		
10. Was the budget prepared according to the standards desired by the chief school administrator?		
11. Are statistics and information for previous years indicated as a means of comparison?.		
12. Is there a summary of receipts and expenditures listed concisely on one page so that the total budget can be quickly seen?		
13. If receipts from athletics or other funds are to be added to the budget, is this shown?		
14. Are there alternate program plans with budgetary changes in the event the budget is not approved?		
15. Has a statement of objectives of the program been included that reflects the overall educational philosophy and program of the total school and community?		
16. Has the budget been prepared so that the major aspects may be viewed readily by those persons desiring a quick review and also in more detail for those persons desiring a further delineation of the budgetary items?		
17. Is the period of time for which the budget has been prepared clearly indicated?		
18. Is the physical education and athletics budget based on an educational plan developed to attain the goals and purposes agreed on by the director and his staff within the framework of the total school's philosophy?		
19. Is the physical education and athletics plan a comprehensive one reflecting a healthful environment, physical education class, adapted, intramural and extramural, and interscholastic program?		
20. Does the plan include a statement of the objectives of the physical education and athletic programs and are these reflected in the budget?		
21. Are both long-range and short-range plans for achieving the purposes of the program provided?		
22. Have provisions been made in the budget for emergencies?		
23. Are accurate records kept on such activities involving expenditures of money as transportation, insurance, officials, laundry and dry cleaning, awards, guarantees, repairs, new equipment, medical expenses, and publicity?		

CHECKLIST FOR BUDGETING AND FINANCIAL ACCOUNTING—cont'd

	Yes	No
24. Are accurate records kept on the receipt of monies from such sources as gate receipts and advertising revenue?		
25. Once the budget has been approved, is there a specific plan provided for authorizing expenditures?		
26. Are specific forms used for recording purchase transactions?		
27. Are purchases on all major items based on competitive bidding?		
28. Are requisitions used in obtaining supplies and equipment?		
29. Are requisitions numbered and do they include such information as the name of the person originating the requisition, when the item to be purchased will be needed, where to ship the item, the description and/or code number, quantity, unit price, and amount?		
30. With the exception of petty cash accounts, is a central purchasing system in effect?		
31. Is the policy of quantity purchasing followed whenever possible and desirable in the interest of economy?		
32. If quantity purchasing is used, are advanced thought and planning given to storage and maintenance facilities and procedures?		
33. Are performance tests made of items purchased? Are state, regional, or national testing bureaus or laboratories utilized where feasible?		
34. Are receipts of equipment and supplies checked carefully?		
35. Is an audit made of all expenditures?		
36. Are specific procedures in effect to safeguard money, property, and employees?		
37. Is there a check to determine that established standards, policies, and procedures have been followed?		
38. Are procedures in operation to check condition and use of equipment and supplies?		
39. Is a financial report made periodically?		
40. Are there proper procedures for the care and maintenance and accountability of all equipment and supplies?		
41. Are accurate records kept on all equipment and supplies, including condition, site, and age?		
42. Have established procedures been developed and are they followed in regard to the issuance, use, and return of equipment?		
43. Have provisions been made for making regular notations of future needs?		

SUMMARY

The management of physical education and athletic programs must be concerned with proper fiscal administration. The lack of money from traditional sources such as a school district's general fund is prompting many organizations to look to government, foundations, the corporate sector, and other sources for help in meeting their fiscal needs. Other organizations are engaging in special fund-raising projects such as raffles to get the help they need. The management of funds also requires a knowledge of such things as how to prepare and implement budgets, how to determine proper costs of equipment and supplies, how to use zero base budgeting and PPBES, and how to provide for fiscal accountability within the organization.

SELF-ASSESSMENT TESTS

These tests will assist students in determining if material and competencies presented in this chapter have been mastered.

1. What are five reasons for fiscal management in physical education and athletic programs?
2. Outline the procedure you would follow in preparing a budget if you were the chairperson of a department of physical education and athletics for a city educational system.
3. Develop a detailed PPBES plan for a department of physical education and athletics.
4. As a business administrator in a school system, what aspects of fiscal management would involve you with the administration of a physical education and athletic program?
5. Formulate 10 policies to ensure sound financial accounting.

REFERENCES

1. Aufesser, P.M., and Mechikoff, R.: Journal of Physical Education, Recreation and Dance **55**:69 August 1984.
2. Clegg, A.A., Jr.: The teacher and manager of the curriculum, Educational Leadership, January 1973, p. 308.
3. Klappholz, L.A.: Physical Education Newsletter, November 1980.
4. Parkhouse, B.L., and Dennison, Maria: ''Pay for play: solution or stopgap?'' Athletic Business, April 1984, p. 12.
5. Roe, W.H.: School business management, New York, 1961, McGraw-Hill Book Company.
6. ''What happens when the money runs out?'' Athletic Purchasing and Facilities, July 1981, p. 44.

SUGGESTED READINGS

- Austin, D.A.: ''Economic impact on physical education,'' Journal of Physical Education, Recreation and Dance **55**:35, May/June 1984.
  Tells how government and many other sources of funds that affect physical education programs have been cut back. It then lists strategies for a lifetime game plan, the main one of which stresses that the way to sustain physical education is to provide excellent instructional programs in this field. The value of being taught to actively engage in physical exercise should be continually stressed since the public is willing to supply funds to accomplish the objectives that result from such programs.

- Bronzan, R.: Fund raising today demands better ideas, Athletic Business, May 1984, p. 12.
  Accents the need to raise for physical education and athletic programs in schools and colleges. Such outside sources need to be tapped if such programs are to survive. Provides suggestions for procuring outside funds.

- Dougherty, N.J., and Bonanno, D.: Management principles in sport and leisure services, Minneapolis, 1985, Burgess Publishing.
  Chapter 6 of this text covers financial management and discusses fiscal aspects such as operating versus capital budgets, types of budgets, preparing and presenting the budget, and sources of funding.

- Jackson, J.J.: Sport administration, Springfield, Ill., 1981, Charles C Thomas, Publisher.
  For sports programs chapter 8 in this text provides information on budgets, the budget process, budget guidelines and format. It also discusses financial control and accounting.

- Lewandowski, D.M.: Shoestrings and shoeboxes, Journal of Physical Education, Recreation and Dance **55**:34, August 1984.
  Provides suggestions how a school without sufficient cash can, through ingenuity plus time, come up with solutions for insufficient space and solutions for insufficient equipment. It also provides many suggestions in chart form for homemade equipment, how items can be constructed, and in what activities they can be used.

- Lopiano, D.A.: New ideas for promotion and fund raising in non revenue sports, Athletic Purchasing and Facilities, October 1983, p. 14.
  Tells how athletic departments can improve fund raising and promotion by combining strategies of business and nonprofit revenue production.

Chapter Eleven

The Purchase and Care of Supplies and Equipment

Instructional Objectives and Competencies to be Achieved
After reading this chapter the student should be able to

- Show why sound supply and equipment management is important and explain the basis on which supplies and equipment should be selected for physical education and athletic programs.
- Discuss the various procedures and principles that should be followed in purchasing supplies and equipment.
- List guidelines for the selection of an equipment manager and for the administration of the equipment room.
- Establish a system for checking, issuing, and maintaining supplies and equipment.
- Justify the need for various types of audiovisual supplies and equipment for physical education and athletic programs.

In the chapter on fiscal management it was shown that much of the money allotted was used to purchase supplies and equipment for physical education and athletic programs. Management has the responsibility for seeing that the supplies and equipment that are purchased will meet program needs, be of good quality, and are acquired via a procedural pattern that represents efficient administration.

Physical education and athletic programs use many supplies and equipment that cost thousands of dollars. *Supplies* are those materials that are expendable and that need to be replaced at frequent intervals, such as shuttlecocks and adhesive tape. *Equipment* refers to those items that are not considered expendable but are used for a period of years, such as parallel bars and audiometers.

Because so much money is spent on supplies and equipment and such materials are vital to the health and safety of participants, to good playing conditions, and to values derived from the programs, it is important that this management phase of the specialized fields of physical education and athletics be considered carefully. The purchase of supplies and equipment should also be related to achieving the objectives designated by PPBES. Physical educators should express their need for equipment and other materials in terms of the goals these aids represent.

Many different sources for purchasing equipment exist, many grades and qualities of materials are available, and many methods of storing and maintaining such merchandise are prevalent. Some of these sources, grades, and methods are good, and some are questionable. To obtain the best value for the money, basic principles of selecting, purchasing, and maintaining need to be understood.

DETERMINING SUPPLY AND EQUIPMENT NEEDS

Supplies and equipment needs vary according to certain influencing factors. These include the programs themselves and the activities offered. Other factors are the facilities, the training rooms, and playing space available. Some organizations have only limited physical education facilities. Under such conditions the supplies and equipment needed differ from those required in settings where spacious accommodations exist. Other factors to consider are the nature of the clientele (age, sex, and number), the money available, the length of playing seasons, and health and safety provisions. Those responsible for purchasing supplies and equipment should carefully study their own particular situations and estimate their own needs objectively and realistically.[6]

In the athletic training area, first aid supplies, scales, examining tables, beds, towels, and sheets will be needed. In the physical education skill area, all types of balls, apparatus, uniforms, timers, and racks will be needed for individual, team, formal, aquatic, dance, and other activities. Different types of materials will be required for interschool and intercollegiate athletic programs, intramural and extramural programs, programs for the handicapped, and class programs.

Physical education supply and equipment needs and the manner by which they are determined vary from organization to organization. For example, an elementary school may be given equipment based on the number of students enrolled. Then, within the parameters of their budget teachers request at the end of each year the equipment and supplies they will need the following year. Another procedure that might be followed in a high school where various units of different activities constitute the program would be to have an inventory of supplies at the conclusion of each teaching unit. In athletic programs inventories are usually taken and purchase requests instituted at the end of each sport season such as at the end of the football season.

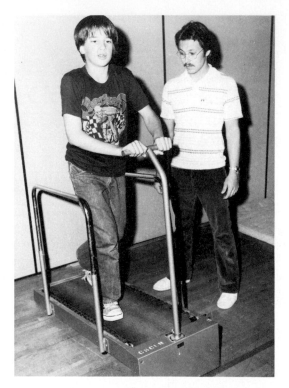

Portable treadmill for development of cardiovascular fitness.

A third procedure that is followed in cities and school districts is, in the interest of economy, to have all supplies and equipment ordered through a central office for all schools within the city or district. In such cases, items are frequently kept in a warehouse where they can be obtained as needed.

GUIDELINES FOR SELECTING SUPPLIES AND EQUIPMENT

Selection should be based on local needs. Supplies and equipment should be selected because they are needed in a particular situation and by a particular group. Items should be selected that represent materials needed to carry out the program as outlined and that represent essentials to fulfilling program objectives.

Selection should be based on quality. In the long run, the item of good quality is the cheapest and the safest. Bargain goods too often represent inferior materials that wear out much earlier. Only the best grade of football equipment should be purchased. A study was conducted on football deaths that occurred during a 25-year period and found that many of these deaths had resulted from the use of inferior helmets and other poor equipment. What is true of football is also true of other activities.

Selection should be made by competent personnel. The persons selecting the supplies and equipment needed in physical education and athletic programs should be competent. Performing this responsibility efficiently means examining many types and makes of products, conducting experiments to determine economy and durability, listing and weighing the advantages and disadvantages of different items, and knowing how each item is going to be used. The person selecting supplies and equipment should be interested in this responsibility, have the time to do the job, and be able to perform the function efficiently. Some organizations have purchasing agents who are specially trained in these matters. In small organizations the chairperson, director, or coach frequently performs this responsibility. One other point is important: regardless of who the responsible person may be, the staff member who uses these supplies and equipment in his or her particular facet of the total program should have a great deal to say about the specific items chosen. He or she is the one who understands the functional use of the merchandise.

Selecting should be continuous. A product that ranks as the best available this year may not necessarily be the best next year. Manufacturers are constantly conducting research to produce something better. There is keen competition among them. The management therefore cannot be complacent and apathetic,

Gymnastic room with equipment.

for new equipment. Management will need to weigh such factors in making its decision.

Selection should consider the handicapped. The handicapped and members of other special populations need special types of equipment to participate in many of the activities that are a part of the physical education program. Equipment is needed for such aspects of the program to perform perceptual-motor activities, to stretch and strengthen certain muscle groups, to correct postural faults, to develop balance, and to develop physical fitness.

Arnheim and Sinclair[1] discuss equipment and supplies for special populations. They include information on topics such as ordering equipment, maintenance of equipment, unsafe equipment, supervision needed, and storage space.

Selection should consider acceptable standards for athletic equipment.[4] The stamp of approval of the National Operating Committee on Standards for Athletic Equipment (NOCSAE) should be on football helmets. This will ensure that the helmet has been properly constructed and injury will be less

thinking that because a certain product has served them well in the past, it is the best buy for the future. Instead, the search for the best product available must be continuous.

Selection should consider service and replacement needs. Items of supplies and equipment may be difficult to obtain in volume. On receipt of merchandise, sizes of uniforms may be wrong, and colors may be mixed up. Additional materials may be needed on short notice. Therefore one should select items that will be available in volume, if needed, and deal with business firms that will service and replace materials and take care of emergencies without delay and controversy.

Selection should consider whether old equipment can be reconditioned successfully or whether new equipment should be purchased. Management should make this decision based on factors such as safety, cost, and suitability for effective use in activities where the item is required. In some cases, if old equipment is repaired, it may be costly; therefore it is better to buy new equipment. If the safety of participants is in question, the decision definitely should be

Laundry for washable supplies.

Nautilus exercise equipment.

Rolling equipment cart, one of several designed for specific classes of the physical education program. These are stored in the equipment room and transported to activity areas by student helpers.

```
ORIGINAL                                      REQUISITION FORM
(To Superintendent's Office)
                          BOARD OF EDUCATION
                          ————, NEW YORK
                                              DATE_____
The following supplies, equipment, or services are required for the use of
_____
                                    Teacher or Department
                                              _____
                                                     Signed
```

Quantity	Description—give complete information	Purpose	Cost Unit	Total

PURCHASE REQUISITION

Comment:

Purchase requisitions are generally initiated by a school or department to cover requirements which are needed during the school year and which are to be purchased from a supplier. Requisition should be made out in duplicate:

1. Original sent to business office for processing
2. Duplicate retained in initiating school or department

APPROVED

Superintendent of Schools

Fig. 11-1. Purchases requisition.

likely to occur. The NOCSAE researches athletic equipment and encourages acceptable standards in manufacturing athletic equipment. They also distribute this information to various organizations and individuals in the interests of safety, utility, and legal considerations. Furthermore, they provide an opportunity for individuals and organizations to consider problems regarding various aspects of athletic equipment and how they can be solved.

Selection should consider trends in athletic uniforms.[5] The emerging trends in athletic uniforms also should be taken into consideration. Some significant changes in uniforms include ventilated mesh cloth for players' uniforms, school colors for coaches' uniforms, more casual basketball uniforms (for example, shirts are worn outside pants), screen-printed lettering, one-piece wrestling uniforms, and pullover tops in baseball. The management also should be familiar with various types of material such as nylon filament, stretch nylon, cotton, acrylic, and polyester.

GUIDELINES FOR PURCHASING SUPPLIES AND EQUIPMENT

Purchases should meet the organization's requirements and have management approval. Each organization has its own policy providing for the pur-

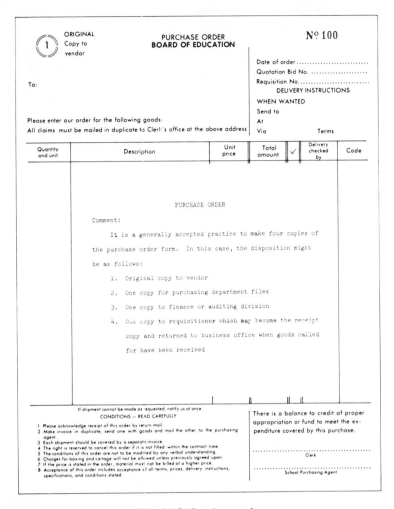

Fig. 11-2. Purchase order.

chase of supplies and equipment. It is essential that the prescribed pattern be followed and that proper management approval be obtained. Requisition forms that contain descriptions of items, amounts, and costs (Fig. 11-1), purchase orders that place the buying procedure on a written or contract basis (Fig. 11-2), and voucher forms that show receipt of materials should all be used as prescribed by regulations. The physical education manager and staff members should be familiar with and follow all the local purchasing policies.

Purchasing should be done in advance of need.[2] The main and bulk purchases of supplies and equip-ment for physical education and athletic programs should be completed well in advance of the time the materials will be used. Late orders, rushed through at the last moment, may mean mistakes or substitutions on the part of the manufacturer. When purchase orders are placed early, manufacturers have more time to carry out their responsibilities efficiently. Goods that do not meet specifications can be returned and replaced, and many other advantages result. Items needed in the fall should be ordered not later than the preceding spring, and items desired for spring use should be ordered not later than the preced-ing fall.

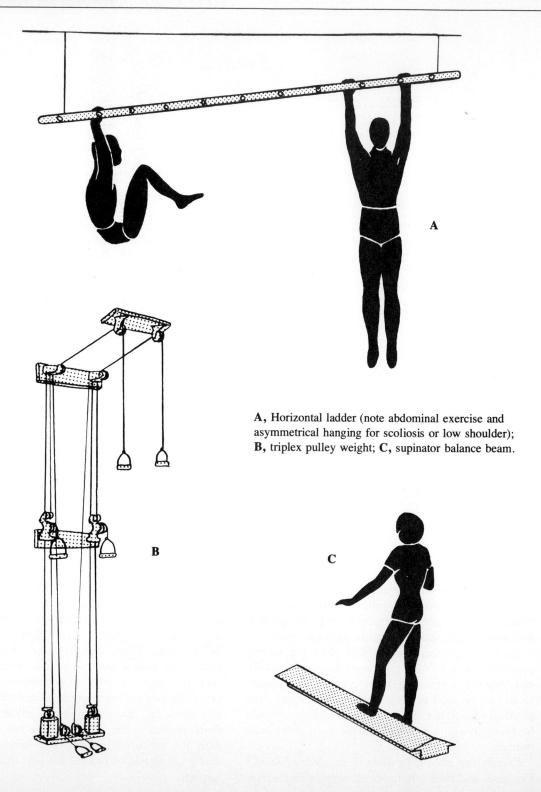

A, Horizontal ladder (note abdominal exercise and asymmetrical hanging for scoliosis or low shoulder); **B,** triplex pulley weight; **C,** supinator balance beam.

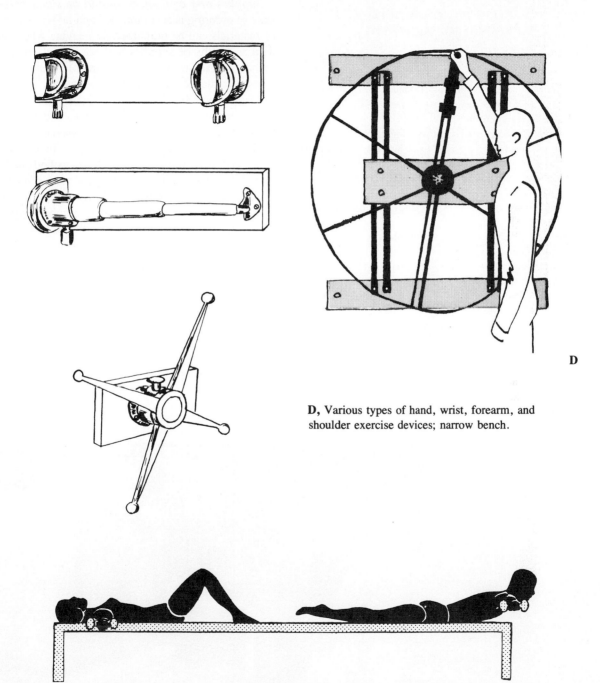

D, Various types of hand, wrist, forearm, and shoulder exercise devices; narrow bench.

> **· STEPS TO CONSIDER IN PURCHASING EQUIPMENT**
>
> *Initiation.* A request is made for equipment to fulfill, augment, supplement, or improve the program.
>
> *Review of request.* The proper management personnel approve or disapprove request after careful consideration of need.
>
> *Review of budget allocation.* A budget code number is assigned after availability of funds in that category has been determined.
>
> *Preparation of specifications.* Specifications are prepared in detail, giving exact quality requirements, and made available to prospective contractors or vendors.
>
> *Receipt of bids.* Contractors or vendors submit price quotations.
>
> *Comparisons of bids to specifications.* Careful evaluation is made to determine exact fulfillment of quality requirements.
>
> *Recommendations are made.* The business administrator prepares specific recommendations for approval.
>
> *Purchase order to supplier.* After approval, a purchase that fulfills the requirements at a competitive price is made.

Supplies and equipment should be standardized. Ease of ordering is accomplished and larger quantities of materials can be purchased at a saving when standardized items of supplies and equipment are used. Standardization means that certain colors, styles, and types of material are ordered consistently. This procedure can be followed after careful research to determine what is the best, most reliable, and most serviceable product for the money. However, standardization of supplies and equipment should never mean that further study and research to find the best materials to meet program objectives are terminated.

Specifications should be clearly set forth. The trademark, item number, catalog number, type of material, and other important specifications should be clearly stated when purchasing material to avoid any misunderstanding of what is being ordered. This procedure ensures that quality merchandise will be received when it is ordered. It also makes it possible to compare objectively bids of competing business firms. For example, if a particular brand of baseball, basketball, or football is desired, the trademark, item number, and catalog number should be clearly stated. Also, it should be pointed out that no substitutes will be accepted.

Computers are an example of important equipment needed in modern programs of physical education and athletics.

Cost should be kept as low as possible without loss of quality. Quality of materials is a major consideration. However, among various manufacturers and business concerns, prices vary for products of equal quality. Because supplies and equipment are usually purchased in considerable volume, a few cents per unit could represent a saving of many hundreds of dollars to taxpayers. Therefore, if quality can be maintained, materials should be purchased at the lowest cost figure.

Purchases should be made from reputable business firms. In some cases higher management authorities decide the firm from which supplies and equipment are to be purchased. In the event of such a procedure, this principle is academic. However, where the business firm from which purchases will be made is determined by physical education personnel, it is wise to deal with established, reputable businesses that are known to have reasonable prices, reliable materials, and good service. In the long run this is the best and safest procedure to follow.

Central purchasing can result in greater economy. Some school districts and other organizations purchase supplies and equipment for several schools or other groups. In this way they can buy larger amounts at a reduced price per unit. In some cases large school districts standardize their uniforms' colors, thus enabling them to purchase uniforms at lower prices. If desired, this system also makes it possible to have a central warehouse and a common location for orders, contracts, and other records.

Local firms should be considered. The administration's main concern is to obtain good value for money expended. If local firms can offer equal values, render equal or better service for the same money, and are reliable, then preference should probably be given to local dealers over dealers located farther away. If such conditions cannot be met a question can be raised about the wisdom of such a procedure. In some cases it is advantageous to use local dealers, because they are more readily accessible and can provide quicker and better service than firms located farther away.

Bids should be obtained. A sound management procedure that helps eliminate any accusation of favoritism and helps obtain the best price available is competitive bidding. This procedure requires that special forms be distributed to many dealers who handle the supplies and equipment desired (Fig. 11-3). In such cases, the specifics regarding the kind, amount, and quality of articles desired should be clearly stated. After bids have been obtained, the choice can be made. Low bids do not have to be accepted. However, a decision not to honor one must be justified. Such justification could be that a company's reputation is in question, the service rendered is poor, delivery cannot be made on time, or the company is situated at such a great distance that communication is hampered.

Horine[3] discusses the question of whether or not the bidding process is desirable. He points out that this process sometimes increases costs, slows down the purchasing process, discourages bids from local dealers, encourages dealers to cut prices in some way to submit lower bids, and the delivered product may be unsatisfactory.

On the other hand, Horine points out the advantages of such bidding: it stimulates honest competition, resulting in lower prices; it may result in on-time delivery; it can provide for better service; it spreads the purchasing among more vendors; it eliminates favoritism, and it lessens the risk of poorer quality of merchandise.

Gifts or favors should not be accepted from dealers. Some dealers and salesmen are happy to present an administrator or staff member with a new rifle, set of golf clubs, tennis racquet, or other gift if, in so doing, they believe it is possible to get an account. In many cases it may be poor policy to accept such gifts or favors. The reason is that it may place a person under obligation to an individual or firm and can only result in difficulties and harm to the program. A manager or staff member should never profit personally from any materials purchased for use in his or her programs. Therefore such gifts or favors should be scrutinized carefully in light of professional ethics in each case.

A complete inventory analysis is essential before purchasing. Before purchases are made, the amount of supplies and equipment on hand and the condition of these items should be known. This knowledge prevents overbuying and having large stockpiles of materials that may be outdated when they become needed. Inventories in some cases are taken periodically,

NOTICE TO BIDDERS

(For use in advertising)

The board of education of ___(legal name)___ School District

No. ____ of the Town(s) of _____ popularly known

as _____ , (in accordance with Section 103 of

Article 5-A of the General Municipal Law) hereby invites the sub-

mission of sealed bids on _____ for use in the

schools of the district. Bids will be received until _____ on the
                                                       (hour)

_____ day of _____ , 19 ____ , at _____
(date)   (month)   (place of bid

_____ , at which time and place all bids will be publicly opened.
opening)

Specifications and bid form may be obtained at the same office. The

board of education reserves the right to reject all bids. Any bid

submitted will be binding for _____ days subsequent to the date of

bid opening.

                                    Board of Education

                    _____ School District No. ____

                    of the Town(s) of _____

                    County(ies) of _____

                    _____
                              (Address)

                    By _____
                              (Purchasing Agent)

_____
    (Date)

Note: The hour should indicate whether it is Eastern Standard or
      Eastern Daylight Saving Time.

Fig. 11-3. Sample notice to bidders form.

whereas in other cases a perpetual inventory is maintained. In some organizations inventories are taken at such times as the end of a sport season, semester, or on an annual basis. In other organizations the inventory is kept up to date on a continuing basis. Computerized inventories for school districts and other organizations are now in use in many places.

GUIDELINES FOR THE EQUIPMENT AND SUPPLY MANAGER AND EQUIPMENT ROOM

The equipment and supply manager's position is very important. The money spent on uniforms and other supplies and equipment amounts to a large part of an organization's budget. Therefore the person in charge of the equipment and supply room, whether a student or a paid employee, should be selected with care. A qualified person will be able to help make equipment and supplies last longer through proper storage, cleaning, and care. Accountability for equipment will be better assured because a system of good record keeping will be established and less equipment will be lost (Figs. 11-4 and 11-5). Also, a qualified manager will be able to make sound recommendations regarding the purchasing of athletic equipment. In light of such important responsibilities, an equipment manager should be selected who has qualifications such as creative organizational ability, an understanding of

---

STEPS FOR PURCHASING

The Need	Staff identifies need for equipment in program
Consultation	Staff consults with management supporting need for equipment
Staff action	Budget is checked for adequate funds
Requisition	Purchase requisition is initiated and specifications are outlined
Standardization	Purchasing agent meets with staff to see if certain specifications can be agreed on and if standardization is possible
Specifications	Sets up specifications in line with meetings
Bids or quotations	All possible sources are checked to get the best buy
Purchase order	Purchasing officer and designated cosigners sign purchase order; copies go to vendor, warehouse, purchasing agent, and accounting office
Follow-up	Purchasing agent makes a follow-up if equipment is not received when due
Receipt of goods	Warehouse receives goods, checks according to specifications, and returns purchase order with OK
Payment	Purchasing agent and board of education approve purchase for payment, and accounting office pays
Accountability	Goods are sent to the department that is held accountable for equipment
User receives	Staff picks up equipment at designated place

EQUIPMENT ISSUE

Date...

I .... have

accepted school property ....

.... (write in article and its number)

and agree to return it clean and in good condition or pay for said uniform.

Signed ....

H. R. #

Home Phone #   Home Address...

Fig. 11-4. Form for checking out physical education and athletic equipment.

EQUIPMENT CHECKOUT RECORD

Player_____   Home Room_____

Address_____   Phone_____

Class_____ Height_____ Weight_____ Age_____

Parents Waiver_____ Examination_____ Insurance_____

Football   Cross Country   Basketball   Swimming   Wrestling

Baseball   Track   Tennis   Golf

	Out	In	Game Equipment	Out	In
Blocking pads			White jersey		
Shoulder pads			Maroon jersey		
Hip pads			White pants		
Thigh pads			Maroon pants		
Knee pads			Warm-up pants		
Helmet			Warm-up jacket		
Shoes			Stockings		
Practice pants					
Practice jersey					

I hereby certify that I have received the above-listed athletic equipment
and will return same not later than the day following the last game of
the season for the sport checked.

Signature_____

Fig. 11-5. Equipment checkout record.

athletic equipment and supplies and what is needed to maintain them, a willingness to learn, the ability to get along well with people, trustworthiness, the ability to supervise other people effectively, and a willingness to make minor repairs to equipment to make it more serviceable.

The equipment and supply room is an important facility in physical education and athletic programs. It is important to have sufficient space to take care of the various purposes for which such a room exists. Space should be sufficient to store, label, and identify the equipment and supplies needed in the program. An adequate number of bins and racks for equipment will be needed. Also, proper air circulation is important. Space should be sufficient to permit movement for handling the routine functions of issuing equipment and supplies. People working in the room should be able to move with ease throughout the facility. Space should be provided for drying equipment, such as football uniforms that have become wet when practice or games are held in the rain. The equipment and supply room should be well organized and be a model of efficiency and sound organization.

GUIDELINES FOR CHECKING, STORING, ISSUING, AND MAINTAINING SUPPLIES AND EQUIPMENT

All supplies and equipment should be carefully checked on receipt. Equipment and supplies that have been ordered should not be paid for until they have been checked for amount, type, quality, size, and other specifications listed on the purchase order. If any discrepancies are noted, they should be corrected before payment is made. This is an important responsi-

Physical education class in the Huntsville City Schools, Huntsville, Al.

bility and should be carefully followed. It represents a good business practice in an area requiring good business sense.

Supplies and equipment requiring organization identification should be labeled. Equipment and supplies are often moved from location to location and also are issued to participants and staff members on a temporary basis. It is a good procedure to stencil or stamp everything with the organization's identification to check on such material, help trace missing articles, discourage misappropriation of such items, and know what is and what is not departmental property.

Procedures should be established for issuing and checking in supplies and equipment. Considerable loss of material can result if poor accounting procedures are followed. Procedures should be established so items are issued as prescribed, proper forms are completed, records are maintained, and all materials can be located. Articles should be listed on the records according to various specifications of amount, size, or color, together with the name of the person to whom the item is ussued. The individual's record should be classified according to name, street address, telephone, locker number, or other information important for identification. In all cases the person or persons to whom the supplies and equipment are issued should be held accountable.

Equipment should be in constant repair. Equipment should always be maintained in a serviceable condition. Procedures for caring for equipment should be routinized so repairs are provided as needed. All used equipment should be checked and then repaired, replaced, or serviced as needed. Repair can be justified, however, only when the cost for such is within reason. Supplies should be replaced when they have been depleted.

Equipment and supplies should be stored properly. Supplies and equipment should be handled efficiently so space has been properly organized for storing, a procedure has been established for ease of location, and proper safeguards have been taken against fire and theft. Proper shovels, bins, hangers, and other accessories should be available. Temperature, humidity, and ventilation are also important considerations. Items going into the storeroom should be properly checked for quality and quantity. An inventory should be constantly available for all items on hand in the storeroom. Every precaution should be taken to provide for the adequate care of the material so that a wise investment has been made.

Garments should be cleaned and cared for properly. According to the *Rawlings Athletic Handbook*, the care of garments can be considered under four headings. First the new garments; they should be kept in original packing boxes and stored in a cool, dry

---

SUGGESTIONS FOR CLEANING ATHLETIC EQUIPMENT

- The cleaner should be informed concerning the need for special handling of the garments.
- Dry cleaning usually will remove dirt and stains but normally will not remove perspiration. (Some people stress that garments that can be cleaned by soap and water rather than by dry cleaning should be purchased because dry cleaning will not remove perspiration.)
- Garments of different colors should not be laundered together.
- Strong chemicals or alkalies should not be used because they will fade colors and may damage the material.
- A chlorine bleach should not be used.
- Water levels in washing equipment should be kept high if lower mechanical action is desired, but kept low if uniforms are badly soiled, to increase mechanical action. Do not overload washing equipment.
- When using commercial steam press, it is recommended that garments should be stretched back to original size.
- Uniforms and other garments should be dry before being stored.
- Water temperatures above 120° F may fade colors and cause shrinkage.
- Specialized all-automatic athletic laundry facilities that are owned by the organization are recommended as a means of protecting garments against shrinkage, color fading, snags, and bleeding.

Rawlings Sporting Goods Company.

Employee at PepsiCo in Purchase, New York, taking advantage of the equipment subsidized by the company to improve corporate health.

Treadmills in fitness program at PepsiCo in Purchase, New York.

MONTH / TYPE OF ATHLETIC EQUIPMENT

MONTH	FOOTBALL	BASEBALL	BASKETBALL	TRACK
JANUARY	ORDER NEW EQUIPMENT	ORDER NEW EQUIPMENT	PRACTICE FREE THROWS DURING STUDY HALL	ORDER NEW EQUIPMENT
FEBRUARY	ORDER NEW EQUIPMENT	TIME IS RUNNING OUT		TIME IS RUNNING OUT
MARCH	ORDER NEW EQUIPMENT	DELIVERY	TAKE INVENTORY	MAKE PLANS FOR VACATION
APRIL	TIME IS RUNNING OUT	MARK EQUIPMENT	ORDER NEW EQUIPMENT	GO FISHING
MAY	MOW PRINCIPAL'S LAWN		ORDER NEW EQUIPMENT	
JUNE	GO TO SCHOOL BOARD PICNIC	TAKE INVENTORY	ORDER NEW EQUIPMENT	TAKE INVENTORY
JULY	DELIVERY		ORDER NEW EQUIPMENT	
AUGUST	MARK EQUIPMENT	ATTEND COUNTY FAIR	TIME IS RUNNING OUT	
SEPTEMBER			DELIVERY	DELIVERY
OCTOBER		ORDER NEW EQUIPMENT	MARK EQUIPMENT	MARK EQUIPMENT
NOVEMBER	TAKE INVENTORY	ORDER NEW EQUIPMENT		ORDER NEW EQUIPMENT
DECEMBER	ORDER NEW EQUIPMENT	ORDER NEW EQUIPMENT		ORDER NEW EQUIPMENT

Legend:
- ORDER NEW EQUIPMENT
- TIME IS RUNNING OUT
- YOU MAY BE TOO LATE

Athletic equipment buyers' almanac.

area where there is low humidity. Second, during the season garments should be cared for immediately following a game. Before sending them to the cleaner they should be inspected for tears or other defects and repaired as soon as possible. Third, on a trip the garments should be packed for the trip home and then hung up as soon as one returns. If an extended trip is being made, or if the trip home will not take place until the next day, the garments should be hung up for drying after each game is completed. Fourth, between seasons the most important procedure is to take care of the final cleaning, repair, and storage of the garments as soon as the last game has been played and the season is over. Following these procedures will make the garments last longer and look better, and time and money will be saved.

AUDIOVISUAL SUPPLIES AND EQUIPMENT

Audiovisual aids and materials have become an important part of physical education and athletics programs.

A survey among 100 schools, colleges, and many other organizations found that more than one half of them used some form of audiovisual aid in their programs. All of the persons surveyed felt that audiovisual media are valuable supplements to instruction in learning motor skills and in encouraging persons to be physically fit. The survey also found that videotaping is on the increase as an instructional tool. The audiovisual media used most frequently by those persons surveyed included cartridge films, loop films, 16- and 8-mm films, wall charts, slide films, film strips, audio cassettes, and instructional television.

Reasons for increased use of audiovisual materials in physical education and athletic programs

They enable the viewer to better understand concepts and the performance of a skill, events, and other experiences. Using a film, pictures, or other materials gives a clearer idea of the subject being taught, whether it is how a heart functions or how to perfect a golf swing.

They help provide variety to teaching. Motivation is increased, the attention span of students and others is prolonged, and the subject matter is more exciting when audiovisual aids are used in addition to other teaching techniques.

They increase motivation on the part of the viewer. To see a game played, a skill performed, or an experiment conducted in clear, understandable, illustrated form helps motivate a person to engage in a game, perform a skill more effectively, or want to know more about the relation of exercise to health. This is particularly true in video replay, where a per-

---

MANAGEMENT'S CODE OF ETHICS FOR PERSONNEL INVOLVED IN PURCHASING

1. To consider first the interests of the organization and the betterment of the program.
2. To be receptive to advice and suggestions of colleagues, both in the department and in business administration, and others insofar as advice is compatible with legal and moral requirements.
3. To endeavor to obtain the most value for every dollar spent.
4. To strive to develop an expertise and knowledge of supplies and equipment that ensure recommendations for purchases of best value.
5. To insist on honesty in the sales representation of every product submitted for consideration for purchase.
6. To give all responsible bidders equal consideration in determining whether their product meets specifications and the educational needs of your program.
7. To discourage and to decline gifts that in any way might influence a purchase.
8. To provide a courteous reception for all persons who may call on legitimate business missions regarding supplies and equipment.
9. To counsel and help others involved in purchasing.
10. To cooperate with governmental or other organizations or persons and help in developing sound business methods in the procurement of equipment and supplies.

Adapted from New York State Association of School Business officials.

son can actually see how he or she performs a skill and then can compare the performance to what should be done.

They provide an extension of what can normally be taught in a classroom, gymnasium, or playground. Audiovisual aids enable the viewer to be taken to other countries and to experience sporting events in other parts of the United States and the rest of the world. All of these are important to physical education and athletic programs.

They provide a historical reference for physical education and athletics. Outstanding events in sports, physical education, and health that have occurred in past years can be brought to life before the viewers' eyes. In this way the person obtains a better understanding of these fields and the important role they play in our society and other cultures of the world.

Guidelines for selecting and using audiovisual aids

Audiovisual materials should be carefully selected and screened before purchasing and using. Appropriateness for age and grade level of students and others, adequacy of subject matter, technical qualities, inclusion of current information, cost, and other factors are important to know when selecting audiovisual materials.

The management should see that the presentation of materials is carefully planned to provide continuity in the subject being taught. Instructors should select and use materials that amplify and illustrate some important part of the material being covered in a particular course. Furthermore, they should be used at a time that logically fits into the presentation of certain material and concepts.

The management should see that the materials are carefully evaluated after they have been used. Whether materials are used a second time should be determined on the basis of their worth the first time they were used. Therefore they should be evaluated carefully after their use. Records of evaluation should be maintained.

The management should realize that slow motion and stop-action projections are best when a pattern of coordination of movements in a skill is to be taught. When teaching a skill, the physical educator usually likes to analyze the various parts of the whole and also to stop and discuss aspects of the skill with the students.

Exercise equipment in use at PepsiCo's multimillion dollar fitness plant in Purchase, New York.

CHECKLIST OF SELECTIVE ITEMS TO CONSIDER IN THE PURCHASE AND CARE OF SUPPLIES AND EQUIPMENT

	Yes	No
1. Selection of equipment and supplies is related to the achievement of the goals of physical education and athletics.		
2. Equipment and supplies are selected in accordance with the needs and capacities of the participants, including consideration for age, sex, skill, and interest.		
3. A manual or written policies have been prepared regarding the procedure for purchasing and care of all supplies and equipment.		
4. Mechanics of purchasing such as the following are used: requisitions, specifications, bids and quotations, contracts and purchase orders, delivery data, receipt of merchandise, vendor invoices, and payment.		
5. The relationship of functions such as the following to purchasing is considered: programming, budgeting and financing, auditing and accounting, property maintenance, legal regulations, ethics, and philosophy of education.		
6. Principles of purchasing such as the following are adhered to: quality, quantity, storage, inventory, and salvage value.		
7. A close working relationship exists between the department chairperson and school or college business administrator.		
8. Girls and boys have their own equipment and supplies when needed.		
9. Merchandise is purchased only from reputable manufacturers and distributors, and consideration is also given to their replacement and the services provided.		
10. The greatest value is achieved for each dollar expended.		
11. Administration possesses current knowledge of equipment and supplies.		
12. Administration is receptive to advice and suggestions from colleagues who know, use, and purchase equipment and supplies.		
13. The coach of a sport is contacted when ordering merchandise for his or her activity, and specifications and other matters are checked.		
14. The director of physical education and athletics consults with the business administration when equipment and supplies are needed and ordered.		
15. Local regulations for competitive purchasing are followed.		
16. Equipment and supply purchases are standardized wherever possible to make replacement easier.		
17. Administration is alert to improvements and advantages and disadvantages of various types of equipment and supplies.		
18. Brand, trademark, and catalog specifications are clearly defined in the purchase requisitions.		
19. Purchase orders are made on regular school forms.		
20. Functional quality of merchandise and the safety it affords are major considerations.		
21. The inventory is used to plan for replacements and additions.		
22. Complete and accurate records are kept on all merchandise purchased.		
23. New equipment and supply needs are determined well in advance.		
24. New materials and equipment are tested and evaluated before being purchased in quantity lots.		
25. New equipment complies with minimum safety requirements.		

Continued.

CHECKLIST OF SELECTIVE ITEMS TO CONSIDER IN THE PURCHASE AND CARE OF SUPPLIES AND EQUIPMENT—cont'd

	Yes	No
26. Honesty is expected in all sales representation.	____	____
27. State contracts are used when they are available.	____	____
28. Administration is prompt and courteous in receiving legitimate salespeople and businesspeople.	____	____
29. All competitors who sell merchandise are given fair and equal consideration.	____	____
30. Gifts or favors offered by sales people or manufacturers are refused.	____	____
31. Materials received are checked with respect to quality and quantity and whether they meet specifications that have been indicated in school requisitions.	____	____
32. Prompt payment is assured on contracts that have been made.	____	____
33. All orders are checked carefully for damaged merchandise, shortages, and errors in shipment.	____	____
34. Policies have been established for designating procedures to be followed when there is theft, loss, or destruction of merchandise.	____	____
35. People who are issued equipment and supplies are held accountable for them.	____	____
36. Inventories are taken periodically to account for all materials.	____	____
37. A uniform plan is established for marking equipment and supplies.	____	____
38. A written procedure has been established for borrowing and returning equipment and supplies.	____	____
39. A procedure has been established for holding students accountable for merchandise that is not returned.	____	____
40. Proper storage facilities have been provided.	____	____
41. Equipment is cleaned and repaired when necessary before it is ordered.	____	____

The management should see that equipment is properly maintained and repaired. Projectors, record players, television equipment, and other materials need to be kept in good operating condition and operated by qualified personnel to have an effective audiovisual program.

SUMMARY

Physical education and athletic programs spend thousands of dollars on supplies and equipment in order to provide a varied program of activities for their clientele. Since a large expenditure of funds is made for these items, it is important that this management responsibility be carried out in a business-like manner. Supply and equipment needs must be adequately determined, selection accomplished according to sound guidelines, purchasing done in line with organizational requirements, and storage and maintenance of these items provided so that maximum use can be assured.

SELF-ASSESSMENT TESTS

These tests will assist students in determining if material and competencies presented in this chapter have been mastered:

1. Why is supply and equipment management important, and what factors need to be considered regarding this administrative responsibility?
2. List and discuss five principles that should be followed when purchasing supplies and equipment. Apply these procedures and principles to selecting a diving board for a swimming pool.
3. Establish a set of guidelines for the position of equipment manager and the conduct of the equipment room.
4. Prepare an administrative plan that you as chairperson of a physical education and athletic department would recommend for checking, issuing, and maintaining physical education supplies and equipment.

5. Prepare a report on the various types of audio-visual aids that could be used effectively in teaching volleyball.

SELECTED REFERENCES

1. Arnheim, D.D., and Sinclair, W.A.: Physical education for special populations, Englewood Cliffs, N.J., 1985, Prentice-Hall, Inc.
2. Equipment innovations: how they've changed the way we play, Athletic Business, January 1985, p. 40.
3. Horine, L.: Administration of physical education and sport programs, Philadelphia, 1985, Saunders College Publishing.
4. Protective equipment: getting the right fit makes the difference, Athletic Business, March 1985, p. 36.
5. Roberts, J.: Investigate the market before purchasing uniforms, Athletic Business, May 1985, p. 78.
6. Rosandich, T.J.: The purchasing challenge, Athletic Business, June 1985, p. 30.

SUGGESTED READINGS

- "How to select and care for your wrestling, gym mats," Athletic Purchasing and Facilities, September 1982, p. 60.
  Shows how the materials and manufacturing methods that go into today's wrestling and gym mats have made tremendous gains. It also shows how the best mat will break down if not given proper care. The article outlines several suggestions for keeping mats in good repair.
- Rosentsweig, J.: Homemade strength equipment, Journal of Physical Education, Recreation, and Dance **55**:45, January 1984.
  Discusses how homemade strength equipment can be simple and inexpensive. Provides a means whereby many organizations that cannot afford expensive strength machines can develop and use equipment that can still accomplish the goal of developing strength.

Chapter Twelve

Management and the Athletic Training Program

Instructional Objectives and Competencies to be Achieved
After reading this chapter the student should be able to

- Summarize the incidence of injuries among athletes.
- Understand the role of prevention and care of injuries in the athletic program.
- Discuss the qualifications, duties, and responsibilities of team physicians and athletic trainers.
- Discuss some administrative procedures that should be taken to emphasize safety in a school or other organization.

In addition to the functions of fiscal management and facility management, physical educators, directors of athletics, and other members of the management team need to provide for the health of students and athletes. With the increasing number of participants in athletic programs it becomes particularly important to provide proper training, conditioning, and other preventive measures to reduce the number of injuries that may occur in physical education and athletic programs. This chapter is concerned with the nature and scope and the responsibilities of management in providing a sound athletic training program.

The number of athletes injured increases annually. An estimated one million sport injuries requiring hospital treatment occur each year, and many more go unreported. One estimate is that 28% of them are in football, 6.8% in contact sports other than football, and 3.6% in noncontact sports.

More than 1 million boys participate in high school football annually, another 70,000 at college, and still another 200,000 in other organizations. There are an estimated 200,000 to 600,000 football injuries alone—injuries caused by things such as poor football helmets, pads, and other equipment; hazardous playing surfaces; and players returning to action before fully recovering from injuries. Many basketball players suffer sprained ankles, broken bones, and other injuries to the head, elbows, knees, and Achilles tendons. In baseball most injuries occur in arms, legs, feet, heads, and necks; some of these injuries are caused by improper sliding techniques, poor playing surfaces, collisions, and being hit with balls. In track and field muscle pulls, abrasions, and knee and ankle injuries are common. Sprains and fractures plague skiers, and hockey players are injured from body checks and being hit with a puck or stick.

John L. Marshall, orthopedic surgeon at the Hospital for Special Services in New York City has stated that fewer than 10 out of every 100 of the nation's 22,000 high schools have proper medical care for their athletes. A professor of biomechanics in Michigan says that the majority of high schools in his state do not provide adequately for athletic injuries. A survey by the Department of Health, Education, and Welfare reported at least 111,000 serious sports-related injuries each year that cause students to miss at least 3 weeks of school.

As a result of the increasing participation of girls and women in sports, both the number and severity of injuries among female participants have risen.

The most common types of injuries are ankle sprains, knee injuries, and contusions. The least common injuries were those to the breast, head, and neck. When the same data were organized into type of major injuries by sport, the most serious injuries, including major fractures, head injuries, and dislocations, are in basketball, field hockey, softball, and gymnastics.

Medical supervision is essential for all sports participants. Unfortunately, many athletic contests are not adequately supervised medically. Dr. Allan J. Ryan cites his experiences at the University of Wisconsin concerning the lack of medical supervision in high school athletics. In one semester Dr. Ryan encountered 27 male freshmen enrolled in an adaptive physical education program who were suffering from musculoskeletal system defects. Eighteen of these students incurred the defects as a result of athletic competition in football, basketball, and ice hockey.

Football fatalities caused by neck and brain injuries and deaths from heat stroke because of inadequate preventive measures have been reported. Numerous injuries also occur in wrestling. Many reports were cited where boys on wrestling teams endure dramatic weight losses to qualify for lower weight class matches. In many cases communication between physicians and coaches is lacking.

One organization that collects data on athletic injuries is the National Athletic Injury Illness Reporting System (NAIRS). Participating schools receive periodic reports about the number and types of injuries in various sports.

An organization that is very much concerned with equipment standards to reduce injuries in sports is the American Society for Testing and Materials (ASTM), an organization composed of manufacturers, consumers, and technical experts. One of the technical committees of this organization is the National Operating Committee on Standards for Athletic Equipment (NOCSAE). They have a subcommittee that studies the number and types of injuries suffered by female athletes, and they are looking into the use of athletic brassieres for protecting against injuries. The organization also is very much concerned with helmets and face guards for sports such as football, baseball, and hockey.

SECONDARY SCHOOL ATHLETIC INJURIES

Chandy and Grana[2] did a 3-year study of seven sports in 130 Oklahoma secondary schools. The number of male athletes in the survey was 24,485 and the number of female athletes was 18,289. The study showed that female athletes had more and also more severe injuries than did the males. Girls had injuries such as sprains and dislocations, whereas boys had more strains and fractures. Knee injuries requiring surgery were more common among girls than boys. Of the sports studied, basketball had the highest injury rate.

To reduce the number of injuries the study recommended that, particularly among female athletes, a sound conditioning program be established in order to develop strength of the major muscle groups in the lower extremities, particularly those muscle groups that protect the joints.

The study also pointed out that the well-trained, conditioned female athlete is no more susceptible to injuries than male athletes. It is important for all to develop peak levels of strength, power, endurance, and flexibility.

SPORTS MEDICINE

Sports medicine is a rapidly expanding area of health services for athletes. The fact that more than an estimated 17 million persons are injured each year in this country in physical activities and sports has accented the need for this new field. Sports medicine is particularly concerned with how sports injuries occur, how they can be prevented, and the long-range impact they have on a person's performance.

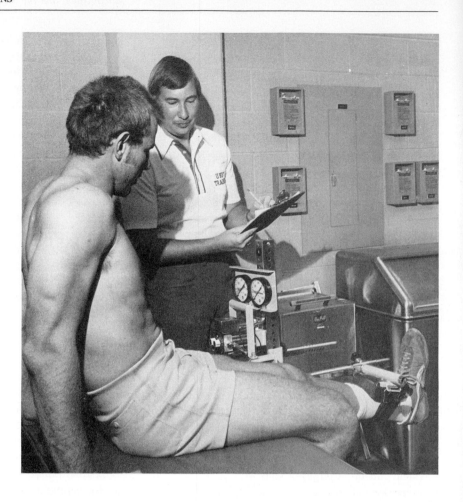

Athletic trainer at work.

Sports medicine is the medical relationship between physical activity and the human body. It is concerned with the scientific study of the effects of physical activity on the human body and of the influence of elements such as the environment, drugs, emotions, intellect, age, and growth on human physical activity. It also is concerned with the prevention of disease and injury and with therapy and rehabilitation.

An institute of sports medicine and athletic trauma has been founded by Dr. James Nicholas, orthopedic surgeon at Lenox Hill Hospital in New York City. The center is concerned with a study of the mechanics, diagnosis, treatment and rehabilitation of physical injuries sustained in organized and unorganized athletics and recreational activities.

Sports medicine has provided new knowledge of sports injuries. For example, Dr. Nicholas has found a relationship between joint flexibility and injury; tight-jointed players are more likely to have muscle and tendon strains than loose-jointed players. On the other hand, loose-jointed players more frequently suffer dislocations. These findings indicate that tight-jointed players should exercise to increase flexibility and loose-jointed players should exercise to firm up the joints. Dr. Nicholas has also found a relationship between flexibility and power. He points out that a person who is extremely flexible will have less strength.

Dr. John Marshall has found that high arches in the foot and tight heel cords are conducive to ankle sprains.

MANAGEMENT'S ROLE IN THE HEALTH OF THE ATHLETE

Although this chapter has implications for all persons who participate in physical education programs, essential health services are especially important for athletes. The growth of sports and athletic programs supports this emphasis.

Physical education and athletic managers are responsible for providing adequate policies to guide the programs in the proper care of and protection of the health of the athlete.

Health services for athletes involve continuous medical attention, sound policies and procedures, and the availability of qualified personnel. A close working relationship should exist among physicians, coaches, trainers, athletic directors, managers, and

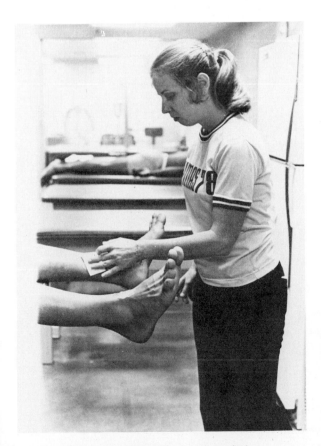

Women athletic trainers are needed.

medical society representatives to protect athletes adequately from injury and harm.

The American Medical Association, through its Committee on the Medical Aspects of Sports, the National Athletic Trainers Association, and athletic organizations such as the National Collegiate Athletic Association, and the National Federation of State High School Athletic Associations, have prepared materials, made recommendations to safeguard the health of the athlete, and outlined first aid procedures for athletic injuries.

Medical supervision of athletes can be improved if management, physical educators, physicians, coaches, and trainers make this a priority. Frequently, coaches lack medical training, and they feel that too much supervision from doctors and nurses will hurt their team's win-loss record. The management must adopt a philosophy of medical supervision that places the individual athlete first and enables him or her to have the best possible medical attention.

Adequate health management in sports is essential because of the physical, physiological, and psychological demands of competition; the problem of treatment and rehabilitation involved in athletic injuries; the increased possibility of infectious diseases caused by lowered resistance; and the close relationship between physical activity and disease and injury.

A survey by Rolnick, which was conducted as part of his doctoral study at New York University to determine the standards of health supervision and how they were implemented, recommended the implementation of nationally and regionally adopted standards governing health aspects of sports, including: (a) a physical examination and medical history for each athlete, (b) medical supervision at all contact sports, (c) ambulance at all contact sports, (d) availability of communication for emergency purposes, (e) athletic facilities that are safe and meet size requirements, and (f) use of noncaustic materials for marking athletic fields.

THE TEAM PHYSICIAN

A team physician must be selected with care. He or she must not neglect team responsibilities because of a growing practice or other commitments. The physician should remain objective and avoid being influ-

SAFEGUARDING THE HEALTH OF THE ATHLETE

A joint statement of the Committee on the Medical Aspects of the American Medical Association and the National Federation of State High School Athletic Associations
A checklist to help evaluate five major factors in health supervision of athletics

Participation in athletics is a privilege involving both responsibilities and rights. The athletes' responsibilities are to play fair, to train and to conduct themselves with credit to their sport and their school. In turn they have the right to optimal protection against injury as this may be assured through good conditioning and technical instruction, proper regulations and conditions of play, and adequate health supervision.

Periodic evaluation of each of the factors will help assure a safe and healthful experience for players. The checklist below contains the kinds of questions to be answered in such an appraisal.

PROPER CONDITIONING helps prevent injuries by hardening the body and increasing resistance to fatigue.

1. Are prospective players given directions and activities for preseason conditioning?
2. Is there a minimum of 3 weeks of practice before the first game or contest?
3. Are precautions taken to prevent heat exhaustion and heat stroke?
4. Is each player required to warm up thoroughly before participation?
5. Are substitutions made without hesitation when players evidence disability?

CAREFUL COACHING leads to skillful performance, which lowers the incidence of injuries.

1. Is emphasis given to safety in teaching techniques and elements of play?
2. Are injuries analyzed to determine causes and to suggest preventive programs?
3. Are tactics discouraged that may increase the hazards and thus the incidence of injuries?
4. Are practice periods carefully planned and of reasonable duration?

GOOD OFFICIATING promotes enjoyment of the game and the protection of players.

1. Are players as well as coaches thoroughly schooled in the rules of the game?
2. Are rules and regulations strictly enforced in practice periods as well as in games?
3. Are officials qualified both emotionally and technically for their responsibilities?
4. Do players and coaches respect the decisions of officials?

RIGHT EQUIPMENT AND FACILITIES serve a unique purpose in protection of players.

1. Is the best protective equipment provided for contact sports?
2. Is careful attention given to proper fit and adjustment of equipment?
3. Is equipment properly maintained and worn, outmoded items discarded?
4. Are proper areas for play provided and carefully maintained?

ADEQUATE MEDICAL CARE is a necessity in the prevention and control of injuries.

1. Is there a thorough preseason health history and medical examination?
2. Is a physician present at contests and readily available during practice sessions?
3. Does the physician make the decision as to whether an athlete should return to play following injury during games?
4. Is authority from a physician required before an athlete can return to practice after being out of play because of disabling injury?
5. Is the care given athletes by coach or trainer limited to first aid and medically prescribed services?

Adapted from Committee on the Medical Aspects of Sports of the American Medical Association.

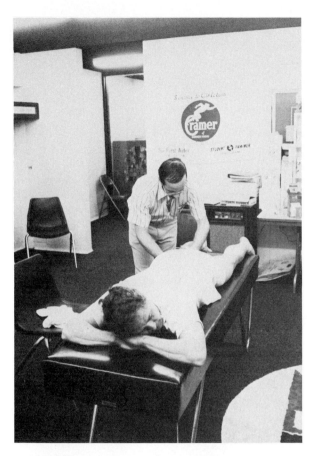

Athletic trainer attending to an athlete's injury.

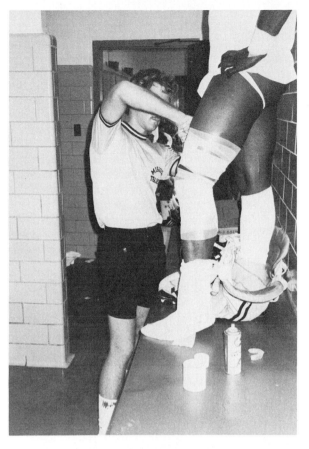

Athletic trainer preparing player for competition.

enced by students, parents, and coaches. If a physician is needed and none is available, the local medical society should be consulted for a recommendation of one or perhaps two physicians who will jointly care for the team. An injured athlete should not return to play until authorized by the team physician.

Many schools will not have a physician present for athletic contests or when injuries occur in physical education classes. Some suggestions for the physical education and athletic management in such cases include the following:

At football and other contact sports if physician cannot be present, have a telephone number where he or she can be called on short notice.

Provide for an ambulance if needed.

Determine the extent of the injury; do not move injured athlete if he or she is unconscious or suffering from a severe injury.

Send for a physician and ambulance, if necessary.

Administer first aid.

Notify parents of nature and extent of injury and procedure you have followed.

Prepare accident report containing all essential data regarding items such as nature and extent of injury, date, time, place, and witnesses. Keep report on file.

Refer to family physician if parents desire.

THE TEAM PHYSICIAN'S DUTIES

- Preparing and compiling medical histories of students, noting injuries and other health conditions.
- Examining athletes, reporting to coaches the results of such examinations, and making recommendations regarding whether or not player can participate, or under what conditions he or she can play.
- Supervising and counseling athletic trainers and working with coaches, athletes, and parents in determining the best course of action to follow.
- Attending home games and also practice, if at all possible.
- Working cooperatively with the athletic trainer and the athletic director in preparing emergency procedures.
- Examining all injuries and making recommendations about the future play of the athlete. The player must receive the physician's approval to play.
- Providing time for students' queries regarding such matters as nutrition, conditioning, and injuries.
- Engaging in in-serevice self-education to keep abreast of the latest in sports medicine and injuries.
- Making recommendations to the athletic director and coaches regarding injury prevention.
- Verifying injuries when required for insurance settlements.
- Making recommendations regarding and helping to select proper protective equipment.

Modified from Parkhouse, B.L., and Lapin, J.

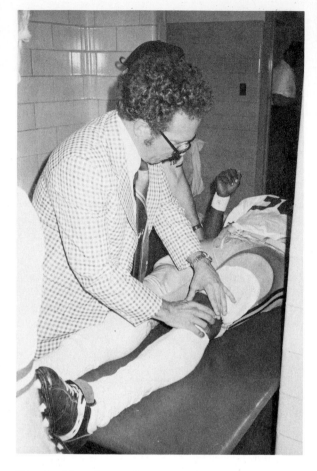

The physician plays an important role in athletic programs.

ATHLETIC TRAINERS

The importance of athletic trainers in sports injury prevention and treatment cannot be overlooked by the management. Unfortunately, in the secondary schools where athletic trainers are most needed, they are poorly represented. Compounding this situation is the inadequate medical and injury prevention training of most coaches. Even if the coach has been well prepared in these areas, he or she does not have sufficient time to carry out both coaching duties and the responsibilities of the athletic trainer.

In 1980, 10.9% of public secondary schools had athletic trainers, but only 5% had National Athletic Trainers Association (NATA) approved trainers. Of the private secondary schools 15.4% had trainers but only 5% of them were NATA approved. On the college level 16.1% of the 2-year colleges had trainers, but only 7% were NATA approved; 40% of the 4-year colleges had trainers with 28% of them NATA approved. With more than 21,000 high schools in the United States it is important to provide an athletic training program that will reduce the number of injuries in sports.

Since there is a lack of properly qualified athletic trainers, it is important that the management see that coaches are provided with in-service training in this area. The injury rate is much higher where qualified trainers are absent and where the coaches have not received proper training in injury prevention. It is estimated that coaches in 75% of the cases make decisions on injuries, and that 47% of the coaches have not even taken a first aid course.

Since most high schools cannot afford a full-time athletic trainer, Porter and associates[3] instituted a pilot program that trained 43 employed teachers to become certified athletic trainers. This program assumed that one way to solve the problem is to train employed teachers to become certified athletic trainers with the objective that they would teach during the day and then serve as athletic trainers after school and on weekends where necessary.

The professional education committee of the NATA outlined a program that included 300 hours of classroom and laboratory instruction over three summers. The program was conducted by the Center for Sports Medicine of Northwestern University Medical School. The students ranged from 21 to 52 years of age, and most of them were physical educators. The curriculum was designed and coordinated by two orthopedic surgeons and an athletic trainer-physical therapist. Thirty-one physicians and 18 certified athletic trainers were lecturers in the program. Seventy percent of the students successfully completed the program and then took the NATA examination; most of them were granted NATA certification. Most of the graduates are now associated in some way with injury prevention.

Traditionally the athletic trainer simply applied ankle wraps and administered first aid to athletes. He or she usually had no special preparation for this role but had learned through on-the-job training. Often such an individual had little scientific knowledge concerning the prevention and care of athletic injuries.

Today, considerable scientific information, such as awareness of biomechanics (that is, how and why certan injuries occur in human motion), is available to help the athletic trainer reduce sports injuries, modify equipment, and care for athletes. Furthermore, knowledge of rehabilitation procedures and ways to prescribe exercise is expanding. As a result of the training needed, a trend today is to hire trainers who

Injured athlete is treated by the athletic training staff.

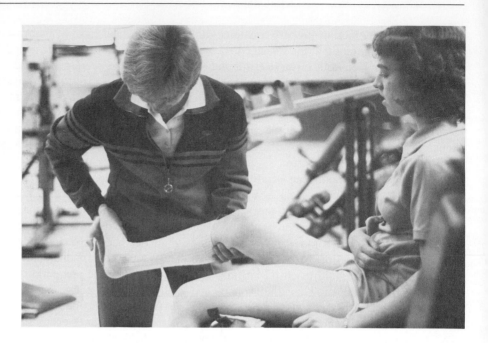

Athletic trainer treats an athlete.

have an undergraduate major in physical education with graduate work in physical therapy or athletic training.

The qualifications for an athletic trainer[1] are both personal and professional. Personal qualifications include poise, good health, intelligence, maturity, emotional stability, compassion, cleanliness, ethics, and fairness. Professional qualifications include a knowledge of anatomy and physiology, conditioning, nutrition, taping, methods for preventing injury, and protective equipment. Furthermore, the athletic trainer should have qualities that provide a harmonious and productive rapport with the team physician, coaches, athletic managers, and the public in general. The trainer must be able to practice good human relations, as well as protect the athletes' well-being.

The National Athletic Trainers Association's (NATA) basic minimum requirements for the professional preparation of athletic trainers are recommended by most experts in the field. These standards include graduating from an approved undergraduate or graduate program that meets specific criteria set forth by the NATA, having a physical therapy degree (such preparation meeting the specific requirements

set forth by the NATA), or serving an apprenticeship that meets NATA specifications. Persons preparing for positions in athletic training should also be certified by NATA. To do this, they must have proper training and pass the NATA certification examination. Important courses in preparing to be an athletic trainer include anatomy and physiology, physiology of activity, kinesiology, psychology, first aid and safety, nutrition, remedial exercises, health, techniques of athletic training, and advanced techniques of athletic training.

The entry of more women into the field is long overdue. Athletic competition among women has increased greatly, and female athletic trainers are needed. The management and physical educators must be made aware of the need for women trainers, and students interested in physical education should be told about the profession of athletic training. With the acceptance of the fact that girls and women can play and compete against men in certain sports, such as swimming, volleyball, and tennis, as well as engage in highly competitive programs of their own, the need for women who have the knowledge and training to handle and prevent sports injuries is vital.

Table 12-1. Checklist for trainer's kit*

Item	Amount	Football-rugby	Basketball-volleyball-soccer	Wrestling	Baseball	Track and cross country	Water polo and swimming	Gymnastics	Tennis
Adhesive tape									
½-inch	1 roll	X	X	X	X	X		X	X
1-inch	2 rolls	X	X	X	X	X		X	X
1½-inch	3 rolls	X	X	X	X	X		X	X
2-inch	1 roll	X	X	X	X	X		X	X
Alcohol (isopropyl)	4 ounces	X	X	X	X	X	X	X	X
Ammonia ampules	10	X	X	X	X	X	X	X	X
Analgesic balm	½ pound	X	X	X	X	X	X	X	X
Ankle wraps	2	X	X		X	X			X
Antacid tablets or liquid	100	X	X	X	X	X	X	X	X
Antiglare salve	4 ounces	X			X				
Antiseptic powder	4 ounces	X	X	X	X	X	X	X	X
Antiseptic soap (liquid)	4 ounces	X	X	X	X	X	X	X	X
Aspirin tablets	100	X	X	X	X	X	X	X	X
Band-Aids (assorted sizes)	2 dozen	X	X	X	X	X	X	X	X
Butterfly bandages (sterile strip)									
Medium	6 dozen	X	X	X	X	X		X	
Small	6 dozen	X	X	X	X	X		X	
Cotton (sterile)	1 ounce	X	X	X	X	X	X	X	X
Cotton-tipped applicators	2 dozen	X	X	X	X	X	X	X	X
Elastic bandages									
3-inch	2 rolls	X	X	X	X	X		X	X
4-inch	2 rolls	X	X	X	X	X		X	X
6-inch	2 rolls	X	X	X	X	X	X	X	X
Elastic tape roll (3-inch)	2 rolls	X	X	X	X	X		X	X
Eyewash	2 ounces	X	X	X	X	X	X	X	X
Felt									
¼-inch	6 by 6 feet	X	X	X	X	X		X	X
½-inch	6 by 6 feet	X							
Flexible collodion	2 ounces	X	X	X	X	X		X	
Foot antifungus powder	2 ounces	X	X	X	X	X	X	X	X
Forceps (tweezers)	1	X	X	X	X	X	X	X	X
Fungicide (salve)	2 ounces	X	X	X	X	X	X	X	X
Germicide (solution)	2 ounces	X	X	X	X	X	X	X	X
Grease (lubrication)	2 ounces	X	X	X	X	X			X
Gum rosin (adherent)	1 ounce	X	X		X	X			X

*Extra amounts of items such as tape and protective padding are carried in other bags.　　*Continued.*
From Arnheim, D.D.

Table 12-1. Checklist for trainer's kit—cont'd

Item	Amount	Football-rugby	Basketball-volleyball-soccer	Wrestling	Baseball	Track and cross country	Water polo and swimming	Gymnastics	Tennis
Heel cups	2			X		X		X	
Instant cold pack	2	X	X	X	X	X	X	X	X
Liniment	2 ounces	X	X	X	X	X	X	X	X
Medicated salve	2 ounces	X	X	X	X	X	X	X	X
Mirror (hand)	1	X	X	X	X	X	X	X	X
Moleskin	6 by 6 feet	X	X	X	X	X		X	X
Nonadhering sterile pad (3 by 3)	12	X	X	X	X	X		X	X
Oral screw	1	X	X	X	X	X	X	X	X
Oral thermometer	1	X	X	X	X	X	X	X	X
Peroxide	2 ounces	X	X	X	X	X	X	X	X
Salt tablets	50	X	X	X	X	X		X	X
Shoehorn	1	X	X	X	X	X			X
Sponge rubber					X				
⅛-inch	6 by 6 sheet	X	X	X	X	X		X	X
¼-inch	6 by 6 sheet	X	X	X	X	X		X	X
½-inch	6 by 6 sheet	X							
Sterile gauze pads (3 by 3)	6	X	X	X	X	X		X	X
Sun lotion	2 ounces	X	X	X	X	X	X	X	X
Surgical scissors	1	X	X	X	X	X	X	X	X
Tape adherent	6-ounce spray can	X	X	X	X	X		X	X
Tape remover	2 ounces	X	X	X	X	X	X	X	X
Tape scissors (pointed)	1	X	X	X	X	X	X	X	X
Tongue depressors	5	X	X	X	X	X	X	X	X
Triangular bandages	2	X	X	X	X	X	X	X	X
Waterproof tape (1-inch)	1 roll						X		

THE TRAINING ROOM

Elaborate training rooms and equipment are not always essential in athletic programs. Indeed, most high schools do not have much in the way of a training room. A private examining room with an examining table, a desk, and a few chairs is a minimum requirement. However, a training room should be provided if possible, for it will serve both physical education and athletic programs as a multipurpose place for first aid, physical examinations, bandaging and taping, reconditioning, treating athletes, keeping records, and other functions concerned with the health of students, athletes, and staff members. The training room should be near the dressing, shower, and athletic areas. A telephone, proper lights, and if possible, equipment for thermal and mechanical therapy, electrotherapy, and hydrotherapy should be provided.

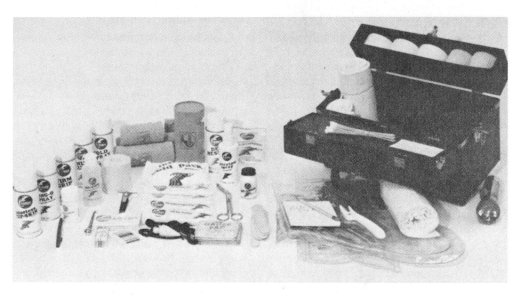

Well-outfitted trainer's kit.

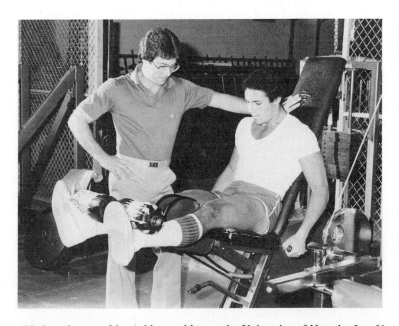

The athletic trainer working with an athlete at the University of Nevada, Las Vegas.

Adequate training room facilities contribute to prevention and care of athletic injuries. Training room, University of Notre Dame.

SELECTED DUTIES OF THE ATHLETIC TRAINER

- To prevent and care for injuries associated with competitive athletics
- To prepare and use an athletic conditioning program
- To administer first aid as needed
- To apply devices such as strapping or bandaging to prevent injury
- To administer therapeutic techniques under the direction of physician
- To develop and supervise rehabilitation programs for injured athletes under supervision of team physician
- To select, care, and fit equipment
- To supervise training menus and diets
- To supervise safety factors involved in facilities and use of equipment

---

If the athletic program involves a great number of sports and participants, it is recommended that special service sections be arranged with low walls or partitions provided if possible. For those institutions that desire more sophisticated facilities, separate sections would include those for taping, bandaging, and orthotics; thermal and mechanical therapy; electrotherapy; hydrotherapy; and a reconditioning section with equipment such as knee exercisers and bicycle exercisers. Of course, there should be a section for storage so adequate training supplies would always be available.

MANAGEMENT, DRUG ABUSE, AND THE YOUNG ATHLETE

The drug abuse problem in the world of professional and college sports is of great concern to Americans. Physical educators and athletic managers should be even more concerned about the young athlete and drug abuse. Drug use and addiction is not limited to adults; it has also snared the younger generation.

The Drug Education Committee of the NCAA has indicated that most athletes bring their drug use habits with them when they come to the college campus. Therefore they conclude that dealing with the problem at the secondary school level may be more effective. As Dr. Roy T. Bergman, team physician for high school teams, Escanaba, Michigan, points out, "(Drugs) have made their way into high school and junior high school athletes and substance abuse among these age groups is on the increase."

Alcohol is the most commonly used drug with 93 out of 100 young athletes 11 to 14 years of age coming in contact with it. Marijuana is the next most common drug used by the young athlete. The United States Department of Health and Human Services has pointed out that approximately 1 out of 3 high school seniors had tried marijuana before reaching high school.

Other agents used by young athletes include cocaine and "uppers" such as amphetamines, caffeine, and ephedrine to pep them up and give them more energy. Anabolic steroids are also being used by these young athletes hopefully to make them bigger and stronger for sports competition.

These drugs are taking their toll among our young athletes. Growth potential and maturity are being hampered. Side effects are causing poor health, and instead of improving athletic performance the drugs are having a deleterious effect by resulting in slower reaction times, improper coordination with poor execution of movement, altered perception of speed, and impairment of motor function in general. In addition, they are also resulting in academic and vocational failure.

Management needs to become involved in establishing measures to cope with this problem. Here is what some schools are doing about the drug problem.

According to a report in the September 1984 issue of *Athletic Business,* the Milton, Wisconsin, School District is coming to grips with drug abuse. Their program is designed to identify those students who come to school under the influence of alcohol or other drugs. If students exhibit overt behavior of drug abuse they are referred to the principal of their school. If

they voluntarily admit use of drugs, they are then referred to a student assistance and counseling program. However, if they claim noninvolvement they are given a urinalysis test; if the test is positive, they are assigned to a state-licensed assessment program. If students refuse to take the test, they are placed on a 3-day suspension and assigned to a licensed assessment program; they must get treatment before returning to school.

The Milton, Wisconsin, program applies to all students including athletes. Players and cheerleaders are informed that the use of alcohol and other drugs is strictly forbidden. They are also told that voluntary self-referral to the student assistance program for drug abuse is not a violation of the athletic code.

Superintendent of Schools Jon C. Platts, in speaking about his school system's drug abuse program says, "We're saying to kids, we want to help. Our primary motive is to have services available to students who have a problem. On the other hand, we want boys and girls to know that if they come to school under the influence of drugs or alcohol, we're going to deal with them very severely."

The Milton, Wisconsin, management recognizes that it is very important to teachers and staff to be well informed. To accomplish this they are given guidelines that include a listing of various modes of behavior that may indicate prevalence of a drug abuse problem. In addition, orientation sessions are provided. Management stresses that good judgment must be used before referring a student to the student assistance program.

The Milton school system administration recognizes that their program may be open to legal challenge, so they have obtained advice from their lawyers to make sure the program is within the law. In respect to the possibility of a legal challenge, the community and the board of education feel that the advantages of the program they have instituted are well worth the risk.

In reflecting on his drug abuse program Superintendent Platts concludes, "We think it is a fair way to approach a very serious problem. We've received correspondence from around the country urging us to stick with it."

The Arkadelphia, Arkansas, School District program for drug abuse is similar in many ways to the Wisconsin program, but is more punitive in nature. Stiff penalties are imposed when students are caught: *first offense*—withdrawal from school for one semester or suspension, *second offense*—suspension for 12 months, *third offense*—permanent expulsion.

Bruce Durbin, Executive Director of the National Federation of State High School Associations that represents 20,000 schools and has 93,000 individual members, feels that a drug program should stress education rather than punishment. Such programs should reach coaches, officials, students, and educators in general.

The state of Minnesota is using an education program with the help of the Hazelden Foundation, the Kroc Foundation, and the Minnesota State High School League. As a team they are sponsoring several projects, such as Chemical Awareness Seminars. This program is building a model for other state associations to follow.

The drug abuse program, called Operation Cork, was founded by Joan Kroc, widow of McDonald's founder Ray Kroc, for the purpose of coping with the problems of athletes and drugs. The Hazelden-Kroc Foundation is investing $7 million in a facility that will focus its efforts on drug education and drug abuse prevention.

MANAGEMENT'S RESPONSIBILITY IN ATHLETIC TRAINING

What is the management's responsibility in preventing sports injuries? The first responsibility is to hire, when possible, physicians, coaches, and trainers who understand sports injuries and how to treat them. These persons should also be aware of preventive measures necessary for sports safety. This may not be a simple job for management because trained personnel are difficult to find. The manager may also run into budget difficulties, proliferation of sports, and established regulations. In addition, schedules may prohibit proper training before athletic competition because sports seasons tend to overlap more and more.

To prevent injuries, complete medical examinations, including blood tests, must be given to each athlete. Athletes who are immature physically, who have sustained previous athletic injuries, or who are inadequately conditioned are all prone to sports injuries. Crash diets and dehydration are injurious to an athlete's health. Training practices based on sound physiological principles are the best way to avoid sports injuries. Of course, proper protective equipment must be used in appropriate sports. Facilities and equipment must be developed with safety in mind, and sports safety regulations must be reviewed. Research also must be conducted to improve sports safety.

Proper conditioning of athletes. Conditioning athletes helps prevent sports injuries. It requires preseason training, as well as proper maintenance during the season, careful selection and fitting of equipment, protective strapping, counseling athletes about nutrition and rest, proper playing surfaces and facilities, and educators who know how to convey correct athletic training procedures and how to coach sports fundamentals.

Conditioning exercises for athletics should be compatible with the athlete's capacity and include a warmup, a progressive exercise routine both in-season and out-of-season, and special exercises to increase strength, flexibility, and relaxation.

Protective sports equipment. Sports equipment that protects vulnerable parts of the athlete's body from injury is important, particularly in such contact sports as football, hockey, and lacrosse. For example, football helmets should be purchased in accordance with standards established by the NOCSAE. The NOCSAE seal on a football helmet indicates that the manufacturer has complied with the best standards available for protection of the head. As basketball and soccer become more aggressive, proper equipment is also vital in these sports.

Protective equipment must be tested for adequacy, keep in good repair, and able to prevent injury. Excellent equipment is needed to protect the head in activities such as football and hockey and to protect the face of the baseball catcher and the goalie in ice hockey and lacrosse. Also, mouth guards, ear guards, and guards to protect the athletes who wear glasses are often necessary. Furthermore, proper equipment to protect the chest, ribs, elbows, knees, and shins is required in certain sports. Shoes should always be

first aid chart for athletic injuries

FIRST AID, the immediate and temporary care offered to the stricken athlete until the services of a physician can be obtained, minimizes the aggravation of injury and enhances the earliest possible return of the athlete to peak performance. To this end, it is strongly recommended that:

ALL ATHLETIC PROGRAMS include prearranged procedures for obtaining emergency first aid, transportation, and medical care.

ALL COACHES AND TRAINERS be competent in first aid techniques and procedures.

ALL ATHLETES be properly immunized as medically recommended, especially against tetanus and polio.

Committee on the
Medical Aspects of Sports
AMERICAN MEDICAL ASSOCIATION

to protect the athlete at time of injury, FOLLOW THESE FIRST STEPS FOR FIRST AID

STOP play immediately at first indication of possible injury or illness.

LOOK for obvious deformity or other deviation from the athlete's normal structure or motion.

LISTEN to the athlete's description of his complaint and how the injury occurred.

ACT, but move the athlete *only* after serious injury is ruled out.

BONES AND JOINTS

fracture Never move athlete if fracture of back, neck, or skull is suspected. If athlete *can* be moved, carefully splint any possible fracture. Obtain medical care at once.

dislocation Support joint. Apply ice bag or cold cloths to reduce swelling, and refer to physician at once.

bone bruise Apply ice bag or cold cloths and protect from further injury. If severe, refer to physician.

broken nose Apply cold cloths and refer to physician.

HEAT ILLNESSES

heat stroke Collapse—with dry warm skin—indicates sweating mechanism failure and rising body temperature.
THIS IS AN EMERGENCY; DELAY COULD BE FATAL. Immediately cool athlete by the most expedient means (immersion in cool water is best method). Obtain medical care at once.

heat exhaustion Weakness—with profuse sweating—indicates state of shock due to depletion of salt and water. Place in shade with head level or lower than body. Give sips of dilute salt water. Obtain medical care at once.

sunburn If severe, apply sterile gauze dressing and refer to physician.

IMPACT BLOWS

head If any period of dizziness, headache, incoordination or unconsciousness occurs, disallow any further activity and obtain medical care at once. Keep athlete lying down; if unconscious, give nothing by mouth.

teeth Save teeth, if completely removed from socket. If loosened, do not disturb; cover with sterile gauze and refer to dentist at once.

solar plexus Rest athlete on back and moisten face with cool water. Loosen clothing around waist and chest. Do nothing else except obtain medical care if needed.

testicle Rest athlete on back and apply ice bag or cold cloths. Obtain medical care if pain persists.

eye If vision is impaired, refer to physician at once. With soft tissue injury, apply ice bag or cold cloths to reduce swelling.

MUSCLES AND LIGAMENTS

bruise Apply ice bag or cold cloths and rest injured muscle. Protect from further aggravation. If severe, refer to physician.

cramp Have opposite muscles contracted forcefully, using firm hand pressure on cramped muscle. If during hot day, give sips of dilute salt water. If recurring, refer to physician.

strain and sprain Elevate injured part and apply ice bag or cold cloths. Apply pressure bandage to reduce swelling. Avoid weight bearing and obtain medical care.

OPEN WOUNDS

heavy bleeding Apply sterile pressure bandage using hand pressure if necessary. Refer to physician at once.

cut and abrasion Hold briefly under cold water. Then cleanse with mild soap and water. Apply sterile pad firmly until bleeding stops, then protect with more loosely applied sterile bandage. If extensive, refer to physician.

puncture wound Handle same as cuts; refer to physician.

nosebleed Keep athlete sitting or standing; cover nose with cold cloths. If bleeding is heavy, pinch nose and place *small* cotton pack in nostrils. If bleeding continues, refer to physician.

OTHER CONCERNS

blisters Keep clean with mild soap and water and protect from aggravation. If already broken, trim ragged edges with sterilized equipment. If extensive or infected, refer to physician.

foreign body in eye Do not rub. Gently touch particle with point of clean, moist cloth and wash with cold water. If unsuccessful or if pain persists, refer to physician.

lime burns Wash thoroughly with water. Apply sterile gauze dressing and refer to physician.

EMERGENCY PHONE NUMBERS		
Physician	Phone:	
Physician	Phone:	
Hospital	Ambulance	
Police	Fire	Other

Fig. 12-1. First aid chart for athletic injuries.

High school girl athlete in the Clark County School District, Las Vegas, Nev., involved in a cross-country activity. Both girl and boy athletes need the care that an athletic training program can provide.

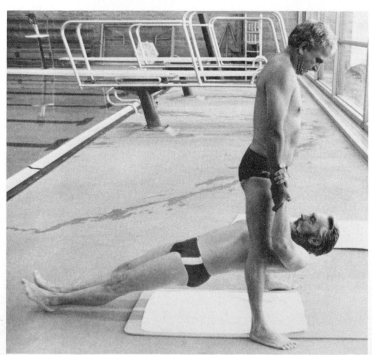

Strength conditioning of upper body in the adult fitness program at the University of Nevada, Las Vegas.

carefully selected to ensure maximum comfort and protection.

Taping, bandaging, and padding. Protective taping, bandaging, and padding can help prevent, as well as care for, athletic injuries. Bandaging is needed at times to protect wounds from infection, to immobilize an injured area, to protect an injury, to support an injured part, to hold protective equipment in place, and to make arm slings and eye bandages. Padding and orthoses are needed to cushion against injury, to restrict the athlete's range of joint motion, and to be used as foot pads. Orthoses can help in knee supports and shoulder braces. Taping, bandaging, padding, and orthoses require special skill and knowledge. They should not be attempted by the untrained.

Nutrition. Proper nutrition is important to the health of the athlete for physical fitness, recuperation from fatigue, energy, and the repair of damaged tissues. The athlete should include proper amounts of carbohydrates, fats, proteins, minerals, vitamins, and water in his or her diet.

Ergogenic aids. Ergogenic aids are supplements or agents that supposedly enhance athletic performance. In other words, they are work-producing aids and are supposed to improve physical effort and performance. They include drugs, food, physical stimulants such as thermal packs or electrical devices, and hypnosis. Some are questionable and unethical.

Coaches, athletic trainers, and physical educators should not use or recommend the use of any substance that may be harmful to the participant. They should endorse only ethically and morally sound training practices. Some athletic associations and sports medicine leaders have taken a strong stand against the use of agents or drugs that enhance performance through artificial means. For example, the use of amphetamines such as Benzedrine to reduce fatigue and of anabolic steroids to gain weight and strength is not approved or condoned. Also, the use of dimethyl sulfoxide, better known as DMSO, is frowned on by most administrators as a means of alleviating injuries.

SAFETY IN ATHLETICS AND PHYSICAL EDUCATION

In light of the increased participation in athletics and physical education, management must give attention to providing for the safety of persons engaging in these activities. Injuries are related not only to actual participation in these activities but also to things such as the equipment provided and the surfacing of athletic fields and playfields.

Accidents are an important consideration in our way of life. The National Safety Council indicates that over 100,000 people die annually as a result of accidents. Another 10 million experience disabling injuries. Accidents are the main cause of death in the range of people 1 to 38 years old, and in the age range of 15 to 24 years more young people die from accidents than from all other causes combined.

Sports participation results in many accidents and injuries. In soccer, for example, the incidence of such injuries as skin abrasions or blisters, contusions, strains and sprains, fractures, knee ligament damage, cartilage tears, and brain concussion is high. In racquetball there are an estimated 7.5 million players and over 850 registered racquetball court clubs. The increase in injuries to the eyes and the facial area has been dramatic. In swimming approximately 8000 drownings a year occur.

Given the large number of participants and accidents, it is recommended that the first management step should be a policy statement prepared by each organization involved in these activities. Written policy has been a valuable tool in enforcing safety regulations.

A second management recommendation is the appointment of an individual who will be responsible for the safety program of the organization. This professional would have responsibilities such as developing policies and procedures, inspecting facilities and equipment, reporting accidents, and conducting safety research. In large organizations such a position would pay for itself in cutting down on the accident rate, the loss of production, and other costs related to accidents and injuries. If a full-time professional cannot be employed, this responsibility should be assigned to a staff member.

A third management recommendation is the development of a proper accident reporting system. According to the National Safety Council, a well-organized accident report is essential to a safety program. The council points out that accident reports help prevent further accidents by getting at the causes of unsafe acts and unsafe conditions and by developing a

DISQUALIFYING CONDITIONS FOR SPORTS PARTICIPATION

Conditions	Contact*	Noncontact endurance†	Others‡
General			
Acute infections:			
Respiratory, genitourinary, infectious mononucleosis, hepatitis, active rheumatic fever, active tuberculosis, boils, furuncles, impetigo	X	X	X
Obvious physical immaturity in comparison with other competitors	X	X	
Obvious growth retardation	X		
Hemorrhagic disease:			
Hemophilia, purpura, and other bleeding tendencies	X		
Diabetes, inadequately controlled	X	X	X
Jaundice, whatever cause	X	X	X
Eyes			
Absence or loss of function of one eye	X		
Severe myopia, even if correctable	X		
Ears			
Significant impairment	X		
Respiratory			
Tuberculosis (active or under treatment)	X	X	X
Severe pulmonary insufficiency	X	X	X
Cardiovascular			
Mitral stenosis, aortic stenosis, aortic insufficiency, coarctation of aorta, cyanotic heart disease, recent carditis of any kind	X	X	X
Hypertension of organic basis	X	X	X
Previous heart surgery for congenital or acquired heart disease	X	X	
Liver			
Enlarged liver	X		
Spleen			
Enlarged spleen	X		
Hernia			
Inguinal or femoral hernia	X	X	
Musculoskeletal			
Symptomatic abnormalities or inflammations	X	X	X
Functional inadequacy of the musculoskeletal system, congenital or acquired, incompatible with the contact or skill demands of the sport	X	X	

*Lacrosse, baseball, soccer, basketball, football, wrestling, hockey, rugby, etc.
†Cross country, track, tennis, crew, swimming, etc.
‡Bowling, golf, archery, field events, etc.
From Committee on the Medical Aspects of Sports, American Medical Association.

DISQUALIFYING CONDITIONS FOR SPORTS PARTICIPATION—cont'd

Conditions	Contact*	Noncontact endurance†	Others‡
Neurological			
History of symptoms of previous serious head trauma or repeated concussions	X		
Convulsive disorder not completely controlled by medication	X	X	
Previous surgery on head or spine	X	X	
Renal			
Absence of one kidney	X		
Renal disease	X	X	X
Genitalia			
Absence of one testicle	X		
Undescended testicle	X		

SUGGESTED SPORTS CANDIDATES' QUESTIONNAIRE

(To be completed by parents or family physician)

Name _____ Birth date _____

Home address _____

Parents' name _____ Tel. no. _____

1. Has had injuries requiring medical attention	Yes	No
2. Has had illness lasting more than a week	Yes	No
3. Is under a physician's care now	Yes	No
4. Takes medication now	Yes	No
5. Wears glasses	Yes	No
contact lenses	Yes	No
6. Has had a surgical operation	Yes	No
7. Has been in hospital (except for tonsillectomy)	Yes	No
8. Do you know of any reason why this individual should not participate in all sports?	Yes	No

Please explain any "yes" answers to above questions:

_____

_____

9. Has had complete poliomyelitis immunization by inoculations (Salk) or oral vaccine (Sabin)	Yes	No
10. Has had tetanus toxoid and booster inoculation within past 3 years	Yes	No
11. Has seen a dentist within the past 6 months	Yes	No

_____

Parent or Physician

From Committee on the Medical Aspects of Sports, American Medical Association.

Women engaged in a fitness program at a spa.

program that results in the removal of such unsafe acts and conditions.

In schools the recommendation is preparation of a school safety handbook, which can contain specific guidelines for maintaining a safe environment, can identify individual responsibilities, and can call attention to safe work practices.

Another management recommendation is the establishment of a safety committee. Safety committees have proved helpful in gaining organizational support for sound safety practices. The functions of such a committee are to develop procedures and implement safety suggestions, to hold regular meetings to discuss safety promotion, to conduct periodic inspections, to conduct accident investigations, to recommend changes in equipment, to eliminate hazards, and to promote safety and first aid training.

SUMMARY

An important responsibility in physical education and athletic management is to provide for the health of participants in activity and athletic programs. This requires establishing policies that will provide for proper medical procedures, seeing that coaches have an understanding and skill in sound athletic training procedures, providing a full-time athletic trainer

when possible, and ensuring that proper uniforms and equipment are provided. The number of injuries that occur in sports programs today requires management to oversee the programs to make sure that sound athletic training practices exist so that such injuries can be kept to a minimum.

SELF-ASSESSMENT TESTS

These tests will assist students in determining if material and competencies presented in this chapter have been mastered.

1. Prepare a report on the nature and scope of injuries that occur to athletes each year in various sports.
2. As a coach of a football or basketball team, what steps should you take in preventing injuries to your players? Describe the procedures you would follow if a player broke a leg in practice.
3. What are the duties of a team physician?
4. Prepare a list of arguments to present to the board of education to justify the addition of an athletic trainer to the school staff. Also indicate the qualifications and responsibilities of the athletic trainer.

REFERENCES

1. Arnheim, D.D.: Modern principles of athletic training, ed. 6, St. Louis, 1985, Times Mirror/Mosby College Publishing.
2. Chandy, T.A., and Grana, W.A.: Secondary school athletic injury in boys and girls: a three-year comparison, The Physician and Sports Medicine **13:**106, March 1985.
3. Porter, M., et al.: The faculty athletic training program: a model, The Physician and Sports Medicine **10:**85, April 1982.

SUGGESTED READINGS

• Avoiding aerobics injuries, Athletic Business **9:**10, March 1985.
  Discusses the fast-growing activity of aerobic dancing and how instructors of this activity are being overloaded with classes with the result that rising injury rates are common.
• Kent, F.: Athletes wait too long to report injuries, The Physician and Sports Medicine **10:**127, April 1982.
  A Canadian survey of 450 amateur athletes with injuries found that nearly one of every two waited five days or more before seeing a physician. The delay can have serious consequences.
• Morris, A.F.: Sports medicine: prevention of athletic injuries, Dubuque, Iowa, 1984, Wm. C. Brown Publishers.
  A text for physical educators and exercise science persons who wish to study the emerging field of sports medicine; the text is written from a physical education perspective.
• Mueller, F.O., and Blyth, C.S.: Fatalities and catastrophic injuries in football, The Physician and Sports Medicine **10:**135, October 1982.
  Compares football fatalities and injuries for the years 1976 through 1981, with earlier data drawing implications for rule and equipment changes that have taken place since 1976.

• Olson, J.R., and Bauer, R.P.: Safety guidelines for gymnastic facilities, Athletic Business **8:**28, July 1984.
  Sets forth guidelines for a safe gymnastic program that includes maintaining constant supervision, conducting regular safety inspections, and making all repairs promptly.
• Olson, J.R., and Hunter, G.R.: Weight training safety guidelines, Athletic Purchasing & Facilities **7:**29, January 1983.
  Guidelines for weight training facilities that guard against unsafe practices, hazardous conditions, and dangerous equipment.
• Roy, S., and Irvin, R.: Sports medicine, Englewood Cliffs, N.J., 1983, Prentice-Hall, Inc.
  A text that is concerned with the prevention, evaluation, management, and rehabilitation of athletic injuries.
• What's new in training room aids? Athletic Business **8:**58, September 1984.
  A comprehensive look at what is available for training rooms from tape to training tables to therapeutic, protective, and rehabilitation devices.
• Wilmore, J.H.: Training for sport and activity, Boston, 1982, Allyn & Bacon, Inc.
  A text that is designed to provide the sport practitioner, the coach, the athlete, the team trainer, and the team physician with a basic understanding of physiological principles underlying physical conditioning and performance in athletics and physical fitness.

Chapter Thirteen

Legal Liability, Risk, and Insurance Management

Instructional Objectives and Competencies to be Achieved
After reading this chapter the student should be able to

- Define each of the following terms: *legal liability, tort, negligence, in loco parentis, save harmless, assumption of risk, attractive nuisance, immunity,* and *insurance management.*
- Indicate the legal basis for physical education programs throughout the United States and the implications this has for making physical education a requirement for all students.
- Discuss recent court interpretations regarding sports product liability, violence, and physical education activities held off-campus.
- Illustrate what constitutes negligent behavior on the part of physical educators and coaches and what constitutes defenses against negligence.
- Identify common areas of negligence in the conduct of physical education and athletic programs, and explain what can be done to eliminate such negligence.
- Appreciate the relationship of Title IX to legal liability in the conduct of physical education and athletic programs.
- Discuss precautions that physical educators can take to prevent accidents and provide for the safety of students and other individuals who participate in their programs.
- Recommend a sound insurance management plan for a physical education and athletic program.

Among the most important management responsibilities of physical education and athletic programs is conducting programs within limits provided by legislation and the law. Unlike other programs that relate to academic pursuits, physical education and athletic programs take place in many more settings where injuries may occur. Therefore every effort must be taken to provide preventive measures that will keep such injuries to a minimum. This includes hiring qualified personnel to conduct activities, purchasing quality equipment, and providing facilities and play areas that are safe. This chapter covers those aspects of legal liability, risk, and insurance management that are pertinent to the administration of physical education and athletic programs.

According to Bouvier's *Law Dictionary,* liability is

"the responsibility, the state of one who is bound in law and justice to do something which may be enforced by action." Another definition states, "liability is the condition of affairs that gives rise to an obligation to do a particular thing to be enforced by court action."

Leaders in physical education and athletics should know how far they can go with various aspects of their programs and what precautions are necessary so they will not be held legally liable in the event of an accident. The fact that approximately 65% to 70% of all school jurisdiction accidents involving boys and 59% to 65% involving girls occur in physical education and recreation programs has some broad implications for this field. Furthermore, the fact that millions of boys and girls and adults participate in athletic programs indicates another management concern for physical educators. It is estimated that every year 1 of 30 to 35 students attending school will be injured. It is alarming to note that physical educators are involved in more than 50% of the injuries sustained by students each year. Furthermore, industrial fitness programs, health spas, and other areas where physical educators are employed involve millions of people where accidents and injuries occur.

When an accident resulting in personal injury occurs, the question often arises about whether damages can be recovered. All employees run the risk of being sued by injured persons on the basis of alleged negligence that caused bodily injury. Such injuries occur on playgrounds, athletic fields, in fitness laboratories, classes, or any place where physical education and athletic programs take place.

The legal rights of the individuals involved in such cases are worthy of study. Although the law varies from state to state, it is possible to discuss liability in a way that has implications for all sections of the country and for any setting in which physical educators work. First, it is important to understand the legal basis for physical education, athletics, and allied areas.

TRENDS IN PHYSICAL EDUCATION AND SPORT LEGAL LIABILITY CASES

Appenzeller,[1] a specialist in physical education and sport legal liability cases, identifies several trends in these areas. These include the modification of the doctrine of governmental immunity in all 50 states, increased possibility of litigation because of a better informed citizenry, a public attitude that groups such as insurance companies and schools have endless sources of revenue, movement toward the doctrine of comparative rather than contributory negligence, an increase in litigation involving discrimination in respect to handicapping conditions, management being included in litigation, and lawsuits where participants were not properly warned that injury could result from their participation.

THE LEGAL BASIS FOR PHYSICAL EDUCATION, ATHLETICS, AND ALLIED AREAS

Surveys concerning physical education requirements by law in elementary, junior, or senior high schools indicate certain interesting facts. Physical education instruction ranging from 1 to 4 years is required in grades nine through twelve in most states. Most states require some type of program in grades seven and eight and at the elementary level. Physical education is required in all grades (one through twelve) in several states.

Legal implications for requiring physical education

One legal implication for schools is that of requiring pupils to enroll in physical education classes. The schools should be flexible enough to provide alternatives for those cases where activities such as dancing are against a student's principles. Where rules and regulations are questioned, a review of the rationale behind the rule or regulation should be provided. It also should be noted that a student may be denied the right to graduate when a required course such as physical education is not taken.

LEGAL LIABILITY

Some years ago the courts recognized the hazards involved in the play activities that are a part of the educational program. A boy sustained an injury while he was playing tag. The court recognized the possibility and risk of some injury in physical education programs and would not award damages. However, it pointed out that care must be taken by both the participant and the authorities in charge. It further implied that the benefits derived from participating in physical education activities such as tag offset the occasional injury that might occur.

The decision regarding the benefits derived from participating in physical education programs was handed down at a time when the attitude of the law was that no government agency, which included the school, could be held liable for the acts of its employees unless it so consented. Since that time a changing attitude in the courts has been evident. As more accidents occurred, the courts frequently decided in favor of the injured party when negligence could be shown. The immunity derived from the old common-law rule that a government agency cannot be sued without its consent is slowly changing in the eyes of the courts so that both federal and state governments may be sued.

Compulsory elements of a school curriculum, such as physical education, prompt courts to decide on the basis of what is in the best interests of the public. Instead of being merely a moral responsibility, safety has become a legal responsibility. Those who uphold the doctrine that a government agency should be immune from liability maintain that payments for injury to constituents are misappropriations of public funds. On the other hand, some persons feel it is wrong for the cost of injuries to fall on one or a few persons; instead, they should be shared by all. To further their case, these persons cite the constitutional provision that compensation must be given for taking or damaging private property. They argue it is unjust for the government to be able to take or damage private property without just compensation on the one hand, yet on the other hand to injure or destroy a person's life without liability for compensation. This position is held more and more by the courts.

The role of immunity is the law in some states. Because school districts are instruments of the state, and the state is immune from suit unless it consents, the state's immunity extends to the districts. Some exceptions are in states such as California, Washington, and New York. However, as has been pointed out previously, the doctrine of immunity is starting to crumble.

Bingham v. Board of Education of Oregon City,

223 P2d 432, handed down by the Supreme Court in Utah in October 1950, involved a 3-year-old child who, while riding her tricycle on the school grounds, fell into some burning embers left on the grounds and suffered severe burns. Adjacent to the playground area the school maintained an incinerator in which rubbish was burned. From time to time embers and ashes were removed and scattered around the adjoining area. The parents sued to recover damages, and the court held that the district was not liable. Judge Latimer wrote the court's opinion:

While the law writers, editors, and judges have criticized and disapproved the foregoing doctrine of government immunity as illogical and unjust, the weight of precedent of decided cases supports the general rule and we prefer not to disregard a principle so well established without statutory authority. We, therefore, adopt the rule of the majority and hold that school boards cannot be held liable for ordinary negligent acts.

The importance of this case is that two judges dissented. The dissenting judges said: "I prefer to regard said principle for the purpose of overruling it. I would not wait for the dim distant future in never-never land when the legislature may act." It was also pointed out that the rule rests on the "immortal and indefensible doctrine" that "the king (sovereign) can do no wrong" and that a state should not be allowed to use this as a shield.

Court activity regarding the principle of governmental immunity has been considerable. In 1959 the Illinois Supreme Court (*Molitor v. Kaneland Community Unit,* District No. 302, 163 N.E. 2d 89) overruled the immunity doctrine. The supreme courts of Wisconsin, Arizona, and Minnesota legislature followed suit, but in 1963 the Minnesota legislature restored the rule but provided that where school districts had liability insurance they were reponsible for damages up to the coverage. The principle of governmental immunity has also been put to the test in courts in states such as Colorado, Iowa, Kansas, Oregon, Pennsylvania, and Utah. However, the courts in some of these states are hesitant to depart from the precedent and furthermore insist that it is the legislature of the state rather than the courts that should waive the rule.[18]

In the case of *Cerrone v. Milton School District*, 479 A. 2d 675 (Pa. 1984) Cerrone had received an injury while wrestling in high school. As a result of a suit against the Milton School District in Pennsylvania the court ruled that the school district was immune from suit as provided by the Tort Claims Act.[4]

In another case, *Kain v. Rockridge Community Unit School District #300*, 453 N.E. 2d 118 (Ill. 1983), a football coach was granted immunity when Kraig Kain sued the Rockridge Community Unit School District for alleged negligent conduct by the coach who played him in a game without observing the required number of practices before participation.[1]

In many of the 50 states school districts have governmental immunity, which means that as long as they are engaging in a governmental function they cannot be sued, even though negligence has been determined. In a few states governmental immunity has been annulled by either legislation or judicial decision. In some states schools may legally purchase liability insurance (California requires and several other states expressly authorize school districts to carry liability insurance) protecting school districts that may become involved in lawsuits, although this does not necessarily mean governmental immunity has been waived. Of course, in the absence of insurance and *save harmless* laws (laws requiring that school districts assume the liability of the teacher, whether negligence is proved or not), any judgment rendered against a school district must be met out of personal funds. School districts in states such as Connecticut, Massachusetts, New Jersey, and New York have *save harmless* laws. Wyoming permits school districts to indemnify employees.

School districts still enjoying governmental immunity usually are either required or permitted to carry liability insurance that specifically covers the operation of school buses.

A strong feeling exists among educators and many in the legal profession that the doctrine of sovereign immunity should be abandoned. In some states students injured as a result of negligence are assured recompense for damages directly or indirectly, either because governmental immunity has been abrogated or because school districts are legally required to indemnify school employees against financial loss. In other states, if liability insurance has been secured, a possibility exists that students may recover damages incurred.

Although school districts have been granted immunity in many states, teachers do not have such immunity. A 1938 decision of an Iowa court provides some of the thinking regarding the teacher's responsibility for his or her own actions (*Montanick v. McMillin*, 225 Iowa 442, 452-453, 458, 280 N.W. 608, 1938):

[The employee's liability] is not predicated upon any relationship growing out of his [her] employment, but is based upon the fundamental and underlying laws of torts, that he [she] who does injury to the person or property of another is civilly liable in damages for the injuries inflicted. . . . The doctrine of *respondeat superior*, literally, "let the principle answer," is an extension of the fundamental principle of torts, and an added remedy to the injured party, under which a party injured by some act of misfeasance may hold both the servant and the master. The exemption of governmental bodies and their officers from liability under the doctrine of *respondeat superior* is a limitation of exception to the rule of *respondeat superior* and in no way affects the fundamental principle of torts that one who wrongfully inflicts injury upon another is liable to the injured person for damages. . . . An act of misfeasance is a positive wrong, and every employee, whether employed by a private person or a municipal corporation owes a duty not to injure another by a negligent act of commission.

Interpretations of special situations of legal liability by the courts

The courts have had cases that resulted in a look at areas such as sports product liability, violence and legal liability, and physical education classes held off campus and legal liability.

Sports product liability[5]

The sale of sporting goods is a multibillion dollar industry today. The fact that many people want to engage in physical fitness and sports activities is one reason for this growth in sales. As a result, the subject of sports product liability has arisen. The term *sports product liability*, according to Arnold,[5] refers to the liability of the manufacturer to the person who uses his or her manufactured product and who sustains injury or damage as a result of using the product.

What is most important to physical educators, athletic directors, and coaches is that they are being named as codefendants in approximately one third of all liability suits involving sports product liability.

Years ago the buyer was responsible for inspecting the product before making the purchase. He or she assumed the risk of injury or damage to property. Today, however, the courts are placing more and more responsibility on the manufacturer to discover weaknesses and defects in the product. The manufacturer is required to exercise due care in designing, manufacturing, and packaging the product. The manufacturer guarantees the product to be safe for consumer use.

According to Arnold, within the last 30 years an estimated 42 states have used the *strict liability doctrine* for some products. Under this doctrine the plaintiff must establish proof that the product contained a defect causing the injury or damage. In addition to this doctrine, a breach of the manufacturer's warranty can also be just cause for awarding damages.

The number of suits involving product liability has increased dramatically in the last few years. One reason is the possibility of a large monetary settlement if an injury has occurred. A result of these large awards is skyrocketing insurance rates.

The June 1985 issue of *Athletic Business* pointed out that sporting goods manufacturers are calling for a national product liability standard that would stabilize the rules under which they operate. However, legislators are having difficulty finding a solution acceptable to both consumers and business. At present the lack of certainty about how cases will be treated contributes to the high cost and the availability of product liability insurance.[11]

Violence and legal liability[8]

An increasing number of injuries occurring in sports contests are not accidental but intentional. When such an act occurs, it is referred to as battery and "involves the harmful, unpermitted contact of one person by another." Carpenter and Acosta point out that courts are making large awards for violence in sports cases.

REDUCING THE RISKS ASSOCIATED WITH SPORTS PRODUCT LIABILITY

Arnold has listed 10 ways that the risks associated with sports product liability may be reduced and that will help when faced with product liability litigation.

- Become involved in collecting pertinent facts and information associated with illness and injury. This procedure can result in discouraging unwarranted claims.
- Purchase the best quality equipment available. Equipment should be carefully evaluated and tested. When purchased, records should be kept regarding such items as date of purchase. Also, reconditioned and repaired items should be recorded.
- Purchase only from reputable dealers. Reputable dealers stand behind their products and provide replacements when called for.
- Use only reputable reconditioning equipment companies that have high standards. For example, the NOCSAE stamp of approval should apply to reconditioned football helmets.
- Follow manufacturer's instructions regarding fitting, adjusting, and repairing equipment, particularly protective equipment. Also, urge participants to wear protective equipment regularly.
- Be careful not to blame someone or something for the injury without just cause. Furthermore, it is best to confine such remarks to the accident report.
- Good teaching and supervising are important. Do not use any drills or techniques frowned on by professional associations and respected leaders in the field.
- An emergency care plan should be prepared and ready to be implemented when needed.
- Insurance coverage for accident and general liability should be purchased or be available to all parties concerned, including athletes, staff members, and schools.
- When and if serious injuries occur, preserve items of evidence associated with the injury, such as pieces of equipment.

Adapted from Arnold, D.E.

APPENZELLER AND ROSS'S RECOMMENDATIONS REGARDING HELMETS

- Purchase only the best equipment.
- Insure that *all* players have the best equipment.
- The coach should see that helmet fits properly.
- The helmet should be inspected weekly.
- In event of injury see that no one removes helmet during transportation to hospital.
- See that helmet is removed safely.
- Both players and parents should be informed about risk involved in using helmet.

Adapted from Appenzeller, H., and Ross, T.

They cite the case of the professional basketball player who was hit in the face with a powerful punch and was awarded in excess of $3 million in damages. The authors also indicate that the courts are attempting to curb violence in sports.

Carpenter and Acosta also point out that the coach is not necessarily free from liability in such cases of violence. They cite two theoretical situations when the coach may be held liable. The first situation is when a coach knows a player is likely to commit a violent act in a sports situation but puts the player into the lineup. In this case the coach is not taking the necessary precautions to protect opponents from harm and injury, and in the event injury occurs, the coach may be found negligent. The second situation is when a coach may instruct a player ''to take X out of the game.'' In this case the player who follows such an instruction is acting as an agent of the coach; as a result, a person who causes battery to be committed (in this case the coach) is just as negligent as the person who commits the act. In both of these cases the coach should exercise leadership and see that he or she and the team conduct themselves in accordance with proper standards of conduct.

Physical education classes held off campus and legal liability[6]

Off-campus physical education activities have become popular in many communities, schools, and colleges. In such cases instruction in the activity may

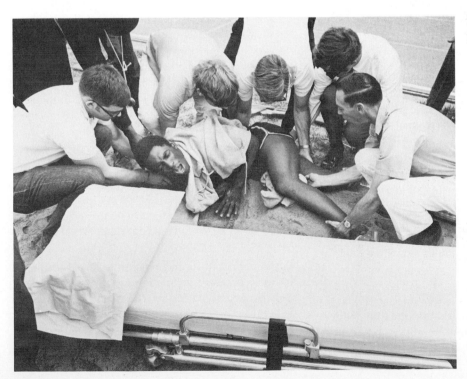

In some cases of injuries and accidents there are questions of legal liability.

be provided by faculty members, or faculty members may only provide supervision, with the activity being instructed by a specialist not associated with the school or university, or no faculty member may be present on a regular basis.

Although instruction may take place in off-campus settings and by nonfaculty members, considerable responsibility and control still rest with the management and staff members of the organization sponsoring these activities. Arnold cites the case of a college that had a person not affiliated with the college teach a course at an off-campus equestrian center. The plaintiff was injured in a fall from a horse while receiving instruction. The plaintiff's attorney argued that the college was vicariously liable for the negligence of the riding academy. The court's ruling went in favor of the college, which did not have to pay damages on the grounds that a master-servant relationship did not exist between the plaintiff and the college. To show such a relationship the plaintiff would have had to prove that, among other things, the college could control the instruction taking place. Furthermore, the court ruled that the agency relationship did not result in the college authorizing the fall leading to the injury and that no complaints had been supplied regarding the instruction given.

Where off-campus physical education activities are conducted, it is of primary concern of whether *due care* is provided. The type of activity offered would indicate the amount of care that should be provided. For example, according to Arnold, bowling in a town bowling alley would not need as much care in most cases as a skiing class. It is the responsibility of the organization and the administration to exercise care and prudence in selecting the sites to be used for off-campus activities, the quality of the instruction, and the supervision provided. Failure to observe proper care can result in negligence on the part of the organization. The administration should also look into other aspects of off-campus activities such as transportation.

TORT

A *tort* is a legal wrong resulting in direct or indirect injury to another individual or to property. A tortious act is a wrongful act, and damages can be collected through court action. Tort can be committed through an act of *omission* or *commission*. An act of omission results when the accident occurs during failure to perform a legal duty such as when a teacher fails to obey a fire alarm after he or she has been informed of the procedure to be followed. An act of commission results when the accident occurs while an unlawful act, such as assault, is being performed.

The National Education Association points out that:

A tort may arise out of the following acts: (a) an act which without lawful justification or excuse is intended by a person to cause harm and does cause the harm complained of; (b) an act in itself contrary to law or an omission of specific legal duty, which causes harm not intended by the person so acting or omitting; (c) an act or omission causing harm which the person so acting or omitting did not intend to cause, but which might and should, with due diligence, have been foreseen and prevented.[16]

The teacher, leader, or other individual not only has a legal responsibility as described by law but also has a responsibility to prevent injury. This means that in addition to complying with certain legal regulations, such as proper facilities, the teacher must comply with the principle that children should be taught without injury to them and that prudent care, such as a parent would give, must be exercised. The term *legal duty* does not mean only those duties imposed by law but also the duty owed to society to prevent injury to others. A duty imposed by law would be one such as complying with housing regulations and traffic regulations. A duty that teachers owe to society in general consists of teaching children without injury to them. For example, it was stated in one case (*Hoose v. Drumm,* 281 N.Y. 54):

Teachers have watched over the play of their pupils time out of mind. At recess periods, not less than in the classroom, a teacher owes it to his charges to exercise such care of them as a parent of ordinary prudence would observe in comparable circumstances.

It is important to understand the legal meaning of the word *accident* in relation to the topic under discussion. According to the Black's *Law Dictionary:*

An accident is an unforeseen event occurring without the will or design of the person whose mere act causes it. In its proper use the term excludes negligence. It is an event which occurs without fault, carelessness, or want of proper circumspection for the person affected, or which could not have been avoided by the use of that kind and degree of care necessary to the exigency and in the circumstance in which he was placed.

Lee v. Board of Education of City of New York in 1941, showed that prudent care was not exercised, and the defendant was liable for negligence. A boy was hit by a car while playing football in the street as a part of the physical education program. The street had not been completely closed off to traffic. The board of education and the teacher were found negligent.

NEGLIGENCE

Questions of liability and negligence occupy a prominent position in connection with the actions of teachers and leaders in physical education and athletic programs.

The law in America pertaining to negligence is based on common law, previous judicial rulings, or established legal procedure. This type of law differs from statutory law, which has been written into the statutes by lawmaking bodies.

Negligence implies that someone has not fulfilled his or her legal duty or has failed to do something that according to common sense reasoning should have been done. Negligence can be avoided with common knowledge of basic legal principles and proper vigilance. One of the first things that must be determined in event of accident is whether there has been negligence.

The National Education Association's report elaborates further:

Negligence is any conduct which falls below the standard established by law for the protection of others against unreasonable risk of harm. In general, such conduct may be of two types: (a) an act which a reasonable man would have realized involved an unreasonable risk of injury to others, and (b) failure to do an act which is necessary for the protection or assistance of another and which one is under a duty to do.[16]

The National Education Association report includes the following additional comment:

The law prohibits careless action; whatever is done must be done well and with reasonable caution. Failure to employ care not to harm others is a misfeasance. For example, an Oregon school bus driver who parked the bus across a drive-

Physical education activities at times lend themselves to injuries that may raise questions of legal liability.

way when he knew the pupils were coasting down the hill was held liable for injuries sustained by a pupil who coasted into the bus (*Fahlstrom v. Denk,* 1933).[16]

Negligence may be claimed when the plaintiff has suffered injury either to self or to property, when the defendant has not performed his or her legal duty and has been negligent, and when the plaintiff has constitutional rights and is not guilty of contributory negligence.[10] The teacher or leader of children in such cases is regarded as *in loco parentis,* that is, acting in the place of the parent in relation to the child.

Because negligence implies failure to act as a reasonably prudent and careful person, necessary precautions should be taken, danger should be anticipated, and common sense should be used. For example, if a teacher permits a group of very young children to go up a high slide alone and without supervision, he or she is not acting prudently. In *Lee v. Board of Education of City of New York,* when the physical education class was held in a street where cars were also allowed to pass, negligence existed.

Four factors of negligence must be proved before a lawsuit can be won. First, there must be conformance to a standard of behavior that avoids subjecting a person to reasonable risk or injury. Second, a breach of duty must be shown. Third, the breach of duty must be the cause of injury to the victim. The final factor that must be proved is that injury did occur.

A verdict by the jury in a California district court points to negligence in football. Press dispatches indicated that the high school athlete who suffered a disabling football injury was brought into court on a stretcher. The award was $325,000 (against the school district) in a suit in which the parent charged the coach "was negligent in having the boy moved to the sidelines *too soon* after he was injured." The newspaper report seemed to imply that the negligence was involved not in the *method* of moving the boy from the field, but rather in the *time* at which he was moved.

An interesting case in which the court ruled negligence occurred in New Jersey. In 1962 a student in the Chatham Junior High School was severely injured in an accident while participating in physical education. The testimony revealed that the physical education teacher was not present when the accident occurred but was treating another child for a rope burn.

A SCHOOL EMPLOYEE MAY BE NEGLIGENT BECAUSE OF THE FOLLOWING REASONS:

- He did not take appropriate care.
- Although he used due care, he acted in circumstances which created risks.
- His acts created an unreasonable risk of direct and immediate injury to others.
- He set in motion a force which was unreasonably hazardous to others.
- He created a situation in which third persons such as pupils, or inanimate forces, such as shop machinery, may reasonably have been expected to injure others.
- He allowed pupils to use dangerous devices although they were incompetent to use them.
- He did not control a third person such as an abnormal pupil, whom he knew to be likely to inflict intended injury on others because of some incapacity or abnormality.
- He did not give adequate warning.
- He did not look out for persons, such as pupils, who were in danger.
- He acted without sufficient skill.
- He did not make sufficient preparation to avoid an injury to pupils before beginning an activity where such preparation is reasonably necessary.
- He failed to inspect and repair mechanical devices to be used by pupils.
- He prevented someone, such as another teacher, from assisting a pupil who was endangered although the pupil's peril was not caused by his negligence.

From Garber, L.O.

However, he had continually warned his class not to use the springboard at any time he was out of the room. (The student was trying to perform the exercise where he would dive from a springboard over an obstacle and finish with a forward roll.) The prosecution argued that the warning had not been stressed sufficiently and that the teacher's absence from the gymnasium, leaving student aides in charge, was an act of negligence. The court ruled negligence and awarded the boy $1.2 million dollars for injuries. His parents were awarded $35,140. On appeal, the award to the boy was reduced to $300,000, but the award to the parents remained the same.

Concerning negligence, considerable weight is given in the law to the *foreseeability of danger*. One authority points out that "if a danger is obvious and a reasonably prudent person could have foreseen it and could have avoided the resulting harm by care and caution, the person who did not foresee or failed to prevent a foreseeable injury is liable for a tort on account of negligence.[11] If a person fails to take the needed precautions and care, he or she is negligent. However, it must be established on the basis of facts in the case. It cannot be based on mere conjecture.

Physical educators must realize that children will behave in certain ways, that certain juvenile acts will cause injuries unless properly supervised, and that hazards must be anticipated, reported, and eliminated. The question raised by most courts of law is: "Should the physical educators have had enough prudence to foresee the possible dangers or occurrence of an act?"

Two court actions point to legal reasoning on negligence as interpreted in one state. In *Lane v. City of Buffalo* in 1931, the board of education was found not liable. In this case a child fell from a piece of apparatus in the schoolyard. It was found that the apparatus was in good condition and that proper supervision was present. In *Cambareri v. Board of Albany*, the defendant was found liable. The City of Buffalo owned a park supervised by the park department. While skating on the lake in the park, a boy playing crack the whip hit a 12-year-old boy who was also skating. Workers and a policeman had been assigned to supervise activity and had been instructed not

to allow rough or dangerous games.

Although there are no absolute, factual standards for determining negligence, certain guides have been established that should be familiar to teachers and others engaged in physical education. Attorney Cymrot, in discussing negligence at a conference in New York City, suggested the following:

1. The person must be acting within the scope of his or her employment and in the discharge of his or her duties in order to obtain the benefits of the statute.
2. There must be a breach of a recognized duty owed to the participant.
3. There must be a negligent breach of such duty.
4. The accident and resulting injuries must be the natural and foreseeable consequence of the person's negligence arising from a negligent breach of duty.
5. The person must be a participant in an activity under the control of the instructor, or, put in another way, the accident must have occurred under circumstances where the instructor owes a duty of care to the participant.
6. A person's contributory negligence, however modified, will bar his or her recovery for damages.
7. The plaintiff must establish the negligence of the instructor and his or her own freedom from contributory negligence by a fair preponderance of evidence. The burden of proof on both issues is on the plaintiff.
8. Generally speaking, in a school situation, the board of education alone is responsible for accidents caused by the faulty maintenance of plants and equipment.[17]

Some states have a save harmless law. For example, in New Jersey the law reads:

Chapter 311. P.L. 1938 Boards assume liability of teachers. It shall be the duty of each board of education in any school district to save harmless and protect all teachers and members of supervisory and administrative staff from financial loss arising out of any claim, demand, suit or judgment by reason of alleged negligence or other act resulting in accidental bodily injury to any person within or without the school building provided such teacher or member of the supervisory or administrative staff at the time of the accident or injury was acting in the discharge of his duties within the scope of his employment and/or under the direction of said board of education; and said board of education may arrange for and maintain appropriate insurance with any company created by or under the laws of this state, or in any insurance company authorized by law to transact business in this state, or such board may elect to act as self-insurers to maintain the aforesaid protection.

Negligence concerning equipment and facilities

Defective or otherwise hazardous equipment or inadequate facilities are often the cause of injuries that lead to court action. If a physical educator has noted the equipment is defective, he or she should put this observation in writing for personal future protection. A letter should be written to the principal and superintendent of schools or other responsible person stating that danger exists and the areas of such danger. The physical educator should keep a copy for evidence in a possible lawsuit. In these cases the courts tend to agree with the student, even if dangerous conditions had been noted. Conditions cannot only be recognized but also must be corrected. Therefore physical educators should see to it that defective equipment is either repaired or discarded.

Negligence concerning instruction

Many cases result from situations concerning instruction in an activity. For example, if a child is injured in a fall from a trampoline, a case might ensue where the child and his or her parents may try to show that instruction had been inadequate. These cases are often found in favor of the student because of the inherent danger of the activity. Other students and their families have sued teachers because they did not follow a class syllabus that many states require of their teachers. Such a syllabus outlines the course content, and if injury occurs in an unlisted activity, then a basis for suit is apparent.

Negligence in athletic participation

Many injuries are related to participation in athletics. Unequal competition is often the cause of athletic accidents. Physical educators should consider sex, age, size, and skill of students in grouping players for an activity.

Defenses against negligence

Despite the fact that an individual is negligent, to collect damages one must show the negligence resulted in or was closely connected with the injury.

The legal question in such a case is whether or not the negligence was the *proximate cause* (legal cause) of the injury. Furthermore, even though it is determined that negligence is the proximate cause of the injury, a defendant may base his or her case on certain defenses.

Proximate cause. The negligence of the defendant may not have been the proximate cause of the plaintiff's injury.

In *Ohmon v. Board of Education of the City of New York,* 99 N.Y.S. 2d 273 (1949), it was declared that when a 13-year-old pupil in public school was struck in the eye by a pencil thrown in classroom by another pupil to a third pupil, who stepped aside, the proximate cause of injury was an unforeseen act of the pupil who threw the pencil and that absence of the teacher (who was stacking supplies in a closet nearby the classroom) was not proximate cause of injury so as to impose liability for the injury on the board of education.

MEASURES TO BE TAKEN TO AVOID CHARGES OF NEGLIGENCE

- Be familiar with the health status of players.
- Require medical clearance of players who have been seriously injured or ill.
- Render services only in those areas where fully qualified.
- Follow proper procedures in the case of injury.
- See that medical personnel are available at all games and on call for practice sessions.
- See that all activities are conducted in safe areas.
- Be careful not to diagnose or treat players' injuries.
- See that protective equipment is properly fitted and worn by players who need such equipment.
- See that coaching methods and procedures provide for the safety of players.
- See that only qualified personnel are assigned responsibilities.
- See that proper instruction is given before players are permitted to engage in contests.
- See that a careful and accurate record is kept of injuries and procedures followed.
- Act as a prudent, careful, and discerning coach whose players are the first consideration.

From *The Coaches Handbook* of the AAHPERD.

Act of God. An act of God is a situation that exists because of certain conditions beyond the control of human beings. For example, a flash of lightning, a gust of wind, a cloudburst, and other such factors may result in injury. However, this assumption applies only in cases where injury would not have occurred had prudent action been taken.

Assumption of risk. Assumption of risk is especially pertinent to games, sports, and other phases of the physical education and athletic program. It is assumed that an individual takes a certain risk when engaging in various games and sports where bodies are coming in contact with each other and where balls and apparatus are used. Participation in such activity indicates that the person assumes a normal risk.

In *Scala v. City of New York,* 102 N.Y.S 2d 709, the plaintiff was injured when playing softball on a public playground, but at the same time was aware of the risks caused by curbing and concrete benches near the playing fields. It was decided that the plaintiff must be held to have voluntarily and fully assumed the dangers and, having done so, must abide by the consequences.

In an action by Maltz (*Maltz v. Board of Education of New York City,* 114 N.Y.S. 2d 856, 1952) against the Board of Education of the City of New York for injuries, the court held that a 19-year-old (who was injured when he collided with a doorjamb in a brick wall 2 feet from the backboard and basket in a public school basketball court and who had played on that same court several times before the accident) knew the basket and backboard were but 2 feet from the wall, had previously hit the wall or gone through the door without injury, was not a student at the school but a voluntary member of a team that engaged in basketball tournaments with other clubs, knew or should have known the danger, and thus assumed the risk of injury.

Contributory and comparative negligence. Another legal defense is contributory and comparative negligence. A person who does not act as a normal individual of similar age and nature would thereby contributes to the injury. In such cases negligence on the part of the defendant might be ruled out. Individuals are subject to contributory negligence if they expose themselves unnecessarily to dangers. The main consideration that seems to turn the tide in such cases is the age of the individual and the nature of the activity in which he engaged.

Contributory negligence has been changed to include the concept of comparative negligence, that is, where the fault is prorated. In other words the plaintiff and the defendant both share at times some of the fault for the injury or damage. In such cases where comparative negligence exists damages are awarded on a prorated basis.

Appenzeller[2] reports that 39 states have adopted the comparative negligence doctrine and that other states are trying to change to this concept.

Contributory negligence is usually a matter of defense, and the burden of proof is put upon the defendant to convince the jury of the plaintiff's fault and of its causal connection with the harm sustained. Minors are not held to the same degree of care as is demanded of adults.[13]

Contributory and comparative negligence have implications for a difference in the responsibility of elementary school teachers and high school teachers. The elementary school teacher, because the children are immature, has to assume greater responsibility for the safety of the child. That is, accidents in which an elementary school child is injured are not held in the same light from the standpoint of negligence as those involving high school students who are more mature. The courts might say that a high school student was mature enough to avoid doing the thing causing him or her to be injured, whereas if the same thing occurred with an elementary school child the courts could say the child was too immature and that the teacher should have prevented or protected the child from doing the act that caused the injury.

Sudden emergency. Sudden emergency is pertinent in cases where the exigencies of the situation require immediate action on the part of a teacher and as a result, an accident occurs. For example, an instructor in a swimming pool is suddenly alerted to a child drowning in the water. The teacher's immediate objective is to save the child. He or she runs to help the drowning person and in doing so knocks down another student who is watching from the side of the pool. The student who is knocked down hits his head on the tile floor and is injured. This would be a case of sudden emergency and, if legal action is taken, the defense could be based on this premise.

LAW SUITS

Law suits only need a complaint to exist. The NCAA Committee on Competitive Safeguards and Medical Aspects of Sports[9] assumes that those who sponsor and govern athletic programs have accepted the responsibility of attempting to keep the risk of injury to a minimum. Because law suits are apt to occur in cases of injury, despite the efforts of athletic educators, attempts should be made to be protected legally. The committee contends that the principal defense against an unwarranted complaint is documentation that adequate measures have been taken and programs have been established to minimize the risk inherent in sports. No checklist is ever complete, but the checklist that follows should serve as a review of safety considerations for those responsible for the administration of interscholastic and intercollegiate sports programs.

CHECKLIST

Preparticipation medical examination. Before an athlete is permitted to participate in organized sports at the high school or college level, he or she should have his or her health status evaluated. An annual update of a student's health history with the use of referral exams when warranted is sufficient. The NCAA Committee on Competitive Safeguards and Medical Aspects of Sports has developed a health questionnaire to assist in conducting a preparticipation medical examination.

Health insurance. Each student-athlete should have, by parental coverage or institutional plan, access to customary hospitalization and physician benefits for defraying the cost of a significant injury or illness.

Preseason preparation. Particular practices and controls should protect the candidate for the team from premature exposure to the full rigors of the sport. Preseason conditioning recommendations from the coaching staff will help the candidate arrive at the first practice in good condition. Attention to heat stress and cautious matching of candidates during the first weeks are additional considerations.

Acceptance of risk. "Informed consent" or "waiver of responsibility" by athletes, or their parents if the athlete is a minor, should be based on an informed awareness of the risk of injury being accepted as a result of the student-athlete's participation in the sport involved. Not only does the individual share responsibility in preventive measures, but also he or she should appreciate the nature and significance of these measures.

Planning and supervision. Proper supervision of a sizable group of energetic and highly motivated student-athletes can be attained only by appropriate planning. Such planning should ensure both general supervision and organized instruction. Instruction should provide individualized attention to the refinement of skills and conditioning. First aid evaluation should also be included with the instruction. Planning for specific health and safety concerns should take into consideration conditions encountered during travel for competitive purposes.

Equipment. As a result of the increase in product liability litigation, purchasers of equipment should be aware of impending, as well as current safety standards being recommended by authoritative groups and purchase materials only from reputable dealers. In addition, attention should be directed to the proper repair and fitting of equipment.

In accordance with the above paragraph, one should know that NOCSAE has established a voluntary football helmet standard that has been adopted by the NCAA, the National Association for Intercollegiate Athletics (NAIA), the National Junior College Athletic Association (NJCAA), and the National Federation of State High School Associations. All new helmets purchased by high schools and colleges must bear the NOCSAE seal. According to NCAA football rules, if a helmet is in need of repair, it must be reconditioned according to the NOCSAE Football Helmet Standard recertification procedures.

Facilities. The adequacy and condition of the facilities used for all sports should not be overlooked. The facilities should be examined regularly. Inspection should include warm-up and adjacent areas, as well as the actual competitive area.

Emergency care. The NCAA guidelines state that

Every precaution must be taken to prevent accidents. Students learn to handle a canoe in water safety course at Cuyahoga Community College in Cleveland, Ohio.

attention to all possible preventive measures will help to eliminate sports injuries. At each practice session or game, the following should be available:

- The presence or immediate availability of a person qualified and delegated to render emergency care to an injured participant.
- Planned access to a physician by phone or nearby presence for prompt medical evaluation of the situation when warranted.
- Planned access to a medical facility—including a plan for communication and transportation between the athletic site and medical facility—for prompt medical services when needed.
- A thorough understanding by all affected persons, including the leadership of visiting teams, of the personnel and procedures involved.

Records. Documentation is fundamental to administration. Authoritative sports safety regulations, standards, and guidelines kept current and on file provide ready reference and understanding. Waiver forms may not prevent law suits, but they help reflect organized attention to injury control.

PRECAUTIONS TO BE TAKEN BY THE PHYSICAL EDUCATOR TO AVOID POSSIBLE LEGAL LIABILITY

- Be familiar with the health status of each person in the program.
- Consider each individual's skill when teaching new activities.
- Group participants together on equal competitive levels.
- Be sure equipment and facilities are safe.
- Organize and carefully supervise the class. Never leave the class unattended—even in emergencies. If an emergency occurs, get a replacement before leaving the room.
- Administer only first aid—never prescribe or diagnose.
- Use only qualified personnel to aid in classrooms.
- Keep accurate accident records.
- Provide adequate instruction, especially in potentially dangerous activities.
- Make sure any injured person receives a medical examination.

Wrestlers at Clark County Schools in Las Vegas, Nev., prevent injury by wearing headgear at practice and in competition.

NUISANCE

Action can be instituted for nuisance when the circumstances surrounding the act are dangerous to life or health, result in offense to the senses, are in violation of the laws of decency, or cause an obstruction to the reasonable use of property.

One source states the following regarding a nuisance:

There are some conditions which are naturally dangerous and the danger is a continuing one. An inherent danger of this sort is called by law a "nuisance"; the one responsible is liable for maintaining a nuisance. His liability may be predicated upon negligence in permitting the continuing danger to exist, but even without a showing of negligence the mere fact that a nuisance does exist is usually sufficient to justify a determination of liability. For example, a junk pile in the corner of the grounds of a country school was considered a nuisance for which the district was liable when a pupil stumbled over a piece of junk and fell while playing at recess *(Popow v. Central School District No. 1, Towns of Hillsdale et al., New York, 1938)*. Dangerous playground equipment available for use by pupils of all ages and degrees of skills has also been determined to be a nuisance *(Bush v. City of Norwalk, Connecticut, 1937)*.

On the other hand, allegations that the district has maintained a nuisance have been denied in some cases; for example, when a small child fell into a natural ditch near the schoolyard not guarded by a fence, the ditch was held not to be a nuisance for which the district would be liable *(Whitfield v. East Baton Rouge Parish School Board, Louisiana, 1949)*. The court said this ditch did not constitute a nuisance; nor did the principle of *res ipsa loquitur* apply. Under this principle the thing which causes the injury is under the management of the defendant and the accident is such that in the ordinary course of events, it would not have happened if the defendant had used proper care.

Mr. Cymrot,[17] attorney at law, in addressing the Health Education Division of the New York City Schools had the following to say about an "attractive nuisance":

Teachers need to be aware of decisions of the courts pertaining to "attractive nuisance," . . . an attractive contrivance which is maintained, alluring to children but inherently dangerous to them. This constitutes neglect. But it is not every contrivance or apparatus that a jury may treat as an "attractive nuisance." Before liability may be imposed, there must always be something in the evidence tending to show that the device was something of a new or uncommon nature with which children might be supposed to be unfamiliar or not know of its danger. Many courts have held, however, that for children above the age of 10 years the doctrine of "attractive nuisance" does not hold. Other children are expected to exercise such prudence as those of their age may be expected to possess.

The following cases point up some court rulings concerning nuisance.

In *Texas v. Reinhardt* in 1913, it was ruled that ball games with their noises and conduct were not a nuisance in the particular case in question and an injunction should not be issued stopping such activity.

In *Iacono v. Fitzpatrick* in Rhode Island in 1938, a 17-year-old boy, while playing touch football on a playground, received an injury that later resulted in his death. He was attempting to catch a pass and crashed into a piece of apparatus. The court held the apparatus was in evidence and the deceased knew of its presence. It further stated the city had not created or maintained a nuisance.

In *Schwarz v. City of Cincinnati, Ohio,* the city had permitted an organization to have fireworks in one of its public parks. The next day a 12-year-old boy was injured after lighting an unexploded bomb he found. The court ruled the permit granted the association was "not authority to create a nuisance . . . not authority to leave an unexploded bomb in the park." The city, which was the defendant in the case, was not held liable.

GOVERNMENTAL VERSUS PROPRIETARY FUNCTIONS

The government in a legal sense is engaged in two types of activity: (1) governmental and (2) proprietary.

The *governmental function* refers to particular activities of a sovereign nature. This theory dates back to the time when kings ruled under the divine right theory, were absolute in their power, and could do no wrong. As such the sovereign was granted immunity and could not be sued without his consent for failing to exercise governmental powers or for negligence. Furthermore, a subordinate agency of the sovereign could not be sued. The municipality, according to this interpretation, acts as an agent of the state in a governmental capacity. The logic behind this reasoning is that the municipality is helping the state govern the people who live within its geographic limits.

Many activities are classified under the governmental function. Functions such as education, police protection, and public health fall in this category.

Regarding public education, the courts hold this is a governmental function and therefore is entitled to state's immunity from liability for its own negligence. As has previously been pointed out, however, the attitude of the courts has changed and has taken on a broader social outlook that in some cases allows reimbursement of the injured.

Proprietary function pertains to government functions similar to those of a business enterprise. Such functions are for the benefit of the constituents within the corporate limits of the governmental agency. An example of this would be the manufacture, distribution, and sale of some product to the public. A cafeteria conducted for profit in a school is a proprietary function. In proprietary functions a governmental agency is held liable in the same manner as an individual or a private corporation would be held liable.

In *Watson v. School District of Bay City,* 324 Mich. 1, 36 N.W. 2d 195, a decision was handed down by the supreme court of Michigan in February 1949. In this case a 15-year-old girl attended a high school night football game. In going to her car she was required to walk around a concrete wall. As she attempted to do this, she fell over the wall and onto a ramp. She suffered paralysis and died 8 months later. The parking area was very poorly lighted. The supreme court held that staging a high school football game was a governmental function and refused to impose liability on the district.

From this discussion it can be seen that education, recreation, and health are governmental functions. Whereas the distinction between governmental and proprietary functions precludes a recovery from the governmental agency if the function was governmental, the federal government and some of the states by legislation have eliminated this distinction.

FEES

Most public recreation activities, facilities, and the like are offered free to the public. However, certain activities, because of the expenses involved, necessitate a fee to stay in operation. For example, golf courses are expensive, and charges are usually made so they may be maintained. This is sometimes true of facilities such as camps, bathing beaches, and swimming pools.

The fees charged have a bearing on whether recreation is a governmental or a proprietary function. The courts in most states have upheld recreation as a governmental function, because of its contribution to public health and welfare and also because its programs are free to the public at large. When fees are charged, however, the whole picture takes on a different aspect.

The attitude of the courts has been that the amount of the fee and whether or not the activity was profit making are considerations in determining whether recreation is a governmental or a proprietary function. Incidental fees used in the conduct of the enterprise do not usually change the nature of the enterprise. If the enterprise is run for profit, however, such as a health spa, the function changes from governmental to proprietary.

LIABILITY OF THE MUNICIPALITY

It has been previously noted that a municipality as a governmental agency performs both governmental and proprietary functions.

When the municipality is performing a governmental function, it is acting in the interests of the state, receives no profit or advantage, and is not liable for negligence on the part of its employees or for failure to perform these functions. However, this would not hold if there was a specific statute imposing liability for negligence. When the municipality is performing a proprietary function—some function for profit or advantage of the agency or people it comprises—rather than the public in general, it is liable for negligence of those carrying out the function.

This discussion shows the importance of conducting recreation as a governmental function.

LIABILITY OF THE SCHOOL DISTRICT

As a general rule the school district is not held liable for acts of negligence on the part of its officers or employees, provided a state statute does not exist to the contrary. The reasoning behind this is that the school district or district school board in maintaining public schools acts as an agent of the state. It performs a purely public or governmental duty imposed on it by law for the benefit of the public; in so doing it receives no profit or advantage.

Some state laws, however, provide that the state may be sued in cases of negligence in the performance of certain duties, such as providing for a safe environment and competent leadership. Furthermore, the school district's immunity in many cases does not cover acts that bring damage or injury through trespass of another's premises or where a nuisance exists on a school district's property, resulting in damage to other property.

LIABILITY OF SCHOOL BOARD MEMBERS

Generally, school board members are not personally liable for any duties in their corporate capacities as board members that they perform negligently. Furthermore, they cannot be held personally liable for acts of employees of the district or organization over which they have jurisdiction on the theory of *respondeat superior* (let the master pay for the servant). Board members act in a corporate capacity and do not act for themselves. For example, in the state of Oregon the general rule about the personal liability of members of district schools boards is stated in 56C.J., page 348, section 223, as follows:

School officers, or members of the board of education, or directors, trustees, or the like, of a school or other local school organization are not personally liable for the negligence of persons rightfully employed by them in behalf of the district, and not under the direct personal supervision or control of such officer or member in doing the negligent act, since such employee is a servant of the district and not of the officer or board members, and the doctrine of *respondeat superior* accordingly has no application; and members of a district board are not personally liable for the negligence or other wrong of the board as such. A school officer or member of a district board is, however, personally liable for his own negligence or other tort, or that of an agent or employee of the district when acting directly under his supervision or by his direction.

However, a board member can be held liable for a *ministerial* act (an act or duty prescribed by law for a particular administrative office) even though he or she cannot be held for the exercise of discretion as a member of the board. If the board acts in bad faith and with unworthy motives, and if this can be shown, it can also be held liable.

LIABILITY OF TEACHERS, LEADERS, AND INSTRUCTORS

The individual is responsible for negligence of his or her own acts. With the exception of specific types of immunity, the teacher or leader in programs of physical education, athletics, and recreation is responsible for what he or she does. The Supreme Court has reaffirmed this principle, and all should recognize its important implications. Immunity of the governmental agency such as a state, school district, or board does not release the teacher or leader from liability for his or her own negligent acts.

In New York a physical education teacher was held personally liable when he sat in the bleachers while two strong boys, untrained in boxing, were permitted by the instructor to fight through nearly two rounds. The plaintiff was hit in the temple and suffered a cerebral hemorrhage. The court said:

It is the duty of a teacher to exercise reasonable care to prevent injuries. Pupils should be warned before being permitted to engage in a dangerous and hazardous exercise. Skilled boxers at times are injured, and . . . these young men should have been taught the principles of defense if indeed it was a reasonable thing to permit a slugging match of the kind which the testimony shows this contest was. The testimony indicates that the teacher failed in his duties in this regard and that he was negligent, and the plaintiff is entitled to recover. (*LaValley v. Stanford*, 272 App. Div. 183, 70 N.Y.S. 2d 460.)

In New York (*Keesee v. Board of Education of City of New York*, 5 N.Y.S. 2d 300, 1962) a junior high school girl was injured while playing line soccer. She was kicked by another player. The board of education syllabus listed line soccer as a game for boys and stated that ''after sufficient skill has been acquired two or more forwards may be selected from each team.'' The syllabus called for 10 to 20 players on each team and required a space of 30 to 40 feet. The physical education teacher divided into two teams some 40 to 45 girls who had not had any experience in soccer. A witness who was an expert in such matters testified that to avoid accidents no more than two people should be on the ball at any time and criticized the board syllabus for permitting the use of more than two

forwards. The expert also testified that pupils should have experience in kicking, dribbling, and passing before being permitted to play line soccer. The evidence showed the teacher permitted six to eight inexperienced girls to be on the ball at one time. The court held that possible injury was at least reasonably foreseeable under such conditions, the teacher had been negligent, and the teacher's negligence was the cause of the pupil being injured.

Teachers and leaders are expected to conduct their various activities carefully and prudently. If this is not done, they are exposing themselves to lawsuits for their own negligence. The National Education Association's report[16] has the following to say regarding administrators:

The fact that administrators (speaking mainly of principals and superintendents) are rarely made defendants in pupil-injury cases seems unjust to the teachers who are found negligent because of inadequate supervision, and unjust also to the school boards who are required to defend themselves in such suits. When the injury is caused by defective equipment, it is the building principal who should have actual or constructive notice of the defect; when the injury is caused by inadequate playground supervision, the inadequacy of the supervision frequently exists because of arrangements made by the building principal. For example, a teacher in charge of one playground was required to stay in the building to teach a make-up class; another teacher was required to supervise large grounds on which 150 pupils were playing; another teacher neglected the playground to answer the telephone. All of these inadequacies in playground supervision were morally chargeable to administrators; in none of these instances did the court action direct a charge of responsibility to the administrator. Whether the administrator in such cases would have been held liable, if charged with negligence, is problematical. The issue has not been decided, since the administrator's legal responsibility for pupil injuries has never been discussed by the courts to an extent that would make possible the elucidation of general principles; the administrator's moral responsibilities must be conceded.

ACCIDENT-PRONE SETTINGS

Because many accidents occur on the playground, during recess periods, in physical education classes, and at sports events, some pertinent remarks are included here from the National Education Association's report.[16]

Playground and recess games

The unorganized games during recess and noon intermissions are more likely to result in pupil injuries than the organized games of physical education classes. Playground injuries may be pure accidents, such as when a pupil ran against the flagpole while playing *(Hough v. Orleans Elementary School District of Humboldt County, California, 1943)*, or when a pupil was hit by a ball *(Graff v. Board of Education of New York City, New York, 1940)*, or by a stone batted by another pupil *(Wilbur v. City of Binghamton, New York, 1946)*. The courts have said in connection with this type of injury that every act of every pupil cannot be anticipated. However, the school district should make rules and regulations for pupils' conduct on playgrounds so as to minimize dangers. For example, it was held to be negligence to permit pupils to ride bicycles on the playground while other pupils were playing *(Buzzard v. East Lake School District of Lake County, California, 1939)*.

Playgrounds should be supervised during unorganized play and such supervision should be adequate. One teacher cannot supervise a large playground with over a hundred pupils playing *(Charonnat v. San Francisco Unified School District, California, 1943)*, and when the supervision is either lacking or inadequate districts which are not immune are liable for negligence in not providing adequate supervision *(Forgnone v. Slavadore Union Elementary School District, California, 1940)*. Pupils are known to engage in fights and may be expected to be injured in fights; it is the responsibility of the school authorities to attempt to prevent such injuries. The misconduct of other pupils could be an intervening cause to break the chain of causation if the supervision is adequate; but when the supervision is not adequate, misconduct of other pupils is not an intervening superseding cause of the injury.

If a pupil wanders from the group during playground games and is injured by a dangerous condition into which he places himself, the teacher in charge of the playground may be liable for negligence in pupil supervision *(Miller v. Board of Education, Union Free School District, New York, 1943)*, although the district would not be liable in a common-law state because of its immunity *(Whitfield v. East Baton Rouge Parish School Board, Louisiana, 1949)*.

Supervision of unorganized play at recess or noon intermission should be by competent personnel. A school janitor is not qualified to supervise play. *(Garber v. Central School District No. 1 of Town of Sharon, New York, 1937.)*

When children of all ages share a playground, extra precautions should be taken to prevent accidents, since some children are more adept in using equipment than others and some playground equipment is dangerous to the unskilled.

Physical education and sports events

Pupil injuries in this area occur when playground or gymnasium equipment is defective, when pupils attempt an exercise or sport for which they have not been sufficiently trained, when there is inadequate supervision of the exercise, when other pupils conduct themselves in a negligent manner, and even when the pupils are mere spectators at sports events.

It has been held that physical education teachers, or the school district in states where the district is subject to liability, are responsible for injuries caused by defective equipment. For example, there was liability for the injury to a pupil who was injured in a tumbling race when the mat, not firmly fixed, slipped on the slippery floor *(Cambareri v. Board of Education of Albany, New York, 1940)*.

Defects in equipment should be known to the physical education instructor. There may be what is called actual or constructive notice of the defect. Actual knowledge is understandable; constructive notice means that the defect has existed for a sufficient time so that the instructor should have known of its existence, whether he did or not. Teachers of physical education should make periodic examination of all equipment at frequent intervals; otherwise they may be charged with negligence in not having corrected defects in equipment that have existed for a sufficient time that ignorance of the defect is a presumption of negligence.

Physical education teachers may also be liable for injuries that occur to pupils who attempt to do an exercise that is beyond their skills. A running-jump somersault is one such instance *(Govel v. Board of Education of Albany, New York, 1944);* boxing is another *(LaValley v. Stanford, New York, 1947);* and a headstand exercise is another *(Gardner v. State of New York, New York, 1939).* All of these exercises were found to be inherently dangerous by the courts, and the evidence showed that previous instruction had been inadequate and the pupils had not been warned of the dangers. However, where the previous instruction and the supervision during the exercise are both adequate, there is no liability so long as it cannot be proved that the teacher is generally incompetent *(Kolar v. Union Free School District No. 9, Town of Lenox, New York, 1939).* These cases suggest that teachers should not permit pupils to attempt exercises for which they have not been fully prepared by warnings of the dangers and preliminary exercises to develop the required skills.

As in other types of pupil injuries, the physical education teacher is not liable if the injury occurred without his negligence. If caused by the negligence of another pupil, the teacher will likely be relieved of liability if the other pupil's misconduct was not foreseeable. Pure accidents occur in sport also, and if there is no negligence there is no liability *(Mauer v. Board of Education of New York City, New York, 1945).*

Sports events to which nonparticipating pupils and even the public are invited raise other problems of liability for the district or the physical education teacher in charge. If the locality is in a common-law state where the district is immune, the charge of an admission fee does not nullify the district's immunity or make the activity a proprietary function as an exception to the immunity rule *(Watson v. School District of Bay City, Michigan, 1949).* If the accident occurs in a state where the district is liable for at least certain kinds of injuries, such as California, the invitation to attend a sports event includes an invitation to the nearby grounds and equipment, imposing liability for injury from hidden glass or other dangers *(Brown v. City of Oakland, California, 1942).* If a spectator is accidentally hit by a ball, however, there is no liability; even when a pupil was injured by being hit by a bottle at a game there was no liability because the misconduct of the other spectator was not foreseeable *(Weldy v. Oakland High School District of Alameda County, California, 1937).*

In its fifteenth year, Boys Night Out pairs 100 boys ages 7 to 12 from single-parent homes with men in the community for an evening of fun and companionship. Pictured are two teams testing their skills at the fooseball table.

COMMON AREAS OF NEGLIGENCE

Common areas of negligence in physical education and athletic activities listed by Begley[7] in a New York University publication are situations involving poor selection of activities, failure to take protective procedures, hazardous conditions of buildings or grounds, faulty equipment, inadequate supervision, and poor selection of play area. Cases involving each of these common areas of negligence follow.

Poor selection of activities. The activity must be suitable to the child or youth. In *Rook v. New York,* 4 N.Y.S. 2d 116 (1930), the court ruled that tossing a child in a blanket constituted a dangerous activity.

Failure to take protective measures. The element of forseeability enters here, and proper protective measures must be taken to provide a safe place for children and youth to play. In *Roth v. New York,* 262 App. Div. 370, 29 N.Y.S. 2d 442 (1942), inadequate provisions were made to prevent bathers from stepping into deep water. When a bather drowned, the court held the state was liable.

Hazardous conditions of buildings or grounds. Buildings and grounds must be safe. Construction of facilities and their continual repair must have as one objective the elimination of hazards. In *Novak et al. v. Borough of Ford City,* 141 Atl. 496 (Pa., 1928), unsafe conditions were caused by an electric wire over the play area. In *Honaman v. City of Philadelphia,* 185 Atl. 750 (Pa., 1936), unsafe conditions were caused by failure to erect a backstop.

Faulty equipment. All play and other equipment must be in good condition at all times. In *Van Dyke v. Utica,* 203 App. Div. 26, 196 N.Y. Supp. 277 (1922), concerning a slide that fell over on a child and killed him, the court ruled that the slide was defective.

Inadequate supervision. Qualified supervisors must be in charge of all play activities. In *Garber v. Central School District No. 1, Town of Sharon, N.Y.,* 251, App. Div. 214, 295 N.Y. Supp. 850, the court held a school janitor was not qualified to supervise school children playing in a gymnasium during lunch hour.

Poor selection of play area. The setting for games and sports should be selected with the safety of the participants in mind. In *Morse v. New York,* 262 App. Div. 324, 29 N.Y.S. 2d 34 (1941), when sledding and skiing were permitted on the same hill without adequate barriers to prevent participants in each activity from colliding with each other, the court held that the state was liable for negligence.

SUPERVISION

Children are entrusted by parents to recreation, physical education, and athletic programs, and parents expect adequate supervision will be provided to minimize the possibility of accidents.

Questions of liability regarding supervision pertain to two points: (1) the extent of the supervision and (2) the quality of the supervision.

Regarding the first point, the question is raised about whether adequate supervision was provided. This is difficult to answer because it varies from situation to situation. However, the answers to these questions help determine this: "Would additional supervision have eliminated the accident?" and "Is it reasonable to expect that additional supervision should have been provided?"

Regarding the quality of the supervision, it is expected that competent personnel should handle specialized programs in physical education, athletics, and recreation. If the supervisors of such activities do not possess proper training in such work, the question of negligence can be raised.

WAIVERS AND CONSENT SLIPS

Waivers and consent slips are not synonymous. A waiver is an agreement whereby one party waives a particular right. A consent slip is an authorization, usually signed by the parent, permitting a child to take part in some activity.

Regarding a waiver, a parent cannot waive the rights of a child who is under 21 years of age. When a parent signs such a slip, he or she is merely waiving his or her right to sue for damages. A parent can sue in two ways, from the standpoint of the child's own rights that he or she has as an individual, irrespective of the parent. A parent cannot waive the right of the child to sue as an individual.

Kaiser[15] points out that, although the courts have a penchant not to enforce liability waivers, they are still helpful in a risk management program since they can

Special care should be provided for sports like scuba diving.

discourage lawsuits and enhance legal defenses by increasing participant awareness.

Consent slips offer protection from the standpoint of showing the child has the parent's permission to engage in an activity.

THE COURTS AND ELIGIBILITY RULES

Traditionally, when eligibility regulations have been challenged, courts have been reluctant to substitute their judgment for the judgments of school athletic associations. In recent years, however, federal judges have been finding eligibility rules unconstitutional, and administrators and physical educators should note this change in court rulings.

Court decisions where eligibility rules have been found to be segregationist have been consistently found unconstitutional. A ruling found that the common practice in Alabama of having racially based athletic associations was unconstitutional, and a specific ruling of the United States Circuit Court ordered the Louisiana High School Athletic Association to admit a private black high school.

Other significant rulings concerning eligibility include a recent federal court order voiding the Indiana High School Athletic Association rule that prohibited married students from athletic participation. Another significant decision involved the Iowa High School Athletic Association and their suspension of a student athlete because he was riding in a car that was transporting beer. The student was not drinking, athletic training was not taking place, and the event occurred in the summer when school was not in session. In addition, no state or federal law was broken. The eligibility law was found to be unreasonable, and the student was reinstated.

TITLE IX AND THE COURTS

Recent years have found the media reporting on numerous cases involving discrimination against women in sports. In 1978 a federal judge in Dayton, Ohio, ruled that girls may not be barred from playing on boys' school athletic teams, even in contact sports such as football and wrestling. In his decision the judge pointed out there might be many reasons why girls would not want to play on boys' teams, such as "reasons of stature or weight, or reasons of temperament, motivation, or interest. This is a matter of choice. But a prohibition without exception based on sex is not." The judge also indicated his ruling would have national implications. The Ohio High School Athletic Association had barred girls from contact sports.

A ruling by the State Division on Civil Rights of New Jersey requires Little League baseball teams to permit girls to play. New Jersey was the first state to have such a ruling. The order also requires that both boys and girls be notified of team tryouts and that both sexes be treated equally.

An amendment to the Education Law of New York State provides that no one may be disqualified from school athletic teams because of sex, except by certain regulations of the state commissioner of education.

Another case involved two women coaches who were denied admittance to the North Carolina Coaching Clinic because of their sex. A lawsuit was instituted by the women against the all-male coaching association.

In Indiana the Indiana Supreme Court ruled that it was discriminatory for a high school to sponsor a boys' team and not a girls' team.

Title IX has legislated that there should be no discrimination by sex. Although it is a federal law, it still is necessary for many girls and women to go to court to ensure their rights under the law.

A Michigan judge's court ruling in 1981 had serious implications for the implementation of Title IX. Federal District Court Judge Joiner ruled that Title IX can only apply to programs that directly receive federal funds. In the case in question, the judge ruled the U.S. Department of Education could not enforce Title IX in the Ann Arbor School District's interscholastic sports program because the program itself did not receive any federal funding.

The United States Court of Appeals for the First Circuit also ruled Title IX is programmatic, and not institutional, in scope. The Court of Appeals ruled that "the only meaningful interpretation of Title IX is that it prohibits sex discrimination in a federally funded education program offered by an educational institution." In support of its decision, the court relied on the language of the statute (including its definition of the term *education institution*), the legislative history of Title IX, and previous court rulings that have addressed the question.

The Supreme Court of the United States ruled on February 24, 1984, that Title IX was intended to apply only to education "programs and activities" that receive direct federal aid. Prior to this decision the interpretation was that if an institution received federal aid all programs within that institution were subject to Title IX regulations. As a result of this decision, *Grove City College v. Bell,* the status of Title IX enforcement remains uncertain.

SAFETY

It is important to take every precaution possible to prevent accidents by providing for the safety of students and other individuals who participate in programs of physical education, athletics, and recreation. If such precautions are taken, the likelihood of a lawsuit will diminish and the question of negligence will be eliminated. Precautions the leader or teacher should take follow:

- Instructor should be properly trained and qualified to perform specialized work.
- Instructor should be present at all organized activities in the program.
- Classes should be organized properly according to size, activity, physical condition, and other factors that have a bearing on safety and health of the individual.
- Health examinations should be given to all pupils.
- A planned, written program for proper disposition of participants who are injured or become sick should be followed.
- Regular inspections should be made of items such as equipment, apparatus, ropes, or chains, placing extra pressure on them, and taking other precautions to make sure they are safe. They should also be checked for deterioration, looseness, fraying, and splinters.
- Overcrowding athletic and other events should be avoided, building codes and fire regulations should be adhered to, and adequate lighting for all facilities should be provided.

- Protective equipment such as mats should be used wherever needed. Any hazards such as projections or obstacles in an area where activity is taking place should be eliminated. Floors should not be slippery. Shower rooms should have surfaces conducive to secure footing.
- Sneakers should be worn on gymnasium floors and adequate space provided for each activity.
- Activities should be adapted to the age and maturity of the participants, proper and competent supervision should be provided, and spotters should be used in gymnastics and other similar activities.
- Students and other participants should be instructed in correctly using apparatus and performing in physical activities. Any misuse of equipment should be prohibited.
- The buildings and other facilities used should be inspected regularly for safety hazards, such as loose tiles, broken fences, cracked glass, and uneven pavement. Defects should be reported immediately to responsible persons and necessary precautions taken.
- In planning play and other instructional areas the following precautions should be taken:

Space should be sufficient for all games. Games using balls and other equipment that can cause damage should be conducted in areas where there is minimum danger of injuring someone. Quiet games and activities requiring working at benches, such as arts and crafts, should be in places that are well protected.

- In the event of accident the following or a similar procedure should be followed:

    a. The nearest teacher or leader should proceed to the scene of the accident immediately, notifying the person in charge and nurse, if available, by messenger. Also, a physician should be called at once if one is necessary.
    b. A hurried examination of the injured person will give some idea of the nature and extent of the injury and the emergency of the situation.
    c. If the teacher or leader is well versed in first aid, assistance should be given (a first aid certificate will usually absolve the teacher of negligence).

    Every teacher or leader who works in these specialized areas should and is expected to know first aid procedures. In any event everything should be done to make the injured person comfortable and reassure the injured until the services of a physician can be secured.

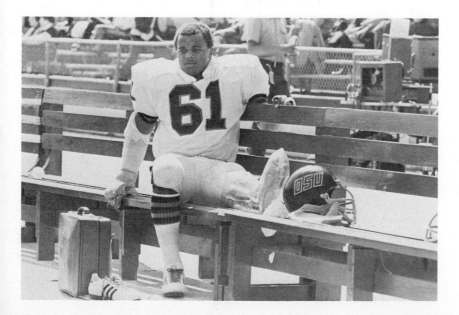

Injured players should receive prompt medical attention and proper treatment.

d. If the injury is serious, an ambulance should be called.

e. After the injured person has been provided for, the person in charge should fill out the accident forms and take the statements of witnesses and file for future reference. Reports of accidents should be prepared promptly and sent to proper persons. They should be accurate and complete. Among other things they should contain information about:

    Names and address of injured person

    Activity engaged in

    Date, hour, and place injury occurred

    Person in charge

    Witnesses

    Causes and extent of injury

    Medical attention given

    Circumstances surrounding incident

f. There should be a complete followup of the accident, an analysis of the situation, and an eradication of any existing hazards.

Thelma Reed, Chairman of Standard Student Accident Report Committee of the National Safety Council, listed the following reasons why detailed injury reports are important for school authorities:

1. Aid in protecting the school personnel and district from unfortunate publicity and from liability suits growing out of student injury cases;

2. Aid in evaluating the relative importance of the various safety areas and the time each merits in the total school safety effort;

3. Suggest modification in the structure, use, and maintenance of buildings, grounds, and equipment;

4. Suggest curriculum adjustments to meet immediate student needs;

5. Provide significant data for individual student guidance;

6. Give substance to the school administrators' appeal for community support of the school safety program;

7. Aid the school administration in guiding the school safety activities of individual patrons and patrons' groups.

INSURANCE MANAGEMENT

Schools and other organizations use three major types of insurance management to protect themselves against loss. The first is insurance for *property*. The second is insurance for *liability protection* when there might be financial loss arising from personal injury or property damage for which the school district or organization is liable. The third is insurance for *crime protection* against a financial loss that might be incurred as a result of theft or other illegal act. This section on insurance management is concerned primarily with liability protection.

Athletic trainer at Tuskegee Institute, Ala.

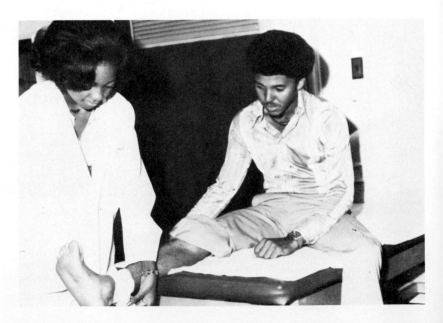

SAFETY CODE FOR THE PHYSICAL EDUCATION INSTRUCTOR

The following safety codes should be followed by the physical education instructor:

Have a proper teacher's certificate in full force and effect.

Operate and teach at all times within the scope of his or her employment as defined by the rules and regulations of the employing board of education and within the statutory limitations imposed by the state.

Provide the safeguards designed to minimize the dangers inherent in a particular activity.

Provide the required amount of supervision for each activity to ensure the maximum safety of all the pupils.

Inspect equipment and facilities periodically to determine whether or not they are safe for use.

Notify the proper authorities forthwith concerning the existence of any dangerous condition as it continues to exist.

Provide sufficient instruction in the performance of any activity before exposing pupils to its hazards.

Be certain the task is one approved by the employing board of education for the age and abilities of the pupils involved.

Do not force a pupil to perform a physical feat the pupil obviously feels incapable of performing.

Act promptly and use discretion in giving first aid to an injured pupil, but nothing more.

Exercise due care in practicing his or her profession.

Act as a reasonably prudent person would under the given circumstances.

Anticipate the dangers that should be apparent to a trained, intelligent person (foreseeability).

From Munize, A.J.

A definite trend can be seen in school districts toward having some form of school accident insurance to protect students against injury. The same is true wherever physical education programs are conducted. Along with this trend can be seen the impact on casualty and life insurance companies that offer insurance policies. The premium costs of accident policies vary from community to community and also in accordance with the age of the insured and type of plan offered. Interscholastic athletics have been responsible for the development of many state athletic protection plans, as well as the issuance of special policies by commercial insurance companies. When it is realized that accidents are the chief cause of death among students between the ages of 5 and 18, it is apparent that some protection is needed.

Common features of school insurance management plans

Some school boards have found it a good policy to pay the premium on insurance policies because full coverage of students provides peace of mind for both parents and teachers. Furthermore, many liability suits have been avoided in this manner.

SOME COMMON FEATURES OF INSURANCE MANAGEMENT PLANS ACROSS THE UNITED STATES

Premiums are paid for by the school, by the parent, or jointly by the school and parent.

Schools obtain their money for payment of premiums from the board of education, general organization fund, or a pooling of funds for many schools taken from gate receipts in league games.

Schools place the responsibility on the parents to pay for any injuries incurred.

Blanket coverage is a very common policy for insurance companies to offer.

Insurance companies frequently offer insurance coverage for athletic injuries as part of a package plan that also includes an accident plan for all students.

Most schools have insurance plans for the protection of athletes.

Most schools seek insurance coverage that provides for benefits whether x-ray films are positive or negative.

Hospitalization, x-ray films, medical fees and dental fees are increasingly becoming part of the insurance coverage in schools.

Other school officials investigate the various insurance plans available and then recommend a particular plan, and the parents deal directly with the company. Such parent-paid plans are frequently divided into two options: (1) they provide coverage for the student on a door-to-door basis (to and from school, while at school, and in school-sponsored activities) and (2) they provide 24-hour accident coverage with premiums usually running to four times higher than the school only policy. The school only policy rates are based on age, with rates for children in the elementary grades lower than those in the higher grades. These policies also usually run only for the school year.

Student accident insurance provides coverage for all accidents regardless of whether the insured is hospitalized or treated in a doctor's office. Medical plans such as Blue Cross and Blue Shield are limited in the payments they make. Student accident insurance policies, as a general rule, offer reasonable rates and are a good investment for all concerned. Parents should be encouraged, however, to examine their existing family policies before taking out such policies to avoid overlapping coverage.

A survey of nine school districts in Ohio disclosed the following practices and problems concerned with selecting an insurance policy for athletics:

1. The chief school administrator was the person who usually selected the insurance company from whom the policy would be purchased.
2. Medical coverage on policies purchased ranged from $30 to $5000 and dental coverage from nothing to $500.
3. The claims collected for one particular type of injury ranged from nothing to $792.30.
4. Companies did not follow through at all times in paying the amount for which the claim was made.
5. Most insurance companies writing athletic policies have scheduled benefit plans.
6. Catastrophe clauses were absent from all policies.
7. Athletes covered ranged from 80% to 100%.
8. In most cases part of each athlete's premium was paid for from a school athletic fund.
9. Football was covered in separate policies.

As a result of this survey the following recommendations were made:

1. Some person or group of persons should be delegated to review insurance policies and, after developing a set of criteria, to purchase the best one possible.
2. Where feasible, cooperative plans with other schools on a county or other basis should be encouraged to obtain less expensive group rates.
3. Criteria for selecting an insurance policy should, in addition to cost, relate to such important benefits as maximum medical, excluded benefits, maximum hospital, dental, or dismemberment, surgical, and x-ray films.
4. The greatest possible coverage for cost involved should be an important basis for selecting a policy.
5. In light of football programs especially, the catastrophe clause should be investigated as possible additional coverage.
6. Deductible clause policies should not be purchased.
7. Dental injury benefits are an important consideration.
8. Determine what claims the insurance company will and will not pay.
9. The school should insist on 100% enrollment in the athletic insurance program.
10. Schools should have a central location for keeping insurance records, and there should be an annual survey to ascertain all the pertinent facts about the cost and effectiveness of such coverage.

Procedure for insurance management

Every school should be covered by insurance. Five types of accident insurance can be used: (1) commercial insurance policies written on an individual basis, (2) student medical benefit plans written on a group basis by commercial insurers, (3) state high school athletic association benefit plans, (4) medical benefit plans operated by specific city schools systems, and (5) self-insurance. Before adoption by any school, each type of insurance should be carefully weighed so the best coverage is obtained for the type of program sponsored.

Athletics and insurance coverage

Some schools and colleges do not provide an athletic insurance program. If a student is injured in an athletic event, the family is then responsible for all medical expenditures. No provision is made for the school

Fitness program for women employees at PepsiCo's plant in Purchase, New York.

or college to reimburse the family for its expense. Of course, the school or college is always open to a lawsuit by the parents in an effort to reclaim expenses. This is expensive for the school or college, for if the claim is settled in favor of the parents, the school's or college's insurance premiums for the next few years are increased. If the lawsuit is settled in favor of the school or college, the insurance company has already placed a sum of money in reserve until the final decision is reached. This is also costly because the premium is increased during the time the money is in reserve. An intangible effect is the damage to the school's or college's public relations.

An alternative is to provide an opportunity for students to purchase athletic insurance or, better yet, for the school or college to purchase a policy for students participating in sports. Of course, the latter is the best method because all students are covered, regardless of their economic status, and the students' liability policy is not subject to suit. Most parents are only interested in recovering monies actually spent, and they are satisfied accordingly. Usually a blanket policy purchased by the school or college can be obtained at a lower unit cost than a policy purchased by individuals. The athletic insurance program can be administered by a local or regional broker, relieving the school or college of going into the insurance business.

It is the responsibility of the director of physical education to supply accurate lists of participating students to the business office before the beginning of sports seasons. It is imperative for the various coaches to be made aware of the types of insurance coverage so when accidents happen, they can inform the athletes of the proper procedure to follow in filing reports and claims. Usually the business office will supply policies for every participant in a covered athletic team. The coach should not only be knowledgeable, but he or she should also show concern for accident victims. This is not only a form of good public relations, but it may also make the difference in the parents' minds concerning a lawsuit. The coaches then must be instructed in the proper attitude to take when such mishaps occur.

School athletic insurance

Athletic protection funds usually have these characteristics: they are a nonprofit venture, they are not compulsory, a specific fee is charged for each person registered with the plan, and provision is made for recovery for specific injuries. Generally the money is not paid out of tax funds but instead is paid either by the participants themselves or by the school or other agency.

In connection with such plans, an individual, after receiving benefits could in most states still bring action against the coach or other leader whose negligence contributed to the injury.

In respect to paying for liability and accident insurance out of public tax funds, the states vary in their practices. Some states do not permit tax money to be used for liability or accident insurance to cover students in physical education activities. On the other hand, the state legislature of Oregon permits school districts to carry liability insurance. This section is stated as follows in the revised code, O.R.S.:

332.180 Liability insurance; medical and hospital benefits insurance. Any district school board may enter into contracts of insurance for liability coverage of all activities engaged in by the district, for medical and hospital benefits for students engaging in athletic contests and for public liability and property damage covering motor vehicles operated by the district, and may pay the necessary premiums thereon. Failure to procure such insurance shall in no case be construed as negligence or lack of diligence on the part of the district school board or the members thereof.

Some athletic insurance plans in use in the schools today are entirely inadequate. These plans indicate a certain amount of money as the maximum that can be collected. For example, a boy may lose the sight of an eye. According to the athletic protection fund, the loss of an eye will draw, say, $1,500. This amount does not come even remotely close to paying for such a serious injury. In this case a hypothetical example could be taken by saying that the parents sue the athletic protection fund and the teacher for $30,000. In some states, if the case is lost, the athletic fund will pay the $1,500 and the teacher the other $28,500. It can be seen that some of these insurance plans do not give complete and adequate coverage.

Bowling as part of the program in the Clark County School District, Las Vegas, Nev.

In many states physical educators need additional protection against being sued for accidental injury to students. Legislation is needed permitting school funds to be used as protection against student injuries. In this way a school would be legally permitted and could be required to purchase liability insurance to cover all pupils.

SUMMARY

Legal liability, risk, and insurance management are important functions of those persons in charge of physical education and athletic programs. It is important that in managing such programs the persons in charge be familiar with the laws and legal basis for physical education and athletic programs and the responsibilities associated with things such as product liability, negligence in the conduct of activities, common areas of negligent behavior, safety precautions necessary to be taken to prevent accidents, and the

The following exercise should provide personal guidance for the administrator as to the establishment of an appropriate degree of prudence commensurate with the professional, as well as legal responsibility of the contemporary administrator in physical education and athletics.

	Degree of compliance			
The prudent administrator:	Always	Frequently	Rarely	Never
1. Seeks to prohibit the situation which may lead to litigation through constant foresight and care inherent in the professional role he/she holds.	——	——	——	——
2. Assigns instructional and supervisory duties concerning an activity to only those people who are qualified for that particular activity.	——	——	——	——
3. Conducts regular inspections of all equipment used and insists on full repair of faulty items prior to use.	——	——	——	——
4. Establishes procedures and enforces rules concerning safe use of equipment and proper fitting of all uniforms and protective gear.	——	——	——	——
5. Has written plans with adequate review procedures to assure that participants do not move too rapidly into areas of skill performance beyond their present skill level.	——	——	——	——
6. Selects opponents for each participant/team with care to avoid potentially dangerous mismatching.	——	——	——	——
7. Establishes and scrupulously enforces rules regarding reporting of illness or injury, to include compilation of written records and names and addresses of witnesses.	——	——	——	——
8. Does not treat injuries unless professionally prepared and certified to do so.	——	——	——	——
9. Regularly updates first aid and emergency medical care credentials.	——	——	——	——
10. Does not permit participation in any activity without medical approval following serious illness or injury.	——	——	——	——
11. Readily recognizes the presence of any attractive nuisance, and initiates firm control measures.	——	——	——	——
12. Posts safety rules for use of facilities, then orients students and colleagues to danger areas in activities, facilities, and personal conduct.	——	——	——	——
13. Does not place the activity area in the control of unqualified personnel for *any* reason.	——	——	——	——
14. Relies on waiver forms not as a negation of responsibility for injury only as a means of assuring that parents/guardians recognize students' intent to participate.	——	——	——	——
15. Does not permit zeal for accomplishment or emotion of the moment to suppress rational behavior.	——	——	——	——
16. Provides in letter and spirit nondiscriminatory programs for all students.	——	——	——	——

From Parsons, T.W.

Continued.

The following exercise should provide personal guidance for the administrator as to the establishment of an appropriate degree of prudence commensurate with the professional, as well as legal responsibility of the contemporary administrator in physical education and athletics.

	Degree of compliance			
	Always	Frequently	Rarely	Never
17. Cancels transportation plans if unable to be thoroughly convinced of the personal and prudent reliability of drivers, means of transportation and adequacy of insurance coverage.	____	____	____	____
18. Does not conduct a class/or practice/or contest without a plan for medical assistance in the event of injury regardless of the setting.	____	____	____	____
19. Holds professional liability insurance of significant dollar dimensions and pertinent applicability to professional pursuits involving physical activity.	____	____	____	____
20. Does not permit excessive concern about legal liability to prohibit the development of a challenging and accountable physical education experience for each participant.	____	____	____	____

provisions that need to be implemented for a sound insurance management program. Furthermore, management should be aware that citizens are becoming increasingly aware of the meaning of laws that concern their programs as well as their individual rights in such matters. As a result, the prospect of litigation is increased. The management therefore should be prepared for possible litigation.

SELF-ASSESSMENT TESTS

These tests will assist students in determining if material and competencies presented in this chapter have been mastered.

1. Without consulting your text, write out a one sentence definition of each of the following terms: *legal liability, tort, negligence, in loco parentis, save harmless law, assumption of risk, attractive nuisance, immunity,* and *insurance management*. Check your definitions with those in the text.
2. Prepare a legal brief for a case in your state that justifies a rule that requires all students in grades 1 to 12 be required to attend physical education classes.
3. Outline recent court interpretations of sports product liability, violence, and physical education activities that are held off campus.
4. Arrange a mock trial in your class. Have a jury, prosecutor, defendant, witnesses, and other features characteristic of a regular court trial. The case before the court is that the coach of a high school football team in the final minutes of a game used a player who had incurred a brain concussion in the first quarter. The player later died from the injury.
5. Survey the physical education and athletic programs at your college and identify any areas of negligence that might exist in the conduct of the programs. If any are found, recommend how they can be eliminated.
6. Discuss some of the legal aspects of women in sports and also of coeducational physical education classes as a result of the passage of Title IX.
7. Prepare a list of safety procedures that should be followed by every physical education teacher and coach to provide for the welfare of all students and players.

8. Prepare a sound insurance management plan for a high school physical education and athletic program. After preparing the plan, check with an insurance broker to get his or her reaction to your plan. Discuss the results with your class.

REFERENCES

1. Appenzeller, H.: Sports and the courts, Physical Education and Sports Quarterly, Proceedings of the Summer Law and Sports Conference, Greensboro, N.C., June 1983, Guilford College.
2. Appenzeller, H.: Sports and the courts: Trends in tort liability, Physical Education and Sports Law Quarterly, Summer Law and Sports Conference, Greensboro, N.C., June 1983, Guilford College.
3. Appenzeller, H., and Ross, T.: Sports and the courts, Summer Law and Sports Conference, Greensboro, N.C., June 1983, Guilford College.
4. Appenzeller, H., et al.: "Sports and the courts," **5**:15 Spring 1985.
5. Arnold, D.E.: Sport product liability, Journal of Physical Education and Recreation **49**:25, November/December 1978.
6. Arnold, D.E.: Legal aspects of off-campus physical education programs, Journal of Physical Education and Recreation **50**: 21, April 1979.
7. Begley, R.F.: Legal liability in organized recreational playground areas, Safety Education Digest, 1955.
8. Carpenter, L.J., and Acosta, R.V.: Violence in sport—is it part of the game or the intentional tort of battery? Journal of Physical Education and Recreation **51**:18, September 1980.
9. Coping with the "Sue Syndrome," The Athletic Educator's Report, August 1980.
10. Dougherty, N.J., and Bonanno, D.: Management Principles in Sport and Leisure Services, Minneapolis, 1985, Burgess Publishing.
11. The fight for reform, Athletic Business **9**:10, June 1985.
12. Garber, L.O.: Law and the School Business Manager, Danville, Ill., 1957, Interstate Printers & Publishers, Inc. (Note: These stipulations also apply to women.)
13. Horine, L.: Administration of Physical Education and Sport Programs, Philadelphia, 1985, Saunders College Publishing.
14. Jensen, C.R.: Administrative Management of Physical Education and Athletic Programs, Philadelphia, 1983, Lea & Febiger.
15. Kaiser, R.A.: Program liability waivers: do they protect the agency and staff? Journal of Physical Education, Recreation and Dance **55**:54, August 1984.
16. National Education Research Division For the National Commission On Safety Education: Who is liable for pupil injuries? Washington, D.C., 1950, National Education Association, p. 5.
17. Proceedings of the City Wide Conference With Principals' Representatives and Men and Women Chairmen Of Health Education, City of New York Board of Education, Brooklyn, N.Y.
18. Shapiro, F.S.: Your liability for student accidents, National Education Association Journal **54**:46, 1965.

SUGGESTED READINGS

• Berg, R.: Catastrophic injury insurance: an end to costly litigation? Athletic Business **8**:10, November 1984.
Discusses the Ruedlinger Plan, a plan endorsed by 48 state high school athletic associations that is designed to provide lifetime care for catastrophically-injured athletes and protection from lawsuits for the schools.
• Bayless, M.A., and Adams, S.H.: A liability checklist, Journal of Physial Education, Recreation and Dance **56**: 49, February 1985.
Provides guidelines for coaches to assist them in evaluating the adequacy of their program to avoid liability-producing circumstances.
• Kaiser, R.A.: Program liability waivers, Journal of Physical Education, Recreation and Dance **55**:54, August 1984.
Discusses the pros and cons of liability waivers and shows how they can discourage lawsuits and enhance legal defenses by increasing participant awareness.
• Potter, G.: Centralia (Wash.) high school's safety list, The First Aider, September 1983.
A set of guidelines for football players in Centralia regarding the proper techniques to practice for maximum safety in the contact phase of the game.
• Stotlar, D.K., and Butkie, S.D.: Who's responsible when a spectator gets hurt? Athletic Purchasing and Facilities **7**:22, April 1983.
Explains how the courts have ruled that spectators at athletic events assume certain risks. However, there are steps managers can and must take to discuss potential negligence on their part.
• Wong, G.M., and Ensor, R.S.: Torts and tailgates, Athletic Business, **9**:46, May 1985.
Pre- and post-game tailgating are popular among sport fans, but institutions can be held liable if reasonable precautions are not taken, particularly those related to alcohol problems.

Chapter Fourteen

Public Relations

Instructional Objectives and Competencies to be Achieved
After reading this chapter the student should be able to

- Define the term *public relations* and its purpose and importance to physical education and athletic programs.
- Understand the relationship of marketing to a public relations program.
- Recognize the needs of various publics in physical education and athletics.
- Describe key principles that should guide a sound public relations program.
- Be familiar with various public relations media and how they can best be used to promote physical education and athletic programs.

Abraham Lincoln once said, "Public sentiment is everything. With public sentiment, nothing can fail; without it nothing can succeed." The management teams of physical education and athletic programs need public recognition that the programs under their jurisdiction are meeting the needs of consumers. In order to accomplish this, the consumer and the public in general should be familiar with, understand, and support the services these programs render. Therefore, to have sound public relations, excellent programs must exist, effective promotion must take place, communication lines with the various publics must be kept open, and media must be used in a manner that effectively presents the objectives of the organization to the public at large.

Public relations is a much defined term. It is commonly defined as the activities and attitudes used to influence, judge, and control the opinion of any individual, group, or groups of persons in the interest of some other individuals. Two characteristics of this program are careful planning and proper conduct, which in turn will result in public understanding and confidence. It includes attempts to modify the attitudes and actions of the public through persuasion and to integrate the attitudes and actions of the public with those of the organization or people who are conducting the public relations program. Public relations is the entire body of relationships that make up our impressions of an individual, an organization, or an idea.

These concepts of public relations help clarify its importance for any organization, institution, or group of individuals trying to develop an enterprise, profession, or business. Public relations considers important factors such as consumers' interest, human relationships, public understanding, and goodwill. In business it attempts to show the important place that specialized enterprises have in society and how they exist and operate in the public interest. In education, it is concerned with public opinion, the needs of the school or college, and acquainting constituents with what is being done in the public interest. It also should acquaint the community with problems that must be solved for education to render a greater service.

Purposes of school relations include: (1) serving as a public information source concerning school activities, (2) aiding the promotion of confidence in the schools or school-related organizations, (3) gathering support for school or organizational funding and programs, (4) stressing the value of education for all individuals, (5) improving communication among students, teachers, parents, and community members, (6) evaluating school and organization programs, and (7) correcting misunderstandings and misinformation concerning the aims and objectives of the school or other organizations.

Physical education and athletics need public relations because the public does not always understand the contributions that these special fields make to young and old people alike. Many persons feel that these fields are appendages to the school programs and are sources of entertainment rather than education. A sound public relations program is needed to correct these misunderstandings.

The goals of physical education and athletics as discussed in Chapter 2 are educational in nature and can be achieved through well-planned and well-managed programs of physical education and athletics. These facts should be communicated to the public through various media as well as through the pursuit of excellence in the programs.

The practice of public relations is pertinent to all areas of human activities, religion, education, business, politics, military, government, labor, and other affairs. A sound public relations program is not hit-or-miss. It is planned with considerable care, and great amounts of time and effort are necessary to produce results. Furthermore, it is not something in which only top management, executives, or administrative officers should be interested. For any organization to have a good program, all members must be public relations conscious.

The extent to which interest in public relations has grown is indicated by the number of individuals specializing in it. A recent edition of the *Public Relations Directory and Yearbook* listed nearly 1500 individuals who are working independently, approximately 5000 who are directors of public relations with business firms, approximately 2000 who are associated with trade and professional groups, and nearly 1000 who are with social organizations. Many of these people are involved in physical education.

Public relations is steadily being recognized for the

Warm-up exercises, food and fitness fair, Washington, D.C.

part it can play in educational, business, or social advancement. All need public support and understanding to survive. Public relations helps obtain these essentials.

MARKETING AND PHYSICAL EDUCATION AND ATHLETIC PROGRAMS

In the past American industry manufactured goods and then put forth every effort to sell them. Today, the management of the more progressive organizations starts with marketing and identifying and trying to satisfy the needs of the consumer. Management is marketing oriented, rather than production oriented. In other words, nothing should be manufactured unless it can be sold. This concept applies to physical education and athletics, as well as to industry.

The term *marketing* includes areas such as analysis, promotion, and coordination. It involves a study of the various factors that relate to getting the public to endorse and buy a product or service. In so doing it tries to find out things such as what goods and services customers want and how best to advise them of what is available. In practical terms marketing has several dimensions, sometimes called the *marketing mix*. These dimensions include consumer research, product planning, pricing, public relations, advertising, promotion, distribution, packaging, and servicing. Management is responsible for coordinating all of these dimensions into an effective program.

A marketing-oriented organization starts with the consumer and his or her needs, which have been identified by sound marketing research. A determination is made between specialization and diversification— whether to stress one or several services or products.

Public relations includes a close liaison with the press. The type of media to be used should be selected with care. Feedback regarding the effectiveness of the program is continuous. Distribution channels extend from the supplier to the consumer. Evaluation is continuous.

In essence, marketing refers to the relationship of the producer to the consumer. In physical education and athletic programs it relates to the various services provided and programs implemented and how well these services and programs meet the needs of the consumer (students, adults, and the population in general). Marketing is the process by which the objectives of the physical education and athletic programs can be best achieved. A marketing strategy that will enable the organization to accomplish its objectives as efficiently as possible should be developed.

THE MANY PUBLICS

For a public relations program to be successful, accurate facts must be presented. To establish what facts are to be given to the public, the management needs to identify the consumers of the product or service.[2] Marketing people call this *market segmentation*. In identifying the consumer they determine the socioeconomic, geographic, and product-service needs of various publics and which ones they wish to direct their efforts toward.

A public is a group of people drawn together by common interests who are in a specific geographic area or are characterized by some other common feature. The people in the United States comprise hundreds of different publics—farmers, organized laborers, unorganized workers, students, professional people, and veterans. The various publics may be national, regional, and local. They can be classified according to race or nationality, age, religion, occupation, politics, sex, income, profession, economic level, or business, fraternal, and educational backgrounds. Each organization or group with a special interest is a public. The community or public relations-minded person must always think in terms of the publics with which he or she desires to promote understanding and how they can best be reached.

To have a meaningful and purposeful community relations program, it is essential to obtain some facts about these various publics, to know their understanding of the professions, their needs and interests, their health practices and hobbies, and other essential information. It is also important to consider what is good for people in general.

Public opinion decides whether a profession is important or not, whether it meets an essential need, and whether it is making a contribution to enriched living. It influences the success or failure of a department, school, institution, business, or profession. Public opinion is dynamic and continually changing. Public opinion results from the interaction of people. Public opinion has great impact, and any group or organization that wants to survive should know as much about it as possible.

To get information on what the public thinks, why it thinks as it does, and how it reaches its conclusions, various techniques may be used. Surveys, questionnaires, opinion polls, interviews, expert opinion, discussions, and other techniques have proved valuable. Anyone interested in community relations should be acquainted with these various techniques.

Public opinion is formed to a great degree as a result of influences in early life, such as the effect of parents, home, and environment; on the basis of people's own experiences in everyday living, what they see, hear, and experience in other ways; and finally by media such as newspapers, radio, and television. It is important not only to be aware of these facts but also to remember that one is dealing with many different publics, each requiring a special source of research and study to know the most effective way to plan, organize, and administer the public relations program.

PLANNING THE PUBLIC RELATIONS PROGRAM[3]

Public relations programs are more effective when they are planned by many interested and informed individuals and groups. Individuals and groups such as school boards, management personnel, teacher, administrators, and citizens' committees can provide valuable assistance in certain areas of the community relations program. These people, serving in an advisory capacity to physical education and athletic departments can help immeasurably in planning a community relations program by following these specific steps:

- Establish a sound public relations policy.
- Identify the services that will yield the greatest dividends.
- Obtain facts about what consumers do and do not know and believe about educational values and needs.
- Decide what facts and ideas will best enable consumers to understand the benefits obtained from good programs and what improvements will increase these benefits.

- Make full use of effective planning techniques to generate understanding and appreciation.
- Relate cost to opportunity for participants to achieve.
- Decide who is going to perform specific communication tasks at particular times.

After the public relations plan is put into operation, it is important to test and evaluate its results and then improve the program accordingly.

PRINCIPLES OF PUBLIC RELATIONS

Principles to observe in developing a public relations program follow:

- Public relations should be considered internally before being developed externally. The support of everyone within the organization, from the top administrator down to the last worker, should be obtained. Furthermore, such items as purpose of program, person or persons responsible, funds available, media to use, and instructional aids to carry on the program should be primary considerations before implementation.
- A public relations program should be outlined and put in writing, and every member of the organization should become familiar with it. The better it is known and understood, the better chance it has of succeeding.
- The persons directly in charge of the public relations program must have complete knowledge of the professional services being rendered; the attitudes of those who are members of the profession and of the organization represented; and the nature, background, and reaction of the consumers and of all the publics directly or indirectly related to the job being performed.
- After all the information has been gathered, a program that meets the needs revealed by research should be developed.
- Adequate funds should be available to do the job. Furthermore, the person or persons in charge of the public relations program should be allowed to spend this money in whatever ways they feel will be most helpful and productive for the organization.
- The formation of a public relations staff will be determined by the needs of the organization, the amount of money available, the attitude of the man-

Wheelchair participants in annual Marine Corps Marathon.

agement, and the size of the organization. If additional staff members are available, special talents should be sought to provide effectively for a well-rounded program.

• Individuals assigned public relations work should stay in the background instead of seeking the limelight, keep abreast of the factors that affect the program, develop a wide acquaintance, and make contacts that will be helpful.

• As a public relations program is developed, the following items should be checked. Is there a handbook or a newsletter to keep members of the organization informed? Is there a system for dispensing information to local radio and press outlets? Is there a booklet, flyer, or printed matter that tells the story of the organization? Do members of the organization participate regularly in community affairs? Are there provisions for a speakers' bureau where civic clubs and other organizations may obtain someone to speak on various topics? Does the organization hold open house for interested persons? Does the organization have a film or other visual material that can be shown to interested groups and that explains and interprets the work?

• A good public relations program will employ all available resources and machinery to disseminate information to the public to ensure adequate coverage.

PUBLIC RELATIONS MEDIA

Many media can be employed in a public relations program. Some have more significance in certain localities than others. Some are more readily accessible than others. Physical educators, athletic directors, and coaches should survey their communities to determine the media that can be used most effectively.

Program and staff

The program and the staff represent the best medium for establishing an effective public relations program. Through activities and experiences provided and the leadership given, much goodwill may be built for any school, college, department, or profession.

Another important consideration is that the most effective community relations occurs on a person-to-person level. This might be teacher to student, student to parent, teacher to citizen, or physical educator to participant. In all cases the participant is an important consideration, indeed the most important means of communication.

Newspapers

The newspaper is one of the most common and useful medium for disseminating information. It reaches a large audience and can be helpful in interpreting physical education and athletics to the public at large. Some questions that might be asked to determine what makes a good news story are: Is the news of interest to the public? Are the facts correct? Is the style direct? Is it written in the third person in non-technical terms, and is it well organized? Does it include news on individuals who are closely related to the school, colleges, or other organization? Does the article have a plan of action, and does it play a significant part in interpreting the program?[1]

When a story is submitted to a newspaper, the following standard rules apply to copy preparation: Prepare all copy in typewritten form as neatly as possible, double-spaced, and on one side of the paper only. The name, address, and telephone number of your organization should be on the first page, in the upper left-hand corner. Also at the top of the first page, but below the address, should be the headline and release date for the story. Paragraphs should be short; if the story necessitates more than one page, write the word *more* at the end of each page. At the top of each additional page, list the name of the story in the upper left-hand corner. The symbols # # # should be placed at the end of the article.

One expert on newspapers has pointed out that the most common reasons for rejecting material include limited reader interest, poor writing, inaccuracies, and insufficient information.

The newspaper represents a medium that can be used effectively by any school or other organization. To be most effective, however, the information should be newsworthy.

Pictures and graphics

Pictures represent an effective medium for public relations. Two words should be kept in mind by the persons who take and select the pictures for publication: *action* and *people*. Pictures that reflect action are more interesting and appealing than still pictures. Furthermore, pictures with people in them are more effective than ones with no people. Usually a few people are better than many. Finally, such considerations as good background, accuracy in details, clarity, and educational significance should not be forgotten.

Educational matters, such as budgets, statistical information regarding growth of school population, information about participation in various school or

Young Ambassadors of Fitness performing in Tacoma, Wash.

college activities, and many other items relating to schools and other organizations can be made more interesting, intelligible, and appealing if presented through colorful and artistic charts, graphs, and diagrams. Pictures and graphics, of course, should relate specifically to the age, grade, or sex that is being publicized.

Magazines

Thousands of popular magazines, professional journals, trade publications, and other periodicals are published today. National magazines such as *Newsweek, U.S. News and World Report,* and *Reader's Digest* are excellent for publicity purposes. However, it is difficult to get stories in such publications because of their rigid requirements and because the editors like to cover the stories with their own staff writers. Many times it is better to suggest ideas to them rather than to submit a manuscript. The public relations person can attempt to interest the editors in some particular work being done and ask them to send a staff writer to cover the story. It might be possible to get a free-lance writer interested in the organization and have him or her develop a story. Someone on the department staff with writing skill can be assigned to write a piece for magazine consumption and then submit it to various periodicals for consideration.

In many cases, it is not necessary to get a story in a national magazine. Many magazines that will provide excellent exposure are geared specifically to one community or one profession. For example, the physical education profession through its *Journal of Physical Education, Recreation and Dance,* will give a program outstanding exposure.

Public speaking

Public speaking can be an effective medium for public relations. Public addresses to civic and social groups in the community, at public affairs, gatherings, and professional meetings afford good opportunities for interpreting a profession to the public. However, it is important to do a commendable job, or the result can be poor rather than good community relations.

To make an effective speech, a person should observe many fundamentals, including mastery of the subject, sincere interest and enthusiasm, interest in putting thoughts rather than the speaker across to the public, directness, straightforwardness, preparation, brevity, and clear and distinct enunciation.

If the organization is large enough and it has several qualified speakers within it, a speaker's bureau may be an asset. Various civic, school, college, church, and other leaders within a community can be informed of the services the organization has to offer. Then, when the requests come in, speakers can be assigned on the basis of qualifications and availability. The entire department or organization should set up facilities and make information and material available for the preparation of such speeches. If desired by the members of the organization, in-service training courses could even be worked out in conjunction with the English department or some experienced person in developing this particular phase of the community relations program.

Discussion groups

Discussion groups, forums, and similar meetings are frequently held in communities. At such gatherings, representatives from the community, including educators, industrialists, business people, physicians, lawyers, clergy, union leaders, and others discuss topics of general interest. This is an excellent setting to clarify issues, clear up misunderstandings, enlighten civic leaders, and discuss the pros and cons of community projects. Physical educators should play a larger role in such meetings than in the past. Much good could be done for these specialized fields through this medium.

Radio and television

Radio and television are powerful mediums because of their universal appeal. These mediums are well worth the money spent for public relations. However, the possibilities of obtaining free time should be thoroughly examined. The idea of public service will influence some radio and television station managers to grant free time to an organization. This may be in the nature of an item included in a newscast program, a spot announcement, or a public service program that uses a quarter, half, or even a full hour.

Some radio and television stations are reserved for

Physical education demonstration, National Conference on Physical Fitness and Sports, Washington, D.C.

educational purposes. This possibility should be investigated. Many schools and colleges have stations of their own that may be used.

Sometimes a person must take advantage of these mediums on short notice; therefore it is important for an organization to be prepared with written plans that can be put into operation immediately. This might make the difference between being accepted or rejected for such an assignment. The organization must also be prepared to assume the work involved in rehearsals, preparation of scenery, or other items essential in presenting such a program.

Radio and television offer some of the best means of reaching a large number of people at one time. Organizations concerned with physical education and athletics should continually use their imaginations to translate the story of their professions into material that can be used effectively by these media.

Many local radio and television stations at the present time will be receptive to people involved in physical education and athletic programs.

Films

Films can present dramatically and informatively such stories as an organization's services to the public and highlights in the training of its leaders. They con-

stitute an effective medium for presenting a story briefly. A series of visual impressions will remain long in the minds of the audience.

Because such a great majority of the American people enjoy movies today, it is important to consider them in any community relations program. Movies are not only a form of entertainment but also an effective medium to use to inform and educate. Films stimulate attention, create interest, and provide a way of getting across information not inherent in printed material.

Movies, slide films, educational television, and other phases of these visual aids have been used by a number of departments of physical education and athletics to present their programs to the public and to interest individuals in their work. Volunteer associations, professional associations, and official agencies in these fields have also used them to advantage.

Posters, exhibits, brochures, demonstrations, miscellaneous media

Posters, exhibits, and brochures are important in any public relations program concerned with physical education and athletics. Well-illustrated, brief, and attractive brochures can visually and informatively depict activities, facilities, projects, and services that a department or organization has to offer as part of its total program.

Drawings, paintings, charts, graphs, pictures, and other aids, when placed on posters and given proper distribution, will illustrate activities, show progress, and present information visually. These mediums will attract and interest the public.

Exhibits, when properly prepared, interestingly presented, and properly located, such as in store window or some other prominent spot, can do much to demonstrate work being done by an organization.

Demonstrations that entertainingly and informatively present the total program of an organization or profession have a place in any community relations program. The main objectives for a physical education demonstration are: (1) to inform the public and provide an outlet for interest in physical education programs by community members, (2) to provide an opportunity for members of an organization to work together toward a common goal, (3) to demonstrate the need and benefit of physical education to all participants, (4) to provide opportunities for the general public to see the physical education program in action, (5) to contribute to the objectives of the organization, (6) to include all participants in the activities, (7) to reflect the needs of the consumer in the present and in the future, and (8) to contribute to the health, social, and emotional well-being of participants and spectators.

Other miscellaneous mediums, such as correspondence in the forms of letters and messages to parents, student publications, and reports, offer opportunities to develop good relations and favorable understanding concerning schools, colleges, and other organizations and the work they are doing. Every opportunity must be used to build good public relations.

PUBLIC RELATIONS IN ACTION

Many examples exist that show effective public relations programs. The President's Council On Physical Fitness and Sports distributes many materials designed to make physical educators, health educators, and the public in general aware of the value of physical fitness and sports. One of their most recent publications is ''A School Physical Education Performance Checklist'' whereby students, parents, physical educators, and others may check how effective their pro-grams are in light of the objectives being sought. (See Performance Checklist.)

The PEPI project

The Physical Education Public Information (PEPI) project is designed to educate the public regarding the vital contribution of physical education to children, youths, and adults. Through the project the use of local media—press, radio, and television—is emphasized as a means of gaining greater public understanding.

In its initial phase the project identified a local PEPI coordinator for each of the nation's 100 largest metropolitan listening and viewing areas (there are now more than 600 PEPI coordinators). The PEPI coordinator's responsibility is to organize and report PEPI activity in his or her area. This means such things as arranging with local radio and television stations for programming.

PEPI was developed by the Physical Education Division of the AAHPERD and funded by the AAHPERD. The President's Council on Physical Fitness and Sports also provides both technical and material support for PEPI.

The basic concepts of the PEPI program include: (1) physical education is a form of health insurance, (2) physical education contributes to academic achievement, (3) physical education contributes to lifetime sports skills, and (4) physical education helps develop a positive self-concept and an ability to both compete and cooperate with others.

The PEPI Action Corps (PAC) was organized to aid PEPI coordinators with public information and media contact. PAC consultants were selected on the basis of their enthusiasm and outstanding achievements on behalf of physical education. Some of the consultants have their own television and radio programs, and all act in an advisory capacity to further the objective of publicizing the benefits of physical education.

National Physical Education and Sports Week was initiated by the PEPI network.

National Physical Fitness and Sports Month

National Physical Fitness and Sports Month was established by the President's Council On Physical Fitness and Sports and is endorsed by the president of

A PERFORMANCE CHECKLIST

Yes   No

☐   ☐   Physical fitness is not a part-time thing. Does your school provide at least one period per day of instruction in vigorous physical activity?

☐   ☐   Play alone won't develop physical fitness. Is a part of each physical education period devoted to activities like running, calisthenics, agility drills and weight training?

☐   ☐   Skill in sport is a valuable social and health asset. Does your school program offer instruction in lifetime sports like tennis, swimming, golf, skiing and jogging?

☐   ☐   Most physical problems can be alleviated if discovered early enough. Does the school give a screening test to identify those students who are weak, inflexible, overweight, or lacking in coordination?

☐   ☐   All children can improve with help. Are there special physical education programs for students with special problems, such as the retarded, the handicapped, and the underdeveloped?

☐   ☐   Testing is important to measure achievement. Are all students tested in physical fitness at least twice a year?

What to do to change the "No" answers to "Yes"

First: Make sure you know what your local school code says about physical education, and what is specified in state laws or regulations.

Then:

1. Speak to the physical education instructor in your child's school. You will find him or her very cooperative and willing to answer your questions.

2. If the physical education instructor can't help, speak to the school principal.

3. If significant changes are needed in the school's priorities or scheduling, try to encourage your parent/teacher organization to support a regular physical education program with an adequate emphasis on physical fitness.

4. If the problem is one of policy in the entire school district, take up the issue with your local Board of Education.

5. If your school is doing all it can at this time, make certain your child gets at least one-half hour of vigorous physical activity every day before or after school.

For additional information or help in setting up a program of vigorous physical activity for your child write:

THE PRESIDENT'S COUNCIL ON
PHYSICAL FITNESS AND SPORTS
Washington, D.C. 20001

---

the United States. May is usually designated as the month, and some goal is set forth to motivate the public into action. In 1986 the slogan was "Shape up America" and showed several groups of people of various ages engaged in vigorous activities to improve their fitness. As a result of this promotion many communities across the country sponsored various physical education and sport activities during the month of May.

Jump-for-Heart

One of the most successful public relations activities of the AAHPERD is the Jump-for-Heart program.

The American Heart Association and the AAHPERD cooperate to sponsor rope-skipping exhibitions, Jump-for-Heart, and Jump-Rope-a-Thons to raise funds. Student groups who have been involved in demonstrations have been very well received. This project has raised considerable money to augment AAHPERD funds.

Public relations in selected United States communities

Oklahoma City physical education teachers accepted the responsibility for developing positive public relations with the faculty, administration, students, and public in general. The public responded and gave physical education programs excellent support and devised money-making projects in order to do things such as installing creative playgrounds, purchasing new supplies and equipment, hiring additional faculty and reducing class size.

In Norfolk, Virginia, an effective public relations program has resulted in community awareness and an outstanding physical education program. School-parent communication, local government and business cooperation, community sponsorship of school programs, effective relations with students and adult participants, and active participation in physical education projects by such groups as the Rotary Club, Cosmopolitan Club and Lung Association have been accomplished.

PUBLIC RELATIONS IN ELEVEN SCHOOL SYSTEMS

A survey was conducted among 11 school systems to determine the nature and scope of their public relations programs. Several questions were asked of physical education personnel through personal interviews.

The policies that govern the programs indicated that the director of physical education and athletics was directly responsible for all public relations releases to the press. All printed material needed the approval of the director and the superintendent of schools before being released. The coaches of interscholastic athletics were responsible for preparing all releases regarding their programs. Each physical educator was urged to recognize that his or her activities were part of the professional and public relations programs of the school.

Communications media used included the physical education program, newspaper, posters, films, public speaking, school publications, newsletter, letters to parents, demonstrations and exhibits, personal contact, pictures, radio, television, window displays, brochures, sports days, and bulletin boards. The five media found to be the most effective in their professional and public relations programs were (1) the total physical education program, (2) personal contact, (3) newspapers, (4) public speaking, and (5) demonstrations and exhibits.

All the directors of physical education and athletics indicated that athletics received more publicity than any other phase of the physical education program. When asked why they thought this was so, some typical comments were: "The public demands it," "It is required because of public interest," and "The newspapers will only accept and print releases on athletics."

When the directors were asked what message they were trying to convey to the public, the following were typical answers: the value of the total physical education and athletic programs, the importance of the programs to the student, recognition and achievement of all students in all areas of physical education and athletics, efforts and energies being expended to give each person a worthwhile experience in physical education and athletics, the role of the physical education and athletic programs in enhancing the health and welfare of the participant, and the aims and objectives of the total physical education and athletic programs.

In summary, the professional and public relations programs in the 11 school districts were conducted in light of the following principles:

- Each physical education and athletic department recognized the importance of an active public relations program.
- Sound policies guided the program.
- Responsibility for public relations was shared by all members of the department, with central authority residing with the director.
- Many different communications media were used to interpret the program to the numerous publics.
- The total physical education and athletic program was recognized as being the most effective medium of professional and community relations.
- Efforts were made to interpret accurate facts about physical education to the public.
- Considerable planning was needed for the effective use of public relations media.

SUMMARY

Public relations is an important responsibility for all who manage physical education and athletic programs. Public support for these programs is essential

Maypole dance provides opportunity for special rhythmical activity in front of townspeople.

if the necessary funds, facilities, staff and other essentials are to be provided. Therefore sound principles should guide the public relations program in a way that will communicate the objectives of these programs to the various publics who are interested. Furthermore, all of the faculty, staff, and members of the organization should be involved in the public relations program.

SELF-ASSESSMENT TESTS

These tests will assist students in determining if material and competencies presented in this chapter have been mastered:

1. As a manager you are conducting a staff meeting in your school. Explain to your staff why you feel that an inservice program in public relations would be valuable to staff members and managers alike.
2. What is meant by the term *marketing* and what are its implications for promoting physical education and athletic programs?
3. What is meant by the fact that physical education and athletics are dealing with not just one but many publics? Identify two different publics and indicate what type of community relations program you would use with each and how they differ from each other.
4. List ten principles that should be observed in a public relations program. How would you apply five of these principles in communicating the importance of a strong physical education program in your school?
5. Prepare a news release to be published or broadcast to the public at large about some event or phase of a physical education or athletic program. Have the class evaluate your news release.

REFERENCES

1. Dougherty, N.J., and Bonanno, D.: Management Principles in Sport and Leisure Services, Minneapolis, 1985, Burgess Publishing.
2. Kraus, R.G., and Curtis, J.E.: Creative Management in Recreation and Parks, St. Louis, 1986, The C.V. Mosby Co.
3. Pangrazi, R.P., and Darst, P.W.: Dynamic Physical Education Curriculum and Instruction For Secondary School Students, Minneapolis, 1985, Burgess Publishing.

SUGGESTED READINGS

- American Alliance for Physical Education, Recreation and Dance. Shaping the Body Politic: Legislative Training for the Physical Educator, Reston, Va., 1985, The Alliance.

  A new publication prepared by the American Alliance Public and Legislative Affairs Office. It offers some helpful advice for educators charged with developing a school public relations program.

- Buturusis, D.: Gaining and keeping support for physical education, Journal of Physical Education, Recreation and Dance **55**:44, August 1984.

  Discusses various ways physical education can achieve public support. Stresses such requirements as direct communication with parents and other segments of population, staff involvement, a quality program, assessing community needs, wise use of media, and speaking at service clubs.

- Coventry, W.F., and Burstiner, I.: Management: A Basic Handbook, Englewood Cliffs, N.J., 1977, Prentice-Hall, Inc.

  Shows how the success of any enterprise largely depends on the caliber and efficacy of the people who staff its managerial slots. In turn, efficient management performance is associated with a thorough grounding in the fundamentals of management and to the development of human and conceptual skills, and communicative proficiency. Covers various aspects of management including public relations.

- Jackson, J.J.: Sport Administration, Springfield, Ill., 1981, Charles C Thomas, Publisher.

  The author presents the theoretical base for a particular aspect of management, including public relations, then links it with specific situations in physical education, sport, and recreation.

- Rolloff, B.D.: Public relations: objectives for physical education, Journal of Physical Education, Recreation and Dance **56**:69, March 1985.

  Sets forth 15 objectives for public relations that, when properly implemented, will achieve public understanding and support for physical education.

- Tenoschok, M., and Sanders, S.: Planning an effective public relations program, Journal of Physical Education, Recreation and Dance **55**:48, January 1984.

  Shows how concerned parents and administrators are more willing to offer support if they know how the physical education program helps their children, what concepts are developed, and why activities are offered. Various techniques are suggested for accomplishing these goals.

- Yiannakis, A.: Sports marketing and fund raising, Journal of Physical Education, Recreation and Dance **55**:20, September 1984.

  Tells how sound marketing techniques can be used to raise money for sport programs—survival strategy for high school sports in particular.

Chapter Fifteen

Office Management

Instructional Objectives and Competencies to be Achieved
After reading this chapter the student should be able to

- Appreciate the importance of the office in the management of a physical education and athletic program.
- Understand and appreciate the role of the computer in accomplishing management tasks.
- Justify the need for office personnel in the management of a physical education and athletic program.
- Identify basic office management procedures that should be used in conducting the affairs of a physical education and athletic program.
- List the records that should be maintained in a physical educator's and athletic manager's office.

The management of physical education and athletic programs know that efficient office management determines to a great extent the success of their programs. Therefore, along with functions such as public relations, facility management, and fiscal accountability, office management is an important administrative function.

Office management has often been neglected by physical educators and managers. Efficient office management indicates a well-run department. The office is the place for first impressions, communication between student and teacher and consumer and business executive, the focus of management duties, and a point of contact for the management and staff.

OFFICE MANAGEMENT TASKS

Office management is responsible for many important tasks, including the following:

Communication. The office is the nerve center of the organization where information is transmitted to staff members and others by means such as face-to-face conferences, the telephone, correspondence, and intercome systems.

Correspondence. The office is the setting for preparing and filing letters for managers and staff members and for handling their incoming and outgoing mail.

Supplies and equipment. The office is the place for requesting, receiving, and disbursing supplies and equipment needed in conducting the organization's various activities.

Processing materials. The office is a central point for duplicating and typing materials pertinent to the management of the program.

Record keeping. The office is the place where records containing information on staff members, students, athletes, and materials are kept.

Report preparation. The office is a place for preparing reports for various staff members, officers and other personnel to whom the management is required to report.

Budget preparation and implementation. The office is where budget information is centralized, where revenues and expenditures are recorded, and where financial reports and summaries are compiled and stored.

Community and public relations. The office is a key communications center for the conduct, planning, and management of community and professional projects that are closely related and important to the achievement of the goals and functions of the organization.

Emergencies. The office is a focal point for meeting day-to-day emergency situations that call for immediate action.

IMPORTANCE OF OFFICE MANAGEMENT

Colleagues, business prospects, new members, students, and visitors frequently have their initial contacts with physical education and athletic departments in the central office. Their reception, the courtesies they are shown, the efficiency with which the office work is carried out, and other operational details leave lasting impressions. Friends are often made or lost at this strategic point.

Center for communications

Office work, broadly defined, is the handling and management of information. The office is usually the place where schedules are arranged and distributed, telephone calls made and received, reports typed and mimeographed, bulletins prepared and issued, conferences arranged and held, appointments made and confirmed, and greetings voiced and exchanged. The office represents the hub of activity around which revolves the efficient functioning of the physical education personnel. Unless these functions are carried out with dispatch, and with accuracy and courtesy, the entire management process begins to break down.

Focus of management duties

The chief management personnel, secretarial assistants, and clerical help constitute the office staff. The filing system, key records, and reports are usually housed in the office. When inventories need to be examined, letters pulled from files, or the chairperson of the department consulted on important matters, the office is frequently the point of contact. Management responsibilities are carried out in the office, making this space a point of focus for the entire organization.

Point of contact for management and staff members

Staff members visit the office regularly. Mailboxes are located there, and telephone calls may be taken in the office. Conferences and appointments with students and visitors often bring staff members to the office. Constant communication takes place between the management and staff members in this setting. The atmosphere in the office can create high staff morale, efficiency, a friendly climate, and a feeling of working toward common goals.

RELATIONSHIP OF MANAGEMENT TO OFFICE STAFF MEMBERS

The management should establish a good working relationship with office staff members. Secretaries and other personnel should have a feeling of belonging and a recognition that they are an important part of the organization. The work each one performs is essential to the achievement of the organization's goals.

Most managers depend heavily on their office staff members to carry out day-to-day duties and routines efficiently and productively. Furthermore, managers are frequently away from their desks on organization assignments, and in their absence the office needs to function in the same manner as when the manager is present. These goals cannot be achieved unless there is an excellent working relationship between the management and office staff members.

In-service education of office staff members. The management should encourage office staff members to engage in in-service education and be aware of the updating of any office procedures. Areas where improvement might take place include typing and shorthand skills, answering telephones, office housekeeping, updating the filing system, simplifying record keeping, and human relations skills.

Sexual harassment of office staff members. Sexual harassment of office staff members is a problem that has been revealed in recent years. Newspaper stories and court cases have described how sexual harassment in business and corporate affairs has been used against women who want promotions, salary raises, and to stay on the job. Managers must recognize that such methods cannot be tolerated. The manager who uses sexual harassment to achieve personal desires is asking for trouble. This trouble may take the form of litigation, public censure, reprimand, or dismissal.

In a few cases managers, seeking to achieve their own personal goals, have been unjustly accused of sexual harassment. The best advice for managers is to behave in such a way that their behavior does not suggest they are making advances toward members of the opposite sex.

OFFICE SPACE

The central office for the physical education and athletic departments should be readily accessible. This office should be near health service and athletic training offices, gymnasiums, exercise rooms, locker rooms, athletic fields, and other facilities of the department.

Most central offices for physical education and athletics should consist of at least three divisions: general reception area, clerical space, and private offices. Other desirable features to be considered are a rest room, storage room, and conference room for staff and other meetings.

General reception area

The general reception area is used by visitors as a waiting room or information center, for staff members who desire to get their mail, have appointments, or wish information, and for office services in general. It should be attractive, with comfortable chairs, bulletin boards, and other items essential to carrying out the necessary administrative routines and creating a warm, friendly atmosphere. A counter or railing

should separate the general waiting room from the rest of the office facilities. This helps ensure greater privacy and more efficient conduct of office responsibilities.

Clerical space

The clerical space should be separated from the general waiting and reception room. It should be equipped with typewriters, files, tables, and telephones. It is often desirable to have a private alcove or office for one or more of the secretaries, depending on the size of the department and office. Privacy is often needed for typing, preparing reports, or for the convenience of visitors and other personnel. There should be ample lighting and sufficient space for freedom of movement so duties can be carried out with a minimum of confusion and difficulty.

Private offices

The chairperson of the department and possibly other staff members, depending on the size of the department, should have private offices. The offices should be large enough so that the persons in charge of management can concentrate on their work without interruptions, have private conferences with students, staff members, or visitors; and in general carry out their duties as efficiently as possible. The offices should be equipped appropriately. Desks should be neat and large enough, with calendars, schedule pads for appointments and conferences, and other essential materials. Filing cabinets, storage cabinets, and other equipment should be provided as needed.

OFFICE PERSONNEL

The number of office personnel depends on the size of the department. The staff can consist of secretaries, stenographers, transcribing machine operators, receptionist, switchboard operator, and typists in a large department. However, the office usually consists of one secretary. In some small schools, student help may be all the personnel available.

The *secretary* should be a good right arm to the chairperson and to the department as a whole. To be most helpful, he or she will be a typist, a stenographer, a public relations representative, will operate

The computer is a valuable tool in the office.

a word processor, computer, photocopier, and duplicating machine, and will see that the office runs smoothly. The secretary will help the chairperson and other staff members remember facts, appointments, and other important information. He or she should know where materials are filed and be able to obtain them quickly, relieve the supervisor of minor details, and see that reports are sent out on time and that accurate records are kept.

A *stenographer* is a typist who can also take shorthand. A stenographer, however, does not have the confidential duties a secretary has. Large departments frequently have stenographic pools where individuals are on call to do work for any staff member having work to be done.

A *transcribing operator* listens to dictated material on a playback mechanism then types the material in accordance with the instructions given.

A *receptionist's* position will vary with the department. In some departments a receptionist is a greeter who presents an attractive appearance and is polite, courteous, and helpful to callers. Some departments

also assign to this person certain typing, filing, and telephone duties, in addition to the reception of callers.

Large departments frequently have *switchboard operators* who cover the phones for many staff members and other personnel. Frequently staff members are not in, and messages are then relayed by the switchboard operator through the prescribed channels.

Office personnel should be selected very carefully. Experience, character, personality, appearance, and ability should play important roles in the selection process. The secretary should have, as a minimum, a high school diploma. An individual who has been through a secretarial course and who has a good background in typing, bookkeeping, English, and secretarial practice is valuable to the department.

The chairperson of the department and other staff members should treat a secretary and other office personnel with respect. Staff members should be patient and see that clerical help know the details of their jobs, should recognize the importance of each, and should appreciate the responsibilities of those positions.

In small elementary schools, high schools, and colleges, the manager may have to rely partially or entirely on students to get some of the clerical work accomplished. In-service education should take place for these students to see that acceptable procedures are followed in filing, typing, mimeographing, maintaining records, and performing other office duties.

EQUIPMENT AND SUPPLIES

Whether or not an office is efficient depends on the equipment and supplies available. The materials needed vary with the size of the organization. In smaller organizations equipment such as computers might be readily available in the central office but not in department offices. Following are some of the items that should be considered:

Adding machine	Paper cutter
Bookcases	Paste
Bulletin boards	Pencil sharpeners
Buzzers	Pencils and pens
Calendars	Reproducing machines
Chairs	Rulers
Clips	Safe
Coat racks	Scissors
Clock	Scrapbooks
Computer	Stamps
Desk baskets	Stapling machine
Desk lights	Stationery and paper
Desk pads	Tables
Desks	Telephone
Dictionaries	Typewriters
Ditto machine	Umbrella rack
First aid cabinet	Wardrobe cabinets
Letter trays	Wastebaskets
Magazine racks	

OFFICE WORK AND AUTOMATION

Whether or not new automated equipment should be installed in the office depends on such factors as the extent of the program the office serves, the amount of clerical work that needs to be done, and the size of the budget.

When considering whether or not more mechanized equipment should be added to the office, five important questions should be asked: (1) *How much labor will it save?* In other words, can it result in the elimination of office personnel or can it result in not having to hire another office worker? (2) *How much time will it save?* Will it provide office personnel with more time to perform other essential tasks? (3) *Will it ensure more accuracy?* Will the machine help eliminate human errors such as those involved in computation tasks? (4) *Will it provide for a more efficient office operation?* (5) *Is the cost of the machine a sound investment?* Will the machine pay for itself in the work it performs? (6) *Will the machine contribute to the morale of office staff members?* Will the machine eliminate some tasks office staff members find difficult or tedious and take an inordinate amount of time?

Automation as used here refers to processing data by some mechanical device or system other than typewriters, adding machines, calculators, and photocopiers. Automation can be used in handling such items as accounts payable, cumulative records, health records, inventories, personnel records, schedules, work requests, and transcripts.

An organization can use automation either by installing its own machines or by working through some business organization that processes educational data for a fee. Also, joining with several other departments or organizations for such a service works well in some situations. Depending on the size of the operation, it may be that with automation a job can be done better, hiring additional personnel can be eliminated, and the cost can be lower.

THE COMPUTER AND OFFICE MANAGEMENT

In 1983 sales of personal computers reached approximately 3.5 million units. The number of desktop computers in schools is estimated to be at least one million. It is predicted that by 1990 65% of all professional, managerial, and administrative workers will be using computers.[1]

The Department of Parks and Recreation in Hartford, Connecticut, realized the potential of the computer in its project Leisure Match. The department developed a computer information service for Hartford residents in order to familiarize them with the many leisure opportunities the city was providing. It enabled interested individuals to match leisure interests to leisure opportunities, helped people to better understand and enjoy new and different leisure experiences, and provided management with a computerized information system that not only resulted in a better program but also contributed to future planning and resource allocation. As a result, *Leisure Match* has stimulated greater use of existing programs and opportunities.[1]

Tenneco Incorporated has a computer system to help achieve the goals of its industrial health and fitness program. The computer has been particularly helpful in areas such as providing demographic and exercise data on employees, in keeping a record of employee activity workouts, fitness and medical testing data, and exercise logging.[1]

The use of the computer is not only taking place in parks and recreation programs and in industrial fitness programs but also to some degree in physical education and athletic programs in various organizations. However, because many staff members are unfamiliar with computers, the full potential of the computer has not yet been realized.

Computer contributions to management

A computer is a machine that can, among other things, program administrative functions in areas such as physical education and athletics. It possesses a memory and when given a set of instructions will perform them at incredible speeds. It can take data concerning physical education and athletic programs and process that information by performing mathematical and logical operations.

The main advantages for management in using a computer include *speed;* it saves a considerable amount of time (for example, the addition that one person could do in 100 days can be done in 10 seconds on a computer). A second advantage is *accuracy;* the computer does not make errors if fed the right information. A third advantage is that it *imposes discipline;* a person must thoroughly understand a problem before programming the computer to give the right answer. A fourth advantage is *versatility;* the computer can add, subtract, multiply, divide, sort, and compare.[1]

Use of computer in physical education program at Riverside-Brookfield High School, Riverside, Ill.

Areas of computer use in management

The computer can be especially valuable in the areas of finance, personnel, programs, and facilities. In the area of finance the computer can be helpful in such management tasks as handling payrolls, inventories, budgets, cost analysis, and general accounting. In the area of personnel the computer can save much clerical work and be of help in such areas as student registration, grade reporting, grade recording, faculty assignments, and staff retention. In the area of programs the computer can assist management in the designing of programs and scheduling of students or other clientele for particular classes. It can record facts concerned with students' interests, faculty availability, complex scheduling, and staff use. In the area of facilities the computer will be an asset for management in providing for the best use of building space, availability of facilities, equipment inventory, cost of building maintenance, and future needs of projected buildings and other facilities.

To be more specific, physical educators are interested in having complete records on faculty and staff regarding names, addresses, phone numbers, teaching background, and teaching loads, and the computer will be an asset in having such records filed away and immediately accessible. Registration of students and class scheduling can be better accomplished. The computer can accurately report which gymnasiums, swimming pools, tennis courts, weight rooms, basketball courts, baseball fields, and other facilities are in use at any particular time. The computer can be used to keep physical fitness records on every student or member of an organization. Instead of keeping individual cards on each person the computer would have a master file of physical fitness data for each person. The computer can keep class attendance records and can be used to compare prices for equipment and supplies.

Computer use in athletics

Many of the management tasks listed above are also part of the athletic program. Other uses for the computer in athletic programs would be the scheduling of games and facilities, data on players in a school or organization, and identifying their weaknesses and strengths. It can keep individual statistics on every team member. In baseball it can keep a record of the team roster, how many games each player participated in, batting and fielding averages, individual records for the team, and other important information. In the area of scouting the computer can keep records on strengths and weaknesses of opposing teams, show what plays and strategies are most effective, and predict probability of success for the various plays that are used in games (Fig. 15-1).

The computer can be used effectively in physical education and athletic programs. It can be programmed to aid in management decision making at all levels. The main point is recognizing that many management tasks, whether concerned with bookkeeping, class scheduling, or record keeping, can be handled by the computer. To be able to apply various programs to everyday management problems will be helpful to the organization. The economy and accuracy of the computer cannot be matched by the clerical staff.

MANAGEMENT ROUTINE

The management routine or manner in which the day-to-day business of the department is carried out by the office represents the basic reason why such a facility exists. Therefore this matter should receive careful consideration.

Office hours

The office should be open during regular hours. This usually means from 8 or 9 AM to 4 or 5 PM. During this time someone should always be present to answer the telephone, greet visitors, and answer questions. Some exceptions to these hours may be made, but even in these cases regular office hours that have been publicized as widely as possible are essential.

Staff members should also have regular office hours when they will be accessible to colleagues and others who would like to see them. These office hours should be posted, office personnel informed, and the schedule carefully observed so requests for information and assistance can be properly handled.

Assignments

All assignments, whether for office personnel or staff members, should be clear, in writing, and properly publicized. Office personnel may be required to set

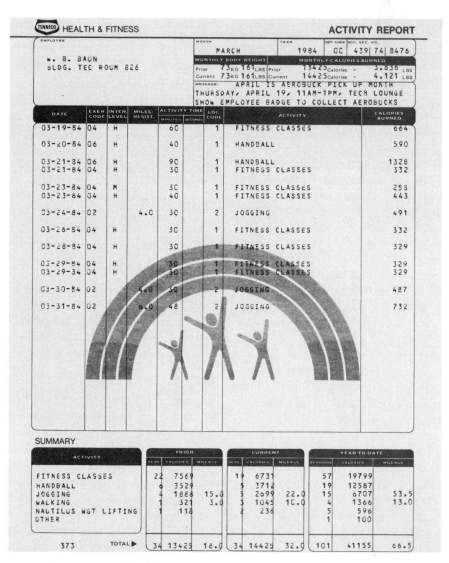

Fig. 15-1. Computer Activity Report used in Health and Fitness Program at Tenneco Inc., Houston, Tex.

clocks, take messages, mimeograph daily or weekly bulletins, distribute minor supplies, check the calendar of events, provide messenger service, or assist in health examinations. These details should be clearly understood and carried out at the proper time. Specific responsibilities should be fixed and a schedule of duties prepared to prevent any misunderstanding.

Correspondence

Correspondence represents a most effective public relations medium. Letters can be written in a cold, impersonal manner, or they can carry warmth and help interpret what a program expects and is trying to do for a student or other person. Letters should be prepared carefully, using proper grammar and a neat manner that meets the highest standards of secretarial practice. If a physical educator must do his or her own letters, these same standards should be met. Letters should convey the feeling that the department is anxious to help wherever possible. Letters should be answered promptly, not placed in a drawer and left for weeks or months. Carbon copies of letters should be made and filed for future reference.

Files and filing

The office should contain steel filing cases for vertical filing. The filing system used depends on the number of personnel involved and the person doing the filing, but in any case it should be simple and practical. Files usually consist of correspondence and informational material. For ease of finding material, some form of alphabetical filing should usually be used, although numerical filing may at times be practical. The alphabetical files can be done on a name or subject basis (for example, ''Brown, Charles A.'' or ''Health Examinations'') using a manila folder for all the material to be filed under the name or subject (Fig. 15-2). Cross references should be included to facilitate finding material. Guide cards can be used to show which divisions of the file pertain to each letter of the alphabet, thus facilitating the search for material.

A visible filing system for any current records and reports that are used constantly proves helpful. These records are usually prepared on cards, and the visible filing case contains flat drawers that show the names or index numbers when pulled outward.

Office files should be kept accurately. The person

GIRLS' PHYSICAL FITNESS TEST RECORD

Name				Grade		Period	
School		Age	Ht.	Wt.	Test 1 Classification		
		Age	Ht.	Wt.	Test 2 Classification		

Test No.	1		2	
Date				
Event	Score	Percentile	Score	Percentile
Modified Pull-Ups				
Sit-Ups (Max 50)				
Broad Jump				
50-yd. Dash				
Shuttle Run				
Modified Push-Ups				
600-yd. Run-Walk				
Softball Throw				
P.F.I.—Average percentile of 5 events				

Fig. 15-2. Girls' physical fitness test records that are kept in office.

filing should be careful to see that the letter or other material gets into the proper folder and that the folder gets into its correct location. Filing should also be kept up to date. A periodic review of the files should be made to weed out material that is no longer pertinent to the department. Files that for any reason are removed from the cabinet should be returned. If one is kept out for any length of time, an "out" sign should be substituted, showing where it is.

Telephone

The use of the office telephone is a major consideration for good departmental public relations. A few simple rules that should be observed follow.

Promptness. The telephone should be answered as promptly as possible. Answering promptly reflects efficient office practice and consideration for the person calling.

Professional purposes. The telephone is installed in an office for professional purposes. Office personnel should not be permitted to talk for long periods of time about personal matters. The telephone should be kept clear for business important to the achievement of professional objectives.

Courtesy, friendliness, and helpfulness. The person answering the phone should be pleasant and courteous and should desire to be of assistance to the caller. This should be the procedure at all times. Such a telephone manner represents a professional responsibility that should be carried out with regularity.

Messages. At times staff members who are being called will not be available. A pencil and telephone pad should be kept at hand for recording calls in such cases, and a definite procedure should be established for relaying these messages to the proper persons.

Appointments

Appointments should not be made unless it is believed they can be kept. Furthermore, all appointments should be kept as close to the time scheduled as possible. Many times the person making an appointment has arranged his or her day with the understanding that the conference will be at a certain time. If this time is not adhered to, it means the schedule has to be altered, and complications frequently arise as a result.

The secretary should keep an accurate list of appointments. If no secretary is available, the staff member should keep his or her own schedule of appointments and check it regularly to see that it is met.

RECORDS AND REPORTS

At times records and reports are not prepared and maintained accurately because the directions given by the chairperson of the department or the staff members are not clear and definite. When complicated reports are to be prepared, oral instructions by themselves will usually not be sufficient. Instead, directions should be written, typed, and distributed. The preparation of a sample will also help ensure better results.

Managers are often responsible for poorly kept records, inaccurate reports, and late submissions. Directions should be clear, with announcements at regular intervals, reminders of when reports are due, and a prompt checking of reports to see if they are all in and whether there are any omissions or other inaccuracies.

A survey was conducted of 21 school systems to determine the types of records that were kept in departmental files for physical education personnel (Fig. 15-3). The results of this survey showed that some of the schools were conscientious in record keeping and others were not. In general, most of the department heads and teachers admitted they should put more time and effort into this phase of physical education administration.

The survey showed that in some schools records were kept in the physical education department, whereas in other schools these same records were kept in another department. For example, in some schools attendance records were kept by the physical education department, but in other schools an attendance officer had complete control. In some schools the physical education department kept records on health; in other schools these records were kept by the school nurse. The same was true regarding budgetary and inventory records. Some heads of physical education departments kept these records, whereas the business manager and principal kept them in other schools.

X denotes records kept	Accident	Adapted program	Application for participation in interscholastic sports	Attendance	Cumulative class record	Equipment	Extracurricular activities	Game reports	Health	Interscholastic sports	Intramurals	Inventory	Medical form for inter-scholastic sports	Medical form for physical education	Parental permission sports	Physical fitness
School 1	X			X	X				X	X	X					X
School 2		X			X			X			X	X			X	X
School 3	X	X		X					X	X					X	X
School 4	X			X		X						X	X	X	X	X
School 5		X			X					X			X		X	X
School 6	X	X		X	X			X			X	X	X		X	X
School 7	X			X								X				X
School 8	X		X	X	X		X		X	X	X	X			X	X
School 9	X			X												
School 10	X			X					X		X		X	X	X	X
School 11	X	X	X	X		X				X	X	X			X	
School 12		X		X		X				X	X	X				X
School 13	X	X	X	X	X		X				X	X				
School 14		X		X							X				X	X
School 15	X		X	X	X	X		X	X	X				X	X	
School 16	X			X					X			X		X		
School 17				X								X			X	
School 18			X						X						X	X
School 19	X			X										X		X
School 20	X			X					X				X		X	X
School 21	X		X	X	X	X	X		X	X	X		X			X

Fig. 15-3. Physical education records used in 21 schools.

CHECKLIST OF SOME IMPORTANT CONSIDERATIONS FOR OFFICE MANAGEMENT

Space and working conditions   Yes   No

1. Does the reception room provide ample space for waiting guests? _____ _____
2. Is the clerical space separated from the reception room so office work is not interrupted by the arrival of guests? _____ _____
3. Are there private offices for the director of physical education and athletics and as many staff members as possible? _____ _____
4. Is there an up-to-date health suite that provides an office and other essential facilities for the school nurse? _____ _____
5. Are there adequate space and equipment for filing? _____ _____
6. Are file drawers arranged so papers can be inserted and removed easily and with space for future expansion? _____ _____
7. Is the office arranged so as many workers as possible get the best natural light, with glare from sunlight or reflected sunlight avoided? _____ _____
8. Has the office space been painted in accordance with the best in color dynamics? _____ _____
9. Have provisions been made so unnecessary noise is eliminated, distractions are kept to a minimum, and cleanliness prevails? _____ _____
10. Is there good ventilation, appropriate artificial lighting, and satisfactory heating conditions? _____ _____
11. Is the value of the computer recognized? _____ _____

Personnel

12. Is a receptionist available to greet guests and answer queries? _____ _____
13. Is there a recorded analysis of the duties of each secretarial position? _____ _____
14. Are channels available for ascertaining causes of dissatisfaction among secretarial help? _____ _____
15. Do secretaries dress neatly and conservatively? _____ _____
16. Do secretaries maintain a desk that has an orderly appearance and clear their desks of working papers each day? _____ _____
17. Do secretaries concern themselves with the efficiency of the office? _____ _____
18. Are secretaries loyal to the department and staff members? _____ _____
19. Do staff members have regular office hours? _____ _____
20. Are appointments kept promptly? _____ _____
21. Is up-to-date reading material furnished for waiting guests? _____ _____
22. Does the office help continually pay attention to maintaining offices that are neat, with papers, books, and other materials arranged in an orderly manner? _____ _____
23. Are the secretaries knowledgeable about departmental activities so that they can answer intelligently queries about staff members and activities? _____ _____
24. Do secretaries wait on guests promptly and courteously? _____ _____
25. Are letters typed neatly, well placed on the sheet, properly spaced, free from erasures, smudge, and typographic errors? _____ _____
26. Is correspondence handled promptly? _____ _____
27. Is the filing system easily learned and is the filing done promptly so the work does not pile up? _____ _____
28. Does the office routine use human time and energy efficiently eliminating duplicate operations or forms? _____ _____
29. Are the most effective and efficient office methods used? _____ _____

CHECKLIST OF SOME IMPORTANT CONSIDERATIONS FOR OFFICE MANAGEMENT—cont'd

Procedures	Yes	No
30. Is the clerical output satisfactory, with work starting promptly in the morning and after lunch, breaks taken according to schedule, and work stoppage taking place as scheduled?	____	____
31. Has a streamlined procedure been developed so telephones are answered promptly, guests are courteously treated, and personal argument and gossiping eliminated?	____	____
32. Are essential records properly maintained and kept up to date?	____	____
33. Have procedures for typing and duplicating course outlines, committee reports, examinations, bulletins, fliers, letters, and announcements been developed to eliminatae uncertainty or confusion on the part of staff members?	____	____
34. Are regular office hours for staff posted and known so office staff members can make appointments as needed?	____	____
35. Are secretaries acquainted with such details as securing films and other visual aids, obtaining reference material, helping in registration, duplicating material, and obtaining additional forms and records?	____	____
36. Is the office covered continuously during working hours?	____	____

Examples of reports and records maintained by the physical education departments include the following:

Health records and reports

Health consultation request
Medical examination record
Health history
Growth records
Excuse forms
Exercise card
Height and weight card
Body mechanics inspection form
Films and visual aids list
Health habits record form
Accident records

Physical education activity, skill, and squad records and reports

Basket card
Physical education record
Field event report card

Physical education test and achievement forms

Physical fitness record
Report to parents
Résumé of personality traits

Citizenship guide sheet
Athletic report

Physical education attendance and excuse records and reports

Squad card attendance record
Appointment slip
Absence report
Change of program

Physical education equipment forms

Padlock record
Equipment record
Equipment inventory and condition report
Lost property report

SUMMARY

Office management is an important consideration in the administration of physical education and athletic programs. It concerns such matters as communication, correspondence, processing materials, record keeping, and public relations. It is the nerve center of the operation; therefore, if the department or other unit of the organization is to be well run, much attention must be given to office management. Things such as space, personnel, equipment, computers, management routine, records, and reports should receive continual attention.

SELF-ASSESSMENT TESTS

These tests will assist students in determining if material and competencies presented in this chapter have been mastered.

1. Why is sound office management essential to effective public relations? What are some important reasons why office management is important to a department of physical education and athletics?
2. In what ways can the computer be used in physical education and athletic programs?
3. As a manager of a large high school physical education and athletic program, describe the office personnel you would need and then justify your request.
4. Establish a set of rules for an effective management routine with respect to (a) office hours, (b) assignments, (c) correspondence, (d) files and filing, (e) telephone, and (f) appointments.
5. Prepare a set of sample records you would want to maintain as part of a small elementary, junior high school, and senior high school physical education and athletic program.

REFERENCE

1. Jensen, M.A.: Computer applications: an introduction, Journal of Physical Education, Recreation and Dance **55:**32, April 1984.

SUGGESTED READINGS

• Asbury, G.: Bringing your operations into the computer age, Athletic Purchasing and Facilities **7:**20, March 1983.
  The assistant athletic director at Stanford University describes a computer-based system for managing facility operations and maintenance and how it has helped turn a $1-million annual budget deficit into a surplus.

• Baun, W.B., and Baun, M.: A corporate health and fitness program: motivation and management by computers, Journal of Physical Education, Recreation and Dance **55:** 42, April 1984.
  Describes how Tenneco uses computers in its industrial health and fitness program to achieve departmental goals and objectives.

• Cicciarella, C.A.: Getting into the computer game: guidelines and pitfalls, Journal of Physical Education, Recreation and Dance **55:**46, April 1984.
  Suggests procedural guidelines for selecting, acquiring, and installing computer hardware and software.

• Coventry, W.F., and Burstiner, I.: Management: A Basic Handbook, Englewood Cliffs, N.J., 1977, Prentice-Hall, Inc.
  A book devoted to management with many implications for office management.

• Dougherty, N.J., and Bonanno, D.: Management Principles In Sport and Leisure Services, Minneapolis, 1985, Burgess Publishing.
  Chapter 8, Computer Utilization, and Chapter 11, Time Management, offer guidelines for use of computers and how management can more efficiently use its time on the job.

• Tontimonia, T.L.: Choosing a computer that fits your needs, Athletic Business **8:**32, October 1984.
  Tells how to choose a computer that fits the needs of any particular organization or program.

• Turner, J.A.: A personal computer for every freshman: even faculty skeptics are now enthusiasts, Chronicle Of Higher Education February 1985.
  Tells how some colleges and universities are providing students with computers and how they are being used.

Appendixes

Appendix A

The Sixth National Conference of City and County Directors of the AAHPERD spent considerable time on the subject of crowd control at athletic contests. A summary of their discussions follows:

APPROACHES TO CROWD CONTROL
Summary of reports: small group discussions

The nature and seriousness of the problems in crowd control have recently become more drastic and bizarre as they have occurred with increasing frequency. They take on the collective character of a deliberate attempt either to ignore or confront the system. This social problem may be impossible to eliminate completely, but an attempt must be made to cope with the immediate symptoms. Our only hope is for imaginative and coordinated efforts by the school administration, the majority of students, and community authorities to promote standards of conduct conducive to continuing spectator sports in comparative tranquility. The alternatives are to allow a disruptive element to completely negate the nature of school athletics, to play with no spectators, or to abandon the activity.

The following will present some causes of crowd control problems and some approaches to solutions.

Some causes of problems

Lack of anticipation of, and preventive planning for, possible trouble

Lack of proper facilities

Poor communication resulting in lack of information

Lack of involvement of one or more of the following: school administration, faculty, student body, parents, community, press, and law enforcement agencies

Lack of respect for authority and property

Attendance at games of youth under the influence of narcotics

Increased attitude of permissiveness

School dropouts, recent graduates, and outsiders

Some approaches to solutions

Develop written policy statements, guidelines, and regulations for crowd control

1. Consult the following before writing policy statements or promulgating regulations: a school administration, athletic director, coaches, faculty members involved in the school sports program, school youth organizations, local police departments
2. Properly and efficiently administer regulations and provide for good communications
3. Constantly evaluate regulations and guidelines for their relevance and effectiveness
4. Make guidelines and regulations so effective that the director of athletics who follows them is secure in knowing he or she has planned with the staff for any eventuality and has sufficient help to cope with any situation that may arise

Provide adequate facilities

1. Plan and design stadiums, fieldhouses, and gymnasiums for effective crowd control
2. Provide for adequate rest room facilities
3. Establish a smoking area when indoor contests are held
4. Complete preparation of facilities before game time

Teach good sportsmanship throughout the school and the community

1. Begin education in good sportsmanship in the earliest grades and continue it throughout school life
2. Make frequent approving references to constructive and commendable behavior

3. Arrange for program appearances by faculty members and students jointly to discuss the true values of athletic competition including good sportsmanship

4. Make use of all news media through frequent and effective television, radio, and press presentations and interviews, commentaries, and frequent announcement of good sportsmanship slogans

5. Distribute a printed Code of Ethics for Good Sportsmanship

6. Include the good sportsmanship slogan in all printed programs at sports events

7. Urge the use of athletic events as an example in elementary school citizenship classes, stressing positive values of good conduct at games, during the raising of the flag, and singing of the national anthem; courtesy toward visitors

8. Involve teachers in school athletic associations, provide them with passes to all sports events, and stress the positive values of their setting an example of good sportsmanship

Intensify communications before scheduled games

1. Arrange for an exchange of speakers at school assembly programs; the principals, coaches, or team captains could visit the opposing school

2. Discuss with appropriate personnel of the competing school the procedures for the game, including method and location of team entry and departure

3. Provide superintendent or principal, athletic director, and coach with a copy of the written policy statement, guidelines and regulations

4. Meet all game officials and request them to stress good sportsmanship on the field

5. Meet with coaches and instruct them not to question officials during a contest; stress the importance of good sportsmanship and that their conduct sets the tone for spectator reaction to game incidents

6. Instruct students what to expect and what is expected of them

7. Schedule preventive planning conferences with local police to be assured of their full cooperation and effectiveness in spectator control

Inform the community

1. Request coaches and athletic directors to talk to service groups and other community groups

2. Invite community leaders (nonschool people) to attend athletic events

3. Post on all available notice boards around town, in factories and other public places, posters showing the Sportsmanship Code of Ethics and Guidelines in brief

4. Release constructive information and positive statements to news media and request publication of brief guidelines on sports pages

5. Provide news media with pertinent information as to ways in which the community may directly and indirectly render assistance in the crowd control problem

Involve law enforcement personnel

1. Police and other security personnel should be strategically located so as to afford the best possible control

2. Law enforcement professionals should handle *all* enforcement and disciplining of spectators

3. Strength in force may be shown by appearance of several policemen, motorcycles, police cruise cars, etc., at and near the site of the game

4. Women police may be stationed in women's rest rooms

5. Civil Defense organizations could patrol parking areas

6. A faculty member from the visiting school may be used as a liaison with police and local faculty in identifying visiting students

7. Attendents, police, county sheriffs, deputies should be in uniform. Uniformed authority figures command greater respect

Use supervisory personnel other than police

1. Select carefully teacher supervisors who are attentive and alert to signs of possible trouble

2. Identify faculty members by arm bands or other means

3. Provide for communication by means of walkie-talkie systems

4. Assign some faculty members to sit behind the visiting fans; this reduces verbal harassment of visitors

5. Employ paid ticket takers and paid chaperones to mingle strategically among the crowd and to remain on duty throughout the game, including half-time

6. Issue passes to junior high physical education teachers to provide more adult supervision

Continued.

APPROACHES TO CROWD CONTROL
Summary of reports: small group discussions—cont'd

Plan for ticket sales and concession stands

1. Arrange for advance sale of student tickets to avoid congestion at the gate
2. Sell tickets in advance only to students in their own schools, and avoid sale of tickets to outsiders and nonstudents
3. Provide for a close check at the gate or entrance
4. Arrange for concession stands to be open before the game, during half-time, and after the game, but closed during actual play
5. Channel the flow of traffic to and from concession stands by means of ropes, or other means; keep traffic moving

Prepare spectators and contestants

1. Encourage as many students as possible to be in the uniforms of the athletic club, pep club, booster clubs, band, majorettes, cheerleaders
2. Bus participants to and from the site of the game
3. Have participants dressed to play before leaving for a game or contest
4. Adhere to established seating capacity of stadiums and gymnasiums
5. Request home team fans to remain in their own stands until visiting team fans have left
6. Try to arrange for a statewide athletic association regulation prohibiting all noise makers including musical instruments except for the school band or orchestra under professional supervision
7. Request the assistance of visiting clubs
8. Educate cheerleaders, student leaders, band captains, pep squads, and faculty supervisors by means of a one day conference program
9. Keep spectators buffered from the playing area as much as practical
10. Request that elementary school children be accompanied by an adult

Miscellaneous

1. Inform and involve school superintendents fully when problems arise in connection with sports events

2. Impose severe penalties on faculty and student leaders guilty of poor conduct
3. Publish the identity of offenders at games and notify parents, if possible; any penalties inflicted should also be noted (Note: If the offense leads to juvenile court action, care should be taken not to contravene laws about publishing names of juvenile offenders)
4. Consistently enforce rules and regulations; this is a necessity
5. Work toward the assumption of responsibility for strong regulation and enforcement of team behavior on the part of the state athletic associations
6. Attempt to work with the courts toward greater co-operation
7. Avoid overstressing the winning of games
8. Discontinue double headers and triple headers
9. After-game incidents away from the proximity of the stadium or gymnasium are out of the control of school officials, but cause bad public reaction

Summary

Sound safety and crowd controls at school athletic functions are a must! Greater concentration on treating the causes of the problem is essential. Preliminary groundwork is the key to good crowd control. Coordination and cooperation of school and law enforcement agencies is the key to success.

Youths should be taught to know what to expect and what is expected of them. Consistent enforcement of rules and regulations in a necessity if youth is to respect authority. Adult behavior should be such that it may be advantageously and admirably emulated by youth whose actions hopefully may result in deserving praise instead of negative criticism and disapproval.

The athletic program is a constructive and valuable school activity. It should be premitted to function in a favorable, healthful, and friendly environment.

Appendix B

CHECKLIST FOR FACILITY PLANNERS

General   Yes   No

1. A clear-cut statement has been prepared on the nature and scope of the program, and the special requirements for space, equipment, fixtures, and facilities dictated by the activities to be conducted.   _____   _____

2. The facility has been planned to meet the total requirements of the program as well as the special needs of those who are to be served.   _____   _____

3. The plans and specifications have been checked by all governmental agencies (city, county, and state) whose approval is required by law.   _____   _____

4. Plans for areas and facilities conform to state and local regulations and to accepted standards and practices.   _____   _____

5. The areas and facilities planned make possible the programs that serve the interests and needs of all people.   _____   _____

6. Every available source of property or funds has been explored, evaluated, and used whenever appropriate.   _____   _____

7. All interested persons and organizations concerned with the facility have had an opportunity to share in its planning (professional educators, users, consultants, administrators, engineers, architects, program specialists, building managers, and builder—a team approach).   _____   _____

8. The facility and its appurtenances will fulfill the maximum demands of the program. The program has not been curtailed to fit the facility.   _____   _____

9. The facility has been functionally planned to meet the present and anticipated needs of specific programs, situations, and publics.   _____   _____

10. Future additions are included in present plans to permit economy of construction.   _____   _____

11. Lecture classrooms are isolated from distracting noises.   _____   _____

12. Storage areas for indoor and outdoor equipment are adequately sized. They are located adjacent to the gymnasiums.   _____   _____

13. Shelves in storage rooms are slanted toward the wall.   _____   _____

14. All passageways are free of obstructions; fixtures are recessed.   _____   _____

15. Facilities for health services, athletic training, health testing, health instruction, and the first aid and emergency-isolation rooms are suitably interrelated.   _____   _____

16. Buildings, specific areas, and facilities are clearly identified.   _____   _____

17. Locker rooms are arranged for ease of supervision.   _____   _____

18. Offices, teaching stations, and service facilities are properly interrelated.   _____   _____

19. Special needs of the physically handicapped are met, including a ramp into the building at a major entrance.   _____   _____

20. All "dead space" is used.   _____   _____

Adapted from Participants in National Facilities Conference, updated by the author.   *Continued.*

CHECKLIST FOR FACILITY PLANNERS—cont'd

General—cont'd	Yes	No

21. The building is compatible in design and comparable in quality and accommodation to other organizational structures. _____ _____

22. Storage rooms are accessible to the play area. _____ _____

23. Workrooms, conference rooms, and staff and administrative offices are interrelated. _____ _____

24. Shower and dressing facilities are provided for professional staff members and are conveniently located. _____ _____

25. Thought and attention have been given to making facilities and equipment as durable and vandalproof as possible. _____ _____

26. Low-cost maintenance features have been adequately considered. _____ _____

27. This facility is a part of a well-integrated master plan. _____ _____

28. All areas, courts, facilities, equipment, climate control, security, etc., conform rigidly to detailed standards and specifications. _____ _____

29. Shelves are recessed and mirrors are supplied in appropriate places in rest rooms and dressing rooms. Mirrors are not placed above lavatories. _____ _____

30. Dressing space between locker rows is adjusted to the size and age level of participants. _____ _____

31. Drinking fountains are conveniently placed in locker room areas or immediately adjacent thereto. _____ _____

32. Special attention is given to provision for the locking of service windows and counters, supply bins, carts, shelves, and racks. _____ _____

33. Provision is made for the repair, maintenance, replacement, and off-season storage of equipment and uniforms. _____ _____

34. A well-defined program for laundering and cleaning of towels, uniforms, and equipment is included in the plan. _____ _____

35. Noncorrosive metal is used in dressing, drying, and shower areas except for enameled lockers. _____ _____

36. Antipanic hardware is used where required by fire regulations. _____ _____

37. Properly placed hose bibbs and drains are sufficient in size and quantity to permit flushing the entire area with a water hose. _____ _____

38. A water-resistant, coved base is used under the locker base and floor mat, and where floor and wall join. _____ _____

39. Chalkboards and/or tackboards with map tracks are located in appropriate places in dressing rooms, hallways, and classrooms. _____ _____

40. Book shelves are provided in toilet areas. _____ _____

41. Space and equipment are planned in accordance with the types and number of participants. _____ _____

42. Basement rooms, being undesirable for dressing, drying, and showering, are not planned for those purposes. _____ _____

43. Spectator seating (permanent) in areas that are basically instructional is kept at a minimum. Rollaway bleachers are used primarily. Balcony seating is considered as a possibility. _____ _____

44. Well-lighted and effectively displayed trophy cases enhance the interest and beauty of the lobby. _____ _____

CHECKLIST FOR FACILITY PLANNERS—cont'd

	Yes	No
45. The space under the stairs is used for storage.		
46. Department heads' offices are located near the central administrative office, which includes a well-planned conference room.		
47. Workrooms are located near the central office and serve as a repository for department materials and records.		
48. The conference area includes a cloak room, lavatory, and toilet.		
49. In addition to regular secretarial offices established in the central and department chairperson's offices, a special room to house a secretarial pool for staff members is provided.		
50. Staff dressing facilities are provided. These facilities may also serve game officials.		
51. The community and/or neighborhood has a "round table"—planning round table.		
52. All those (persons and agencies) who should be a party to planning and development are invited and actively engaged in the planning process.		
53. Space and area relationships are important. They have been carefully considered.		
54. Both long-range plans and immediate plans have been made.		
55. The body comfort of the student and other participants, a major factor in securing maximum learning, has been considered in the plans.		
56. Plans for quiet areas have been made.		
57. In the planning, consideration has been given to the need for adequate recreation areas and facilities, both near and distant from the homes of people.		
58. Plans recognize the primary function of recreation as being enrichment of learning through creative self-expression, self-enhancement, and the achievement of self-potential.		
59. Every effort has been exercised to eliminate hazards.		
60. The installation of low-hanging door closers, light fixtures, signs, and other objects in traffic areas has been avoided.		
61. Warning signals, both visible and audible, are included in the plans.		
62. Ramps have a slope equal to or less than a 1-foot rise in 12 feet.		
63. Minimum landings for ramps are 5 feet × 5 feet, they extend at least 1 foot beyond the swinging arc of a door, have at least a 6-foot clearance at the bottom, and have level platforms at 30-foot intervals on every turn.		
64. Adequate locker and dressing spaces are provided.		
65. The design of dressing, drying, and shower areas reduces foot traffic to a minimum and establishes clean, dry aisles for bare feet.		
66. Teaching stations are properly related to service facilities.		
67. Toilet facilities are adequate in number. They are located to serve all groups for which provisions are made.		
68. Mail services, outgoing and incoming, are included in the plans.		
69. Hallways, ramps, doorways, and elevators are designed to permit equipment to be moved easily and quickly.		
70. A keying design suited to administrative and instructional needs is planned.		
71. Toilets used by large groups have circulating (in and out) entrances and exits.		

Continued.

CHECKLIST FOR FACILITY PLANNERS—cont'd

	Yes	No
Climate control		

1. Provision is made throughout the building for climate control—heating, ventilating, and refrigerated cooling.   _____ _____
2. Special ventilation is provided for locker, dressing, shower, drying, and toilet rooms.   _____ _____
3. Heating plans permit both area and individual room control.   _____ _____
4. Research areas where small animals are kept and where chemicals are used have been provided with special ventilating equipment.   _____ _____
5. The heating and ventilating of the wrestling gymnasium have been given special attention.   _____ _____

Electrical

1. Shielded, vaporproof lights are used in moisture-prevalent areas.   _____ _____
2. Lights in strategic areas are key controlled.   _____ _____
3. Lighting intensity conforms to approved standards.   _____ _____
4. An adequate number of electrical outlets are strategically placed.   _____ _____
5. Gymnasium lights are controlled by dimmer units.   _____ _____
6. Locker room lights are mounted above the space between lockers.   _____ _____
7. Natural light is controlled properly for purposes of visual aids and other avoidance of glare.   _____ _____
8. Electrical outlet plates are installed 3 feet above the floor unless special use dictates other locations.   _____ _____
9. Controls for light switches and projection equipment are suitably located and interrelated.   _____ _____
10. All lights are shielded. Special protection is provided in gymnasiums, court areas, and shower rooms.   _____ _____
11. Lights are placed to shine between rows of lockers.   _____ _____

Walls

1. Movable and folding partitions are power-operated and controlled by keyed switches.   _____ _____
2. Wall places are located where needed and are firmly attached.   _____ _____
3. Hooks and rings for nets are placed (and recessed in walls) according to court locations and net heights.   _____ _____
4. Materials that clean easily and are impervious to moisture are used where moisture is prevalent.   _____ _____
5. Shower heads are placed at different heights—4 feet (elementary) to 7 feet (university)—for each school level.   _____ _____
6. Protective matting is placed permanently on the walls in the wrestling room, at the ends of basketball courts, and in other areas where such protection is needed.   _____ _____
7. An adequate number of drinking fountains is provided. They are properly placed (recessed in wall).   _____ _____
8. One wall (at least) of the dance studio has full-length mirrors.   _____ _____
9. All corners in locker rooms are rounded.   _____ _____

CHECKLIST FOR FACILITY PLANNERS—cont'd

	Yes	No

Ceilings

1. Overhead-supported apparatus is secured to beams engineered to withstand stress.
2. The ceiling height is adequate for the activities to be housed.
3. Acoustical materials impervious to moisture are used in moisture-prevalent areas.
4. Skylights, being impractical, are seldom used because of problems in waterproofing roofs and the controlling of sun rays (gyms).
5. All ceilings except those in storage areas are acoustically treated with sound-absorbent materials.

Floors

1. Floor plates are placed where needed and are flush-mounted.
2. Floor design and materials conform to recommended standards and specifications.
3. Lines and markings are painted on floors before sealing is completed (when synthetic tape is not used).
4. A coved base (around lockers and where wall and floor meet) or the same water-resistant material used on floors is found in all dressing and shower rooms.
5. Abrasive, nonskid, slip-resistant flooring that is impervious to moisture is provided on all areas where water is used—laundry, swimming pool, shower, dressing, and drying rooms.
6. Floor drains are properly located, and the slope of the floor is adequate for rapid drainage.

Gymnasiums and special rooms

1. Gymnasiums are planned so as to provide for safety zones (between courts, end lines, an walls) and for best use of space.
2. One gymnasium wall is free of obstructions and is finished with a smooth, hard surface for ball-rebounding activities.
3. The elementary school gymnasium has one wall free of obstructions, a minimum ceiling height of 18 feet, a minimum of 4000 square feet of teaching area, and a recessed area for housing a piano.
4. Secondary school gymnasiums have a minimum ceiling height of 22 feet; a scoreboard; electrical outlets placed to fit with bleacher installation; wall attachments for apparatus and nets; and a power-operated, sound-insulated, and movable partition with a small pass-through door at one end.
5. A small spectator alcove adjoins the wrestling room and contains a drinking fountain (recessed in the walls).
6. Cabinets, storage closets, supply windows, and service areas have locks.
7. Provisions have been made for the cleaning, storing, and issuing of physical education and athletic uniforms.
8. Shower heads are placed at varing heights in the shower rooms on each school level.
9. Equipment is provided for the use of the physically handicapped.
10. Special provision has been made for audio and visual aids, including intercommunication systems, radio, and television.

Continued.

CHECKLIST FOR FACILITY PLANNERS—cont'd

Gymnasiums and special rooms—cont'd Yes No

11. Team dressing rooms have provisions for:
    a. Hosing down room _____ _____
    b. Floors pitched to drain easily _____ _____
    c. Hot- and cold-water hose bibbs _____ _____
    d. Windows located above locker heights _____ _____
    e. Chalk, tack, and bulletin boards, and movie projection _____ _____
    f. Lockers for each team member _____ _____
    g. Drying facility for uniforms _____ _____
12. The indoor rifle range includes:
    a. Targets located 54 inches apart and 50 feet from the firing line _____ _____
    b. 3 feet to 8 feet of space behind targets _____ _____
    c. 12 feet of space behind firing line _____ _____
    d. Ceilings 8 feet high _____ _____
    e. Width adjusted to number of firing lines needed (1 line for each 3 students) _____ _____
    f. A pulley device for target placement and return _____ _____
    g. Storage and repair space _____ _____
13. Dance facilities include:
    a. 100 square feet per student _____ _____
    b. A minimum length of 60 linear feet for modern dance _____ _____
    c. Full-height viewing mirrors on one wall (at least) of 30 feet; also a 20-foot mirror on an additional wall if possible _____ _____
    d. Acoustical drapery to cover mirrors when not used and for protection if other activities are permitted _____ _____
    e. Dispersed microphone jacks and speaker installation for music and instruction _____ _____
    f. Built-in cabinets for record players, microphones, and amplifiers, with space for equipment carts _____ _____
    g. Electrical outlets and microphone connections around perimeter of room _____ _____
    h. An exercise bar (34 inches to 42 inches above floor) on one wall _____ _____
    i. Drapes, surface colors, floors (maple preferred), and other room appointments to enhance the room's attractiveness _____ _____
    j. Location near dressing rooms and outside entrances _____ _____
14. Training rooms include:
    a. Rooms large enough to administer adequately proper health services _____ _____
    b. Sanitary storage cabinets for medical supplies _____ _____
    c. Installation of drains for whirlpool, tubs, etc. _____ _____
    d. Installation of electrical outlets with proper capacities and voltage _____ _____
    e. High stools for use of equipment such as whirlpool, ice tubs, etc. _____ _____
    f. Water closet, hand lavatory, and shower _____ _____
    g. Extra hand lavatory in the trainer's room proper _____ _____
    h. Adjoining dressing rooms _____ _____
    i. Installation and use of hydrotherapy and diathermy equipment in separate areas _____ _____
    j. Space for the trainer, the physician, and the various services of this function _____ _____
    k. Corrective exercise laboratories located conveniently and adapted to the needs of the handicapped _____ _____

CHECKLIST FOR FACILITY PLANNERS—cont'd

	Yes	No

15. Coaches' room should provide:
    a. A sufficient number of dressing lockers for coaching staff and officials
    b. A security closet or cabinet for athletic equipment such as timing devices
    c. A sufficient number of showers and toilet facilities
    d. Drains and faucets for hosing down the rooms where this method of cleaning is desirable and possible
    e. A small chalkboard and tackboard
    f. A small movie screen and projection table for use of coaches to review films

Handicapped and disabled

Have you included those considerations that would make the facility accessible to, and usable by, the disabled? These considerations include:

1. The knowledge that the disabled will be participants in almost all activities, not merely spectators, if the facility is properly planned.
2. Ground-level entrance(s) or stair-free entrance(s) using inclined walk(s) or inclined ramp(s).
3. Uninterrupted walk surface; no abrupt changes in levels leading to the facility.
4. Approach walks and connecting walks no less than 4 feet wide.
5. Walks with gradient no greater than 5%.
6. A ramp, when used, with rise no greater than 1 foot in 12 feet.
7. Flat or level surface inside and outside of all exterior doors, extending 5 feet from the door in the direction that the door swings, and extending 1 foot to each side of the door.
8. Flush thresholds at all doors.
9. Appropriate door widths, heights, and mechanical features.
10. At least 6 feet between vestibule doors in series, i.e., inside and outside doors.
11. Access and proximity to parking areas.
12. No obstructions by curbs at crosswalks, parking areas, etc.
13. Proper precautions (handrails, etc.) at basement-window areaways, open stairways, porches, ledges, and platforms.
14. Handrails on all steps and ramps.
15. Precautions against the placement of manholes in principal or major sidewalks.
16. Corridors that are at least 60 inches wide and without abrupt pillars or protrusions.
17. Floors that are nonskid and have no abrupt changes or interruptions in level.
18. Proper design of steps.
19. Access to rest rooms, water coolers, telephones, food-service areas, lounges, dressing rooms, play areas, and auxiliary services and areas.
20. Elevators in multiple-story buildings.
21. Appropriate placement of controls to permit and to prohibit use as desired.
22. Sound signals for the blind, and visual signals for the deaf as counterparts to regular sound and sight signals.
23. Proper placement, concealment, or insulation of radiators, heat pipes, hotwater pipes, drain pipes, etc.

Continued.

CHECKLIST FOR FACILITY PLANNERS—cont'd

Swimming pools   Yes   No

1. Has a clear-cut statement been prepared on the nature and scope of the design program _____ _____
   and the special requirements for space, equipment, and facilities dictated by the activities to be conducted?

2. Has the swimming pool been planned to meet the total requirements of the program to _____ _____
   be conducted as well as any special needs of the clientele to be served?

3. Have all plans and specifications been checked and approved by the local board of _____ _____
   health?

4. Is the pool the proper depth to accommodate the various age groups and types of _____ _____
   activities it is intended to serve?

5. Does the design of the pool incorporate the most current knowledge and best experi- _____ _____
   ence available regarding swimming pools?

6. If a local architect or engineer who is inexperienced in pool construction is employed, _____ _____
   has an experienced pool consultant, architect, or engineer been called in to advise on design and equipment?

7. Is there adequate deep water for diving (minimum of 9 feet for 1-meter boards, 12 feet _____ _____
   for 3-meter boards, and 15 feet for 10-meter towers)?

8. Have the requirements for competitive swimming been met (7-foot lanes; 12-inch black _____ _____
   or brown lines on the bottom; pool 1 inch longer than official measurement; depth and distance markings)?

9. Is there adequate deck around the pool? Has more space been provided than that _____ _____
   indicated by the minimum recommended deck/pool ratio?

10. Does the swimming instructor's office face the pool? And is there a window through _____ _____
    which the instructor may view all the pool area? Is there a toilet-shower-dressing area next to the office for instructors?

11. Are recessed steps or removable ladders located on the walls so as not to interfere with _____ _____
    competitive swimming turns?

12. Does a properly constructed overflow gutter extend around the pool perimeter? _____ _____

13. Where skimmers are used, have they been properly located so that they are not on walls _____ _____
    where competitive swimming is to be conducted?

14. Have separate storage spaces been allocated for maintenance and instructional equip- _____ _____
    ment?

15. Has the area for spectators been properly separated from the pool area? _____ _____

16. Have all diving standards and lifeguard chairs been properly anchored? _____ _____

17. Does the pool layout provide the most efficient control of swimmers from showers and _____ _____
    locker rooms to the pool? Are toilet facilities provided for wet swimmers separate from the dry area?

18. Is the recirculation pump located below the water level? _____ _____

19. Is there easy vertical access to the filter room for both people and material (stairway if _____ _____
    required)?

20. Has the proper pitch to drains been allowed in the pool, on the pool deck, in the _____ _____
    overflow gutter, and on the floor of shower and dressing rooms?

21. Has adequate space been allowed between diving boards and between the diving boards _____ _____
    and sidewalls?

22. Is there adequate provision for lifesaving equipment? Pool-cleaning equipment? _____ _____

CHECKLIST FOR FACILITY PLANNERS—cont'd

	Yes	No
23. Are inlets and outlets adequate in number and located so as to ensure effective circulation of water in the pool?	_____	_____
24. Has consideration been given to underwater lights, underwater observation windows, and underwater speakers?	_____	_____
25. Is there a coping around the edge of the pool?	_____	_____
26. Has a pool heater been considered in northern climates in order to raise the temperature of the water?	_____	_____
27. Have underwater lights in end racing walls been located deep enough and directly below surface lane anchors, and are they on a separate circuit?	_____	_____
28. Has the plan been considered from the standpoint of handicapped persons (e.g., is there a gate adjacent to the turnstiles)?	_____	_____
29. Is seating for swimmers provided on the deck?	_____	_____
30. Has the recirculation-filtration system been designed to meet the anticipated future bathing load?	_____	_____
31. Has the gas chlorinator (if used) been placed in a separate room accessible from and vented to the outside?	_____	_____
32. Has the gutter waste water been valved to return to the filters, and also for direct waste?	_____	_____

Indoor pools

	Yes	No
1. Is there proper mechanical ventilation?	_____	_____
2. Is there adequate acoustical treatment of walls and ceilings?	_____	_____
3. Is there adequate overhead clearance for diving (15 feet above low springboards, 15 feet for 3-meter boards, and 10 feet for 10-meter platforms)?	_____	_____
4. Is there adequate lighting (50 footcandles minimum)?	_____	_____
5. Has reflection of light from the outside been kept to the minimum by proper location of windows or skylights (windows on side walls are not desirable)?	_____	_____
6. Are all wall bases coved to facilitate cleaning?	_____	_____
7. Is there provision for proper temperature control in the pool room for both water and air?	_____	_____
8. Can the humidity of the pool room be controlled?	_____	_____
9. Is the wall and ceiling insulation adequate to prevent "sweating"?	_____	_____
10. Are all metal fittings of noncorrosive material?	_____	_____
11. Is there a tunnel around the outside of the pool, or a trench on the deck that permits ready access to pipes?	_____	_____

Outdoor pools

	Yes	No
1. Is the site for the pool in the best possible location (away from railroad tracks, heavy industry, trees, and dusty open fields)?	_____	_____
2. Have sand and grass been kept the proper distance away from the pool to prevent them from being transmitted to the pool?	_____	_____
3. Has a fence been placed around the pool to assure safety when not in use?	_____	_____
4. Has proper subsurface drainage been provided?	_____	_____
5. Is there adequate deck space for sunbathing?	_____	_____

Continued.

CHECKLIST FOR FACILITY PLANNERS—cont'd

Outdoor pools—cont'd	Yes	No
6. Are the outdoor lights placed far enough from the pool to prevent insects from dropping into the pool?	_____	_____
7. Is the deck of nonslip material?	_____	_____
8. Is there an area set aside for eating, separated from the pool deck?	_____	_____
9. Is the bathhouse properly located, with the entrance to the pool leading to the shallow end?	_____	_____
10. If the pool shell contains a concrete finish, has the length of the pool been increased by 3 inches over the official size in order to permit eventual tiling of the basin without making the pool too short?	_____	_____
11. Are there other recreational facilities nearby for the convenience and enjoyment of swimmers?	_____	_____
12. Do diving boards or platforms face north or east?	_____	_____
13. Are lifeguard stands provided and properly located?	_____	_____
14. Has adequate parking space been provided and properly located?	_____	_____
15. Is the pool oriented correctly in relation to the sun?	_____	_____
16. Have windshields been provided in situations where heavy winds prevail?	_____	_____

Appendix C

The Computer

The computer is made up of (1) *input units* that feed data into the system, (2) *a central processor* that is in charge of the processing function and is capable of storing large amounts of data, and (3) *output units* that create records and reports.

Communication with the computer is done through input/output devices. These devices can send and/or receive information. Data from an input device passes through the processing unit where it is analyzed and sent to the output devices. Input/output devices include the following:

Keyboard. An input device, the keyboard is the typewriter-like component. As the numbers, symbols, and letters of the keyboard are punched, the computer converts them into binary language to be interpreted by the central processing unit. The information that is typed is displayed on the monitor.

Monitor. This output device usually comes with the computer. Information is displayed on the monitor. It can be purchased in black and white, amber, or color.

Modem. This input/output device is capable of converting information into a form that can be transmitted and received over ordinary phone lines. In this way the computer can interface with other computers.

Printer. This is strictly an output device. Information is transmitted to the printer and a copy is made.

Central processing unit. This unit interprets and executes programs with their series of instructions. The control unit determines what instructions are to be executed. It controls and coordinates input data and operates the computer and its input/output devices. Thus it is the brain of the computer, controlling all its functions. The arithmetic/logic unit performs

mathematics and makes decisions as directed by the control unit. The mathematical portion performs subtraction, multiplication, and other arithmetic functions. The logic portion performs decision-making functions. Before the computer can perform any of the above operations the data must be stored in the central memory. Input/output devices such as the keyboard convert the symbols typed into a binary code to be interpreted; the material is then stored in the central memory until retrieved by the control unit.

Disc drives. Information is stored on rotating disks that in many ways look like phonograph records. The data is stored on the disks as sequences of magnetized spots appearing on concentric circles. There are two main types of disk drives, the floppy and the hard.

The floppy disk is flexible and sealed in a square jacket with a hole in the center. The drive spins the disk. The surface of the disk is covered with magnetic oxide. Each sector of the disk is divided into tracts accessed through the head access hole, an oblong hole in the disk jacket. The drive has a magnetic head that is positioned along the tracks of the disk. As the disk spins, different sectors of the track pass beneath this magnetic head. In this manner data on the disk are read. This form of access is called random access since it will allow the operator to quickly find any piece of information at any time.

The hard disk is more expensive than the floppy disk; however, it can store more information. It can locate files faster and can feed them into the computer or onto the screen at a faster rate than floppy disks, thus providing instant access.

Software. Computer programs include a detailed series of instructions that request the computer to fulfill specified commands. These software programs are the single most important component of a computer system. Before purchasing any computer hardware, management should consider the software that is available. For instance, if management plans to use the computer to create, grade, and record test scores, it is important to shop for the specific programs that are needed to fulfill these requirements and then purchase the computer system that is compatible with the software. Without the needed software the computer is useless, unless management can program it themselves.

Basic pieces of software are widely recommended and used by most computer users. When needs become more specific, software becomes more difficult to find.

Program. This is a series of instructions that are given to the computer and will provide the answer desired and solve the problem in question. It is a group of related routines designed to solve a given problem. If a program cannot be found for the particular problem a person wishes to solve, one option is to write a program. However, a major time commitment is needed to accomplish such a task—similar, as one person has said, to learning the equivalent of a foreign language. Of course, it may be possible to hire someone to write the needed program, but this could involve a sizable sum of money.

Hardware. Hardware is the physical equipment that is involved in the operation. It is the computer itself and its various attachments. Hardware is the vehicle that allows information to be put into the system. It usually consists of the keyboard, monitor, disk drive, printer, and modem. Besides these basic items management can purchase several other pieces of hardware such as a voice speech synthesizer, music synthesizer, and card reader. Additional equipment can add efficiency to the system.

Word processor. The word processor allows the user to type, edit, and save any document. Each page of type can be rearranged as desired by simply giving it the correct instructions. For example, the user can select various formats such as size of text or the number of lines between sentences. Also, the user may make several copies of the same letter with a few minor changes in each, such as different names, addresses or figures, which can be automatically inserted by the word processor as it prints the text.

Appendix D

The Adapted Program and Physical Education for Handicapped Persons

Some terms used in relation to programs for handicapped persons need to be defined. These terms are *impaired, disabled, handicapped, exceptional person,* and *adapted physical education.*

Impaired: This refers to an identifiable organic or functional condition; some part of the body is actually missing, a portion of an anatomical structure is gone, or one or more parts of the body do not function properly or adequately.

Disabled: This refers to a limitation or restriction of an individual, because of impairments, in executing some skills, doing specific jobs or tasks, or performing certain activities.

Handicapped: Handicapped individuals, because of impairment or disability, are adversely affected psychologically, emotionally, or socially, or in a combination of ways.

Exceptional person: The exceptional person, because of some physical, mental, emotional, or behavioral deviation may require a modification of school practices or an addition of some special service to develop his or her maximum potential.

Adapted physical education: The Committee on Adapted Physical Education defines adapted physical education as a diversified program of developmental activities, game, sports, and rhythms suited to the interests, capacities, and limitations of students with disabilities who may not safely or successfully engage in unrestricted participation in the vigorous activities of the general physical education program.

Objectives for the adapted program

Physical education can be valuable to the atypical and handicapped individual in many ways. It can help in identifying deviations from the normal and in referring students to proper individuals or agencies, when necessary. It can provide the atypical person with a happy, wholesome play experience. It can help the student achieve, within his or her limitations, physical skill and exercise. It can provide many opportunities for learning skills appropriate for the handicapped person to achieve success. It can help correct conditions that can be improved. It can help individuals protect themselves from injuries and conditions that might occur as a result of participating in physical education activities. Finally, physical education can contribute to a more productive life for the handicapped individual by developing those physical qualities needed to meet the demands of day-to-day living.

Scheduling the adapted program

Before scheduling a student in the adapted program, one needs a thorough understanding of the boy's or girl's atypical condition and the type of procedure that will best meet his or her total development.

Because of the shortage of funds, space, and staff, many scheduling difficulties arise concerning the adapted program. Many times equipment has to be improvised, special groups must be scheduled within the regular class period, and staff members have to devote out-of-school time to this important phase of the total physical education program. Unfortunately, some teachers solve the problem by sending the exceptional student to study hall or letting him or her observe from the bleachers, thus failing to provide a modified program.

Some physical education leaders feel that scheduling atypical children and youth in separate groups is not always satisfactory. Many educators who have studied this problem feel the atypical student in many cases should take his or her physical education along with nonhandicapped students and, to provide for the handicapping condition, the program should be modified and special methods of teaching used. In such cases, the administrator should make sure that the modification of the program for the student is physically and psychologically sound. Sometimes mental and emotional defects can be minimized if the teacher acquaints other students with the general problems of the handicapped person and encourages their cooperation in helping the student make the right adjustment and maintain self-esteem and social acceptance.

In larger schools it sometimes has been possible to schedule special classes for students with some types of abnormalities. Also, special schools have been established for the severely handicapped. These two procedures have not always proved satisfactory, mainly because of the feeling that the handicapped should be scheduled with nonhandicapped students for social and psychological reasons and also because PL 94-142 requires it in many cases.

In some smaller schools and colleges where a staff problem exists, students needing an adapted program have been scheduled in a separate section within the regular physical education class period. In some cases group exercises have been devised together, with the practice of encouraging pupils to assist one another in the alleviation of their difficulties. These methods are not always satisfactory but, according to the schools and colleges concerned, are much better than not doing anything about the problem. In other schools and colleges atypical pupils have been scheduled during special periods, where individual attention can be given to them.

The procedure any particular school or college follows in scheduling students for the adapted program will depend on PL 94-142, the school's educational philosophy, finances, facilities, and the needs of the staff and students.

Selecting activities for adapted physical education

Activities should be selected for the adapted physical education program with the needs of the atypical student in mind after consulting proper medical authorities. The IEP will indicate activities that should be provided. The activities selected should develop worthwhile skills, maintain a proper state of organic fitness, and consider the social and emotional needs of the student. In no case should an activity ever aggravate an existing injury or atypical condition. Of course, all activities should be appropriate to the age level of the student and be ones in which he or she can find success. As far as possible and practical, activities should reflect the regular program of physical education offered at the school or college. The fewer changes made in the original activity, usually the more the atypical person feels that he or she is being successful and not different from the other students. Activities should contribute to the development of basic movements and skills. There should be as much group activity as possible, because the socializing benefits of participation are important in providing students with a feeling of belonging.

The teacher in the adapted program

In the United States today several institutions offer specialization in adapted physical education programs. The specialist in adapted physical education usually has a master's degree or a doctorate and has taken courses in special education, psychology, sociology, and other allied areas, as well as in adapted physical education.

It is also important that physical educators and classroom teachers be given the opportunity to take courses in adapted physical education so they will be able to approach their students with greater understanding. Course work in adapted physical education should also be made available to undergraduates.

The teacher of adapted physical education should also understand the student with the atypical condition—the various atypical conditions, their causes, and treatment. The teacher should like to work with students who need special help and be able to establish a good rapport to instill confidence in the work that needs to be done. The teacher should appreciate the various mental and emotional problems confronting an atypical person and the methods and procedures that can be followed to cope with these problems. The teacher must in some ways be a psychologist, creating interest and stimulating motivation toward physical activity for the purpose of hastening improvement. The teacher should be sympathetic to the advice of medical personnel. She or he should be willing to give corrective exercise under the guidance of physicians and to plan the program with their help. It is also necessary to know the implications of medical and other findings for the adapted physical education program, to be familiar with the medical, psychological, or other examinations of each student, and, with the help of the physician, psychologist, social worker, or other specialist, to work out a program that best meets the needs of the student.

Mainstreaming

Mainstreaming means that handicapped persons receive their education, including physical education, with persons who are not handicapped, unless the nature of the handicap is such that education in the regular classroom or gymnasium setting cannot be achieved satisfactorily, even with the use of supplementary aids and services. The federal law does not mean that all handicapped children will be a part of the regular class. It does mean that those handicapped students who can profit from having their physical education with regular students should be assigned to regular classes.

Management principles that apply to mainstreaming

Some management principles that should apply and guide the mainstreaming concept follow:

All students should be provided satisfactory learning experiences, whether they are nonhandicapped or handicapped.

Class size should be such that all students can receive an adequate educational offering and effective teaching.

Facilities should be adapted to meet the needs of all students, including the handicapped (such as providing ramps, if necessary).

Mainstreaming should be used only for those students who can benefit from such a practice. In other words, some handicapped students may benefit more from special classes.

Periodic evaluation should take place to determine objectively the effectiveness of mainstreaming in terms of students' progress.

Adequate supportive personnel, such as a speech therapist or a person trained in physical education for the handicapped, should be provided for handicapped students.

The administration should support the program and make it possible for those teachers involved in such a program to have the necessary instructional supplies, space, time, and resources necessary to adequately do the job required.

Adequate preservice and in-service teacher preparation should be provided for all teachers who will be involved in working with handicapped students.

To ensure full public support, the school should carry on an adequate public information program to ensure that parents, the community, and the general public are aware of the program, its needs, and what it is doing for children.

A concept of mainstreaming being favored by more educators today is that of providing educational services for handicapped students in the "least restrictive environment." In essence, this means that a handicapped child is placed in a special class or a regular class or is moved between the two environments as dictated by his or her abilities and capabilities. Furthermore, the school assumes the responsibility of providing the necessary adjunct services to ensure that handicapped students perform to their optimum capacity, whether integrated into the regular program or left in a special class.

Physical education is an area where much can be done for handicapped students if they are mainstreamed, provided the physical educators in charge understand the needs of handicapped individuals and the type of programs that will best meet those needs. Whether or not the program is successful depends on the teacher and his or her ability to individualize the program to meet the needs of each student in the class. It is essential to select the program of activities carefully, to begin where the student is at present, and to let the capabilities of the individual determine his or her progress (Fig. 1).

The physical educator should use several approaches in teaching various types of handicapped students. A thorough medical examination should be a first step. Personal assistance will be needed from time to time. Modification of the activities will be necessary in many cases. Rapid progress in skill development should not be expected. Handicapped students should feel they have achieved and are successful in their efforts. Complete records on each student

<figure>

LOS ANGELES CITY SCHOOL DISTRICTS
Health Education and Health Services Branch—Auxiliary Services Division
Corrective Physical Education Section

CORRECTIVE PHYSICAL EDUCATION ACTIVITY GUIDE
A Guide for the Teacher and Physician
In Planning a Restricted Program of Physical Education

Pupil_____ Date_____

School_____ Corrective Phys. Ed. Teacher_____

I. TYPES OF MOVEMENTS	OMIT	*MILD	**MODERATE	UNLIMITED	REMARKS
Bending					
Climbing					
Hanging					
Jumping					
Kicking					
Lifting					
Pulling					
Pushing					
Running					
Stretching					
Throwing					
Twisting					

II. TYPES OF EXERCISES	OMIT	*MILD	**MODERATE	UNLIMITED	REMARKS
Abdominal					
Arm					
Breathing					
Foot					
Head					
Knee					
Leg					
Trunk					
Relaxation					

III. TYPES OF POSITIONS	LIMITED	UNLIMITED
Lying supine		
Lying prone		
Sitting		
Standing		

IV. TYPES OF ACTIVITIES	YES	NO
Competitive sports		
Games——Sitting		
Games requiring standing but no running or jumping		
Officiating		
Swimming		
Coeducational activities		
Social dancing		
Square dancing		
Sports and games		

Recommended until_____ 196_

Remarks:

_____
Signature of Physician

*Very little activity.
**Half as much as the unlimited
  program.

</figure>

Fig. 1. A guide for planning restricted physical education program for students.

should be kept, with notations concerning the nature of the handicap, recommendations of the physician, and appropriate and inappropriate activities.

Each handicapped student must be made to feel a part of the physical education program. For example, mentally retarded children should gain self-confidence, and physically handicapped students should have fun meeting the challenges that certain activities and exercises provide. In addition, the activities should be challenging and at the same time rewarding for the development of positive self-esteem. Some handicapped students should be taught leisure time activities and ways to play. The need for physical fitness should be stressed. Finally, it is important to stress safety, not to underestimate a student's abilities, and to remember that many handicapped children have a short attention span, tire easily, and are easily distracted.

Suggested management procedures for implementing PL 94-142

Cole and Dunn* have suggested the following management procedures for implementing PL 94-142:

- Develop task forces on a local and regional basis and appoint people who know about the law to leadership positions.
- Appoint someone with responsibility to implement the law and also see that the implementation processes are prescribed in writing.
- Establish a series of workshops to orient administration and staff personnel to the various components of the law and implementation procedures.
- Request information about the law and its implementation from organizations concerned with special education.
- Simulate team placement conferences so that administration and staff may become better informed of their responsibilities, the instructional strategies involved, and other administrative details in providing for handicapped students.
- Prepare a brochure on the program for parents, outlining their rights and the rights of children under the law. Also, explain procedures that may be used and programs under consideration.

- Organize workshops for administrative and staff personnel to familiarize them with different instructional strategies for individualizing instruction and to acquaint them with the relationships between learning style characteristics and these instructional strategies.
- Visit schools that are already providing excellent programs under PL 94-142, find out what practices are successful, and get suggestions for implementing the program.
- Develop a curriculum that meets the needs of various types of handicapped students, including the preparation of such features as learning packages, contract activity packages, multisensory instructional packages, and resource lists for teachers.
- Involve parents and students in the provision of resources and in helping handicapped students.
- Decide carefully which students will be mainstreamed and which ones will not be.
- Encourage all teachers to individualize instruction so that handicapped students will be integrated into their classes as easily as possible.
- Have all teachers, whether teaching regular or special classes, participate on the reevaluation team.
- Simplify instructional materials so that they may be easily understood by the students.
- Participate in regional, state, and national conferences on the implementation of PL 94-142 to discover new techniques and means of instruction that have proved to be effective in other schools.

Suggested organizational structures for handicapped students

Various organizational structures have been suggested to provide for students with varying degrees of handicapping conditions. Some students may have severe handicaps, and some may have mild handicaps. The organizational structure selected should meet the needs of each student.

Some organizational structures that should be considered include the following:

- Students placed in special classes
- Students placed in regular classes, with or without supported services

---

*Adapted from Cole, R.W., and Dunn, R.

- Students placed in special classes for part of the school day
- Students placed in a special residential school
- Students provided for at home
- Students placed in regular classes with supplementary services provided
- Students placed in special schools that are a part of the public school system
- Students provided for by using a special diagnostic program

Puthoff suggests that the following four organizational structures should be considered in physical education:

Integrated or combined class. Handicapped students are placed in regular classes with modifications made where necessary in respect to goals, activities, and methodology. Individualized instruction is provided and based on a student's needs, interests, goals, and present status. Individual activities, such as track and field and gymnastics, are suggested, because performance in these activities does not affect the success or failure of other students, as is the case with team sports.

Dual class structure. Handicapped students are placed in an integrated class setting part of the time and in a setting where they can concentrate on their individual needs the rest of the time. Such an arrangement is not to be thought of as remedial instruction. Instead, individual special needs are met when the students are not in an integrated class setting.

Separate class. Handicapped students are placed in a class separate from the regular physical education class. The reasons for this type of classification could be that students are not yet ready for the regular class or that their handicap is too severe to permit them to participate with nonhandicapped students. Handicapped students who are assigned permanently to separate classes, however, would be in the regular school setting and would have the opportunity to interact with nonhandicapped students during noninstructional hours and experiences. In this way they would not be separated from their nonhandicapped counterparts by being in a separate school.

Flexible model plan. Handicapped students are placed in regular classes when they can safely and successfully participate in the activities provided and are placed in a separate class when more individualized instruction and experiences are needed because of their handicap.

Suggested instructional strategies for teaching handicapped students

In addition to organizational structures, there is a need to consider what methods will be the most effective methods of teaching handicapped students. Again, as with organizational structures, these methods will vary with the nature of the handicap each child has.

Puthoff[*] lists four instructional strategies that can be used when teaching physical education to handicapped students:

Modification of content. The goal in teaching the handicapped student is to individualize instruction (Fig. 2), modifying such elements as goals, behavioral objectives, and activities to meet individual differences. Instructional objectives can be differentiated according to each student's needs, skills, and knowledge. Behavioral objectives can be differentiated in respect to learning outcomes and competencies expected from the handicapped child. Individual selection of activities or modification in these activities can be provided to meet the needs of students.

Modification of learning rate. The learning rate for the handicapped student can be modified so that the student sets his or her own pace of learning.

Teaching and learning style options. The amount of time a teacher spends with each student can be differentiated. This is based on the premise that some students will require more teacher help than others. Furthermore, visual aids and other techniques will enable some students to move ahead independently in achieving their instructional goals.

Internal class environmental settings. Within a class the teacher can create different settings to provide for the needs of each handicapped student. For example, opportunities may exist to use methods that involve large and small group instruction, independent study, and an open gymnasium.

---

*Puthoff, M.

INDIVIDUALIZED EDUCATIONAL PROGRAM

I. Student name __John Doe, Jr.__ Date of birth __1-24-61__ Age __16__ School divisions __Stony Point__

Parent/guardian __Mrs. John Doe__ Date of eligibility __6-15-77__ Date of IEP implementation __9-6-77__

Address __1736 Bay Street__ Categorical identification __E.M.R.__

II. Present level of performance (summary data)

Academic:

Piat		AAHPER Physical Fitness Test (Refer to charts/age group)	
Reading recognition	2.3	Items	
Reading	3.6	Pull-up/flexed arm hang	5
Spelling	2.0	Sit-ups (flexed legs)	41
Reading comprehension	4.8	Shuttle run	10.1
Mathematics	4.2	50 yard dash	6.7
General knowledge	5.9	600 run-walk	1:55
		Standing broad jump	6'9"

Key Math
  3.8
Dolch Sight
Word Inventory
  263 words mastered

Behavior:

John is very shy and lacks physical fitness. There is little eye contact with others. He is well mannered. John gets discouraged easily when working in language areas. He performs well in math. His social skills are limited. John is interested in wood-working. Carpentry may provide a setting for advancement and training after he has obtained the necessary prevocational orientation.

III. Long-term goals

1. All items on the *AAHPER Physical Fitness Test* will increase to the 50th percentile (above satisfactory) by the end of the school year.

2. a. To increase sight word vocabulary and survival words.
   b. To increase skills in reading through spelling skills and decoding skills.
   c. To increase math processes skills to include banking and savings.
   d. To demonstrate planning of careers, duties of specific jobs, and survival forms of applications.
   e. To provide instruction in local, state, and national governments.
   f. To increase self-confidence and social adaptability.

Continued.

Fig. 2. Example of an IEP prepared by Virginia Department of Education.

VI. Participants

Date	Signature of persons present	Relationship to student
9-1-77	Mrs. Ann Long	Guidance Counselor
9-1-77	Mrs. Louise Green	EMR Teacher
9-1-77	Mr. George Dean	Physical Education Teacher
9-1-77	Mrs. John Doe	Parent
9-1-77	Ms. Matilda Snodgrass	Psychologist
9-1-77	Mr. Oscar Rinklefender	Director of Special Education

I GIVE PERMISSION FOR MY CHILD ___John Doe___ to be enrolled in the special program described in the individualized education program plan. I understand that I have the right to review his/her records and to request a change in his/her individualized education program at any time. I understand that I have the right to refuse this permission and to have my child continue in his/her present placement pending further action.

I did participate in the development of the individualized education program.   YES __X__ NO ___

I did not participate in the development of the individualized education program, but I do approve of the plan.

     YES ___ NO ___

__9/1/77__   __Mrs. John Doe__
Date   Signature of parent/guardian

I DO NOT GIVE PERMISSION FOR MY CHILD _____ to be enrolled in the special education program described in the individualized education program. I understand that I have the right to review his/her records and to request another placement. I understand that the action described above will not take place without my permission or until due process procedures have been exhausted. I understand that if my decision is appealed, I will be notified of my due process rights in this procedure.

_____   _____
Date   Signature of parent/guardian

Fig. 2, cont'd. Example of an IEP prepared by Virginia Department of Education.

IV. Education and/or related services

	Date to begin	Anticipated completion date	Environment	Location	Personnel
E.M.R.					
Physical education	9-6-77	Through high school	4 periods – self-contained	Virginia High School	Mrs. Green
Vocational orientation	9-6-77	Through grade 10	½ period per day regular	Virginia High School	Mr. Dean
	9-6-77	Through high school	½ period regular	Virginia High School	Vocational Rehabilitation W.I.N. Program

V. Short-term objectives

Objectives	Methods	Special materials and equipment	Dates Begun	Completed	Continuation and/or modification
P.E.	Establish warm-up stations to be used for following activities:				
1. Student's performance levels should show improvement in efforts to reach the 50th percentile	1. To perform sit-ups three times per week	Tape, stop watch, horizontal bar	9/6	5/4	Mastered/ Maintain
	2. To perform pull-ups three times per week		9/6	5/4	Cont./Inc. No. per week
	3. To perform shuttle-run two times per week		9/6	5/4	Cont./Inc. No. per week
	4. To run three 50-yard wind sprints per week		9/6	5/4	Cont./Modif. No.
	5. To jump vertically 1 minute three times per week		9/6	5/4	exercise
	6. To run one 600-yard run-walk per week		9/6	5/4	Mastered/ Continue
Academic					
1. To master Dolch sight vocabulary and survival words	Cover and write method	Flash cards, word finds, crossword puzzles	9/15	6/3	Continue/ increase
2. To spell and define 10 words per week			9/15	6/3	Modify
3. To, etc.			9/15	6/3	Continue

Fig. 2, cont'd. Example of an IEP prepared by Virginia Department of Education.

Credits

Chapter 1 P. 4, University of Nevada, Las Vegas; p. 6, President's Council on Physical Fitness and Sports; p. 9, Robert F. George, U.S. Olympic Training Center, Colorado Springs, Colorado; p. 11, Bob Thomason, Tenneco, Inc.

Chapter 2 Pp. 24-25, President's Council on Physical Fitness and Sports; p. 38, Don Adee.

Chapter 3 P. 64, John Tasker, Arnold College Division, University of Bridgeport, Conn., Parents and Friends Association of Mentally Retarded Children; p. 69, Le Moyne Coates; pp. 84-86, adapted from Piscopo, J.: Quality instruction: first priority, *The Physical Educator 21:* 162, 1964.

Chapter 4 P. 91, from Jones, T.R.: Needed—a new philosophical model for intramurals, *Journal of Health, Physical Education, and Recreation 43:* 34, 1971; p. 92, President's Council on Physical Fitness and Sports; p. 94, Cosom, Minneapolis, Minn.; p. 100, from Hyatt, R.W.: *Intramural sports: organization and administration,* St. Louis, 1977, The C.V. Mosby Co.; p. 101, Youth Services Section, Los Angeles City Schools; pp. 102-104, from Hyatt, R.W.: *Intramural sports: organization and administration,* St. Louis, 1977, The C.V. Mosby Co.; p. 106, from Intramurals for Senior High Schools, The Athletic Institute, Chicago, Ill.; p. 107, from Hyatt, R.W.: *Intramural sports: organization and administration,* St. Louis, 1977, The C.V. Mosby Co.; p. 108, from Intramurals for Senior High Schools, The Athletic Institute, Chicago, Ill.; p. 110, Division of Municipal Recreation and Adult Education, Milwaukee Public Schools, Milwaukee, Wisc.; pp. 114-115, from Matthews, D.O.: Intramural administration principles, *The Athletic Journal 46:* 82, 1966. Reproduced courtesy *The Athletic Journal,* adapted and updated 1979.

Chapter 5 P. 124, American Alliance for Health, Physical Education, Recreation, and Dance. 1900 Association Dr., Reston, Va.; pp. 125, 126, Cramer Products, Inc., Gardner, Kan.; p. 130, Iowa State University, Ames, Iowa; pp. 131, 140, Cramer Products, Inc., Gardner, Kan.; pp. 146-147, National Council of Secondary School Athletic Directors: Evaluating the High School Athletic Program, Washington, D.C., 1973, American Association for Health, Physical Education, and Recreation; p. 155, National Collegiate Athletic Association.

Chapter 6 P. 168, Evelyn Navarro, Tenneco, Inc.; p. 171, The Forbes Magazine Fitness Center, New York; p. 176, Dow Health and Physical Education Center, Hope College, Holland, Mich.; p. 181, Westwood Home, Clinton, Mo.

Chapter 7 Pp. 190, 191, 193, University of Nevada, Las Vegas; p. 196, Smith College, Northampton, Mass.; p. 200, Cramer Products, Inc., Gardner, Kan.; p. 201, from Seyle, H.: *Stress without distress,* New York, 1974, Signet; p. 209, Omaha Public Schools.

Chapter 8 P. 220, Oak View Elementary School, Fairfax, Va.; p. 224, Office of Public Relations, Smith College, Northampton, Mass.; p. 225, State University College at Potsdam, N.Y.; p. 227, from American Alliance for Health, Physical Education, Recreation, and Dance: Test items in the AAHPERD Health-Related Physical Fitness Test, AAHPERD update, June 1980; p. 229, from Abernathy, R., and Waltz, M.: Toward a discipline; first steps first, *Quest,* monograph II, p. 3, April, 1964.

Chapter 9 P. 238, Dave Black; p. 240 (top), Robert F. George; p. 240 (bottom), Dave Black; p. 242, Trinity College, Hartford, Conn.; p. 250, AAHPERD; p. 256, Scholastic

Coach; p. 258, from The Athletic Institute and AAHPERD: *Planning facilities for athletics, physical education, and recreation*. Flynn, Richard B., editor, North Palm Beach, Fla., 1985. The Athletic Institute; p. 259, University of Notre Dame; pp. 260, 261, from Auxter, D., and Pyfer, J.: *Principles and methods of adapted physical education and recreation*, ed. 5, St. Louis, 1985, Times Mirror/Mosby College Publishing; p. 264, A, Shaver & Co., Salina, Kan., B, Educational Facilities Laboratories, New York; p. 268, Houston Sports Association, Inc., Houston, Texas.

Chapter 10   P. 272, Cramer Products, Inc., Gardner, Kan.; p. 283, from Clegg, A.A., Jr.: The teacher and the manager of the curriculum, *Educational Leadership,* January 1973, p. 308; p. 288, Martha Swope.

Chapter 11   P. 296, California State University, Audio Visual Center, Long Beach, Calif.; pp. 297, 298, University of California at Irvine; p. 299 (top), Nautilus Sports/Medical Industries, DeLand, Fla.; p. 299 (bottom), University of California at Irvine; pp. 302, 303, from Auxter, D., and Pyfer, J.: *Principles and methods of adapted physical education and recreation*, ed. 5, St. Louis, 1985, Times Mirror/Mosby College Publishing; p. 304, Clark County School District, Las Vegas, Nev.; p. 306, from School Business Management Handbook Number 5. The University of the State of New York, Albany, N.Y.; p. 308, from Bucher, C.A., and Koenig, C.R.: *Methods and materials in secondary school physical education*, ed. 6, St. Louis, 1983, Times Mirror/Mosby College Publishing; p. 310, Rawlings Sporting Goods Company; p. 311, Martha Swope; p. 312, from How to Budget, Select, and Order Athletic Equipment, Chicago, The Athletic Institute; p. 313, adapted from the New York State Association of School Business Officials: Code of Ethics for School Purchasing Officials; p. 314, Martha Swope.

Chapter 12   Pp. 320, 322, University of Nevada, Las Vegas; p. 322, adapted from Committee on the Medical Aspects of Sports of the American Medical Association and the National Federation of State High School Athletic Associations: Tips on Athletic Training XI, Chicago, The American Medical Association; p. 323, Cramer Products, Inc., Gardner, Kan.; p. 324, modified from Parkhouse, B.L., and Lapin, J.: *The woman in athletic administration,* Santa Monica, Calif., 1980, Goodyear Publishing Co., Inc.; p. 324, 325, Cramer Products, Inc., Gardner, Kan.; p. 326, Riverside-Brookfield High School, Riverside, Ill.; p. 327, from Arnheim, D.D.: *Modern principles of athletic training,* ed. 6, St. Louis, 1985, Times Mirror/Mosby College Publishing; p. 329, Cramer Products, Inc., Gardner, Kan.; p. 334, Institute of Aerobics Research, Dallas, Texas; pp. 336-337, from Committee on the Medical

Aspects of Sports, American Medical Association: A guide for medical evaluation of candidates for school sports, Chicago, 1966, The Association; p. 337, from Committee on the Medical Aspects of Sports, American Medical Association: A guide for medical evaluation of candidates for school sports, Chicago, 1966, The Association, p. 2. Reprinted with permission of the American Medical Association.

Chapter 13   P. 344, adapted from Arnold, D.E.: Sport product liability, *Journal of Physical Education and Recreation 49:* 25, November/December 1978; p. 345 (box), adapted from Appenzeller, H., and Ross, T.: Sports and the courts, Summer Law and Sports Conference, Greensboro, N.C., June 1983, Guilford College; p. 345 (figure), Cramer Products, Inc., Gardner, Kan.; p. 347, Tom and Faye Sitzman, Omaha, Neb.; p. 348, from Garber, L.O.: *Law and the school business manager,* Danville, Ill., 1957, Interstate Printers & Publishers, Inc.; p. 350, from *The coaches handbook* of the AAHPERD; p. 359, Boys and Girls Club, Las Vegas, Nev.; p. 361, University of Nevada, Las Vegas; p. 363, Cramer Products, Inc., Gardner, Kan.; p. 365, from Munize, A.J.: The teacher, pupil injury, and legal liability, *Journal of Health, Physical Education, and Recreation 33:* 28, 1962; p. 367, Martha Swope; p. 369, from Parsons, T.W.: What price prudence? *Journal of Physical Education and Recreation 50:* 45, January 1979. Courtesy American Alliance for Health, Physical Education, Recreation, and Dance, 1900 Association Dr., Reston, Va.

Chapter 14   P. 373, President's Council on Physical Fitness and Sports; p. 376, U.S. Marine Corps, courtesy of President's Council on Physical Fitness and Sports; pp. 377, 379, 381, President's Council on Physical Fitness and Sports; p. 383, Oak View Elementary School, Fairfax, Va.

Chapter 15   P. 388, Clark County School District, Las Vegas, Nev.

Appendixes   Pp. 403-412, adapted from Participants in National Facilities Conference: Planning areas and facilities for health, physical education and recreation, revised 1965, The Athletic Institute, updated by the author, 1979; p. 419, adapted from Cole, R.W., and Dunn, R.: A new lease on life for education of the handicapped: Ohio copes with PL 94-142, *Phi Delta Kappan 59:* 3, September 1977; p. 420, Puthoff, M.: Instructional strategies for mainstreaming. In *Mainstreaming physical education,* National Association for Physical Education for College Women and The National College Physical Education Association for Men, Briefing 4, 1976.

Index